ANALYTICAL EXPOSITION

OF

THE EPISTLE OF PAUL THE APOSTLE

TO

THE ROMANS.

BY JOHN BROWN, D.D.,

SENIOR MINISTER OF THE UNITED PRESBYTERIAN CONGREGATION, BROUGHTON PLACE, EDINBURGH, AND PROFESSOR OF EXEGETICAL THEOLOGY TO THE UNITED PRESBYTERIAN CHURCH.

Αἱ ἐπιστολαὶ τοῦ Παύλου πνεύματος εἰσι μέταλλα καὶ πηγαί· μέταλλα μὲν, ὅτι χρυσίου παντὸς τιμιώτερον ἡμῖν παρέχουσι πλοῦτον· πηγαὶ δὲ, ὅτι οὐδέποτε ἐπιλείπουσι· ἀλλ' ὅσον ἂν κενώσῃς ἐκεῖθεν, τοσοῦτον, καὶ πολλῷ πλέον, ἐπιῤῥεῖ πάλιν.—CHRYSOSTOM.

NEW YORK:
ROBERT CARTER AND BROTHERS, 530, BROADWAY.
1857.

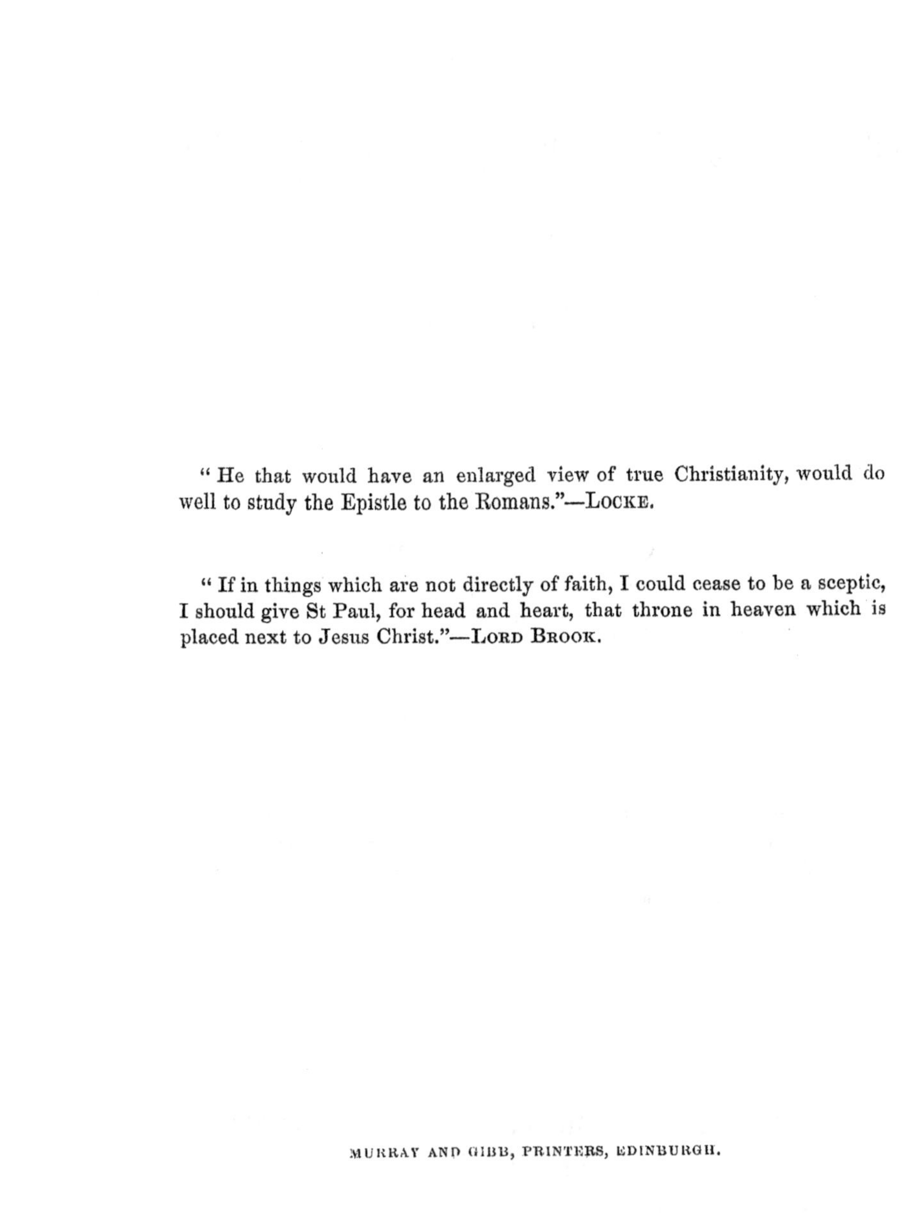

"He that would have an enlarged view of true Christianity, would do well to study the Epistle to the Romans."—Locke.

"If in things which are not directly of faith, I could cease to be a sceptic, I should give St Paul, for head and heart, that throne in heaven which is placed next to Jesus Christ."—Lord Brook.

MURRAY AND GIBB, PRINTERS, EDINBURGH.

TO

THE VERY REV. JOHN LEE,

D.D., M.D., LL.D., SS.T.P., VP.R.S.E.,

PRINCIPAL OF THE UNIVERSITY OF EDINBURGH, DEAN OF THE CHAPEL ROYAL.

My Dear Principal,

This Dedication, while expressive of high respect for your remarkable endowments and acquirements, for the distinguished station these have won for you, and for the exemplary manner in which you perform its duties, is chiefly meant by me, as I believe it will be chiefly valued by you, as a token of personal regard from one of your oldest friends.

It is just about sixty years since we first met, as fellow-students, in the halls of that University over which you now preside. Though necessarily a good deal separated by the widely different spheres of duty we have been called to fill, we have never, during that long period, lost sight of each other, nor ever looked towards each other with any feeling but respect and good will; and now, at its close, we are so happy as to find, amid the shipwrecks of many literary and ecclesiastical friendships on all sides, that in our case the liking of youth has ripened into the esteem of age—to be perfected, let us hope, in the friendship of heaven.

Believe me to be,

My Dear Principal,

Yours respectfully and affectionately,

JOHN BROWN.

ὁ ἀγαπητὸς ἡμῶν ἀδελφὸς Παῦλος κατὰ τὴν αὐτῷ δοθεῖσαν σοφίαν ἔγραψε ὑμῖν . . . λαλῶν . . . περὶ τούτων ἐν οἷς ἐστὶ δυσνόητά τινα.—Πετ. 'Επ. Δευτ. Γ. ιέ, ιϛ'.

"No doubt Paul's writings *do* contain 'things hard to be understood;' but that is a reason why Christians should take the more pains to understand them, and why those who are commissioned by the chief Shepherd for that purpose, should the more diligently explain them to their flocks."—WHATELY. *Essays on the Writings of St Paul*, Ess. ii. sect. 2.

contained in this Epistle, of the doctrine and law of Christ, and of the arguments in support of the one, and the motives to comply with the other; and to do this, in such a form as to convey, so far as possible, to the mind of the general reader, unacquainted with any but the vernacular language, the evidence on which I rest my conviction, that such is the import of the apostle's words.

In carrying out this plan, I have, as a matter of course, confined myself chiefly to what may be termed Logical or Analytical Exposition. To the unlearned, grammatical interpretation can only, within narrow limits, be made intelligible, and within still narrower bounds, interesting; and the force of evidence by which a particular conclusion is come to, on grammatical principles, they can scarcely at all appreciate. From similar causes, they can derive but little advantage, even from what is termed Historical interpretation.

But, among this class, there are to be found not a few who, in the exercise of a sound mind, are equally good judges as the learned, as to the clearness of a statement, the appositeness of an illustration, the point of an antithesis, the weight of an argument, and the force of a motive; and when they are made to see that, without using undue freedom with the words of the inspired author, in a translation which they have reason to think upon the whole faithful, the book is made to appear to have one grand object successfully prosecuted by a set of appropriate means; that, while a considerably complicated, it is a singularly harmonious, piece of thought; they not only obtain a clearer view of the meaning, but a deeper conviction that this must be the meaning of the inspired writer, than could be produced on such minds in any other way. And this is a result earnestly to be desired—carefully sought for—for it is of infinite importance, not only that such minds should be brought in contact with what is the mind of God in His word, but into conscious contact with it, so as that they may know and be sure that this is the meaning of the revelation made to them.

This logical or analytical exposition has, in the present instance, been erected on the basis of a carefully conducted grammatical and historical interpretation. Without this it would be a mere castle in the air. The analysis was not first made from a superficial view of the text, or borrowed from some previous exposition, and then the Epistle made to suit the analysis; but, after ascertaining, as far as possible, the meaning of the separate words and phrases, by grammar and history, there has been an honest attempt to bring out, by analysis, satisfactory proof that these words and phrases embody a closely connected discussion of one great subject, that there runs through the Epistle a deep, strong, clear, stream of connected thought—that the statements are perspicuous—the illustrations apposite—the argument sound—and the motives appropriate and cogent.

I am not unaware that, from the fact that the human mind is itself logical, there is a hazard of an analytical expositor creating, instead of discovering, order. But I trust there will not be found much of this kind of paralogism in the following work; for I am sure I have guarded against such a tendency; and I have a deep and solemn conviction that there is no worse or more dangerous way of "adding to the words of this Book," than by first putting into the text, and then bringing out of it, our own preconceived notions, and that he who consciously does so, does it at a tremendous risk.

While the leading character of the exposition is intentionally analytical, I have by no means scrupulously avoided either grammatical or historical remark, where it seemed requisite to subserve my main purpose; and I shall be seriously disappointed if those who study the Epistle, that they may become "wise unto salvation," have reason to complain of the work as but little fitted to guide them in the exercises of the inner life, or to minister motives to the duties, and support and consolation amid the trials and sorrows of the outward life.

The growing study of the writings of the Apostle Paul, and especially of the Epistle to the Romans, appears to me one of the most promising signs of our times. "His labours," as Archbishop Whately says, "can never be effectually frustrated, except by their being kept out of sight. Whatever brings Paul into notice will ultimately bring him into triumph." I rejoice in the great accession that has, since I first began to study his writings, been made to the means of understanding him, in the elaborate and acute, though doctrinally very unsound, grammatical commentary by Fritzsche, as well as in the safer illustrations of Tholück and Olshausen, Stuart and Hodge, Peile and Alford; and I cannot altogether regret that the suggestion of the able writer just quoted, that there might be more undesirable things than "a plausible attack on Paul's writings," has been realized.

Oxford has had the credit, or discredit, of giving origin to a work of this description, distinguished by considerable ability of various kinds, but betraying, on the part of the author, an incapacity of forming a just judgment equally of the apostle and of himself. I

ANALYTICAL EXPOSITION

OF THE

EPISTLE OF PAUL TO THE ROMANS.

"Cum epistola haec Pauli ad Romanos, unica totius Scripturæ sit methodus, et absolutissima epitome Novi Testamenti, seu Evangelii, quod ipsa certe, vel sola breviter et purissime tradit; dignam sane existimo, quae non modo ab omnibus Christianis imbibatur a teneris, edidiscaturque ad verbum, sed et quæ assidua et perpetua meditatione, ceu ruminata et concocta, haud aliter atque probe digestus cibus, in intima animi viscera trajiciatur. Tam dives autem hæc epistola est spiritualium opum thesaurus, et ceu opulentissimum quoddam copiæ cornu, ut millies perlegenti semper occurrat novum aliquid; adeo ut hæc lectio longe omnium utilissima, quod in eruditione rerum sacrarum, cognitione Christi, discenda natura fidei, omnium spiritualium affectuum vi cognoscenda, altius provehat, subinde tibi inter manus crescat, semperque major, jucundior, preciosior, opulentior seipsa fiat."—LUTHERUS, Præf. in Ep. ad Rom.

"Subtilis est Paulus, ingeniosus, sententiisque abundans, sed parcus sæpe verborum; et conjuncta in eo est summà sententiarum varietas et crebritas, et cum disputationis concitatione, quæ abundantium et ferventium Scriptorum propria est; et cum orationis ubertate quam eloquentia gignit, ex animi commotione et pietate nata."—FRITZSCHE. The following character of Varro by Cicero might seem intended for Paul:—"Præceps quædam, et cum idcirco obscura quia peracuta, tum rapida et celeritate caecata oratio: sed neque verbis aptiorem cito alium dixerim, neque sententiis crebriorem."—*Brut.*, 76.

PREFACE.

THE interpretation of ancient writings, such as the Phædo of Plato, the Poetics of Aristotle, the Cato Major of Cicero, or the Epistle to the Romans of Paul, is necessarily a work of some complexity and difficulty. To its right performance, it is requisite to be so acquainted with the language in which the work is written, as to be familiar with the principles of its construction, and the meaning of its words and phrases; to know the peculiar circumstances and habits of thought of the writer, and of those for whom his work was primarily intended, both of which are likely, in some degree, to have influenced him in his use of the language; and, moreover, to be able to determine, on sound principles, the subject and method of the work, the object which the writer has in view, and the means which he employs for gaining it. We are warranted, then, to expect, in an expositor, a competent knowledge of Grammar, of History, and of Logic, as without these he cannot rightly perform his functions; and to hold that an exposition, of any of the sacred books, to be thoroughly satisfactory, must be at once Grammatical, Historical, and Logical. This is requisite, whether the main object be the unfolding of principles or the illustration of the influence of these principles, in moulding the character and guiding the conduct; whether the exposition be intended to be doctrinal, or experimental, or practical, or, as it should be, all these combined.

To produce such an Exposition of the Epistle to the Romans would be to bestow, on the church and on the world, a boon of inappreciable value. Such a work remains to be executed; and its accomplishment may well be an object of ambition to Christian scholars of the highest abilities, and the most extensive attainments. Much, indeed, that is valuable, has been written on this marvellous book; but a complete Exposition of it is still a desideratum. "Multum adhuc restat operis, multumque restabit."[1]

It is more than forty years since the Epistle to the Romans became to me an object of peculiar interest, and the subject of critical study. At that time I

[1] Seneca, Ep. 64.

wrote considerably ample illustrations of it, with such helps as were within my reach. These were comparatively scanty. In addition to my Greek Testament, Lexicon, and Concordance, Poli Synopsis, a book which it would be difficult to praise beyond its merits, Bengel's Gnomon, and Koppe's Annotations, with Whitby, Locke, and Taylor, formed my principal critical apparatus. Since that time, many Exegetical works, of great and varied merit, have appeared, having for their object the Exposition of this Epistle. Besides those most valuable helps to the study of the New Testament generally—Robinson's Lexicon, Winer's Grammar of the New Testament Idioms, and Davidson's Introduction to the New Testament—I need only mention the works of Tholuck, Böhme, Fritzsche, Olshausen, Stuart, Hodge, Turner, Barnes, and Alford. These works, and an endless variety of illustrations of particular passages in the Epistle, in the Opuscula of German Exegetes, many of them of great value, have been carefully consulted by me; and my illustrations, corrected and enlarged by an increasing acquaintance with the inexhaustible subject, have, in substance, been repeatedly, though in different forms, presented to Christian congregations, and to classes of Theological Students.

Under the impression that I might be able to shed

some new light on the general design of the Epistle, and on some of the more important and obscure passages in it, I, at one time, entertained the design of either publishing, or leaving for publication, an Exposition which might have some claim to the threefold appellation of a Grammatical, Historical, and Logical Commentary. The work is still, however, so far from being what I think it ought to be, that, at my advanced period of life, I cannot reasonably expect to be able to complete it, in the way that could be desired, and I have, therefore, given up, not without a struggle, this long and fondly cherished expectation.

Yet I am unwilling to go hence without leaving some traces of the labour I have bestowed on this master-work of the apostle—without contributing some assistance, however limited, toward the production of what, whenever produced, will mark an era in the history of Scriptural Exegesis—a Complete Exposition of the Epistle to the Romans. Forbidden to build the temple, I would yet do what I can to furnish materials to him who shall be honoured to raise it.

For the last twelve months, my principal occupation has been, so to condense and remodel my work, as to present, in the fewest and plainest words, what appears to me the true meaning and force of the statements, have no doubt that important and salutary results will spring out of Professor Jowett's most unseemly attack on Paul, as an apostle, as a thinker, as a writer, and as a man. Paul's enemies "may assail him" (I again avail myself of Dr Whately's words), "but they will not only assail him in vain, but will lead, in the end, to the perfecting of his glory and the extension of his Gospel. They may scourge him uncondemned, like the Roman magistrates at Philippi; they may inflict on him the lashes of calumnious censure, but they cannot silence him; they may thrust him, as it were, into a dungeon, and fetter him with their strained interpretations; but his voice will be raised, even at the midnight of anti-Christian darkness, and will be heard effectually; his prison doors will burst open as with an earthquake, and the fetters will fall from his hands; and even strangers to Gospel truth, will fall down at the feet of him, even Paul, to make that momentous inquiry, 'What shall I do to be saved?'"

The following work is not written in a polemical spirit, nor for sectarian objects. It is quite possible, however, that some portions of it may provoke animadversion, and lead to controversy. At my age, it would be absurd to give a pledge, which could scarcely have been wisely given at any stage of life, of replying to any such animadversions, however deserving in themselves of such notice; but, in all good faith, I promise that I will carefully read and consider any suggestions which may expose the deficiencies and mistakes which, I have no doubt, are to be found in the book—count myself, in no common measure, a debtor to him who enables me to supply the one, and correct the other, and take care that, should these illustrations ever be presented to the world in a re-impression, such favours shall be at once improved and acknowledged.

It would be injustice to my own sense of obligation, to conclude this Preface without acknowledging the kind and valuable assistance of my esteemed friend, the Reverend Peter Davidson, in carrying this work through the press. The omission of such a recognition would be the less pardonable, as this is not the first, nor the second time, that he has, in this way, been "my helper."

JOHN BROWN.

Arthur Lodge,
July 1857.

CONTENTS.

PART THIRD.

PART FOURTH.

ANALYTICAL EXPOSITION.

PRELIMINARY REMARKS—DESIGN OF THE WORK—DIVISION OF THE EPISTLE.

THE Epistle to the Romans is the nearest approach of anything in the inspired volume to a systematic view of Christianity. The design of the following work is to present, with as much conciseness as is compatible with perspicuity, such a view of the statements and illustrations, of the doctrine and law of Christ, contained in that remarkable composition, as may at once induce the conviction that, apart from its undoubted claims to Divine inspiration, it deserves to be regarded as a piece of deep and close thinking instinct with appropriate emotion, on the most important subjects which can occupy the human faculties; and, at the same time, lead, on the part of Christians at large, to the devotement of a measure of attention to its study, in some degree proportioned to its doctrinal and practical value.

Such a study of this Divine book, were it to become general, would not only soon tell powerfully on the improvement of individual character, but, through this best of channels, would lead to the attainment of the great purposes of Christianity, both within the pale of the Church and beyond it. It was what Paul believed and felt that made him what he was:

in the degree in which men believe and feel *that*, they will be like him; and when men are generally like Paul, there will be little to wish for the Church or for the world.

The Prolegomena, usually prefixed to commentaries, would be here out of place. The reader may be amply furnished with the information he may wish, as to the author, origin, authenticity, inspiration, and literature of the Epistle, in the commentaries of Tholuck, Stuart, and Hodge, and in the Introductions to the New Testament by Michaelis, Hug, Schott, Horne, and Dr Samuel Davidson; which last work contains a full and accurate statement of the results of the latest inquiries on these subjects. Rambach's "Introductio Historico-Theologica in Epistolam Pauli ad Romanos," to which is appended Luther's truly "Aurea Prefatio," is warmly recommended to the student. Its matter and spirit are equally admirable; the latter, especially, furnishing a striking contrast to that of some of the later German interpreters,[1] whose acuteness and learning we would gladly secure at any price short of the taking along with them their unduly high estimate of themselves, and their unduly low estimate of the sacred books and their authors.

The Epistle to the Romans, in its general plan, resembles the other Pauline epistles. After the Salutation and a few introductory statements, we have a set of doctrinal discussions, followed by a number of practical exhortations, and the Epistle is concluded by a variety of miscellaneous remarks. The parts of the Epistle, then, are four—INTRODUCTORY, DOCTRINAL, PRACTICAL, and CONCLUDING.

The introductory part occupies the first seventeen verses of the first chapter;—the doctrinal reaches from the eighteenth verse of the first chapter, down to the end of the eleventh chapter;—the practical begins with the twelfth chapter, and ends with the thirteenth verse of the fifteenth chapter;—and the concluding portion occupies the rest of the Epistle. Each of these parts naturally resolves itself into a variety of subdivisions.

[1] Rückert and Fritzsche may be considered as favourable specimens of the class of exegetes referred to.

PART I.

INTRODUCTORY.

THE Salutation and the Introduction proper are the two sections of the first division; the Salutation being included in the first seven verses, and the Introduction in the following ten verses.

SECTION I.

SALUTATION.

CHAPTER i. 1–7.—Paul, a servant of Jesus Christ, called to be an apostle, separated unto the gospel of God (which he had promised afore by his prophets in the holy Scriptures) concerning his Son Jesus Christ our Lord, which was made of the seed of David according to the flesh, and declared to be the Son of God with power, according to the Spirit of holiness, by the resurrection from the dead; by whom we have received grace and apostleship, for obedience to the faith among all nations, for his name; among whom are ye also the called of Jesus Christ: to all that be in Rome, beloved of God, called to be saints: Grace to you, and peace, from God our Father, and the Lord Jesus Christ.

In the salutation the writer describes himself by his name "Paul," and by his office "a servant of Jesus Christ,[1] called[2] to be an apostle,[3] separated," set apart "to" declare "the

[1] Jos. i. 1; Jud. ii. 8; Psal. cxxxii. 10.

[2] κλητὸς may be construed either by itself as if it were a substantive, or in construction with ἀπόστολος. In the first case it would correspond with "grace" (ver. 5) in the other with "apostleship."

[3] See article *Apostle* in Kitto's Cyclopædia.

Gospel of God"[1]—good news which come from God,[2] which He had announced, as to be proclaimed at a future season, by His prophets in the sacred writings,[3] and which have for their great subject "His Son Jesus Christ our Lord," who, as to His human nature, was a descendant of David;[4] but who as to His higher nature—the Divine—"the Spirit of Holiness"[5] was, and, "by the resurrection from the dead,"[6] was clearly proved[7] to be, "the Son of God."[8]

Having stated that from *Him* he had received what he accounted "a grace"—no common favour,[9] the office of "apostleship"—an office the object of which was to bring mankind of all nations, Romans among the rest, to believe the truth respecting this illustrious person, and yield to Him the obedience due to that name above every name, which he had "obtained by inheritance," "Lord of all;"[10] he, in the exercise of the authority connected with that office, addresses this letter to the Society of Christians, which, by means with which we are not acquainted, had been formed in Rome,[11] the capital of the Gentile world, describing them as "called of Christ Jesus, beloved of God, and called to be saints";[12] and invokes on them all heavenly and spiritual blessings—"grace and peace from God our Father and from the Lord Jesus Christ,"[13] the love of God and of Christ, in its manifestations and effects.

[1] *εὐαγ· Θεοῦ·* Θ· is the *gen. auctoris*, not *subjecti*, as is plain from what follows *περὶ κ.τ.λ.*

[2] Ver. 1. [3] Ver. 2. [4] Ver. 3.

[5] The antithesis between *κατὰ σάρκα* and *κατὰ πνεῦμα ἁγιωσύνης* fixes both the reference and the meaning. 1 Tim. iii. 16; Heb. ix. 14; 1 Pet. iii. 18.

[6] Matt. xxii. 31; Acts xvii. 32, xxiv. 21, xxvi. 23; 1 Cor. xv. 12, 13, 21, 42; Heb. vi. 2. *ἐκ* omitted *causa euphoniæ*.

[7] Theophylact explains *ὁρισθέντος* as = *ἀποδειχθέντος, βεβαιωθέντος, κριθέντος*.

[8] Ver. 4. [9] Eph. iii. 8. [10] Ver. 5. [11] Ver. 6.

[12] The appellations given to Christians are borrowed from those given to the old *peculium* of God, the Israelitish people. Comp. Exod. xix. 6 with 1 Pet. ii. 9; Num. xvi. 3; Deut. xiv. 1, 2, with 1 Tim. iii. 15; Deut. xxxii. 19; xxxiii. 3 with Phil. ii. 15; 1 John iii. 1, 2, 10; v. 1.

[13] Ver. 7.

SECTION II.

INTRODUCTION PROPER.

CHAPTER i. 8–17.—First, I thank my God through Jesus Christ for you all, that your faith is spoken of throughout the whole world. For God is my witness, whom I serve with my spirit in the Gospel of his Son, that without ceasing I make mention of you always in my prayers; making request (if by any means now at length I might have a prosperous journey by the will of God) to come unto you. For I long to see you, that I may impart unto you some spiritual gift, to the end ye may be established; that is, that I may be comforted together with you, by the mutual faith both of you and me. Now I would not have you ignorant, brethren, that oftentimes I purposed to come unto you (but was let hitherto), that I might have some fruit among you also, even as among other Gentiles. I am debtor both to the Greeks and to the Barbarians, both to the wise and to the unwise. So, as much as in me is, I am ready to preach the gospel to you that are at Rome also. For I am not ashamed of the gospel of Christ: for it is the power of God unto salvation to every one that believeth; to the Jew first, and also to the Greek. For therein is the righteousness of God revealed from faith to faith: as it is written, The just shall live by faith.

In the Introduction the apostle expresses devout gratitude for the conversion of the Romans to the faith of Christ, and for the notoriety that so important a fact, as the formation of a Christian Church in the imperial city, had gained throughout the world;[1] assures them, in an appeal to God as Him whom he worshipped in his spirit according to the Gospel of His Son,[2] that his regard for them expressed itself in unceasing prayers,[3] and particularly in a request that, if it were the will of God, he might have an opportunity of personal intercourse with them,[4] that he might gratify an earnest wish to be useful to them in establishing them by the communication of some spiritual gift,[5] and in the hope that such

[1] Ver. 8.

[2] Ver. 9.

[3] λατρεύω properly refers to religious worship. Matt. iv. 10; Acts vii. 7, 42, xxiv. 14, xxvi. 7; Heb. ix. 14; Rom. i. 25; 2 Tim. i. 3; Phil. iii 3.

[4] Ver. 10.

[5] Ver. 11.

an interview would contribute to his comfort and advantage, as well as to theirs.[1] He informs them that he had frequently intended to visit them, but had hitherto been prevented;[2] that, feeling that his apostolic mission laid him under obligations to promote the spiritual welfare of men of all countries and in all states of civilization,[3] he was exceedingly desirous of an opportunity of preaching the Gospel at Rome, in the hope that the same blessed effects might result from his labours there as at other places.[4] The principal cause of this anxious desire was his deep conviction of the transcendent excellence of the Gospel, and of its altogether peculiar efficacy in promoting the highest interests of mankind.[5] It might be supposed that he, a Jew, and therefore a natural object of dislike and contempt to Romans, might shrink from bringing before the notice of a people, characterized at this time equally by the pride of real supremacy of dominion, and of fancied superiority in refinement and wisdom, the strong statements and uncompromising claims of the new religion; but it was far otherwise: "I am ready," says he, "to preach the Gospel at Rome: for I am not ashamed of the Gospel of Christ."[6]—*i.e.* 'I count it my highest glory to proclaim it: and I may well so count it: for it is "the power of God unto salvation to every one that believeth;" and it is so because "therein is the righteousness of God revealed from faith to faith."'[7]

These words form the close of the introduction, and they bring forward the great subject of the Epistle—"The righteousness of God." On this account there are no two verses in the Epistle that have stronger claims on our attentive consideration than the 16th and 17th of the first chapter; and an additional reason for looking at them somewhat closely is, that their meaning seems generally misapprehended, or at best but very imperfectly understood.

[1] Ver. 12. The 12th verse is a beautiful example of the apostle's delicacy of feeling.

[2] Ver. 13. See Paley's Horæ Paulinæ, ch. ii. No. 3.

[3] Ver. 14. [4] Ver. 15. [5] Ver. 16.

[6] An example of the figure μείωσις or Litotes. [7] Ver. 17.

The Gospel, which is the revelation of the grace of God to man in the mission of His Son, is "the power of God unto salvation to every one that believeth." The object of the Gospel is salvation—the salvation of men; their deliverance from the state of degradation, danger, and misery, into which sin has brought them; their deliverance from guilt or condemnation, from ignorance and error, from depravity and suffering in all their forms—complete everlasting deliverance from all these. This is what the Gospel proposes to effect:—it proposes to confer on man an extent and variety of enduring blessing of which mere human philanthropy never dreamed, and to the attainment of which all the most powerful ameliorating agencies, such as philosophy and commerce, government and education, are not merely altogether inadequate, but utterly unfitted. But the Gospel *has*, *is*, POWER to effect such a salvation; it meets all man's wants as a rational, active, fallen, immortal being, and provides for the supply of these wants. It has that in it which can make foolish man wise, sinful man holy, miserable man happy. It has that in it which can make man's endless being a source of indefinite improvement in knowledge, excellence, and happiness.

This power of the Gospel is not intrinsic, but is derived from its author. It thus has, and is, "power unto salvation," for it is "the power of God." It is His instrument—formed by Him, wielded by Him. It is *He*—He alone that saves. The knowledge of truth—the pardon of sin—the transformation of the mind and heart—good hope—eternal life,—these are all *His* gifts. Who but He could give them? "Their greatness speaks their author."[1] But while He is their author, the Gospel is the instrumentality suited to the constitution and circumstances of man, by which God communicates these benefits. The Gospel is God's efficacious means of saving man: that is the meaning of "the Gospel is the power of God unto salvation." This Gospel is not only powerful, but *all* powerful. There is no man, however degraded, guilty, depraved, and miserable, that it cannot save.

[1] George Herbert.

But the Gospel can act only according to its nature. It is Gospel—good news; but good news from the very nature of the case must be heard, understood, believed, in order to their imparting satisfaction. The Gospel is a revelation of divine truth—and while it can, while it certainly will save all that believe it—it cannot save those who are ignorant of it—who neglect it, who misapprehend it, who reject it—who do not understand and believe it. The Gospel is "the power of God unto salvation to every one that believeth:" in other words—"The Gospel believed is God's effectual method of saving mankind." In this we find a very good reason both why Paul should not be ashamed of the Gospel, and why he should wish to preach it. It is the appointed and the effectual method for making men—without reference to nation or country, or measure of previous guilt, depravity, and misery—truly happy. Is this a thing to be ashamed of? And it is by being believed that it can alone serve its purpose; therefore, who that is called to so high and holy an office would not be "ready" to preach it? How can men be saved through an unheard, unbelieved Gospel? and how are they to hear it, how are they to believe it, if it is not made known to them.[1]

The apostle has thus very satisfactorily, in the 16th verse, accounted for his not being "ashamed of the Gospel of Christ:" let us now attend to the account he gives in the 17th, of the way in which the Gospel is what he declares it to be—God's effectual method of making those who believe it holy and happy. "The Gospel is the power of God unto salvation to every one that believeth—for therein is the righteousness of God revealed from faith to faith." These words are, I am afraid, very imperfectly understood by most who read them. Indeed, as they stand in our version, it would be very difficult to bring a distinct meaning out of them. "The righteousness of God" is a phrase which, in the New Testament, is ordinarily employed in a somewhat peculiar way; being almost

[1] See chap. x. 11–15.

uniformly used in reference to the subject of the sinner's justification before God.[1] "Righteousness," with the Apostle Paul, usually signifies justification—sometimes viewed as a privilege bestowed by God—sometimes a benefit enjoyed by men. The Gospel is said, in opposition to the law, which is the ministration of condemnation and death, to be "the ministration of righteousness"—that is justification—and, "of the Spirit."[2] Christians are said to be "of God in Christ Jesus, righteousness, sanctification, and redemption"[3]—*i.e.* justified, sanctified, and redeemed. They are said to be "made the righteousness of God in Christ Jesus"[4]—*i.e.* they are justified in the sight of God as united to Christ Jesus. The long description of "the righteousness of God," in the concluding paragraph of the third chapter of this epistle, exactly suits the Divine method of justification, and it suits nothing else; I therefore consider "the righteousness of God" here, as meaning God's way of treating a sinner as if he were just, in consistency with his own righteousness—'the Divine method of justification.' The words, "from faith,"[5] or "by faith," should be connected with "the righteousness of God," and not with the word "revealed:" The righteousness of God by faith is revealed, or the righteousness of God is revealed as of faith—*i.e.* In the Gospel a revelation of the Divine method of justification by faith is made. The concluding clause, "to faith,"[6] is equivalent to —"in order to faith,"—or, "that it may be believed." The complete sentiment in the 17th verse is—"In the Gospel there is a revelation of the Divine method of justification by faith, made in order to be believed;" and the apostle's assertion is—"It is this which fits the Gospel for being what it is —God's effectual means of saving all who believe."

Nor is it difficult to perceive that it is indeed so, and that it

[1] See Storr. Opusc. I. Voorst Annotat. Rom. i. 17; iii. 21, 22, 25, 26; x. 5. Zimmermann Com. de vi et sensu, Δικαιοσύνη Θεοῦ. Winzer. program. de voce. δίκαιος, δικαιοσύνη, et δικαιοῦν. Stuart's Comment. Fritzsche, in loc.

[2] 2 Cor. iii. 8, 9. [3] 1 Cor. i. 30. [4] 2 Cor. v. 21. [5] ἐκ πίστεως.

[6] εἰς πίστιν. For a similar use of εἰς, see chap. x. 10.

could not be otherwise. Nothing could be an effectual means of saving sinful man, that did not embrace "a method of justification;" for man's sin is the cause of all that he needs to be delivered from. Deliverance from the condemning sentence of the divine law is then the fundamental blessing of his salvation. So long as he continues under the curse, he can neither be holy nor happy. It is equally plain that an efficient means for saving man must embrace and disclose the *divine* method of justification. Humanly devised methods of justification can serve no purpose. It is God, whose law we have offended, who must decide whether there is to be any way of justification for man, and if so, what that way of justification is to be. Men's methods of justification increase guilt instead of removing it. Still farther, a method of justification in any other way than "by faith"—a method in which such a condition in the form of working, as would have been consistent with the Divine honour to enact—would not have suited fallen man. With him, where this is law, there is sure to be transgression; so that a method of justification by works could never have done him any good. If he is to be justified at all, he must, in believing, receive as a free gift, what he never can earn as the stipulated reward of stipulated labour. And, finally, as a great part of the benefits of a method of justification must arise from the moral effect of its details on the mind of the justified sinner, this Divine method of justification must be revealed, that it may be believed, and thus become influential in saving men, by making them holy and happy. The Gospel then has every thing necessary for its purpose which such an instrument can have—a method of justification—the Divine method of justification—a method of justification by grace, not by merit—by faith, not by works; and a revelation of all this, in plain terms, and with abundant evidence, so that it may be believed, and by being believed, become effectual for saving man. This Divine method of justification by faith, revealed in the Gospel, is the great subject in the sequel, and with the announcement of it, concludes the introductory part, of the Epistle.

PART II.

DOCTRINAL.

The doctrinal part of the epistle, which, beginning at the 18th verse of the 1st chapter, ends with the 11th chapter, may be divided into two great sections. In the first of these, the necessity of the Divine method of justification is proved; and in the second, its nature, and influence, and results are illustrated.

SECTION I.

OF THE NECESSITY OF THE DIVINE METHOD OF JUSTIFICATION, FROM THE UNIVERSAL STATE OF CONDEMNATION AND MORAL HELPLESSNESS OF FALLEN MAN.

Chapter i. 18–iii. 20.—For the wrath of God is revealed from heaven against all ungodliness and unrighteousness of men, who hold the truth in unrighteousness; because that which may be known of God is manifest in them: for God hath showed it unto them. For the invisible things of Him from the creation of the world are clearly seen, being understood by the things that are made, even his eternal power and Godhead; so that they are without excuse: because that, when they knew God, they glorified Him not as God, neither were thankful; but became vain in their imaginations, and their foolish heart was darkened. Professing themselves to be wise, they became fools, and changed the glory of the uncorruptible God into an image made like to corruptible man, and to birds, and four-footed beasts, and creeping things. Wherefore God also gave them up to uncleanness through the lusts of their own hearts, to dishonour their own bodies between themselves: who changed the truth of God into a lie, and worshipped and served the creature more than the Creator, who is blessed for ever. Amen. For this cause God gave them up unto vile affections: for even their women did change the natural use into that which is against nature: and likewise also the men, leaving the natural use of the woman, burned in their lust one toward another; men with men working that which is unseemly, and receiving in themselves that recompence of their error which was meet. And even as they did not like to retain God in their knowledge, God gave them over to a reprobate mind, to do those things which are not convenient: being filled with all unrighteousness, fornication, wickedness, covetousness, maliciousness; full of envy, murder, debate, deceit, malignity; whisperers, backbiters, haters of God, despiteful, proud, boasters, inventors of evil things, disobedient to parents, without understanding, covenant-breakers, without natural affection, implacable, unmerciful: who, knowing the judgment of God, that they which commit such things are worthy of death, not only do the same, but have pleasure in them that do them. Therefore thou art inexcusable, O man, whosoever thou art that judgest: for wherein thou judgest another, thou condemnest thyself: for thou that judgest doest the same things. But we are sure that the judgment of God is according to truth against them which commit such things. And thinkest thou this, O man, that judgest them which do such things, and doest the same, that thou shalt escape the judgment of God? Or despisest thou the riches of His goodness, and forbearance, and long-suffering; not knowing that the goodness of God leadeth thee to repentance? But after thy hardness and impenitent heart treasurest up unto thyself wrath against the day of wrath and revelation of the righteous judgment of God; who will render to every man according to his deeds: to them who, by patient continuance in well-doing, seek for glory, and honour, and immortality, eternal life; but unto them that are contentious, and do not obey the truth, but obey unrighteousness, indignation and wrath, tribulation and anguish, upon every soul of man that doeth evil, of the Jew first, and also of the Gentile: but glory, honour, and peace, to every man that worketh good; to the Jew first, and also to the Gentile: for there is no respect of persons with God. For as many as have sinned without law, shall also perish without law; and as many as have sinned in the law, shall be judged by the law; (for not the hearers of the law are just before God, but the doers of the law shall be justified. For when the Gentiles, which have not the law, do by nature the things contained in the law, these, having not the law, are a law unto themselves; which show the work of the law written in their hearts, their conscience also bearing witness, and their thoughts the mean while accusing or else excusing one another;) in the day when God shall judge the secrets of men by Jesus Christ, according to my Gospel. Behold thou art called a Jew, and restest in the law, and makest thy boast of God, and knowest His will, and approvest the things that are more excellent, being instructed out of the law; and art confident that thou thyself art a guide of the blind, a light of them which are in darkness, an instructor of the foolish, a teacher of babes, which hast the form of knowledge and of the truth in the law. Thou therefore which teachest another, teachest thou not thyself? thou that preachest a man should not steal, dost thou steal? thou that sayest a man should not commit adultery, dost thou commit adultery? thou that abhorrest idols, dost thou commit sacrilege? thou that makest thy boast of the law, through breaking the law dishonourest thou God? For the name of God is blasphemed among the Gentiles through you, as it is written. For circumcision verily profiteth, if thou keep the law: but if thou be a breaker of the law, thy circumcision is made uncircumcision. Therefore if the uncircumcision keep the righteousness of the law, shall not his uncircumcision be counted for circumcision? And shall not uncircumcision which is by nature, if it fulfil the law, judge thee, who by the letter and circumcision dost transgress the law? For he is not a Jew, which is one outwardly; neither is that circumcision which is outward in the flesh: but he is a Jew, which is one inwardly; and circumcision is that of the heart, in the spirit, and not in the letter; whose praise is not of men, but of God. What advantage then hath the Jew? or what profit is there of circumcision? Much every way: chiefly, because that unto them were committed the oracles of God. For what if some did not believe? shall their unbelief make the faith of God without effect? God forbid: yea, let God be true, but every man a liar; as it is written, That thou mightest be justified in thy sayings, and mightest overcome when thou art judged. But if our unrighteousness commend the righteousness of God, what shall we say? Is God unrighteous who taketh vengeance? (I speak as a man) God forbid: for then how shall God judge the world? For if the truth of God hath more abounded through my lie unto His glory; why yet am I also judged as a sinner? And not rather, (as we be slanderously reported, and as some affirm that we say,) Let us do evil, that good may come? whose damnation is just. What then? are we better than they? No, in no wise: for we have before proved both Jews and Gentiles, that they are all under sin; as it is written, There is none righteous, no, not one: there is none that understandeth, there is none that seeketh after God. They are all gone out of the way, they are together become unprofitable; there is none that doeth good, no, not one. Their throat is an open sepulchre: with their tongues they have used deceit: the poison of asps is under their lips: whose mouth is full of cursing and bitterness: their feet are swift to shed blood: destruction and misery are in their ways; and the way of peace have they not known: there is no fear of God before their eyes. Now we know, that what things soever the law saith, it saith to them who are under the law: that every mouth may be stopped, and all the world may become guilty before God. Therefore by the deeds of the law there shall no flesh be justified in His sight: for by the law is the knowledge of sin.

Laying a deep foundation for his argument in the principles, that the Supreme Ruler is displeased at impiety and injustice,[1] and that all mankind have—from the frame of

[1] Ver. 18.

nature, the dispensations of Providence, the constitution and working of their own minds, to say nothing of early revelations which ought to have been preserved, and fragments of which were to be in part found among all nations—the means of obtaining such a knowledge of God as ought to lead them to venerate and obey Him; the apostle proceeds to show what a career of departure from God, by ignorance, and error, and idolatry, and injustice, and cruelty, and impurity, the race of man had run.[1]

The details in the latter part of the first chapter of the downward course of mankind, are absolutely frightful, and we might have been apt to suspect the apostle of exaggeration, were there not abundant evidence, in the pages of contemporary pagan literature, that the darkest features of the picture are drawn from life.[2]

In establishing his charge against the human race, he avails himself of the striking fact, that mankind were often self-condemned, allowing in themselves practices which they censured in others,[3] and states the great principle on which the moral government of God is founded, and which will regulate those sentences which will fix the final state of mankind, that responsibility is proportioned to advantage, and that every man will receive according to his deeds. The privileges of those who have enjoyed a Divine revelation, being an aggravation of guilt, will be no shield from punishment; and the disadvantages of those who have been destitute of a Divine revelation, though they lessen guilt, will by no means secure impunity.[4]

That part of the apostle's argument, illustrative of the principle that "there is no respect of persons with God," is of so much importance in itself, and is in general so completely misapprehended, that it may serve a good purpose to say a few words in the way of unfolding its meaning and force.

[1] Ver. 19–32.

[2] See Tholuck "On the Nature and Moral Influences of Heathenism, especially among the Greeks and Romans."—Biblical Cabinet xxviii.

[3] Chap. ii. 1.

[4] Ver. 2–11.

The passage I refer to is contained in the 11th, 12th, 13th, 14th, and 15th verses of the second chapter, "There is no respect of *persons* with God."[1] "He renders to every man according to his *work;*" taking into equitable consideration the means which every individual has enjoyed of knowing "what is good, and what God has required of man." "As many as have sinned without law,[2] shall also perish without law."[3] They who have not enjoyed a Divine revelation shall be punished for their *sins,* but their punishment shall not be what it would have been had they enjoyed a Divine revelation. "And as many as have sinned in the law"—under the law—"shall be judged by the law."[4] They who enjoyed a Divine revelation will be considered guilty in every case in which they have transgressed the law, and shall be subjected to the punishment the law denounces against their transgression. An unimproved revelation—a violated law deepens guilt, aggravates punishment. The wicked Jew was a privileged person here, but his privilege will be no shield to him in the day of judgment. It is not "the hearing of the law," the having possessed Divine revelation, that can do a man any good in the day of the revelation of the righteous judgment of God. If a claim for reward is presented, it must rest on "the doing of the law," on the revelation being rightly improved.[5]

There can thus be no doubt that those who have had a revelation are proper subjects of a final judgment. But how does it accord with the Divine justice, that they who have had no such revelation, should yet be judged and punished? The apostle's answer to this question is in the 14th and 15th verses. "For when the Gentiles which have not the law, do by nature the things contained in the law, these, having not the law, are a law to themselves, which show the work of the law written in their hearts; their conscience also bearing witness, and their thoughts the meanwhile accusing or else excusing one another."

[1] Ver 11.

[2] *ἀνόμως* is usually = *παρανόμως*. Here it is — *χωρὶς νόμου*. *ἔννομος* and *ἄνομος* are contrasted, 1 Cor. ix. 20, 21.

[3] Ver. 12. [4] Ver. 12. [5] Ver. 13.

This is the reason for what the apostle had said in the first clause of the 12th verse, "As many as have sinned without law, shall also perish without law." It has generally been supposed that the apostle asserts, in the 14th verse, that the Gentiles, who had not a written revelation of God's will, did by nature the duties required in the written revelation which the Jews possessed. It is quite plain that this, as a general assertion, is not true—is indeed the very reverse of true—is notoriously false. Did the Gentiles generally "love God with all their heart, and soul, and strength, and mind, and did they love their neighbour as themselves?" You have the answer to this question in the end of the previous chapter. And even with regard to such rare exceptions as Socrates, with what large limitations must we use the words before we can say that even they did the things contained in the law, in the sense of performing the actions it prescribes? Besides, what bearing would such a statement, even supposing it to be true, have on the proof, that they who have not the law shall perish without law. The truth is, the phrase 'to do *the things of the law*,' which our translators have unwarrantably rendered to "do the things *contained in* the law," describes not the yielding of obedience to the law, but the performing of the functions of the law.[1] The proper business of law is to say, "This is right, that is wrong—you ought to do this, you ought not to do that—you will be rewarded if you do this, you shall be punished if you do that." To command, to forbid, to promise, to threaten —these are "the things of the law," or "the work of the law," as it is in verse 15. The apostle's assertion is this,—an assertion exactly accordant with truth, and directly bearing on his argument,—'The Gentiles who have no written

[1] Aristot. Rhet., 1, 15, 7, has *οὐ γὰρ ποιεῖ τὸ ἔργον τὸ τοῦ νόμου*, does not do the office of the law. It seems a phrase similar to *ποιεῖν τὰ τοῦ πατρὸς*, to act the part of a father. "*τὸ ἔργον τοῦ νόμου*, non est id quod lex jubet, sed id quod lex facit. Quid facit lex? Jubet, convincit, damnat, punit. Hoc ipsum facit Ethnicus quidam, simul ac incipit adolescere."—CAPPELLUS. An able defence, by Dr W. Peddie, then a student, of this mode of exegesis is to be found in the Christian Monitor, vol. v., p. 485.

Divine law, perform by nature, from their very constitution, to themselves and each other, the functions of such a law. They make a distinction between right and wrong, just as they do between truth and falsehood. They cannot help doing so. They often go wrong by mistaking what is right and what is wrong, as they often go wrong by mistaking what is true and what is false. But they approve themselves and one another when doing what they think right; they disapprove themselves and one another when they do what they think to be wrong; so that, though they have no written law, they act the part of a law to themselves. This capacity, this necessity of their nature, distinguishes them from brutes, and makes them the subjects of Divine moral government. In this way they show "that the work of the law"—not the work required by the law, but the work which the law does—is "written in their hearts," enwoven in their constitution, by the actings of the power we call conscience, which is a constituent part of human nature. It is just, then, that they should be punished for doing what they knew to be wrong, or might have known to be wrong; it is just that they who sinned without law should perish, though it would not be just to punish them for what, in consequence of their not having the law, they could not have known to be wrong. The Gentile sinner, as well as the Jewish sinner, is justly condemned, and if not pardoned, must, ought, and will be, punished—proportionally punished.'

The charge of guilt is brought home to the Jew with great force in the concluding part of the second chapter, from the 17th verse to the end: and the refuges of lies, in which he was accustomed to seek for shelter, are swept away as by an overflowing flood of eloquent argument. Thus the fact, on which the necessity of such a restorative scheme as the Divine method of justification is based, is established as to the race of man in both its constituent parts; those who had a revelation, and those who had none—the Jews and the Gentiles.

In the beginning of the third chapter, the apostle shows that what he has said is in no way inconsistent with the fact, that the

Jews possessed great advantages above the Gentiles. "To them were committed the oracles of God."[1] These words are commonly supposed to mean,—'They were made the depositories of the Divine revelation,'—as the Psalmist says, "He showeth His word unto Jacob: His statutes and His judgments to Israel. He hath not dealt so with any nation."[2] This was no doubt a great distinguishing privilege, but the course of the apostle's reasoning seems to make it evident that it is not to this he refers, but to what he states more fully in other words in chap. ix. 3, "To them pertained the promises." "With them were established the oracles of God." Peculiar promises were made to the Jews as a nation. But might the Jewish objector say—If, according to your doctrine, we Jews are all under the condemning sentence of God's law for our unbelief and disobedience, how can we be the better for these promises? And must not God's pledged faith or faithfulness be forfeited?[3] No, says the apostle, God will fulfil His promises to them to whom they are made. He will show Himself true, whoever be unfaithful. The unbeliever may well exclude himself from the enjoyment of the promises, but there will be a believing Israel to whom the promises will be performed.[4] This is illustrated, at great length, in the ninth chapter of the epistle. In answer to the suggestion, that the Jews should not be punished because their unfaithfulness served but as a foil to set off the faithfulness of God,[5] the apostle answers, that, on the same principle, that might be denied which the Jews held very fast, to wit, that God would "judge," that is, condemn, punish "the world"[6]—the Gentiles; for their sins, as well as those of the Jews, would be overruled to the display of His glory and the attainment of His purposes; and that this principle, followed out to its fair consequences, leads to the monstrously absurd and shockingly impious conclusion—"Let us do evil that good may come."[7]

While the apostle thus admits that Jews were more highly

[1] Chap. iii. 1, 2. [2] Psalm cxlvii. 19, 20. [3] Ver. 3.
[4] Ver. 4. [5] Ver. 5. [6] Ver. 6.
[7] Ver. 7, 8.

privileged than Gentiles, he holds, that in reference to the great question of justification before God, the former were "in no wise better" than the latter.[1] And he might well do so; for he had, in the two preceding chapters, clearly "proved that both Jews and Gentiles are all under sin." He then clothes in language, borrowed from a great variety of passages in the Old Testament, the judgment to which he had been conducted in reference to the state and character of fallen man. "There is none righteous, no, not one; there is none that understandeth; there is none that seeketh after God. They are all gone out of the way, they are together become unprofitable; there is none that doeth good, no, not one. Their throat is an open sepulchre: with their tongues have they used deceit: the poison of asps is under their lips: whose mouth is full of cursing and bitterness: their feet are swift to shed blood. Destruction and misery are in their ways: and the way of peace have they not known. There is no fear of God before their eyes."[2] The language of these passages of Scripture, referring most of them to certain individuals, in various ages, is used by the apostle, as a man speaking under the inspiration of the Holy Ghost, to describe the true spiritual state of the fallen race. This is what men, left to themselves, unchanged by Divine influence, are and ever have been.

On the general principle that "whatsoever law says, it says to them who are under law," he comes to the conclusion that "the whole world"—all mankind, must have a verdict of "guilty before God" recorded against them.[3] The revealed law proclaims, "Cursed is every one who continueth not in all things written in the book of the law to do them;" and the law of nature, in the human conscience, proclaims, 'He who does what he knows to be wrong—he who does not what he knows to be right, deserves to be punished.' No man under the revealed law has continued in all things written in the book to do them. No man under the natural law has always done what he knew to be right, always avoided what he knew to be

[1] Ver. 9. [2] Ver. 10-18. [3] Ver. 19.

wrong. On the principles of the revealed law, and on the principles of natural law, the Jew and the Gentile are equally brought in guilty before God, and are equally exposed to "the wrath of God which is revealed from heaven against all ungodliness and unrighteousness of men, who hold the truth in unrighteousness."

Man, every man, thus is condemned and needs a method of justification. His relations towards God are out of order—they are full of danger—they need to be re-adjusted in order to his being safe, for he is "condemned, and the wrath of God abides on him."

But may not man, by his own exertions, be restored to the Divine favour, which he undoubtedly has lost? May he not be justified "by the deeds of the law?" by obedience to the law which he has violated? The thing, says the apostle, is demonstrably impossible—"By the law is the knowledge of sin."[1] 'The law proves and pronounces man to be a sinner.' How can it then acquit or justify him? It says, Thou deservest punishment, how then can it say thou deservest reward? "As many as are of the works of the law," who seek justification by these works, "are under the curse; for it is written, Cursed is every one who continueth not in all things written in the book of the law to do them."[2] The state of the sinner is one of utter moral helplessness. The law does nothing—can do nothing—in reference to its violator, but condemn and curse him. Can any expectation be more obviously absurd than that that law, whatever it may be to the innocent and obedient, should be to the sinner the instrument of justification?

"No hope can on the law be built
Of justifying grace;
The law, which shows the sinner's guilt,
Condemns him to his face.

"Silent let Jew and Gentile stand,
Without one vaunting word;
And, humbled low, confess their guilt
Before heaven's righteous Lord."

[1] Ver. 20. [2] Gal. iii. 10.

Such is the substance of the first great section of the doctrinal part of the Epistle to the Romans. The object of this section is plainly to show, that apart from "the righteousness of God" which the Gospel reveals, there is no hope for man—none for the race—none for the individual. No human being can be saved in consistency with the Divine justice, on the principles of violated law. Every man has violated God's law, every man deserves punishment; and, but for "the righteousness of God by faith," every man must be punished. Put that out of view, and look forward to "the day of the revelation of the righteous judgment of God." The whole race are there. But "all have sinned, all have lost the approbation of God," none have "obeyed the truth," all have "obeyed unrighteousness." What, then, but for the Divine method of justification, must have awaited the whole sinning race but "indignation and wrath," "wrath to the uttermost," "tribulation and anguish," "everlasting destruction from the presence of the Lord and from the glory of His power."

Such, then, were mankind as a race—such was man, as an individual, in the days of the Apostle Paul. It is a question of deep interest, How far does his description of the world, and of the individual men of the first century, apply to the world and individual men of the nineteenth? Except so far as "the righteousness of God," the Divine method of justification, operating through the Gospel which reveals it, has directly or indirectly influenced the state of the race and individuals, we must answer to the question, "What, then, are we better than they? No, in no wise." Look at our world. Is it not in open rebellion against its Maker? Does it not lie enslaved under the wicked one? Fearful as were the impieties, and impurities, and cruelties, of the ancient pagan world, would it be difficult to find parallels to the foulest of them in the pagan world of our own time? Is there not reason to fear that there is as much idolatry and impurity to be found in modern Rome as in ancient Rome? What is the moral character of the great cities of the most civilized countries on our earth—of such cities as Paris, London, New York, New Orleans? How much shameless vice prevails in our own city? I am a believer in the progress of human society. I believe that things in reference to our race, as a whole, are better, aye, much better, than they were in the days of the Apostle Paul, and that the amelioration is to be traced to the mediate or immediate influences of Christianity; but assuredly, we have abundant evidence that the wickedness of man is still great upon the earth, that the earth is still corrupt before God,—that the earth is still full of violence; and in the fact, that from the employment of the best means of improvement for so many centuries, results so inadequate have been obtained, we have a very strong proof of the refractory nature of the materials to which they have been applied.

The state of the world would be altogether hopeless, in a religious and moral point of view, were it not for that Gospel which reveals and applies the righteousness of God. Just in the degree in which that Gospel is believed among men will there be moral improvement. The believers are "transformed by the renewing of their minds;" and, in a great variety of ways, their internal change operates in the way of producing a salutary external change on the character and conduct of those who do not believe. It is Christianity, chiefly, that has raised our nation from the condition of painted savages, to its height of civilisation and greatness. The world will never be made moral but by being made Christian. The world will never be cured of idolatry, and gross impurity, and barbarous cruelty, but by the Gospel—that "mystery which was kept secret from former ages, but is now manifested—being made known by the Scriptures of the prophets, according to the commandment of the everlasting God, to all nations for the obedience of faith." That—that alone—can do it. Let us show that we are not ashamed of the Gospel, by employing it for the purpose of converting the world; for it alone is the power of God to salvation to every one that believeth: for therein is a revelation of the Divine method of justification given that it may be believed—and if to be believed, assuredly that it may be proclaimed to those who are ignorant of it.

And as to the individual man of the nineteenth century, is he not in state and character just what the man of the first century was? There were then, as there are now, men pardoned, and purified, washed, sanctified, justified;—there were such men under the former economy, but they had all become so by the "righteousness of God,"—a system which came into operation immediately on the fall of man. All who have been pardoned, all who have been sanctified, have been so through the great sacrifice on which this method of justification is based, through the good Spirit whose influence it secured, and through the faith of the truth respecting the saving character of God manifested in these two inseparable gifts. Originally they were all guilty and depraved, "children of wrath," slaves of sin, "even as others." And is it not still true that every man is a sinner—that every man has violated God's law, and incurred its curse, and by depravity utterly unfitted himself for communion with God in holy happiness. Such is the universal condition of man, and it must remain his perpetual condition, but for "the righteousness of God" which the Gospel reveals. Such is the original state of every child of Adam. Continuing in this state he is lost, utterly lost, lost for ever. There is no deliverance from this state but through "the righteousness of God;" there is no interest in the pardoning, justifying, sanctifying, saving influences of "this righteousness of God," but by the belief of the truth in reference to it. It is under the new economy manifested to *all*, but it takes effect only on *all that believe.* He that believeth is not condemned: *he* can never come into condemnation. He that believeth not is condemned already, and if he continues an unbeliever, the wrath of God must abide on him. It is an unspeakable privilege to have this "righteousness of God" revealed to us, but that privilege will produce only increased guilt, deeper punishment, if the truth revealed is not by faith brought into the mind and made influential over the heart. That truth, believed by the individual, secures the salvation of the soul. That truth, generally embraced by the world, would effect that regeneration, to produce which, philosophy, and government, and civilisation, and education, have so long laboured in vain.

SECTION II.

THE RIGHTEOUSNESS OF GOD, OR, THE DIVINE METHOD OF JUSTIFICATION.

CHAPTER III. 21–CHAPTER XI. 36.

I NOW proceed to the second great section of the doctrinal part of the Epistle, which may receive for its title—"Of the Divine Method of Justification." It begins at the 21st verse of the third chapter, and ends at the close of the eleventh; and resolves itself into a considerable number of sub-sections. —The first, which occupies the close of chapter iii., from ver. 21, may be entitled, "A General Account of the Divine Method of Justification."—The second fills the fourth chapter, and may be entitled, "The Testimony of the Law and the Prophets to the Divine Method of Justification, as 'without Law,' 'by Faith'—'the Faith of Christ'—and 'upon all them that Believe.'"—The third section is contained in the fifth chapter, and has for its subject—"The Divine Method of Justification 'Free'—'by God's Grace'—'through the Redemption that is in Christ Jesus.'"—The fourth occupies the whole of the sixth and seventh chapters, and the eighth chapter down to the 17th verse. The subject is, "The Bearing of the Divine Method of Justification on the Spiritual Transformation of Man."—The fifth section fills the remaining part of the eighth chapter, and may be entitled—"The Consistency of the Sufferings of the present time, to which Believers are Exposed, with the Reality and Permanence of the Blessings secured to them by the Divine Method of Justification."—The sixth and last of these sub-divisions has for its subject, "The Relations of Mankind, viewed as divided into Jews and Gentiles, to the Manifested Divine Method of Justification," and occupies the whole of the ninth, tenth, and eleventh chapters. We proceed to the examination of these in their order.

§ 1. *A General Account of the Divine Method of Justification.*

CHAPTER III. 21–31.—" But now the righteousness of God without the law is manifested, being witnessed by the law and the prophets; even the righteousness of God, which is by faith of Jesus Christ unto all and upon all them that believe; for there is no difference: for all have sinned, and come short of the glory of God: being justified freely by His grace, through the redemption that is in Christ Jesus; whom God hath set forth to be a propitiation through faith in His blood, to declare His righteousness for the remission of sins that are past, through the forbearance of God; to declare, I say, at this time His righteousness; that He might be just, and the justifier of him which believeth in Jesus. Where is boasting then? It is excluded. By what law? of works? Nay; but by the law of faith. Therefore we conclude, that a man is justified by faith without the deeds of the law. Is He the God of the Jews only? is He not also of the Gentiles? Yes, of the Gentiles also: seeing it is one God which shall justify the circumcision by faith, and uncircumcision through faith. Do we then make void the law through faith? God forbid: yea, we establish the law."

It were unreasonable to expect, in an epistolary composition, the formal method of a professedly regular treatise; yet, in this first sub-section, we shall find almost all the topics brought forward which are discussed at large in the sequel, and brought forward, too, in nearly the same order in which they are there discussed. These eleven verses bear, to the remaining part of the section, a relation very similar to that which the laying down of the method does to the body of a treatise, or the stating the leading divisions and sub-divisions, the heads and particulars, as they are called, does to the rest of a pulpit discourse. The leading features of the Divine method of justification, as here sketched, are these:—(1.) It is "without the law"[1]—apart from law—not by law; (2.) It is "witnessed by the law and the prophets;"[2] (3.) It is "by the faith of Jesus Christ;"[3] (4.) It is now "manifested to all;"[4] (5.) It takes effect "on all them that believe;"[5] (6.) It treats all mankind as on the same level in reference to it;[6] (7.) In reference to man, its character is gratuitousness;[7]

[1] Ver. 21. [2] Ver. 21. [3] Ver. 22. [4] Ver. 22, 23.
[5] Ver. 22. [6] Ver. 22. [7] Ver. 24.

(8.) In reference to God, its character is graciousness;[1] (9.) It is "through the redemption that is in Christ Jesus;"[2] and this its most characteristic feature is strikingly exhibited in that view of His propitiatory sacrifice, contained in the Gospel, which shows how, both in the times that are past and in the times that now are, the claims of justice were reconciled with the exercise of mercy, and how God is the just God, while He justifies him that believeth in Jesus.[3] From these general views of the Divine method of justification, the apostle concludes—(1.) That this Divine method of justification excludes all boasting;[4] (2.) That a saving interest in it can be obtained by believing—by believing without the works of the law—and can only be thus obtained;[5] (3.) That it is equally necessary and equally sufficient for all men, whether they be Jews or Gentiles;[6] and (4.) That, far from making void the law, without which—apart from which—it is, it establishes it.[7]

He who understands these statements—who attaches a clear and just idea to each of these descriptions—will have a distinct, and, so far as it goes, accurate view of the Divine method of justification; and will be prepared for proceeding with advantage to the apostle's more extended illustrations. Such a clear apprehension of the elementary principles of the doctrine of Christian justification, is far from being so common as might be imagined. Many suppose they have it, who are lamentably destitute of it. Let us take care that we possess it. Much that is deficient and wrong in inward experience and in practical conduct among professors of Christianity, is to be traced to imperfect and mistaken views on this subject. I will endeavour in the sequel, in as plain and few words as I can select, to express to you what appears to me the apostle's meaning in these propositions; and we will find, I am persuaded, that they are not expressions, as some may be apt to consider them, merely of nice dialectical distinctions, but statements of truths which have a vital connection with men's becoming truly holy and happy—truths stated in the form best

[1] Ver. 24. [2] Ver. 24. [3] Ver. 25, 26. [4] Ver. 27.
[5] Ver. 28. [6] Ver. 29, 30. [7] Ver. 31.

fitted to remove the mistakes, which men are naturally disposed to fall into with regard to the method of justification, and which, if persisted in and acted on, will assuredly be fatal to their highest interests.

STATEMENT 1. *The Divine Method of Justification is "without the Law."*

The first thing the apostle says, in reference to "the righteousness of God," or the Divine method of justification, is, that it is "without the law,"[1] or rather "without law;" the apostle not referring merely to the law of Moses, but to law in general—to the principle of all law, human and divine: "the man that doeth the things contained in a law shall live in them—by them." This is not the principle of the Divine method of justifying sinful men. It is the principle of the method of the justification of holy angels; it was the principle of the method by which man, continuing innocent and obedient, would have been justified. But the Divine method of justification for sinners is "without law"—*i.e.* it stands apart from law; it is founded on other principles; it is characterized by different qualities. When our Lord says, that without Him His disciples can do nothing,[2] He means that, separate from Him, they can do nothing. In like manner, when the apostle says, the Divine method of justification is "without law," he means that it is something quite distinct and different from law. It is not, like law, the offspring of equity, it is the offspring of sovereign grace; and all its details are in beautiful harmony with its origin and corresponding nature. It indeed "magnifies law and makes it honourable;"[3] it does not make it void, but establishes it. But, as a method of justification, it stands apart from it. It could not have answered its purpose otherwise. Law is, in its nature, fitted to be the principle of the justification of the innocent and obedient. It has served its purpose in the case of the elect angels; it would have served its purpose in the case of innocent and obedient

[1] χωρὶς νόμου. [2] John xv. 5. χωρὶς ἐμοῦ.
[3] Isa. xlii. 21.

man. But law, as a method of justification for sinners, has become " weak through the flesh." Man's guilt and depravity make it, in the nature of things, impossible that the law should be the means of his justification and final happiness. It *can* do nothing, with regard to him, but pronounce condemnation and secure punishment. No modification of law would serve the purpose of justifying the sinner. Indeed, the law of God, all perfect, does not admit of being modified. Every attempt to do so, instead of establishing the law or saving the sinner, dishonours the law, and deludes and destroys the sinner. Yet all the mistaken notions of the Divine method of justification are just modifications of the method of justification by law. All who do not, in an enlightened faith of the truth, submit to the righteousness of God—God's method of justification—all who have any concern about being justified, in going about to establish their own methods of justification, however various in their details, " seek justification, as it were, by the works of the law:"[1] hence the importance of our clearly and fully apprehending the meaning of the apostle's assertion, that the Divine method of justification is 'apart from law;' that in its principle and in its details, it is altogether different from legal justification.

We can conceive of a method of justification in which the obedience of the individual is, strictly speaking, the *ground* of obtaining the Divine favour,—the Divine favour being the stipulated reward, his obedience the stipulated work: or we may conceive of a method of justification, in which the ground of justification is something else than the man's own obedience—say the obedience unto death of the incarnate Son; but the *means* by which the individual obtains a personal interest in it, is his own obedience, his doing some stipulated work in order to his having the advantage of that ground of justification. In neither of these cases would the method of justification be " without law." Now, in both these respects the Divine method of justification is "without law"—apart from

[1] Rom. ix. 32.

law. Neither its ground nor its means are *legal*. According to the Divine method of justification, obedience is neither the *ground* nor the *means* of justification. Nothing can be plainer than the apostle's words, in ver. 28 of this chapter, "A man is justified without the deeds of the law;" except, perhaps, his words in Gal. ii. 16, "A man is not justified by the works of the law."

Obedience is not, cannot be, the *ground* of the sinner's justification. If obedience be the ground of the sinner's justification, it must either be perfect, or imperfect but sincere, obedience.—Perfect obedience to the Divine law cannot be the ground of the sinner's justification, for two reasons—(1.) There is no such thing to be found among men. There is not, there never was, there never will be, such a just mere man as doeth good and sinneth not; not that even perfect obedience is a physical impossibility, but men, who are in the flesh, cannot please God in anything, far less in everything; and (2.) Though such obedience existed for the future, in the case of the sinner, it could not be the ground of justification, for *he* is condemned already. Such obedience may prevent further condemnation, but it cannot procure immunity from punishment deserved for previous offences.—Imperfect but sincere obedience cannot be the ground of the sinner's justification, for two reasons also—(1.) From its imperfection, that is, its mixture with sin, it is unfit for this purpose; and (2.) No man but a justified man—a man already in favour with God—can yield really sincere obedience to God—that is, obedience rising out of cordial esteem and love of the Divine character and law.

Obedience can as little be the *means* as the *ground* of the sinner's justification. Perfect obedience cannot; for, as we have seen, there is no such thing to be found among men. Sincere but imperfect obedience cannot; for we have seen that there is no sincere obedience but among the justified. Nothing can be the means of obtaining its own cause. In all the extent of meaning, then, that belongs to the very comprehensive phrase, the righteousness of God is "without law;" the Divine method of justification stands apart from law.

STATEMENT 2. *The Divine Method of Justification is witnessed by the Law and the Prophets.*

The apostle's second statement, in reference to the Divine method of justification, is, that it is "witnessed by the law and the prophets." The Jews used to call the five books of Moses "the law," and the other inspired books of their canon "the prophets;" so that the apostle's assertion is that the Divine method of justification, revealed in the Gospel, is "witnessed" in the Old Testament Scriptures. Not merely was the Gospel, in which this method is revealed, "promised afore by God's prophets in the Holy Scriptures,"[1] but in these Scriptures a testimony is given respecting this "righteousness of God." The Divine method of justification had been in operation since after the fall of man; and though, to a great extent, a "mystery"—a concealed thing, till *He* came who is "Jehovah our righteousness,"[2] many of its most distinctive features were dimly revealed; and, in comparing these intimations with the full revelation, we cannot help seeing that they refer to the same Divine economy of the exercise of grace in consistency with righteousness. The apostle seems to have meant something more than that some account of the Divine method of justification is to be found in the Old Testament—he appears to intimate that it is there witnessed to as being "without law;" its two great principles being to be found there, to wit, that the ground of the sinner's justification is not his own doing and suffering, but the doing and suffering of another, and that the means of the sinner's justification is not working but believing. The first of these principles is the very soul of the whole substitutionary services of the Mosaic law, and is stated in as plain principles by the Prophet Isaiah as by any of the evangelists or apostles.[3] The second principle was exemplified in the case of Abraham,[4] and the pas-

[1] Rom. i. 2.
[2] Jerem. xxiii. 6.
[3] Isa. liii. 5, 6, 8, 10, 11, 12.
[4] Gen. xv. 6.

sage quoted at the 19th verse of the first chapter, from the Prophet Habakkuk, shows how the prophets "witnessed" it.

STATEMENT 3. *The Divine Method of Justification is "by the Faith of Christ."*

The apostle's third statement is, that the Divine method of justification is "by the faith of Christ." "The faith of Christ" may, according to the usage of the New Testament, signify either "the truth about Christ revealed to be believed"—that is, the Gospel; or "the belief of that truth"—that is, the faith of the Gospel. In both cases the Divine method of justification is "by the faith of Christ." It is by the Gospel of Christ, not by the law of Moses, that this method of justification gains its object; and it is by believing the truth about Christ, not by yielding obedience to any law, that the sinner, according to this method of justification, is justified. The latter seems to express the apostle's precise meaning here, for, in the strictly parallel passage in the Epistle to the Galatians, chap. ii. 16, "the faith of Jesus Christ" is contrasted, not with "the law," but with "the works of the law." We consider the apostle, then, as here saying, 'According to the Divine method of justification, men are justified by believing the truth respecting Jesus Christ, exhibited in the Gospel as the propitiation for sin.' When he says, that "this Divine method of justification" is thus "by the faith of Christ," he by no means intends, what some have supposed him to mean, that, in this method, faith holds the same place as obedience does in the method of justification by law—that the sinner is justified on the ground of his faith. We shall have an opportunity of showing, by and by, that the passage on which this hypothesis chiefly rests, "Faith is imputed" or counted "for righteousness,"[1] rightly interpreted, lays no foundation for any such conclusion. It is enough at present to remark, that "faith," however you may understand the word, cannot be the ground on which God justifies the sinner. It is neither perfect obedi-

[1] Rom. iv. 5.

ence, nor does it in any way give satisfaction for sin. Viewed in its true meaning as, the counting true what God says, on abundant evidence that God says it, it obviously can have no merit; viewed as equivalent to reliance on the work of Christ, it is an entire relinquishment of reliance on itself, or anything else; and, viewed as the seminal principle and substance of obedience, justification by faith would become but another form of that justification by law, which we have shown to be utterly foreign to the genius of that Divine method that stands apart from law. What the apostle states here, and so often and so plainly elsewhere, is, that the faith of the truth about Christ is the only and the certain way in which an individual sinner can realize for himself the benefits of this Divine method of justification; that we are justified by faith—only by faith; that, as our Lord says, "He that believeth not is condemned, and the wrath of God abideth on him." "He that believeth is not condemned; he shall not come into condemnation."[1] Thus faith, while not the ground, is the means, the only means, of the sinner's justification.

In thus making the faith of the truth about Christ the only link for connecting the sinner with the ground of justification, which the Divine method of justification furnishes, we have a striking display of the manifold wisdom of God. (1.) Such an arrangement agrees with the gratuitous character of the economy. Its being by faith shows that it is of grace. What credit can any sane man take to himself for believing well-accredited truth? (2.) It corresponds with, and illustrates the generosity of the Divine character. Its language is, 'Trust me, and your expectations, however high, will be surpassed. Refuse to trust me, after the manifestation I have given of my disposition to forgive and bless, and I *cannot* bestow on you my favour.' (3.) The faith which is the means of justification, is the instrument of sanctification; and, (4.) There does not appear to be any other conceivable way of putting a being like man in possession of the blessings of a justified state, a peaceful conscience, and a holy heart.

[1] John iii. 18, 36; v. 24.

STATEMENT 4. *The Divine Method of Justification is " now manifested to all."*

The fourth statement of the apostle is, that the Divine method of justification is "*now* manifested to all."[1]—The Divine method of justification, originating in the eternal purpose of mercy, came into operation as soon as it was required, immediately after the fall of man; and its exercise was, from its nature and object, accompanied with a partial revelation. That revelation became more extensive and distinct as ages moved on. The testimonies of the law are more obscure than the testimonies of the prophets. The revelation was confined to a comparatively small part of mankind—the original revelation to Adam and Noah being soon lost, or so corrupted as to become equivalent to no revelation—and, after the call of Abraham, the revelations being in a great measure limited to his descendants in the line of Isaac and Jacob. But "now,"—now that the Messiah is come in the person of Jesus Christ, the incarnate Son of God—the Divine method of justification is manifested to all. The method is "manifested," made evident, by the great events having taken place on which the Divine method of justification is founded. Not in a figure, but in reality has been offered up the great sacrifice of expiation, on which all human justification rests; and the whole of the facts in reference to this event and its design, and the manner in which it is to accomplish this design, have been made the subject of a plain revelation, which may be translated into all languages, and carried into all nations; and those into whose hands it is come are charged, not only to keep it carefully and to transmit it to their children pure and entire, as the Jews were, with regard " to the law and the prophets," but to use every suitable means for its becoming universally known. The Gospel, in which it is contained, is to be preached to every nation under heaven; and " by the commandment of the Everlasting God," the " mystery, which was hid from former ages

[1] δικαιοσύνη θεοῦ πεφανέρωται, ver. 21; εἰς πάντας, ver. 22.

and generations," is to be "made known among all nations for the obedience of faith." [1]

STATEMENT 5. *The Divine Method of Justification takes effect "upon all that believe."*

The fifth statement made by the apostle is, that this Divine method of justification is "on all them that believe"—*i.e.* it takes effect not on all to whom it is addressed or made known, not on any of them, unless they believe it.—This rises out of its nature, as a method of justification by *believing*—a method suited to man's rational nature. It does not work like a charm. No man is justified by merely having in his possession the Bible in which this method is revealed. No man is justified by it, by being only a hearer of the Gospel in which it is set forth. But every man who believes the revelation about it, is personally interested in the benefits it conveys. It takes effect on every believer. It cannot take effect on the unbeliever; and it cannot but take effect on the believer. The Jew with the law cannot be justified unless he believes. The Gentile without the law, if he believes, is justified. All believers shall—none but believers can—be justified by this "righteousness of God."

STATEMENT 6. *The Divine Method of Justification treats all Men as on a level.*

The sixth statement by the apostle is, that this Divine method of justification treats all its subjects, as on a level. "There is no difference; for all have sinned, and come short of the glory of God."—This does not deny that there may be, that there are differences—great differences among men, even among believers. It merely states that, in reference to justification, there is no difference. This Divine economy takes no notice of the artificial distributions of men, nor even of their comparative moral distinctions. It relates to man *the sinner*.

[1] Rom. xvi. 25, 26.

Its direct object is to deliver from guilt; and though all are not equally guilty, in the sense of having committed the same number of crimes of the same heinousness and aggravation—there is a great difference here—yet all are guilty; all are condemned, though not to the same measure of punishment, yet to such a measure of punishment as to them will be perdition—hopeless perdition, if the sentence is not repealed. "They have all sinned—they have all come short of the glory,"[1] the approbation "of God."[2] They have all violated the law—they have all incurred its penalty—they are all, what to rational creatures is the most dreadful of all evils, the objects of the judicial displeasure and the moral disapprobation of God. This method of justification deals with men not as Jews or Gentiles, not as possessing or being destitute of a Divine revelation, not as being comparatively harmless or enormously wicked—but as *men*, as *sinners*. All need it, equally need it, for they must perish without it; and it is equally suitable, equally fitted to be efficacious to all—the Gentile as well as the Jew—the chief sinner as well as the man not far from the kingdom of God.

STATEMENT 7. *In reference to Man, the character of the Divine Method of Justification is gratuitousness.*

The seventh statement is that in reference to man, the character of this Divine method of justification is gratuitousness. Those who are justified by it are justified "freely."—Nothing like an equivalent is required, or can, if offered, be accepted in the case of this justification. Forgiveness and acceptance under this economy are the "gift of God." There is—there can be no cause of justification in the sinner. The blessings conferred are, in no sense, nor degree, for value received or to be received. Man cannot be profitable to God, as man may be to man.

[1] Luke xiv. 10; John v. 41, 44, xii. 43; Rom. v. 2, vi. 4; 2 Cor. vi. 8; 1 Thes. ii. 6.

[2] Ver. 23.

STATEMENT 8. *In reference to God, the Character of the Divine Method of Justification is Graciousness.*

The next—the eighth statement is of a kindred signification, yet still bears a very important, distinct meaning. In reference to God, the character of the Divine method of justification is gracious sovereignty. They who are justified by it are "justified by God's grace."[1]—The blessings conferred, and the method of conferring them, originated in self-moved sovereign benignity. They could not originate in anything else. Interest was out of the question. His glory and happiness are, like Himself, eternal and independent. Justice demanded any thing but men's justification. They deserved punishment; they never could deserve any thing else. To the questions, Why is there a Divine method of justification for sinning men rather than for sinning angels?—Why are any of the fallen race justified?—Why is there a plan of justification revealed to all, and taking effect on all that believe?—the only answer is, It is "according to the good pleasure of His will,"[2] "which He purposed in Himself"[3]—"the riches of His grace."[4] He has mercy, because He wills to have mercy; He has compassion, because He wills to have compassion.[5]—These two statements are, as we have remarked, closely connected, yet still distinct. In the first the apostle looks to the recipient of justification, and says, It is "free"—there is no cause of it in man. In the second he looks to the author and bestower of justification, and he says, It is "by God's grace"—there is no cause of it in God but sovereign kindness.

STATEMENT 9. *The Divine Method of Justification is "Through the Redemption that is in Christ Jesus.*

The ninth statement by the apostle is, that this method of justification is "through the redemption that is in Christ Jesus."—Redemption, which properly signifies deliverance by the pay-

[1] Ver. 24. [2] Eph. i. 5. [3] Eph. i. 9.
[4] Eph. i. 7. [5] Rom. ix. 15.

ment of a ransom, is sometimes used in reference to the deliverance itself thus obtained; at other times to the act of deliverance by the payment of the ransom. It seems here used in the latter sense; for justification is not so much *through* redemption, in the former sense, as a part—the fundamental part of it, while it is through the payment of the ransom that the justification is enjoyed: that is its ground. The whole method of Divine justification is framed with a reference to this great fact. Redemption, in the sense of the deliverance, is "in Christ Jesus," inasmuch as it is only in union with Him that this deliverance can be enjoyed. Redemption, in the sense of the act of ransoming, is said to be "in" or by "Christ Jesus," because He paid the ransom. The general truth taught us is that, according to the Divine method of justification, the ransom paid by Jesus Christ is the ground of the sinner's justification—is *that* which makes it just in God to justify the ungodly. The justification which the righteousness of God brings near to men, is not mere amnesty. It is pardon and acceptance granted in consequence of something having taken place, which answers all the demands of the Divine moral government, as well as, aye infinitely better than, the infliction of the penalty would have done. That something, which all created wisdom would have sought for in vain, is found in the perfect obedience to death of the incarnate Son of God—in His submitting to take the place of man, and expose Himself to those evils which are the manifestation of the displeasure of God against the sin of man. He Himself, in His all-perfect humanity—doing and suffering all that the righteous governor held necessary for the vindication of His holy law from the dishonour done to it by the sins of men, till on the cross, yielding up His Spirit, He could say, "It is finished,"—was the ransom that laid the foundation for unlocking the fetters of guilt and delivering from the slavery of sin and Satan.

This central truth of Christianity is further illustrated in the words that follow, in which the apostle shows that the manifestation of the Divine method of justification, in the Gospel, is effected by that Gospel setting forth Jesus Christ as a propitiatory sacrifice, in the atoning, expiatory efficacy of which men are interested by believing: this wonderful dispensation, lying at the foundation of this method of justification, both as it was exemplified, before the offering of the great sacrifice, by God, in the exercise of "forbearance," remitting sins for which, as yet, there had been made no atonement; and as it is exemplified *now*, under the new economy, in His being and appearing to be just and the justifier of him that believeth in Jesus—that Just One who gave Himself, in the room of the unjust, a ransom—a sacrifice that He might bring them to God. It would require more space than our plan affords, to show, by a minute analysis, how this meaning may be brought out of the 24th, 25th, and 26th verses. I would only remark, that I consider "the righteousness of God," in these verses, as having the meaning which it has in every other part of the paragraph; and "the declaring" of that righteousness by "setting forth" Jesus Christ "a propitiation through faith in His blood," as being equivalent to the "revelation of the righteousness of God" in the Gospel, in chapter i. 17, and the "manifestation of the righteousness of God to all," in verses 21, 22, of this chapter.

To some it may appear that entire gratuitousness and sovereign graciousness, both as we have shown, distinctive features of the Divine method of justification, do not harmonize very well with these statements. But, if our plan admitted, it would not be difficult to show that this thought springs from misconception. It might be shown (1.) That, in the most extensive view which we can take of the Divine government, every dispensation is an act of justice; and, therefore, if justice and grace are incompatible, there can be no such thing as a display of grace. (2.) That it does not appear possible that a sinner should be justified without the exercise of grace, whatever compensation might be made for his sin. (3.) That what is an act of justice in one view, may be an act of grace in another. The same Divine dispensation may be an act of justice to one person, and an act of grace to another; what to him who paid the ransom is justice, may be grace, pure grace, to him for whom it was paid. (4.) That when a person voluntarily contracts an obligation, by the promise to bestow a blessing which he was in no way bound to confer, the bestowal of that benefit—while the discharge of an obligation on the part of him who confers it—is not less an act of bounty to the person who receives it, than if the obligation to give had never been contracted by the promise to give. (5.) Finally, that the person who paid the ransom being "God manifest in flesh," there is—there can be, no claim of right for the justification of the sinner, extrinsic of the Divinity.

From these nine propositions respecting the Divine method of justification, the apostle draws four conclusions, with which he shuts up this bird's-eye view of the subject, before he enters on the illustration of its various parts and bearings.

CONCLUSION 1. *That the Divine Method of Justification excludes boasting.*

The first of these conclusions is, that this Divine method of justification excludes boasting. "Where is boasting, then? It is excluded. By what law? By the law of works? Nay, but by the law of faith."[1]—It is quite plain that the method of justification excludes all boasting on the part of those who are interested in it. Justification is a free gift, originating in sovereign favour. The person who enjoys it cannot boast of himself, for he is a mere recipient; he cannot boast over those who along with him enjoy it, for it is equally undeserved in every case; he cannot boast over those who do not enjoy it, for what was *He* better than they? *Who* made them to differ? The apostle especially fixes the mind on the fact that the Divine method of justification being a law of justification not by works, but by faith, leads to this result—the exclusion of boasting. The full expression is found in chapter ix. 31, "law of righteousness" or law of justification. How does the Divine method of justification exclude boasting? It

[1] Ver. 27.

does so because it is a law or method of justification by faith. If it had been a law or method of justification by works, it would not have done so. If the condition of justification had been some work, it matters not what, he who had done it might boast of having done it—he might compare himself with others who also had done it, and please himself with the thought that he had done it better than they; he might compare himself with those who had not done it, and plume himself on his superiority to them. But all this boasting is excluded. In believing plain truth, accompanied with sufficient evidence, he has received a gift. That is the whole matter. What is there to glory of in this?

CONCLUSION 2. *That an interest in the Divine Method of Justification can be obtained by Faith without the Works of the Law, and can only be thus obtained.*

The second conclusion is, that a saving interest in this Divine method of justification can be obtained by believing without the works of the law. "Therefore we conclude," or we judge then "that a man is justified by faith without the works of the law."[1]—Without believing the truth respecting Christ and the way of salvation through Him, a man cannot be justified. No ceremonial atonement, no external privilege, no act of obedience, singly or combined, can restore a sinner to the enjoyment of the Divine favour. The man who does really believe the true Gospel, shall be, is justified—"justified from all things"—however numerous, however aggravated his sins. And this, without the works of the law. We can suppose what, indeed, some men calling themselves *Christian* ministers do, in substance, teach—that God, having in view the justification of man as a gratuitous gift on the ground of Christ's merits, might still have suspended the grant on the performance of a certain measure of obedience to the law. The righteousness of God might have been on all who discovered a teachable disposition, and who, to a certain extent, kept the law of God.

[1] Ver. 27.

But this is not "the righteousness of God;" this is not the Divine method of justification. It is "to him that worketh not but believeth that righteousness is imputed"—to him alone.[1]

CONCLUSION 3. *That the Divine Method of Justification is equally necessary, equally suitable, equally sufficient for all Men, whether Jews or Gentiles.*

The third conclusion is, that it is equally necessary and equally sufficient for all men, whether they be Jews or Gentiles. —Is the God who is revealed in this method of justification, the peculiar exclusive property of the Jews?[2] Had it been a method of justification by circumcision, or keeping the law of Moses, that might have been the case. But it is a method of justification by faith, something that men, as men, are capable of—something which nothing can supply the place of in this method of justification. There is but one God and one method of justification; and it equally suits, and is equally effectual in, Jews and Gentiles. God "justifies the circumcision *by* faith, and the uncircumcision *through* faith."[3] The distinction thus marked may be made plainer to an English reader thus:—He justifies the Jew not as a Jew, but as a believer; and as to the Gentile, He will not exclude him from justification because he is a Gentile; let him believe, and, like the believing Jew, he will be equally "justified freely by God's grace, through the redemption that is in Christ Jesus." If the Jew is justified, it is not because he is a Jew, but a believing man; and if the Gentile remains in condemnation, it is not because he is a Gentile, but because he is an unbelieving man.

CONCLUSION 4. *The Divine Method of Justification does not make void, but establishes the Law.*

The fourth and last conclusion is, that this Divine method of justification, far from making void the law, apart from which

[1] Rom. iv. 5. [2] Ver. 29. [3] Ver. 30.

it stands on its own peculiar basis, establishes the law. In the all-perfect righteousness of Jesus Christ, it secures honour to the law, both in its precepts and sanctions, such as it never could have obtained in any other way; and in its effects on the justified person, it secures from him a kind and extent of obedience that could not otherwise have been obtained. As the apostle afterwards says—"God sending his Son in the likeness of sinful flesh, and for sin"—that is, a sacrifice for sin has done what the law could not do, because it was weak through the flesh, "has condemned sin in the flesh; so that "the righteousness of the law,"—the requirements of the law, "are fulfilled in us who walk not after the flesh but after the spirit."[1] Such is the general view which the apostle gives of "the righteousness of God"—the Divine method of justification.

Now, this is not a piece of abstract speculation. It is a statement of indubitable, because Heaven-revealed, facts. It is a statement of facts in which every one of us has the deepest personal interest. Every one of us needs to be restored to God's favour, for every one of us has forfeited it. If not thus restored, the consequence must be utter ruin—hopeless perdition; for what else, what less can be the meaning of "God's wrath to the uttermost abiding" on a human being? We *may* be restored to the Divine favour. This is the method of restoration—the only method of restoration. They who have not yet availed themselves of it have no time to lose. It secures the interests of eternity, but it is only in time we can secure an interest in *it*. There is no Divine method of justification for condemned men in the future state, any more than for condemned angels. By this method of justification, the boon must, according to its nature and ours, be received as a gift in the belief of the truth in reference to it. He who attempts to gain it in any other way will not only lose it, but add to his guilt, deepen his perdition. "The plea of

[1] Rom. viii. 4.

works," in every form, either as the ground or the means of justification,—

> "The plea of works, as arrogant and vain,
> Heaven turns from with abhorrence and disdain;
> Not more affronted by avowed neglect,
> Than by the mere dissembler's feigned respect.
> What is all righteousness that men devise?
> What but a sordid bargain for the skies?
> But Christ as soon would abdicate His own,
> As stoop from Heaven to sell the proud a throne."

> "Accept it only and the boon is yours:
> And sure it is as kind to smile and give,
> As, with a frown, to say—'Do this and live.'
> Love is not pedlar's trump'ry, bought and sold:
> God *will* give freely or He *will* withhold.
> He stipulates indeed, but merely this—
> That man will freely take an unbought bliss—
> Will trust Him for a faithful generous part,
> Nor set a price upon a willing heart."[1]

The whole of the Divine method of justification, in its own nature and in its intended influence, is contained in these words—"Freely ye receive, freely give."

Let those who have in the faith of the truth submitted to "the righteousness of God," who have embraced cordially the Divine method of justification, avail themselves of all its advantages, and carefully regard the obligations which grow out of it. What do they owe to Him in whose grace the whole wonderous plan originates, and to Him who, by giving Himself to be the propitiation for our sins, opened a way for this grace to reign through righteousness to their eternal life. How should they value for themselves that record, by the faith of which they obtain and retain all the blessings of this Divine method? and how should they labour to communicate it to others, by whom the Divine method of justification is equally needed, for

[1] Cowper.

whom it is equally suited, and who *can* be interested in it only by knowing and believing the truth? Knowing that "all things are of God" in this method of justification, and that "of God are they in Christ righteousness"—"the righteousness of God in Him"—let them learn not to glory in His presence, or if they glory, to glory only in the Lord; and, finally, let them see that they possess, in ever increasing measure, the only satisfactory evidence of personal interest in this Divine method of justification, in the law being established as to its great object in their experience, in its righteousness being fulfilled, in their walking not after the flesh but after the spirit. Justification is not sanctification, but the one cannot exist without the other. Where there is justification, there is, there must be, sanctification.

I conclude these illustrations with a serious question. Exposed as we all are to the righteous displeasure of Almighty God—that wrath, the power whereof not man nor angel knows—where have we sought—where have we found a refuge? That refuge must be "a righteousness"—a justification. There are many refuges of lies; there is but one secure refuge. There are many methods of justification; there is but one Divine, and therefore efficacious, method of justification. Abraham, David, Isaiah, Paul, sought and found shelter there. It is "the everlasting righteousness" which Messiah the Prince has brought in.[1] It is brought near even to "the stout-hearted, far from righteousness."[2] And the worst of them in the belief of the truth may say, 'It is for me —"Surely in the Lord have I righteousness and strength;"' and if he does so in good earnest, "In the Lord he shall be justified, and in the Lord shall he glory."[3] Happy they who have submitted to this righteousness, who "*have* this righteousness, not of the law, but by the faith of Christ, the righteousness of God which is by faith."[4]—"Lift up your eyes to the heavens and look upon the earth beneath, for the heavens shall vanish away like smoke, and the earth shall

[1] Dan. ix. 24. [2] Is. xlvi. 12. [3] Is. xlv. 24, 25. [4] Phil. iii. 9.

wax old like a garment, and they that dwell therein shall die in like manner—the moth shall eat them like a garment, and the worm shall eat them like wool; but my salvation shall be for ever, and my righteousness shall not be abolished—my righteousness shall be for ever, and my salvation from generation to generation."[1]

To quote the judicious Hooker—an appellation appropriate, at least, in this instance—"Oh, that our hearts were stretched out as tents, and the eyes of our understanding were as bright as the sun, that we might thoroughly know the riches of the glorious inheritance of saints, and what is the exceeding greatness of His power towards us whom He accepteth as pure and holy through our believing! Oh, that the Spirit of the Lord would give this doctrine entrance into the stony and hard heart which followeth the law of righteousness, but cannot attain to the righteousness of the law; who therefore stumble at Christ, are bruised, shivered to pieces as a ship that has run itself upon a rock! Oh, that God would cast down the eyes of the proud, and humble the souls of the high-minded, that they might at length abhor the garments of their own flesh, that cannot hide their nakedness, and put on the faith of Christ, as he did put it on who said, 'Doubtless, I think all things but loss for the excellent knowledge' sake of Christ Jesus my Lord, for whom I have counted all things loss, and do judge them to be dung that I may win Christ and be found in Him, not having mine own righteousness, which is of the law, but that which is through the faith of Christ, even the righteousness which is of God through faith!' Oh, that God would open the ark of mercy wherein this doctrine lieth, and set it wide before the eyes of poor afflicted consciences, which fly up and down on the water of their affliction, and can see nothing but only the deluge of their sins, wherein there is no place to rest their feet! The God of pity and compassion give you all strength and courage, every

[1] Is. li. 6, 8.

day, and every hour, and every moment, to build and "edify yourselves" in this most pure and "holy faith."[1]

§ 2. *The Divine Method of Justification, as "without Law," "by Faith," "the Faith of Christ"—"witnessed by the Law and the Prophets."*

CHAPTER IV.—"What shall we then say that Abraham our father, as pertaining to the flesh, hath found? For if Abraham were justified by works, he hath whereof to glory, but not before God. For what saith the scripture? Abraham believed God, and it was counted unto him for righteousness. Now to him that worketh is the reward not reckoned of grace, but of debt. But to him that worketh not, but believeth on Him that justifieth the ungodly, his faith is counted for righteousness. Even as David also describeth the blessedness of the man, unto whom God imputeth righteousness without works, saying, Blessed are they whose iniquities are forgiven, and whose sins are covered. Blessed is the man to whom the Lord will not impute sin. Cometh this blessedness then upon the circumcision only, or upon the uncircumcision also? for we say that faith was reckoned to Abraham for righteousness. How was it then reckoned? when he was in circumcision, or in uncircumcision? Not in circumcision, but in uncircumcision. And he received the sign of circumcision, a seal of the righteousness of the faith which he had yet being uncircumcised: that he might be the father of all them that believe, though they be not circumcised; that righteousness might be imputed unto them also: and the father of circumcision to them who are not of the circumcision only, but who also walk in the steps of that faith of our father Abraham, which he had being yet uncircumcised. For the promise, that he should be the heir of the world, was not to Abraham, or to his seed, through the law, but through the righteousness of faith. For if they which are of the law be heirs, faith is made void, and the promise made of none effect. Because the law worketh wrath: for where no law is, there is no transgression. Therefore it is of faith, that it might be by grace; to the end the promise might be sure to all the seed: not to that only which is of the law, but to that also which is of the faith of Abraham, who is the father of us all (as it is written, I have made thee a father of many nations), before Him whom he believed, even God, who quickeneth the dead, and calleth those things which be not as though they

[1] Ser. II. on Jude 17-21, § 28, Works, Hanbury's Edition, vol. iii., p. 495.

were: who against hope believed in hope, that he might become the father of many nations, according to that which was spoken, So shall thy seed be. And being not weak in faith, he considered not his own body now dead, when he was about an hundred years old, neither yet the deadness of Sarah's womb: he staggered not at the promise of God through unbelief; but was strong in faith, giving glory to God; and being fully persuaded that what He had promised He was able also to perform. And therefore it was imputed to him for righteousness. Now, it was not written for his sake alone, that it was imputed to him; but for us also, to whom it shall be imputed, if we believe on Him that raised up Jesus our Lord from the dead; who was delivered for our offences, and was raised again for our justification."

I proceed now to the second sub-section, under the head, "Of the righteousness of God." It occupies the whole of the fourth chapter, and may receive for its title, "The Divine Method of Justification, as 'without Law,' 'by Faith,' 'the faith of Christ,' and 'upon *all* them that Believe,' 'witnessed by the Law and the Prophets;' or, "The Testimony of the Law and the Prophets in reference to the Divine Method of Justification, as 'without Law,' 'by Faith,' 'the faith of Christ,' and 'upon *all* them that Believe.'"

The first testimony which the apostle adduces to the Divine method of justification, as "without law," "by faith," "upon *all* them that believe," is taken from "the Law"—that is, from the Pentateuch, and from the first book in it, and consists of the history of the manner in which Abraham, the friend of God, the head on earth of the holy family—'the sons of God,' as contradistinguished from the ungodly, 'the sons of men'—the pattern of the manner in which God deals with all the members of the household, was justified. The form in which the apostle presents his argument is peculiar, but it will bear close examination, and will be found a wide-reaching, and a thoroughly conclusive one. It is as if he had said, 'Let us appeal to Abraham, and see how he was justified; for, that *he* was justified—that he was an object of the special favour of God—there can be no doubt. What, then, shall we say of Abraham, *our* father—the father of all the people of God—as to justification? Shall we say that he "obtained"[1] that justification which, without doubt, he possessed—shall we say that he obtained this "as pertaining to the flesh?"[2] Did he derive it from anything external? Did he obtain it through circumcision, or through animal sacrifice, or through any outward privilege or service? In other words, shall we say that *he* was "justified by works?" If he had been justified by works, he would have had whereof he might glory. He would have found in himself something that laid a foundation of self-exultation, as having distinguished him from others, who were not justified, as a fit object of the Divine special favour; for, as the apostle said, in the close of the last section, the law of works—the method of justification by works—does not exclude, it leaves room for boasting.[3] But Abraham had nothing to glory of before God, and, therefore, could not be justified by works.[4] So *says* the apostle. But where is his proof? It is not far to seek. "Abraham hath not whereof to glory before God." For what saith the Scripture? "Abraham believed God, and it was counted to him for righteousness."[5] The Scripture represents Abraham as justified by believing; and this representation proves at once that justification is by faith, and is without the law. The passage quoted by the apostle here, and elsewhere, is to be found in the 6th verse of the fifteenth chapter of Genesis.

The first thing we must do here is to inquire into the meaning of these words, and then to evolve the apostle's argument based on them. It is the more necessary to inquire into their meaning, that they have been often misunderstood. One class of interpreters have supposed the inspired historian to say—'Abraham believed God; he did not disregard His communications; he listened to Him, and showed a disposition to credit what He said to him, and do what He bade him; and God, instead of requiring from Abraham,

[1] Chap. xi. 7.

[2] Chap. iv. 1. The phrase, "according to the flesh," is connected, not with "our father," but with "found."

[3] Chap. iii. 27. [4] Ver. 2. [5] Ver. 3.

who, no doubt, was a sinner, atonement for the past, and perfect obedience for the future, balanced the account by setting down this faith, this believing, as if it had been the righteousness, the satisfaction and obedience, which the law demanded, and treated him accordingly.' Others, seeing that this makes faith void, turns promise into law, faith into works, and directly opposes what the apostle is establishing, have held that the historian's narrative is this—'Abraham believed God; he trusted in God that the great promise made to him respecting "a seed"—"the seed of the woman who was to bruise the head of the serpent"—"a seed in whom all the nations of the earth were to be blessed"—would be fulfilled; and God imputed—reckoned—to him the *righteousness* of this glorious person who was the object of his faith, that is, the holiness of His human nature, His obedient life, and His expiatory death, for his righteousness, on the ground of which he was justified. This is, no doubt, substantially sound doctrine, but it is not correct interpretation; there is no way of fairly bringing these thoughts out of these words, which refer, not to the *ground*, but to the *means*, of justification.

What, then, is their meaning? So far as I can see, it is this: Abraham believed what God revealed to him—he counted it true, and he counted it true just because God had revealed it to him. That is the plain meaning of "Abraham believed God." So far all is clear enough. But what was it that God reckoned or imputed to Abraham? what is meant by God's reckoning it to him? and what by God's reckoning it to him "for righteousness?" Now, to the first question I think there can be only one answer. It was Abraham's believing that was reckoned to him. It seems quite unnatural to say that the object of his faith was reckoned to him, whether by that object you mean the Divine testimony or the subject of the Divine testimony. But what are we to make of the expression, 'God reckoned Abraham's faith or believing to him?' In the Hebrew language, when a mental act is said to be reckoned to a person, the meaning is, the person is reckoned to have exercised it; if an action is reckoned to him, the meaning is, he is reckoned to have performed it; if a privilege is reckoned to him, he is reckoned to possess it. If sin is reckoned to a man, the meaning is, he is reckoned a sinner; if righteousness or justification is reckoned to him, he is reckoned to be righteous or justified; if faith or believing is reckoned to a man, he is reckoned a believer. Faith was reckoned to Abraham plainly by God,—*i.e.* 'God reckoned Abraham a believer:' and so He well might; for He saw his heart, and knew that he not only professed faith, but possessed it.

It only remains to find out what 'reckoning Abraham a believer for righteousness' means. The expression is literally, '*unto* righteousness;'[1] or, according to the ordinary meaning of that word in the epistle, unto justification. "Unto justification" is just equivalent to, 'so that he was justified.' That is plainly the meaning of the phrase in chapter x. 10, "With the heart man believeth unto righteousness," or justification —believeth so as to be justified; in other words, is justified through believing.

The inspired narrative of Abraham's justification thus consists of three parts, or, taking in what is necessarily implied, of four parts:—(1.) God made a revelation to Abraham; (2.) Abraham believed that revelation; (3.) God reckoned Abraham to be, what he was, a believer; and (4.) Reckoning him a believer, He justified him. The ground of justification is not *here* before the apostle's mind. It comes forward prominently enough afterwards. All that he has in view just now is, to prove that the Divine method of justification, as exhibited in the case of Abraham, was "without law," and "by faith."

And how does he prove this? You have his proof in the 4th and 5th verses. The gist of the argument may be given in a very few words,—'The language of this narrative does not at all suit the case of a man justified by law; it exactly suits the case of a man justified simply by believing.' "To him that worketh is the reward reckoned not of grace, but of

[1] εἰς δικαιοσύνην.

debt."[1] When a man receives a stipulated reward for a piece of stipulated labour, he has got no favour, he has got what he worked for. Had this been Abraham's case—had he done something in order to obtain the Divine favour—the record of his justification would have been couched in other terms. It would have been—'Abraham obeyed in leaving Chaldea at the command of the Lord, or in offering up his son Isaac, or in submitting to circumcision; and his obedience was reckoned to him, and thus he was justified.' On the other hand, the language of the narrative exactly suits the case of a man who, in the belief of the truth, receives justification as a free gift. The man is *un*godly—undeserving of God's favour; he does not perform a service to buy back the Divine favour; he believes a declaration of God, indicating kind regard to him; and, reckoned by God a believer—for he is one—he is treated by Him as if he were a righteous person.[2] Such was Abraham; such is the story of his justification; and thus does the *Law*—the Pentateuch—witness to the Divine method of justification, as "without law," and "by faith."

The Prophets give the same testimony. The apostle appeals to "the prophet David."[3] The Psalms formed a part of that division of the Old Testament Scriptures which the Jews termed the Former Prophets, just as Genesis formed the first part of what they termed the Law. The passage which the apostle refers to is the 1st verse of the thirty-second Psalm. When David describes the blessed man—that is, the justified man, the object of God's favour, which is life, happiness—he describes him as a person whom God reckons righteous, or justified "without works."[4] He does not describe him as a man who has never sinned; nor, as a man who has made atonement for his sin; nor, as a man who, as a reward of his obedience, or on consideration of his repentance, has obtained forgiveness. He describes him as a sinner—a freely forgiven sinner—a sinner who is justified merely because God has imputed or reckoned righteousness to him, without his working.

[1] Ver. 4. [2] Ver. 5. [3] Acts. ii. 30. [4] Ver. 6.

His words are, "Blessed are they whose transgressions are forgiven, whose sins are covered. Blessed is the man to whom the Lord will not impute sin"[1]—will not reckon *guilty*, in the sense of exposed to punishment, on account of sin. Is not this just the Divine method of justification, "not by law" but "by grace?"—not the earnings of desert, but the gift of free kindness? And is not this testimony of the Prophets a clear and conclusive one?

But the Divine method of justification, according to the apostle, is not only "without law," and "by faith,"—it is also "upon *all* them that believe." And the same testimony from the law, which, as we have seen, establishes the first two of these principles, confirms also the third. Does this blessedness of being justified, says the apostle, come on "the circumcision"—the Jews—only? or does it come "on the uncircumcision"—the Gentiles—also? "We say that faith was reckoned to Abraham for righteousness"[2]—that he was justified, not by working, but by believing. This proves that all of whom Abraham is the pattern and spiritual father must be justified in the same way. But Abraham was the head of the circumcision. It might seem, then, that the argument can go no farther than to prove that Jews are justified by faith. But, says the apostle, what were the circumstances of Abraham when he is declared to have been justified? Was he a circumcised or an uncircumcised man? "How"—in what circumstances, "was faith reckoned to him?" Was he reckoned a believer unto justification "when he was in circumcision or uncircumcision?" The answer is easy: "Not in circumcision, but in uncircumcision."[3] The period referred to (which the apostle seems to have selected, not as the date of Abraham's justification, but as the time when an express declaration was given of his being justified by faith) was fourteen years previous to the institution of circumcision; and this shows that circumcision had not only nothing to do with Abraham's justification, but nothing to do with the justification of those of

[1] Ver 7, 8. [2] Ver. 9. [3] Ver. 10.

whom he was the spiritual father. This was no accidental occurrence. It was so ordered, "that he might be" fittingly "the father of all who believe, though they should not be circumcised;" that it might be indicated that justification was for *them* equally with their circumcised brethren; and that it might be indicated that, if he was the spiritual father of believing circumcised persons, he was so on the ground, not of their circumcision, but of their faith.[1]—This is the statement contained in the 10th verse, the second half of the 11th, and the whole of the 12th verse.

The parenthetical clause in the beginning of the 11th verse (for it is obviously parenthetical, and the not marking it as such has obscured the passage) is intended to meet the question, "What profit is there in circumcision." And the reply is substantially, While circumcision can have no causal or instrumental connection with justification—for Abraham was justified before he was circumcised,—that sign, that mark, which was at once an outward badge of a race, and the emblematical expression of spiritual truth, was to Abraham a token, a seal, of the fact that he was a justified person through believing at the time he received it; and a confirmation to all, in all succeeding ages, of the great truth—that the restoration of a sinful man to the Divine favour is entirely independent of external privileges, or personal services or sacrifices. Thus is the principle that the Divine method of justification is "upon *all* them that believe," and only on them that believe, "witnessed to by the law," in the history of Abraham's justification.

The apostle follows up the argument in the sequel of the chapter. The promise that Abraham should be the heir, possessor of Canaan, was to him and to his seed according to the law of circumcision; but the higher promise, "that he should be the heir of the world," was "through the righteousness of faith." The apostle, if I mistake not, refers to the promise, "I will be thy God;" for he who has God for his own "inherits all things:"[2] he who is an heir of God is of course an heir of

[1] Ver. 11. [2] Rev. xxi. 7.

the universe, which is God's: "All things are yours," says the apostle, of the class here referred to, "whether Paul, or Apollos, or Cephas, or the world, or things present, or things to come; all are yours; for ye are Christ's, and Christ is God's;"[1] and, what is equally true, 'Christ is yours, and God is Christ's.' This promise was not to Abraham as a circumcised person, nor was it to his circumcised descendants *as such*, nor was it confined to them; this promise was to him as a man justified by believing, and it was to his descendants, whether natural or merely spiritual, as men justified by believing.[2] If Abraham's descendants were by obedience to the law to obtain this promised blessing, then there would be no use for that faith on which, according to the original constitution as revealed to Abraham, everything hung; and indeed the promise would be of none effect, for it never could be performed, being suspended on what is an impracticable condition with fallen men. "Law"—that is, the system which holds out God's favour as a reward to man's work—"worketh wrath;"[3] *i.e.* it leads not to Divine approbation, but to Divine disapprobation—to displeasure and punishment. It does so in consequence of man's inveterate tendency to transgress. Justification, to suit fallen man, must be something placed beyond the hazards of such a system as law. All men who are under *law* are under the curse. Where there is law, there is, there will be transgression. Free them from curse without entirely transforming their nature, and keep them under law as a system of justification, and they will soon be under the curse again, soon forfeit the promised blessing. The Divine method of justification, to serve its purpose, must be a gratuitous, not a legal system. It must be without law—apart from law—taken out of the sphere of law. Justification is something which, if obtained at all, must be freely given; and man, as he cannot procure it for himself, so, if he really possess it, he cannot forfeit it. The blessing could not have been secured for one of the seed, if it had not been absolutely gratuitous—by grace;

[1] 1 Cor. iii. 21–23. [2] Ver. 13. [3] Ver. 15.

and that it might be and appear to be of grace, it is by faith—obtained, retained by, or rather in, believing. And all this is so to the end—for the purpose, that the promise—the promised blessing of a free justification and its results, might be sure—might be secured to all the *seed*—all the spiritual descendants of Abraham; not only to those of them who, besides being believers, were his natural posterity, but to those of them also who were his seed only as walking in the steps of his faith:[1] a blessing conferred, in the exercise of sovereign mercy, on sinners, and received by them in believing. What is to prevent that becoming the inheritance of all the seed? It is happily placed beyond the possibility of their losing it. It is "hid with Christ in God."[2]

To complete his argumentative illustration, that the Divine method of justification is without works, by faith, upon *all* that believe, drawn from the narrative of Abraham's justification, the apostle adverts to the fact that Abraham was something more than a private individual. He was a public character. He was the head of the Israelitish people; but this was not all. He was the head of a spiritual family, of which his natural descendants by Isaac were a type. "Before men," he was only the father of those who descended from him; but "before God"—in the estimation of God, he was "the father of all believers."[3] He was, in a still higher sense than the Apostle Paul, "a pattern to them who should afterwards believe to life everlasting."[4] His justification was, if I may use the expression, normal. He was constituted the head of a spiritual family whose relation to him originated not in natural descent, but in believing; and to whom, as to himself, was secured, through believing, all the blessings included in and springing out of the peculiar favour of God: as the apostle says in his Epistle to the Galatians, "They which are of faith, the same are the children of Abraham. And the Scripture, foreseeing that God would justify the heathen through faith, preached before the Gospel," or rather, announced beforehand

[1] Ver. 16. [2] Col. iii. 3. [3] Ver. 17. [4] 1 Tim. i. 16.

the glad tidings to Abraham—" In thee"—along with thee, in the same manner with thee, " shall all nations be blessed. So then they that be of faith are blessed with"—along with, in the same way with, " faithful," believing, " Abraham."[1]

The apostle appeals to Gen. xvii. 5, as warranting him to say Abraham is the father of *all* believers: " I have made thee a father of many nations"—a promise fulfilled both in its literal and in its typical reference. He then describes that faith of Abraham by which, according to the inspired narrative, he was justified, for the purpose, apparently, of enabling his readers more distinctly to understand *how* they, as his spiritual seed, were justified. *Whom* did Abraham believe? *What* did Abraham believe? *Why* did Abraham believe? And what was the character of Abraham's faith?—*Whom* did he believe? He believed *God*, as infinitely powerful—who could quicken the dead, and who had merely to will that beings and events should be, and they immediately came into existence.[2] *What* did he believe? What God was pleased to reveal. What is mentioned here is, that he should become the father of many nations; but that was but a part, a small part, of what was revealed and what he believed. He believed in effect—for this was the sum of what God revealed to him—that one of his descendants was to be the promised Saviour of men; and that both he and his spiritual seed were to be saved by faith in Him. The revelation was comparatively indistinct; but this was its purport. *Why* did Abraham believe this? Just because God had said it. He had no other ground for it. Everything else would have led him to doubt or disbelieve it. And what were the *characteristics* of Abraham's faith? It was firm faith: he was " fully persuaded that what God had promised he was able to perform,"[3] and would certainly perform. It was hopeful faith: he " believed in hope," though what he expected was a thing " against hope"[4]—beyond hope,—what, but for God's promise, it would have been madness to hope for. It

[1] Gal. iii. 6-9. [2] Ver. 17. [3] Ver. 21. [4] Ver 18.

was faith that no seeming impossibilities could shake. "He staggered not at the promise of God through unbelief, but was strong in faith, giving glory to God."[1] Thus did Abraham believe. Such was his faith. And *therefore*, because Abraham thus believed, faith was reckoned to him;[2] God reckoned him, accounted him, treated him, as what he was indeed—a believer; and *thus* Abraham was justified.

Now, as Abraham is a public character, "the father of us all," this narrative of his justification by believing is put on record in the inspired book, which is to be the rule of faith and manners to all men, in all ages, not only—not principally, "for his sake"—to do him honour, but for the sakes of those who should live when the Divine method of justification by faith, exemplified in the case of Abraham, should in the Gospel be revealed, manifested to all, that it might be believed, and take effect on *all* them that believe, whether Jews or Gentiles. Faith will be reckoned to every man to justification, who, like Abraham, believes God—making known the method of justification, simply on God's own authority—so believes as to trust the Divine promise, and in the face of all difficulties expect its performance, in the way of Divine appointment.[3]

The God who was revealed to Abraham as the God who quickeneth the dead, is made known to us, to whom the Divine method of justification is revealed, manifested, declared, as "the God who raised up Jesus our Lord from the dead."[4] That Jesus, our Lord, is His incarnate only begotten Son, on whom He had laid all our iniquities, making Him sin —a sin-offering—in our room,—whom He "delivered" up as a sacrifice, "the just in the room of the unjust, for," that is, 'on account of,' "our offences"—our violations of His law, and whom He has "raised up" from the dead, to the throne of the universe—the highest place in heaven, "for our justification,"[5] —that is, I apprehend, not 'that He may justify us,' though

[1] Ver. 20. [2] Ver. 22. [3] Ver. 23.
[4] Ver. 24. [5] Ver. 25.

that is true too, but in contrast with "He delivered Him for, or on account of, our offences," He "raised Him on account of that which justifies us," that which is our justification—the only ground of our justification—the substantial righteousness on account of which we are treated as righteous,—that is, the obedience to the death of this Lord Jesus.[1] The form, then, in which "the righteousness of God" comes before our minds is substantially this: "God in Christ is reconciling the world to Himself, not imputing to men their trespasses, seeing He has made Him who knew no sin to be sin in our room, that we might be made the righteousness of God in Him;"[2] and being "well pleased for His righteousness' sake," He has, as "the God of peace, brought again from the dead our Lord Jesus, that great Shepherd of the sheep, by the blood of the everlasting covenant," and "set Him at His own right hand;"[3] while in the Gospel He "sets Him forth a propitiation through His blood by faith," proclaiming Himself "the just God and the Saviour,"—"just, and the justifier of him that believes in Jesus."[4] To him who believes this, his faith will be reckoned unto justification. "He will be blessed, by being justified along with—in the same way as, believing Abraham."[5] Such is the apostle's argumentative illustration, that the Divine method of justification, "without law," "by faith," and taking effect "on *all* them that believe," is attested—"witnessed by the law and the prophets."

The account contained in this section of the faith of Abraham, is a very fit means of giving clear views—views easily applied to practical and experimental purposes—of justifying faith. On no subject is it of more importance to have distinct and accurate notions, than on the way in which a guilty human being, righteously condemned on account of his sins,

[1] The full antithesis is—He was delivered on account of our παραπτώματα, offences, which were our κατάκρισις, condemnation, and raised again on account of His own δικαίωμα, righteousness, which is our δικαίωσις, justification.

[2] 2 Cor. v. 19, 21.

[3] Heb. xiii. 20; Eph. i. 20.

[4] Rom. iii. 25.

[5] Gal. iii. 9.

may obtain the forgiveness of sins, and be treated by a righteous God as if he were a righteous person. That there is such a method, is a truth clearly revealed in Scripture; and it is also distinctly stated, that it is only through the knowledge and belief of what God has revealed respecting this method of salvation, that the individual sinner can obtain a personal interest in it, and in the invaluable benefits which it secures —which it alone can secure.

It is not, then, wonderful that, among those who profess to consider the New Testament as a Divine revelation, that *faith*, which holds so prominent a place in that Divine method of justification which it unfolds, should have been made the subject of most serious investigation; though there is cause both for wonder and regret that much of this investigation has tended rather to perplex than to explain, to obscure than to illustrate.

One of the principal causes of those indistinct and erroneous views of faith, and of course of the Divine method of justification by faith, is, if I mistake not, to be found in the tendency of the human mind to regard abstract terms or notions as real existences. Faith is often spoken of and thought of as something separate or separable from the mind in which it exists—some agent in it, instead of what it really is, the mind itself in a particular state, or acting in a particular way. The attempt to explain what faith is, in a general abstract way, without keeping constantly in view the simple truth, which yet some learned divines seem never to have got a glimpse of, that faith is just a man believing, has exceedingly darkened a subject which in itself is certainly not peculiarly difficult, and just and distinct views of which are most intimately connected both with man's holiness and his comfort.

The best, and perhaps the only way, of guarding against such confused and perplexing views of faith is, when we think of the subject, to bring before our mind some individual believer, and then, by reflecting on *whom* he believed, *what* he believed, *why* he believed, and what influence his believing had on his dispositions and conduct, we will soon arrive at clear and definite ideas of what faith is—ideas easily explicable to others, and easily applicable to practical purposes in our own experience. We escape out of a world of shadows into a world of realities.

It is in this way, as we have seen, that the Apostle Paul explains the nature, and operations, and influence of faith, in the section of his Epistle to the Romans which we have been considering. He does not set before our minds the abstract notion of Faith; he does not tell us about a historical faith, as distinguished from a confidential faith—a faith of the head, as distinguished from a faith of the heart; he enters into no discussion as to whether faith be an operation of the mind, or a *state* of the mind—whether it be a mental act or a mental habit—whether it be a capacity or a faculty—whether it belong to the department of the understanding or of the will—whether it be merely a matter of the intellect or merely a matter of the affections, or both, and if both, which has the initiative—whether the mind is active or passive in believing, or whether it is not in some measure both, and if so, in what degree it is active, and in what passive;—all these questions which philosophers and divines have delighted to agitate, are put aside, and the apostle places full before the mind "Abraham the believer." He tells us *whom* he believed, *what* he believed, and on what evidence he believed it; and he tells us that, if we believe *Him* whom Abraham believed, if we believe what Abraham believed, if we believe on the same kind of evidence on which Abraham believed, God will deal with us as He dealt with Abraham. He will reckon us believers; and, reckoning us believers, He will treat us as if we were righteous, and bless us with all heavenly and spiritual blessings.

The two questions which are fitted most deeply to interest the awakened sinner on this subject—and I believe no other person will get much good from agitating such questions—are, What is the *object* of the faith by which a man is justified? and what is the *ground* of that faith?—in other words,

What is it that is to be believed in order to justification, and *on what evidence* is that to be believed? And a satisfactory answer to these two questions will be found in the true answer to these two other *questions*—What did Abraham, who was justified by faith, believe? and, Why did he believe what he did believe?—on what evidence did he believe it?

What did Abraham believe? He believed what God revealed to him respecting the way of salvation. We are not to restrict Abraham's faith, spoken of in this section, to the revelation that he was to have a son by Sarah; that through that son he was to become the father of many nations; and that, along with him, in his seed all the nations were to be blessed. We know from the best authority that Abraham was aware that these promises referred to a great Deliverer, who had been promised to man from the beginning, and that "his seed" was the same person as "the seed of the woman." "Your father Abraham," said our Lord to the Jews, "rejoiced to see my day, and he saw it and was glad." The truth revealed respecting the salvation of lost mankind was the object of Abraham's faith. That truth came in the form of promise. The testimony then was, "This is a faithful saying, and worthy of all acceptation," that the seed of the woman shall bruise the head of the serpent; and that in Abraham's seed, in the line of Isaac, all the nations of the earth shall be blessed. What was the precise extent of Abraham's explicit knowledge of the meaning of these declarations, is more than we can particularly explain. But so far as he apprehended their meaning, he firmly believed them. He expected salvation through their accomplishment.

The object of the faith by which a man is justified is in every case materially the same. It is what God has revealed respecting the way of salvation. To us the testimony is, "This is a faithful saying, and worthy of all acceptation, that Jesus Christ came into the world to save sinners, even the chief." "God hath so loved the world as to give his only begotten Son, that whosoever believeth in Him might not perish, but might have eternal life." "This is the testimony—the record—which God hath given us, that He hath given to us eternal life, and this life is in his Son."[1] The truth revealed by God respecting the salvation of mankind was the object of Abraham's faith, and it is the object of the faith of all in every age who are justified. He who does not believe this truth, whatever else he may believe, is not, cannot be justified.

The second question is, What was the ground of that faith which Abraham had, and by which he was justified? On what evidence did he believe the testimony made to him? Was it because he had been taught these things from his infancy? Was it because he had received them by tradition from his fathers? Was it because he had been convinced of them by rational argument? No; it was simply because he believed that the testimony he had heard was *God's* testimony. He had no reason for believing it, but that God had said it, and in that he found abundant reason for believing. To have believed what he did believe, if God had not said it, would have been presumption and madness. But he had satisfactory evidence that God had said it; and therefore alone did he believe it.

It is just so with the man who, through believing, in every age is justified. The truth he believes cannot, from its nature, be demonstrated on rational principles. It is in the form of a testimony; and the testimony of no number of *men*, however accomplished, can lay a foundation for believing what God will do in a matter that depends entirely on His sovereign good pleasure. He has abundant evidence, of a great variety of kinds, that this testimony is the testimony of God; but he believes the truth of the things contained in the testimony entirely on the authority of the Divine witness. Had it been any but God who gave the promise, Abraham could not have believed it. Had it been any but God who gives the testimony in the Gospel revelation to the believing sinner, he feels that he could not have believed it either. In both cases, it is a "setting to the seal that God is true,"—perceiving that

[1] 1 Tim. i. 15; John iii. 16; 1 John v. 11.

to do anything else would be to treat Him as a liar. If, then, we are to form our notions of what justifying faith is from the example of Abraham—and surely this is the purpose for which it is brought forward—the conclusion we rest in is this: 'The faith by which a man is justified is the considering as true what God has revealed respecting the way of salvation, because He has revealed it,—the knowing and being sure of *this*, for *this* reason.'

May every one of us thus believe the truth to justification —thus believe to the saving of the soul, and know from our happy experience that, "being thus justified by believing" "that God raised from the dead our Lord Jesus, who was delivered for our offences, and raised again for our justification," "we have peace with God and free access to Him,"—stand by faith in the state of favour into which our faith has introduced us,—"rejoice in hope of the glory of God," "a hope that maketh not ashamed," and "joy in God through our Lord Jesus Christ, by whom we have received the reconciliation."

§ 3. *The Blessings secured by the Divine Method of Justification are "free," "by God's grace," "through the Redemption that is by Christ Jesus."*

CHAPTER V.—Therefore, being justified by faith, we have peace with God through our Lord Jesus Christ: by whom also we have access by faith into this grace wherein we stand, and rejoice in hope of the glory of God. And not only so, but we glory in tribulations also: knowing that tribulation worketh patience; and patience, experience; and experience, hope; and hope maketh not ashamed: because the love of God is shed abroad in our hearts by the Holy Ghost, which is given unto us. For when we were yet without strength, in due time Christ died for the ungodly. For scarcely for a righteous man will one die; yet peradventure for a good man some would even dare to die. But God commendeth His love toward us, in that, while we were yet sinners, Christ died for us. Much more then, being now justified by His blood, we shall be saved from wrath through Him. For if, when we were enemies, we were reconciled to God by the death of His Son; much more, being reconciled, we shall be saved by His life. And not only so, but we also joy in God through our Lord Jesus Christ, by whom we have now received the atonement. Wherefore, as by one man sin entered into the world, and death by sin ; and so death passed upon all men, for that all have sinned: (For until the law sin was in the world: but sin is not imputed when there is no law. Nevertheless death reigned from Adam to Moses, even over them that had not sinned after the similitude of Adam's transgression, who is the figure of Him that was to come. But not as the offence, so also is the free gift. For if through the offence of one many be dead, much more the grace of God, and the gift by grace, which is by one man, Jesus Christ, hath abounded unto many. And not as it was by one that sinned, so is the gift; for the judgment was by one to condemnation, but the free gift is of many offences unto justification. For if by one man's offence death reigned by one ; much more they which receive abundance of grace, and of the gift of righteousness, shall reign in life by one, Jesus Christ:) therefore, as by the offence of one judgment came upon all men to condemnation ; even so by the righteousness of one the free gift came upon all men unto justification of life. For as by one man's disobedience many were made sinners ; so by the obedience of one shall many be made righteous. Moreover, the law entered, that the offence might abound: but where sin abounded, grace did much more abound: that as sin hath reigned unto death, even so might grace reign through righteousness unto eternal life by Jesus Christ our Lord.

The fifth chapter of the Epistle to the Romans obviously divides itself into two paragraphs of nearly equal length—the one reaching from the beginning of the chapter to the 11th verse, and the other from the 12th verse to the end of the chapter. But it has one great subject—that stated in the closing verse, "grace reigning through righteousness unto eternal life by Jesus Christ our Lord:" in other words, it takes up the topic started at the 24th verse of the third chapter, "Being justified freely by His grace through the redemption that is in, or by, Jesus Christ." This third sub-section may be entitled, "The blessings secured and conferred by the Divine method of justification, 'free,' 'by God's grace,' 'through the redemption that is in Christ Jesus'—*i.e.* undeserved—not wrought for by man, bestowed by God in the exercise of sovereign mercy entirely on account of the ransom paid by Jesus Christ." If I mistake not, everything in the chapter goes to the illustration of these closely connected distinctive features, of the Divine method of justification.

The first part of the section is employed in an enumeration and description of some of the principal blessings which are secured and conferred by the Divine method of salvation, and this enumeration and description is so managed as to bring out, in strong relief, both that they are entirely gratuitous, and that they are bestowed entirely in consequence of that propitiatory sacrifice of Himself which Jesus Christ offered as the ransom for sinners. "Therefore being justified by faith,"—or rather, 'being then justified by faith,' for the words do not express a logical inference, but an established connection—"Being then justified by faith, we have peace with God through our Lord Jesus Christ."[1] We "who believe in God, who raised up Jesus Christ our Lord from the dead, who was given for our offences, and raised again for our justification," have faith "reckoned to us for justification." We are "jusfied;" our sins are pardoned; and we are treated as righteous on the ground of "the redemption," or ransom, which was paid when Jesus Christ was delivered as a propitiatory sacrifice for our offences; and which was proved to be complete and acceptable when He was raised from the dead by the mighty power of God. Here is nothing *done*, but much *received*, on the part of man; and on the part of God, what is there but an act of sovereign kindness, harmonized with righteousness by the redemption that is in Jesus Christ?

And "being thus justified, we have peace with God *through our Lord Jesus Christ*." God is the enemy of man the sinner. Man the sinner is, he cannot but be, the object of the holy disapprobation, the subject of the just condemnatory sentence, of God. And on the other hand, man the sinner is the enemy of God; "an enemy in his mind by wicked works," set in opposition to God's holy and benignant purposes. But, being justified by believing, the state of war becomes a state of peace on both sides—God is pacified, and the sinner is reconciled: and this "through our Lord Jesus Christ," who was given for our offences, and raised again for our justification. *With* that pro-

[1] Chap. v. ver. 1.

pitiatory sacrifice, which was the divinely appointed and every way suitable ransom for man, God is well pleased; and *through* that propitiatory sacrifice, He is well pleased with every sinner who, in believing, accepts the atonement or reconciliation. He was angry; but His "anger is turned away." The sinner's happiness was opposed to the ends of His holy government: it is so no longer. He is just in justifying him; and the same ransom, viewed as the subject of a well-accredited revelation believed under the influence of the Holy Spirit, destroys the enmity of the sinner's heart. God and the believing justified sinner are then at one; the quarrel is entirely made up. And here, too, man is simply a receiver; God is a gracious bestower; and it is entirely through Jesus Christ, as the propitiatory ransom, that man thus receives, and God bestows peace.

But this is not all. Not only have we, "being justified by faith, peace with God through our Lord Jesus Christ"—we have also by Him "access"—that is, to God.[1] "Access *to* God" is more than peace *with* God. It indicates not only a state of security *from* God, but a state of intimate and endearing friendship and fellowship *with* Him. The justified sinner is not only freed from all hazard arising from God's righteous displeasure, but, as an object of His peculiar favour, admitted to "see His face," to "dwell in His presence," to "go boldly to the throne of grace." He enjoys, and knows that he enjoys, the fatherly love of God. This, too, is "by Jesus Christ," "delivered for our offences, raised again for our justification." We are "made accepted in the beloved," even "in Him, in whom we have redemption through His blood, the forgiveness of sin;" and this, too, is "according to the riches of God's grace."[2]

This access to God the justified sinner enjoys by faith in reference to *this* grace—the grace which reigns through righteousness, or the manifestation of that grace in this gracious economy—the righteousness of God.[3] It is "precious faith

[1] Ver. 2. [2] Eph. i. 6, 7.

[3] *πίστις εἰς*—faith in reference to. *πιστεύειν εἰς τι*, 1 John v. 10.

in the righteousness of our God and Saviour"—in the truth respecting the Divine method of justification, that enables the sinner, through the new and living way, to draw near with a true heart, with assured confidence, having his heart sprinkled with the blood of the propitiatory sacrifice by which atonement was made.

By this faith the justified sinner "stands."[1] The interest which he has obtained in the justifying, pacifying, access-procuring influence of the Divine method of justfication, is not of a transient but of a permanent kind; he can never come into condemnation—God never can be again his enemy—he can never again be God's enemy. The way to the throne of grace is always open, and the Father of Mercies is ever ready to supply all his need by blessing him with all heavenly and spiritual blessings.

"Standing" in the enjoyment of this state of favour, the sinner justified by believing "rejoices in hope of the glory of God." "The glory of God" seems here to mean, as in chapter iii. 23, the approbation of God. The reference is to the heavenly state; but it is to that as a state of perfect conformity to the will and image of God. The ultimate object of the believer's hope is to be, in character, conduct, and condition, just what God would have him to be. This he hopes for, seeing God has promised it; and he knows that by the atonement of His Son, the influence of His Spirit, and the instrumentality of His Word and Providence, He is carrying forward such a transformation, which He will perfect in the day of the Lord; and in this hope the believer rejoices, glories, exults. Amid a deep sense of deficiency and fault, it fills him with unutterable gladness, to think that he will one day be "unblameable and unreprovable" in His presence, and be as holy and happy as the infinitely holy and good God could wish him to be.

And such is the influence of this hope, all grounded on the

[1] ἑστήκαμεν, *remain*, in opposition to *move from*, or *stand*, in opposition to *fall*.—John viii. 44; 1 Cor. x. 12; xv. 1; Eph. vi. 13; Gal. v. 4; Rev. ii. 5.

redemption in Christ Jesus, all received in believing, that the afflictions to which he is exposed by the profession and acting out of his faith, instead of depressing him, do in the measure of that faith increase his exultation, as they strengthen instead of destroying his hope. "We glory in tribulations also,[1] knowing"—that is, 'seeing we know'[2]—"that tribulations" in us who are justified by believing "*work*"[3]—lead to—"patience,"[4] or rather, perseverance: however severe, they do not, as in the case of the false professor, produce apostacy; they make us hold the faster by the Saviour, and by the faith which makes Him known to us. And this perseverance "works"—leads to—"experience,"[5] that is, trial or proof: it proves the reality of our faith; it proves that we possess the faith we profess, and that our faith is the faith which overcomes the world. And this proof "works"—leads to—hope, increased hope, not by changing or adding to its foundation, but by showing that we have indeed built on that foundation. So that we may well glory in tribulations which, in this way, instead of destroying or even shaking the hope in which we glory, invigorate it.

And further, we exult in this hope of the glory of God, for we know that it is a hope that shall not "make ashamed."[6] It will not disappoint us. We shall obtain what we hope for, and find in it all, far more than all, we expected. And we know this, "for the love of God is shed abroad in our hearts by the Holy Ghost given to us." The love of God is, here, God's love to us, not our love to God. This is plain: for (1.) It is not our love to God, but His love to us, that secures that our hope shall not make us ashamed; and (2.) It is God's love to us, and not our love to God, that the apostle proceeds immediately to illustrate. The meaning of the affirmation is, We know that God loves us, and we know this

1 Ver. 3.
2 1 Cor. xv. 58; 2 Cor. i. 7; iv. 14.
3 Chap. iv. 15.
4 Luke viii. 15; xxi. 19; Rom. viii. 25; xv. 4; 1 Thes. i. 5; 2 Thes. iii. 5; Heb. x. 36; xii. 1; James i. 3, 4; v. 11; Rev. ii. 2; iii. 10.
5 Ver. 4.
6 Ver. 5.

through the operation of Divine influence: the Holy Ghost has made us know and believe it. And how has He done this? Is it by giving us individually a direct testimony to the fact that God loves us? No; it is by leading us really to believe the Gospel record. "Hereby perceive we the love of God, because HE, God's Son, laid down his life for us." "In this was manifested the love of God toward us, because that God sent His only begotten Son into the world, that we might live through Him." "Herein is love, not that we loved God, but that He loved us, and sent His Son to be the propitiation for our sin." How can we believe this, and doubt that God loves us? We know and are sure of this love; for we know and are sure that when we were "without strength" and "ungodly," incapable of helping ourselves, undeserving of God's help, Christ saved us by dying in our room.[1]

And surely this is satisfactory proof. It were incredible that a merely just, strictly honest, man should find anybody ready to ransom his life by the sacrifice of his own. Such a mark of regard may, as the highest proof of human love, be given to a good, a benevolent man, by one whom he has laid under peculiar obligations. But what is this to the proof which God has given of His love to us? We were not *good*—we were not even *just*—we were sinners, righteously condemned persons; yet for us Christ, who is the incarnate God,—"God manifest in flesh"—died.[2] If this do not prove love, what can?

But is it not possible that God should cease to love us, and thus our hope of His glory be disappointed and make us ashamed? The thing is impossible. (1.) If, when we were in circumstances the most calculated to excite despair, "*sinners*"—condemned, "enemies"[3]—persons regarded with displeasure, God manifested love, He assuredly will not cease to love, and

[1] Ver. 6. [2] Ver. 7, 8.

[3] "ἐχθροὶ may either be active, as Col. i. 21, or passive, as Rom. xi. 28. But here the latter meaning only can apply, for the apostle is speaking of the death of Christ, and its effects, as applied to all time, not merely to those believers who lived: and those unborn at the death of Christ could not have been ἐχθροὶ in the active sense."—ALFORD.

manifest love, now that, "justified" by His grace, we are in circumstances every way fitted to encourage hope.[1] (2.) If we have already received the strongest possible proof of God's love, surely He will not withhold any other proof of love necessary to our happiness. He who gave us His Son cannot refuse us His heaven.[2] (3.) If He gave the highest proof of His love when we were in the worst conceivable circumstances, He will not withhold proofs of His love, which, however extraordinary, are not to be compared to this, when we are brought into far more favourable circumstances. He who gave His Son for us when enemies, will not withhold His heaven from us when we are reconciled to Him.[3] And finally, (4.) If consequences so full of blessing, so expressive of love, flowed from the death of Christ, surely every blessing needful for our complete and eternal happiness may be expected from the power of His endless life.[4] Well then may the sinner justified by believing "rejoice in the hope of the glory of God"—a hope which tribulations strengthen instead of destroying—a hope which cannot be disappointed, because founded on the clearly demonstrated love of the unchangeable God. And this joyful hope, like "the peace" and "the access," which are secured by "the righteousness of God"—the Divine method of justfication, is graciously bestowed by God, freely received by man, through the redemption that is in Christ Jesus.

There is still another and higher privilege secured by this Divine method, with which the apostle concludes his wonderful enumeration. "And not only so"—that is, not only being justified by believing, have we solid peace, and free access, and joyful hope—but "we joy," exult, "in God through our Lord Jesus Christ, by whom we have now received the atonement," or rather, the 'reconciliation.'[5] The justified person stands in a new and peculiar relation to God. He has a personal interest in that sum and substance of all the exceeding great and precious promises, "I will be thy God." 'I will be to thee, I

[1] Ver. 9. [2] Ver. 10. [3] Ver. 9, 10. [4] Ver. 10.

[5] Ver. 11. The English word originally signified reconciliation, at-onement, the being at one.

will do for thee, all that may be expected from the infinite perfections of the Godhead—infinite power, eternal and unchangeable wisdom, righteousness, faithfulness, and love.' And in God thus related to him, the believer joys, exults, glories. The language of his heart is, "God is the portion of my inheritance. My God is my glory. My soul makes her boast in God. In God is my salvation and my glory: the rock of my strength; and my refuge is in God. My flesh and my heart faileth; but God is the strength of my heart, and my portion for ever." And this relation to God, and this gloriation in Him, are "through our Lord Jesus Christ;" through His mediation do we obtain and enjoy these blessings. Through Him we receive the reconciliation. His propitiatory sacrifice was the ransom. His Spirit is the author of that faith which interests us individually in the ransom, and makes us partakers of the blessings which it procures. And we *now* receive the reconciliation. The enjoyment of the full and entire approbation of God, as perfectly holy, is something future, and is the object of hope; but the reception of the reconciliation is something present. "We *now* receive the reconciliation," and this enables us *now* to "rejoice in God." This result of the righteousness of God is thus, like all the rest, "freely, by God's grace, through the redemption that is in Christ Jesus."

To show *how* entirely justification, and the peace with, and access to God, and the permanence of these blessings, and the joyful hope of God's glory, and the triumphant exultation in God Himself, which are secured by justification, are owing to "the redemption that is in Christ Jesus," seems the object of the apostle in the concluding paragraph of the fifth chapter; and he prosecutes this object by instituting a comparison and contrast between the way in which man originally became guilty, through the sin of Adam, and the way in which mankind become righteous—are justified—through the redemption in Christ Jesus—His obedience to death, which, as a propitiatory sacrifice, is our ransom. The justification of the believer is as entirely the result of this obedience, without reference to his own good works, as certain evils, to which all mankind are exposed, are entirely the result of the first sin of the first man, without reference to their personal transgressions of the Divine law.

It is of great importance that we should distinctly apprehend both the subject and object of the important paragraph now before us. The *subject* is justification—restoration to the Divine favour—and that on which it rests. The apostle is not contrasting a condition of righteousness generally, including both state and character, relation and disposition, with a condition of sinfulness, in an equally extended sense; he is not contrasting a state of sanctification with a state of depravity: he is contrasting a state of security *from* punishment, and of happiness, as contrasted with a state of liability *to*, certainty *of*, punishment and misery—a state of favour with a state of wrath—a state of justification with a state of condemnation—a state of secured happiness with a state of impending ruin. And the *object* he has in view is to illustrate the former by the latter—to show that there is a strong analogy, in one of the most peculiar features of the way in which it is procured, to an equally peculiar feature of the way in which its opposite was incurred; and that is—That as *all* men are, in certain points, treated as if they were sinners entirely on account of the first sin of the first man, Adam, *so* all men who are justified are treated as if they were righteous entirely on account of the obedience to death of Him of whom the first man was an image—the Lord from heaven: and *thus*, even *thus*, is the Divine method of justification "through the redemption that is in Christ Jesus."

All the evil that befalls mankind, either in the present or the future world—all the multifarious forms of guilt, depravity, and misery—may, in one point of view, be considered as originating in the first sin of the first man. Directly or indirectly, they all flow from this source. Some of these evils are realized, however, only through the individual, in his own person, becoming an actual violator of the Divine law, and are realized by him in the degree in which he does so. There are others that come directly on the race, as the manifestation of the displeasure of God at the first sin: Death, including in that dreadful word man's loss of immortality, as an embodied being; a life longer or shorter, it might be, but liable to disease, doomed to death, and the greater loss of that holy Divine influence which is the soul of the human soul, the principle of its true excellence and highest happiness. These—mortality and destitution of spiritual goodness—come equally on all men, without reference to personal acts of guilt; and these are the evils, the manner of incurring which the apostle employs as an illustration of the manner in which the great blessing of justification is obtained for man. This seems plain from the apostle's object, for evils not resulting entirely from Adam's sin, would not have corresponded with blessings resulting entirely from our Lord's obedience; and it appears also from his stating that the evils he refers to are not only incurred, but undergone, by the whole of the race, even by those of them who are "to reign in life by Christ Jesus;" and further, from his obviously contrasting the judgment of the one offence, which is executed, with the judgment of the many offences, which is graciously removed in justification.

The apostle's analogical illustration of the manner in which the Divine method of the justification of mankind is through the redemption that is in Christ Jesus—that is, His obedience to death, by the manner in which mankind came into a state of condemnation through the disobedience of Adam, is contained in the paragraph from ver. 12 to ver. 19; and it consists of a statement—(1.) Of the fact on which the analogy proceeds; (2.) Of the points in which it does not hold; and (3.) Of the points in which it does hold.

The *fact* is stated in the 12th verse: "Wherefore, as by one man sin entered into the world, and death by sin; and so death passed upon all men, for that all have sinned."[1] The word "wherefore" is either equivalent to, 'Since these things are so—since Jesus Christ was so given for our offences, as that we are justified by Him—since by Him we have peace with and access to God—since by Him we receive the recon-

[1] *ἥμαρτον* is explained, ver. 19, as = *κατεστάθησαν ἁμαρτωλοί.*

ciliation—in one word, since we are justified by the redemption that is in Him, it follows that there is a very remarkable coincidence between the way in which we are justified and the way in which we became guilty;' or it is to be understood, as it sometimes is, as equivalent to, 'In reference to this matter'—our receiving the reconciliation,—it is, "as by one man sin entered into the world." The sentence is plainly what is called elliptical—something is wanting to make out its meaning; and the supplement last noticed seems the simplest.

Now, what is the fact which is to illustrate our entire indebtedness to the work of Christ for our justification? It is this: "By one man"—that is plainly the first man—"sin entered into the world." The meaning is not, sin then first began to exist in the universe. Devils had sinned, Eve had sinned, before Adam sinned. The words, "sin came into the world," refer not so much to Adam's sin, as to the consequence of Adam's sin. To be in the world marks what is common. By one man sinning, sin—guilt—became a world-wide thing; and so did death, for death came along with guilt: where there was guilt there was death, and where there was death there was the evidence of guilt; and thus death became not only common, but universal among mankind; for all men have sinned, all men are guilty—so guilty as to die. All mankind are exposed to death in consequence of the first sin of the first man; all men are treated as guilty on account of that one offence.

The proof of this fact, on which the apostle's analogical illustration rests, is contained in the 13th and 14th verses: "For until the law sin was in the world: but sin is not imputed when there is no law. Nevertheless death reigned from Adam to Moses, even over them that had not sinned after the similitude of Adam's transgression." If I mistake not, the apostle's argument is perplexed by the meaning given in our version to the particle rendered "until." It is often used to signify 'during,' or 'while:' as Acts xxvii. 33, "While the day was coming on;" Heb. iii. 13, "Exhort one another *while* it is called to-day." Understanding it so here,[1] this seems the apostle's argument: 'During the law—the Mosaic law—sin was so in the world that men died—all men died. All men were treated as criminals by being put to death.' But it might be said, Their being under the law accounts for this—it was the law that killed them. The apostle might have said, No, death was not the sanction of the Mosaic law: premature violent death was, not simple death. The men condemned to die would of their own accord have died; and men died beyond Judea as well as in it. But, instead of taking that ground, he rises to the state before the law, and taking along with him the principle, "where there is no law there is no transgression," he, as it were, says, It surely was not the law that killed the men who lived from Adam to Moses. Yet they died—they all died. Death reigned over them. But was it not the sentence of what may be termed *natural* moral law, that doomed them? No, not that either, says the apostle; death reigned even over those who had not sinned after the similitude of Adam's transgression, by doing what they knew to be wrong. This interpretation, which refers "those who did not sin after the similitude of Adam's transgression" to infants and idiots, seems to me the only one which, agreeing to the natural sense of the words, brings out the force of the apostle's argument.[2] The true account of death in them is the true account of death in all men. They die entirely on account of the first sin of the first man, without reference to their own personal violations of the Divine law. Such is the fact and the evidence.

Let us now see in what points the analogy between the economy of condemnation and that of justification does not hold. Adam is, in this very remarkable event, appealed to as a figure—a type of Him who is to come; but the type, though striking, is not perfect. The points where the analogy does

[1] ἄχρι. We are not singular in our view of the particle. Origen, Chrysostom, Theodoret, Augustine, Erasmus, Krebs, Beausobre, Koppe, Fritzsche, and others, explain it thus here.

[2] *Vide* Hodge *in loc.*; Hill's Lectures, ii., 394; Edwards' Works, ii., 303, where our exegesis is clearly stated, and powerfully sustained.

not hold, are thus stated by the apostle in the 15th, 16th, and 17th verses: "But not as the offence, so also is the free gift. For if through the offence of one many be dead; much more the grace of God, and the gift by grace, which is by one man, Jesus Christ, hath abounded unto many. And not as it was by one that sinned, so is the gift: for the judgment was by one to condemnation, but the free gift is of many offences unto justification. For if by one man's offence death reigned by one; much more they which receive abundance of grace, and of the gift of righteousness, shall reign in life by one, Jesus Christ." I do not think these verses are the statement of an argument, but merely an affirmation. They are true, viewed as an affirmation; but it would not be easy to make a conclusive argument out of them.

The first of these verses is a general assertion that the justifying economy transcends the condemning economy. "The free gift," or gracious interposition, to which we owe our deliverance from guilt, is not as "the offence," the transgression of Adam, by which we all became guilty; the one does not in every point correspond to the other. No, it far transcends it. Of "the offence" this is the sum that has been said: "By this offence of one man many are dead"—or many die through it; and if the free gift had been *as* this, it would have just been said, 'By the free gift many are made alive, or live.' But it is much more than this. "The grace of God"—the sovereign mercy of God, in which all originates—and "the gift by grace" —the Divine economy of dispensing forgiveness, "which is by"—through—"one man, Jesus Christ,"—these are not merely adequate, in their good effects, to the bad effects of the offence, but they "have much more abounded to a great multitude." The points of resemblance here, you will perceive, are two: The offence is by one man, and issues in evil to a multitude; the free gift is by one man too, and issues in good to a multitude. The point of contrast is, 'The amount of good resulting from the free gift, to those interested in it, is much greater than the amount of the evil directly and solely derived from the offence.'

The two succeeding verses illustrate this general principle, and show—(1.) That the free gift delivers not only from the evil incurred by the offence, but from other evils; and (2.) That the free gift raises those who are interested in it to a higher state of happiness than they would have enjoyed had the offence never occurred. The natural supplement of the ellipsis, in the beginning of ver. 16, is "the judgment," "Not as the judgment through one that sinned is the gift." "The judgment" is the sentence of the law in reference to the offence; this sentence was "through one that sinned;" it went forth on all men, through the medium of our first parent, when he sinned. Now, says the apostle, "the gift is not as this judgment." "The gift" is the free sentence of forgiveness, which, in the justifying economy, takes the place of the righteous sentence of condemnation under the condemning economy. The apostle shows in what the dissimilitude consists: "the judgment was by one to condemnation, but the free gift is of many offences to justification." The first clause here is somewhat dark, from a word not having been supplied that ought to have been supplied, and from the particle, rightly rendered *of* in the second clause, being rendered *by* in the first. The apostle's meaning is plain when you read, "for the judgment"—the righteous sentence, "was of one offence"—the first offence of the first man, of course, "to condemnation;" "but the free gift"—the gracious sentence, "was of many offences to justification." The sentence, condemning men to death, was grounded on the first sin of the first man. Had there been just a correspondence, and no more, there would have been a reversal of that sentence, and no more. Other offences, against which other sentences had gone forth, must still be encountered. But "the blood of Jesus Christ cleanseth from all sin;" the gracious sentence of remission removes all iniquities.

But this is not all. Not only are their other offences as well as the first offence remitted, but the justifying economy raises those interested in it to a higher place than that from which they were hurled by the condemning economy. "By one man's offence, death reigned by one." By the transgression of one man—Adam, death not only prevailed but reigned,—that is, *all* men died through means of him, the transgressor. But what is the other side of the contrast? Is it, 'By one man's obedience men are brought back from the death into which the one man's offence plunged them?' No, it is something much more than this: "Much more shall they who receive abundance of grace, and of the gift of righteousness, reign in life by Jesus Christ." "The abundance of grace" is just equivalent to abundant grace—an overflow of Divine kindness. "The gift of righteousness" is a further description of this abundant grace: "the gift of righteousness" is the gift of justification—full, free justification, justification by God's grace—the gift of God. To "receive" this is to be interested in it: it is to "have it," as the apostle says;[1] and it is "*upon* all them that believe," only on them. Now, says the apostle, these persons "shall reign in life"—they shall live and reign.[2] They shall enjoy a state as far—infinitely further—above the paradisaic life lost by the offence, as royal life is supposed to be above ordinary life, and this they shall enjoy by one, Christ Jesus. They will be indebted—entirely indebted—to Him for it all.

The apostle now states the points in which the analogy holds: this he does in the 18th and 19th verses. "Therefore as by the offence of one, judgment came upon all men to condemnation, even so by the righteousness of one, the free gift came upon all men to justification of life. For as by one man's disobedience many were made sinners, so by the obedience of one shall many be made righteous." In the margin of your Bibles, you will find "one offence" for "the offence of one," and "one obedience" for "the obedience of one." That in the margin is the better rendering, as is indeed generally the case. In the 18th verse, he compares the *unity* of the offence with the unity of the obedience; and in the 19th, the *singularity* of

[1] Phil. iii. 9.

[2] Horace, Epist. i. 10, says, "Vivo et regno," *i.e.* beatissime vivo.

the offender with the singularity of the obeyer. You will observe also, that in verse 18 there are two considerable supplements printed in the italic character—"judgment came," and "the free gift came." A shorter supplement—for some supplement is necessary—would have equally served the purpose. "As it was by one offence upon all men to condemnation, so is it by one righteousness on all men to justification of life;" or, to give the apostle's idea more in the English idiom, 'As by one offence all men were condemned, so by one righteousness are all men justified so as to live.' To complete the sense, you must supply the word 'death' in the first clause, so as to correspond with the word "life" in the second. 'Well, then, as by one offence all men were condemned so as to die, so by one righteousness all are justified so as to live.' "The one offence" is Adam's first sin; "the one righteousness" is the one unbroken great act of obedience of our Lord, commenced in his birth, terminated on the cross —an act embracing the whole demands of the law. On the ground of the first is condemnation ending in death; on the ground of the second, justification ending in life.

There is a difficulty in the phrase "*all men.*" We know most certainly that, though all men, on the ground of the one offence, are condemned so as to die, all men are not, on the ground of the one obedience, justified so as to live. Had the expression been *all*, then it might have meant the two totals of the two bodies of which Adam and Christ are respectively the heads; as when it is said, "In Adam all die—in Christ all are made alive" with the resurrection of life; that is, "All in Adam die"—"all in Christ are made alive." But the phrase is "*all men,*" and therefore I apprehend we must explain it on a principle not unfrequently adopted in Scripture. In both cases the effects are not confined to particular classes of men: men of all descriptions, young or old, rich or poor, Jew or Gentile, learned or unlearned, are to be found involved in the condemning power of the offence and the justifying power of the obedience.

In the 19th verse, the contrast is between the "singularity," the "oneness," of the individuals by whom respectively men are "made sinners" and "made righteous." "By"—through "the disobedience of one man," Adam, "many," even the whole race, were, by a Divine constitution, "made sinners," reckoned guilty—constituted, in a particular sense of the term sinners, liable to the punishment of sin; on the other hand, by the obedience of one—the faultless, perfect satisfaction given to the demands of the Divine law by our Lord, many—a multitude that no man can number out of all nations, and kindreds, and peoples, and tongues, are "made"—constituted, "righteous," that is, are justified, *entirely* on the ground of this all-perfect righteousness.

Such is the analogy between the condemnatory economy through Adam, and the justificatory economy through Christ Jesus. The fact on which it rests is, 'All men are treated as sinners, within certain limits, entirely on the ground of the first sin of the first man.'—The evidence of that fact is, 'All men *died* during the Mosaic law, but the Mosaic law did not kill them. This is plain, for men died before the law as well as under it; nor can you account for their death as the sanction of *natural* moral law, for those died—infants and idiots—who were not capable of violating it. The account of death in them is the true account of death in all men. They are reckoned guilty in consequence of the first sin of the first man, and therefore die.'—Men owe their justification as entirely to Christ as they did their original condemnation to Adam.—The saving efficacy of Christ's obedience is greater, however, than the condemning efficiency of Adam's disobedience. It delivers not only from the evils directly resulting from Adam's sin, but from those contracted by personal transgressions; and it raises to a higher height than that from which we were precipitated.—Still, however, the analogy is striking and extensive. On the one hand, there is one man, Adam; on the other, one man, Jesus Christ: on the one hand, offence or disobedience; on the other, righteousness and obedience: on the one hand, one offence; on the other, one righteousness: on the one hand, a righteous sentence; on the other, a gracious sentence: on the one hand, the righteous sentence denounces condemnation; on the other, the gracious sentence pronounces justification: on the one hand, there is condemnation issuing in death; on the other, there is justification issuing in life: on the one hand, there is a multitude of men of all descriptions; on the other, a multitude of men of all descriptions: in fine, on the one hand, there is a multitude of men of every description, condemned and dying, entirely on account of the one offence of the one man Adam; on the other, a multitude of men of every description, justified and living, entirely on account of the righteousness of the one man Jesus Christ. So full of meaning is the enunciation that "the reconciliation is AS by one man sin entered into the world, and death by sin." [1]

All this illustration is drawn from the original constitution of things and the violation of it. In the two concluding verses, further illustration of the Divine method of justification is drawn from the state of things which followed this violation.[2] "Moreover, the law entered that sin might abound, but when sin abounded then did grace much more abound; that as sin has reigned unto death, even so might grace reign through righteousness unto eternal life." The apostle seems here to follow out the thought transiently noticed at verse 16—The "free gift" of forgiveness is "not only of the one offence,"—of which, and of its direct results he has hitherto been speaking —but "of many offences to justification." Whence came these "many offences?" One unacquainted with human nature might suppose that the consequences of the one offence, in the reign of universal death, were so dreadful, that there would be no more offending. The apostle's account is, "The law," or rather, Law, "entered." These words have received two applications, either of them expressive of an important truth, though not equally suiting the apostle's object—which is to show how the offence abounded, or was multiplied, and how the Divine method of justification meets all those multiplied offences. It has been supposed that "Law" here means, as at verse 13, the law of Moses; in which case

[1] Ver. 12. [2] Ver. 20, 21.

the statement is—The Law in due time, indeed, was introduced: but that did not undo the effects of the first offence. If the *design* of the law be in the apostle's eye, he says 'the law entered, *in order* that it might be apparent that the offence—sin, did abound:' "By the law is the knowledge of sin. If the *effect* of the law be in his view, then he says—'it entered, *so that* the offence abounded.' With fallen man, where there is law, there will be transgression.

There are, however, serious difficulties in interpreting law here, of the Mosaic law. The apostle says 'law,' not 'the law.'[1] The word, translated 'entered,'[2] means 'entered silently,' or 'stole in'—a phrase very indescriptive of the magnificent giving of the law to Israel at Sinai. Besides, it is natural to expect something that came closely after the first offence and its disastrous consequences, and something involving all mankind, during the great part of their history; whereas the law was not given till more than 2500 years after the fall, and was an economy confined to a single, and comparatively a small, nation.

It seems, then, more natural to refer law entering—to the moral law silently taking the place of the positive constitution under which man was placed very soon after his creation, and which, on the fall, ceased to exist except in its consequences. No longer does Adam stand in the place of his children: every man is henceforth entirely answerable for himself.[3] This is *law*, and it entered silently—the word seems to be chosen as a contrast to the mode of giving the Mosaic law. Now, what was the effect of this? did men strictly obey the law? No; "the offence abounded"—was multiplied. Adam's first son killed his brother; and by the time of Noah, "the earth was full of violence." "And God saw the wickedness of man that it was great on the earth, and that every imagination of his heart was only evil and that continually."[4] And after the flood things soon became equally bad; and even when *the* law came, the people to whom it came did not keep it. In their case, too, the offence abounded or was multiplied. I think it

[1] νόμος, not ὁ νόμος.
[2] παρεισῆλθεν. Gal. ii. 4; comp. 2 Peter ii. 1.
[3] Gen. iv. 7.
[4] Gen. ii. 8, vi. 5, 12, 13.

not unlikely that, under the general phrase 'the entering of law,' the apostle might have in view all law—including moral, Jewish, and even civil law. Whenever *law* came in, it led not to uniform or even ordinary obedience, but to extended transgression. The idea then seems to be—things have been made a great deal worse for man since the fall.

But however bad they have become, the grace of God, in the Divine method of justification, is fitted to rectify them—"where sin abounded, grace did much more abound." The free mercy of God has made provision for the pardon, not only of the first offence, but of all offences. "That as sin has reigned unto death, even so might grace reign through righteousness unto eternal life, by Jesus Christ our Lord."[1] "*That*" may mark either the design or the effect of the saving economy: this was so arranged, and so done, *in order that*, or *so that*, etc. Both are true. This was His purpose from everlasting; and it shall stand, and He will do all His pleasure. Sin, as a powerful tyrant, is represented as reigning unto death—it is literally *in*[2] death—death being the present actual condition of fallen man; grace, as an omnipotent sovereign, reigning through righteousness—the righteousness of God *unto*[3] "eternal life"—that being the state to which the reign of grace is to conduct all her subjects.

Take the substance of this statement in a sentence—"Since a multitude of men of all descriptions become guilty and die, through Adam; and since a multitude of men of all descriptions are justified not only from the guilt contracted in Adam, but also from the guilt contracted by themselves, and are not only restored to the life which Adam forfeited in Paradise, but raised to a royal, eternal life with Christ Jesus; surely if sin has reigned in death over all men, grace reigns more gloriously over her subjects, through righteousness unto eternal life; surely though sin has reigned, grace does much more reign—and all this through Jesus Christ our Lord. The holy law, sprinkled with the blood of His accepted sacri-

[1] Ver. 21. [2] ἐν. [3] εἰς.

fice, is the throne of grace: "In Him we have redemption through His blood, the forgiveness of sins according to the riches of God's grace." This, then, is the apostle's illustration of his statement—"Justified freely by God's grace through the redemption that is in Christ Jesus."

And now, is not this a plan of salvation worthy of Him who is Love, and who alone hath wisdom? Is it wonderful that the angels should desire to look into it? Is it not of all monstrous incongruities the greatest that *men*, who have the deepest interest in it, should, of all intelligent creatures, be the least affected by it? Say, my brethren, do we not stand in need of such a salvation? Are we not mortal? Are we not condemned? Does not the wrath of God rest on us? Must we not die—must we not perish, unless thus saved? Innumerable offences compass us about. And is there any other way of deliverance? None; and none is needed, for here is salvation exactly suited to our circumstances. Is there an "offence"—"many offences?" Here is an "obedience" that overbalances them all. Is there a righteous sentence of condemnation? Here is a gracious sentence of free remission. Is there death a thousand times merited? Here is eternal life—held out to the most guilty as 'the gift of God through Jesus Christ our Lord." Will, then, any be so impious, so mad, as to reject this salvation, so freely offered for their acceptance?

What grateful acknowledgments are due from all the saved to the God of salvation, and to His beloved Son Jesus! "Herein is love, not that we loved God, but that He loved us, and sent His Son to be the propitiation for our sins."[1] "God commendeth His love towards us, in that, while we were yet sinners, Christ died for us."[2] Let this love constrain us, to show our gratitude by our obedience. Influenced by these mercies of God, let us present ourselves "a living sacrifice, holy, acceptable unto God, which is our reasonable service—our rational worship."

[1] 1 John iv. 10. [2] Rom. v. 8.

§ 4. *The Bearing of the Divine Method of Justification on Spiritual Transformation.*

The fourth sub-section under the head 'Of the Divine Method of Justification,' is considerably longer than any of the preceding, reaching from the beginning of the sixth chapter to the middle of the 17th verse of the eighth. Its subject is 'The Bearing of the Divine Method of Justification, on Sanctification—of the Change of State, on the Change of Spiritual Condition and Character.' Its text, among the outlines contained in the first sub-section, may be considered as chapter iii. 31: "Do we make void the law through faith? God forbid: yea, we establish the law."

In this section the apostle shows, first, that justification is necessary to sanctification, and secures it. This he does from the beginning of the sixth chapter to the 4th verse of the eighth; and then he shows that sanctification is the evidence, the only satisfactory evidence, of a man's being interested in the Divine method of justification. Let us endeavour, then, to follow out the apostle's illustrations of these two important and somewhat difficult topics, embracing as they do the whole subject of the connection of justification and sanctification—of the change of relation and disposition, of state and character —the legal and the personal change which the religion of Christ is designed to effect in man—a subject involving almost all that is most peculiar both in doctrinal and experimental Christianity.

A. *Justification is necessary to Sanctification, and secures it.*

The apostle enters on the subject by an interrogation, very naturally rising out of the discussions contained in the previous sub-sections,[1]—"What shall we say then? Shall we continue in sin, that grace may abound?"—'If we are treated as

[1] Chap. vi. 1.

righteous, not on the ground of our own doings and sufferings, but entirely on the ground of the doings and the sufferings of another; if we obtain a personal interest in these justifying doings and sufferings, not by working but believing; if our personal merits have no more causal influence on our being justified and saved, than our personal demerits had on our being condemned and dying in Adam; if the grace of God, through Jesus Christ, be more powerful to pardon and to save, then guilt, whether hereditary or personal, be to condemn and destroy; then, is it not a fair inference from all this, that we *may*, without hazard, "continue in sin"—go on in sin; nay, on the principle which all this seems to enfold, that doing evil is the way to make good come—the grace of God abounding more, through our sin, to God's glory—are we not encouraged to say, "Let us continue in sin, that grace may abound?"' Thus, very early, did men of corrupt minds "turn the grace of God into lasciviousness;" and thus, too, did many enemies of the Gospel build up an argument against its Divine original.

The apostle rejects the suggestion with abhorrence, and shows that it arises out of an entire misconception of the nature and working of the Divine method of justification.[1] "God forbid. How shall we, that are dead to sin, live any longer therein?" The purport of the apostle's reply to the blasphemous suggestion has, I think, been very generally misapprehended. Some consider it as equivalent to, 'We have undergone a *real* as well as a *relative* change. We have become as dead persons in reference to sinful desire and action, and we have professed this in submitting to baptism.' But that does not at all meet the difficulty, in the case either of the abuser or the denier of the Gospel. The point in question is the *tendency* of the Divine method of justification, not by works, by the faith of Christ, through the redemption that is in Christ Jesus; and the answer, 'We are bound to be holy; we have admitted our obligation; and we are habitu-

[1] Ver. 2.

ally holy,' does not meet it. The adversary might say, 'No doubt such is your obligation, but how can that obligation consist with your doctrine? If you are indeed, in a moral sense, dead to sin, it is more than was to be expected from that doctrine of yours; and whatever you have engaged to do, this is what that doctrine warrants, encourages, and we doubt not will end in leading you to do—"to continue in sin that grace may abound."'[1]

The apostle takes up different ground altogether. He sets himself to show that the Divine method of justification is at once necessary to sanctification, and secures it. He shows, first, that the Divine method of justification establishes such an union or intimate relation between those who are its subjects and Jesus Christ, both in His death and in His restored life, as secures that anything like habitual unholiness of heart and life cannot take place; and as, besides, furnishes the strongest motives and encouragements to the cultivation of universal holiness. This occupies him to the 13th verse of this chapter. He then shows that that state of freedom from law, and subjection to grace, into which, according to the Divine method of justification, the believer is brought—far from leading to say, 'Let us sin, since we are not under the law but under grace'—is necessary to and sufficient for securing sanctification—making it plain, from his own past experience, that law cannot make a bad man good; and from his present experience, that law cannot make a good man better; and showing how, in securing freedom from condemnation, and an adequate spiritual influence, the Divine method of justification, which is a system not of law but of grace, furnishes all that is necessary to begin and perfect the work of spiritual transformation in the mind of man. This is the subject of the apostle's discussion, from the 14th verse of the seventh chapter to the end of the 4th verse of the eighth chapter. Let us endeavour to trace out the thread, sometimes a fine and en-

[1] Fraser's Scripture Doctrine of Sanctification, a Commentary on Rom. vii.–viii. 4, is well worth studying. The old Scottish divine is "rude in speech, yet not in knowledge."

tangled one, of the apostle's illustration of this most important subject.

1. *The Union with Christ, in His Death and Life, implied in the Divine Method of Justification, secures that the Justified Person shall not continue in Sin.*

CHAPTER VI. 1–13.—" What shall we say then? Shall we continue in sin, that grace may abound? God forbid. How shall we, that are dead to sin, live any longer therein? Know ye not, that so many of us as were baptized into Jesus Christ were baptized into His death? Therefore we are buried with Him by baptism into death; that like as Christ was raised up from the dead by the glory of the Father, even so we also should walk in newness of life. For if we have been planted together in the likeness of His death, we shall be also in the likeness of His resurrection: knowing this, that our old man is crucified with Him, that the body of sin might be destroyed, that henceforth we should not serve sin. For he that is dead is freed from sin. Now, if we be dead with Christ, we believe that we shall also live with Him: knowing that Christ, being raised from the dead, dieth no more; death hath no more dominion over Him. For in that He died, He died unto sin once; but in that He liveth, He liveth unto God. Likewise reckon ye also yourselves to be dead indeed unto sin, but alive unto God through Jesus Christ our Lord. Let not sin therefore reign in your mortal body, that ye should obey it in the lusts thereof: neither yield ye your members as instruments of unrighteousness unto sin: but yield yourselves unto God, as those that are alive from the dead, and your members as instruments of righteousness unto God."

Before proceeding to the analysis of this paragraph, I will lay down what, after a good deal of consideration, appear to me the elementary principles of the first of these argumentative illustrations of the proposition, that by faith the law is not made void, but established, and that a free, full forgiveness, entirely on the ground of the obedience of Jesus Christ—the redemption that is in Him—instead of encouraging to continue in sin, absolutely secures true holiness both of heart and life.

It is of importance, on many accounts, to understand the *genesis*—the natural history of sin, in the sense of depravity. Depravity plainly can have no existence in an innocent creature. That were a contradiction in terms. In an innocent, rational, responsible creature, there may be, probably there must be, principles which make him susceptible of temptation. Till, however, temptation is yielded to, there is no depravity, as there is no guilt. The first act of a voluntary Being yielding to temptation is the beginning both of guilt and of depravity. It is "the transgression of the law;" and without Divine intervention, the abnormal, disordered state produced in the mind and heart proceeds, sin multiplies, and depravity grows. As a matter of course, that Divine influence, leading to good—the token of God's complacency in His innocent creature—is withdrawn from the sinning creature. The delusion in reference to the Divine character, in which transgression originates, extends and deepens. Evil influence from without the mind works now unopposed. Thus man, the transgressor, becomes the slave of sin; and while he continues a condemned criminal, he cannot be emancipated.

The Christian scheme of spiritual transformation is the only one that meets, or indeed even contemplates, the difficulties of the case. It begins at the beginning. It makes provision for such a change in man's relations, as lays a solid foundation for a change in his character. "The righteousness of God"—the Divine method of justification—is that provision. In reversing the sentence of condemnation, it unlocks the fetters of depravity, secures an influence to sanctify, superior in power to the influence either from within or from without to deprave, and provides suitable motives to induce the man to mortify sin and cultivate holiness. The obedience unto death of the incarnate Son, as the substitute of sinners—vindicating the rights, illustrating the excellence of the violated law, and brought to bear on the individual in his believing a Divine testimony respecting it, is in substance this Divine method, which, *therefore*, is at once the necessary and the sufficient cause of sanctification. If the two corresponding Divine arrangements—that Jesus Christ, God's Son, as the representative of man, should die as a victim and rise in the enjoyment of the Divine favour; and that the believing sinner should, on his believing, become so connected with this death and life as to be brought under their *influence*, in all the extent of meaning belonging to that word,—if these two corresponding Divine arrangements are understood, the antinomian abuse of the Divine method of justification, and the objection of the infidel, grounded on the supposition that the antinomian abuse is the true tendency of that method, are seen to be equally unfounded, and "faith" appears indeed, not to "make void," but to "establish the law." There is secured such a death in reference to sin, as makes it impossible that the man interested in the Divine method of justification should continue to live in it. The leading thought is, guilt is the source and perpetuator of depravity; deliverance from guilt is the full and perennial fountain of sanctification.

To the question, "Shall we continue in sin"—shall we continue under guilt, by, when pardoned, contracting new guilt, by committing new sin—"that grace may abound?" the apostle replies, "God forbid"—let it not be. "How shall we, that are dead to sin, live any longer therein?"[1] The general meaning of the phrase rendered "dead to sin," is not difficult to perceive, but the precise signification is not quite so easy to be apprehended. It may signify 'dead *by* sin'—put to death by guilt in the person of our representative, when He was delivered for our offences; or it may signify, 'become to sin as a dead slave in reference to his master'—freed from the power of guilt both to condemn and to deprave. The two things signified are intimately connected: the second is the necessary result of the first. The apostle's question is equivalent to an assertion, that the believing sinner's relations to *guilt* have been so changed, as that it can no longer exercise over him its former influence.

Having made this assertion, he proceeds to illustrate it. He shows that, according to the Divine method of justification, all who are interested in it are so intimately related to Jesus Christ—so "in Him," as to have, as it were, died in Him—

[1] Ver. 2. The preposition ἐν is used in the same way as when demoniacs are said to be ἐν πνεύματι ἀκαθάρτῳ, and when the world is said κεῖσθαι ἐν τῷ πονηρῷ.

been buried in Him—been raised in Him, and as to live in Him. It shows, further, that the death of Christ, in which all who are justified by believing are interested, was a death *by* sin, or *to* sin; that the life to which Christ is raised, and to which they in Him are also raised, is a life *by* God, or *to* God; and that the efficacy of Christ's death—as a deliverance from the legal power of guilt, in consequence of His dying as a victim, proved by His resurrection and unending life—renders it absolutely impossible that the justified should continue under the depraving, any more than under the condemning, influence of sin. This is the general line of the apostle's argumentative illustration, to the end of the 14th verse of this chapter.

"Know ye not," says he[1]—'Are you not aware that it is one of the first principles of the oracles of Christ, that all who are united to Him are united to Him as having died, been buried, and raised again, and living a new and an endless life?' The phrase "baptized into Jesus Christ,"[2] occurs only here and in Gal. iii. 27, and cannot be understood of the baptism by water, for a plain reason, that baptism *into* Jesus Christ is uniformly represented as connected with what we know most certainly is often dissociated from, and in no case necessarily connected with, water baptism. "Baptism into Christ" is that of which water baptism is the emblem—that union to Jesus Christ, which is connected with the belief of the truth which baptism emblematically represents, and of which, when submitted to by a person of mature age, it is the solemn profession. He who is baptized into Jesus Christ is he who is united to Him by faith. Now, it is one of the things most surely believed among Christians, that he who is

[1] Ver. 3.

[2] Pronomen ὅσοι *quotquot* vulgo tantundem valere dicitur *quantum*. Adjectivum *omnes*. Mihi vero auctor non inconsiderate, pronomen quod exceptionem ferebat, usus esse videtur."—VON HENGEL. I agree in the remark though not in the use VON HENGEL makes of it; for I do not think the implied antithesis is between *baptized* and *not baptized*, but between *baptized* and baptized *into Christ*.

thus united to Christ is united to Him as having died, and been buried; and that he has been so united, that as Christ, raised up from the dead, lives a new life, "through the expressed approbation" (for that is, I think, the meaning of "glory" here too, as well as in ver. 2 and in chap. iii. 23) "of the Father," the believer, united to Him, may also "walk in newness of life"[1]—may, in principle and conduct, be a new man, enjoying the glory, the approbation, of God.

This union reaches to the life as well as to the death; "for," says the apostle,[2] "if we are planted in the likeness of His death"—that is, if I mistake not, 'if we are, *as it were*, partakers of His death'—"we shall also be in the likeness of His resurrection"—'we shall also be partakers of His resurrection.'[3] Our state as to sin is what might be expected in a person who had died, and who has risen again, and who lives, as it were, in union, with Jesus Christ.

"Knowing this," that is, for we know this,[4] "that our old man was crucified with *Christ*, that the body of *sin* might be destroyed, that henceforth we should not serve sin." "Our old man"[5] is the depraved system of our fallen nature, that wrong mode of thinking, feeling, and acting, which characterises man born of the flesh. That was crucified along with Christ: the meaning of this remarkable phrase is, 'when Christ died on the cross as the victim of sin, that took place which secured the destruction of this system in the case of all united to Christ.'

"That the body of sin might be destroyed, that henceforth we should not serve sin." "The body of sin" is, I apprehend, the mass of guilt which Jesus, as the victim for men, bore, and bore away on the cross. The destruction of that body is the

[1] Ver. 4. [2] Ver. 5.

[3] May not *σύμφυτοι* be construed with *τοῦ θανάτου*, and *τῆς ἀναστάσεως* and *τῷ ὁμοιώματι* be regarded = *ἐν παραβολῇ*, Heb. xi. 19, *as it were*; *σύμφυτος* is construed with the genitive by Nonnus *σύμφυτος εἰμι τοκῆος*, Par. xiv. 10. 'The death and resurrection spoken of by the apostle are not a death and resurrection like those of Christ Jesus.' It is of the real death and resurrection of Christ that they are *τῷ ὁμοιώματι—σύμφυτοι.*

[4] Ver. 6. [5] Eph. iv. 22; Col. iii. 9.

same thing as the " finishing of transgression, the making an end of sin"—the bearing our sins to the cross and leaving them there—the " putting away of sin." This was the direct effect of the atonement completed in the crucifixion, and it refers to a change of relation; and this looks forward to another effect, referring to a change of character, that believers united to Christ, as having thus destroyed " the body of sin," " might not be the servants, the slaves of sin"—might not live under the demoralizing influence of guilt, which had been fully expiated, and, as it were, annihilated.

This statement is confirmed by the general proposition announced in ver. 7, " For he who is dead is free from sin." ' He who has died *by* sin, *for* sin, has been justified from the sin by which, for which, he died." " The wages of sin are death," and he who has fully received these wages, is discharged, is free from that master. Sin—guilt—has no more to do with him. Till the condemning sentence is executed, the man is subject to sin, both in its power to condemn and in its power to deprave; but let the penal consequences be fully endured, let the demands of the law be met, by due and complete satisfaction, and the man is at once delivered from its condemning power and its depraving influence, which depends as we have seen above, on its condemning power. Now, in this way, all that are in Christ—all that are "justified freely through the redemption that is in Christ Jesus," have died, not indeed in their own persons, but in the person of their surety; and, *therefore*, are delivered from the reign of sin—from its power to condemn, and, therefore, also from its power to rule in the heart and life.

In the sixth and seventh verses the apostle has shown how union with Christ, in His death, necessarily secures deliverance from the demoralizing influence of a state of guilt. He now goes forward to show, that the union with Christ, in His restored life, affords further security for the same result. " Now, if we be dead with Christ we believe that we shall also live with him."[1] "To live with Christ" here, is to be so

[1] Ver. 8.

united to Christ that the principles of spiritual activity and enjoyment are the same in justified persons as they are in the perfected Redeemer, the risen Saviour. "Their life is hid with Christ in God."[1] *They* do not so much live as *Christ* lives in them.[2] They are in reference to sin as if they had died with Christ, and now lived with Him. Find out the leading characters of Christ's new life, and you will find out the leading characters of the *Christian's* new life. "If we be dead with Christ," or have died with Christ, His death is past; "We shall live with Him," His life is present and future, and so shall ours in Him be. These two things are indissolubly connected. Christ's resurrection and restored life were the merited reward of His death *by* sin, *for* sin. It was because Christ died *by* sin, *for* sin, and thus made full satisfaction for it, that He was raised from the dead and crowned with immortal life—life in the glory of God, in the full possession of the entire approbation and complacency of God. Now, if this be the true state of the case, all who are united to Christ as dying, must be united to Christ in living, and have their interest in what He secured by dying.

To complete this argument, from the union of Christians with Christ in His death and life, for the holy tendency of the Divine method of justification, the apostle goes forward to notice the immortal endurance and the peculiar character of that life, rising out of the peculiar character of that death of which it was the result and the reward. "Knowing"—that is, for we know, it is this that gives us assurance—that "having died with Christ, we shall also live with Him:" we know "that Christ being raised from the dead, dieth no more, death hath no more dominion over Him: for in that He died, He died unto sin once, but in that He liveth, He liveth unto God."[3] Christ being raised from the dead "dieth no more," *shall* never, *can* never, again submit to death. "He was dead, but He is alive again, and lives for ever more."[4] The second clause, "death hath no more dominion over Him," is not mere repe-

[1] Col. iii. 3. [2] Gal. ii. 20. [3] Ver. 9, 10. [4] Rev. i. 18.

tition. It assigns the reason why He shall not, why He cannot, ever die. It was because He bore our guilt that death had dominion over Him. It was only *thus* that death could be permitted to touch that Holy thing born of the virgin, the Son of God. But having fully met our responsibilities by dying for us, death, the law's officer, has no more authority over Him.

And this rises out of the nature of His death and of the life which follows—"For in that He died He died unto sin, once." "For in that He died," is just equivalent to, 'as to His death. "He died *to* or *by* sin"—that is, His death was a death to sin or by sin. For Christ to "die *to* sin, was to be completely freed from the reign of sin. But, it may be asked, how could Christ be made free from the reign of sin? Was He ever subject to it? The answer is, As to the depraving influence of sin, Christ never was subject to it—"He knew no sin;" but as to the penal power of sin—what the apostle styles "sin reigning unto death"—no one ever knew, experimentally knew, *that* as He did; He was subject to it in consequence of God's "making Him, though He knew no sin, to be sin for us." In all mere creatures capable of moral action, the penal reign and the depraving, prevailing influence of sin, seem to be, in the nature of things, inseparable. In the case of our Lord, they were as necessarily separated. Christ, occupying the place of sinners, was subjected to that reign of sin unto death which they had incurred; and, by sustaining the full punishment awarded by the great Lawgiver and Moral Ruler, He delivered Himself, and all whom He represented, from this penal reign, which, owing to the absolute singularities of His case, was not in Him as it is in all men beside, accompanied by its depraving influence.

To this mode of interpreting the phrase rendered, "died to sin," I have but one objection, which is, that it gives to the word death, in the second clause, a figurative sense; while in all the rest of the passage, except here, and perhaps in the second verse, the word bears its plain literal signification.

Supposing that "died *by* sin" is the preferable rendering, the apostle's meaning is not materially different:—With regard to His death, Christ died "by sin," that is, He died 'on account of sin'—through the condemnatory power of sin. His death was expiatory. He suffered what sin deserved. This mode of interpretation has the advantage of giving a uniformity of meaning to the word 'death' throughout the whole paragraph.

This death to sin, or this death by sin, was "once." This indicates how completely Christ's death, in which His people are united with Him, answered its purpose in delivering both Himself and them from the reign of sin and of death. The constantly returning deaths of the Mosaic victims intimated their inadequacy to take away sin. The "offering of the body of Jesus Christ once for all,"[1] indicates the completeness of the sacrifice. "Such a High Priest became us, who is holy, harmless, undefiled, separate from sinners, and made higher than the heavens; who needed not daily to offer sacrifice for the sins of the people; for this He did once—once for all—when He offered up Himself."[2] When He bare the body of our sins in His body to the tree, there to destroy it by a complete expiation, "He suffered once for sin, the just for the unjust."[3]

Christ's *life*, in which the believer has the same interest as in His death, equally secures that he cannot continue in sin. "In that He liveth He liveth unto God." The phrase rendered, "liveth to God," admits of two translations—*to* God, *by* God. To live *to* God, as appears from chap. xiv. 6–8, is to live devoted to God. Christ's new life is a life devoted to the promotion of the Divine glory, and if *Christians* have fellowship with Him in that life, how can they live in sin? "Because He lives they live also,"[4] and His life is the pattern of their life. "To live *by* God," which sense the words will bear, conveys the same idea as "raised from the dead by the glory of God." His new life is continued as well as begun by

[1] Heb. x. 10. [2] Heb. vii. 26, 27. [3] 1 Pet. iii. 18. [4] John xiv. 19.

expressed approbation and complacency of God; and they, united to Him, partake with Him of this complacency, which must secure for them those supplies of Divine influence which, in their design, tendency, and effect, go to prevent them from continuing in sin. This last mode of interpretation has the advantage of keeping the contrast between the death and the life more exact. In the former case, it is a moral, mystical, spiritual, figurative life, contrasted with a real, literal death; in this case, both death and life have their proper signification.

The sum of the whole matter is this. All who are interested in the Divine method of justification are so related to Jesus Christ, "as delivered for our offences, and raised again for our justification," that His death is, as it were, their death—His life, their life; and if Jesus Christ have, by once dying, expiated completely all the sins of those who believe in Him, and, as a proof of this, live for ever by, and in the enjoyment of, the Divine special favour, then must not they who died in Him, and live in Him, be delivered from the penal reign of sin, which, in the person of their Surety, they have sustained, and from that depraving influence too, which, in their case, though not in His, is necessarily connected with its penal dominion?

In the 11th, 12th, and 13th verses, the apostle presses on the Roman Christians, as a motive and encouragement to universal holiness, the doctrine he had taught regarding their security from the continuance of that depraving power of sin, which is connected with its penal reign. "Likewise reckon ye also yourselves to be dead indeed *to*, or *by*, sin; but alive *unto*, or *by* God, through—or rather *in* Jesus Christ our Lord"[1] (for it is rather Christ's headship than His mediatorship that is referred to here). The belief of this, in his apprehension, lay at the root of their progressive sanctification. The particles, "Likewise also," would have been better rendered, 'And thus.'[2] The apostle does not call on the believing Romans

[1] Ver. 11.

[2] Οὕτω καί.

"to die to sin, or to live to God." That is technical, but not scriptural phraseology. The death to sin, and the life to God, he here speaks of, are not duties to be performed, but privileges enjoyed in consequence of union with Christ, laying a foundation for the performance of all duties. The words before us are an assertion, that it is the believer's duty to be fully persuaded that he is so interested in Christ's death and life, and united to Him, that he has died *by* sin, *to* sin, and lives *by* God, *to* God. It is as if he had said, 'Since, according to the Divine method of justification, you are, by believing, united to Christ, and since He died by sin and liveth by God, you have died by sin in Him, you in Him live by and to God. And it is of much importance that you firmly believe and habitually consider these truths.' It is by the influence of these truths believed that the moral transformation, which was secured by the expiatory death and the new life of Jesus Christ, is carried forward. This verse is in meaning precisely parallel with the remarkable passage in the beginning of the fourth chapter of the First Epistle of Peter.[1]

Believing, holding fast, this truth, "Let not sin" *therefore* reign in your mortal bodies, that ye should obey it in the lusts thereof." 'Do not allow guilt, in its depraving influence, to reign, to exercise an influence, over your mortal bodies—that is, over you while in this mortal body. Sin reigns no more, through death, over your Lord's glorified body: it will have no power over your glorified bodies; but even now, in the mortal body—the body that must die because of sin, it is unbecoming that you should allow sin to exercise a power of which it has been legally deprived—its power to create alienation from God—moral disorder. In your embodied state act like—what you are—persons who are united to Christ in His death and in His life. Do not obey sin; do not yield to its natural influence to estrange you from God, "in," or by, "the lusts," the natural desires, of the body. Let those natural principles be regulated, not by the influences of sin—a state

[1] 1 Pet. iv. 1, 2.

of condemnation, but by the influences of righteousness—a state of justification.' 'Let it not be so,' says the apostle—'it is your own fault if it be so. If any man sin, it is his own fault, for he is laid under no physical necessity of sinning; for a believer to sin is doubly his fault, for he is furnished in abundance with all that is necessary for obedience.'

The apostle proceeds with his exhortation. "Neither yield ye your members as instruments of unrighteousness unto sin; but yield yourselves to God, as those who are alive from the dead; and your members as instruments of righteousness unto God."[1] 'Do not allow your members—your faculties, your powers of action—to be under the demoralizing influence of *sin*—guilt, a state of condemnation. In the belief of the great truth just stated, assert your freedom. Refuse to *guilt* the employment of your faculties; for assuredly the work they will be set to will be unrighteousness—what is opposed to the holy, just, good will of God, as expressed in His law. On the contrary, in the belief of this truth, devote yourselves to God as your reconciled Father and God in Christ, as those whom He has in Christ raised from the dead, in consequence of His having died for them, the just in the room of the unjust, and to whom He has given a new life—a proof of His love—fitting them for His service; and let all your faculties, brought under the influence of your new state, become instruments of righteousness in the service of God.' In other words, "Walk at liberty, keeping His commandments."

It must never be forgotten that this exhortation is not addressed to all men indiscriminately, but only to those who have believed the Gospel, and are justified by believing. It is not true of unbelieving sinners that they are "dead to sin and alive to God in Christ Jesus our Lord;" and the apostle certainly would never encourage, far less command, any man to believe a lie. Besides, if unregenerate sinners could be brought, without first believing the Gospel testimony, to believe that they, as individuals, though strangers to the truth by which

[1] Ver. 12.

alone they can be transformed by the renewing of the mind—are secured from all the effects of the condemning sentence of the law, through the death and life of Jesus Christ—this persuasion would certainly lead them to say, "Let us continue in sin, that grace may abound."

On this subject, I am afraid that a good deal of perplexed and dangerously mistaken thinking prevails. It has not been uncommon, with a certain class of preachers, to call on sinners to believe that they are in a safe state; that they need only to believe that they are saved, and they are saved—to believe that they are in Christ, and that they are dead to sin and alive to God in Him. Now, there is strange confusion of thought here. This is all wrong; for, to call on a man to believe *this*, who does not first of all believe God's testimony respecting His Son, is to call on him to believe a lie—to believe something not only for which he has no evidence—but against which he has overwhelming evidence if he would but attend to it. The Gospel testimony is not, that I, as an individual, am secure of salvation, but that "God is in Christ Jesus reconciling the world to Himself, not imputing to men their trespasses; seeing He has made Him who knew no sin to be sin in our room, that we might be made the righteousness of God in Him." To him who does not believe this, it is the same, so far as saving consequences are concerned, as if no atonement had been made. Of him it cannot be said that he is united to Christ, either in dying or in living, for he is "without Christ,"—apart from Him, not united to Him at all.

The truth on this infinitely important subject is briefly this: In the Gospel God has given a plain well-accredited testimony respecting the way of salvation for sinners through the mediation of His Son. Do you ask me what that testimony is? I answer, it is substantially—"God has given to us eternal life, and this life is in His Son."[1] "God so loved the world, that He gave His only begotten Son, that whosoever believeth in Him might not perish, but have everlasting life;

[1] 1 John v. 11.

for God sent His Son into the world, not to condemn the world, but that the world through Him might be saved."[1] It is the duty of every person who hears this well-accredited testimony of God to believe it. He who believes it is, by believing it, united to Jesus Christ. He "*has* the Son," in whom is eternal life. God becomes his God. He is dead *by*—*to*—sin, he is alive *by*—*to*—God, in Christ Jesus; and it is his duty, for it is the very truth most sure, to reckon himself thus dead *by*—*to*—sin, thus alive *by*—*to*—God.

It is only the believing sinner who is thus interested in the justifying, sanctifying efficacy of the atonement, and it is only he who can be properly called on to reckon himself so. At the same time, it is the duty, the immediate, the primary duty, of every sinner, who hears the Gospel, to believe *it;* and, in believing it, all the blessings of the Christian salvation are secured to him, and it is now his duty to believe *that.* "This reckoning, on the part of the ungodly who have believed in Jesus, says an able German interpreter, is no comforting self-deceit, but is a spiritual operation, fully true, answering throughout the aim of Christ, without which true sanctification, and especially that thorough humility and divestiture of all selfishness, is impossible."[2]

But for a man continuing in unbelief thus to reckon himself, is high presumption, for it is to believe what God has not revealed, and to expect what God has never promised; and when an unbeliever succeeds in working himself up to something like a persuasion of this, he is but involving himself in deeper delusion, and his persuasion will have anything rather than a sanctifying influence on his mind. For a believer thus to reckon himself, is but to set to his seal that God is true; for him to doubt it is in a high degree sinful; and just in proportion as he keeps this truth steadily in view, will be his progress at once in solid comfort and universal holiness.

I dare bid no impenitent sinner believe directly that he is

[1] John iii. 16, 17.

[1] Olshausen.

dead *by*—dead *to*—sin, alive *by*—alive *to*—God, because he is united to Him who died *by* sin and lives *by* God; but I not only dare, but I do most earnestly, invite and exhort, entreat and command, by the authority of God, and the mercies of the Lord Jesus Christ, the guiltiest of our guilty race to accept, in the faith of the truth, an all-accomplished Saviour and a complete salvation, and have no hesitation in assuring him that, however guilty, depraved, and unworthy, he shall never perish, but have everlasting life, if he but believe the Divine testimony. God is his God. Christ is his Saviour. He has died in Christ; he has risen in Christ. He lives in Christ, and he shall live in Him, with Him, for ever; and it is at once his present privilege and his immediate duty, as a believing sinner, to "reckon himself dead indeed unto sin, and alive unto God through Jesus Christ our Lord."

2. *The Freedom from Law, and the Subjection to Grace, implied in the Divine Method of Justification, secures that the Justified Person shall not continue in Sin.*

CHAPTER VI. 14–VIII. 4.—" For sin shall not have dominion over you: for ye are not under the law, but under grace. What then? shall we sin, because we are not under the law, but under grace? God forbid. Know ye not, that to whom ye yield yourselves servants to obey, his servants ye are to whom ye obey; whether of sin unto death, or of obedience unto righteousness? But God be thanked, that ye were the servants of sin; but ye have obeyed from the heart that form of doctrine which was delivered you. Being then made free from sin, ye became the servants of righteousness. I speak after the manner of men, because of the infirmity of your flesh: for as ye have yielded your members servants to uncleanness, and to iniquity unto iniquity; even so now yield your members servants to righteousness unto holiness. For when ye were the servants of sin, ye were free from righteousness. What fruit had ye then in those things whereof ye are now ashamed? for the end of those things is death. But now, being made free from sin, and become servants to God, ye have your fruit unto holiness, and the end everlasting life. For the wages of sin is death; but the gift of God is eternal life through Jesus Christ our Lord. Know ye not, brethren (for I speak to them that know the law), how that the law hath dominion over a man as long as he liveth? For the woman which hath an husband is bound by the law to her husband so long as he liveth; but if the husband be dead, she is loosed from the law of her husband. So then if, while her husband liveth, she be married to another man, she shall be called an adulteress: but if her husband be dead, she is free from that law; so that she is no adulteress, though she be married to another man. Wherefore, my brethren, ye also are become dead to the law by the body of Christ; that ye should be married to another, even to Him who is raised from the dead, that we should bring forth fruit unto God. For when we were in the flesh, the motions of sins, which were by the law, did work in our members to bring forth fruit unto death. But now we are delivered from the law, that being dead wherein we were held; that we should serve in newness of spirit, and not in the oldness of the letter. What shall we say then? Is the law sin? God forbid. Nay, I had not known sin but by the law: for I had not known lust, except the law had said, Thou shalt not covet. But sin, taking occasion by the commandment, wrought in me all manner of concupiscence. For without the law sin was dead. For I was alive without the law once; but when the commandment came, sin revived, and I died. And the commandment, which was ordained to life, I found to be unto death. For sin, taking occasion by the commandment, deceived me, and by it slew me. Wherefore the law is holy, and the commandment holy, and just, and good. Was then that which is good made death unto me? God forbid. But sin, that it might appear sin, working death in me by that which is good; that sin by the commandment might become exceeding sinful. For we know that the law is spiritual; but I am carnal, sold under sin. For that which I do I allow not: for what I would, that do I not; but what I hate, that do I. If then I do that which I would not, I consent unto the law that it is good. Now then, it is no more I that do it, but sin that dwelleth in me. For I know that in me (that is, in my flesh) dwelleth no good thing: for to will is present with me; but how to perform that which is good I find not. For the good that I would I do not: but the evil which I would not, that I do. Now, if I do that I would not, it is no more I that do it, but sin that dwelleth in me. I find then a law, that, when I would do good, evil is present with me. For I delight in the law of God after the inward man: but I see another law in my members warring against the law of my mind, and bringing me into captivity to the law of sin which is in my members. O wretched man that I am! who shall deliver me from the body of this death? I thank God, through Jesus Christ our Lord. So then with the mind I myself serve the law of God, but with the flesh the law of sin. There is therefore now no condemnation to them which are in Christ Jesus, who walk not after the flesh, but after the Spirit. For the law of the Spirit of life in Christ Jesus hath made me free from the law of sin and death. For what the law could not do, in that it was weak through the flesh, God sending His own Son in the likeness of sinful flesh, and for sin condemned sin in the flesh; that the righteousness of the law might be fulfilled in us, who walk not after the flesh, but after the Spirit."

Let us now proceed to the consideration of the second proof, that justified persons cannot live in sin—continue in sin.[1]

"For sin shall not have dominion over you: for ye are not under the law, but under grace." It has been common among interpreters to consider these words as finishing a paragraph rather than beginning one—as very intimately connected with the sentence in ver. 12 and 13, that immediately precedes them—as, indeed, containing a reason for what the apostle says there, or a motive and encouragement to the mode of conduct which he recommends. "Let not sin reign"—yield not your members to it as its instruments; on the contrary, "yield yourselves to God, and your members to Him as His instruments; *for* sin shall not have dominion over you." This is no doubt excellent sense; the consideration, that sin shall not have dominion over the believer, being one of the strongest motives, both as exhibiting obligation and encouragement, which can be proposed to the believer to avoid sin and to practise duty. But the motive to the duty enjoined in the 12th and 13th verses is to be found in the 11th verse, and in the preceding context. It gives more concinnity to the apostle's argument to consider a new paragraph as commencing with the 14th verse, in which he proceeds to another branch of the same great subject. He has concluded one most satisfactory proof, that men justified by believing cannot continue in sin; and he here enters on another and equally satisfactory one. The 14th verse hangs by the 1st and 2d. We, justified by believing, cannot continue in sin, "for sin shall not have dominion over us;" and the reason of that is, "for we are not under the law, but under grace." As that union to Christ, in His death and life, implied in the Divine method of justification, secures that we shall not continue in sin; so that freedom from law, and that subjection to grace, which it equally implies, secures that sin shall not have dominion over us.

[1] Ver. 14.

(1.) *General Illustration of the Argument.*[1]

There are three points which must be cleared, to give full illustration to the apostle's argument. What is it for sin to "have dominion" over a man? What is it to be "not under law, but under grace?" And, How does the not being under law, but under grace, secure that "sin shall not have dominion" over the man who is so? "*Sin*" is here plainly personified. The results of being in a state of sin are represented as the effects of regal power or influence. In this epistle we read of two different kinds of power or dominion, which sin, personified, is represented as possessing and exercising over men. In chapter v. 21, we read of "sin reigning unto death." The meaning of that is, 'Men are punished with death on account of sin.' At the 12th verse of this chapter we read of "sin reigning over men's mortal bodies, so that they obey it in their lusts"—*i.e.*, in the exercise of their natural desires. The meaning of that is, 'Men act under the depraving influence of sin.' The truth is, that, in the first of these passages, sin, or guilt, is viewed as securing punishment, according to the principles of the Divine government. In the second, it is viewed as producing and perpetuating depravity, according to the principles of the human constitution. The question, In which of these closely related, but still quite distinct senses, is the dominion of sin to be understood here? is not difficult to answer. The apostle's object is plainly to show how deliverance from guilt delivers also from depravity—how the method of justification secures sanctification. To say, sin shall not condemn you, justified persons, is nothing to the point: his argument requires the assertion, sin shall not continue to deprave you; and when we look into the subsequent discussions, we find that they all bear on this point.

Now, this deliverance from the depraving dominion of sin is represented by the apostle as secured by the Divine method of justification, inasmuch as it delivers from subjection to law,

[1] Chap. vi. 14.

and brings into subjection to grace. "Sin shall not have dominion over you, *for* ye are not under the law, but under grace."[1] The contrast here is not properly between the law of Moses and the Gospel of Christ, as two Divine economies: it is between law and grace, as the principles of two methods of justification—what the apostle calls "the law of works," and "the law of faith," which is by grace. For an innocent being to be under law, as in the case of Adam, is to have his final acceptance and salvation suspended on his obedience to the law under which he is placed: for a guilty man to be under law, is to be condemned to punishment for disobedience; while the obligation to perfect obedience continues unchanged, every new act of disobedience incurring new guilt, and exposing to increased punishment; and while deliverance from that punishment is utterly hopeless, being unattainable except by the impracticable means of at once fully enduring the punishment denounced, and perfectly complying with all the preceptive requisitions of the law. This is to be under the law; and the apostle declares that all the justified by faith are not thus under the law, and because they are not *thus* under the law, "sin shall not have dominion over them."

But they are not only not under law, they are "under grace." "Grace" is free favour. The system of justification under which they are placed dispenses pardon, acceptance, and salvation, not as the specified rewards of specified services —wages for work done—but as free gifts; not something which we are to merit by our doings and sufferings, but enjoy as the result of the free sovereign mercy of God, finding its way to guilty man through the redemption that is in Christ Jesus.

How the being not under the law, but under grace, secures that sin shall not have dominion over the man interested in the Divine method of justification, is fully explained in the discussion, from the beginning of the seventh chapter to the 4th verse of the eighth chapter.

[1] Ver. 14.

(2.) *Popular Illustration of the Incompatibility of a State of Justification and a State of Subjection to the Dominant Power of Sin.*[1]

Before proceeding to this somewhat difficult and abstruse subject, the apostle, in the closing paragraph of the sixth chapter, gives a short popular view of the entire incompatibility, the utter opposition, of the two states of sin and justification, which are considered to be united in the supposed case of the justified man who continues in sin. To suppose a man really justified, and yet habitually living under sin, is to suppose one of the grossest absurdities and self-contradictions. "What then?" says the apostle, after having asserted that the justified are not under law, but under grace—"What then? Shall we sin, because we are not under law, but under grace?"[2] 'Shall we abuse our privileges? shall we take encouragement to *sin* because pardon is free? Were we to do so, we should behave in the most inconsistent and absurd way; but if we are really not under law, but under grace, we cannot act such a part; deliverance from law, subjection to grace, is that which alone can free man from the bondage of depravity, and enable him to walk at liberty, keeping God's commandments.' The first of these principles is illustrated in the remaining part of this chapter; the second, in the seventh chapter, and first four verses of the eighth.

This, then, is the theme of the paragraph, beginning at the 16th verse, and ending with the chapter. To sin, because we are not under the law, but under grace—to take encouragement to live in sin from our being freely justified—would be the most enormous and loathsome of all self-contradictions and absurdities. "Know ye not, that to whom ye yield yourselves servants to obey, his servants ye are to whom ye obey; whether of sin unto death, or of obedience unto righteousness? But God be thanked, that ye were the servants of sin; but ye have obeyed from the heart that form of doctrine which was

[1] Chap, vi. 15-23. [2] Ver. 15.

delivered you. Being then made free from sin, ye became the servants of righteousness."[1] The apostle represents the two opposite influential states of sin—guilt or condemnation, and of righteousness or justification, as two masters, so opposed to one another as that you cannot at the same time serve both, but that in the degree to which you are subject to the one, you are—you must be—free from the other. He who, under the influence of a state of guilt, lives an unholy life, whatever profession he may make, is a condemned man; he is the slave of guilt. He only who, under the influence of justification, lives a holy life, is a justified man; he is the servant of righteousness. There are just these two masters—just these two influential states. Every man must serve one of them—every man must be under the influence of guilt and condemnation, or of justification. The two influential states stand thus in antithesis: sin or guilt, leading to death; obedience, leading to righteousness or justification.[2] To complete the antithesis, you must look into the following verses. You will find, on the one side, sin—*i.e.* guilt or condemnation, the slavery of the devil, uncleanness and iniquity, death; on the other, obedi-

[1] Ver. 16–18.

[2] This is one of those imperfectly expressed antitheses which we not unfrequently meet with in the apostle's writings: for example, Chap. iv. 15—"Because the law worketh wrath: for where there is no law, there is no transgression"—*but where there is law, there is transgression.* Chap. viii.—"We are debtors, not to the flesh, to live after the flesh"—*but to the spirit, to live after the spirit.* The force of the apostle's statement, in both cases, rests on the implied, but not expressed, part of the antithesis.

The complete antithesis here is, παρακοή—ὑπακοή; ἁμαρτία—δικαιοσύνη; αἰσχύνη—ἁγιασμός; θάνατος—ζωή. Disobedience leads to condemnation, and condemnation to shameful conduct, and shameful conduct to death; obedience, which is here *faith*, ver. 17, leads to justification, and justification to holiness, and holiness to life. We naturally expect here that ἁμαρτία εἰς θάνατον should have been contrasted with δικαιοσύνη εἰς ζωήν—but it may account for the peculiarity of the phraseology, that the apostle is speaking of δικαιοσύνη as a state exerting moral power, and this it does through ὑπακοή, which is here equivalent to πίστις. ὑπακοή εἰς δικαιοσύνην is = πίστις εἰς δικαιοσύνην, and it is as the δικαιοσύνη διά πίστεως, that the δικαιοσύνη Θεου, transforms men by the renewing of their minds.

ence, righteousness or justification, the service of God, holiness, eternal life—all direct opposites.

The one influential state or master is "*Sin*"—the state of guilt and condemnation. He who is in this state must feel its influence, and reach its end. He who serves this master must do his drudgery—iniquity, and receive his wages—death. The other influential state is "obedience unto righteousness"—that is, as I apprehend, unto justification. The obedience here is not doing the works of the law, by which no man can obtain righteousness or be justified; it is not the holiness which is represented in the 22d verse as the fruit of a justified state; it is something that naturally precedes justification, while holiness follows it. This expression, "obedience unto righteousness," would have been extremely puzzling, had not the apostle himself explained it in the 17th verse. It is "the obeying from the heart the form of doctrine which had been delivered unto them." Whether you understand the words rendered "the form of doctrine which was delivered to you," as meaning 'that system of doctrine which has been taught you,' which the English words signify—or 'that doctrine into which, as a mould, you have, by believing, been cast, so as to have your characters formed by it,' which the original words seem to indicate,—there can be no doubt that "the form of doctrine" is just the Gospel; and that "obeying" this form of doctrine from the heart, is just really—cordially, "believing" this Gospel. "Faith reckoned unto righteousness," or justification, and "obedience unto righteousness," or justification, as explained by the apostle, are equivalent expressions. The influential state is justification by believing; and the obedience of the heart to the form of doctrine—that is, the faith of the Gospel by which men are justified receives prominence, seeing by it justification exerts its transforming influence—the doctrine being the mould into which, by believing, the mind, softened by Divine influence, is poured, so as to take on it the image of the new man.

These, then, are the two great influential spiritual states—a state of guilt, into which you enter by sinning—a state of justification, into which you enter by believing. 'You must then,' says the apostle, 'be under the influence of one of these states—you must be the servants of one of these masters. You once were under the power of the first—"ye were the servants of sin"—you were under the practical, the depraving influence of guilt and condemnation: ye are so no longer; and blessed be God for the change.' The phraseology is here peculiar, but the meaning is plain. "God be thanked, ye were the servants of sin; but ye have obeyed from the heart the form of doctrine delivered to you, or into which you have been delivered."[1] Not that the apostle thanked God that they ever had been the servants of sin, but that he thanked Him that they were so no longer; and his gratitude for their emancipation was increased by thinking of the debasing slavery in which they had been previously involved. By believing the Gospel, they had been justified; and by the same faith of the Gospel, their justified state was exerting its influence, in transforming them by the renewing of their mind. By thanking God for the change, the apostle acknowledges *Him* as its author. "Faith is the gift of God." It is the act of man too, but the act of man acted on by God. Men purify their souls "in obeying the truth *through the Spirit*."[2]

Now, says the apostle, "being made free from sin, ye became the servants of righteousness."[3] To be freed from sin, is just the reverse of being the servants of sin, and signifies, to be delivered from the prevailing depraving influence of a state of guilt and condemnation. "Righteousness" I consider here as bearing its ordinary sense in this epistle—'justification;' and to be the servant of justification, is just to be under the influence of a justified state in reference to our temper and conduct. The apostle's assertion in this verse seems to be, that deliverance from the depraving influence of a state of guilt, and subjection to the sanctifying influence of a state of justification, go together, and are equally effected by the faith of the Gospel. It is impossible to be freed from the power of

[1] Ver. 17. [2] 1 Pet. i. 22. [3] Ver. 18.

guilt and condemnation, and to be brought under the power of justification, but by the obeying from the heart the form of doctrine—that is, believing the Gospel; and, on the other hand, it is impossible to believe the Gospel without being freed from the demoralizing power of guilt, and subjected to the sanctifying influences of pardon and acceptance.

The first part of the 19th verse is evidently parenthetical, and ought to have been so marked. It interrupts the current of thought, and is obviously introduced as an account of, or an apology for, the apostle's employing, in this paragraph, a much more popular and familiar kind of illustration and proof, than he does either in the paragraph that precedes or in that which follows it. It is as if he had said, 'I am adopting a popular mode of teaching—speaking "after the manner of men," to meet the necessities of the less spiritually intelligent of my readers, "because of the infirmities of your flesh"—because you are so much under the influence of things seen, that it is only by way of comparison that you can be made to apprehend things unseen.' He speaks here to that portion of the Roman Christians who were not so spiritual as others of their brethren, who in comparison were "carnal," as "babes in Christ."[1] He requires to be a spiritual man to enter fully into Paul's illustrations of the influence of justification on sanctification—from the union which subsists between the justified and Christ, in his death, resurrection, and new life—and from the different tendencies of a state of subjection to law, and of a state of subjection to grace. In the first part of the sixth chapter, and in the seventh, down to the fourth verse of the eighth, "he speaks wisdom among them who are perfect"—he feeds those of full age with "strong meat;" but in this paragraph he gives "milk to babes."[2] The figurative illustration which he here gives of the absurdity of supposing that a justified man should continue habitually an unholy man, drawn from the different, the opposite origin, nature, tendencies, and consequences of a state of guilt and a state of

[1] 1 Cor. iii. 1. [2] Cor. ii. 6; Heb. v. 13, 14.

justification, is what any man of ordinary good sense, if he but attend to it, cannot but perceive the force of. Here, as everywhere, the apostle is a pattern for the Christian teacher. He is not to forget that there are babes among those whom he is teaching: and he is to give them the only food they can relish and digest; but neither is he to forget that all are not babes. The man of mature age and disciplined spiritual faculties, must not be overlooked; and the babe must be wisely accustomed to the use of stronger food, that he may the sooner become a man.

In the latter part of this verse, the apostle prosecutes his popular illustration. "For as ye have yielded your members servants to uncleanness, and to iniquity unto iniquity; even so now yield your members to righteousness unto holiness."[1] "Uncleanness and iniquity," as contrasted with "righteousness," is the impure and lawless state of guilt, as contrasted with righteousness—the state of justification, a state conformable to the holiness and justice of the Divine nature and law. Previously to their conversion, the Roman Christians had yielded their members—their faculties, to the influence of that state, leading to practical lawlessness or iniquity,—so becoming, as it were, its servants. 'Now,' says the apostle, 'as you have done this but *now* are justified, it is meet that ye should yield your members to the influence of your new state, leading to practical holiness,—"so becoming, as it were, *its* servants."' The force of the particle *as*, is either to describe the manner in which the justified person ought to yield himself to the practical influence of his new state, as entirely as he had yielded himself to the practical influence of his former state—that he should seek to be as free from the influence of the former, as he had at an earlier period been free from the latter; or, to indicate a motive, "*since*" you formerly yielded yourselves freely, fully, solely, up to the practical influence of a state of guilt, therefore now you should yield yourselves freely, fully, solely, to the practical influence of a state of justification.

[1] Ver. 19.

In the first case, the 20th and 21st verses are the illustration of the thought; but, for reasons which will speedily become apparent, we are rather inclined to prefer the second mode of interpretation.

The idea seems to be, 'You ought to feel your former readiness to yield to the immoral influences of your old spiritual state, as a reason why you should now as readily yield to the moral influences of your new state: you ought to do so, "for when ye were the servants of sin, ye were free from righteousness."'[1] These words are ordinarily considered as meaning, 'When you were the slaves of sin, ye were in no degree subject to holy principle'—ye were utterly depraved; or, understanding the terms "sin" and "righteousness" as we do, 'When you were under the influence of a state of guilt, ye were completely uninfluenced by a state of justification.' The objection—and it is a strong one—to this mode of exposition is, that it gives to the word rendered "free," a sense which nowhere else belongs to it. Our word 'free' means, not merely 'emancipated,' but 'destitute of'—not merely 'in possession of liberty,' but 'unaffected, uninfluenced by.' The word in the original merely expresses liberty as opposed to slavery. It is difficult to see what meaning could be attached to the phrase, 'ye were in a state of liberty from righteousness:' for subjection to righteousness is liberty; and when man is the self-sold slave of sin, the claim of righteousness is not annulled, not weakened. I am inclined, then, to think that the apostle's meaning is given in these words: "When ye were the servants of sin—of guilt, ye became free—ye were emancipated, by righteousness"—by justification. This meaning of the word "free," as equivalent to "freed," is not unexampled. In John viii. 33 we have, "Ye shall be *made free;*" and in Rom. vii. 3 we have, "*freed* from that law," "the law of her husband." In both these places it is the same word as here; and *there* it is doubtless rightly rendered. It is justification that frees men from the dominant influence of guilt, as well

[1] Ver. 20.

as from its penal power. How absurd, then, to suppose that it should tend to strengthen and perpetuate the very bond which it, and it alone, can loose.

In the two following verses, the 21st and 22d, the apostle continues to contrast a state of sin with a state of justification, to show that they are so utterly incompatible, as that in the degree in which a man is subject to the one, he is free from the other. "What fruit had ye then in those things of which ye are now ashamed? for the end of these things is death. But now being freed from sin and become servants to God, ye have your fruit unto holiness, and the end is everlasting life."[1] The word "fruit" sometimes signifies pleasure or advantage resulting from a particular course; at other times, practical consequence, of whatever kind. The first part of the 21st verse admits of two modes of pointing and construction, which bring out senses considerably different. According to the mode of pointing and construction adopted by our translators, the meaning is, 'What advantage did you derive from these depraved pursuits in which ye were once engaged, but of which ye are now ashamed?' The answer left to be supplied is, 'None—absolutely none: for the end of these things is death—destruction.' Many of the best commentators, however, both ancient and modern, construe and point the passage differently,[2] thus: they put the point of interrogation immediately after the word *then*, which contrasts with "*now*" in the beginning of the 22d verse—"What fruit had ye then?" What was the practical effect of that state of subjugation to guilt in which you then were? The answer is—"Things of which you are now ashamed;" 'moreover'—or, '*and*,' you have good reason to be ashamed of them, "*for* the end of these things is death."' Here is their former state—the state of sin, the fruit of that state, and the end of it, corresponding with their new state—the state of righteous-

[1] Ver. 21, 22.

[2] Syriac Version, Theodoret, Theophylact, Luther, Melancthon, Koppe, Flatt, Tholuck, Ruckert, Kölner, Olshausen, Lachmann, Griesbach, De Wette.

ness and *its* fruit and end, as these are stated in the 22d verse: *Then*, ye were the servants of sin, the fruit of which was what you are now ashamed of, the end of which was death: *Now*, ye are free from sin—the servants of God; the fruit—the practical result, is holiness; and the end—the ultimate result, is eternal life—complete and unending happiness. How absurd, then, to think that this latter state can encourage men to continue in the former state!

The concluding verse of the chapter hangs from the two statements: The end of a state of subjection to sin is death; The end of a state of subjection to righteousness 'is eternal life:' "for the wages of sin is death, but the gift of God is eternal life, through Jesus Christ our Lord."[1] These are the final terminations of the two states. Guilt conducts through a shameful course of sin to death—eternal death; righteousness conducts through an honourable course of holiness to life—eternal life; and all under the law must reach the first fearful termination, "for death is the wages of sin," which the law awards to man the sinner; and none but those under grace can reach the second glorious goal, for "eternal life" cannot be obtained by man but as "the gift of God" —the expression of His free favour, "through Jesus Christ our Lord."

Now of the things which the apostle has spoken in this paragraph, this is the sum. The spiritual states of mankind exercise so powerful an influence over their character, conduct, and condition, that they may be fitly personified as their masters. There are two such great spiritual conditions: that of sin, guilt, and condemnation; and that of righteousness, justification, pardon, and acceptance. These are directly opposed to one another in their influence as well as in their nature. No man can be under the dominant influence of both at the same time. Believers were once under the influence of a state of guilt—they were "in sin," and the "servants of sin." Believers are now under the influence of a state of

[1] Ver. 23.

righteousness or justification—they are the servants of righteousness. They were brought into that state by the obedience of the truth—the faith of the Gospel. It was *God* who effected the change, and He is to be thanked for doing so. Thus they were made free from sin—delivered from its habitual dominant influence, and became servants of righteousness—were subjected to the dominant influence of a justified state; and it is therefore most meet that, as in their former state they yielded their faculties to the influences of the impure and lawless state of guilt, to be employed by it as their master in the work of iniquity, so now they should yield their faculties to the influence of righteousness—a justified state, as their master, to be employed in holiness. It is most meet; for it is righteousness or justification that has delivered them from sin, guilt, and its depraving influence. The practical effect of yielding to the influence of sin was shameful conduct, and its final result, if unopposed, would have been everlasting destruction; while, on the other hand, the practical effect of yielding to the influence of a state of justification is holiness, and its final result is eternal life; and that it is so is the consequence of the Divine method of justification, by which you are not under law, but under grace; "for the wages of sin is death," which *law* awards man the sinner, "but the gift of God is eternal life"—a gift which grace confers on the believing sinner "through Jesus Christ our Lord." Can, then, a believer of the truth respecting the Divine method of justification, say "Let us continue in sin, that grace may abound?"—or, "Let us sin because we are not under the law, but under grace?" Nothing can be more absurd.

Such is the apostle's popular illustration of the incompatibility of a state of justification with a state of continuance in sin. He takes up the second part of his more profound illustration of this principle at the beginning of the 7th chapter, and prosecutes it to the 4th verse of the 8th chapter.

What the apostle says, in the paragraph which we have been illustrating, is well calculated to destroy the delusive confidence of those who please themselves with the thought, that they are in a state of favour with God, while they live in the love and practice of sin in some of its forms. Such characters are, I am afraid, far from being rare among professors of what is termed evangelical Christianity. They appeared early, so early as the apostle's times; and they are not yet extinct. Such persons are in extreme danger; and their hazard is the greater that, unaware of it, they are saying to themselves, "Peace and safety." Hell has no torments more intense than those reserved for the abusers of the Gospel—the presumptuous claimants of the privileges of a state into which they prove that they have never passed, by being destitute of the character which it uniformly produces; and their damnation will be as obviously just as intolerably severe. Most anxiously would I chase such men from their refuges of lies, not to drive them to despair, but to shut them up to the faith of the Gospel, and to "good hope through grace." If any man is conscious that he is living in sin, let him rest assured that, in this single fact, he has stronger evidence that he is unbelieving, and of course unjustified, than he possibly can have in any other way, that he has believed and is in a state of justification. But why will he not now believe? Why will he not receive "the gift of righteousness"—of justification, brought near, in the word of the truth of the Gospel, to him "far from righteousness?" Be it known to you, even to you despisers or abusers of the Gospel, who may have turned the grace of God into lasciviousness, and acted out the principle, "Let us continue in sin that grace may abound,"—be it known, that to you, even to you believing, all the blessings of a justified state—among the rest, freedom from the predominance of sin in any form—are ready to be communicated. Obey now, from the heart, the form of doctrine delivered to you; and though formerly the servants of sin, you shall be made free by that justification which is "not to him that worketh, but to him who believeth on Him that justifies the ungodly."

How completely does the Divine method of justification secure holiness! how powerfully does it oblige all under its influence to cultivate holiness! Without it, there can be no such thing as holiness in the heart of fallen man. He who is interested in it is, as a matter of course, renewed in the whole man —created in Christ Jesus to good works. The sovereign grace of God, and the infinite atonement of Jesus Christ, are the only solid foundation, not only of human hope and happiness, but of human holiness. "Other foundation can no man lay than that which is laid—Jesus Christ."[1] Receive the truth as it is in Jesus, and ye shall be justified—sanctified—saved. They who hope for heaven without holiness, or for holiness without justification, or for justification without faith, must each of them be equally disappointed. This is the order in which heaven's blessings are bestowed: heaven on the holy, holiness on the justified, justification on the believer. All the blessings of the Christian salvation are free gifts, but they can be obtained only according to this due order.

The faith of the Gospel is the portal of the Christian salvation. The gate is wide open; and the guilty children of men are invited to enter, and participate in all the blessings of the "everlasting covenant, ordered in all things, and sure."[2] "Ho, every one that thirsteth, come ye to the waters, and he that hath no money; come, yea come, buy wine and milk without money and without price. Wherefore do you spend money for that which is *not* bread, and your labour for that which satisfieth not? Hearken diligently unto me, and eat ye that which is good, and let your soul delight itself in fatness. Incline your ear, and come unto me; hear, and your soul shall live; and I will make with you an everlasting covenant, even the sure mercies of David."[3]

If men, after all, *will* continue in unbelief and sin—will not come to Christ that they may have life, their destruction is absolutely certain; for the wages of sin is death; and, in their case, these wages will be fully earned, for they have heard that eternal life is the gift of God through Jesus Christ our Lord, and they have scornfully put away from them

[1] 1 Cor. iii. 11. [2] 2 Sam. xxiii. 5. [3] Isa. lv. 1–3.

the highest blessing God has to bestow—a holy, happy eternity, equally the purchase of His Son's blood and the free gift of His own sovereign mercy. "Without holiness no man shall see the Lord."[1] But the most unholy need not despair of being admitted into heaven; for, as there is pardon for the guiltiest, there is sanctification for the most depraved. If the sinner who hears the Gospel is shut out from the marriage feast for want of a wedding garment, it will be because he would not, in the faith of the truth, put it on. The sinner under the Gospel can find *his* way to perdition only by trampling under foot the atoning, justifying blood of the Son of God, and doing despite to the transforming, sanctifying influence of the Spirit of God. Miserable maniac, "it is hard for thee to kick against the pricks." Remember, if you will not have the gift, you must have the wages. Oh, is there any comparison? On the one hand, hard work, as you well know this service of sin to be—harder wages, as ere long you shall know; on the other, the gift of God, grace on grace, all heavenly and spiritual blessings, to be gratefully received and improved. How *can* men halt between two opinions here!

(3.) *More Particular Illustration of the Argument.*[2]

The illustration of the principle, "Sin shall not have dominion over *you*," *i.e.*, those who are the subjects of the Divine method of justification, "for ye are not under the law, but under grace," commences with the 1st verse of the seventh chapter, and ends with the 4th verse of the eighth. The apostle takes up the two statements in their order. "Sin shall not have dominion over you, for ye are not under the law;" and "sin shall not have dominion over you, for ye are under grace." The first of these is illustrated from the 1st to the 24th verse of the seventh chapter; the second, from the 25th verse of that chapter to the 4th verse of the eighth.

[1] Heb. xii. 14.

[2] Chap vii. 1–viii. 4.

The first four verses of the seventh chapter are occupied with a statement and illustration of the fact, that believers are delivered from law in consequence of their union with Christ, in order to their becoming holy. The purport of the next paragraph, from verse 5 to verse 13, seems to be, to show that such a deliverance from law was necessary for this purpose, by a reference to the past experience of the believing Romans, and especially to his own, while unregenerate; and the design of the succeeding paragraph appears to be to establish the same truth, by a reference to his experience as a regenerate man: the object of the first being to show that law cannot make a bad man good, but, though from no fault in it, that it exasperates, extends, and perpetuates the power of sin over him; and of the second, to show that law cannot make a good man better, but that it leaves him hopelessly to struggle with remaining depravity. From the 25th verse of the seventh chapter to the 4th verse of the eighth, the apostle illustrates the statement, "Sin shall not have dominion over you, for ye are under grace," by showing that grace, through the incarnation and sacrifice of Jesus Christ, God's Son, effectuates that which law could not do, in that it was weak through the flesh—destroying the power of sin over men, and leading them to fulfil the righteousness of the law, by walking not after the flesh, but after the spirit; thus making it clear that the Divine method of justification by faith does not make void, but, on the contrary, establishes the law.

This general outline of the apostle's course of thought, in this portion of his illustration of the bearing of the Divine method of justification on the moral, spiritual transformation of man—what we usually call sanctification, may be of some use in guiding us into just views both of the meaning of particular expressions, and of the design and bearing of particular statements and arguments, which might otherwise seem obscure or even unintelligible.

a. "Sin shall not have dominion over you, for ye are not under the law."[1]

1. *The Divine Method of Justification delivers from Law.*[2]

The apostle begins with laying down a general principle, which, he says, must be familiar to all acquainted with law, as those to whom he was writing were: ("I speak to them who know the law, or rather, who know law—I speak to civilised, not barbarous men), that the law, or law, hath dominion over a man as long as he liveth."[3] The principle seems to be this, which holds of law generally—of the Jewish law, of the Roman law, of all law: Law binds a man as long as he lives, no longer. There is no question here about the repealing of a law. The law is supposed to remain in force; and the statement is substantially, Death frees a man from the obligation of a law to which he is rightfully subject; nothing else can. Law binds the living, not the dead. The application of this principle comes by and by. Law, as the principle of justification, has dominion over a man, till, by union to Christ, the propitiatory victim for sin, he become as a dead man in reference to the law.

In the 2d and 3d verses, the apostle gives an instance in which death dissolves legal obligation. "The woman which hath a husband is bound by the law to her husband so long as he liveth; but if the husband be dead, she is loosed from the law of her husband: so then if, while her husband liveth, she be married to another man, she shall be called" (reckoned to be, for she is) "an adulteress; but if her husband be dead, she is free from that law; so that she is no adulteress though she be married to another man." The woman referred to becomes dead to the law of her husband, not by her own, but by his death—is as completely removed from under its power as if she herself had died. She is "loosed from the law of her husband," —that law has no more dominion over her, as to it she is as it were dead. The general law of a husband remains unrepealed

[1] Chap. vii. 1-24. [2] Chap. vii. 1-4. [3] Chap. vii. 1.

—it has lost none of its power over its proper subjects, but it has no dominion over her: she is out of its limits.

The bearing of the general principle announced in ver. 1, and of the example given in ver. 2, 3, on the present subject—the believer's freedom from *law* as the principle of justification and sanctification, is stated in ver. 4. "Wherefore," or, thus then, "my brethren, ye also are become dead to the law by the body of Christ; that ye should be married to another, even to Him who is raised from the dead, that ye should bring forth fruit unto God." 'You are, according to the principles of the Divine method of justification, as completely delivered from law, as a dead man is from the law he was subject to when alive, or as the woman whose husband is dead is from the law which bound her to her husband. It is not by law that you are to be justified, sanctified, or saved.'

This freedom from law believers obtain, not by their own death, but by, or "through, the body of Christ." "The body of Christ" may either signify his literal body—the body born of the Virgin, in which He "bore our sins on the tree;"[1] or it may mean the mystical body of Christ—"the Church, which is His body"[2]—all true believers, viewed as represented by Him. In the first case, the meaning is, 'Our freedom from the law is the result of what Christ did and suffered in our room.' It is in consequence of His having been made sin for us, that we are made the righteousness of God in Him. It is in consequence of His having become a curse in our room, that we are delivered from the curse of the law. Our salvation is secured by His having brought in an everlasting righteousness. In the second sense, the meaning is, 'In consequence of our being Christ's body, we are freed from the law.' We are considered as if we had done what He did, and obtained what He obtained. In Him, we obeyed, suffered, and died. "He bore our sins." "He was wounded for our transgressions, He was bruised for our iniquities: the chastisement of our peace was on Him; and by His stripes we are healed." "He died for

[1] 1 Pet. ii. 24. [2] Eph. i. 23.

us."[1] The meaning is substantially the same, though I apprehend the first mode of interpretation is the preferable one. "The body of Christ" seems here quite equivalent to the phrase in the Epistle to the Colossians, "reconciled in the body of His flesh through death."[2] We are "*sanctified* by the offering of this body of Christ once for all."[3] He "abolished in His flesh the enmity, the law of commandments." He "nailed the handwriting that was against us to the cross."[4] The death of Christ, in which we are one with Him, was a death which answered all the law's demands. It killed Him, and killed us in Him ('ye are put to death' is the literal rendering of the phrase);[5] so that if we are in *Him*, the law has, it can have, no demands on us as a method of justification.

This freedom from the law by union to Christ in His death, was in order to our union with Christ in His new life, procured by His death as a living, life-giving covenant head, that we might be brought into a relation to Him similar to that in which we previously stood to the law. They who are under law look, though they look in vain, for justification and sanctification by its means. They hope to enter into life by keeping the commandments, expecting both a title to, and a fitness for, final happiness from their personal obedience. The law is their hope and dependence. Now, to be Christ's—married to Christ, is to have our happiness identified with His; to place our dependence for all we need on Him; to expect to be justified by His righteousness, sanctified by His Spirit, saved *in*, *by*, Him "with an everlasting salvation."

It is obvious, then, that we must be completely freed from the law in order to our being thus married to Christ. If we are under the law, we are condemned; if we are in Christ, we are justified. We cannot be both. If we are under the law, we are seeking for salvation by our own doings; if we are in Christ, we are saying, "Surely in the Lord have we righteousness and strength." We cannot be doing both. We must be

[1] Isa. liii. 5; Rom. v. 8. [2] Col. i. 22. [3] Heb. x. 10.
[4] Eph. ii. 15; Col. ii. 14. [5] ἐθανατώθητε.

dead to—free from the law, in order to our being united to Christ. The freedom from the law here affirmed of believers, and their union with Christ in death and life, mentioned in the former paragraph, are thus most intimately connected. It is our union to Him as dying the victim for sin, that gives us freedom from the law; it is our union to Him as raised from the dead by "the glory"—the expressed approbation, of His Father, that brings us into a state of *grace*.

The grand design and the certain result of this freedom from the law, in consequence of dying *to* it, dying *by* it, *in* Christ Jesus, and this marriage relation to Jesus Christ, are, that believers may and do bring forth fruit to God. "The bringing forth fruit," describes the practical results of that which is represented as the tree or plant. The Spirit is represented as producing fruits in holy dispositions and conduct. The peculiar relation between believers and Christ, is here represented as intended to lead to practical results of a sanctifying kind. The wild olive grafted into the good olive tree partakes of its root and fatness, and produces corresponding fruits. The believer married to Christ brings forth fruit to God—is formed to a character, and distinguished by a conduct, which God approves.

To "bring forth fruit to God," is the same thing as to "live to God." The design and the certain effect of the believer's freedom from law, secured by the Divine method of justification, is not that they may live in sin, but that they may live to God.

2. *This Deliverance from Law is necessary in order to Sanctification.*[1]

(1.) *Law cannot make a Bad Man Good.*[2]

The apostle proceeds to show that this deliverance from law is *necessary*, for this purpose: that it not only does not encourage sin, but is essential to holiness; for, in the case of fallen man, a state of subjection to law, as the principle of justi-

[1] Chap. vii. 5-24. [2] Chap. vii. 5-13.

fication, is a state of subjection to sin; and, in order to our living to God, we must become dead to—free from, the law.

In illustration and proof of this, the apostle appeals to the experience of the Roman Christians that it was indeed so. "For when we were in the flesh, the motions of sins, which were by the law, did work in our members to bring forth fruit unto death. But now we are delivered from the law, that being dead wherein we are held" (or rather, as it is in the margin, we being dead to that in which we were held), "that we should serve in newness of the spirit, and not in the oldness of the letter."[1]

"We" here plainly refers to believers—we who were in the flesh, but are so no longer—we who are now "in the spirit." "The flesh" is equivalent to the state in which all men are born, and continue till they are born again. It is of similar import with "the old man,"—a state in which men are chiefly affected by things that are sensible and present, seen and temporal.

Now, says the apostle, when we were in this state, what was the effect of the law on us, who were then under it—did it make us holy? No; "the motions of sin which were by the law, did work in our members to bring forth fruit unto death."

"The motions of sin" seem to signify the sinful propensities of our fallen nature—its tendencies to evil, the bias to error, the disposition to sin, the forming design, the rising desire, of evil.

These motions of sin are said to be "by the law." That obviously means more than that we had such motions, when we were under the law. Some have supposed, that by "the motions of sin" being "by the law," the apostle means that these evil propensities were discovered by the law, and refer to ver. 7 as an illustration. But this is not satisfactory; for the law serves this purpose, to those who are delivered from it, in even a higher degree than it ever does to them while they are under it. The word which must be supplied to bring out

[1] Ver. 5, 6.

the sense, seems to be 'excited,' or 'called forth into exercise:' "The motions of sin," or the sinful propensities, "which were" *excited*, or called forth into exercise, "by the law."

The law has no tendency to excite sinful propensities in innocent, holy creatures. But the apostle is not speaking of innocent, holy creatures: he is speaking of men "in the flesh"—of unregenerate, depraved men; and there can be no doubt that in them sinful propensities are excited, called out to exercise, by the law. Instead of subduing sinful affections in a depraved heart, the law irritates them. The sinner finds himself curbed and checked by the law, and is filled with displeasure at the law and the Lawgiver. The strictness of the precepts of the law, and the severity of its sanctions, make him fret against its Author, and form harsh thoughts of that inflexible justice and immaculate purity which are essential elements of the Divine character. Displeasure at the holiness of the law is direct enmity against God; and enmity against God is at once the worst of "the motions of sin," and the fruitful parent of all others.

These sinful propensities, called forth into exercise by means of the law, "did work in the members," or rather, put forth their energy by "the members"—*i.e.*, as I have already explained it, 'by the various faculties of our nature:' they exerted themselves by means of our understanding, imagination, affections, and all the different capacities of thought and feeling and action of which we are possessed.

And thus exerting themselves, "they brought forth fruit unto death:" they led to practical consequences—to the external manifestation of themselves in a course of action, the end of which, under the Divine government, could be nothing but death—destruction. Such was the influence of law on the apostle and the Roman Christians when they were "in the flesh." The tendency and effect was anything but sanctifying.

With this state the apostle contrasts their present state—as delivered from the law, and being in the Spirit: "But now we are delivered from the law, that being dead wherein we were held; that we should serve in newness of spirit, and not in the oldness of the letter."

"We"—that is, we believers, who once were in the flesh, and under law—'we, now in the spirit, are delivered from law—*i.e.*, we have been completely delivered from the condemning sentence of the law, and we are brought into a state in which our everlasting happiness is not suspended on our own personal obedience as its meritorious condition.'

This deliverance from the law rises out of our death to it. The words in our translation represent the law as dead; but there is no doubt the reading followed in the marginal rendering is the preferable one[1]—"We being dead to that by which we were held." The reference is to what the apostle, in the 4th verse, calls our death to the law "by the body of Christ." Our freedom from the law arises from Christ, as our representative, having settled our accounts with the law on the cross—in which settlement of accounts we obtain a personal interest by believing.

Now, we are thus delivered from the law, in consequence of this death to the law, not that we may continue in sin, and live as we list, but that we should do, what we never would have done under the law, "serve"—*i.e.*, 'serve God, yield obedience to God'—"in newness of spirit, not in the oldness of the letter." "Newness of spirit" is equivalent to a new spirit, or in a new and spiritual way; not in the old, spiritless, literal way in which men under the law serve. Whatever obedience the man under the law yields, is the obedience of a slave; the obedience of the man delivered from the law is the obedience of an affectionate son. Disobedience—not obedience of any kind, is the general character of those in the flesh under the law; and the exceptional cases of obedience have the character of heartless literality. Obedience is the prevailing character of the man in the spirit, delivered from law; and his obedience is spiritual obedience—the obedience of the mind and the heart; he walks at liberty, keeping God's commandments; and,

[1] ἀποθανόντες.

"delivered from the hands of his enemies, serves Him without fear, in righteousness and holiness, all the days of his life."[1]

On hearing such a statement, as to the effect of the law on men in the flesh, and the necessity of being delivered from it, it might very naturally suggest itself to a depraved man—'Then the law is more in fault than I am; I am fully as much to be pitied as blamed.' Or an opponent to Paul's doctrine might say, 'Your system cannot be true, for it transfers the guilt from the sinner to the law.' A most satisfactory answer, by anticipation, is given to both these objections in the paragraph from the 7th to the 13th verse. "What shall we say then? Is the law sin? God forbid. Nay, I had not known sin, but by the law: for I had not known lust, except the law had said, Thou shalt not covet. But sin, taking occasion by the commandment, wrought in me all manner of concupiscence. For without the law sin was dead. For I was alive without the law once; but when the commandment came, sin revived, and I died. And the commandment, which was ordained to life, I found to be unto death. For sin, taking occasion by the commandment, deceived me, and by it slew me. Wherefore the law is holy, and the commandment holy, and just, and good. Was then that which is good made death unto me? God forbid. But sin, that it might appear sin, working death in me by that which is good; that sin by the commandment might become exceeding sinful."

"What shall we say then?" This is the apostle's ordinary way of introducing an objection. "Is the law sin?"[2] The phraseology is peculiar. The meaning may be, Is the law a bad thing? or, is the law in fault—is *it* to blame? It seems rather to be, Is then the law the cause of sin? or, as the apostle expresses it in Gal. ii. 17, "the minister of sin?" We find a similar expression in the book of the prophet Micah,[3] where "Samaria" is said to be "the transgression," or sin, "of Jacob," and "Jerusalem" is said to be "the high-places of

[1] Luke i. 74, 75.

[2] Lex index peccati, non genetrix.—AMBROS.

[3] Chap. i. 5.

Judah"—the meaning apparently being, that the idolatries of the two metropolitan cities were the principal cause of the idolatry of the two kingdoms. The force of the objection may be thus stated: 'If sinful propensities be excited by the law, is not the law the cause of sin?'

To this question the apostle replies by an indignant negative. "By no means"—'Let it not be;' and he goes on to show, first, how the law cannot be the cause of sin; and, secondly, how the law, though not the *cause* of sin, was yet the *occasion* of calling forth into active operation "the movements of sins"—the depraved propensities of our nature.

He does the first in the conclusion of the 7th verse, and the second in the eighth verse. "Nay"—*i.e.*, 'So far from law being sin'—"I had not known sin, but by the law: for I had not known lust, except the law had said, Thou shalt not covet." The apostle here illustrates his principles from his own experience. Many learned interpreters strangely suppose that the apostle here, and in the consequent context, down to the end of the chapter, personates some other individual, or rather class of individuals; some supposing that he speaks in the name of the Jewish people, and gives an account of their moral state, first before the law, and then after the law was given, in order to show that the Gospel was necessary in order to make men holy; others, that he personates an individual, first ignorant of the law, and then instructed in the law, to serve the same purpose. But there is not the slightest hint, in the whole discussion, that the apostle is not speaking in his own person; though, no doubt, much that he says is substantially applicable to other men similarly placed. There is no reason to doubt that the apostle's object is to show, from his own experience, both before and after conversion, that a state of subjection to law is, in the case of a being like fallen man, whether in his wholly lapsed or partially restored state, inconsistent with true holiness.

It may be asked, why Paul here turns suddenly from the common experience of himself and the Roman Christians to his own individual experience—why the *we*, of the 5th and 6th verses becomes here I, and with one exception, in ver. 14, continues so to the end of the chapter? The true account of the matter seems to be this. He is about to make statements of what passes within—of the working of the law on the human heart. "He is about to depict the work of the law, by an example which will set it forth in vivid colours, in detail, in connection with sin in a man. What example, then, so apposite as his own?"[1] In these discussions the apostle might have said, "Verily we speak what we do know, and testify what we have seen."

"The law is not sin; on the contrary, I had not known sin but by the law." Interpreters have found it difficult to fix the precise meaning of the expression, 'to know sin.' Some suppose that it signifies to know what *is* sin. 'I had not known accurately what is and what is not sin, but for the law, for what is sin but "the transgression of the law?"' Men ignorant of the law mistake as to what is duty and what is sin—putting evil for good, and good for evil. Others suppose that it signifies to know what sin *is*. 'I had not known how inconceivably bad a thing sin is, but for the law showing me, in its precepts, how opposite sin is to the Divine character and will, and, in its tremendous sanction, how malignant a thing that must be against which the God of love threatens such fearful evils.' Others still suppose that it signifies to be personally convinced of sin—to know that I myself am a sinner; and to know what, as a sinner, I am and deserve. It is the light of the law brought into the conscience that does all this. The man ignorant of the law has no just conceptions of his own character and condition as a sinner—he is scarcely aware that he is a sinner at all.

I do not see the necessity of confining it to any one of these different meanings, or rather phases of the same meaning. To know sin is, I apprehend, just equivalent to knowing the truth about sin—and that comprehends all; and it is plainly true, that this knowledge of sin, in all its extent, is by the law

[1] Alford.

—cannot be but by the law; and it is as plainly true, that if the law be calculated thus to give the knowledge of sin, it cannot be the cause of that, the true character of which, as most criminal, loathsome, and destructive, it so clearly unfolds, and the commission of which it so strongly forbids and so awfully denounces.

The apostle illustrates the general principle, that "by the law is the knowledge of sin," or that he would not have known sin but by the law—by a particular example drawn from his own experience—"for I had not known lust, except the law had said thou shall not covet."

A good deal of obscurity has been cast over this passage, by a want of uniformity in rendering on the part of our translators. The same word is rendered "lust," in the 7th verse, and "concupiscence" in the 8th; and the cognate verb is here rendered "covet." The words should have been uniformly rendered. The meaning is inordinate forbidden desire—"I had not known lust except the law had said thou shalt not lust; but sin, taking occasion by the commandment, wrought in me all manner of lust."

"To know lust," is a phrase which must be explained in conformity to the general phrase it is intended to illustrate—"to know sin." 'I had not known, perhaps, that unrestrained desire was a sin at all (the Jewish Rabbins taught that it was not); most assuredly I had not known it to be the great sin it is, and I had not known that I was the guilty person I know myself to be in consequence of indulging it, had it not been that the law in the tenth commandment of the decalogue had explicitly forbidden inordinate desire, in the precept "Thou shalt not covet" or lust.'

The apostle seems here to refer to the manner in which the true knowledge of sin came into his mind and heart by means of the law. Saul of Tarsus, the pupil of Gamaliel, was,—"after the righteousness of the law"—according to the manner in which the Jewish teachers judged, "blameless." He looked at the law "in the oldness of the letter." The law to him was an outside thing. When viewed in that light, he was a strict doer of the law. He had no God but Jehovah; he abominated idolatry; he had never profaned the sacred name nor desecrated the sacred day. He was an exemplary relative—he had never committed murder, or adultery, or theft, or perjury—none of these first nine commandments, thus understood, touched him, or brought home the charge of guilt to him: but when his eyes were opened to the meaning of the tenth commandment, 'Thou shalt not desire that which is forbidden,' and he saw what a new light it shed over the whole law as a spiritual thing, then he knew that lust was sin, and that he was a sinner and a great one.

This commandment, though it plainly could not be the cause of sin, was, in the case of the apostle, the occasion of sin—"the motions of sins were by this law." When convinced of the sinfulness of inordinate desire in all its forms, did he immediately and for ever abandon it? Alas! for this purpose, "the law was weak through the flesh." On the contrary, "Sin, taking occasion by the commandment, wrought in me," says he, "all manner of concupiscence"—*i.e.*, forbidden, inordinate desire.

"Sin" is here generally understood as equivalent, not to guilt, but depravity—man's bias to evil personified. This does not originate in the law, but it takes occasion from the law, to manifest and exert itself in a way in which, otherwise, it might not have done. In the case of Paul, it took occasion, by the commandment—this commandment, 'Thou shalt not desire that which is forbidden'—to excite, in a more than ordinary degree, desire after what was forbidden. Paul was at this time an unjustified and an unregenerate man—a man "under the law," "in the flesh." By the meaning of the tenth commandment opening on his mind and conscience, he was made to see the criminality of inordinate desires, the first tendencies of the heart to evil. Now, what was the consequence? Did he cease to desire what was forbidden? On the contrary, these desires which, like hidden vipers, had, unopposed, scarcely been noticed by him, now swarmed in every corner of his heart, hissing with indignation at the law which doomed them to death. The injunction seemed a hard saying not to be borne; and the whole inner man rose in rebellion against it. It is a striking figure of a late German interpreter—"as a rapidly flowing river rolls calmly on, so long as no obstruction checks it, but foams and roars when any hindrance stops it: just as calmly does the sinful element in human nature find its course through the man, so long as nothing comes to stem it; but when the Divine commandment rises as a dyke of adamant across its progress, then the man feels the force of an element, of the dominion of which he had no adequate conception." A chemical compound liquid appears perfectly pellucid, without colour or smell, till a particular foreign substance is added to it, when in a moment it begins to effervesce violently, becomes opaque, exhibits a very decided colour, and sends forth the most pestiferous fumes.

I am much inclined to interpret "sin" here, as generally in the epistle, of a state of guilt and condemnation and spiritual helplessness. In the case of a man under the influence of this state—especially consciously under its influence—the effect described by the apostle in his own case is exactly what must take place on his obtaining a clear view of the requisitions and sanctions of the law, while ignorant and unbelieving respecting the Divine method of justification.

The concluding clause of the 8th verse, and the 9th, 10th, and 11th verses, contain a further illustration of the strange facts which the apostle had just stated. "For without the law sin was dead; for"[1] (rather 'but' or 'and') "I was alive without the law once;[2] but when the commandment came, sin revived, and I died. And the commandment, which was ordained to life, I found to be unto death. For sin, taking occasion by the commandment, deceived me, and by it slew me."

[1] δέ.

[2] These words have been supposed to mean—"The Jewish nation, during the period of their history previously to the giving of the law, thought themselves entitled to life in consequence of the covenant with Abraham—not being aware of any law punishing sin with death."—Dr DAVID RITCHIE, after Dr JOHN TAYLOR. Certainly, on the principle of interpretation here assumed, "anything may be made to mean anything."

Here, as I apprehend, "sin" is still the condemned helpless state of the sinner personified. This state is said to be "dead without law"—*i.e.*, to have been uninfluential while the person was without law, whatever that may mean. This statement is plainly not to be understood absolutely but comparatively. Both the phrase "without the law," or 'without law,' and the term "dead," must be understood with limitations, but these limitations are easily defined. No human, no created being, whether innocent or guilty, is or can be without—apart from, law. The creature must be subject to the will of the Creator. It is law which has made him a sinner, in the sense of a condemned person; for "where there is no law there can be no transgression: for sin is the transgression of the law."[1] "The strength of sin is the law;"[2] and the law which condemns still commands. "Without law"—here means plainly without such a knowledge of the law, in its requisitions and sanctions, as carries to the conscience a sense of the meaning and authority of the law, and, of consequence, a conviction of guilt and danger. When the sinner is thus "without law," and in the degree in which he is so, "sin is dead." A condemned state cannot be altogether an inert or dead state. No; "the word of God," the curse of His law, which creates this state, is a "quick and powerful" thing.[3] It binds the sinner in chains to the judgment of the great day. It shuts him out from Divine sanctifying influence, and gives him over to the influences of the evil spirit, of his own depraved nature, and of the course of this present evil world.

But, while working powerfully, the condemned state works silently, where the law is unknown, or only superficially known. There is little of felt struggling against the precepts of the law, for they are but imperfectly known, and their spirituality not at all apprehended; and there is little feeling of remorse or alarm, for the true nature and desert of sin are not at all understood. "When a strong man armed keepeth his palace, his goods are in peace."[4] The condemned state, while the law

[1] 1 John iii. 4. [2] 1 Cor. xv. 56. [3] Heb. iv. 12. [4] Luke xi. 21.

is kept in abeyance, neither makes the man so determinedly and sensibly depraved, nor so deeply miserable, as he becomes when the law "comes to him," and he knows what is *sin*, and what sin *is*—knows that *he* is a sinner, and feels that he is utterly indisposed to obey the law's precept, utterly incapable of enduring the law's penalty, and as unable to escape beyond the obligation of its precepts, and the reach of its adjudged punishments. Apart from law, the guilty state of man is comparatively inert or dead, as to the production of sinful propensity or painful feeling.

In this state, says the apostle, I once was: "I was alive without the law once," and then sin was dead. There never was a time when the apostle was without law—without *the* law. He very early obtained an extensive and accurate knowledge of the letter of the form of law under which he was placed—the Mosaic. But that was quite consistent with being "without the law," in the sense of not understanding its spirituality and true extent, and feeling the power, both of its precepts and of its threatenings, in the conscience. This was Paul's state down to the day when he went to Damascus.

Now, when he was thus without law, "sin was dead." Not that his state of condemnation did not exert a depraving influence over him, and an influence utterly inconsistent with true rational happiness; but its influence was in a great degree unfelt. He had no adequate idea of what sin *is;* he had no idea that much was sin that is sin. He was not aware that *he* was a chief sinner—scarcely aware that he was a sinner at all. He had no risings of heart against the strictness and spirituality of the law, for he was ignorant of them. He was not wrung with remorse, nor terrified with the prospect of justly merited, certainly coming, destruction. As a late German expositor expresses it—"He had no consciousness of sin as something alien from—opposed to his true nature. He was so impregnated with sin that he did not regard it, a foreign element, dwelling in him." The abominations of the Hottentot's kraal and person have no existence to him. He is not aware of them.

And while sin was thus dead, he was alive. Some would interpret these words, "I was alive without the law once"—'I once lived without law;' but there is no sense in which that was true, for there never was a time when Paul was not under the law; and we have no reason to think there ever was a time when he acted a lawless part. On the contrary, at the very time here referred to, touching "the righteousness of the law"—*i.e.*, external obedience to the law of Moses, "he was blameless."[1] Paul's *life* here is contrasted both with *sin's death*, and with his *own death* when sin *revived*. When sin was *dead*, he was *alive*; when sin *revived*—became alive, he *died*.

It is obvious, then, that the word "alive" must be understood, not absolutely, but in consistency with the connection in which it occurs. It most certainly does not mean "spiritually alive;" for, at the period referred to, he was, in this sense, as it were, twice dead. It means, 'I was "alive"—in a good, comfortable, desirable state, in my own estimation, to my own feeling.' In the period referred to, Paul enjoyed much self-complacency; he had no doubt of the goodness of his state before God, or of the excellence of his dispositions and character. He rejoiced in false hopes of eternal life; and he would have started with astonishment, as well as indignation, had any one told him that he was "dead in sin"—condemned already, and in constant hazard of the righteous judgment of God.

But an important change came over Paul's views of himself. "The commandment came, sin revived, and he died." There can be no doubt that "the commandment" here signifies the tenth commandment of the decalogue: "Thou shalt not covet"—thou shalt not desire that which is forbidden. That commandment "came." The expression is very picturesque. The commandment had always been there, and Paul was doubtless as familiar with its words as with those of any other of the commandments. But, at a time distinctly marked in his recollections, and which he should never be able to forget

[1] Philip. iii. 6.

throughout eternity, that dead, lifeless form of words, without him, assumed life and power, and entered into his mind and heart. He was made to understand it, not merely as forbidding the wish to obtain unlawfully the wife or the property of his neighbour—of neither of which wishes had he likely ever been conscious, but as giving a spiritual character to the whole law, and making it, what he had never thought of it as being, "a discerner of the thoughts and intents of the heart."[1] It had the activity and power of a thunder-bolt. It carried home the conviction, 'Thou art a sinner, and a great one, righteously condemned of God.' "Cursed art thou, for thou hast not continued in this thing—in anything, written in the book of the law to do it."

The consequence of this entrance of this commandment, quick and powerful, was, "Sin revived, and I," says Paul, "died." "Sin revived." It should have been otherwise: overawed by the holiness and majesty of the law, the depraving influence of sin should have been extinguished. But it was not so, and, according to the constitution of fallen human nature under the Divine government it could not be so. The sinful, guilty, condemned state of man, displayed its true influence—its power to deprave, its power to make miserable. Paul, the sinner, finding himself condemned for what he had been accustomed to think scarcely matters of moral import, feeling on his inmost thoughts and desires a bridle, which he had been unconscious of, and was not at all disposed to submit to, became sensible of a measure of enmity against God and His law, of which he had never previously been aware.

And, while "sin" thus "revived," Paul "died." He *died* in a sense corresponding to that in which he had *lived* when he was "once without the law." He became a dead man, in his own estimation—a condemned criminal; and he became a miserable man in his inmost consciousness. Severe as the law was, he could not, eagerly as he might wish it, think it unjust. Remorse took the place of self-complacency, and a

[1] Heb. iv. 12.

fearful looking for of judgment, of hope of a place in the kingdom of God. The law and his own heart, which formerly had had no quarrel, but had, in his estimation, been always on the best terms, seemed now utterly irreconcilable; and nothing seemed to remain for him but irreversible condemnation, hopeless depravity, everlasting destruction. This is what the law, in the form of the tenth commandment, did to the apostle—this is all it could do for him; and this is what it will do—this is all it can do, for any unregenerate man, when it comes to him in the clear light of its holy, just, spiritual requisitions, and in the irresistible thunder-bolts and lightning-flashes of its righteous denunciations.

The law, when it thus came, did not—it could not, make him either holy or happy. On the contrary, says the apostle, "The commandment, which was ordained to life, I found to be unto death."

"The commandment" here, as throughout the whole passage, is the tenth commandment: "Thou shalt not covet"—thou shalt not desire that which is forbidden. This commandment is said to have been "ordained to life." "*Ordained*" is a supplement, as you will observe from its being printed in italics. The idea is, that the tendency and design of the commandment were "to life"—that is, as is plain from the connection, to the making men happy. This commandment, and indeed every part of the Divine law, was intended and calculated to promote the happiness of an innocent man. His inclinations would correspond to its requisitions; and to him the path of duty would be the path of pleasure. This commandment especially, which goes to the securing in the mind and heart conformity with the will of God, would secure, if complied with, that all duty, however laborious, should be delightful.

But, in consequence of the state into which sin brings men, the case is completely altered; "and the commandment, which was to life," was in fact "found to be unto death." The apostle's meaning here does not seem at all to be—'That the law, which, had it been fulfilled, would have sentenced man to life, now, in consequence of being violated, sentenced him to death'—though that too is a truth, and an important one; but that the law, originally fitted to make man happy, corresponding as it did with the apprehensions and convictions of a holy mind, and the dispositions and desires of a holy heart, was now found, in consequence of its opposition to the false judgments and depraved moral principles of fallen man, to be to unregenerate men a source of misery. These words give us a very impressive view of the misery of man in his unregenerate state. The best things are the occasion of evil to him. Prosperity does not produce gratitude but pride. Adversity irritates rather than humbles. The law which is to life, is found to be to death. Even "the Gospel of salvation" is "a savour of death unto death;" and the foundation of hope "a stone of stumbling and a rock of offence." How infatuated are those men—and they are the prodigious majority of mankind, even in countries where revelation is most generally known—who live at ease, while all things, even the best things in heaven and on earth, are working together for their destruction!

The manner in which he had found the law to be unto death, is thus described by the apostle. "For sin, taking occasion by the commandment, deceived me, and by it slew me." "Sin" retains its meaning. It is the personification of the state of guilt, condemnation, and helplessness, in which the sinner is placed. Sin is an abstract term; and can only by a figure be represented as doing anything. When sin is said to do anything, the meaning is, some intelligent agent, in consequence of being in the state into which transgression brings intelligent moral agents, acts, or is acted upon, in a particular way. The apostle's meaning is, 'In consequence of my being a guilty, and therefore a depraved being, the law, which should have guided me, deceived me; the law, which should have contributed to my happiness, made me miserable.'

"Sin, taking occasion by the commandment," 'Thou shalt not covet,' "deceived me." In an innocent man, the only tendency of the commandment is to guide into truth and holiness. It would naturally excite in his mind such thoughts as these—'God is a spirit, he must be spiritually worshipped.

All external service is valuable only so far as it is the expression of the state of the mind and heart. How wise—how good is God, to guard against what alone can lead to actual transgression—to enjoin what gives interest and life to all external acts of service!' But what is the train of thought it naturally excites in man, the sinner? 'I am forbidden to desire what I cannot but desire. I am condemned for desiring what I cannot but desire. Can it be so? Can this be the Divine law? And if it be, is it not impracticably rigid, utterly unreasonable? To what purpose is it to attempt to keep such a law? to satisfy such a lawgiver?' These are some of the false views which a discovery of the purity and extent of the spiritual law of God occasions in the mind of sinful man. Thus does sin take occasion by the commandment to *deceive* men.

But the apostle represents sin as not only having taken occasion by the commandment to deceive him—to lead him into fatally mistaken views of the law and the lawgiver—but also as by this law "having *slain* him." The general idea is—made me miserable, very miserable—put me to death. It is not properly the condemning power which, according to the Divine law, sin exercises over the sinner that is here referred to. That sentence is passed whether the sinner be aware of it or not; and if he is not removed beyond the sphere of its operation, it will in due time be fully executed in the eternal world. What is spoken of here takes place in this world "when the commandment comes" to the sinner. When an innocent being, like a holy angel, has the spiritual law of God brought strongly under his notice, it gives him nothing but delight. He sees in it the glories of the Divine character, and rejoices in being subject to a law so like its Author, holy, just, and good. It excites no remorse or fear, for the law has never been violated by him—no struggling, for his whole heart goes along with it. But how different is it with the sinner, and just because he is a sinner! How different was it with Saul of Tarsus! He was slain by the law—slain by the law in consequence of his being in a state of "sin"—guilt, condemnation, helplessness. The law made him miserable. It deprived him of the enjoyment of his previous self-complacency. It obliged him to see that he was a sinner, and a great one—as to his state, a condemned criminal, instead of an object of Jehovah's favour; and—as to his character—instead of a keeper of God's commandments, a holy person—a man whose inward dispositions were most powerfully opposed to the requisitions of the Divine law, and whose whole inner life had been a course of rebellion against it. It filled him with remorse, it agitated him with alarm. It made him feel not only that *hell* was his doomed portion, but gave him a foretaste of its miseries in the experience of a state of unquelled rebellion against the Divine will. This the law did; nor could it do anything else. It had no promise of pardon to offer. The very greatest encouragement it could give to obedience was, It will be better for you to obey than to disobey; for every new act of disobedience will lay you open to increased punishment: more—heavier stripes, in the one case than in the other. But it could furnish no influence adequate to contend with the influence of evil spirits, of his own sinful nature, or of the course of the world. It could not possibly deliver from the dominion of sin.

In the connective particle, "Wherefore," or 'Thus then,'[1] with which the 12th verse commences, the apostle plainly refers to the whole discussion, from the beginning of the 7th verse—"Is the law sin?" and concludes from that discussion, that though the law, in consequence of the influence of sin, had deceived and killed him, that was in no degree the fault of the law or the lawgiver. It was entirely the result of that state into which he had brought himself by sin, and was the manifestation of the inconceivably malignant and destructive nature of sin. "Wherefore the law is holy, and the commandment holy, just, and good. Was then that which was good made death to me? God forbid. But sin, that it might appear to be sin, working death in me by that which is good; that sin by the commandment might become exceeding sinful."[2]

[1] ὥστε—μέν.

[2] Ver. 12, 13.

"The law" is just what we commonly call the moral law—th whole of those requisitions which God makes on His intelligent creatures, the sum of which is contained in the two precepts, "Thou shalt love the Lord thy God, with all thy heart, and soul, and strength, and mind," and "Thou shalt love thy neighbour as thyself," and the leading branches of which are to be found in the decalogue; with those appropriate sanctions—the promise of reward, and the threatening of punishment, folded up in these pregnant words—"He that doeth these things shall live by them," and "The soul that sinneth, it shall die." In the case of Paul, it was that law as unfolded in the Old Testament Scriptures.

The word "holy" is here used in one of the most common of its secondary senses, as equivalent to faultless or perfect. It is as if the apostle had said: From what has been stated, it is quite plain, that in all these deplorable results, no fault attaches to the law. The law is every way fitted to serve its own purposes. Its requisitions are not too extensive—its sanctions are not too severe. It forbids nothing but what is wrong and mischievous; it requires nothing but what is right and salutary. It appoints nothing but what is just. In its nature, design, and tendency, it is worthy of its all wise, all holy, all benignant Author.[1] If it has become the occasion of guilt, and depravity, and misery, the fault is neither with Him nor with it; and it is no disparagement to it, that it is incapable of doing what it never was intended to do, and what, indeed, is incompatible with its nature and design.

What is true of the law in general, is true of the particular commandment, which, in the case of the apostle, had wrought all manner of concupiscence, and been the occasion which sin employed to deceive and slay him. "The commandment is holy, and just, and good." The commandment, "Thou shalt not covet," was not to blame, though it wrought in the apostle all manner of concupiscence. The result proves that the commandment was much called for, not that it was in any way

[1] See "The equity and benignity of the Divine law."—*Plain Discourses.*

faulty. Suppose a man a rebel at heart against the government under which he lives, and strongly disposed and addicted to practices that certain laws, to which, for some reason, he has not had his attention particularly directed, decidedly prohibit under severe penalties, which he has unconsciously incurred. Let us suppose the administrators of the law, who may have been too facile—to bring the real state of the case before the man's mind, to show him that the law opposes his strongest inclinations—that by breaking it he has already incurred very serious responsibilities, and that, if he do not mean to draw down on his head accumulated vengeance, he must henceforth abstain from what has become, as it were, a second nature to him; would not that man's becoming very unhappy, and a more determined rebel, at least in heart, than before, be the natural result of such a disclosure—but supposing the law a wise and good one, would *it* be in any degree to blame for this.

The epithets, "just and good," are explicatory of "holy"—faultless. The commandment is "holy"—faultless, being both just and good.

"Just," is another word for right and equitable. Had the commandment been an unjust one, it could not have been holy, faultless. If laws are unreasonable and unrighteous, he who imposes them is more in fault than he who violates them. But the commandment, "Thou shalt not covet"—thou shalt not desire that which is forbidden, is not an unjust law: it is only requiring from man obedience suited to his nature as an intelligent, moral agent. "God is a spirit," and therefore it is meet that by His rational creatures He be worshipped, not only in external observances, but in the submission of the understanding and of the heart. The God who made man capable of thinking and wishing, has surely a right to regulate him in the use of these faculties. Indeed, if the commandments which forbid certain overt acts are just, the commandment which forbids the desire of what is prohibited, must be so also; for, "out of the heart are the issues of life." If the heart be habitually wrong the life cannot be right.

But the commandment is not only "just," but "good." "Good," here means what is fitted to produce happiness. This is obvious from the term being contrasted in the next verse with "death," which, from the connection, clearly signifies misery. The commandment, "Thou shalt not covet," is obviously fitted, in a high degree, to promote man's happiness. Whence the painful struggles between inclination and conscience—whence the difficulties of performing duty, whence the misery of a self-condemning mind—but from my not complying with this commandment? To the man who yields obedience to this commandment, none of God's commandments can be grievous. His will is in conformity to God's will, and he has entire satisfaction in doing it. "Wisdom's ways to him are ways of pleasantness, and all her paths are peace."

This last assertion of the apostle, that "the commandment is *good*"—benignant in its tendency—might appear to some not very consistent with what he had just stated in reference to the result of this commandment coming to him. "Sin revived—I died." Sin, reinvigorated by the commandment, "deceived me and slew me by it." This difficulty the apostle meets and removes in the 13th verse—"Was then that which is good made death to me? God forbid. But sin, that it might appear sin, working death in me by that which is good; that sin by the commandment might become exceeding sinful."

By "that which is good," we are to understand the law, the excellence of which he has just declared—"The law is holy, and the commandment holy, both just and good;" and by being "made death," we are to understand—being the cause of that miserable state which was occasioned by it, and which he describes as his dying—his being put to death—slain. The apostle's meaning is not, 'Is the law, so benignant in its tendency when obeyed, the cause of the misery of the sinner, inasmuch as when disobeyed it denounces adequate punishment on him, and secures the infliction of it?' "Death" here, is the death the apostle died "when the commandment came to him." The figurative word death here, does not denote what is termed *legal* death, a state of condemnation—for in that he was like others,—being by nature a child of wrath; nor does it mean what is termed *spiritual* or *moral* death, a state of depravity—for in that he was likewise from his youth upward; but it means that state of misery produced by the conviction of righteous condemnation for sin, irresistibly forced on the mind—sin of which the man was previously unaware, and of which he does not, cannot, cordially repent—that remorse, that fear, that sense of unsubdued, apparently irrepressible, and ever growing opposition of heart to the requisitions of the Divine law, resulting from the law being apprehended by the mind and conscience in its spirituality and extent, and irrelaxable inflexibility and obligation. The question is—"Was then that law, so benignant in its design and tendency, the cause of the extreme misery into which I was plunged" when "the commandment came to me?"

To this question the apostle answers by a strong negative: "God forbid"—let it not be; and then proceeds to show what was the true cause of this death—this misery. "But sin, that it might appear sin, working death in me by that which is good; that sin by the commandment might appear exceeding sinful." There seems to be something very perplexed in the construction of this sentence; and, indeed, as it stands in our version, I rather think it is impossible to extract an intelligible sentiment out of it. The obscurity rises from not repeating the phrase—"was made to me," or, "has become death to me"[1]—after sin. Insert these words, and all is plain. "Was then that which was good made death to me? God forbid. But sin" *was made death to me,* "that sin might appear sin, working death in me by that which is good; that sin by the commandment might appear exceeding sinful." Not the law, but the state of sin in which fallen man lies, is the true cause of that increased activity of sinful propensities, and of that deep felt, varied wretchedness, produced in an unre-

[1] ἐμοὶ γέγονε.

generate man, when the meaning and authority of the Divine law manifest themselves to his mind and conscience. And this fact proves, and is by the arrangements of the Divine moral government intended to prove, how malignant a thing this state of sin is, how morally detestable, how fearfully destructive.

The particle rendered "that,"[1] may signify either 'so that,' or 'in order that;' it may point out either the result or the design of the fact, that the law, through the influence of sin, is the occasion of giving permanence and new activity to depraved principle, and destroying peace, and producing misery. The meaning may be either—'It was sin that thus produced misery, so that sin appears to be what it is—sin. Its true nature and tendency are manifested by working death by that which is good, *so that* sin by the commandment manifests itself to be exceeding sinful—malignant and detestable above all conception;' or, 'This arrangement, that such results do and must arise from the law coming to the carnally secure, unregenerate man, is intended by God *for the purpose* of manifesting the true character of man's fallen state as guilty and morally helpless.' The last, which includes the first, is most probably the apostle's meaning.

The law was never intended as the means of justification or of sanctification to unregenerate man. It is utterly unfit for answering these purposes; but it is fitted, and it is intended, in its operation on unregenerate man, to show how hopelessly depraved and miserable man is and must be, so long as he continues under the condemning sentence of the Divine law, shut out by it from the only influence which can transform the sinful, miserable being into a holy, happy one. What must be the malignity of that which not only neutralizes the salutary influences of the law on a being constituted as man originally was, but converts the law's condemning sentence, intended to deter from sin, into the fetter which binds the sinner in hopeless captivity to depravity, and the law's precepts,

[1] ἵνα.

which were intended to guide in the way of willing, happy obedience to the Supreme Sovereign, into the means of exasperating rebellious feeling, and making the miserable rebel the executioner of the sentence against himself!

Sin does in this way appear in its true colours—"working death by that which is good"—that which is in itself only good in its nature and tendency. Sin, by the commandment, does appear to be, in the apostle's emphatic language, exceedingly, *i.e.* in the highest degree,[1] sinful, literally "a sinner."[2] The guilty helpless state of man termed "*sin*," in opposition to the state termed "righteousness," or justification, is proved by the law to be the exhaustless source of depravity and misery. The law thus, so far from securing that sin shall not have dominion over unregenerate man, secures that it shall have dominion over him, and makes no provision for regenerating him. It proves, indeed, that a man must be delivered from *law*, considered as a method of obtaining salvation, in order to obtain either justification or sanctification. Such, as we apprehend, is the apostle's argumentative illustration drawn from his own experience, that law cannot make a bad man good.

It is a natural question, At what period of Paul's life did he experience these workings of mind which he so graphically describes here? It is impossible to reply to that question with unhesitating confidence that our answer is the true one. But it does appear exceedingly probable that they refer to the inner history of those three memorable days after the Lord met him in the way, during which "he was without sight, and did neither eat nor drink."[3] It does not seem at all likely, when we consider the previous state of his mind—that of a well-taught, thoroughly principled, pharisaic Jew—that the entire revolution in his sentiments and feelings, necessary to his embracing Jesus Christ as his Saviour and Lord, took place in a moment. He had not only no idea of his needing the salvation which Jesus Christ came to procure and bestow, but he had no distinct idea of what that salvation was. How

1 καθ' ὑπερβολήν. 2 ἁμαρτωλός. 3 Acts ix. 9.

Jesus Christ, supposing him to be the Messiah, could have met with the fate He had met, must have appeared to him incomprehensible. The very fact, by which the object of His mission was gained, must have seemed to him the clearest of all evidence that He never had any such mission. It was not one mistake that needed to be corrected: the whole frame of a well-compacted system of opinions, strongly held, and of habits deeply rooted, had to be destroyed.

We may suppose the state of agitation produced by the miraculous vision to have in some measure ceased. In his solitary chamber in Damascus, shut out by his blindness from external objects, and bodily appetite extinguished by mental activity, some such train of thought as this may probably have passed through his mind:—'Is this delusion? Was it a dream? No. I distinctly saw the Man of Nazareth amid the radiance of heavenly light. I distinctly heard His voice. I can as soon doubt of my existence as this. But if I have indeed seen and heard Him speaking from heaven—What is He? What am I? He who died on the cross is the Son of God in heaven—and what am I? To this day I have believed myself a blameless, an accomplished worshipper of the true God, and an heir of all the blessings of His peculiar people. How can I reconcile my firmest convictions with what I have seen and heard?' This naturally led to introspection. He began to examine himself; and we can conceive him going over the whole decalogue, viewing the requisitions in the letter with the eye of a Jew, and saying, "All these I have kept from my youth up:"—I never had any God but Jehovah; I never bent my knee to an idol; I never profaned the sacred name, or desecrated the sacred day; I have been a dutiful relative; I have never been guilty of murder, or adultery, or theft, or perjury, or any thing approaching them; I have never desired the wife or property of my neighbour; "touching the righteousness which is in the law I am blameless." But a new light burst on his mind as to the meaning of the tenth commandment—'Thou shalt not desire what is forbidden.' He saw that thoughts and dispositions, desires and feelings, were within the range of the law's obligation, and the whole law took a new character. Everything appeared valuable, or valueless, as it was, or was not, an expression of inward principle—of a right state of mind and heart towards God. He now saw himself in a new light. He was most unwillingly constrained to reckon his former estimate of himself utterly false—he was brought in "guilty before God." He felt he was a sinner, and a great one. But his rebellious heart rose against the law and the Lawgiver, and he and the law had the fearful battle, here so strikingly described, till the conviction he rested in was—'I am a sinner, deeply guilty, deeply depraved, thoroughly miserable;' and till the question came from the inmost depths of his spirit—"What must I do to be saved?" Out of this thick darkness broke forth the light. Then came to him, by divine revelation, the doctrine of the Gospel, which he says he "first of all received"—"That Christ had died for our sins, according to the Scriptures."[1] A calming heavenly radiance diffused itself over the dark, troubled ocean of his thoughts. All things seemed made new. He now saw what was the kind of salvation he needed, and that the salvation obtained on the cross by the God Man was that salvation. He felt that it was something not to be wrought for, but received—the gift of God through Jesus Christ. The storm was turned into a calm. He believed that the blood of Jesus Christ, God's Son, cleanseth from all sin—that *He* was the Lamb of God bearing, and bearing away, the sins of the world—his sins. He understands now how Christ must suffer, and then enter into glory. "Behold he prayeth!"—prayeth to the God and Father of Jesus Christ, God in Christ reconciling the world to himself. He feels the bands of sin for ever broken, and "sin has not dominion over him, for he is not under the law, but under grace." Henceforth he "walks at liberty, keeping God's commandments;" "serving in a new spirit, and not in oldness of the letter."[2]

[1] 1 Cor. xv. 3.

[2] "I am much inclined to suppose that the apostle had in his memory, and that he here vividly portrays, the feelings of his own mind in the

Thus Paul found liberty and holiness, and so must we if we ever obtain them. "As in water face answers to face, so does the heart of man to man." Few have ever, probably, thought out and felt out the struggle as the apostle did; but something parallel to this—essentially the same as this, has been the experience of every one to whom the law has been, in the highest sense the terms are capable of, "a schoolmaster, bringing them to Christ." They all know what "shut up"[1] to the faith means. None ever entered into the shelter of sovereign mercy, always open, till the avenger of blood was close on him, and every other door of escape shut against him. It is at once the most voluntary and the most compulsory thing a man ever does in his life: he enters with all his heart, yet he is compelled to come in. In our natural state we are, we cannot but be, under the law; and that law to us is a broken law, armed for vengeance—weak to justify, to sanctify, or to save. While forbidding and denouncing all sin, it binds us, as with chains of adamant, in the vile subjection to which we have voluntarily submitted—chains which nothing but the grace of God, operating through the atonement and Spirit of Christ, can unloose. From the law we have nothing to hope. If we seek justification, it can only condemn and curse us. If we seek holiness, it can tell us what we ought to be and do, and what we ought not to be and do: it can tell us what will be the consequence of obedience and of disobedience; but it cannot make us what it requires us to be; it cannot enable us to do what it requires us to do; it cannot change our inclinations; it cannot renew our heart. Most impressively does the apostle show that the law, even when apprehended in its meaning and authority by the unregenerate mind, cannot make holy. It terrifies, but it does not conciliate; it exasperates the disease it cannot cure. It may

period, by him never to be forgotten, between his being struck to the ground near the gates of Damascus, and his receiving peace of mind by faith in his gracious Redeemer."—PYE-SMITH (*Pref. to Stuart's Comment. on the Romans.*)

[1] Gal. iii. 22–24.

to a certain extent produce external homage, but it cannot secure the obedience of the heart.

The way in which depraved man is to become holy is a profound mystery to the great body even of the professors of Christianity. They seem to imagine that for this purpose no more is necessary than that they should be made distinctly to apprehend the precepts and sanctions of the Divine law; and that the perception of the innate beauty and excellence of its requisitions, connected with a feeling of the power of the world to come in the terrors of threatened punishment and the hope of promised recompense, called forth by the belief of revelation, are quite enough to check the propensity to sin, and form the man to the love and practice of every virtue. All these things are important, nay necessary, in their own place; but, as motives to holiness, they can operate effectually only on the mind of the man who has become, in the apostle's phrase, "dead to the law, and married to Christ." The great end for which the Scriptures set before our minds the precepts and the sanctions of the Divine law, is to destroy our legal hopes through the law, to make us "dead to the law," and induce us to flee for refuge "to lay hold upon the hope set before us"[1] in the Gospel. It is "of God that we are in Christ both righteousness and sanctification;"[2] we cannot be sanctified but in Him and by Him; and according to the Divine method of salvation, He must be our justifier in order to his being our sanctifier. He cannot be our justifier while we seek for righteousness by the works of the law; for He is "the end of the law for righteousness to every one that believeth." And the faith which connects us with Jesus Christ as the Lord our righteousness, necessarily implies in it an entire renunciation of our own righteousness, which is of the law. If we seek to be justified by the law, Christ can be of no effect to us as a quickening, transforming spirit. On the other hand, if we are justified by the faith of Christ, the law has no power to condemn, and the demoraliz-

[1] Heb. vi. 18. 1 Cor. i. 30.

ing influence of its condemnatory sentence of course ceases to operate. The obstacles in the way of holiness are removed, a channel is opened for transforming influence, and the man is placed in circumstances in which all the motives to holiness can exert their full force.

The passage we have been considering furnishes important practical instruction to two classes of men. It teaches those who are persuaded that without a thorough spiritual transformation they are undone—that without holiness no man can see the Lord—what course they must follow if they would secure this most important of all attainments. Let them believe in the Lord Jesus, that, united to Him, they may experience the transforming power of His atonement and Spirit. Holiness is the gift of God, through Jesus Christ our Lord. This passage also teaches those who profess to be savingly connected with Christ Jesus, how to test the genuineness of their profession. It gives them two marks by which to try themselves. If they are indeed "married to Christ," they are, in the first place, free from the law; they are habitually relinquishing all dependence on anything they have done, or can do—anything done in them, or by them, as the ground of their hope; and, in the second place, they are bringing forth fruit to God, serving not in the oldness of the letter, but in newness of spirit. Wherever either of these distinguishing characters is wanting, the profession of union to Christ is self-delusion or hypocrisy.

It concerns every man to examine himself by these tests, and tremble, lest he should be found at last among those who, professing to rely on Christ alone, have still been going about to establish their own righteousness, not submitting to the righteousness of God; or among those who, professing to be in Him as the true vine, are yet utterly barren of the fruits of righteousness, which are by Him to the praise and glory of God. Happy is the man who in his own experience has a commentary on these words of the apostle: "I through the law am dead to the law, that I may live to God. I am crucified with Christ: nevertheless I live; yet not I, but Christ lives in me; and the life I live in the flesh, I live by the faith of the Son of God, who loved me, and gave Himself for me."[1] This is the great mystery both of Christian justification and sanctification. He is—he only is, at once the enlightened divine, and the happy man, *to* whom, *in* whom this mystery of God and of the Father and of Christ is revealed—who knows and is sure that of God he is in Christ justified, sanctified, redeemed—complete in HIM.

Blessed be God, that what the law could not do, in that it was weak through the flesh, God has done by sending His Son in the likeness of sinful flesh, and as a sacrifice for sin. Let the man to whom the commandment has come in its power and fearful revelations—who is convinced of his guilt and depravity, and feels that all his exertions to bring his heart and life into conformity with the law, whose essential requirement is love, end only in new discoveries of the inveteracy of his enmity,—let him open his ear to the testimony of the Gospel, and his heart to the soothing purifying influence of the great sacrifice, and the transforming spirit which it reveals. Believe that "God," the author of that holy law, "is in Christ reconciling the world to Himself, not imputing to men their trespasses, seeing He has made Him who knew no sin to be sin in our room, that we might be made the righteousness of God in Him."[2] Believe this, and you cannot but love Him; and loving Him, you will love His law, which is but a picture of Himself; you will find that the constraining influence of the love of God and his Son, can do what all the precepts and curses of the law could never have done. It will still the war within; it will give "the peace of God, that passeth all understanding;" it will make you "delight in the law of the Lord after the inner man." This grace of God will teach you to deny ungodliness and worldly lusts, and to live soberly, righteously, and godly. Influenced by the mercies of God, you will purify yourselves from all filthiness of the flesh and spirit, and perfect holiness in the fear of God. Being in Christ Jesus, and freed from condemnation by the law of the spirit of life in Him, you will

[1] Gal. ii. 19, 20. [2] 2 Cor. v. 19, 21.

be free from the law of sin and death; and the righteousness of the law will be fulfilled in your walking not after the flesh, but after the spirit. Delivered out of the hands of your enemies by Him who is the horn of salvation, raised up in the house of God's servant, David, you will serve God without fear, in righteousness and holiness, all the days of your life. Never shall any man gain the victory over the worst of all enemies—sin, dwelling in him, reigning over him—but by faith in the atonement, and by the Spirit of Jesus Christ—by the blood of the Lamb, and the word of His testimony. This is the Christian doctrine of sanctification, the true grace of God. Let us stand in it, and rejoice in hope of the glory of God.

I cannot leave the subject, without urging on all the question, Have you felt the power of the law to produce alarm, and its powerlessness to produce solid peace? There is no state more dangerous than one of false security. Anything is better than saying, Peace, peace, when there is no peace. These are weighty words of our Christian poet,—

> "He has no hope, who never had a fear,
> And he who never doubted of his state,
> He may perhaps—perhaps he may, too late."[1]

Happy is he who has felt the power of the Divine word to wound and to heal, to kill and to make alive; who has been constrained to say, in reference to both these modes of operation, "What a word is this!" who has within himself a witness to the truth of the declaration of the faithful witness, "It is the spirit that quickeneth: the flesh profiteth nothing; the words that I speak unto you they are spirit, and they are life;" and of that of His holy apostle, "The letter killeth, but the spirit maketh alive." There is deep truth in Ralph Erskine's paradox: "Law-death; Gospel-life"—death *by* the law, *to* the law; life *by* God, *to* God: and all by the death and the life of Christ, who, in that he died, died by, to sin once,

[1] Cowper.

and in that he liveth, liveth by, to God for ever. In His death, we died; and because He lives, we shall live also.

(2.) *Law cannot make a good Man better.*[1]

Few passages of Scripture have given occasion to more discussion among interpreters and theologians, than that which comes now under our consideration. The question, Whether the apostle speaks here in his own person, and details his own inner history at the time he wrote this epistle; or whether he personates the character, and describes the experience, of a man in a state of unregeneracy? has often been agitated, and much ingenuity and learning have been employed in support of both of these hypotheses. In the heat of controversy respecting this point, most of the disputants, on both sides, seem to have overlooked altogether, or, at any rate, to have paid but little attention to, the object of the apostle in introducing this very remarkable paragraph,—a circumstance obviously of the greatest importance, and which, if clearly ascertained, might probably go far towards the satisfactory resolution of a question, not, perhaps, peculiarly difficult in itself, but rendered so, in no ordinary degree, by the perplexed and jarring opinions of contending commentators.

The apostle's object, in the whole of this chapter, seems to be to show that Law—the system that makes obedience the proper condition of life, affords no effectual means for delivering fallen man from the dominion of sin—in other words, for making him holy; so that it is absolutely necessary, in order to his sanctification, that a man should be delivered from law, as a method of obtaining life, and be brought under *grace*, by being interested in "the righteousness of God by faith"—the Divine method of justification by believing—the system by which life is the gift of God through Jesus Christ.

In that part of the seventh chapter which we have already analysed, we find the apostle showing from his own past ex-

[1] Chap. vii. 14–24.

perience, "while in the flesh"—*i.e.*, while in an unregenerate state, that law, even when exercising its fullest influence on him—when seen by him in the spirituality of its meaning, and felt by him in the power of its authority—so far from suppressing the movements of depraved propensity, proved the occasion of exciting them into a state of increased activity and exasperation; so that, so far from becoming better and happier, he became sensibly more depraved and more wretched. This was the natural result of the union of a partially enlightened conscience with a thoroughly depraved heart. The general truth, which is based on this piece of inner history, is, that no unregenerate man, under the law, though it should exert its utmost influence, can, through its instrumentality, obtain dominion over sin. On the contrary, if he continue under law, he must continue under sin. The deliverance from law is necessary to the existence of true holiness in a being like fallen man.

What follows is a statement—still made in the first person, as of himself, but in the present time—of certain inward movements, in some respects similar to, in others very decidedly different from, those described in the preceding context. Had it been the apostle's object to show still further the powerlessness of the law to deliver from sin, by giving the history of a stage in conviction, previous to conversion, more advanced than that described above, he would naturally have continued to use the past time, only intimating that what he was now to say referred to a period posterior to that of which he had just delineated the experiences. But, instead of this, he at once makes a transition from the past to the present, and continues to speak in that time to the end of the discussion. Speaking of his experience, in common with the Roman believers, he had said, "We *were* in the flesh"—*i.e.*, we are so no longer; but here, "we *know*"—not 'we knew,' that the law is spiritual: 'We know now, what we did not know when in the flesh.' Speaking of his own personal experience, he had said, "I *was* alive," "I *died*," "I *was* deceived," "I *was* slain," by sin, through means of the law: but here it is—"I *am* carnal;" "I *do* what I allow not;" "I *consent* unto the law that it is good;" "I *find* a law, that when I would do good evil is present with me;" "I *delight* in the law of God after the inward man;"—expressions clearly descriptive of his thoughts and feelings at the time he was writing. Now, what could be the apostle's object in making these statements, the sum of which is—'I have a supreme approbation and esteem of, and a cordial delight in, the law of God, which I know to be spiritual; but I am far from being perfectly conformed to that holy law—there are propensities in my nature which struggle, and too often with success, against the native influence of my habitual state of mind in reference to that law; and the state of mental conflict—civil war, thus produced, occasions me deep uneasiness?' I can conceive no other object he could have in view, but to carry forward his demonstration that the law could not make a being like fallen man holy. As it could not initiate holiness in the unregenerate man, so it cannot promote and perfect holiness in the regenerate man.

His former illustration is substantially this—'When I was an unregenerate man, wholly depraved, I found that the law, though it could show me what was right and what was wrong, and command me to avoid what was wrong and do what was right, and threaten, and condemn, and curse me if I did not comply with its injunctions, could not eradicate my depraved inclinations, but rather irritated and exasperated them, so that, remaining under law, I never could have become holy.' His subsequent illustration is, I apprehend, substantially this—'And even now that I am a regenerate person—even now that I am brought under influences which, while under the law, never could have affected me—influences which make me love and delight in the spiritual law, and hate whatever violates it—I still feel that I am but imperfectly renewed; I experience the constant influence and the too frequent prevalence of depraved principles; and the struggle to which these opposing principles give rise occasions deep and painful feeling. Were I under law, I could anticipate nothing but constant warfare, frequent defeat, ultimate overthrow. But I know from whence to look for deliverance—not from law, but from grace; and I joyfully thank God, who, through Jesus Christ, has delivered, will continue to deliver, and will in due time give complete deliverance.'

Taking this view of the matter, we readily see the place which the paragraph holds in the apostle's argument, and perceive that, as he has proved from his own *past* experience that law cannot make a bad man good, he now proves from his *present* experience that law cannot make a good man better; and the force of the argumentative illustration stands out in very strong relief when we recollect that, though the regenerate man is delivered from law and brought under grace, by his union to Christ, and can never be again brought under the one, nor removed from under the other; yet, through his own unbelief, by losing sight of that truth, by the belief of which his deliverance has been effected, and in the continued belief of which he only can enjoy the comfort and advantage of having been thus delivered, he often does think and feel as if he were under the law, and not under grace; and thus, to a great degree, subjects himself to the moral influence of being under the law, and deprives himself of the felt moral influence of his being under grace. This is the great cause of that carnality—that felt helplessness under sin—that doing what he does not allow, but hates—that very imperfect conformity to the law, to the goodness of which he habitually consents, and in which, in the inner man, he delights, of which the apostle so bitterly complains. Legality is the great enemy to sanctification; and it is the realization, by faith, of the state of freedom from law and subjection to grace, which can alone sustain under, and give ultimately complete victory in, these painful struggles. It must be obvious to every reflecting person, that this view of the paragraph has at least this recommendation, that it gives coherence and consistency to the apostle's argument. Whether it be supported by the passage itself, must be ascertained by a more close examination of its various parts.

The particle "For," connects the whole paragraph it introduces, not with what immediately precedes, but with the general object of the discussion, stated ver. 4. Men must be freed from the law that they may become holy. The first proof of this is introduced by *For*, ver. 5 : that proof ends in ver. 13. An additional proof is contained in the rest of the chapter, and is naturally introduced by *For* also.[1] Its force, as I apprehend it, is—'Another proof that men must be freed from the law in order to their becoming holy, is, that as law cannot make a bad man good, it cannot make a good man better.

"We know that the law is spiritual"[2]—that is, 'We who were once in the flesh, know now what we did not know then, we know that the law is spiritual—that is, not only a director of conduct, but "a discerner of the thoughts and intents of the heart," requiring, in reference to God, not only external worship, but supreme love as the habitual principle of conduct; in reference to man, not only just and humane treatment, but cordial unselfish good-will.' Now, looking at the law in that aspect, the apostle says : How imperfectly am I conformed to this law! "I am carnal." Had the apostle been comparing his present with his former self, he would have said, I am not *carnal* in the sense in which I once was so, I am spiritual. If he had compared himself with his weaker brethren, whom, in the Epistle to the Corinthians, he calls "carnal,"[3] and of whom he says, they "walked as men," he would have said, I am not carnal in the sense in which they are carnal, I am spiritual. But when he speaks of himself with a reference to the spiritual law of God, he says, "I am carnal." "Things seen and temporal" have an undue influence over me. My thoughts, and feelings, and desires, are far from being in entire conformity with that spiritual and very broad law. This humble estimate of himself rose out of the increased moral and spiritual perspicacity and sensibility which the apostle now possessed. Worldly men have often

[1] We have a similar construction in 1 Pet. iv. 1-6. γάρ, in ver. 6, hangs by the exhortation in ver. 1, as well as γάρ in ver. 3.

[2] Ver. 14.

[3] 1 Cor. iii. 1, 3.

expressed their astonishment at the humiliating acknowledgements which pious men make in reference to themselves, and have accounted for them on the supposition, either that they were not sincere in making them, or that they were conscious of some great crime which the world knew nothing of, or of some very depraved inclination which never has had an opportunity of manifesting itself in act; while the true account of the matter is, that the man of the world is, in reference to spiritual things, blind and insensible, whereas the religious man has his "senses" in some measure "exercised to discern spiritual good and evil." Thus the man of the world continues to maintain a very good opinion of himself—thinks he has a very good heart, even when his conduct is in many respects greatly objectionable; and the religious man, while all but faultless in the estimation of those who know him best, deeply feels and readily acknowledges that the testimony of God respecting the human heart is true of his: "The heart is deceitful above all things, and desperately wicked."[1]

The expression, "sold under sin," seems even a stronger one than "carnal." It has been compared with the sacred historian's description of Ahab, the king of Israel—"who sold himself to work wickedness in the sight of the Lord."[2] But the phrases are not at all of equivalent meaning. The one is the calm record of the historian, that the Israelitish king was so distinguished by habitual, persevering, determined disobedience, that he seemed as if he had given up all his faculties to be employed in the violation of the Divine law. The other is the expression of the apostle's deep regret that his heart and life were not entirely spiritual—in perfect accordance with the Divine law, and that he felt as if he were the slave of a tyrant who employed him in work which he abhorred. His prevailing desire was perfect conformity to the holy, just, and good law; yet he felt that much was wanting, much was wrong. How different is the apostle's account of himself here—"Sold under sin"—from his account of the unregene-

[1] Jer. xvii. 9. [2] 1 Kings xxi. 20, 25.

rate in the 6th chapter, "servants of sin, yielding themselves its servants, and their members as its instruments of unrighteousness." The language of complaint and deeply stirred spiritual feeling must be cautiously, if it is to be fairly, interpreted. Because Job said, and meant what he said, "Behold I am vile"[1]—we must not conclude that he was a very bad man. The only fair inference is, that he had clear perceptions and deep feelings, in reference to the claims of the Divine law and the imperfect manner in which, in his heart and life, he had answered them.

But the apostle explains his own meaning in the verse that follows: "For that which I do I allow not: for what I would, that I do not; but what I hate, that do I."[2] This seems the ground on which the apostle complains that he is "Carnal, sold under sin." "I do that which I do not *allow*." That may mean—as the word rendered "allow," properly signifies, '*know*'—'I am sometimes hurried, by the influence of external things on my natural propensities, into inward and outward acts, of whose true nature I am not aware.' This is true, I believe, of every good man. But the word *know* is used in Scripture as equivalent to *approve*, as in Psalm i. 6, "The Lord *knoweth*"—approveth, "the way of the righteous;" Hos. viii. 4, "They made princes, and I *knew* it not"—I approved not their conduct. Matt. vii. 23—"I never *knew* you"—I never approved of you; and this seems its meaning here—'I do that which I do not approve of.' Habitually to do what we do not approve of, is a characteristic of a state of unregeneracy; but there is not a just man on earth who does not occasionally, alas! but too frequently, do what he cannot, what he does not, habitually approve of. Whether we are to understand the expression in the one way or the other, will not long continue a reasonable subject of doubt.

The apostle's second statement is—"I do not that which I would." The apostle, as he states at ver. 21, would do good—willed to do good. His prevailing desire was to be

[1] Job xl. 4. [2] Ver. 15.

and do good—to be entirely conformed to the Divine law. Such a prevailing will to do good does not exist in the unregenerate mind; for "the imagination of the thoughts of man's" unchanged "heart are only evil continually."[1] There is no such "*will*," as is here described, in fallen man, till God "work it in him of His good pleasure."[2] He who habitually would do good, ordinarily does good. But though this is the truth, it is not less true, that he who habitually would do good, may occasionally, may often, not do the good he habitually would—wills to do. The apostle was conscious of neglect of duty, of not doing what he ought to have done—what he habitually willed to do.

Nay, more than this, the apostle says—"I do what I hate." He hated sin—all sin, he hated it as sin—opposition to the holy, just, good law of God. The regenerate alone *thus* hate sin. Unregenerate men may disapprove of many forms of sin—they may absolutely loathe certain forms of it, but their habitually living in sin is the proof that they love sin in many forms, and that in no case do they hate it as sin. Yet, notwithstanding this hatred of sin, the apostle was conscious that, under the influence of temptation and remaining depravity, he occasionally did what he habitually abhorred; and on this account he was made to abhor himself. The sum of what is said in these verses is this—'I am conscious of being but imperfectly conformed to the law which is spiritual; I feel fettered by remaining sinful propensities. What I habitually approve, I by no means always do—what I habitually will and wish to do, I by no means always do; nay, I but too frequently do what I habitually hate.' This is the only meaning which the undoubted facts, in reference to the constitution of the human mind, permit us to draw out of the words; for a man, who habitually does what he habitually disapproves and even hates, and habitually does not what he habitually wills, and wishes, and delights in, would be a psychical monster—an absolute incongruity and impossibility.

[1] Gen. vi. 5. [2] Phil. ii. 13.

The prevailing judgments and volitions of the mind, and desires and dispositions of the heart, mark the character. It is on this principle that the apostle draws the conclusions contained in the 16th and 17th verses: "If then I do what I would not, I consent unto the law that it is good. Now then, it is no more I that do it, but sin that dwelleth in me." The meaning seems to be, 'If in doing wrong, I do what I habitually will and wish not to do, *that*—not my doing wrong in itself, but its being in opposition to my habitual wish and will, though not to my will and wish, at the moment of transgression—is a proof that "I consent to the law that it is good;" that in the settled convictions of my mind, and the habitual dispositions of my heart, I regard the law, known to be spiritual, in a way very different from what I did when I was in the flesh; I regard it as in every way good—not only holy and just, but good—good for man, good for me. The apostle's estimate of the law was that of the Psalmist, "Thy law is good: therefore my soul loveth it."

The apostle draws a further conclusion from the fact, that his non-conformities to the law were exceptions to the prevailing convictions of his mind, and dispositions of his heart, in reference to the law: "Now then, it is no more I that do it, but sin that dwelleth in me."[1] It is plain that these words must not be understood as an attempt to escape from the responsibilities of these occasional violations of the Divine law, in opposition to a habitual will and wish to yield obedience, by transferring them to something that was in him, but not of him—some distinct spiritual agent, which he terms, "Sin that dwelt in him." The senselessness and the impiety of such an attempt are equally out of keeping with the character of the apostle. He *could* not talk such blasphemous nonsense. But how *are* the words to be understood? They are, I think, a strong and enigmatic statement of the conclusion to which his premises fairly led him, that these occasional exceptional violations of the Divine law were not the true exponents of his

[1] Ver. 17.

character; that notwithstanding these, he, "in his mind," was, as he says in the 26th verse, "a servant of the law of God." This was his true, his habitual character, though he still acted occasionally, and but too often, as if he were "the slave of the law of sin," under the influence of the flesh—his fallen nature, but imperfectly destroyed by the influence of his new state and nature. "Sin dwelling in the apostle," is just a name for the measure of ignorance and error and worldly depraved propensity, which, notwithstanding the change that had come over him, still remained. When Paul, speaking of his apostolic labours, says, "Not I, but the grace of God that was with me,"[1] he does not mean to say he did not perform these labours, but that he performed them under the influence of the grace of God. When he says, "I live; yet not I, but Christ liveth in me;"[2] he means merely, that to Christ he was indebted for the origin and maintenance of his new and better life. And here he means not to deny that he did these things, but to assert that he did them under an influence which was no longer the dominant one in his mind. This is the only consistent, intelligible meaning which the words can bear. "Sin dwelling in a man"—depravity, is an abstract quality. It cannot act. It is the man to whom the quality belongs that acts. Had Paul said, it is not I, but Satan—the Devil, or one of his subordinate agents, who does these things, that would have been an attempt to exculpate himself; but no such meaning can attach to the words he employs. Suppose a good man, say Cranmer, from the terror of a violent death, should make a temporary denial of the faith, would not every one distinctly understand what I meant when I said, speaking of such a mournful event, 'It was not Thomas Cranmer, but his fear, that dictated that recantation?'

The facts stated by the apostle, painful as they were, fully warranted this conclusion. The renewed character was his true character: he could only be considered as acting a consistent part when he did what was good, for that was what he

[1] 1 Cor. xv. 10. [2] Gal. ii. 20.

consented to—what he willed and wished, what he delighted in; of course, what he habitually did. His deviations from that course—his not doing what he would—his doing what he would not, what he hated—were exceptions, to him very painful ones, from the general rule, and to be accounted for, but by no means excused, by the remaining depravity of his nature.

The language deserves particular attention. Sin once "*reigned* over" the apostle; now it only "*dwells* in" him. That by "sin dwelling in" the apostle, we are not to understand any separate agent to whom the blame of occasional deviations from duty was to be imputed, but *himself*, so far as he was still under the influence of natural depravity, is very plain from the words which follow: "For I know that in me (that is, in my flesh) dwells no good thing: for to will is present with me; but how to perform that which is good I find not."[1] You will notice the difference between the *I* in the 17th verse, and the *me* in the 18th. It is not the *I*, in the 17th verse, that commits sin; and in the *me*, of the 18th, there is nothing but sin. How is this? The *me*, in the 18th verse, is equivalent to "*my flesh*"—my nature as unrenewed; the *I*, in the 17th verse, to '*my spirit*'—my nature as renewed. "The spirit," in this sense, and "the flesh," are often personified by the apostle, and are much the same as "the old man," and "the new man." These terms describe not living agents, but frames of thought and feeling—the one, "the flesh," natural to man; the other, "the spirit," produced by the operation of the Holy Ghost through the influence of truth believed. "The old man" is wholly corrupt; "the new man" is "after the image of Him who created him"—holy. The old man can do nothing but sin; the new man sinneth not, he cannot sin, "for he is born of God, and his seed remains in him."[2] These two moral persons, figurative men, exist together in the real Christian man. He was originally all *flesh*, there was nothing else in him. Now, the new man, the spirit, has been formed within him. The tendency of the spirit is to destroy the flesh; the

[1] Ver. 18. [2] 1 John iii. 9.

invigoration of the new man is the weakening of the old man. The two frames of mind and disposition are really antagonistic; and though they may, and do, exist in the same mind, they are ever leading and drawing in opposite directions. As the apostle says, "The flesh lusteth against the spirit, and the spirit against the flesh: and these two are contrary the one to the other."[1] When the Christian acts entirely under the influence of the Spirit, he does not sin; when he acts entirely under the influence of the flesh, he does nothing but sin; and when he acts, as he generally does, under their joint influence, his temper—conduct, is good or evil in the degree in which the one or the other prevails: but he is equally a responsible being when acting in all these various ways.

Having made these remarks, which, if understood, will carry light through the whole discussion, let us look at the apostle's words: "For I know that in *me* (that is, in my flesh) dwelleth no good thing." This is illustrative of the phrase, "Sin dwelleth in me." It is as if he had said—'Yes, sin, though it does not reign as it once did, still dwells in me; for I know, both from the declarations of God's word and from my own experience, that nothing spiritually good dwells in my nature, unchanged by Divine influence. And it is in consequence of this that, while "to will is present with me, how to perform that which is good I find not."' The meaning of these words is, not that the apostle had nothing but a bare will—an ineffectual desire to do good, but that, owing to sin dwelling in him, his habitual will and desire to do good were not so effectual as they should have been—as they would have been in a perfectly holy person. The work really done did not correspond to his will; the flesh prevented him doing much that he willed, and gave a character of imperfection even to what he did. His will, under the influence of the Spirit, was to "*run* in the ways of God's commandments;" but the flesh presented many obstacles and stumbling-blocks,

[1] Gal. v. 17.

which impeded his progress, and sometimes made him stumble and fall.

This state of things was most painful to the apostle; and we find him—under the influence of that law of our nature, familiar to us all, which makes the heart, when oppressed with care, to take a melancholy pleasure in brooding over the cause of its griefs, and gives the tongue a mournful license to repeat its sorrows—reiterating, with scarcely a change of a word, what he had said in the 15th and 16th verses. It was no mere matter of argument, no dialectic subtlety—it was the subject of heartfelt experience and deep sorrow. "For the good that I would I do not: but the evil which I would not, that I do. Now, if I do that I would not, it is no more I that do it, but sin that dwelleth in me."[1] Nothing could express more touchingly the dreary uniformity of this struggle, which, without hope of termination or final success, the regenerate man must maintain with the remaining depravity of his nature, had he no help but what the law gives—were he not under another, an altogether different kind of influence, that of grace. How to the life is this picture! "When a Christian first gives his heart to God, and sees the beauty of holiness, and feels devout joy, he says, in the ardour of his 'first love,' I *will* keep thy commandments—*all* thy commandments. Even after temptation has prevailed, and made him taste the bitterness of remorse, he resolves on new obedience with redoubled ardour; he knows good and evil, and he will not return to folly. Experience convinces him that human resolution is weak; that the heart is very deceitful; that sin dwelleth in him—is wedded to mortality. The past makes him tremble for the future, and even assures him that temptation will return; that he may—probably will, fall in some measure before it; and that all his days on earth must be stained by sin, saddened by penitential sorrow."[2]

In the 21st verse, the apostle appears to give us a general deduction from the particular facts stated in the preceding

[1] Ver. 19, 20. [2] Charters.

verses: "I find then a law, that, when I would go good, evil is present with me."[1] The original words are somewhat perplexed in their construction, and admit of a variety of translations and interpretations. Some would read them, 'I find that to me, willing to do good, the law is present as the occasion of evil.' But this does violence to the construction, is no deduction from what goes before, and breaks entirely the coherence of the apostle's illustration. Others would read them—'I find, then, that evil is present with me, wishing to do good, according to the law;' while a third class prefer this rendering—'I find then, according to the law, that to me, wishing to do good, evil is present.' The sense given by our translators seems, on the whole, the preferable one—'I find it then a law, that, when I would do good, evil is present with me;' or, more literally thus—'I find it then a law with me, willing—*i.e.*, when willing, to do good, that evil is present with me.'

The word "*law*" is here—as well as in the 23d verse, and in chap. iii. 27, and probably, too, in chap. x. 31—used with a signification considerably different from that which the apostle usually gives to it. It seems employed very much in the same way as in the English phrases, 'the laws of nature,' 'the laws of vision,' 'the laws of the human constitution,' 'the laws of thought.' We say that it is by a law of nature, which we call gravitation, that stones fall to the ground, and that the earth moves round the sun; and that it is by a law of the human mind, that the mental perception of the meaning and evidence of a statement or proposition is productive of belief. Our meaning is, that these things take place with a regularity and certainty similar to that which results from the operation of *law*, properly so called. "I find then a law," is just equivalent to, 'Thus I experience this to be the ordinary course of things with me; I find it, as it were, the law of my present imperfectly renewed state, "that, when I would do good, evil is present with me."'

The idea which these words seem most naturally to suggest,

[1] Ver. 21.

is this: 'That if, at any particular time, the apostle was specially desirous to do good, then, in a remarkable degree, the depraved principles of his fallen nature were sure to exert themselves.' That this is often the experience of a regenerate man, there can be no doubt. When he is very desirous of performing some piece of spiritual duty—say meditation, prayer, or thanksgiving—it is no uncommon thing for vain, absurd, vile thoughts to rush in on his mind as a deluge, so that he is constrained to say with the Psalmist, "I am as a beast before Thee."[1]

But the fact referred to by the apostle seems to be one of a more general kind. 'I find it to be the general law of my present state, as a regenerated but an imperfectly sanctified man, that, though I habitually wish to do what is good, I am constantly liable, from the remaining depravity of my nature, to act in a manner inconsistent with the ordinary tenor of my volitions and desires, and, of course, of my conduct too.' Two facts, of an opposite character, are represented as ascertained by the apostle, and together forming the law of his present imperfect state: the one, that he willed to do that which is good; the other, that, though he did so, evil was present with him.

These two facts he proceeds to illustrate in the two following verses: "For I delight in the law of God after the inward man: but I see another law in my members warring against the law of my mind, and bringing me into captivity to the law of sin which is in my members."[2]

The inward or inner man is not here, the *soul* in opposition to the *body;* or the higher powers of our nature, such as reason and conscience, in opposition to the lower powers of our nature, such as appetites and passions. The phrase is to be found only in two other passages of Scripture,[3] and there, as well as here, seems to signify not merely the mind, but the regenerate mind. It appears to mean exactly the same thing as "the mind," which, in the next verse, is contrasted with the *flesh* and its members, and which is obviously not tho body and

[1] Psalm lxxiii. 22.
[2] Ver. 22, 23.
[3] 2 Cor. iv. 16, and Eph. iii. 16.

its members, but corrupt human nature and its faculties. He willed what was good, for, "according to his inner man"—the most central portions of his intellectual and moral being, reason, and conscience, and moral affection, influenced by the Holy Spirit—he "delighted in the law of the Lord." This is very strong language. It expresses not merely, like the words, "I consent to it that it is good," a calm, rational approbation of the law as reasonable and just, and calculated to produce happiness, but a cordial satisfaction with it as divinely beautiful, excellent, and benignant. Not merely had he no wish that the precepts of the Divine law were less strict, or its sanctions less stringent, but he delighted in contemplating it as a picture of the moral excellence of its Author, and rejoiced that he and all the intelligent universe were under its righteous, benignant sway. He sympathized with the Psalmist when he says, "Oh how love I Thy law! Thy word is very pure; therefore Thy servant loveth it. The law of Thy mouth is better to me than thousands of gold and silver."[1]

So much for the one fact. Had there been nothing to interfere with this delight, how happy, how holy, would the apostle have been! But there is another fact—"Evil is present with me." I have stated the law of my renewed nature; "but I see another law in my members warring against the law of my mind, and bringing me into captivity to the law of sin which is in my members." "The members" and "the flesh" are materially the same thing—human nature as depraved: only, when it is called the flesh, we think of it as a whole; when it is termed "the members," we think of the faculties, capacities—modes of operation by which it is distinguished. "I find a law in my members," is equivalent to, 'in the operation of the faculties of my depraved nature, I find an order of things which works with the regularity of law. This order of things is directly the reverse of that now established by the good Spirit in my renewed mind.' According to that law, he habitually delighted in the law of the

[1] Psalm cxix. 72, 97, 140.

Lord, and of course yielded to it a cheerful, willing obedience. This is the law of the new creation, just as it is the law of nature that the sun should shine by day. But then—as by another law in nature, originating in other causes, the sun is sometimes eclipsed and darkened, when, according to the general law, he should be shining, so also—in consequence of the influence of remaining depravity, the best man is always liable to fall, and but too frequently does fall.

"The law in his members"—the ordinary course of things in reference to the operations of his mind, so far as still under the influence of depravity, was, "that evil was present to him:" there was still ignorance and error in the understanding—a tendency to judge wrong, and perversity in the will—a tendency to choose wrong, and a corresponding evil bias in all the faculties. This law in the members warred with the law of the mind. The language is highly figurative, but it is by no means obscure. The two orders of things were opposed to each other, and each developed itself according to its nature. The apostle's figurative statement is, in plain literal language: 'I find, in consequence of my remaining depravity, that I am often indisposed to, and prevented from, the doing of that to which the Holy Spirit and the principles of my new nature incline me as good; and that, on the other hand, I am often inclined to, and led to do, that to which the Holy Spirit and the principles of my new nature indispose me.' It is just the sentiment expressed in the Epistle to the Galatians, which I have already had occasion to refer to,—"The flesh lusteth against the Spirit, and the Spirit against the flesh: and these are contrary the one to the other; so that ye cannot do the things that ye would."[1]

But the apostle states, not only that the law in the members makes war on the law of the mind, but that it sometimes succeeds in bringing him into captivity. "The law of sin" seems an idiomatic expression for the sinful law—that order of things which prevails in human nature as fallen—as sinful, expressly

[1] Gal. v. 17.

opposed to the holy law of God. This sinful order of things is always opposed to the holy order of things in the mind and sometimes prevails; and the renewed man becomes, as it were, its captive, or is by it made sin's captive. We should sadly misinterpret these words, as well as teach what in philosophy is the height of absurdity, and in divinity most false and dangerous doctrine, if we were to say that they intimate, that when a regenerate man sins, he sins against his will, or, in other words, is forced to sin. A sin without will, against will, is a contradiction in terms. But we are to understand two things: first, that the regenerate man may fall into sin—does fall before temptation; and, secondly, that, when he does so, he acts not indeed in opposition to his will at the moment, evilly biased, but in opposition to the general course of his convictions, volitions, and inclinations. The apostle also intimates, that in consequence of the habitual prevalence of renewed sentiment and feeling, these occasional deviations from rectitude, in heart and in life, in thought and inclination, are felt by the regenerate man to be a very great evil; and that occasional subjection to depraved principle is considered by him as the most intolerable and degrading species of captivity.

Such, then, is Paul's account of his own spiritual state—his inner history, as a regenerate man. He habitually approves, and loves, and practises holiness, as enjoined in the Divine law. He is in a very different state from that in which he was when "in the flesh"—when "the motions of sins, which were by the law, did work in his members to bring forth fruit unto death." Yet still he is far from being perfect; under the influence of remaining depravity, he still occasionally violates the Divine law. He is always exposed to temptation, and in danger of falling. He is in a state of continual warfare, and sustains occasional defeats. These occasion deep sorrow and earnest desires of complete deliverance from what is felt to be the worst of evils.

These feelings are very strongly expressed in the 24th verse: "O wretched man that I am! who shall deliver me from the body of this death?" It has been usual with the class of interpreters, with whom we substantially agree in our views of this paragraph, to view it as descriptive of the apostle's habitual feeling, and of the habitual feeling of every regenerate man. I cannot help thinking this a mistake. Generally, the apostle felt himself to be a very happy man—"triumphing in Christ"—"joying in God, through Christ, by whom he had received the reconciliation." In the warfare referred to, the regenerate man is generally the victor; and he has great delight when he finds himself strong in the grace of his Lord—a conqueror, and more than a conqueror, through Him that loves him. But this is the expression of his feeling when he has been foiled, or when, in a melancholy hour, he allows his mind to be so occupied with his own weakness, and the power of his spiritual enemies, as to lose sight of the promise of final complete triumph, or of the grace and power of Him that has made that promise. It is then he breathes out, from the very bottom of the heart, "O wretched man that I am! who shall deliver me from the body of this death?"[1]

"The body of this death," may, with equal propriety, be rendered, "this body of death;"—this body of death being equivalent to this deathful body—this body productive of mischief and misery. Now, what are we to understand by this? Not our mortal body, though the term of deliverance from this deathful body, and that of our parting with our mortal body, will be contemporaneous; but what the apostle calls "the body of sin"—"the flesh," "the old man," "sin that dwelleth in us." It is not improbable that there is, in this expression, an allusion to the custom referred to by the poet when speaking of the treatment of captives by their cruel conquerors—

"The living and the dead, at his command,
Were coupled, face to face, and hand to hand,
Till, chok'd by stench, in loath'd embraces ty'd,
The lingering wretches pin'd away and died."[2]

"Who shall deliver me?" Obviously law cannot; and the

[1] Ver. 24. [2] Virgil Aeneid, viii. Dryden's Translation.

illustration of this seems to be the direct object of the apostle in giving this picture of the working of his mind as a regenerate man. As an unregenerate man, he had found that law could not initiate a life of true sanctification. As a regenerate man, he had found it could neither promote nor perfect that life. The place which law, in the hand of Christ, has in promoting sanctification, though important, is secondary. "Mere objective and authoritative exhibition of truth respecting men's duties cannot sanctify."[1] Something more powerful than a statement of what is duty, and why we should perform it, is requisite to make even regenerate men obey the Divine will. But "law" here, deliverance from which is necessary, according to the apostle, to the commencement and progress of sanctification, is what divines have termed 'law as a covenant'—law making obedience the proper condition of life. Suppose a regenerate man under law in this sense, and you make his struggles hopeless, and deprive him of the most powerful motives to persevere in them. It deserves to be remarked, too, that though a truly regenerate man can never, in fact, be brought again under the law as a covenant, he may, by losing sight of those truths, through the belief of which he obtained deliverance from it, deprive himself to that extent of the felt sanctifying influence of that deliverance; and indeed may, by not realizing his deliverance, think and feel, in reference to himself, as if he were under the law. In the degree in which he does so, his sanctification must be impeded. A legal mode of thinking and feeling gives the principles of depravity an advantage which otherwise they could not have, and occasions many a struggle, and many a fall, which a stronger faith in a more habitual realization of freedom from law, and subjection to grace, would have prevented. It is the clear perception, the firm faith, of those truths respecting the grace of God in Christ Jesus, which gives deliverance from the law as a covenant, both in its condemning power and in its influence over the feelings and character: This, in the hand of the

[1] Hodge.

Spirit, is the grand instrument of Christian sanctification;[1] and they greatly err who would substitute for this a belief (which may or may not be well founded) of the individual's personal deliverance from law and subjection to grace—a belief which, if unfounded, can only delude and produce false confidence, and, if well founded, operates salutarily, chiefly, from its growing out of the faith of the Gospel and its necessary results.

The apostle, in the pathetic inquiry "Who shall deliver me?" expresses earnest desire to be delivered; he indicates also a conviction that law cannot deliver him; but he does not intimate despair of deliverance. He knew who had delivered—who would deliver, who had begun—who would perfect, the good work. "I thank God," he says, "through Jesus Christ our Lord." He has delivered. What the law could not do, He, in his grace, has accomplished.

It deserves notice that there is another, and perhaps preferable, reading: "The grace of God through Jesus Christ our Lord;" in which case the words are at once the answer of the question "Who shall deliver me?" and the text of the discussion, down to verse 4 of the next chapter, as to how *grace* delivers from sin.

This is the hinge which connects the two parts of the apostle's discussion—"Sin shall not have dominion over you:" and "for ye are not under the law." "Sin shall not have dominion over you: for ye are under grace." The first is finished; the other now commences, and reaches to the 4th verse of the next chapter.

The Apostle Paul, here as elsewhere, sets himself up as an "ensample to all those who should believe to life everlasting." With John Newton,[2] I believe the picture, in its great outlines, to be applicable to the most holy Christian on earth; and that the more advanced he is he will the more readily recognise

[1] Tit. iii. 4–8. Note the reference and force of τούτων and ἵνα, and ταῦτα, in ver. 8.

[2] Cardiphonia.

the likeness. Those who have believed through grace are apt to suspect that they have believed in vain, that their faith is not genuine—not the faith of God's elect, because it does not produce all the effects they hoped and wished from it in making them holy. But this passage teaches them, that it is by the prevailing bent of the will that the real character is to be ascertained. It is our duty to desire, and to endeavour, to be as holy as the holy angels; but we must not conclude that we are not holy at all, though we never should be quite like them till we be where they are. We cannot be too deeply humbled on account of sin dwelling in us, and giving so many proofs that it does dwell in us; but we must not give up our hope that we are among the "sanctified in Christ Jesus" because we are not better than the Apostle Paul, nor refuse to acknowledge God's workmanship in our hearts till it be completed in heaven. That is pride under the guise of humility.

The man who can intelligently and honestly use the apostle's language, has no doubt cause, like him, to mourn, but he has also cause to rejoice. If he is obliged to say sometimes, "Wretched man that I am! who shall deliver me?" he may also say, "I thank God, through Jesus Christ." The good work is begun; it will proceed; it will be perfected in the day of Christ. The Christian, even after a shameful defeat, may yet say, "Rejoice not against me, O mine enemy: though I fall I shall arise." God brings good out of this struggle so painful—a struggle which, as we have seen, marks the Christian as an object of blame as well as of pity. The struggle is within. The Christian feels it in himself—he does not see it in his Christian brother; and, as Mr Newton says, judging of him by what he sees, and of himself by what he feels, in lowliness of heart he esteems others better than himself. He learns to warn, to pity, to bear with others; and nothing more habitually reconciles a Christian to the thought of death than the experience of this warfare. Death is unwelcome to nature; but then, and not till then, the conflict will cease. The flesh will be put off with the body. Then we shall sin no more. Is not this worth dying for?

But the most regular formalist, and the most accomplished hypocrite, would discover a lamentable degree of self-ignorance were they to apply the apostle's words to themselves. "Let not him that is deceived trust in vanity." Let no man conclude, because he disapproves many sins which he yet goes on to commit, that he is animated by the spirit of the apostle. His external conduct was most exemplary, and he kept his heart with diligence. Though he complained of being carnal, he neither walked nor warred after the flesh, nor made provision for it, to fulfil its lusts. If a man condemns sin, and yet lives in it, he condemns himself, and God will condemn him out of his own mouth. Such a man cannot say in truth, "It is not I that do it, but sin that dwelleth in me." His conduct shows that sin not only dwells in him, but reigns over him. He loves sin, and his pretended or apparent aversion to it is merely aversion to the misery which he fears will flow from it. He goes on in opposition to the remonstrances of his conscience; and if God do not grant him repentance, his conscience will be his tormentor for ever. He may now, perhaps, succeed, in some measure, in stupifying conscience and excusing his conduct to his own mind, seeking an excuse or palliation in what is indeed an aggravation of his guilt; but when God shall punish him, he shall be speechless—he shall have nothing to answer: the tremendous words, "You knew your duty, and you did it not," shall be inscribed indelibly in letters of living fire on his conscience; and through eternity he shall continue to learn the meaning of the declaration, "Be not deceived; God is not mocked: whatsoever a man soweth, that shall he also reap."

An acquaintance with the letter of the Holy Scriptures is a blessing or a curse, according as it is connected with a true or a false view of their meaning. In the first case, it is an attainment of high value, and may become the instrument of indefinite improvement in knowledge and in holiness. In the second, it is one of the most dangerous talents a man can possess, either for himself or for others, as it enables him to make the worse appear the better reason, both to their minds and his own, and thus to fortify them in error, and confirm them in wickedness. The more extensive such a man's knowledge is, and the greater his ingenuity, just the more thoroughly and systematically is he likely to be in the wrong, and just so much more improbable is his being reclaimed from error. So true is the remark of our Christian poet,—

> "Of all the arts sagacious dupes invent,
> To cheat themselves, and gain the world's consent,
> The worst is Scripture warp'd from its intent."[1]

Almost every passage of Scripture, when misunderstood, is liable to be abused. But there are particular passages which, when misapprehended, are sure to be abused. In the writings of the Apostle Paul there are, as his apostolical brother informs us, passages which "the unlearned and unstable wrest to their own destruction." The passage we have been considering is one of them.

Led astray by the sound of some of its words, it has been no uncommon thing for persons who, under a profession of religion, lead an unholy life, to endeavour to turn it to account as a help to self-delusion. They have sought, by its means, to get rid of the disagreeable feelings of responsibility and remorse, and to conjoin two things which God never meant should go together,—indulged sin, and a comfortable opinion of their own spiritual state and prospects. They confound the struggles of the flesh and the Spirit, to which they are strangers, "not having the Spirit," with the contest between inclination and conscience, with which they are but too familiar; and concluding, in a sense in which the apostle never intended it, that because their conscience lifts up a feeble ineffectual protest when they violate God's law, it is not they but indwelling sin that is in fault, they look on themselves as fitter objects of pity than of blame, and say peace, peace, to themselves, when there is no peace.

[1] Cowper.

The best way of preventing or exposing this very loathsome form of practical antinomianism is, to point out as distinctly as possible the true meaning of the apostle's expressions, so that, while they answer the purpose they were meant to serve—to sustain the true Christian in his struggle with in-dwelling sin, and show him both where he cannot, and where he may find strength to conquer it—they may not be perverted into the means of delusion and ruin on the part of the false-hearted professor, but that he may be driven out of the refuge of lies which he endeavours to find in God's word, and that that word may be clearly seen to be "profitable for doctrine, and for reproof, and for correction, and for instruction in righteousness."

To gain these objects, the preceding observations are intended, and it is hoped that they are not altogether unfitted to serve their purpose. May the good Spirit render them effectual, and may it never happen to the author and his readers, according to the true proverb, "If the blind lead the blind, both shall fall into the ditch." On the contrary, may he be enabled "rightly to divide the word of truth," and may they be enabled to "receive with meekness that word," which, if "engrafted" into the mind or heart, is able to save the soul.

The question referred to in the opening of the section, Of whom does the apostle speak? may be considered, I think, as settled. The apostle speaks of himself—of himself as regenerate. This is the plain meaning of the words. Much is said, which can in truth be said of no unregenerate man—nothing is said but what every regenerate man must acknowledge to be true of himself. Suppose the two opposed states of feeling to be co-existent and habitual, and the man described is an impossibility — such a man never existed, and never can exist. Suppose the sinful state habitual and predominant, and the better state but occasional, the man described is a hypocrite and self-deceiver. Suppose the holy state habitual and predominant, and the sinful state occasional, and the man described is the true Christian—who, though transformed by the renewing of his mind, knows by painful inward evidence that he has not attained, neither is already perfect.

β. "*Sin shall not have dominion over you, for ye are under grace.*"[1]

The words that immediately follow the inquiry, "Who shall deliver me from the body of this death,"[2]—"I thank God, through Jesus Christ our Lord"—seem to be the commencement of the illustration of the second part of the apostle's declaration, "Sin shall not have dominion over you: for ye are under grace;" and the illustration of this thesis closes at the end of the 4th verse of the eighth chapter. The words, "I thank God, through Jesus Christ our Lord," are not exactly those we should have expected after those which immediately precede them. We should have looked for an expression of sorrow and depression rather than of joy and exultation, a prayer rather than a thanksgiving. Their introduction seems very abrupt, and the sentence is plainly elliptical; something must be supplied to bring out a distinct meaning—"I thank God, through Christ Jesus," '*who delivers me*,' or, '*for deliverance*.' And as these words seem strangely to follow what goes before, there seems but little connection between them and those that follow: "So then with the mind I myself serve the law of God, but with the flesh the law of sin."

It is right to remark that, besides the reading which has been followed by our translators, there are two others, either of which has considerable claims to be preferred to it. The first, which is now generally adopted by critics, is, "Thanks be to God, through Jesus Christ our Lord."[3] This is in meaning quite co-incident with the received reading, and labours under the same difficulties of interpretation with it. The second, "The grace of God, through Jesus Christ our Lord,"[4] which has not so much external evidence of genuine-

[1] Chap. vii. 25–Chap. viii. 4.
[2] Ver. 24.
[3] χάρις τῷ Θεῷ.
[4] Ἡ χάρις τοῦ Θεοῦ.

ness as either of the other two (though by no means destitute of such evidence, not only appearing in some Greek MSS. of note, but being the reading followed by the vulgate translator, who probably made his version at a time nearer the apostolic age than the date of any existing Greek MS.), has yet so much internal evidence, that I am disposed to adopt it: "Wretched man that I am! who shall deliver me from the body of this death? The grace of God, through Jesus Christ our Lord." This is just what we might look for. It is an answer, and a true answer, to the question, "Who shall deliver me?" There is no abruptness here, and there is no need of supplying anything to make out a complete sense. It is the natural link between what goes before and what follows. The apostle has shown that law cannot deliver; he now goes on to show that grace *can*, that grace *does*, deliver. The first clause, then, of the 25th verse, read thus, "The grace of God, through Jesus Christ our Lord, delivers me from the body of this death," is the text of the short paragraph which ends at ver. 4 of next chapter.

There are some difficulties arising from some of the connective particles which the apostle uses; but the course of thought seems very clearly defined—'This is the state of things with me as a partially renewed man. "With the mind"—*i.e.*, so far as I am a renewed man, so far as I am under Divine influence, "I serve the law of God"—I am conformed to its spiritual, holy, just, good requisitions. "With the flesh," however—that is, so far as I am not renewed, so far as I am under the influence of my unchanged fallen nature, "I serve the law of sin"[1]—I am carnal and unholy. It was not from law, but grace, that in my mind I became a servant, a willing servant, of the law of God; and it is not to law, but to grace, that I look for deliverance from the sin which still dwells in my flesh, and sometimes makes me a captive. Law could not deliver me from this bondage, because it could not pardon the sins I was constantly contracting, nor could it

[1] Ver. 25.

secure me the help of an influence which would enable me successfully to struggle with, and ultimately to conquer, depraved principle. Grace does both. There is no condemnation to them who are in Christ Jesus, and there is a law of the spirit of life in Christ Jesus which delivers me from the law of sin and death; and both this freedom from condemnation, and this powerful delivering influence, grace bestows—*i.e.*, God, in the exercise of grace, bestows through the mediation of His Son. By the incarnation and sacrifice of His own Son, He has laid a secure foundation for so destroying the power of sin in the case of those who are in Christ Jesus, and who show that they are so by walking, not after the flesh, but after the spirit; so that the righteousness which the law requires, but cannot furnish, shall be fulfilled in them, they being completely delivered from the depraving influence of sin, and made completely holy—a result which the law never could have effected, in consequence not of any deficiency or fault in it, but on account of the depravity of man, "in that it was weak through the flesh."' Such is, I cannot doubt, the apostle's course of thought. Let us examine it a little more minutely.

"The grace"—the free favour "of God," in which the Divine method of justification originates, and of which it is so striking a manifestation, delivers the believer from the demoralizing influence of sin. Every believer—even the most advanced in holiness, such as the Apostle Paul—stands in need of this deliverance. He has been delivered—but he has been only partially delivered. "So then," says the apostle, looking back to the description contained in the last paragraph, "with my mind I serve the law of God:" so far as I am transformed by the renewing of the mind, "I serve the law of God"—I am what that law requires me to be—I think, and feel, and act in conformity with it; but while this is true, it is as true that "with my flesh I serve the law of sin:" so far as I am conformed to this world—so far as my nature remains unrenewed, "I serve the law of sin"—I am regulated by that order of things which originates in my natural state as guilty, helpless, and depraved, and which prevails with the regularity and force of law in unregenerate man. The deliverance I possess I owe not to law, but to grace; and the deliverance I need, I expect not from law, but from grace; and I do expect that grace will deliver—completely deliver me, since it has made provision for this, by exerting itself in the Divine method of justification.

What the believer wants, and what the law cannot give him, is, in the first place, deliverance from the curse—pardon, a state of acceptance with God; and, in the second place, an influence powerful enough to counteract and overpower the depraving influences from without and within to which he is exposed. Now grace, as reigning "in the righteousness of God," does both.

1. *Grace furnishes a justifying righteousness.*[1]

That it secures the first, is strongly asserted in the first verse of the eighth chapter—"There is therefore now no condemnation to them who are in Christ Jesus." There should have been no division of chapters here; these words are most closely connected with those which go before them. They are the statement of what is most fundamental in the way in which grace delivers the believer from the power of remaining depravity, and show how exactly the remedy suits the disease, as described in the close of the preceding verse. It is difficult to perceive the precise nature of the connection indicated by the particles, "therefore" and "now."[2] "Therefore," does not intimate that what is contained in this verse is a logical inference from what goes before, for no connection of this kind can be traced. It is the same particle that is rendered *so* in the preceding verse, and its force seems something like this: As from the previous description of the believer's experience, that "with the mind he serves the law of God,

[1] Chap. viii. 1.

[2] *ἄρα νῦν* plainly contrasted with *ἄρα οὖν* in the preceding verse.

and with the flesh the law of sin," so from the previous description of the righteousness of God—the Divine method of justification, it appears that according to it, "there is no condemnation to them who are in Christ Jesus." "*Now*" and "*then*," are plainly contrasted, though how, is not so clear; probably somewhat in this way, 'Thus then, looking to myself, I find,' etc. 'Thus now, looking to the Divine method of justification as manifested, I find that,' etc.[1] The words, "who walk not after the flesh, but after the spirit," are, I believe, universally, by critics, considered, as not belonging to the first verse, but borrowed from the end of the fourth verse, which is their proper place.

The statement then is, 'The grace of God, through Christ Jesus, shall deliver from the power, and even existence, of the depraving influence of sin, for it secures that there is no condemnation to them who are in Christ Jesus." To be "in Christ Jesus," is to be so related to Christ Jesus that His death is, as it were, our death, His life our life. To those who are thus "in Christ Jesus," there is no condemnation. The word *is*, you will see, is a supplement. The sentiment is, there is not, shall not be, cannot be, any condemnation. They were condemned—they were "children of wrath even as others;"[2] but having been united to Christ by believing, their condemnation has been completely and for ever removed. "He that believeth is not condemned"—he "shall not come into condemnation,"[3] for he is in Christ. Who can condemn him whom God has justified on the ground that Christ has died for him, the just in the room of the unjust.[4] The believer is "made the righteousness of God in Him," who was "made sin in his room."[5] "Of God he is in Christ Jesus righteousness."[6] It is the grace of God that has secured this. We are

[1] A learned friend remarks: "νῦν is *temporal;* οὖν is *inferential;* ἄρα οὖν = matters, or the case being so (οὖν), as a fitting sequence (ἄρα), I serve, etc. ἄρα νῦν = accordingly now; accordingly (ἄρα), *at this stage* of matters, *now* since Christ has died for us, etc. (νῦν)."

[2] Eph. ii. 3. [3] John iii. 18; v. 24. [4] Rom. viii. 33, 34.

[5] 2 Cor. v. 21. [6] 1 Cor. i. 30.

"justified freely by God's grace."[1] In what other source could this justification of a sinner originate?

In thus securing freedom from condemnation, grace also secures freedom from depravity. It could be obtained in no other way. A condemned sinner, remaining such, cannot become holy. Men must be redeemed from the curse in order to their obtaining any spiritual blessing; and he who in being justified is installed in the favour of God, is, as a matter of course, secured of all spiritual blessings.

2. *Grace furnishes regenerating and sanctifying influence.*[2]

But to the deliverance from "the body of death"—that is, "sin dwelling in us," there is necessary a change of character as well as a change of relation; and to this, inward influence in the operation of the Divine Spirit, as well as external performance in the atoning work of the Divine Son, is necessary. These things are closely connected, and the grace which secures the one secures also the other. It is to this I apprehend the apostle refers when, in the 2d verse, he says, "For the law of the spirit of life in Christ Jesus hath made me free from the law of sin and of death."

The connective particle, "for,"[3] is either equivalent to 'moreover,' or it hangs by the first clause of the 25th verse of the last chapter—'The grace of God by Jesus Christ delivers from sin, not only as it frees from condemnation, but also as it furnishes transforming sanctifying influence.' Deliverance from "the law of sin and death," is certainly the same thing as deliverance from "the body of this death"—or from "sin dwelling in us," or from "the law in the members" called "the law of sin," which in the members wars against the law of the mind. That *law* is just the order of things which prevails with the regularity of a law in human nature as depraved, and is productive of nothing but sin and death—guilt, depravity, misery. It is strange that some very excellent interpreters should understand by "the law of sin and of death"

[1] Rom. iii. 24. [2] Chap. viii. 2. [3] γάρ.

the Divine law, in its covenant form. No doubt that law, in this form, can neither justify nor sanctify a condemned sinner, but binds him in guilt, and irritates instead of extinguishing his depraved propensities. But we cannot bring ourselves to believe, that he who so emphatically pronounces that law "holy, and just, and good," and who so carefully guards against the supposition, that it "is sin,"[1] or "becomes death,"[2] could, especially without a word of explanation, call it "the law of sin and death." Besides, what the apostle is here illustrating is not freedom from the law—his discussion on that subject is closed—but freedom from sin. His thesis here is not 'grace delivers from the law, but 'grace delivers from sin.' And how does it deliver? Not only is there no condemnation to them who are in Christ Jesus, but there is to them a quickening spirit. The economy of grace is the ministration not only of righteousness—that is, justification, but of spiritual life—that is, sanctification.[3] "The law of the Spirit of life in Christ Jesus delivers from the law of sin and death."

"The Spirit of life" is here, I apprehend, a designation of the Holy Spirit, the third person of the Godhead, who is the author of all true spiritual life or holiness in human nature—'the living, the life-giving Spirit.' This is the sense in which the word "Spirit" is generally employed in the context. "The law of the Spirit of life" has, by some interpreters, been considered as descriptive of the Gospel; but the contrast between this "law," and "the law of sin and death," seems to fix the true meaning of the phrase. It describes, if I mistake not, the new order of things established in the mind by the Spirit of life, who is given to all true believers in consequence of their being redeemed from the curse of the law. The just views, firm convictions, holy dispositions, produced in the heart by the Holy Ghost, through the instrumentality of the truth believed, deliver from the false views and unholy dispositions which characterize our fallen nature. The one order of things supersedes the other; and just as the law of spring

[1] Chap. vii. 7. [2] Chap. vii. 13. [3] 2 Cor. iii. 8, 9.

contends with the law of winter, till it end in the establishment of the law of summer and autumn, does the law of spiritual life contend with the law of spiritual death, till, through the process of progressive sanctification, it end at last in the perfection of heaven. The force of the expression rendered "hath made free," is "delivers"—"hath delivered" —"does deliver"—"will deliver." It describes what the law of life habitually does—it acts according to its nature.

It is doubtful whether the phrase, "in Christ Jesus," is to be construed with the designation "Spirit of life," or with the word "deliver." In the first case, it signifies the Spirit who is "*in* Christ Jesus"—dwells in Him without measure. In the last, it indicates that our deliverance by the Spirit is enjoyed in union with Christ Jesus. It is as "in Christ Jesus" that there is no condemnation to us; and it is as "in Christ Jesus" that we are delivered from the law of sin and death by the law of "the Spirit of life." Thus, then, does the grace of God, by giving them at once a justifying righteousness and a quickening Spirit, deliver those whom the law could not deliver.

3. *How Grace furnishes a Justifying Righteousness and Sanctifying Influence.*[1]

The wonderful means by which God, in the exercise of His grace, thus delivers men from the depraving influences of their fallen state, are detailed by the apostle in the 3d and 4th verses: "For what the law could not do, in that it was weak through the flesh, God sending His own Son in the likeness of sinful flesh, and for sin condemned sin in the flesh; that the righteousness of the law might be fulfilled in us, who walk not after the flesh, but after the Spirit." A slight transposition brings out the sense more clearly: "For God, sending His Son in the likeness of sinful flesh, and for sin, hath condemned sin in the flesh, that the righteousness of the law might be fulfilled in us, who walk not after the flesh, but after

[1] Chap. viii. 3, 4.

the Spirit; which the law could not do, in that it was weak through the flesh." "For" is illustrative: it is equivalent to, 'This is the way in which God, in the exercise of His grace, delivers from the power of sin—a work which, in consequence of the depravity of human nature, law has not accomplished—never could accomplish.'

The great work which God, in the exercise of His grace, is represented here as accomplishing, through the incarnation and sacrifice of His Son—"the condemning of sin in the flesh, with the intention and to the effect of the righteousness of the law being fulfilled in men, who walk not after the flesh, but after the Spirit"—is plainly the same thing as the delivering of men from the dominion of sin. Sin is here personified, as in so many other passages in the epistle; and few things are of more importance than a correct apprehension of this personification. "Sin" is the state of guilt and helplessness into which transgression brings man—a state opposed equally to a state of innocence and a state of justification. This state has a powerful influence over the character and circumstances of men, in preventing good and producing evil. That is represented by the power of a tyrannical usurper over his slaves. Sin has dominion over men, employing them in its degrading service, and rewarding them with destruction. For this tyrant to be so condemned, that his slaves are set at liberty, is, in plain words, to have the obstacles in the way of man becoming holy, rising out of his natural state of condemnation and moral helplessness, removed, and to have effectual means of his becoming holy brought into operation. The tyrant is brought to justice; he is stripped of his usurped power; he is condemned to die; so that the requisitions of the law, as to character and conduct, are now fulfilled in those who were once his helpless slaves.

Some have supposed that "the flesh," in the clause under consideration, designates our Lord's human nature; and that the expression, "in," or, as they render it, "by the flesh," describes the means by which the condemnation of sin was effected. That, no doubt, was the flesh of Christ—His human nature, offered in sacrifice—"the body of His flesh through death," as Paul expresses it in the Epistle to the Colossians;[1] but thus to understand the phrase is to depart from the natural meaning of the words, and it is to make the apostle unnecessarily repeat the same statement; for he had, in a former clause, stated that "God condemned sin by sending His Son in the likeness of sinful flesh, and for sin."

The influence of man's guilty, helpless state, to perpetuate and increase his depravity, has already been in some measure illustrated. But, as it is a subject of very great importance, and by no means well understood, even among those who count themselves well-informed Christians, a few additional remarks may be useful. The guilty man is the declared object of the Divine judicial displeasure. Being so, he is, as a matter of course, excluded from those Divine influences which are the source of all real holiness in created natures; for how can God bestow, on the object of His judicial displeasure, that sanctifying, blissful influence, which is the most important blessing He can bestow on the objects of His paternal favour? Nor is this all: unguided by the influence of the good Spirit, the principles of man's nature are left to develop themselves under powerful malignant influences—those of the present evil world, and of him who is its god and prince; so that "evil men" naturally "wax worse and worse."[2]

This would be the result of a state of guilt, even if the individual were entirely unaware of the fact that he was thus guilty and condemned. But this is not the case with mankind. In no case, probably, is the condemned sinner entirely unaware of his condition. In many instances it is brought full before him. He knows that "the wages of sin are death," and that he has earned them, and that justice requires that in due time they be paid him in full tale. A knowledge of this sharpens his enmity against the God who condemned him; and this enmity is the exhaustless source of all manner of wickedness. Thus a state of guilt depraves the human

[1] Col. i. 22. [2] 2 Tim. iii. 13.

character. "Sin reigns in men's mortal bodies, and they obey it in its lusts. They yield themselves its servants, and present their members to it as instruments of unrighteousness."[1]

The destruction of this power, as if by a judicial process—the regularly putting down of this irregular power, is the work which the apostle represents God as having, in His grace, performed. This is a work which "the law could not do," and "could not do, in that," or, because, "it was weak through the flesh."

It may be of use, in preparing us for clearly understanding what the apostle means by this statement, to inquire for a moment what the law can do. With respect to the innocent, it can inform them of their duty, and urge them to its performance by salutary fear and joyful hope, while they are in a state of probation; and when that state is finished, it secures for them complete and unending happiness. All this Adam would have experienced had he persevered in integrity. But, as none of the children of men are innocent, it more nearly concerns us to know what are the powers of the law in reference to the guilty. It denounces their condemnation, and secures their punishment; and, while it condemns for the past, it still insists on perfect obedience for the future, on pain of redoubled destruction, but without promise of reward. All it holds out, in the way of encouragement, is, The less sin, the less suffering. This is what the law can do; and it is all that it can do.

It is plain, then, that it cannot so condemn sin in the flesh, as that the righteousness of the law may be fulfilled in fallen men. It cannot make man, guilty and therefore depraved, holy. It cannot repeal its own sentence of condemnation, which binds men under the fetters of depravity. It has no power to wrest from sin the power to destroy with which it has invested it. It makes no provision for mitigating the penalty, or for dispensing with it altogether, or for enabling

[1] Rom. vi. 12, 13.

a man to bear it. We have already showed at length that, while the sentence of condemnation continues in force, man cannot be holy. The law furnishes no adequate means for opposing the powerfully depraving influence of evil spirits and a world lying in wickedness. It cannot so enlighten the mind, or renew the will, or spiritualize the affections, as to secure habitual holiness. It can command to be holy, but it cannot create us anew unto good works. It presents no motive sufficient to move an unregenerate mind from sin toward true holiness.

The reason assigned for this want of power, on the part of the law, is, that "it is weak through the flesh." That the law is inefficacious, does not arise from any inherent defect in its original constitution. The law is well fitted to answer the ends for which it was designed—to preserve man in a state of innocence, and to lead him, through progressive degrees of excellence, to moral perfection. The event proved that the law did not make transgression impossible; but its precepts and sanctions were admirably fitted to keep man good and make him better. How, then, has law lost its power? It has become weak through the flesh. It has become inefficient through the depravity of human nature. How it has become so is easily understood. It shows fallen man what is sin and what is duty; but then he loves sin and hates duty; and mere command, however explicit and authoritative, cannot change inclination. The very circumstance of an action, to which I am inclined, being forbidden, inflames the desire of committing it. The law condemns and curses the sinner for his transgression. Now, what is the natural effect of this on an unregenerate person? Informing him of his doom, but giving him no reason to hope that he can escape that doom, it may irritate him to madness, it may sink him in despair, but it can do nothing in the way of making him holy. The radical principle of holiness—love to God, cannot be excited by law in an unregenerate heart, however much it may be cherished by it in a regenerate one. On the contrary, the strictness of its precepts, and the severity of its penalty, exasperate the sinner's resentment against the Lawgiver, who thwarts his strongest inclinations, and consigns him for yielding to them to hopeless misery. The sun, which, in the temperate regions of the earth, diffuses a comfortable warmth and a vegetative influence, burns up under the equator the fruits of the earth and generates disease: thus the law, though remaining unchanged, is to innocent man fruitful in producing holiness, but to depraved man productive only of sin and misery. Or, to illustrate the subject by a figure still more appropriate: the laws of this country may have power to restrain from crime those who have a principle of honesty or of honour, or who, though destitute of such principles, have yet property or character to lose; but they may fail to influence a man who is equally destitute of principle, property, and reputation—who has already incurred their severest penalty, and has nothing to expect from them but an ignominious death. What power, but to torment and destroy, have the laws of this country over the miserable, condemned murderer, who, without a ray of hope, is in his dungeon waiting for the hour of his execution?

But "what the law could not do," God has accomplished. He has "condemned sin in the flesh;" and He has done so by "sending His own Son in the likeness of sinful flesh, and for sin." In other words, He has done it by that sacrifice of His incarnate Son, which forms the basis of the Divine method of justification: that propitiation, in which His righteousness is declared, that He is "the just God and the Saviour"—"Just, and the justifier of him that believeth in Jesus."[1] The statement here is substantially the same as that made already by the apostle—that "our old man was crucified with Christ, that the body of sin might be destroyed, that we should not serve sin."[2] That which was completed on the cross laid a sure foundation for the complete deliverance from sin of all who, by faith, are united to Him who hung there a victim for sin, "the Just in the room of the unjust."

[1] Rom. iii. 25, 26. [2] Rom. vi. 6.

Of all the works of God, both in the natural and the moral world, it may be said, "His ways are not our ways, His thoughts are not our thoughts." The means which He employs to gain His ends are always the best possible; but they are often such as it never could have "entered into the mind of man to conceive." Had man been called on to conjecture what method God was likely to adopt to gain the great end referred to in the text, it is difficult to say what opinion he would have formed; but certainly the truth would never have occurred to his mind—the apparently most presumptuous thought never could have arisen, that this object was to be gained by the mission, incarnation, and vicarious sacrifice of God's "only begotten Son." Yet thus "it became Him, for whom are all things, and through whom are all things," to "condemn sin in the flesh."

By Divine appointment, the second person of the sacred Trinity, assumed human nature, and in that nature presented Himself as a sin-offering to expiate human transgression. When God is said to have sent His Son "in the likeness of sinful flesh," the meaning is—that the Son, by the appointment of the Father, assumed human nature free from sin, but labouring under those infirmities, not moral, which are the effects of sin—liability to suffering and death. When it is said He sent Him "for sin," the meaning is—He sent Him to be a sacrifice for sin. The phrase translated "for sin"[1] is often used, in the Greek translation of the Old Testament Scriptures, as equivalent to a sin-offering;[2] and it occurs in this sense also in the Epistle to the Hebrews: "In burnt-offerings and sacrifices for sin Thou hast had no pleasure."[3] The phrases in the original are the same. In the last passage, in order to make sense in English, it is necessary to supply the word 'sacrifices;' and it would have contributed much to the perspicuity of the passage before us, had the same mode of translation been adopted—"God sending His Son in the likeness of

[1] περὶ ἁμαρτίας.

[2] Lev. iv. 3; Numb. viii. 8; Psalm xxxix. (lxx.) 6.

[3] Heb. x. 6, 8, 18.

sinful flesh, and a sacrifice for sin, condemned sin in the flesh."

By the Son of God being a sacrifice for sin, is to be understood His doing and suffering what, in the estimation of the Supreme Legislator, was necessary and sufficient to expiate the sins of men—to lay a foundation for the removal of the sentence of condemnation, and the restoration of man to the Divine favour, and all its blissful consequences. For this purpose, it behoved Him to take the place of fallen man, assume his responsibilities, do what he was bound to do, and suffer what he deserved to suffer. Now, this was what the incarnate Son of God actually did. As "the Lamb of God," He "bare," and bare away, "the sin of the world." "He bare our sins in His own body on the tree." "He died for our sins." "He suffered for sins, the Just in the room of the unjust." "He gave Himself for us, an offering and a sacrifice for a sweet-smelling savour to God." "His blood cleanses from all sin;" and "In Him we have redemption through that blood, even the forgiveness of sins."[1]

That the vicarious obedience, suffering, and death of the incarnate Son, are the effectual means of man's deliverance from the depraving influence of sin, is the doctrine of the passage before us; and not of this passage only, but of many other passages of Scripture. Take the following as examples: "For their sakes I sanctify Myself"—*i.e.*, devote Myself as a sacrifice for sin, "that they also may be sanctified through the truth." "Our old man is crucified with Christ." "He gave Himself for us, that He might redeem us from all iniquity, and purify unto Himself a peculiar people, zealous of good works." "Forasmuch as ye know that ye were not redeemed from your vain conversation, received by tradition from your fathers, by such corruptible things as silver and gold, but by blood, precious blood, the blood of Christ, as of a lamb without blemish and without spot." "Who Himself

[1] John i. 29; 1 Cor. xv. 3; 1 Pet. ii. 24, iii. 18; Eph. v. 2; 1 John i. 7; Eph i. 7.

bare our sins in His own body on," or 'to,' "the tree, that we, being dead to sin, should live to righteousness." They who are without blame before the throne of God, came there in consequence of their having "washed their robes, and made them white in the blood of the Lamb."[1]

How this sacrifice of the incarnate Son of God effected this purpose, is to a certain degree explained to us in the holy Scriptures. That sacrifice is represented as the payment of the penalty of sin in the room of those who are saved by it, and of course laid a foundation for the removal of the curse from them. "Christ has redeemed us from the curse, having been made a curse for us."[2] It was such a manifestation of the righteousness of God, and the evil of sin, as that, on its ground, God appeared just in justifying the ungodly.

Till that curse is removed, as we have seen, there can be no holiness in man, for the Divine influence necessary to produce holiness cannot, in consistency with the Divine righteousness, find its way into his heart. On the other hand, God cannot, in consistency with His character as the Father of those who are united to Christ by believing—and thus interested in the saving effects of the atonement—allow them to remain the slaves of sin.

Moreover, it is as a reward of His self-sacrificing service in the cause of God's glory and man's salvation, that the Son of God is put in possession of all power to destroy the works of the devil in the hearts of those who are united to Him.

Still further, by the atonement, a channel is opened into the hearts of all believers for the sanctifying influence of the transforming Spirit. "Christ hath redeemed us from the curse of the law, by becoming a curse in our room," not only "that the blessing of Abraham"—a full and free justification, "might come on us," but that we may "receive the promised Spirit by faith."[3] It has thus become an act of faithful-

[1] John xvii. 19; Rom. vi. 6; Tit. ii. 11, 14; 1 Pet. ii. 24; Rev. vii. 15.
[2] Gal. iii. 13. [3] Gal. iii. 14.

ness and justice, on the part of the God of peace, not only, in the exercise of His grace, to forgive us our sins, but also, by the influence of His Spirit, to "cleanse us from all unrighteousness;"[1] and it is in virtue of His sacrifice that Jesus, "exalted a Prince and a Saviour, gives repentance," and "sheds forth abundantly" the renewing, sanctifying, Spirit on men.[2]

Finally, the truth with regard to this vicarious sacrifice for sin—stated in a plain, well-accredited Divine revelation, is—in the hand of the Divine Spirit, the great instrument for destroying the power of sin in the hearts of men—furnishing, as it does, the most impressive displays of the beauty and excellence, of holiness, and the hatefulness and malignity of sin, the most powerful dissuasives from sin, and the most powerful motives to duty. It is thus that God "condemns sin in the flesh, which the law could not do, because it was weak through the flesh." It is thus that the grace of God delivers from the body of death, from which the law could not deliver. It is thus that "faith does not make void, but establishes the law"—getting for the law what the law never could have got for itself, full satisfaction for its violation, in the sacrifice of the incarnate Son, and genuine, cheerful, ultimately perfect conformity to its spirit and injunctions, in the character and conduct of those who are by faith united to Him, and made partakers of the sanctifying, as well as atoning, efficacy of His sacrifice—the righteousness of the law being fulfilled in them "who walk not after the flesh, but after the Spirit."

This was at once the object and effect of the condemning of sin in the flesh, by the sacrifice of the incarnate Son of God. God thus condemned sin in the flesh, in order that the righteousness of the law might be—and so that the righteousness of the law actually is, and shall be—fulfilled in us, who being justified by believing, "walk not after the flesh, but after the Spirit." "The righteousness of the law"[3] here, is the righte-

[1] 1 John i. 9. [2] Acts ii. 33; v. 31. [3] δικαίωμα.

ous requisition of the law—love to God, love to man, holiness of heart and life; and by that righteousness being fulfilled in us—*i.e.*, in us believers—in us who are interested in the Divine method of justification, I understand that complete conformity to this righteous requisition, which will ultimately, through the condemnation of sin by the Saviour's sacrifice, be produced in every believer. From the moment in which he becomes interested in the Divine method of justification, the sanctifying influence of the atonement begins to operate on him, and it will continue to operate on him till it has completely destroyed the influence of sin, and made him all that the holy law requires him to be—"sanctified wholly, in the whole man, soul, body, and spirit"—cleansed "from all filthiness of the flesh and of the spirit," and having holiness perfected in the fear and love of God.

Some very good interpreters, understand by the phrase "the righteousness of the law," all the preceptive and sanctionary demands of the law, which were fully met by our Lord in His obedience unto the death, and which, as He stood in our place, may be considered as fulfilled in us, as represented in Him. But this interpretation is objectionable, not only because it gives a very unnatural meaning to the words, but because it seems quite foreign to the design of the apostle in the whole section, which is to show that the grace of God, by the sacrifice of Christ, has secured that holiness in man, which the law could not secure.

The concluding words, "who walk not after the flesh, but after the Spirit," are appended, though not necessary to complete the sentence, to mark who the individuals are that really enjoy the sanctifying influence of the Divine method of justification, and thus to introduce the subject of the next sub-section of the epistle—'That, as justification is necessary to, and secures sanctification, so sanctification is the only satisfactory evidence of justification.' As a man must be justified in order to be sanctified—as, if a man be justified, he certainly shall be sanctified—so a man must be sanctified in order to prove that he is justified. Justification is necessary to the existence of sanctification; sanctification is equally necessary to the evidence of justification. It is quite according to the apostle's custom to introduce, in the concluding clause of a paragraph, what is to be the subject of the succeeding one. We have instances of this in chap. v. 12, and in chap. vi. 14.

The remarks which we have been led to make on this section of the Epistle to the Romans, must, if understood, clear those doctrines, which are generally termed evangelical, from the imputation that sometimes, through malignity—more frequently, we should hope, through ignorance—has been cast on them as unfavourable to the interests of holiness.

It must also be obvious, to every considerate reader, that these doctrines are by no means, as they have often been represented, mere speculative opinions—points on which it matters not much what sentiments we entertain, being remotely, if at all, connected with human duty or happiness. On the contrary, it must appear, that they enter into the very essence of the Christian religion, and that, if that religion be true, the person who does not know and believe them cannot be wise, good, or happy. God forbid that we should account none Christians who do not agree exactly with us in our mode of expressing ourselves on this important subject—the ground of justification, the source and means of sanctification; but we hesitate not to say, that hope, placed any where but on the grace of God, through the redemption that is in Christ Jesus, will assuredly make men ashamed; and that, when men attempt to cultivate virtue, without reference to the expiatory sacrifice, the justifying righteousness, and the transforming Spirit of Jesus Christ, "in the day they may make their plant to grow, and in the morning make their seed to flourish, but the harvest shall be a heap in the day of grief and of desperate sorrow."[1] Or, to change the figure, they who see to light the fire of holy affection any where but at the altar on which was offered the great sacrifice, may "compass them-

[1] Isa. xvii. 11.

selves about with sparks, and walk in the light of their own fire; but this shall they have of the hand of the Lord, they shall lie down in sorrow."[1]

Let those who are still the slaves of sin reflect on the misery and danger of their situation. Let them beware of continuing in carnal security, and beware also of seeking deliverance except in the way in which God has promised to bestow it. True holiness is to be found only in Christ. In the Gospel He is set forth as a propitiation in His blood, which cleanseth from all sin. The most guilty and depraved is made welcome, in the faith of the truth, to rely on this atonement, and relying on the atonement, he will find redemption from all his iniquities—he will be "washed and sanctified," as well as "justified in the name of our Lord Jesus, and by the Spirit of our God."

And let those who, by the grace of God, through the influence of the great atonement, have obtained a partial deliverance from the power of sin, look for the perfection of the great work from the same cause, and through the same means by which it was begun, "For all things are of God by Jesus Christ."[2] Let them seek, with ever-increasing earnestness, renewed, enlarged, supplies of Divine influence, as the gift of God communicated to men, through the sacrifice and intercession of His Son. Never let them forget that they owe their sanctification, as well as their justification—their new character, as well as their new state—to God's sending His Son, in the likeness of sinful flesh, a sacrifice for sin; and that "of God are they in Christ Jesus (who of God is made unto them wisdom), righteousness, sanctification, redemption," —justified, sanctified, and redeemed, "That no flesh should glory in God's presence," but that, according as it is written, "He that glorieth, let him glory in the Lord."[3] Yes, to Him who spared not His Son, but delivered Him up for us all, and to Him that loved us and washed us from our sins in His own blood, and hath made us kings and priests to God, even His

[1] Isa. l. 11. [2] 2 Cor. v. 18. [3] 1 Cor. i. 30, 31.

Father—to Him that sitteth on the throne, and to the Lamb, ascribed be all the glory[1]—equal and undivided, by the Church on earth and the Church in heaven, for ever, and ever—world without end—*Amen.*

B. *Sanctification is the Evidence of Justification.*

CHAPTER VIII. 5–17.—"For they that are after the flesh do mind the things of the flesh; but they that are after the Spirit the things of the Spirit. For to be carnally minded is death; but to be spiritually minded is life and peace. Because the carnal mind is enmity against God; for it is not subject to the law of God, neither indeed can be. So then they that are in the flesh cannot please God. But ye are not in the flesh, but in the Spirit, if so be that the Spirit of God dwell in you. Now, if any man have not the Spirit of Christ, he is none of His. And if Christ be in you, the body is dead because of sin; but the Spirit is life because of righteousness. But if the Spirit of Him that raised up Jesus from the dead dwell in you, He that raised up Christ from the dead shall also quicken your mortal bodies by His Spirit that dwelleth in you. Therefore, brethren, we are debtors, not to the flesh, to live after the flesh. For if ye live after the flesh, ye shall die; but if ye through the Spirit do mortify the deeds of the body, ye shall live. For as many as are led by the Spirit of God, they are the sons of God. For ye have not received the spirit of bondage again to fear; but ye have received the Spirit of adoption, whereby we cry, Abba, Father. The Spirit itself beareth witness with our spirit, that we are the children of God: and if children, then heirs; heirs of God, and joint heirs with Christ."

The subject of that division of the doctrinal part of the epistle, in the exposition of which we are engaged, is substantially this proposition, "The righteousness of God"—*i.e.*, the Divine method of justification, originating entirely in the free grace of God, based entirely on the atonement of Christ, and suspended, as to the communication of its blessings, not on working but on believing—so far from having a sinister influence on the interests of true holiness, is the only means by which true holiness can be produced, promoted, and perfected, in human nature. This embraces the whole important topic of the connection between justification and sanctification. The

[1] Rev. i. 5, 6.

apostle takes up the subject under two heads. *First*, Justification is necessary to, and secures sanctification; and *Second*, Sanctification is the evidence of being justified. An unjustified man cannot be holy—an unsanctified man *is* not justified. The first of these heads of argument occupies the apostle from the beginning of the sixth chapter to the 4th verse of the eighth. The discussion of the second begins at the 5th verse, and ends, I rather think, in the middle of the 17th verse of that chapter.

The apostle makes the transition, according to a custom common with him, in the end of the sentence which concludes the illustration of the first point. The Divine method of justification secures holiness, for it, and it alone secures for fallen man that which is at once necessary and sufficient to make him holy—a state of acceptance with God, and a predominant sanctifying influence. "There is no condemnation to them who are in Christ Jesus," and "The Spirit of life in Christ Jesus makes them free from the law of sin and death;" and this is the character of those who are thus interested in "the righteousness of God"—"They walk not after the flesh, but after the Spirit."[1] These, and these only, are the justified ones. These, and these only, are the objects of the Divine favour; and for any other man to suppose that he is a justified person, would be fearful presumption, fatal delusion.

The course of the apostle's thought seems to be this. They who are in the flesh cannot be pleasing to God; they who are in the Spirit cannot but be pleasing to Him. The unsanctified must be and are unjustified; the sanctified are and must be justified. With the illustration of these points he mixes up, according to his manner, practical remark and exhortation. To understand the paragraph aright, it is of importance to remark that it is throughout antithetic, though in a number of cases only one side of the antithesis is expressed. This is a characteristic of the apostle's writings, and, if the interpreter keep it not steadily in view, he will often do the

[1] Ver. 4

inspired writer injustice, by giving an imperfect view of his meaning.

"To walk after the flesh," is to exert the various activities of our nature, under the influence of that frame of thought and feeling which is natural to fallen man, till he be born again. "To walk after the Spirit," is to exert the various activities of our nature under the influence of the frame of thought and feeling which is produced by the Holy Spirit through the belief of the truth. All interested in the righteousness of God, habitually do not act in the first way, habitually do act in the second.

Now, says the apostle, "They that are after the flesh do mind the things of the flesh, and they that are after the Spirit the things of the Spirit."[1] They who are "in the flesh," or "after the flesh," are the same persons as they who "walk after the flesh;" and they who are "after the Spirit," the same as those who "walk after the Spirit." The difference is, the flesh and Spirit are represented, in the first case, as abiding actuating principles; and, in the second, as embodied and exemplified in actual disposition and behaviour. The two together complete each of the two opposite characters—the carnal and the spiritual.

The carnal man "minds the things of the flesh." "The things of the flesh," are such objects of thought and choice and pursuit and enjoyment, as are suited to the faculties and affections of human nature in its fallen and unchanged state. To "mind" these things, is to make them the principal subjects of thought—the principal objects of affection. The apostle's declaration then is, carnal men prove themselves to be what they are, by making things suited to their unrenewed nature the great subjects of thought and objects of affection. In many cases, the bias of the corrupted mind leads the individual to think much of, and to delight in the grosser works of the flesh, enumerated by the apostle in the Epistle to the Galatians;[2] but, in many other cases, there is, owing to a

[1] Ver. 5. [2] Chap. v. 19-21.

variety of causes, a strict abstinence from these, yet still the mind is employed entirely about present and sensible things, and the heart is supremely placed on present and sensible objects. The most morally accomplished worldling is at heart as thoroughly carnal as the most reckless profligate. The flesh may often be refined and purified while it remains flesh still; the best of those who are "of the flesh" still mind exclusively earthly things.

"The things of the Spirit." By the Spirit must be understood either the Holy Spirit, or perhaps, rather, that new frame of thought and feeling produced by His operation; for "That which is born of the Spirit is spirit;"[1] and, according as you understand this term, you must understand, by "the things of the Spirit," either such things as the Spirit reveals and enjoins, or such things as are agreeable to that new nature of which the Spirit is the author—the realities of religion and eternity, "things unseen and eternal." They who are "after the Spirit *mind*" these things. They are the principal subjects of their thoughts, the principal objects of their affections. They who are spiritual are "delivered from the present evil world," and brought under "the power of the world that is to come." They "seek the things that are above, where Christ sits at God's right hand." They "mind," "set their affections on things that are above, and not on things on the earth."[2] They look at every thing in its relation to God and eternity. They think on the things which are "true, and honest, and just, and pure, and lovely, and virtuous, and of good report." They do not indeed mind the things of the Spirit with that intensity and perseverance with which they ought; but still the habitual tenor of their sentiments and affections is spiritual, and the "cleaving of their souls to the dust"[3] is the subject of sincere and deep regret to them. Their treasure is in heaven, and their heart is there also.

The apostle proceeds to use this remark for the purpose of showing that the unsanctified man is not a justified man, and

[1] John iii. 6. [2] Col. iii. 1, 2. [3] Psal. cxix. 25.

that the sanctified man undoubtedly is so. "For to be carnally minded is death, but to be spiritually minded is life and peace."[1] "For" marks what follows as illustrative of what he has just said. The being carnally minded, in verse 6, or the carnal mind, in verse 7, which are two versions of the same word, is just the same thing as the minding of the things of the flesh. This is death. He who is characterized by it is in a state of "death"—a state of insensibility and inactivity as to the highest objects of his nature, and a state of misery. A rational, immortal being, employing his powers and seeking happiness entirely in things seen and temporal, cannot be happy, in the true sense of the word. The carnal mind indicates spiritual death, and produces unhappiness here, and leads to eternal death, to hopeless misery hereafter.

On the other hand, the spiritual mind is "life and peace." The man who is characterized by it is alive and active in reference to God and eternity, and the very course of thought, and feeling, and conduct which is connected with it, gives inward satisfaction, true happiness, "Life and peace in conjunction," as Howe beautifully says, "not raging life, not stupid peace, but a placid, peaceful life, and a vital, vigorous rest and peace. It is not the life of a fury, nor the peace of a stone—it is life that hath peace in it, and peace that hath life in it."

It is a natural inference then, that the carnally-minded man is not a justified man; for, as we have seen, the justified man lives with Christ to God, and, instead of the misery of which death is the expression, he has peace with God, and rejoices in hope—rejoices in God,[2] and the spiritually-minded, identifies himself with the justified, man, by that life and peace which grow out of "the mind of the Spirit." But the apostle does not leave us to infer this conclusion, he draws it himself in the words that follow—"Because the carnal mind is enmity against God, for it is not subject to the law of God, neither indeed can be."[3]

"The minding of the flesh"[4] is "enmity against God."

[1] Ver. 6. [2] Chap. v. 1, 11; vi. 8, 10. [3] Ver. 7. [4] φρόνημα τῆς σαρκός.

"Enmity" is just a strong expression for 'hostile'—opposed to. As the word enmity sometimes signifies hatefulness, some have supposed that the apostle's idea is—' the carnal mind, the mind of the flesh, the minding of the flesh, to be carnal-minded—for all these are the same thing—is hateful to God: and how can it be otherwise? "It is not conformed to His law," it never can be conformed to it; so that it is plain that he who is under its influence, cannot be the object of the Divine complacency. He cannot be a justified person. He must be in condemnation. This is a very clear, close course of thought; but the turn of the expression seems to require us to follow our translators' rendering. "The carnal mind," or "the minding of the flesh," is enmity — that is, very hostile — indicates enmity in the heart in which it dwells. The minding of the flesh is directly opposed to the Divine will, which is, that man should seek and find happiness, not in the flesh, but in the Spirit.

The second clause of the 7th verse is explicatory of the first. How can it but be hostile to God, when "it is not conformed to the law of God, neither indeed can be?" The law is just the expressed will of God. The minding the flesh is not conformed to that expressed will. To mind the flesh is to worship the world and its god. It is thus directly opposed to the great fundamental principles of the law. "The Lord our God is one Lord." "Thou shalt have no other gods before Me." "Thou shalt worship the Lord thy God, and Him only shalt thou serve." And thus it is not only not conformed, but not conformable to the Divine law. "How can snow be warmed? By making it cease to be snow," as Augustine well says. No modification of the minding of the flesh can be reconciled with the Divine law. It is a thing not to be mended but destroyed. There is no possibility of man, under the dominant influence of the carnal mind, yielding acceptable obedience to God. Well then might the apostle draw the conclusion—"So then they that are in the flesh cannot please God."[1] By "in the flesh," the

[1] Ver. 8.

apostle sometimes signifies nothing more than to be "in the body," in this mortal life, as when he says, "For me to abide in the flesh is more needful for you"[1]—"Though we walk in the flesh, we do not war after the flesh;"[2] but here it plainly signifies to be under the habitual influence of our unchanged nature. While they continue thus in the flesh, they cannot be the objects of God's approbation. They must be the objects of His disapprobation. It is plain that they are not justified persons.

The other side of the antithesis is not expressed, but the ellipsis may easily be supplied. 'For the spiritual mind, the minding of the Spirit, is not hostile to, but in accordance with God; for it is subject to His law, and it cannot be otherwise. So then, they that are in the Spirit, must please God.' The "minding of the Spirit" is something that entirely falls in with God's designs, and therefore must be well-pleasing to Him. It is in entire conformity with His law, requiring supreme love to God; and in the measure in which any man "minds the things of the Spirit," he cannot but yield cheerful obedience to the Divine law. So that it is plain that such a man is an object of the Divine favourable regard.

In the words that follow, the apostle applies the statements he had made to those to whom he was writing. "But ye are not in the flesh but in the Spirit, if so be that the Spirit of Christ dwell in you."[3] To be "in the flesh" is to be under the dominant influence of the flesh; to be "in the Spirit" is to be under the dominant influence of the Spirit. The declaration seems equivalent to—'Though the carnally-minded, being spiritually dead, and directly opposed to the Divine will, cannot be the objects of the Divine complacency, it is otherwise with you; ye being not in the flesh but in the Spirit, are spiritually alive—in a state of peace, and objects of the Divine complacent regard.' Their possession of this unfleshly, spiritual character, is attributed to the Spirit of Christ dwelling in them. It is so with you, "if so be that the Spirit of Christ

[1] Phil. i. 24. [2] 2 Cor. x. 3. [3] Ver. 9.

dwell in you." "The Spirit of Christ" is the Holy Spirit, who may receive this appellation for various reasons—His essential relation to Christ as a person of the Godhead, His dwelling in Christ without measure, and His being sent by Christ as Mediator. It is likely the last idea which the apostle expresses. The Holy Spirit is given to believers, in consequence of Christ's having redeemed men from the curse of the law, having become a curse for them.[1] The use of the particle translated, "if so be,"[2] does not express doubt. Its force is perhaps as justly expressed by "since," as many interpreters have done; at any rate, it is not more than equivalent to 'if—as I doubt not,' or 'if really.' It is meant to express the important truth, that the spiritual character can be formed only by the permanent influence of the Holy Spirit, for that seems the meaning of the phrase—who dwelleth in you.

The apostle proceeds to say, "Now," or "But, if any man have not the Spirit of Christ, he is none of His."[3] This is still the same general truth: it is the sanctified only that are the justified. If any man, whatever his profession may be, does not make it evident that he "has the spirit of Christ," by his being not in the flesh, not after the flesh, walking not after the flesh, but being in the Spirit, after the Spirit, walking after the Spirit, he is not one of Christ's peculiar people—not one of those who have, in His life and death, that union with Him which is implied in the Divine method of justification.

"And," or rather 'But,'[4] "if Christ be in you, the body is dead because of sin; but the Spirit is life because of righteousness."[5] "But," or 'and,' "if the Spirit of Him that raised up Jesus from the dead dwell in you, He that raised up Christ from the dead shall also quicken your mortal bodies by His Spirit that dwelleth in you."[6] These words, standing in opposition to the last clause of the 9th verse, seem equivalent to a declaration, that if Christ by His Spirit really dwelt in them, so influencing them as that they were "in the Spirit"

[1] Gal. iii. 13, 14. [2] εἴπερ. 2 Thess. i. 6. [3] Ver. 9.
[4] δέ. [5] Ver. 10. [6] Ver. 11.

and not "in the flesh," then were they secure of all the blessings arising from being in Christ; for though their bodies were mortal and must die, in consequence of that state of condemnation and helplessness into which the sin of the first man brought the race, yet they should enjoy even now the blessings of spiritual life, and in due time, their mortal—their dead bodies, should revive and become immortal.

The words, "the body is dead because of sin," have by some been referred to the mortification of sin; as if it were—'the body is dead in respect of sin;' and others have interpreted them as equivalent to, 'the body is spiritually dead'—as synonymous with—"with my flesh I serve the law of sin." But insurmountable objections lie in the way of both these interpretations.

"If Christ be in you," is plainly the same thing as 'if ye have the Spirit of Christ.' But "to be in Christ," and "to have Christ in us," though uniformly descriptive of the same individuals, do not mean the same thing. The first refers to relation, the second to character. We are so "in Christ" as that when He died we died, when He lives we live. Christ is so "in us" as that, by His Spirit, through His Word, He so transforms us, that we are His living images. His thoughts and feelings become ours. We think, feel, and act like Him. The first is the cause of the second. It is because we are "in Him" that He is "in us."

"The body is dead because of sin;" the body even of those who are in Christ, and in whom Christ is, must die because of sin—the state of sin—condemnation induced by the first sin of the first man. "It is appointed to men once to die."[1] The sentence must be executed—"Dust thou art, and unto dust shalt thou return."[2] "But the spirit is life because of righteousness;" the spirit lives, enjoys true life with the living One, from whose communion sin had cut it off; and enjoys this "because of righteousness,"—the state of justification induced by the obedience of Him of whom Adam was a type.

[1] Heb. ix. 27. [2] Gen. iii. 19.

And even this is not all. "He that raised up Christ from the dead," on account of that which justifies His people—His finished work, "will," at the appointed time, "also raise up their mortal" and "dead bodies." The resurrection of the bodies of believers is represented as rising from their connection with the Holy Spirit as well as with our Lord Jesus. "If the Spirit of Him who raised up Jesus from the dead dwell in you, He who raised Christ from the dead shall also quicken your mortal bodies through—by, His Spirit who dwelleth in you;" or, as it is on the margin, "because of His Spirit who dwelleth in you." It is difficult to say which of the two readings (for they are different readings,[1] not merely renderings), is preferable. Each of them brings out a good and appropriate sense. The meaning in the first case is, that the resurrection of believers will be effected through the operation of the Holy Spirit. The meaning in the second is, that the indwelling of the Spirit in the bodies of believers here is one of the reasons why they are to be raised up. That body which was hallowed by the inhabitation of the Holy Spirit, shall not be allowed to remain for ever under the dominion of death. The sacred edifice shall not always be in ruins, but shall be rebuilt in a style of magnificence and beauty worthy of its Divine inhabitant.

The 9th, 10th, and 11th verses may be considered as the apostle's illustration of his assertion, that the minding of the spirit is life and peace, just as the preceding verses are of the assertion, that the minding of the flesh is death; and, as equally with these, bearing on the object of the paragraph, which is to show that sanctification is the proof of justification.

The next two verses contain an important practical inference, drawn from what he had said: "Therefore, brethren, we are debtors, not to the flesh, to live after the flesh"—this is one side of the antithesis; the other is, "but we are debtors to the Spirit, to live after the Spirit." "For if ye live after the flesh, ye shall die: but if ye through the Spirit do mortify the deeds of the body, ye shall live."[2]

[1] διὰ τοῦ ἐνοικοῦντος αὐτοῦ πνεύματος. διὰ τὸ ἐνοικοῦν αὐτοῦ πνεῦμα.

[2] Ver. 12, 13.

"The flesh" and "the Spirit" are here personified. The term "debtor," is often used as equivalent to, 'one under obligation;' a debt to do the whole law is an obligation to do the whole law. In this sense believers are not debtors to the flesh, but they are so to the Spirit. "The flesh" has no right to rule or guide. Viewed as equivalent to man's animal and sentient nature, the flesh is to be governed and guided: it is the proper subject of obligation. Viewed as this nature under the influence of depravity, it is not to be obeyed, but resisted and mortified. "The spirit"—whether that mean the frame of mind produced by the Holy Spirit, or the Holy Spirit Himself, the author of that frame—is alone entitled to rule the man. The believer is bound to act according to his new nature, which is an embodiment of the Divine will.

But from the context this seems not to be the sense in which the phrase is used here. To be debtor to another, is often used as equivalent to having received favours from him; and, consequently, being under obligations to show gratitude by seeking to please him. An example of this we have at chap. xv. 26, 27. The apostle's meaning seems to be: 'It is plain, from what has been said, that you have derived no such advantage from the flesh as to make it reasonable in you to yield yourselves up to its influence; and that you have derived such advantage from the Spirit, as to make it reasonable that you should submit yourselves to its influence.' What had they obtained from the flesh? "When they were in the flesh," and because they were in it, "the motions of sin, which were by the law, did work in their members to bring forth fruit unto death." The law, as to its power to do good, was made "weak by the flesh." "The minding of the flesh is death," and "they who are in the flesh cannot please God." The flesh had done them nothing but mischief. It might have given them some temporary gratification, but it had done, it could do, them no permanent good: it had done them much harm. They owed it no acknowledgment—no service. To regulate, according to it, their sentiments and habits, dispositions and pursuits, would be absurd. But they were debtors to the Spirit, to live after the Spirit. Christians owe to the Spirit all that is good in their character, happy in their circumstances, and glorious in their hopes. It is the "law of the Spirit of life in Christ Jesus that makes them free from the law of sin and of death." "The minding of the things of the Spirit is life and peace." It is in consequence of the Spirit's taking possession of the mind that, while the body continues mortal, and must die, the spiritual part of our nature becomes in the highest sense living—capable of, and disposed to, activities and enjoyments of the most exalted kind; and it is because the mortal body is tenanted by the Spirit, that it is at last to become immortal, and, like its occupant, spiritual. It was plainly the dictate of gratitude and reason, that they should yield themselves up to the guidance of an agency which had produced so much good—which had produced nothing but what was good.

The obligations of believers not to live after the flesh, but after the Spirit, arising from the consideration of the certain issues of these two courses respectively, are strongly stated in the words that follow: "For if ye live after the flesh, ye shall die: but if ye through the Spirit do mortify the deeds of the body, ye shall live."[1]

To "live after the flesh," is to allow the principles of human nature, unchanged by the Holy Spirit, to govern the character and to guide the conduct. The consequence of this, says the apostle, "is death"—in all the extent of meaning that belongs to that word. He who lives after the flesh is dead while he liveth, and his course must end in the second death; and this is true of all who live after the flesh, whether grossly immoral or not. The apostle does not hesitate to say this to those whom he was addressing. He trusted they were in the Spirit, and he knew that, if they were, they would not live after the flesh; but he might be mistaken, and he wished them to be impressed with this truth, that whatever they professed,

[1] Ver. 13.

whatever they seemed to be, if they lived after the flesh, the end of those things must be death.

If, on the other hand, they lived after the Spirit, and through the Spirit mortified the deeds of the body, they should certainly live. To "live after the Spirit," is to regulate our whole inner and outer life in conformity with the new nature produced by the Holy Ghost. He who does so will "mortify the deeds of the body." "The deeds of the body," does not mean the natural functions of the human body, such as eating, and drinking, and sleeping, or its natural likings and dislikings. These are to be regulated, not mortified, by the Spirit. The expression, "the deeds of the body," is, however we may account for such a sense, equivalent in meaning to the "working of the law of sin in the members;" "our members that are on the earth;" "the lusts of the flesh;" "the deeds of the old man." Indeed, in some of the MSS., the word *flesh* is used instead of body. To "mortify" these, is to put them to death—not to extirpate the natural principle, but to put an end to its undue measure and wrong direction. This can be done only "by the Spirit." The wrong way of thinking and feeling can be put down only by being mastered by the right way of thinking and feeling.

The end, the certain end, of such a course is "*life*," in all the extent of meaning belonging to that word. The capacities for, and tendencies to, the activities and enjoyments of the highest kinds of life that the human being is capable of, will grow throughout the immortality which is his inheritance. Surely, then, it is very plain that nothing is more unreasonable and wrong than to live after the flesh; nothing more reasonable and right than to live after the Spirit; and nothing more absurd than to suppose that an economy like that of the Divine method of justification, which sets these principles in so clear a light, can lead men to say, "Let us continue in sin that grace may abound."

Returning from this practical digression, if it can indeed be accounted one, the apostle proceeds with the great object of the paragraph—to show that none but those who are holy in heart and in life are actually interested in the Divine method of justification—presenting the subject under a different aspect, and accompanies it with a new illustration, "For as many as are led by the Spirit of God, they are the sons of God."[1]

"For," introduces a reason for, or an illustration of, what had been just said. "They who are led by the Spirit," are they who "live by the Spirit," "walk after the Spirit," and "by the Spirit mortify the deeds of the body." Now, says the apostle, these, and these only, are "the sons of God." To be "the sons," or children, "of God," is a figurative expression often used in Scripture respecting good men; and according as it is descriptive of relation, or of character, it indicates either that God regards and treats them as His children, or that they regard and treat Him as their Father. In the passage before us, it is plainly used in the former of these senses, and is equivalent in meaning to, 'they—they only, are the objects of the complacent regards of God. They only are justified persons.' As many, and no more, as are led by the Spirit to live in the Spirit, and by the Spirit to mortify the deeds of the body, are objects of the Divine favour. The sanctifying influence of the Holy Ghost in the new nature, showing itself in holy dispositions and actions, is a satisfactory evidence, and nothing else is a permanently satisfactory evidence, that a person is in a justified state.

But the Spirit attests the justified state, or the filial relation of believers, not only by making them holy, but also by making them happy. This, if I mistake not, is the import of the 15th verse—"For ye have not received the spirit of bondage again to fear; but ye have received the Spirit of adoption, whereby we cry, Abba, Father." Some good interpreters understand these two appellations as equally belonging to the Holy Spirit: the one describing His influence on the mind by the commands and threatenings of the law; the other, His influence on the mind by the declarations and promises of the

[1] Ver. 14.

Gospel. I doubt, however, not only whether the apostle has called, or could call, the Holy Ghost "the spirit of bondage," for he says, "Where"—*i.e.*, wherever, "the Spirit of the Lord is, there is liberty;"[1] but also, whether slavish fear of God's wrath can, in any proper sense, be represented as His work. I consider the word "spirit" here, as describing a frame of mind; as when Isaiah speaks of "a spirit of deep sleep;"[2] and our apostle, of "the spirit of a sound mind."[3] "The spirit of bondage," is a slave-like spirit—a spirit of dislike and fear, the spirit with which the slave regards his task-master and his work.

The word translated "adoption"[4] is, in signification, quite equivalent to sonship. "The spirit of adoption" is the spirit with which dutiful children regard their father, and the employments he is pleased to assign to them—a spirit of love and confidence, producing tranquillity of mind, and cheerful obedience and submission.

'Now,' says the apostle, 'ye Roman Christians, who are in the Spirit, have received from Him, not a servile, but a child-like disposition, to free you from the alarming terrors, and the reluctance to duty, which once possessed your mind. "Ye have not received the spirit of bondage again to fear."' Whether they had been converted from Gentilism or Judaism, they had previously been under this servile spirit, which is a character of fallen humanity. The views which a man unenlightened in the truth takes of God, must produce uneasiness; and whatever services such men render, are the reluctant and melancholy task work of a slave. But they had received a child-like disposition. They had been made to love God, and to trust in Him. The Holy Spirit, given to them, had "shed abroad the love of God in their hearts"—had enabled them to understand and believe the revelation He had made of His love to men, in the incarnation and sacrifice of His Son; and this had produced love of His infinite excel-

[1] 2 Cor. iii. 17.
[2] Isa. xxix. 10.
[3] 2 Tim. i. 7.
[4] υἱοθεσία.

lence, confidence in His mercy, peace and joy in believing. The spirit of bondage led them to fear and tremble; but the spirit of sonship led them to cry, "Abba, Father."

The meaning is plain: this spirit led them to regard God with the delightful feelings of love and confidence with which a child regards his father, and led them to express this in deeply reverential, yet, at the same time, free-hearted, affectionate prayer. Nor is it difficult to account for the peculiar form of the apostle's expression. "Abba" is a Chaldaic word, signifying 'father'—a word which it is said slaves were prohibited from using towards the head of the family—a word appropriated to the children. Syro-Chaldaic was a language with which Paul, as a Jew, was very familiar—likely the language spoken in his father's family; though, in outer intercourse, Greek would be commonly used. The idea he meant to express was, that they who were in the Spirit had the temper of children, and showed it in the way in which they addressed God. Now, what could be more natural than for him to use the word, to which his ear was most accustomed, as the expression of filial regard, and which he had likely a thousand and a thousand times addressed, both to his earthly and his heavenly Father, as an expression of happy confidence and entire love? and then, recollecting that many of those to whom he was writing did not understand the Syro-Chaldaic language, he adds a translation in a tongue more familiar to them. Though we cannot consider the term, "Spirit of adoption," as here a designation of the Holy Spirit, we consider the temper it describes as the result of His influence; for it is in consequence of God's sending forth the Spirit of His Son into the hearts of Christians that they cry, "Abba, Father."[1]

This spirit—this disposition, is in itself an evidence that we are the children of God—that we are in a state of acceptance with Him. "The Spirit itself," or, the same Spirit, "beareth witness with our spirits that we are the children of God." "The Spirit itself," may signify the Holy Spirit; or, if it be the

[1] Gal. iv 6.

same as "the Spirit of adoption," still, as that spirit is the work of the Holy Spirit, He testifies by it. These words may, with more propriety, be rendered, "beareth witness *to* our spirits;" for there is no testimony of our spirits spoken of in the context. The cordial love, the supreme veneration, the entire confidence in God, which the Holy Spirit produces in the mind, and which together form the Spirit of adoption, bear witness to our spirits —testify to our own minds that we are indeed the children of God. It is so different from the spirit with which we used to regard God, that we cannot doubt that the spirit, which is given to the children of God only, has been given to us. An affectionate, dutiful child has in his own bosom the proof of the peculiar relation in which he stands to his father. There is nothing harsh in a particular disposition being represented as bearing testimony to the mind in which that disposition exists. We say, 'My heart or my conscience tells me this is right or wrong.' There is, no doubt, a danger of our confounding an enthusiastic feeling with this testimony of the Spirit of adoption; but that does not, in the slightest degree, affect the facts, that there is such a spirit of adoption produced by the Holy Spirit, and that He does by it give such a testimony. It is to no purpose for a man to deny such a testimony, because *he* has never been conscious of it. There is likely too good a reason. He has not received the Spirit of adoption, and how can he have its testimony? A French philosopher, speaking of a particular kind of sensations, says— "Those who are so unhappy as never to have had such sensations, either through weakness of the natural organ, or because they have never cultivated them, will not comprehend me." And the apostle, in reference to such matters, has said, "The natural man receiveth not the things of the Spirit of God, for they are foolishness unto him; neither can he know them, for they are spiritually discerned."[1] The Spirit testifies by His saving work; and if men will not submit to be saved by Him, how can they have His testimony?

[1] 1 Cor. ii. 14.

In testifying to believers being sons, the Spirit of adoption testifies to their being heirs—the latter being the necessary consequence of the former. In testifying to their being in a justified state, He testifies to their possession of the blessings of a justified state: "And if children, then heirs, heirs of God, and joint heirs with Christ."[1] The apostle's argument, which loses nothing from being clothed in figure, is in plain words,—'If we are dear to God, we shall be blessed by God. If we are children, He will treat us as children—as *His* children.' To be an "heir of God" is to be secured of everything, in the compass of the universe, that is necessary to our happiness—to "inherit all things." This is the apostle's commentary: "All things are yours; whether Paul, or Apollos, or Cephas, or the world, or life, or death; all are yours; for ye are Christ's, and Christ is God's."[2] But they are not only "heirs of God," but "joint heirs with Christ." These words convey two ideas: that the same blessings which Christ enjoys shall be conferred on them; and that they shall enjoy these blessings in consequence of their connection with Christ.

Such, then, is the testimony which the Holy Spirit bears, by the Spirit of adoption, to the justified state of believers; and thus concludes the apostle's illustration, at once of the principle—sanctification is the proof of being justified, and of the general subject of the bearing of the Divine method of justification on the spiritual transformation of human nature. The apostle, in accordance with a method peculiar to him, attaches to the end of the sentence, with which he completes his illustration of one point, a clause indicative of what is to be the subject of the next paragraph—"If so be that we suffer with Him, that we may be glorified together with Him."

Let us endeavour to turn to practical account, in the way of self-examination, the apostle's illustration of the thesis, 'Sanctification is the evidence of being justified.' Let each of us seriously ask himself the question, Am I in a state of

[1] Ver. 16. [2] 1 Cor. iii. 21–23.

condemnation or in a state of acceptance? Do I walk after the flesh? Do I mind the things of the flesh? Am I habitually opposed in my temper and conduct to the law of God? Do I live after the flesh? Am I not led by the Spirit? Am I habitually under the influence of the spirit of bondage, producing the fear that has torment? Then there can be no doubt I am yet in a state of condemnation. I am not, and if I continue in this state, I cannot be, an object of complacency to God. I am in a state of spiritual death; and, continuing in it, I must ere long be in a state of eternal death. I am not a child of God, and have no part in the children's inheritance. These questions, especially as explained by the preceding remarks, should not, if there be honesty of purpose, be difficult to answer. Nor should the antithetic inquiries be more hard of resolution Do I live in and after the Spirit? Do I walk after the Spirit? Do I mind the things of the Spirit? Does the Spirit of God dwell in me? Have I the Spirit of Christ? Do I, through that Spirit, mortify the deeds of the body? Am I led by the Spirit? Have I received the Spirit of adoption? Does that Spirit lead me to holy, reverential confidence in prayer, and bear testimony to my mind that I am a child of God? Then I am in a state of spiritual life, which shall be in due time perfected in life eternal. Then I please God; I am Christ's; I am a son of God, and "if a son, then an heir, an heir of God, a joint heir with Christ Jesus."

It is of infinite importance that we should come to a right conclusion on this question. If we are still condemned, there is no time to lose. Let death, which may take place at any time, intervene, and the sentence becomes irrevocable. All things are ready for the passage of condemned men into a justified state. The atonement has been made. The Spirit is being shed forth abundantly. The plain, well-accredited testimony is constantly being proclaimed, by faith in which all the blessings procured by the atonement, and conferred by the Spirit, may—assuredly shall, be ours. Then there shall be no condemnation to us, seeing we are in Christ Jesus; and the law of the Spirit of life in Christ Jesus will deliver us from the law of sin and death.

If we have reason to conclude that we are not condemned—reason to hope that we shall never come into condemnation, let us prove by our conduct that the charge of a demoralizing influence in the Divine method of justification is a slander, by showing that "the kindness of God our Saviour," manifested in saving us through the atonement of his incarnate Son, "not by works of righteousness which we have done," or can do, "but according to His mercy"—sovereign grace—"by the washing of regeneration, and the renewing of the Holy Ghost, shed on us through Jesus Christ our Saviour, revealed in the Gospel and believed by us, has taught us to be "careful to maintain good works"—leading us to "deny ungodliness and worldly lusts, and to live soberly, righteously, and godly, in this present world; while looking for the blessed hope, and glorious appearing of the great God and our Saviour Jesus Christ; who gave Himself for us, that He might redeem us from all iniquity, and purify to Himself a peculiar people, zealous of good works." Thus let us make our calling and election—our pardon and justification, sure, by "adding to our faith, virtue; and to virtue, knowledge; and to knowledge, temperance; and to temperance, patience; and to patience, godliness; and to godliness, brotherly-kindness; and to brotherly-kindness, charity." Thus will we, walking in the light, as God is in the light, have fellowship with the Father and the Son, and the blood of Jesus Christ, God's Son, shall cleanse us from all sin; and at last, washed, and sanctified, and justified, in the name of our Lord Jesus, and by the Spirit of our God, an abundant entrance shall be ministered to us into the everlasting kingdom of our Lord and Saviour Jesus Christ; and we shall continue to learn, throughout eternity, what these words mean, "And if sons, heirs; heirs of God, and joint-heirs with Christ Jesus."

§ 5. *The Afflictions to which, in the present state, the Justified are exposed, are not inconsistent with the reality and permanence of that Special Divine Favour which, as Justified, they enjoy.*

Chapter viii. 17–37.—"If so be that we suffer with him, that we may be also glorified together. For I reckon, that the sufferings of this present time are not worthy to be compared with the glory which shall be revealed in us. For the earnest expectation of the creature waiteth for the manifestation of the sons of God. For the creature was made subject to vanity, not willingly, but by reason of Him who hath subjected the same in hope; because the creature itself also shall be delivered from the bondage of corruption into the glorious liberty of the children of God. For we know that the whole creation groaneth and travaileth in pain together until now; and not only they, but ourselves also, which have the first-fruits of the Spirit, even we ourselves groan within ourselves, waiting for the adoption, to wit, the redemption of our body. For we are saved by hope: but hope that is seen is not hope: for what a man seeth, why doth he yet hope for? But if we hope for that we see not, then do we with paitence wait for it. Likewise the Spirit also helpeth our infirmities: for we know not what we should pray for as we ought; but the Spirit itself maketh intercession for us with groanings which cannot be uttered. And he that searcheth the hearts knoweth what is the mind of the Spirit, because he maketh intercession for the saints according to the will of God. And we know that all things work together for good to them that love God, to them who are the called according to His purpose. For whom He did foreknow, He also did predestinate to be conformed to the image of His Son, that he might be the first-born among many brethren. Moreover, whom He did predestinate, them He also called; and whom He called, them He also justified; and whom He justified, them He also glorified. What shall we then say to these things? If God be for us, who can be against us? He that spared not His own Son, but delivered Him up for us all, how shall He not with Him also freely give us all things? Who shall lay any thing to the charge of God's elect? It is God that justifieth; who is he that condemneth? It is Christ that died, yea rather, that is risen again, who is even at the right hand of God, who also maketh intercession for us. Who shall separate us from the love of Christ? shall tribulation, or distress, or persecution, or famine, or nakedness, or peril, or sword? (As it is written, For thy sake we are killed all the day long; we are accounted as sheep for the slaughter.) Nay, in all these things we are more than conquerors, through Him that loved us. For I am persuaded, that neither death, nor life, nor angels, nor principalities, nor powers, nor things present, nor things to come, nor height, nor depth, nor any other creature, shall be able to separate us from the love of God, which is in Christ Jesus our Lord."

A new sub-section, being the fifth, seems to me to commence in the middle of the 17th verse, and reaches to the end of the chapter. It may be entitled, "The afflictions of those interested in the Divine method of justification, not inconsistent with the reality and security of that peculiar Divine favour of which it assures them." The topic is broached, and briefly, though strikingly illustrated, in the 3d, 4th, and 5th verses of the fifth chapter. It is fully discussed in the paragraph on the illustration of which we are about to enter. The words, "If so be that we suffer with Him, that we may be also glorified together with Him," which in our version forms the last half of the 17th verse, are plainly, at least as closely, connected with those which follow them as with those which precede them. It is difficult to find a very distinct idea in them, viewed as connected with what goes before. It seems to be this: that we shall be heirs of God, and joint-heirs with Christ Jesus, if we so suffer with Christ Jesus as to be ultimately glorified together with Him. But, from the first clause of the verse, it is obvious that the apostle suspends the security of our heirship, or fixed *relation*, not on contingent circumstances—not on our suffering in a particular temper or cause, but on our being sons. The words, then, are to be considered as standing by themselves. Had it not been for the connecting particle in the next verse, I would have connected them with it so as to form a complete sentence: 'If so be that we suffer with Him that we may be also glorified together, I reckon that the sufferings of the present time are not worthy to be compared with the glory that shall be revealed.' But the inflexible rules of grammar forbid this.

The sentence is elliptical, but the ellipsis is easily supplied. "If so be that we suffer with Christ Jesus, *it is* in order to our being glorified together with Him." We have a construction of precisely the same kind in the 6th verse of the first chapter of the Second Epistle to the Corinthians—"Whether we be afflicted," *it is* "for your consolation and salvation"—or, "whether we be comforted," *it is* "for your consolation and salvation." You will notice, *it is* is a supplement in each of these clauses: And just so here.

The multiplied and severe afflictions to which believers in Christ were exposed, in consequence of their faith in Him, no doubt appeared to many ill to harmonise with the apostle's declaration, that they were the objects of the peculiar and unchanging favour and complacency of God. Surely such sufferings seemed to indicate something else than that they who sustained them were the peculiar favourites of heaven. The conclusion they were ready to come to respecting the servants, was that which had been come to with regard to the Master—"stricken, smitten of God, and afflicted." The apostle meets this natural misconception of the Divine dispensations, and shows, by a variety of considerations, that no afflictions, however severe, were at all inconsistent with the reality and security of that favour of God, which is the peculiar privilege of those who are interested in the Divine method of justification.

1. *They Suffer, with Christ, and that they may be Glorified together with Him.*[1]

The first of these considerations is, that the fellowship of Christians with their Master, in time—on earth, in His sufferings, is in order that they may have fellowship with Him through eternity, in heaven, in His glory. The apostle meets the objection of the world, not by denying the fact on which it rests, but by showing that they misapprehended its cause and design. The objection might find utterance in language like this—'These are indeed glorious things which you proclaim about those whom ye call, justified by the faith of Christ; sons of God; heirs of God; joint-heirs with Christ Jesus. But what are these but swelling words of vanity?

[1] Chap. viii. 17.

Where is the blessedness of which you speak? Christians are poor, despised, miserable creatures, and are so *because* they are *Christians*. If they have fellowship with their Master, whom you call the Son of God, it is not in the glory, you say, He now enjoys, but in the sufferings which we know He did endure when He was on earth.'[1] To such an objection what could be a more appropriate and sufficient answer than what follows: "If so be we suffer"—if (as there can be no doubt) we suffer, we suffer "with Christ;" and we suffer with Him, "that we also may be glorified with Him."[2]

Christians "suffer:" they have sufferings as men, they have sufferings as Christians; and the afflictions of the Christians of the primitive age were peculiarly numerous and severe. In becoming Christians, they did not cease to be men; and on becoming Christians, they were distinctly told, that he who would be Christ's disciple must renounce himself, and take up the cross—that "in the world they should have tribulation,"[3] —and that "through much affliction they must enter into the kingdom of God."[4]

These sufferings were "sufferings with Christ"—borne in common with Him. This is true even of the ordinary afflictions of life. He bore these as well as they; and as borne by them, they indicate a fellowship with Him in His sufferings. These sufferings are not indeed to them, as they were in His case, penal and expiatory; but still Christians have this in common with their Lord, that they submit patiently to, they

[1] In the Octavius of Minucius Felix, c. xiii., we have a specimen of the scoffings referred to. "Quid post mortem impendeat miseri dum adhuc vivitis aestimate. Ecce pars vestrum et major et melior, ut dicitur, algetis, opere, fame laboratis: et Deus patitur, dissimulat; non vult, non potest opitulari suis. Ita aut invalidus aut iniquus est. Tu qui immortalitatem posthumam somnias, cum periculo quateris, cum febribus ureris, cum dolore laceraris, nondum conditionem tuam sentis? nondum agnoscis fragilitatem? invitus miser infirmitates argueris nec fateris. Sed omitto communia. Ecce vobis, minae, supplicia, tormenta, etiam non adorandae sed subeundae cruces: ignes etiam quos et praedicitis et timetis: Ubi Deus qui subvenire reviviscentibus potest viventibus non potest?"

[2] Ver. 17. [3] John xvi. 33. [4] Acts xiv. 22.

acquiesce cheerfully in these afflictions, as righteous appointments of God—expressions of His displeasure at sin. He, though personally not liable, submitted to them, as a portion of the divinely appointed means by which the atonement was to be made; and they, though freed from them as penal evils by their connection with Christ, still submit to them, as manifestations of God's displeasure against sin, as well as the means of their spiritual improvement. They have a still closer fellowship with Christ in the sufferings to which as Christians they are exposed: they are treated as He was treated, and for the same reasons; and they have His sympathy in all their sufferings.

This view of affliction is peculiarly fitted to reconcile the Christian mind to suffering. There is a felt suitableness in it. "It is enough for the disciple that he be as his Master."[1] "I would rather," said one of the Christian fathers, "fall with Christ than reign with Cæsar." The sufferings of Christ have sanctified and sweetened the sufferings of His people.

This is not, however, the leading idea here: that is, 'These sufferings, with Christ here, are in order to our being glorified together with Him hereafter.' There are two thoughts here, each well fitted to reconcile Christians to the sufferings of the present time—*first*, they who suffer with Christ shall be glorified with Him; and, *second*, the suffering with Him is in order to their being glorified together with Him.

To be "glorified with Christ," is to be made partakers of His glory: it is to be made "like Him," seeing Him as He is—conformed to Him in soul, and even in body. Their vile bodies are to be fashioned like unto His glorious body, and they are to shine forth along with Him "as the sun in the kingdom of His Father." "It is a faithful saying, if we be dead with Him, we shall also live with Him; if we suffer with Him, we shall also reign with Him."[2] This is surely enough to reconcile to suffering.

[1] Matt. x. 25.

[2] 1 John iii. 2; Phil. iii. 21; Matt. xiii. 43; 2 Tim. ii. 11, 12.

But this is not all. The design of these sufferings is, "that we may also be glorified together with Him." Not that in the new economy these sufferings are in any degree meritorious, so as to purchase for us our future happiness, but that they form an important part of that system of discipline by which we are prepared for it. They together "work out for us a far more exceeding and eternal weight of glory."[1] "It became Him, for whom are all things, and by whom are all things, in bringing many sons to glory, to make the Captain of their salvation perfect through sufferings;"[2] and by a somewhat similar course of trial does He conduct all His followers to fellowship with Him in His glory. "The trial of their faith, which is more precious"—more valuable, and more availing than the trial of gold, that, if carried very far, ends in the perishing of the thing tried—"will be found unto praise and honour and glory at the appearing of Jesus Christ."[3] Every trial will be found to have improved the character—made it more capable of the celestial glory, and nothing but the dross shall have perished. The afflictions of the justified are not only to be followed by glory, but they are the appointed and appropriate path to it.

2. *There is an immeasurable disproportion between the present Suffering and the coming Glory.*[4]

In the next verse, the apostle asserts the immeasurable disproportion between the sufferings of the present and the glories of the future state, to which they are not only introductory, but preparatory. "For I reckon that the sufferings of the present time are not worthy to be compared with the glory which is to be revealed in us."[5] This is the second proof that the afflictions to which Christians are exposed, however severe, are not inconsistent with the reality and permanence of that peculiar Divine favour, which the Divine method of justification secures for its subjects.

[1] 2 Cor. iv. 17. [2] Heb. ii. 10. [3] 1 Pet. i. 7.
[4] Chap. viii. 18-25. [5] Ver. 18.

"For" is here *illustrative.* "The glory that shall be revealed in us"—rather "to us," towards us, in reference to us,[1] is the glory of Christ, to be manifested in His conduct towards His people at the consummation of all things. It is a general name for the beatitude and grandeur to be then bestowed on them, viewed as a display of His glory—of His glorious power, wisdom, and grace. *He* is to be "glorified in His saints, and admired in all them that believe,"[2] when He presents *them* to Himself, "a glorious church, not having spot or wrinkle, or any such thing,"[3] and gives them full possession of "the inheritance, incorruptible, undefiled, and that fadeth not away."[4] This is "the grace that is to be brought to them at the coming of their Lord." Weighed in the balance with this, all affliction which might be necessary as preparation for it, seemed to the apostle not worthy to be taken into the account—less than nothing, and vanity. "The sufferings of the present time" are not light to any Christian; they were peculiarly heavy in the primitive age. No man ever bore a heavier load of them than the apostle; and they were often long continued. His whole life was a life of suffering; yet, heavy as they might be in themselves, they were light in comparison with that weight of glory, which nothing but the support of an Omnipotent arm could enable a created spirit to sustain; long continued as they might be, they were but momentary, in comparison with the eternity during which this glory was to rest on him.

The apostle seems to have allowed his mind to dwell on the blissful idea of "the glory to be revealed," till his whole soul was penetrated with a sense of its inconceivable grandeur; and he gives vent to his feelings in the sublime, though somewhat obscure, paragraph that follows:—"For the earnest expectation of the creature waiteth for the manifestation of the sons of God. For the creature was made subject to vanity, not willingly, but by reason of Him who hath subjected the same in hope; because the creature itself also shall be delivered

[1] εἰς ἡμᾶς. [2] 2 Thess. i. 10. [3] Eph. v. 27. [4] 1 Pet. i. 4.

from the bondage of corruption into the glorious liberty of the children of God. For we know that the whole creation groaneth and travaileth in pain together until now: And not only they, but ourselves also, which have the first-fruits of the Spirit, even we ourselves groan within ourselves, waiting for the adoption, *to wit*, the redemption of the body."[1]

Interpreters have differed as to the design for which this paragraph is introduced by the apostle—some affirming that his object is to illustrate the *certainty*, and others the *greatness*, of the blessedness which awaits the objects of the Divine favour at the consummation of all things. There can be little reasonable doubt that the last is the apostle's object. It is intended to illustrate and to confirm his estimate of the comparative unimportance of the sufferings to which at present they are exposed. It is as if he had said—Thus I reckon, and I may well so reckon, *for* the event we look for is one of transcendent magnitude. Our deliverance is connected with the deliverance of an enslaved world. The day of our redemption will be the jubilee of the universe.

This passage is confessedly a difficult one; but it deserves notice, that, like most other portions of Scripture, which, for whatever reason, are hard to be understood, none of the primary principles of Christian faith or duty are involved in its interpretation.

Considerable obscurity is cast on it by the somewhat confused and inaccurate manner in which it has been construed and translated in our version. It may surprise some to be told that it is precisely the same word[2] which is translated "creature" in the 19th, 20th, and 21st verses, and "creation" in the 22d. The phrase—"the earnest expectation of the creature waiteth," though a strictly literal translation of the original words, conveys no distinct idea to an English ear. The meaning is—'the creature, earnestly expecting, waiteth;' or, 'the creation, in expectation, waiteth.' The whole of the 20th verse, with the exception of the concluding words, "*in hope*,"

[1] Ver. 19–23.

[2] ἡ κτίσις.

is parenthetical, and is plainly thrown in to show how the creation comes thus earnestly to expect and wait for "the manifestation of the sons of God." The words, "in hope," should be connected with the 21st verse; and the particle rendered "because," should receive its at least equally common rendering, "that;" and the whole verse be considered as the continuation and conclusion of the sentence commenced in the 19th. In the propriety of these changes, almost all critical interpreters are agreed. The passage, construed and translated in conformity to them, would run thus:—"For the creation, in earnest expectation, waiteth for the manifestation of the sons of God (for the creation was made subject to vanity, not willingly, but by reason of Him who hath subjected it thereto"), "in hope that the creation itself also shall be delivered from the bondage of corruption into the glorious liberty of the children of God; for we know that the whole creation groaneth and travaileth in pain together until now."

It would not comport with the purpose of these illustrations, to enter into a statement and discussion of all the different opinions which have been entertained respecting the meaning of this passage. I will content myself with stating the only two opinions that appear to me probable, and giving you the reasons that induce me to prefer the one to the other.

It must be plain to every person, that the interpretation of the passage depends chiefly on the meaning attached to the word translated "creature" and "creation," and which certainly should have uniformly been rendered by one or other of these words. The word primarily and properly signifies the act of creating.[1] By a natural enough transition, it comes to signify that which is created. It sometimes, and especially when connected with the adjective 'all' or 'every,' signifies the created universe—the world—the whole frame of nature; and sometimes it is restricted to one particular class of creatures, and signifies the whole of them—for example, of men, just as our English word "world" is employed. In the first

[1] Rom. i. 20.

of these senses—that of the whole frame of nature—the universe of creatures, it occurs at least in two passages of the New Testament Scripture: "The first-born of every creature"[1]—*i.e.*, as I apprehend, 'the Prince of the whole creation, the Lord of the universe;' and "the beginning of the creation of God"[2]—'the first principle, author, or rather, perhaps, ruler, of the creation of God.' It occurs in this sense in a number of passages in the Apocryphal books.[3] In the second of these senses—the whole of human creatures—it occurs also repeatedly in the New Testament: "Preach the Gospel to every creature,"[4] or, to the whole creation—to all men; "The Gospel which is preached to every creature under heaven,"[5] or, to the whole creation—*i.e.*, to all men under heaven. It is quite plain, then, that the word "the creature," or "creation," "every creature," and "the whole creation," may, so far as the usage of the inspired writers is concerned, be interpreted either of the whole frame of nature—the universe of creatures, or of mankind at large.

There is no other use of the term at all applicable to the subject, that can be supported. Whether it signifies the one or the other of these two things in the passage before us, must be determined by considering which of them best suits the context and the design of the apostle. Interpreters, equally learned, are to be found on both sides, as might be naturally expected in such a case; each mode of interpretation has its recommendations, and each its difficulties.

Those who consider the phrase, "the creature," or "the creation," 'every creature,' or 'the whole creation,' as descriptive of the human race in general, explain the passage as follows: 'The whole race of man is earnestly expecting and waiting for the manifestation of the sons of God—for that period when the glory (spoken of in ver. 18) is to be revealed in *them*, and they are thus clearly shown to be what *they*

[1] Col. i. 15. [2] Rev. iii. 14.
[3] Judith ix. 12, xvi. 14; Wisd. ii. 6, v. 17, xvi. 24, xix. 6.
[4] Mark xvi. 15. [5] Col. i. 23.

are—the sons of God; and it is doing so in the hope that the whole race shall then be delivered from that subjection to vanity under which it at present groans (the word "vanity" being equivalent to frailty, mortality, corruption—a state of things not original to them—not induced by any act of their will, but by an appointment to which they are reluctantly subject); and not only so, but that, delivered from this bondage of corruption, all men shall be introduced into the glorious liberty of the children of God—their complete and everlasting deliverance from death and the grave, and their immortal, unchanging life of blessedness. The state of suffering of the human race, and the intensity of its desires for deliverance, are delineated, in the 22d verse, under the figures of "groaning and travailing in pain even until now."'

This mode of interpretation seems to me to labour under insurmountable difficulties. It is not in accordance with facts that the whole human creation—that the entire race of man, in all ages, or in any age, has expected a period when the sons of God shall appear to be what they are, and when they themselves shall be delivered from the bondage of corruption and made fellow-heirs with the sons of God, of their peculiar privileges. The great body of mankind has, in almost every age, been profoundly ignorant as to the great events here described. Heathens have not expected—they do not expect, the manifestation of the sons of God. They have, in general, no hope of being delivered from the bondage of corruption. There is a natural fear of death, and a natural desire of the continuation of life, which is all but universal among men; but there is not—there never was, a general hope of immortality, far less of a resurrection, among the heathen nations. It by no means removes the difficulty, to say that they expect and hope for these things implicitly in the same way as they have been represented to desire the Messiah. It may be doubted whether the passage referred to[1] is a prediction referring to the Messiah at all; and, if it be, its probable meaning is — that

[1] Hag. ii. 7.

Messiah, when He came, should be an object of affectionate desire to the Gentiles as well as to the Jews. Besides, the interpretation under review goes on a principle quite irreconcilable with numerous most explicit declarations of Scripture—that the whole human race, without exception, are to be made ultimately happy. There shall be two companies before the throne of eternal judgment; and, after the final doom is pronounced, the one shall "go into everlasting punishment," and the other "into life eternal."[1]

For these and other reasons, which might have been adduced, I am disposed to prefer the ancient mode of interpretation, which considers 'the creation,' and 'the whole creation,' as referring to the frame of nature, apart from man—the irrational and inanimate creation. In interpreting the greater part of the paragraph on this principle, there is no difficulty whatever. The world in which we live has become "subject to vanity"—to vicissitude, decay, and dissolution. This phraseology seems to intimate that it was not originally so. We have but little information as to the state of the irrational and inanimate creation previously to the fall of man through sin; but we have reason to think that an important change to the worse has taken place. This we know—that, in its present state, our world is exposed to vicissitude and change, and is doomed to dissolution. "Vanity of vanities, all is vanity." Everything is fluctuating. Processes of change, more rapid or more slow, are everywhere perceptible. "Even the mountain falling cometh to nought, and the rock is removed out of its place: the waters wear the stones, and the things which grow out of the dust of the earth, are washed away."[2] The animal tribes are exposed to many severe sufferings; and we know that, as "the world which once was, being overflowed with water, perished," so "the heavens and the earth which are now, are kept in store, reserved unto fire in the day of judgment and perdition of ungodly men; when the heavens shall pass away with a mighty noise, and the elements shall melt

[1] Matt. xxv. 46. [2] Job xiv. 18, 19.

with fervent fire, and the earth also, and the works which are therein, shall be burnt up."[1]

Into this state the creation was brought, "not willingly"—not of its own accord. 'Will' cannot properly be ascribed to the frame of nature, irrational and inanimate; but the meaning is, that this subjection to vanity did not arise out of its original constitution. It is abnormal, and was superinduced by the will of "Him who subjected it." Some interpreters consider this appellation as denoting Adam, others Satan; but there seems no valid reason of doubt that God is meant. Whatever occasioned this change, the omnipotent will of God alone could cause it. The world became "subject to vanity" when He proclaimed, "Cursed is the ground for thy sake."[2]

Now, this state of subjection to vanity is not to continue for ever. The creation is to be delivered from the bondage of corruption—this state of subjection to change, decay, and dissolution. There is to be "a new heaven and a new earth, wherein Righteousness is to dwell,"[3] and where Stability and Peace shall, under her protection, make their abode. The earth which now is, is materially the same as the earth that was previous to the deluge; and the earth that shall be after the conflagration, shall be materially the same as the earth that now is; so that its re-formation may be considered as a deliverance of the frame of nature from the bondage of corruption. We know but little of the new earth; but we know that it shall "*remain* before the Lord,"[4] no longer "subject to vanity."

As to the brute tribes, if they are to be included in the expression, "whole creation," the phraseology does not necessarily imply their resurrection; though this is not the absurd idea or impossible event which superficial thinkers are apt to suppose it. It merely implies, that if there are irrational creatures in that better state of things, they shall not be exposed to the sufferings to which they are exposed in the present state.

[1] 2 Peter iii. 5, 10.
[2] Gen. iii. 17.
[3] 2 Peter iii. 13.
[4] Isa. lxvi. 22.

But the whole creation is not only to be "delivered from the bondage of corruption," but its various constituent parts are to be introduced to a new and higher state of being: they are to be "delivered—into the glorious liberty of the children of God." The phrase is elliptical, some such word as inducted must be supplied. "The liberty of the children of God," is freedom from evil in all its forms, and the enjoyment of the corresponding good; and when the children of God obtain this liberty in its perfect form, the whole creation shall enter on a state in which nothing is deficient or wrong—a state of perfection suited to its nature. The new earth will not be less perfect and beautiful than the paradisaical—probably incomparably more so.

Some good interpreters have supposed subjection to vanity to refer to the creatures become the occasions and instruments of sin, and their deliverance to the removal of this state of things; but though this principle of interpretation leads to some pleasing, useful thoughts, it is too limited to be a satisfactory key to the passage. All that we have said is plain enough, quite accordant with other passages of Scripture, and all tends to show the transcendent magnitude of that glorious deliverance which Christians are secured of, by the Divine method of justification, and in comparison with which the apostle considers the afflictions of the present time as nothing.

But what are we to make of such expressions as the frame of nature earnestly expecting, hoping, and waiting for the period when the sons of God are to be manifested, and when itself is to be delivered from the bondage of corruption; and testifying the ardour of its expectation, by stretching out the neck, groaning, and travailing in pain? It is plain, that in a literal sense, these phrases are quite inapplicable to the creation, in the sense in which we understand the term. The apostle here uses, as he does in other places, the figure of speech which rhetoricians call personification. He ascribes life and reason to inanimate and irrational creatures. This is no uncommon thing, even in the language of ordinary life.

We say, when the fields are parched and riven with burning drought, that they are thirsty, and are opening their mouths for the drink that is necessary to refresh them. In a fine summer day, when everything looks beautiful, we say Nature smiles. Instances of this kind in Scripture are very frequent. You will find them Gen. iv. 10; Lev. xxvi. 34; Psalm xix. 1; xcvi. 11, 12; xcviii. 7, 8; cxiv. 3–6; Hab. iii. 10; James v. 4. These are but specimens.

But then, in all Scriptural personifications, true and important meaning is embodied; and here we are taught, in a highly poetical and beautiful manner, that at the period when the manifestation of the sons of God is to take place, which is at the time of the redemption of the body, a glorious change to the better is to take place on the frame of nature, and that were it endowed with sense and reason, it would expect and wait for it, and that there are appearances which, to a poetic mind, naturally assume the aspect of the expression of such sentiments; earthquakes, volcanoes, furious tempests, desolate wildernesses, seem the utterances of nature's sufferings, and desires, and anticipations. The whole paragraph is a highly poetical, but, at the same time, a perfectly intelligible representation of this truth, that the final deliverance of the people of God from evil is to be connected with a great and most favourable change in the general frame of nature.

There is, indeed, one difficulty connected with this mode of interpretation, but it is not a formidable one. It may seem strange that, in the midst of an important discussion, the apostle should at once rise from plain prose into the highest regions of poetry. The solution of the difficulty is in the nature of the subject, and the deep interest the apostle had in it. The thought of the glory to be revealed, stirred the very depths of his soul, and called forth its sublimest thoughts and most impassioned emotions. These could not find natural utterance in anything but poetical language. On the supposition that the language is figurative, all is in harmony with the laws of the human mind; but if it is not, as is supposed, by those who apply the passage to *men* generally, I do not see how the apostle can be defended against the charge of gross exaggeration.

In the verses that follow, the apostle states, that the great event—"the glory to be revealed," "the manifestation of the sons of God"—"the deliverance from the bondage of corruption," for which even the irrational and inanimate creation seemed to long, was regarded with deep intelligent interest, and looked forward to with earnest desire by those who, like him and the believing Romans, had, in the Spirit, obtained an earnest of the blessings then, only then, to be fully enjoyed: "And not only *they*, but ourselves also, which have the first-fruits of the Spirit, even we ourselves, groan within ourselves, waiting for the adoption, to wit, the redemption of the body."[1] The word *they* is a supplement; the phrase rendered "not only," is the same as that which in the first paragraph of the fifth chapter is repeatedly rendered "and not only so." If any supplement was inserted, it should have been the whole creation; "And not only does the whole creation groan and travail in pain, but even we ourselves, who have received the first fruits of the Spirit, while waiting for the adoption, the redemption of the body, groan within ourselves."

The "first fruits of the Spirit" is a figurative expression. "The first fruits," literally, denotes a portion of the best of the first ripe grain solemnly devoted to God. The word, when used metaphorically, always implies the idea of excellence, connected with the idea that the persons or things to which it is applied, form a part of an assemblage of persons or things, and have a priority, in time or in dignity, to their associates. "The first fruits" of "the lump" of the Jewish nation,[2] seems to mean their patriarchs. When Christ is called "the first fruits of them who sleep," the idea is, He was the first who rose from the dead to die no more, and His resurrection is necessarily connected with theirs.[3] Epenetus[4] is termed the first fruits of Achaia to Christ, *i.e.*, the first

[1] Ver. 23.
[2] Rom. xi. 16.
[3] 1 Cor. xv. 20.
[4] Rom. xvi. 5.

Achaian convert. There is thus no difficulty in finding the meaning of "first fruits," used figuratively.

But what are the "first fruits of the Spirit?" By "the Spirit," we are to understand the Holy Spirit, with His gifts and influences; and His first fruits may be considered as descriptive either of a portion of His gifts and graces, viewed in reference to the whole of His gifts and graces to be communicated to the Church, or of the gifts and graces of the Spirit generally, as first fruits of the full harvest of holy happiness to be enjoyed by Christians at the consummation of all things. In the first case, "we who have the first fruits of the Spirit," means, we the apostles or primitive Christians, who first in order of time received the gifts of the Holy Ghost. In the latter case, it means we Christians who, in the sanctifying and comforting influences of the Holy Spirit, enjoy the first fruits of the holy happiness we expect to enjoy in heaven.

We prefer the latter mode of interpretation, for the following reasons. What the apostle describes here is not peculiar to apostles or primitive Christians, but is common to all Christians, expecting and waiting for full salvation, and in the meantime groaning within themselves. It gives more force to the apostle's contrast; not only does the enslaved creation groan, but we, though partially delivered, groan; and it accords with the description, which the apostle elsewhere gives us, of the Holy Spirit, as "the earnest of the inheritance until the redemption of the purchased possession."[1] In the enlightening, sanctifying, comforting influences of the Holy Spirit, Christians have the first fruits of final salvation. These are a portion of it; for what is heaven but perfect knowledge, holiness, and happiness? and in them, too, they have evidence that in due time they shall have the whole of what they have now the earnest.

Now, in these circumstances, they are expecting and waiting for the adoption—the redemption of the body. "The adoption," is the state of mature, manifested, Divine sonship

[1] Eph. i. 14.

that is identified with "the redemption of the body." I cannot doubt that this means the resurrection of the body; not, as some would have it, "deliverance from the body of sin," or from the mortal body—or the redemption of the Church, the mystical body of Christ. The resurrection had already, at verse 11th, been spoken of as the completion of the deliverance by Christ. It is when the saints become "the children of the resurrection," that in their complete nature—soul and body—perfected, they are, and are recognised to be, "the children of God."[1] That is the state of mature sonship.

With the "first-fruits"—the gifts and graces of the Spirit, Christians are made truly, but not completely, happy; and the enjoyment of these leads them to expect and wait for what has been distinctly promised to them; but while waiting, expecting, they groan as well as the creation. They too still suffer from the state which sin has introduced. They are saved, but they are not completely saved. Their desire is expressed in groans. It is the expression of present suffering, as well as coming, complete deliverance. The phrase—"within ourselves," is somewhat obscure. It seems equivalent to—we deeply, though patiently, groan; our suffering is intense, our desires ardent. It is probably too intended to suggest the thought, that our longings are very different from those of the whole creation. Theirs is an unconscious, ours an intelligent desire.

The verses which follow explain how it is that they who have the first-fruits of the Spirit expect and groan. The reason is, their salvation, in its complete form, is a future, not a present thing—the object of hope, not of enjoyment. *It is not present*, therefore they groan. *It is future*, therefore they hope. "For we are saved by hope: but hope that is seen is not hope: for what a man seeth, why doth he yet hope for? But if we hope for what we see not, then do we with patience wait for it.[2]

"We are saved by hope" does not mean, 'that it is through the influence of hope, founded on faith, on our mind, that we persevere in faith and holiness, and thus obtain full salvation.'

[1] Luke xx. 36. [2] Ver. 24–25.

This is true, but it is not to the apostle's purpose. What he means is, 'We are saved, in the full extent of that word, not immediately, but prospectively; so that we cannot so justly say that we are saved, as that we hope to be saved.' "The salvation that is in Christ with eternal glory," is to be looked and longed for, and will be brought to us at the coming of our Lord Jesus. "Now hope that is seen is not hope." *Hope* here is the thing to be hoped for, and *seen* is equivalent to realized. A blessing which we were expecting, when realized, ceases, as a matter of course, to be hoped for. It loses its distinctive character and name. It is no longer a hope, it is an enjoyment. "For what a man seeth, why doth he yet hope for?" A state of complete enjoyment puts an end to all hope but the hope of its continuance.

This is not, however, the state of Christians here. They are hoping for what they do not see. They are expecting something different from, something better than, any thing they have experienced. "It does not yet *appear* what they shall be."[1] They know much about their future salvation, but it is by faith, and not by sight; and therefore they expect, and patiently expect it. It is future, therefore they groan. It is certain, therefore they wait, patiently wait. So that, in the circumstances of their present state, there is nothing which should perplex and harass the Christian, and make him doubt of the certainty and security of the love of God to him in Christ Jesus.

How abundant are the consolations thus provided for true Christians, amid the afflictions of life, however complicated and severe! They suffer with Christ. They shall be glorified together with Him. And they suffer with Him, in order that they may be glorified with Him.

Their sufferings, however heavy, however protracted, do not deserve to be compared with the exceeding and eternal weight of glory. They may look forward with confidence to an event which will fill the universe with gladness. But none of all

[1] 1 John iii. 2.

the creatures will be so happy as they—the redeemed of the Lord, the manifested sons of God.

How thankful should they be for the first-fruits of the Spirit, and how diligent in seeking a larger measure of them!

How important is it for them to take just views of their present condition, to remember habitually that the highest blessings their nature is capable of, are future; that if they would not be disappointed, they must make *them* the great object of hope! The hopes, even of Christians, are often misplaced; and those of them that are rightly placed, are interrupted and feeble. If a man place his hopes in things seen and temporal, he may reckon on disappointment. He may often not get what he expected; and he shall never obtain, even in that which he does get, the satisfaction he anticipated from it. Steady hope, founded on firm faith, will not prevent a man from feeling the afflictions of life, or from groaning under them; but it will enable him to expect and to wait—nay, it will enable him to rejoice in his tribulations, for he regards them as steps towards the glory of God, in the hope of which he exults.

Let those who profess to have the hope of the Gospel seriously examine whether the hope they cherish be indeed the hope of the Gospel; and, to ascertain this, to inquire—what is its foundation, and what are its effects?

Let those who have good hope through grace seek to "abound in hope through the power of the Holy Ghost;" and for this purpose, let them often meditate on the great object of hope, eternal life; and on the only ground of hope, the sovereign grace of God, finding its way to sinful man through the mediation of His Son, made known in the word of the truth of the Gospel. And let them often too "bow their knees to the God of hope, the God and Father of our Lord Jesus Christ, that He may give them the spirit of wisdom and revelation in the knowledge of Him, that the eyes of their understanding being enlightened, they may know what is the hope of His calling, and what the riches of the glory of His inheritance in the saints." Thus shall they be enabled, though groaning, to endure bravely, and wait patiently, as seeing Him and that which is invisible, till the seen shall give way to the unseen, the temporal to the eternal; and then they shall find that "Hope maketh not ashamed." They expect much, but they shall obtain more; they shall receive exceeding abundantly above all that they could ask or think. It is not merely what eye has never seen, ear never heard, but what never entered, never could enter, into the heart of man to conceive, that "God hath prepared for him that waiteth for Him."[1] This is the "salvation that is in Christ, with eternal glory."

And all this may be yours, poor thoughtless sinner, miserable self-deceiver, base hypocrite, open profligate, if *now*, in the faith of the truth, you receive Him, who is our *hope*, as He is our *peace*, "made of God" to men, "wisdom, and righteousness, and sanctification, and redemption." But it must be *now*. The Master will, ere long, in reference to each of you, rise up and shut to the door—by the hand of death. How soon may this be, how suddenly! And then there is no hope for you, false or true, throughout eternity. Nothing but intolerable suffering, and a certain fearful looking for of its uninterrupted, unending continuance. Turn to the stronghold. Prisoner of hope! The Avenger is out, and on thy track, and may at any moment overtake or intercept thee. "Escape for thy life," for thy soul's life! Flee! "Look not behind thee." The gate is open; nor man, nor angel can shut it. No safety without—no danger within.

3. *Suitable Spiritual Aids are furnished under Affliction.*[2]

A third and powerful consideration, showing that "the sufferings of the present time" do not affect the reality and security of the blessings connected with a personal interest in "the Divine method of justification," is adduced in the 26th verse—'Under these afflictions, Christians are furnished with suitable spiritual aids and supports.' "Likewise the Spirit also helpeth our infirmities: for we know not what we should

[1] Isa. lxiv. 4. [2] Chap. viii. 26, 27.

pray for as we ought; but the Spirit itself maketh intercession for us with groanings which cannot be uttered. And He that searcheth the hearts knoweth what is the mind of the Spirit, because He maketh intercession for the saints according to the will of God."[1]

The force of the word "likewise" seems to be—'Not only does hope lead us patiently to wait for deliverance from our afflictions; spiritual aids are also afforded us for the same purpose.'

The term "infirmities," or, as is now generally admitted to be the better reading, "infirmity," does not seem to have a reference to moral deficiencies, but to afflictions, and particularly to afflictions rising out of the faith and profession of Christianity. This appears from the following passages:—"If I must needs glory, I will glory of the things which concern mine infirmities."[2] "Of such an one will I glory: yet of myself I will not glory, but in mine infirmities."[3] "He said, My grace is sufficient for thee; for My strength is made perfect in weakness" (infirmity, the same word). "Most gladly therefore will I rather glory in my infirmities, that the power of Christ may rest upon me. Therefore I take pleasure in infirmities"—what follows explains what he means by that phrase—"in reproaches, in necessities, in persecutions, in distresses, for Christ's sake: for when I am weak" (infirm), "then am I strong."[4]

Now, the apostle here describes a peculiar kind of spiritual help, which Christians were secured of, in the state of infirmity or affliction in which they are placed, in the present time. It is of importance that we should ascertain, as exactly as possible, the phase of affliction which the apostle has in his eye. The persons he is speaking of are justified persons—who, through faith, have peace with God, and free access to Him—who have received, not the spirit of bondage, but of adoption, and habitually regard God as their Father. They know His name, and have confidence in Him. They are

[1] Ver. 26, 27. [2] 2 Cor. xi. 30. [3] 2 Cor. xii. 5. [4] 2 Cor. xii. 9, 10.

sure of all that is good for them from Him, for the asking. Why, then, should they ever be perplexed and unhappy, however afflicted? Why should they not "be anxious for nothing, but in everything with prayer and supplication, with thanksgiving, make their requests known to God?" and if they do so, assuredly "the peace of God, which passeth all understanding, shall keep their hearts and minds in Christ Jesus."[1] But here is the difficulty: they often, in their infirmity, "do not know what they should ask as they ought." They know—for "this is the confidence they have in Him, that if they ask anything according to His will, He heareth them"[2]—that "whatsoever they ask, believing, they shall receive." But what is according to the will of God, they often but very dimly descry—sometimes cannot at all perceive; and they often experience a great deficiency of that faith and holy desire, which they know to be essential to acceptable prayer. Could they but find their way to their Father's throne, and pour out requests consciously agreeable to His will, and in the assurance of being heard, any affliction could be borne. This seems to have been exactly the state of the Psalmist, when he said, "This is my infirmity."[3]

Now, says the apostle, "the Spirit helpeth our infirmity," or "our infirmities." We have spiritual aids, suited to our circumstances, in our infirmity. It has been doubted whether "the Spirit" here be the Holy Spirit, personally considered, or the spirit as opposed to the flesh—the spirit of adoption—the new nature. It does not much matter which interpretation is adopted; for, if it be the Spirit personally, it is the Spirit working by the instrumentality of the new frame of dispositions which He has formed and sustains; and if it be the new nature, it is that frame of thought and feeling, as influenced by Him whose work it is.

The expression deserves notice: "The Spirit itself helpeth our infirmity"—aids us, in the very distressed state to which he refers, "by groanings that cannot be uttered." "The

[1] Phil. iv. 6, 7. [2] 1 John v. 14. [3] Psalm lxxvii. 10.

Spirit *itself*"[1]—the very same words used of the Spirit of adoption[2]—"maketh intercession for us, with groanings which cannot be uttered." The help is most appropriate; it is just what we need. We feel as if we could not pray; but the Spirit prays for us—in us, not, it may be, in articulate words, but "with groanings which cannot be uttered."

What is the meaning of these words, supposing the reference to be to the spirit of adoption—the spirit, in opposition to the flesh? Let us take the apostle himself as an example. On a certain occasion, he was in a state of great infirmity and affliction. He was a prisoner, and might at any time become a condemned prisoner. He had eager desires to depart and be with the Lord; but he had also a deep interest in the cause of Christ, and would willingly do and suffer anything to promote it. He was "in a strait between two." For a time, it would seem, he did not know what to pray for. "What I should choose," he says, "I wot not." His new nature led him to groan in earnest desire that Christ might be glorified in his life or in his death, though not able to say whether he should pray for the one or the other. And "He that searcheth the heart"—God, knew—observed, "the mind of the Spirit"—the workings of his new nature, and gave the apostle deliverance from the afflicting uncertainty as to what he was to ask, by making it plain to him that it was more needful for the Church that he should continue in the flesh, and giving him the assurance that he should so "abide and continue for a season."[3]

The force of the concluding clause, according to this mode of interpretation, is confirmatory: "for," or 'because,' "He," or 'it'—the Spirit, "does" thus "make intercession for the saints" (literally) "according to God"—*i.e.*, 'agreeably to the will of God.' The desires which grow out of the renewed mind, even when the individual cannot distinctly express them, will bring down blessings—the appropriate blessings. "Sighs can convey any thing to Him."[4] The new creature is

[1] *αὐτὸ τὸ πνεῦμα.* [2] Ver. 16. [3] Phil. i. 19-25.

[4] George Herbert.—*The Bag.*

God's own creature, and He understands it thoroughly—better than it does itself. The sobbings of His child have to Him a distinct meaning; and, while the very utterance of them gives relief, how much greater a support is it to know He regards them all; and that "what is good He will give!" Such is the meaning, if by the Spirit, we understand the Spirit of adoption.

If, as many most learned and devout interpreters think, "the Spirit" here is to be understood personally of the Holy Spirit, the meaning is not materially different. The Holy Spirit assists us—helps our infirmity—helps us when we are infirm, and especially when, under our infirmities, we do not know what to pray for as we ought. He excites the right desire, in the due degree; and He enables us to utter it, if not in eloquent, or even articulate words, in earnest groanings. When the Holy Spirit is said to "make intercession for us with groanings," it plainly means, He enables us thus to make intercession for ourselves—just as, when sent as "the Spirit of God's Son" into the hearts of Christians, He is said to "cry Abba, Father"[1]—*i.e.*, He makes them "cry Abba, Father." He gives them true filial affection, and enables them to express it. He is, as Fenelon says, "the soul of our soul." It is a good remark of Augustine: "The Holy Spirit does not groan in Himself—with Himself, as a person of the Trinity; but He groans in us when He makes us groan."[2] The entire distinctness, in nature, form, and design, of this intercession of the Holy Spirit, from the intercession of Christ, must be obvious on the slightest reflection.

Now, this deep internal groaning for blessings needed, but the precise nature of which is not distinctly perceived, is the work of the Holy Ghost. What it expresses is a part of "the mind of the Spirit," of which the apostle speaks in the beginning of the chapter. "God knows the mind of the Spirit," however it is expressed. He distinguishes it, even in His own

[1] Gal. iv. 6.

[2] "Non Spiritus Sanctus in semetipso, apud semetipsum, in illa trinitate gemit, sed in nobis gemit, quia gemere nos facit."—*Tract.* vi. *in Joh.* § 2.

people, from "the mind of the flesh:" He will not answer desires, uttered or unuttered—utterable or unutterable, that come from "the mind of the flesh," which in none can be pleasing to Him—which, in His people, is peculiarly displeasing to Him; but He will lend His ear to the prayer which is the expression of the desire which comes from "the mind of the Spirit." The concluding clause has the same force as in the former mode of interpretation—it is confirmatory: "for the Spirit does thus make intercession for the saints, according to the will of God."

Surely, then, afflictions, under which Christians have such helps, are no proofs that they are not the objects of the peculiar love of God: they are strong proofs of the very reverse. Beautifully and impressively does the venerable Moses Stuart[1] say: "The Christian who reads this passage with a spirit that responds to the sentiment which it discloses, cannot avoid lifting up his soul to God with overflowing gratitude for His mercies. Here we are 'poor, and wretched, and miserable, and blind, and naked, and in want of all things.' We are 'crushed before the moth; we all do fade as a leaf, and the wind taketh us away.' We are often in distress, and darkness, and perplexity—in straits from which we can see no escape, no issue: even in far the greater number of cases we know not what will be for our ultimate and highest good, and so know not what we should pray for as we ought; but then the Spirit of the living God is present with all the true followers of the Saviour; He excites desires in their souls of liberation from sin and present evil, of heavenly blessedness and holiness, greater than words can express. The soul can only vent itself in sighs, the meaning of which language is too feeble to express. Often do we not know enough of the consequences or designs of present trials and sufferings, even to venture on making a definite request with regard to them; because we do not know whether relief from them is best or not. The humble Christian, who feels his need of chastise-

[1] Comment. on the Ep. to the Rom., *in loc.*

ment, will very often be brought to such a state. Then, what a high and precious privilege is it, that our unutterable sighs should be heard and understood of Him who searches the heart! Who can read this without emotion? Such are the blessings purchased for sinners by redeeming blood; such the consolations which flow from the throne of God for a groaning and dying world."

4. "*All things shall work together for their good.*"[1]

The apostle proceeds now to bring forward a fourth consideration, still more comprehensive than any which has preceded it, to show that "the sufferings of the present state" are not inconsistent with the near relation to God in which Christians are by justification placed, or with the reality and security of the blessings which grow out of that state. "And we know that all things work together for good to them that love God, to them who are the called according to His purpose. For whom He did foreknow, He also did predestinate to be conformed to the image of His Son, that He might be the first-born among many brethren. Moreover, whom He did predestinate, them He also called; and whom He called, them He also justified; and whom He justified, them He also glorified."

The last consideration arose out of the aids which Christians have under their afflictions: that which now comes under review is derived from the consequences which shall certainly result from them—"We know that all things work together for good to them that love God."[2]

It is of them only whom God loves, and who love God, that the apostle is speaking—of those who, being justified by faith, have peace with God, and who have, by the Spirit of life in Christ Jesus, had that mind of the Spirit formed in them, of which love to God is the primary feature, and which He cannot but love. The apostle, in the whole of this discussion,

[1] Chap. viii. 28–30. [2] Ver. 28.

makes it plain that he is speaking of those who are interested in the Divine method of justification, and who prove themselves to be justified by being sanctified. To those then who supremely love God, as made known in the way of salvation, regarding Him as infinitely estimable, and infinitely kind, He declares that all things work together for good.

The "all things" refer plainly to the whole of the things the apostle is speaking of—"the sufferings of the present time." Whatever befals the Christian contributes, directly or indirectly, to the promoting and the securing of his final happiness. Every thing will ultimately prove to be beneficial to him. Many things occur to him that are in their own nature prejudicial, which neither he nor any of his fellow-men can consider in any other view, or as likely to be productive of any advantageous consequence. Still, however, it is true—"No evil shall happen to the just."[1] No affliction, however severe, however long continued, however apparently disastrous, and even ruinous, but shall be made to contribute to his spiritual improvement and everlasting salvation. Poverty, reproach, persecution, the loss of property, reputation, and life—all these things may happen to him—all these things are in themselves evil, but all of them in his case shall become the means of good.

It has sometimes been asked, "Does sin work for the believer's good?" The question is an impertinent one, for it is the sufferings of the present time that the apostle is exclusively speaking of. The uneasiness connected with 'sin dwelling in us' is one of these sufferings, one of the chief of them; and certainly that uneasiness does work for good. It would be the reverse of good for a Christian to have no painful feelings connected with remaining, depraved principle, manifested in occasional criminal conduct. In its own nature, sin is only evil, and cannot be productive of good, though the consequences of sin, both in inward feeling and external event, have often greatly conduced to the good of the Christian.

[1] Prov. xii. 21.

The language of the apostle is peculiar, and deserves attention: he not only says all things shall work, but "all things shall work *together* for good;" they shall not only operate, but co-operate. It is the wise connection of one thing with another that secures the desired result. There are many things in the case of many a saint which, taken by themselves, could produce nothing but evil. The envy of Joseph's brethren, by itself, had no tendency but to destroy him. Left to the natural effect of that one evil thing, he would have died in the pit; but, along with another great evil—his being sold as a slave to the Midianites—it wrought together with other things, in themselves only evil in their separate tendency, to the great good which resulted from Joseph's becoming lord of all the land of Egypt. Every one of these calamities was a link in the chain which led him to so high a condition of honour and usefulness. This is the triumph of the wisdom and the power of Divine providence. Man finds it difficult to make one thing, in its nature evil, produce good. God makes innumerable evils so modify each other, that out of them all He brings a good, which it seems equally impossible that, before their accomplishment, they should have been conducive to, and after it, that it could have been realized without their instrumentality.

Now, "we know" this, says the apostle. It is not a matter of opinion; we are absolutely certain of it. And how did he, and those to whom he wrote, know it? They knew it because God had said it; and they were persuaded that "He was not a man that He should lie, nor the son of man that He should repent." His declarations are numerous, and most explicit. Take these examples:—"The Lord God is a sun and shield; He will give grace and glory; and no good thing will He withhold from them that walk uprightly."[1] "The path of the just is as the shining light, which shineth more and more unto the perfect day."[2] And the faith founded on these Divine declarations was, no doubt, greatly confirmed by the recorded

[1] Psal. lxxxiv. 11. [2] Prov. iv. 18.

history of the Divine dispensations to such men as Joseph, and David, and Daniel, which so clearly show, that all the ways of the Lord were mercy and truth to them, and that in faithfulness He afflicted them.

But the ground on which the apostle rests the declaration here, seems chiefly that which is indicated in the close of the 28th verse, and forms the subject of the 29th and 30th verses. "All things shall work together for good to them that love God, to them who are the called according to God's purpose"—literally, 'to them, being the called according to God's purpose,' *i.e.* 'to them, because they are "the called according to God's purpose."'

"The called" is one of the distinctive appellations of the spiritual people of God, borrowed, like the most of these, from an appellation of Israel according to the flesh. Abraham was *called* out of Ur of the Chaldees, Israel *called* out of Egypt, to the enjoyment of peculiar privileges. The called under the better covenant are 'called out of darkness into light'—out of slavery into freedom. By a Divine invitation, accepted under Divine influence, they are brought into the possession of high privileges, and higher hopes—"called to eternal life, unto the kingdom and glory of God," "to the obtaining of the glory of our Lord Jesus Christ,"[1] and to the fellowship of God's dear Son.

They are said to be called "according to God's purpose." Their calling is not the result of anything in them laying a foundation for so high a favour: it is the consequence of Sovereign purpose—the "eternal purpose which God purposed in Himself." As the apostle says, in the Second Epistle to Timothy, God calls them, "not according to their works, but according to his own purpose and grace, which was given them in Christ Jesus before the world began."[2] Their being thus called secures that "all things shall work together for their good." How it does so, the apostle proceeds to show—"For whom He did foreknow, He also did predestinate to be

[1] 1 Tim. vi. 12; 1 Thess. ii. 12; 2 Thess. ii. 14; 1 Cor. i. 9.
[2] 2 Tim. i. 9.

conformed to the image of His Son, that He might be the first-born among many brethren."[1]

"Whom He did foreknow," is plainly an imperfect expression. It looks back to the words immediately preceding:—"Whom He did foreknow" are plainly "the called according to God's purpose;" and the phrase is equivalent to—'whom He did foreknow, as to be called according to His purpose.' The word translated "foreknow" has, by some interpreters, been considered as meaning simply, to foresee; by others, to love—regard with peculiar favour; by others, to fore-appoint. The last here, as well as in 1 Peter i. 2, and elsewhere, seems to be its meaning. "Whom God fore-appointed to be called, He also predestinated"—fore-appointed, "to be conformed to the image of His Son."

This conformity to the image of His Son was the great end of their calling. To be conformed to Christ, is to be made like Him, and to be made like Him as the sons of God—to be formed to that filial character by which He is distinguished, and to be made partakers of that happiness and glory which He, as "the first-born" of the family of God, enjoys—to be made perfectly holy and happy. Even here they "put on Christ;" "the mind that was in Him" is in them; and they are in the world as He was in the world;"[2] and "when He shall appear, they shall be like Him"—even their vile bodies being changed and fashioned, so as to be "like unto his glorious body." "As they have borne the image of the earthy" Adam—the first man of the earth, "so shall they bear the image of the heavenly" Adam—"the Lord from Heaven."[3]

This determination has for its object the glory of the Saviour, as well as the happiness of the saved—"that He might be the first-born among many brethren"—that He might be glorious and happy in having so numerous, glorious, blessed a family. "First-born among many brethren" must be viewed as one appellation. The predestination and calling have for their

[1] Ver. 29. [2] Rom. xiii. 14; Phil. ii. 5; 1 John iv. 17.
[3] 1 John iii. 2; Phil. iii. 21; 1 Cor. xv. 49.

object, that His glory, and excellence, and happiness might be imparted to a vast multitude, and still all the glory, excellence, and happiness appear to be coming forth from Him. God calls His people to glory. He appoints His Son, as their elder brother, to lead them to glory. In bringing them to glory, He is determined to conform them to the image of His Son—to make them like Him; and the ulterior object is, to reflect transcendent glory on Him whom He delights to honour, and who "in all things must have the pre-eminence," that He might "see of the travail of His soul, and be satisfied"—"see His seed, and prolong His days," and at last present to the Father, the children given Him "a glorious church," completely conformed to His own image, "not having spot, or wrinkle, or any such thing."[1]

To this conformity in glory to the Saviour, a conformity in suffering is necessary; and this, as well as the other, was the object of the predestination of God. It is the purpose of God—a purpose hanging on no contingency, that all His called ones shall be conformed to the image of His Son, first in suffering, and then in glory. Nothing can interfere with the execution of this purpose. This is "the good of God's chosen,"[2] and all things must work together for it. God's counsel "shall stand, and He will do all His pleasure"—all "the good pleasure of His goodness," in the final happiness of His chosen.[3]

The saving acts of the Divine mind, in reference to His people, are all linked together in an indissoluble chain. "Moreover, whom He did predestinate, them He also called; and whom He called, them He also justified; and whom He justified, them He also glorified."[4] The use of the indefinite *past* in all the verbs here, is to be accounted for, either on the principle that what is matter of Divine purpose is just as certain as if it had taken place, or that the intention is to express what God uniformly does. In this case, as we use the present rather than the past for such indefinite statements, the words

[1] Col. i. 18; Isa. liii. 10, 11; Eph. v. 27.
[2] Psal. cvi. 5.
[3] Isa. xlvi. 10; 2 Thess. i. 11.
[4] Ver. 30.

might have been rendered—"Whom God predestinates, them He also calls; whom He calls, them He also justifies; and whom He justifies, them He also glorifies."

The work of mercy originates in God predestinating certain individuals to be conformed to the image of His Son. This is called "His purpose according to election," His sovereign purpose, His determination, for which no reason can be found out of Himself,—with regard to which we must say, "He has mercy, because He wills to have mercy." He thus chooses them before the foundation of the world, and "predestinates" them "to the adoption of children."[1]

Now, "whom He thus predestinates, He calls" to the fellowship of His Son. By the word of the truth of the Gospel, He invites them to participate in the blessings provided through the mediation of Christ, which He has destined for them, and by His good Spirit He induces them to accept of the invitation, by believing the Gospel.

"Whom He" thus "calls, He justifies." He pardons them; He receives them into favour; He deals with them as if they were righteous. All who obey the call, believe the Gospel; and it is by the faith of the Gospel that men are justified. The Divine method of justification is "by faith;" it takes effect on "all them that believe."

And "whom He thus justifies, He glorifies." Glorification is often considered as but another name for the heavenly state; but, though it undoubtedly embraces this, it is by no means to be confined to it. The glorifying of Christians, seems quite synonymous with the conforming of them to the image of Christ. He is the model of their glory. To be like Him, is to be glorious. The being made like Christ, in holiness and in happiness, is the ultimate design of God in predestinating them. And this is to be truly illustrious and honourable. Even in this world, Christians are thus glorified. They are like mirrors reflecting His glory.[2] They are made to think like Him, to feel like Him, to act like Him. They are

[1] Eph. i. 4, 5. [2] 2 Cor. iii. 18; iv. 6.

admitted to fellowship with Him in His Spirit, and in His enjoyments: His joy is in them. The glory which the Father gives Him, He gives them;[1] and in the world to come, they shall be completely conformed to Him in soul, body, and spirit; they shall "appear with Him in glory;"[2] they "shall sit with Him on His throne,"[3] and "reign with Him for ever and ever;[4]" thus receiving a "far more exceeding, and an eternal weight of glory."

Some have felt as if there were an omission in the enumeration. They would have expected that it should have been—whom He justifies, them He also sanctifies; and whom He sanctifies, them He also glorifies: but it is obvious that there is nothing wanting. Glorification, in the apostle's mode of viewing the subject, embraces, as its fundamental and most important part, sanctification. No incongruity could be greater in his estimation than an unsanctified man being a glorified man.

There is thus an inseparable connection between the blessings of the Christian salvation. They that have evidence that they are called, cannot consistently doubt that they have been predestinated—that they are justified, that they shall be glorified; and if so, it is surely unreasonable in them to repine at the sufferings of the present time, or to doubt that all things shall work together for their good. That God, who from everlasting designed for them salvation in Christ, with eternal glory, may surely be safely intrusted with all their concerns in life and death. To His eternal mind all things were present when He predestinated them to life; and He formed His gracious plan for gaining His object in such perfect wisdom, that nothing should happen to those who should be "heirs of salvation," which He would not so overrule as to make it conduce to their ultimate advantage. Whatever befalls them is the result of His appointment; and He surely appointed nothing in this world to do real injury to those on whom He had determined to bestow absolute blessedness in the next. He

[1] John xvii. 22. [2] Col. iii. 4. [3] Rev. iii. 21.
[4] 2 Tim. ii. 12; Rev. xxii. 5.

who so loved them as to appoint them, before all ages, to final happiness, may surely be trusted with conducting them through this world in the way best fitted for their arriving in safety, and in the state of due preparation, at its complete enjoyment, according to the purpose purposed in Himself from eternity.

He assigns them their place in the world, appoints their mutual relations—aware of all the trials they must undergo, all the conflicts they must engage in, all the enemies they must encounter, all the difficulties they must overcome—and provides them with the needed, seasonable aid. Nothing can befall them, outwardly or inwardly, which He has not taken into the account; so that nothing can disturb His established order, or make its modification necessary. Under His guidance all things must work for the real good and ultimate salvation of those who, predestined to everlasting bliss, have been called into the fellowship of His Son, justified by His grace, and are in progress towards being, in soul, and body, and condition, conformed in glory to their Lord and Head.[1]

5. *Nothing can be wanting to their welfare for whom God hath given His Son.*[2]

The fifth consideration which the apostle brings forward, to show that the afflictions of the present time are not inconsistent with the blessings of a justified state, is, that nothing can really injure those whom God loves so dearly, that He has given His son to die for them; and that, therefore, nothing can be wanting that is calculated to promote their real welfare. "What shall we say then to these things? If God be for us, who can be against us? He who spared not His own Son, but delivered Him up to the death for us all, how shall He not with Him also freely give us all things?"[3] The apostle seems at a loss for language to express his conceptions and feelings, in reference to the security of the people of God amid all the afflictions of the present time. The paragraph,

[1] Benecke. [2] Chap. viii. 31, 32. [3] Ver. 31, 32.

from the beginning of this down to the end of the chapter, is one of the noblest bursts of eloquence in any language.[1] It is not unlikely that Longinus, the heathen critic, refers to this, among other passages, when he includes Paul of Tarsus among the great orators.[2]

The words, "What shall we say to these things?" may either be considered as equivalent to—What shall we say in addition to these things? What more need be said—what more can be said, to show the security and happiness of Christians amid all their sufferings? Or to—What shall we say in opposition to these things? Can any representation of sufferings, however numerous, severe, complicated, and continued, destroy the force of these considerations? The first is probably the true interpretation, and the second clause is as it were the answer. "What shall we say in addition to these things?" This one thing we will say—and it is the sum and substance of all that has been said, of all that can be said, on the subject—"If God be for us, who can be against us?" And that God is for us cannot be doubted, when we reflect what He has done for us.

By "God being for us," we are to understand, the reverse of His being against us—not at variance with us, but reconciled to us; not our enemy, but our friend; on our side against all our enemies; on our side in reference to all our interests. Now, "If God be for us, who can be against us?" The emphasis is on the word *God*. Who is HE? The infinitely powerful, wise, righteous, faithful, and kind one. How can they be in real danger, or real misery, who have infinite power to guard them, infinite wisdom to guide them, infinite holiness and benignity to be their portion for ever? The question does not imply that God's justified ones shall have no enemies. They have to contend with flesh and blood, and with principalities and powers too—the rulers of the darkness of this world, spiritual wickedness in high places. But it does imply that none can successfully oppose them, or safely attempt to injure

[1] "Quid unquam Cicero dixit grandiloquentius."—ERASMUS.

[2] Longin. *Frag.* p. 260. Pearce, Lond. 1752.

them. He who destroys them must be stronger than the Omnipotent, and must overreach the All-wise. The people of God do, indeed, sometimes seem to fall in the contest; but, like their Lord, death to them is "the way of life." The enemies of the saints have seemed to obtain a triumph when they have laid the martyr in a bloody grave. But what saith the Spirit? "Blessed are the dead who have died in the Lord; for they rest from their labours, and their works do follow them."

It is plain, then, that "if God be for the justified amid all their afflictions," none can with effect be against them. But is it equally plain that God is for them? The apostle supplies the evidence. "He that spared not His own Son, but delivered Him up for us all, how shall He not with Him also freely give us all things?" The argument here is materially the same as that in the fifth chapter, ver. 8–10. To bring it fully before our mind, let us attend first to the premiss, then to the conclusion, and then point out the force of the argument.

The premiss is, "God spared not His own Son, but delivered Him up for us all." The expression "spared not," is plainly borrowed from Gen. xxii. 12, where it is used to express Abraham's readiness to offer up Isaac in sacrifice at the command of God. The purport of the apostle's argument restricts the words "*us* all," to all justified by believing. This is not one of the passages in which the general reference of the atonement is stated. *Us all*, plainly refers to those predestinated, and called, and justified, and glorified. The whole discussion refers to them only. God spared not His Son—His own Son—a person one in nature with Himself, and infinitely dear to Him. He spared Him not; He did not withhold Him; He did not refuse to allow Him to undertake our apparently hopeless cause. There is here what grammarians call a negative phrase with a positive meaning. He spared Him not, is equivalent to, He freely gave Him. Some have

[1] Rev. xiv. 13.

supposed that the phrase refers not only to the free gift of the Son to be the Saviour, by the Father as the God of all grace, but also to the Father's not dealing, as righteous judge, more gently with Him in the character of the victim for human guilt, than if He had not been His own Son. As it has been expressed, "He not only did not spare Him from being a sufferer, but He did not spare Him when He suffered." This is a truth, but it may be questioned whether the phrase means so much. It is implied, however, in the second clause, "He delivered Him up for us all." He devoted Him to be a sacrifice for the sins of men: "God so loved the world, that He gave His Son to be lifted up as Moses lifted up the serpent in the wilderness." He was "delivered for our offences"—devoted as a sacrifice in our room, for the salvation of all the justified ones.

The conclusion from this premiss is, "God will freely with Him give us all things;" that is, God will, in connection with Him, give us, without desert on our part, *freely*—in the exercise of abundant grace on His part, all things that are necessary for our happiness.

The force of the argument is obvious. (1.) He has already given us the highest proof of His love: He will not withhold inferior manifestations when necessary. (2.) He has showed that He loved us when we were in circumstances the least likely to be objects of His love: He will not cease to do so, now that He has brought us into much more favourable circumstances. Through the atonement of His Son, applied to us, we are no more the objects of His judicial displeasure; through the effectual operation of His Spirit in us, we are the objects of His moral complacency. (3.) His object in giving His Son was our complete salvation. So great a sacrifice could not be made at a peradventure. All who by faith are interested in the atoning efficacy of Christ's atonement, must then be secure of salvation. It is in effect the same argument as that in chap. v. 8 10.

What strong, abundant, everlasting consolation, has God thus provided for them who have "fled for refuge to lay hold on the hope set before us in the Gospel"—the hope "that entereth into that within the veil"—the hope of complete salvation, in free intercourse with, close resemblance to, the Holy, Holy, Holy, ever-blessed God, in being "conformed to the image of His Son"—the great end of God in predestinating, calling, and justifying men! They can never lose their place in the Divine favour; they shall assuredly at last be fully conformed, in body and soul, to Jesus Christ, and enjoy with Him, through eternity, the felicities and honours of the manifested sons of God; and all the afflictions of life, however numerous, varied, complicated, severe, and enduring, shall be made conducive to the gaining of this glorious result. Happy are the people who are in such a state as this. Happy are the people whose God is the Lord. Well may they go on their way rejoicing, with the high praises of the Lord in their mouth, "I will hope continually, and will yet praise Thee more and more. My mouth shall show forth Thy righteousness, and Thy salvation all the day: for I know not the numbers thereof. I will go in the strength of the Lord God: I will make mention of Thy righteousness, even of Thine only."[1]

Let it be remembered, however, that, by a most merciful and wise arrangement, this consolation cannot be enjoyed by the Christian unless he lives in the faith, and under the influence of the truth. The losing sight of, or distrusting, or resisting the practical influence of the truth, would all interfere with the Christian's legitimate enjoyment of these rich comforts—so fitted to sustain him in weakness, to uphold him in temptation, to make him not only patient but joyful in tribulation, and to enable him to meet death not only with composure, but with triumph. Would you enjoy these comforts, and yet not run the fearful hazard of delusion, take the apostle's advice,—"By patient continuance in well-doing, seek for glory, and honour, and immortality."[2] By faith and patience, seek the promised inheritance. "Make your calling and your election sure, by adding to your faith, virtue, and knowledge, and temperance, and patience, and godliness, and

[1] Psalm lxxi. 14-16. [2] Rom. ii. 7.

brotherly-kindness, and charity; knowing that in doing these things ye shall never fall, but so an entrance shall be ministered to you abundantly into the everlasting kingdom of our Lord and Saviour Jesus Christ."[1]

6. *The Author and ground of Justification, secure the final happiness of the Justified.*

In the 33d verse we have the subject presented to us in a somewhat different aspect. The apostle states and argues the irreversibility of the sentence of justification, from the consideration of the party who pronounces it, and the grounds on which it is pronounced. It is pronounced by the Supreme Judge, and it proceeds on the ground of the completed and accepted sacrifice of Jesus Christ: "Who shall lay anything to the charge of God's elect? It is God that justifieth. Who is he that condemneth? It is Christ that died, yea rather that is risen again, who is even at the right hand of God, who also maketh intercession for us."

By many interpreters, the 33d, 34th, and 35th verses are viewed as a series of questions. Thus: "Who shall lay anything to the charge of God's elect? Shall God, who justifies? Who is he that condemneth? Is it Christ who died? who rose again? who is even at the right hand of God? who also maketh intercession for us? Who shall separate us from the love of Christ? Shall tribulation? or distress? or persecution? or famine? or nakedness? or peril? or sword?" No doubt the idiom of the language permits this; but it would be very strange to have eighteen questions following each other without anything in the form of answer. This mode of construction does not materially change the meaning; and the force and beauty of the passage as a piece of composition is certainly not improved by it. We follow the construction preferred by our translators.

"Who shall lay anything to the charge of God's elect?" The "elect" here are those interested in the Divine method

[1] 2 Pet. i. 5-11.

of justification—those whom God predestinates, and calls, and justifies, and glorifies. The term "elect" is, probably, equivalent here, as it is in some other parts of the New Testament, to 'selected,' or "called, according to God's purpose;" for what the apostle says of them here, is not true of them *as elect*, in the ordinary sense of the term, as synonymous with predestinated; for, previously to their calling and justification, God's law brings the same charge against them as against those who are never called and justified. It condemns them—justly condemns them. The Ephesians, who were "chosen in Christ before the foundation of the world," and "predestinated unto the adoption of children," were yet "by nature children of wrath, even as others."[1] But when election goes forth into calling and justification, then the challenge may fearlessly go forth, "Who shall lay anything to the charge of God's elect?"

As the question, "Who can be against us?" does not imply that the Christian has no enemies, but only that his enemies, however numerous, powerful, and crafty, shall not be able to effectuate his ruin, so the question, "Who shall lay anything to the charge of God's elect?" or, 'Who shall bring an accusatory charge against them?' does not imply that they shall never be accused, but that no accusation that may be brought against them shall ever be so established, as to reverse the sentence of justification which has gone forth in their favour.

This is plain; for "it is God who justifies them." Their Justifier is the ultimate authority in the universe—the supreme and universal Judge: He whose law they had violated, whose displeasure they had excited, whose curse they had incurred—HE has justified them. The "one Lawgiver, who is able to save and to destroy,"[2] has declared that, having believed in the name of His Son, "they are not condemned, and shall never come into condemnation;"[3] that they are "justified from all things;"[4] that He has "forgiven them all

[1] Eph. i. 4, 5, ii. 3.
[2] James iv. 12.
[3] John iii. 18, v. 24.
[4] Acts xiii. 39.

trespasses,"[1] and will "remember their iniquities no more."[2] He has "justified them freely by His grace, through the redemption that is in Christ Jesus;"[3] and the sentence He has passed, no power in the universe can reverse or invalidate. He declares that *He* will not reverse it, and who else can?

"Who is he that condemneth?" It is not unlikely that the apostle, in using these words, had in his mind the noble defiance in Isaiah l. 7, 8—"The Lord God will help me; therefore I shall not be confounded. He is near that justifieth me; who will contend with me? let us stand together: who is mine adversary? let him come near to me." These are the words of the Messiah; but all who are interested in "the righteousness of God" may safely use His language—"Who can condemn whom God justifies?" He who is the supreme and only Potentate—who alone has right to pronounce on men's spiritual state, and character, and destiny—who alone can carry such sentences of condemnation or acquittal into execution—He has justified; and the condemnation of all other beings could, in opposition to His sentence, avail nothing. Their condemnation, so far as the Christian's highest interests are concerned, are empty words.

Though we knew, then, nothing more than that the supreme Judge had pronounced a sentence of irreversible justification on them who are in Christ Jesus, this should be enough to satisfy us that their happiness is secure; but the apostle turns the attention, not only to the fact that such a sentence has been passed by Him who alone has the right to pass it, but also to the ground on which this sentence proceeds. The question, "Who is he that condemneth?" looks forward as well as backward. "It was Christ that died," and He is "risen again;" He sits "at God's right hand;" He "makes intercession." An all-availing atoning sacrifice has been offered. There has been death, and such a death as redeems—pays the ransom for the transgressions which could not be expiated under the first covenant.[4] "Christ died," is clearly

[1] Col. ii. 13.
[2] Heb. viii. 12.
[3] Rom. iii. 24.
[4] Heb. ix. 11-23.

here equivalent to, 'He was "delivered up for us all;" He "died for *us*"—in our room; "He died for our sins;" He "was delivered for our offences." He came in "the likeness of sinful flesh, and became a sin-offering."'

Now, it was *Christ* who thus died. And who is Christ? As to His person, He is God's own Son—as the apostle, in the beginning of the next chapter, says, "God over all, blessed for ever;"[1] and as to His office, He is *Christ*, the Messiah, the anointed One—the divinely-appointed, qualified, and accredited Saviour. "His blood" (for it is the blood of God's Son) "cleanseth us from all sin;"[2] and "in Him"—"who is the image of the invisible God, the first-born of every creature," the Prince of the creation—"we have redemption through His blood, the forgiveness of sin."[3] His obedience unto death, in their place, forms sufficient foundation, in the estimation of the Supreme Ruler, for a sentence of justification going forth in favour of those in whose room He stood.

Of this we have abundant evidence; for He who "died for our sins, according to the Scriptures," has "risen again, according to the Scriptures."[4] He who was "delivered for our offences," has been "raised again for our justification."[5] Had Christ not risen, we had been yet in our sins. His remaining in the grave would have been a proof that His interposition had not been effectual: it would have been a proof that He was not what He declared Himself to be. But "God has raised Him from the dead, and given Him glory, that our faith and hope might be in God,"[6] as "the God of peace"[7]—the pacified Divinity—the "just God and the Saviour"[8]—"just, and the justifier of him who believeth in Jesus."[9] Still further, He "sits at God's right hand"—that is, He reigns along with God[10]—has "all power in heaven and in earth"[11]—is "Lord of all;"[12] and it is appointed that He shall "judge

[1] Rom. ix. 5. [2] 1 John i. 7. [3] Col. i. 14, 15.
[4] 1 Cor. xv. 3, 4. [5] Rom. iv. 25. [6] 1 Pet. i. 21.
[7] Heb. xiii. 20. [8] Isa. xlv. 21. [9] Rom. iii. 26.
[10] 1 Cor. xv. 25. [11] Matt. xxviii. 18. [12] Acts x. 36.

the world in righteousness."[1] This is Christ. How can they be condemned, then, for whom He died? To crown all, He "maketh intercession for us." He continues, in His exalted state, to interpose in their behalf; He appears in the presence of God for them as their advocate; the merits of His atonement are ever before the eye of the Supreme Judge —for He is in the circle of the throne a Lamb as it had been slain; and "He is able to save them to the uttermost, seeing He thus ever lives to make intercession for them."[2]

7. *Conclusion of this Argument.*[3]

The apostle shuts up this illustration of the reality and security of the believer's interest in Christ, rising out of the Divine method of justification, notwithstanding all the calamities to which, during the present time, they may be exposed, in the following overwhelming burst of inspired eloquence: "Who shall separate us from the love of Christ? shall tribulation, or distress, or persecution, or famine, or nakedness, or peril, or sword? (As it is written, For Thy sake we are killed all the day long; we are accounted as sheep for the slaughter.) Nay, in all these things we are more than conquerors, through Him that loved us. For I am persuaded, that neither death, nor life, nor angels, nor principalities, nor powers, nor things present, nor things to come, nor height, nor depth, nor any other creature, shall be able to separate us from the love of God, which is in Christ Jesus our Lord."[4]

In order to the understanding of this passage, so replete with consolation to genuine Christians amid the calamities of the present state, it is of primary importance that we attach the true meaning to the phrases, "the love of Christ" and "of God," and separation from that love. "The love of God," or "of Christ," is an expression which, when taken by itself, may signify either the love of God or Christ to us, or our love to Him. In the following passages, it is our love to

[1] Acts xvii. 31.
[2] Rev. v. 6; Heb. vii. 25.
[3] Chap. viii. ver. 35–39.
[4] Ver. 35–39.

God that is meant: "Ye pass over the love of God"[1]—*i.e.*, 'the duty of love to God.' "I know you, that ye have not the love of God in you."[2] "The Lord direct your hearts into the love of God."[3] "Whoso keepeth His word, in him is the love of God perfected."[4] "This is the love of God, that we keep His commandments."[5] In the following passages, it is the love of God or Christ to us that is meant: "The grace of our Lord Jesus Christ, and the love of God, be with you all."[6] "That He would grant you to know the love of Christ, which passeth knowledge."[7] "Hereby perceive we the love of God, because *He* laid down His life for us."[8] "In this was manifested the love of God towards us, because God sent His only begotten Son into the world, that we might live through Him."[9] In some passages the reference seems doubtful; but, in most of these cases, a little attention to the context will determine it.

In the case before us, interpreters have been divided in their opinions. Some insist that the love of Christ, and of God in Christ, is the love which Christians entertain to Christ, and to God in Christ, and that separation from that love means ceasing to love Christ and God; and that the apostle's sentiment is, that no sufferings, however severe and long continued —that no influence, however strong, whether human or diabolical—that no change of circumstances, whether prosperous or adverse, should ever induce them to abandon their Saviour, or forget their obligations to their redeeming God. They consider the apostle as saying in effect—'Since we derive such numerous and precious blessings from God, through Jesus Christ—since we are indebted to the Gospel of Jesus Christ for all our peace, and hope, and joy—nothing shall ever induce us to apostatize.' In support of this view of the passage, it has been urged, that the events mentioned are all of a kind fitted to shake our attachment to Christ, but by no means to alter, except by increasing, Christ's attachment to

[1] Luke xi. 42. [2] John v. 42. [3] 2 Thes. iii. 5.
[4] 1 John ii. 5. [5] 1 John v. 3. [6] 2 Cor. xiii. 14.
[7] Eph. iii. 19. [8] 1 John iii. 16. [9] 1 John iv. 9.

us—as we love our friends most when suffering, especially when suffering for us. 'There was no need,' say they, 'to tell Christians that the sufferings to which they were exposed, for Christ's sake, would never abate His affection for them; but there was great need to press on them the truth, that, considering the benefits they had derived, and hoped yet to derive from Him, no sufferings should induce them to abandon His cause.'

This view of the passage, however ingenious, will be found, when carefully examined, to be not at all satisfactory. It is quite plain that the great design of the whole section is, to show that the afflictions of the present time are not inconsistent with the justified state of Christians, or, in other words, with their being the objects of the peculiar affection of God and of Christ. And there is no trace of the supposed transition from God's love to us, to our love to God. "The love of Christ," in the 33d verse, is doubtless substantially the same thing as "the love of God in Christ Jesus our Lord" in the 39th,—an expression which admits fairly of no other meaning than the love of God manifested to us through the mediation of Jesus Christ. To explain the phrase, as has been done, of our love to God on account of Christ Jesus, is entirely to disregard the analogy of Scripture phraseology. We hold it then as certain, that the love of God here, is God's love to us; and the love of Christ, Christ's love to us.

It is now for us to inquire what it is to be separated from this love of Christ, and of God in Christ, and to show how the events referred to, whatever be their tendency, shall not be able to effect this separation. A being or event may be said to separate us from the love of God in two ways. It may be said completely to remove us from it, if it can alter the Divine determination to save us, or place us in circumstances in which it becomes, in the nature of things, impossible for us to enjoy the blessings of the final salvation; or it may be said to remove us partially and temporarily from the love of God, if it can intercept from us all manifestations and tokens of the Divine love. Now the apostle's declaration seems to embrace both these ideas, and implies, that in no sense can any of the sufferings of the present time separate Christians from the love of God. The apostle personifies them, and asks *who*, not *what*, shall separate us from the love of Christ? Without expecting a completely distinct signification in each of the different words here used to describe the sufferings of the present time, we naturally look for, in them, taken complexly, a description of the various afflictions to which the primitive Christians were exposed. And we find this.

They might be exposed to "tribulation"[1]—vexation from without, multiplied and severe sufferings from their enemies, in consequence of which they might be involved in "distress"[2]—inward anxiety,—placed in such perplexing circumstances that they should not know what course to take. Nay, they might be "persecuted,"[3]—they might be driven from their homes and pursued by their sanguinary foes; and while in this persecuted state, they might suffer from want of food, and even be reduced to "famine;"[4] they might be deprived of the shelter both of house and of clothing, and exposed in "nakedness"[5] to the rigours of winter. In these circumstances, they might be in constant "peril"[6] of still severer sufferings, and it was no improbable thing that a violent death by the "sword"[7] might close the scene. This is no overcharged picture of what the primitive Christians often suffered in consequence of their attachment to the cause of Christ. What the apostle says of himself and his apostolic brethren, was true also of many of their disciples: "We are made a spectacle to the world, to angels, and to men. Even unto this present hour we both hunger, and thirst, and are naked, and buffeted, and have no certain dwelling-place; reviled, and persecuted, and defamed, we are made as the filth of the world, and the offscourings of all things."[8]

In describing the varied sufferings to which Christians were exposed, the apostle quotes a passage from the Old

[1] θλῖψις. [2] στενοχωρία. [3] διωγμός.
[4] λιμός. [5] γυμνότης. [6] κίνδυνος.
[7] μάχαιρα. [8] 1 Cor. iv. 9–13.

Testament scriptures as peculiarly applicable to them: "As it is written, For Thy sake we are killed all day long, we are counted as sheep for the slaughter." This passage is cited from the 44th Psalm, ver. 22, according to the Greek version generally in use among the Jews of that time. It seems to refer originally to those who suffered persecution under the Syro-Macedonian kings, and is introduced by the apostle as a graphic representation of the state of the primitive followers of Christ. The meaning is plain. It marks strikingly the character of the sufferings—sufferings for the cause of God—sufferings inflicted for refusing to obey men rather than God—"for Thy sake;" their continuance and severity—"all day long;" and sufferings to the death—"killed;" and the barbarity of the persecutors and helplessness of their victims—"counted like sheep for the slaughter." This description was equally accurate in its primary and its secondary application. It was perhaps introduced by the apostle, to suggest the thought that a suffering state was not a new thing to the people of God, and no way inconsistent with their peculiar and endearing relation to Him.

To all these sufferings, the apostle intimates that Christians might not improbably be exposed; but to the question, Shall any, shall all, of these separate them from the love of Christ, or of God in Christ? his reply is, "Nay, in all these things we are more than conquerors through Him that loved us." "Nay," they cannot separate us from the love of God or of his Son. They cannot prevent the Christian from obtaining the final happiness which this love has prepared for him. "Oh how great is the goodness which God has laid up for them that fear and love Him!"—that is, "reserved in heaven" beyond the reach of their enemies.[1]

These afflictions cannot alter the Divine determination. "His covenant will He not break, nor alter the word that has gone out of His mouth." His promise is sure: "I give unto My sheep eternal life, and they shall never perish, neither

[1] Psa. xxxi. 19; 1 Pet. i. 4.

shall any pluck them out of My hand. My Father, who gave them Me, is greater than all; and none can pluck them out of My Father's hand."[1]

They cannot bring the Christian into circumstances which would make his obtaining the final salvation impossible. They cannot *destroy* his being; they can kill his body, but they cannot touch his spirit. They cannot induce him to apostatize. If they could, they might shut him out of heaven; for he who permanently turns back, turns back to perdition. But this, by the arrangements of Divine grace, is impossible. Tribulation in him works, not apostacy, but perseverance. When in danger of apostatizing, Christ prays for him, and he is "kept by the power of God through faith unto salvation."[2]

They cannot even come between him and this love, in the way of intercepting its manifestations in the midst of his sufferings. The afflictions of Christians are indeed themselves tokens of the Divine love. It is because God loves them that He thus tries them, and employs these afflictions as means of increasing their happiness. These will not be allowed to hurt them—they will do them good. And Christians know, or may know this, for it has been very plainly stated in the Scriptures of truth. In the midst of their afflictions they have often the most delightful manifestations of the Divine love, in sustaining them under their afflictions, and in the manner in which He alleviates and removes them. How strong was the sense Daniel had of the love of God in the den of lions! How far were Paul and Silas from being "separated from the love of Christ," when they, with bruised and bleeding bodies, were thrown into the inner prison, and had their feet made fast in the stocks![3] Samuel Rutherford, in his letters, speaks often of his season of banishment and imprisonment at Aberdeen as a time of bright sunshine as to Divine enjoyment.[4] And most Christians, I believe, can from their

[1] John x. 28, 29. [2] 1 Pet. i. 5. [3] Acts xvi. 25.

[4] "My Lord Jesus is kinder to me than ever He was; it pleaseth Him to dine and sup with His afflicted prisoner. A king feasteth me, and His spikenard casteth a sweet smell. I dare not say but my Lord Jesus hath

own experience testify, that as "their afflictions"—especially afflictions for Christ—"abound, their consolations in Christ have"—aye, have "much more—abounded."[1] No, He is not unmindful of His sick children—His suffering friends.

The only way in which "the sufferings of the present time" may seem to come between the Christian and the love of God and Christ, is when he falls before them as a temptation, or in unbelief sinks under them. Then a cloud comes between him and the light of his Father's countenance. But the cloud is not the affliction, but the sin; and it is a merciful arrangement that it is so. The want of comfort tells him that something is wrong. He has not far to seek for the cause; and when it is removed, he sees clearly that God rests in His love, and that the sufferings of the present time are perfectly powerless to separate from that love those who are the objects of it.

But even this is not all. Not only does the apostle give us a strong negative to the question, Shall *any*, shall *all* of these separate us from the love of Christ? he adds, "In all these things we are more than conquerors through Him that loved us." The designation, "Him that loved us," refers to Jesus Christ. This is the appellation given Him in the Apocalyptic doxology, "To Him that loved us." How well He deserves the appellation appears from the sequel of that doxology—"and hath washed us from our sins in His own blood, and hath made us kings and priests unto God, even to His Father."[2] Instead of the afflictions of life separating Christians from *His* love, His love makes them more than con-

fully recompensed my sadness with His joys, my losses with His own sweet presence. I find it a sweet and rich thing to exchange my sorrows with Christ's joys, my afflictions with the sweet peace I have with Himself."—Epist. 18. "I am, in this house of my pilgrimage, every way in good case. Christ is most kind and loving to my soul. It pleaseth Him to feast with His unseen consolations a stranger and an exiled prisoner. I would not exchange my Lord Jesus for all the comfort out of heaven. His yoke is easy, and His burden is light."—Epist. 31.

[1] 2 Cor. i. 5. [2] Rev. i. 5, 6.

querors over these evils. These afflictions not only do not injure them, but they are converted into means of advantage, and this by an influence which comes from Christ, and proves that He loves them. These afflictions are not only no evidence that God and Christ do not love us, they are proofs that they do. To them who are justified by believing, "tribulation works patience, and patience experience, and experience hope;" so that they may well "glory in tribulations."[1] When afflicted, they remember that "whom the Lord loves He chastens, and scourges every son whom He receives;" and that "if they were without chastisement, of which all the children are partakers, then would they be bastards, and not sons."[2] Instead of preventing their final happiness, these afflictions prepare them for it. "The more they toil and suffer here, the sweeter rest will be." "The trying of faith worketh patience," and when "patience has had its perfect work," then is the Christian "perfect and entire, wanting nothing." So that "blessed is the man that endureth temptation; for, when he is tried, he shall receive the crown of life which the Lord has promised to them that love Him."[3] This is not only to raise above the deleterious influence of affliction, but to turn it into a source of blessing—a proof of God's love, instead of an evidence of His dislike; and this the Christian owes to Him who loves him. It is, as the apostle says in his epistle to the Philippians (ch. i. 19), "through the supply of the Spirit of Christ" that the suffering of the present time "turns to the Christian's salvation."

The apostle had already asserted, in strong terms, the immutable security of the happiness of the man justified by believing. We might have thought that he had said all that needed to be said—indeed, all that well could be said—when he had said that tribulation, and distress, and persecution, and famine, and nakedness, and peril, and sword, could do nothing in the way of depriving him of that love of Christ, and of God in Christ, which was the source and the security of his happiness,

[1] Rom. v. 3–5. [2] Heb. xii. 6–8. [3] James i. 3, 4, 12.

but, on the contrary, went to establish what they seemed fitted to destroy. But, as if he had said nothing corresponding to the dignity of the subject, he, in a still higher strain of sacred eloquence, declares his firm persuasion, that nothing within the wide bounds of the created universe could endanger their happiness: "For I am persuaded that neither death nor life, nor angels, nor principalities, nor powers, nor things present, nor things to come, nor height, nor depth, nor any other creature, shall be able to separate us from the love of God, which is in Christ Jesus our Lord."

Christians are the objects of the love of God as well as of His Son. The idea is the offspring of a bastard, technical theology, and not of the New Testament revelation, that we are more indebted for final happiness to the Son than to the Father. "The Father Himself loveth you," says our Lord.[1] Nor are we to suppose that love the result of the Son's interposition in our behalf: the Son's interposition in our behalf was the result of this love. "God so loved the world, as to give his only-begotten Son" "to be the Saviour of the world."[2] Yet it is through the mediation of the Son that this love of the Father is manifested to men. His love to his people is love in, or by, Christ Jesus. It is only in consequence of the incarnation and sacrifice of the Son, that the Father can bestow on men tokens of His love. They are "accepted in the Beloved"—on the ground of His atonement they receive the Spirit, and are "blessed" by the "God and Father of our Lord Jesus Christ," "with all heavenly and spiritual blessings in Him."[3]

The classification deserves notice. It consists of two pairs and two triads placed alternately: "Death and life"—"angels, principalities, and powers"—"things present and things to come"—"height and depth, and every creature."

Of this "love of God in Christ Jesus," the man justified by believing can never be deprived. The apostle enumerates all existing things, all possible things, and declares

[1] John xvi. 27. [2] John iii. 16. [3] Eph. i. 6; Gal. iii. 14; Eph. i. 3.

that none of them can separate the Christian from the love of God.

Neither "death nor life" can separate Christians from the love of God. It is difficult to say what is the precise import of the terms "death and life" here. Some consider them as equivalent to things that are dead, and things that are alive. Neither inanimate nor animate beings—nothing in the whole compass of the creation—can separate us from the love of Christ, and of God in Christ. Others, who consider separation from the love of God as meaning forfeiting the love of God by apostacy, look on death and life as synonymous with the fear of death and the love of life. While others, with whom we are disposed to agree, consider death as descriptive of the dying of the persons spoken of, and life, of their living. In this sense, death shall not separate them from the love of God and of Christ; but, on the contrary, carry them to the full enjoyment of its blessed effects. They shall never know how God has loved them till they die and go into His presence, where are rivers of pleasure for evermore: there they see His face, and there He shews them His "marvellous loving-kindness." Death separates from our earthly friends—it separates our soul from our body; but it does not, it cannot, separate from the love of God. However apparently untimely and painful the death of the saint may be, it is the appointment of Divine love, and promotes his true happiness. It is the Father of mercies calling home his expatriated child to the better country, to dwell in His house, and walk in the light of His countenance. Nor can life separate the Christian from the love of God. His life is spent in a world which is a scene of revolt against God, full of snares and temptations, difficulties and afflictions; but whatever in the course of life he may lose, assuredly he shall not lose the love of God. "Whether he lives, he lives to the Lord; whether he dies, he dies to the Lord: living and dying, he is the Lord's."[1] There are not many things which God has pledged Himself not to take from His people in this world,

[1] Rom. xiv. 8.

but there is one worth them all—"My loving-kindness will I not take from thee:"[1] property, reputation, relations, reason, may all be lost in life, but this, the life of life, cannot be lost, even when life itself is, as it must be, lost.

"Angels" cannot separate us from the love of God. Angels are either bad or good; and neither can separate us from the love of God. Bad angels—devils—earnestly desire to do this: they are ever endeavouring to do it; but all their endeavours shall be in vain. "Satan shall be bruised" shortly "under the feet"[2] of the people of God; and neither his ensnaring temptations, nor his malicious charges, can affect the security of their condition, or make any alteration in the love of God towards them. There is no reason to fear any attempt on the part of the elect angels to separate us from the love of God; for "are they not all ministering spirits, sent forth to minister to them who shall be heirs of salvation?"[3] But though this be the truth, there is no incongruity in the apostle making the supposition of their making such an attempt, and stating what the result would be. "If an angel from heaven," says he, in his epistle to the Galatians, "should preach unto you another gospel than that which we have preached, let him be accursed."[4] And here he declares that all the power of all the angels of God, though they "excel in strength," is powerless to deprive a single believing sinner of his share in the special love of God.

"Principalities and powers" cannot separate us from the love of God. Some consider the words 'principalities and powers,' as explanatory of angels, and referring here, as they seem to do in some other places, to the distinctions which exist in "the host of God"—"the armies of heaven."[5] I rather think that "principalities and powers" are contrasted with angels in the same way as death is with life, and things present with things to come. In this case, the words refer to magistrates, civil authorities.[6] These were generally most hostile to

[1] Isa. liv. 10. [2] Rom. xvi. 20. [3] Heb. i. 14. [4] Gal. i. 8, 9.
[5] Gen. xxxii. 1, 2; Eph. vi. 12; Col. ii. 15. [6] Tit. iii. 1.

the people of God in the primitive age, and inflicted on them many and severe evils. But though the kings of the earth could rob, and oppress, and torture, and murder them, they could not touch their most precious treasure—they could not imperil their highest interests—they could not separate them from the love of God.

"Things present" cannot separate Christians from the love of God. None of the events of the present state can do this. Neither health nor sickness, neither riches nor poverty, neither obscurity nor aggrandizement; no personal circumstance, and nothing in the state of things around the saint of God, whether in the physical or in the moral world—no earthquake or deluge—no revolution or war—no change in church or in state, can affect his highest interest; no conceivable conjuncture of circumstances can dissolve, or even weaken, the band of love which binds God to them.

"Things to come" cannot separate Christians from the love of God. None of the futurities of time, none of the futurities of eternity, none of the events which follow death—not the personal judgment, nothing that shall take place in the separate state—not the resurrection of the body, not the general judgment, none of its results throughout eternity, can separate the believer from the love of God.

Neither "height nor depth" shall be able to separate the Christian from the love of God. The last pair referred to things as existing in time; this refers to things as existing in space. It is somewhat difficult to say what is the precise meaning of these words. Some understand the words metaphorically, considering "height" as designating exalted station and prosperous circumstances, and "depth," affliction and depressed circumstances. As Job says, xxiv. 24, "They are exalted for a little time, but are brought low." As David says, "Out of the depths have I cried to Thee." "They are minished, and brought low: yet setteth He the poor on high." And Paul speaks of "deep poverty." Others consider "height" as designating the heavenly bodies, and "depth" as the earth, and what is under the earth,—the terms in conjunction being equivalent to the created universe. This is a common enough use of the terms in Scripture. "The day-spring from on high"[1]—literally, from the height. "A sign in the depth or in the height above."[2] "He ascended on high"—"He who had descended to the lower parts of the earth"—the upper and lower worlds.[3] No being that exists—no event that takes place in heaven, or earth, or hell, can prevent the Christian from obtaining the happiness which the love of God has destined for him.

Is there any created being—any supposable event, not comprehended in the apostle's enumeration? Reflect and consider. You will find there is not one; but, lest any should be supposed to be not included in his comprehensive catalogue, he adds, "Nor can any other creature" separate us from the love of God in Christ Jesus our Lord. And if they cannot do this, they can do us no substantial or permanent injury. The love of God is the Christian's treasure. Rob him of this, and you make him poor indeed. Possessed of this, let the created universe depart, he has lost nothing: and there is nothing in the unlimitable regions of space—nothing in the unending ages of duration—that can prevent his attaining his final happiness, or make it insecure after it is attained.

Of this most consolatory, most ennobling truth, Paul was fully convinced, "I am persuaded." It is not a matter of opinion, but of assured faith. "He believed, and therefore spake." He had, indeed, the most satisfactory evidence for it—the promise and oath of Him who cannot lie. And we may have—if it be not our own fault—the same evidence which he had. Every believer of the Gospel not only may, but ought, to apply the heart-cheering declaration to himself. What the apostle says here, he says not as an apostle, but as a believing sinner; and every one who like him has, by believing, been "justified freely by God's grace, through the redemption that is in Jesus Christ," may, without presumption, adopt his language.

[1] Luke i. 78. [2] Isa. vii. 11. [3] Psalm lxviii. 18; Eph. iv. 9, 10.

Some have proposed the question, 'But will not *sin* separate us from the love of God?' To those who amuse themselves with this question as a kind of theological puzzle, we would hint that they may easily find a fitter and safer intellectual play-string, and that they may too late discover how hazardous it is to handle thoughtlessly such edge-tools. And of those who look on the subject in a somewhat graver aspect, we would seriously inquire whether they would really wish, whether they would think it a privilege, that they should be secure and safe while committing sin? and, if so, whether they have not abundant evidence, in this mode of thinking, that they have as yet neither part nor lot in Him whose name is Jesus, "because He saves His people," not *in* their sins, but "*from* their sins?" The question referred to has been, with almost equal incaution, answered by a simple negative and a simple affirmative. Some have said distinctly, No; but in saying so they must have forgotten much that is in the word of God. Sin, wherever it exists, is the object of the Divine abhorrence—God hates it everywhere—nowhere more, nowhere so much, as in His own people. The road of sin is the road to hell. Whosoever turns back, turns back towards perdition. Sin would be the ruin of the Christian, did not the Divine method of justification, though it does not make sin an impossibility, on the part of those interested in it, make it impossible that they should continue in a course of sin, and secure that they shall be kept by faith unto salvation. Still, to the very persons the apostle is here speaking of, He proclaims, "If ye live after the flesh, ye shall die."

Some have replied to the question with, if possible, a further deviation from the truth, by a simple affirmative, 'Yes; though nothing else in the universe can separate you from the love of God, your own sin can. There is no security, there can be no security, given you against this.' Alas! alas! then for the stability of Christian comfort, for the power of Christian motive, for the progress of Christian holiness, for the attainment of the Christian salvation, if this were the truth,—if the whole were this, 'God will save you from the power of external causes of separation from His love, if you only take care of the internal ones.' Well has it been said,[1] "This is to offer me only a drop of water when, fainting with thirst, I need a copious draught." Ten thousand thousand enemies without are not half so strong as the one within. And if God's gift of His own Son has not secured the restraining and sanctifying influence, for His children, which shall assuredly enable them to "crucify the old man with his lusts," and "put on the new man," then is the work not only incomplete, but it never will be completed. But assuredly Christ did die to redeem us from the dangers of this most powerful of our enemies, as well as from all other hazards of being separated from the love of God. Were it otherwise, we might abandon all the hopes the Gospel inspires, and give ourselves up as after all lost, hopelessly lost. But "the foundation of God standeth sure." "Our old man was crucified with Him." "I give unto My sheep eternal life, and they shall never perish, neither shall any pluck them out of My hand. My Father, who gave them Me, is greater than all, and none can pluck them out of My Father's hand. I and My Father are one." "If, when we were enemies, we were reconciled to God by the death of His Son, much more, being reconciled, we shall be saved by his life."[2]

The abundant consolation and good hope which these glad tidings of great joy are fitted to communicate, can, however, be legitimately enjoyed only in the faith of the Gospel going forth in its appropriate effects. It is under the clear, warm sunshine of faith, working by love, that that sweet salutary plant, the full assurance of hope, opens its blossoms and matures its fruits. In the cold, damp, dingy atmosphere of spiritual declension, this flower of paradise withers and hangs its head. And fearful is the delusion, appalling the impiety, inconceivable the hazard, of him who, from godless speculation on theological dogmas, has succeeded, in some measure, in making indulged sin consistent, it may be, even with an exult-

[1] Stuart. [2] John x. 28–30; Rom. v. 10.

ing assurance of his own final salvation. Groundless fears are distressing and undutiful, dishonouring to God and injurious to him who indulges them; but unfounded or ill-founded confidence is still more God-dishonouring, soul-ruining. "Fearing" and "Feeble-mind" suffered loss from their want of confidence in the Lord of the pilgrims; but they were true pilgrims, and got safe home. But "Self-will" and "Too-bold" were but pretenders to the pilgrim-character, and never reached the celestial city; and "Vain-confidence" fell into a deep pit, and was dashed to pieces by his fall.[1]

He is the happy man, he only, who "knows whom he has believed, and is persuaded that He will keep that which he has committed to Him against that day;" and who, with unshaken confidence in the infinite atonement of Christ, the omnipotent influence of the Holy Spirit, the exceeding great and precious promises of the Gospel, the unrepealed and unrepealable oath of God, constrained by the mercies of God, lays himself on the altar of God as "a living sacrifice," and having counted all things loss for Christ, "holding fast the righteousness which is of God by faith, does this one thing, forgetting the things that are behind, reaching forth to those that are before, presses to the mark for the prize of the high calling of God in Christ Jesus," and "keeps himself in the love of God, by building himself up on His most holy faith, praying in the Holy Spirit, and looks for the mercy of our Lord Jesus unto eternal life."[2]

May this be the happiness of us all. And "now may the God of hope fill us with all joy and peace in believing, that we may abound in hope, through the power of the Holy Ghost."[3] And "unto Him who is able to keep us from falling, and to present us faultless before the presence of His glory with exceeding joy; to the only wise God, our Saviour, be glory and majesty, dominion and power, both now and ever. Amen."[4]

[1] Pilgrim's Progress. [2] Phil. iii. 8, 9, 13, 14; Jude 20, 21.
[3] Rom. xv. 13. [4] Jude 24, 25.

§ 6. *The Relation of the manifested Divine Method of Justification to the Israelites, and the other Nations of Mankind.*

CHAPTERS ix., x., xi.—"I say the truth in Christ, I lie not, my conscience also bearing me witness in the Holy Ghost, that I have great heaviness and continual sorrow in my heart. For I could wish that myself were accursed from Christ for my brethren, my kinsmen according to the flesh: who are Israelites; to whom pertaineth the adoption, and the glory, and the covenants, and the giving of the law, and the service of God, and the promises; whose are the fathers, and of whom, as concerning the flesh, Christ came, who is over all, God blessed for ever. Amen.

Not as though the word of God hath taken none effect. For they are not all Israel which are of Israel: neither, because they are the seed of Abraham, are they all children: but, in Isaac shall thy seed be called; that is, They which are the children of the flesh, these are not the children of God: but the children of the promise are counted for the seed. For this is the word of promise, At this time will I come, and Sarah shall have a son. And not only this; but when Rebecca also had conceived by one, even by our father Isaac, (for the children being not yet born, neither having done any good or evil, that the purpose of God according to election might stand, not of works, but of Him that calleth,) it was said unto her, The elder shall serve the younger. As it is written, Jacob have I loved, but Esau have I hated.

What shall we say then? Is there unrighteousness with God? God forbid. For He saith to Moses, I will have mercy on whom I will have mercy, and I will have compassion on whom I will have compassion. So then it is not of him that willeth, nor of him that runneth, but of God that showeth mercy. For the Scripture saith unto Pharaoh, Even for this same purpose have I raised thee up, that I might show My power in thee, and that My name might be declared throughout all the earth. Therefore hath He mercy on whom He will have mercy, and whom He will He hardeneth. Thou wilt say then unto me, Why doth He yet find fault? for who hath resisted His will? Nay but, O man, who art thou that repliest against God? Shall the thing formed say to Him that formed it, Why has thou made me thus? Hath not the potter power over the clay, of the same lump to make one vessel unto honour, and another unto dishonour? What if God, willing to show His wrath, and to make His power known, endured with much long-suffering the vessels of wrath fitted to destruction: and that He might make known the riches of His glory on the vessels of mercy, which He had afore prepared unto glory, even us, whom He hath called, not of the Jews only, but also of the Gentiles?

As He saith also in Osee, I will call them My people, which were not My people; and her beloved, which was not beloved. And it shall come to pass, that in the place where it was said unto them, Ye are not my people; there shall they be called the children of the living God. Esaias also crieth concerning Israel, Though the number of the children of Israel be as the sand of the sea, a remnant shall be saved: for He will finish the work, and cut it short in righteousness; because a short work will the Lord make upon the earth. And as Esaias said before, Except the Lord of Sabaoth had left us a seed, we had been as Sodoma, and been made like unto Gomorrha.

What shall we say then? That the Gentiles, which followed not after righteousness, have attained to righteousness, even the righteousness which is of faith; but Israel, which followed after the law of righteousness, hath not attained to the law of righteousness. Wherefore? Because they sought it not by faith, but as it were by the works of the law: for they stumbled at that stumbling-stone; as it is written, Behold, I lay in Sion a stumbling-stone and rock of offence: and whosoever believeth on Him shall not be ashamed. Brethren my heart's desire and prayer to God for Israel is, that they might be saved. For I bear them record, that they have a zeal of God, but not according to knowledge. For they, being ignorant of God's righteousness, and going about to establish their own righteousness, have not submitted themselves unto the righteousness of God. For Christ is the end of the law for righteousness to every one that believeth. For Moses describeth the righteousness which is of the law, That the man which doeth those things shall live by them. But the righteousness which is of faith speaketh on this wise, Say not in thine heart, Who shall ascend into heaven? (that is, to bring Christ down from above;) or, Who shall descend into the deep? (that is, to bring up Christ again from the dead.) But what saith it? The word is nigh thee, even in thy mouth, and in thy heart: that is, the word of faith which we preach; that if thou shalt confess with thy mouth the Lord Jesus, and shalt believe in thine heart that God hath raised Him from the dead, thou shalt be saved. For with the heart man believeth unto righteousness; and with the mouth confession is made unto salvation. For the Scripture saith, Whosoever believeth on Him shall not be ashamed. For there is no difference between the Jew and the Greek; for the same Lord over all is rich unto all that call upon Him. For whosoever shall call upon the name of the Lord shall be saved.

How then shall they call on Him in whom they have not believed? and how shall they believe in Him of whom they have not heard? and how shall they hear without a preacher? and how shall they preach except they be sent? as it is written, How beautiful are the feet of them that preach the Gospel of peace, and bring glad tidings of good things! But they have not all obeyed the Gospel: for Esaias saith, Lord, who hath believed our report? So then faith coming by hearing, and hearing by the word of

God. But I say, Have they not heard? Yes verily, their sound went into all the earth, and their words unto the ends of the world. But I say, Did not Israel know? First, Moses saith, I will provoke you to jealousy by them that are no people, and by a foolish nation I will anger you. But Esaias is very bold, and saith, I was found of them that sought Me not; I was made manifest unto them that asked not after Me. But to Israel he saith, All day long I have stretched forth My hands unto a disobedient and gainsaying people.

I say then, Hath God cast away His people? God forbid. For I also am an Israelite, of the seed of Abraham, of the tribe of Benjamin. God hath not cast away His people which He foreknew. Wot ye not what the Scripture saith of Elias? how he maketh intercession to God against Israel, saying, Lord, they have killed Thy prophets, and digged down Thine altars; and I am left alone, and they seek my life. But what saith the answer of God unto him? I have reserved to Myself seven thousand men, who have not bowed the knee to the image of Baal. Even so then at this present time also there is a remnant according to the election of grace. And if by grace, then is it no more of works; otherwise grace is no more grace. But if it be of works, then is it no more grace; otherwise work is no more work. What then? Israel hath not obtained that which he seeketh for; but the election hath obtained it, and the rest were blinded (according as it is written, God hath given them the spirit of slumber, eyes that they should not see, and ears that they should not hear) unto this day. And David saith, Let their table be made a snare, and a trap, and a stumbling-block, and a recompence unto them: let their eyes be darkened, that they may not see, and bow down their back alway.

I say then, Have they stumbled that they should fall? God forbid: but rather through their fall salvation is come unto the Gentiles, for to provoke them to jealousy. Now, if the fall of them be the riches of the world, and the diminishing of them the riches of the Gentiles; how much more their fulness? For I speak to you Gentiles, inasmuch as I am the apostle of the Gentiles, I magnify mine office; if by any means I may provoke to emulation them which are my flesh, and might save some of them. For if the casting away of them be the reconciling of the world, what shall the receiving of them be, but life from the dead? For if the first-fruit be holy, the lump is also holy; and if the root be holy, so are the branches. And if some of the branches be broken off, and thou, being a wild olive-tree, wert graffed in among them, and with them partakest of the root and fatness of the olive-tree; boast not against the branches: but if thou boast, thou bearest not the root, but the root thee. Thou wilt say then, The branches were broken off, that I might be graffed in. Well; because of unbelief they were broken off, and thou standest by faith. Be not high-minded, but fear: for if God spared not the natural branches, take heed lest He also spare not thee. Behold therefore the goodness and severity of God: on them which fell, severity; but toward thee, goodness, if thou continue in His goodness; otherwise thou also shalt be cut off.

And they also, if they abide not still in unbelief, shall be graffed in: for God is able to graff them in again. For if thou wert cut out of the olive-tree, which is wild by nature, and wert graffed contrary to nature into a good olive tree; how much more shall these, which be the natural branches, be graffed into their own olive tree? For I would not, brethren, that ye should be ignorant of this mystery, (lest ye should be wise in your own conceits,) that blindness in part is happened to Israel, until the fulness of the Gentiles be come in. And so all Israel shall be saved; as it is written, There shall come out of Sion the Deliverer, and shall turn away ungodliness from Jacob: for this is my covenant unto them, when I shall take away their sins. As concerning the Gospel, they are enemies for your sakes: but as touching the election, they are beloved for the fathers' sakes. For the gifts and calling of God are without repentance. For as ye in times past have not believed God, yet have now obtained mercy through their unbelief; even so have these also now not believed, that through your mercy they also may obtain mercy. For God hath concluded them all in unbelief, that He might have mercy upon all.

O the depth of the riches both of the wisdom and knowledge of God! how unsearchable are His judgments, and His ways past finding out! For who hath known the mind of the Lord? or who hath been His counsellor? or who hath first given to Him, and it shall be recompensed unto him again? For of Him, and through Him, and to Him, are all things: to whom be glory for ever. Amen."

A new branch of the subject is obviously introduced in the beginning of the ninth chapter, the various ramifications of which employ the apostle to the end of the eleventh chapter, where his most elaborate doctrinal exposition of the Divine method of justification is brought to a close. The general subject of this section is the relation which the manifested righteousness of God has to the Israelitish people, and to the other nations of mankind. It is in effect an illustration of these words in the third chapter, ver. 29, 30, "Is He the God of the Jews only? Is He not also of the Gentiles? Yes, of the Gentiles also: seeing it is one God that shall justify the circumcision by faith, and the uncircumcision through faith." There is a striking resemblance, yet at the same time an important difference, between the discussion with which the apostle introduces,[1] and that with which he concludes, his illustration of the Divine method of justification.[2] In the former, the relation of the Israelitish people and the Gentile nations to the Divine method of justification, previously to its manifestation, is exhibited; in the latter, the relation of the same parties to the Divine method of justification, now that it has been manifested. The sum of the first statement is, 'Both Jews and Gentiles have, by violating the law of God, incurred the Divine displeasure, and, being incapable of reinstating themselves in the Divine favour which they have lost, stand in absolute need of such a restorative economy as "the righteousness of God"—the Divine method of justification.' The sum of the second is—'The advantages to be derived from the Divine method of justification have been presented equally to Jews and Gentiles for reception in the faith of the Gospel, and have been enjoyed by those, whether Jews or Gentiles, who have believed—by them only.'

The immediate results of the *manifestation* to all of "the righteousness of God"—the exhibition of the Divine method of justification in the Gospel—a plain, well-accredited Divine revelation, fitted and intended for all mankind—were very different from what we would have been apt to anticipate; very different from what those who were furnished with the best means for forming a judgment, by being in possession of the previous revelations of the Divine will, actually did anticipate. We might have been apt to suppose, that what was so deeply and universally needed, would be universally received with gratitude and gladness by Jews and Gentiles; and that, in the faith of the truth, they would all accept "the gift of righteousness"—the full and free justification that is "by God's grace, through the redemption that is in Christ Jesus." The Jews actually did expect that the benefits arising from the coming of the Messiah would be conferred on all Israelites, and, if not their exclusive possession, would be partici-

[1] Chap. i. 18–iii. 20. [2] Chap. ix. 1–xi. 36.

pated in by the Gentiles only on their renouncing Gentilism and merging themselves in the Holy Nation. How different were the results both from our anticipations and theirs! Justification—restoration to the Divine favour, and the blessings which accompany and flow from it, were presented as a free gift equally to Jews and Gentiles, to be received by them in the belief of the Gospel. What was the result? The Jews, with comparatively few exceptions, refused, on these terms, to accept of the proffered blessings, and were, in consequence, not only excluded from their enjoyment, but severely punished for this last and greatest of their sins, their rejection of the Messiah and His salvation. The Gentiles, in great numbers, believed the Gospel, and, through this belief, without becoming Jews, entered on the enjoyment of the heavenly and spiritual blessings, which it is the object of the Divine method of justification to secure and bestow on men. No Jew was excluded from these blessings but by his unbelief: no Gentile, who believed, failed to obtain them. Such was the state of things immediately on the Divine method of justification being manifested. Such, substantially, is the state of things still, after the lapse of eighteen centuries. A few Jews, having embraced the Gospel, enjoy the blessings of the Christian salvation. The great majority of Christians, whether nominal or real, are of Gentile origin. The body of the Jewish nation is unbelieving, and suffering the consequences of their unbelief. But it is not to be so always. "The fulness of the Gentiles" is to "come in" at the appointed time. The nations generally—that is, the great body of mankind, of all nations, are to embrace Christianity. "The blindness in part," which has happened to Israel, is then to cease; and to them, generally embracing, in the faith of the Gospel, Him whom their fathers had crucified and they hitherto rejected, the ancient oracle, "all Israel shall be saved," shall be verified; and God after having in the unfathomable depth of the riches both of His wisdom and knowledge, concluded—shut up Gentiles and Jews in succession in unbelief—that He might show what man is; that He may show what He is—will have mercy on both—putting them equally, and in perpetuity, in possession of the blessings of "the common salvation."

These are the great facts as to the relation in which Jews and Gentiles stand to the manifested Divine method of justification, to the statement and illustration of which the apostle devotes the ninth, tenth, and eleventh chapters of this epistle. Previously to his entering upon the statement and illustration I have just referred to, he vindicates, in opposition to Jewish prejudices, the Divine conduct in thus excluding the great body of Israel from the blessings bestowed by the Messiah, and in inflicting on them evils so dreadful as are implied in being accursed by Christ. This, if I mistake not, is his object from the beginning of the ninth chapter down to the 29th verse. For the purpose of vindicating God in excluding some—the majority—of the Israelites from the enjoyment of the blessings procured and bestowed by the Messiah, after expressing his sorrow for them,[1] he appeals to the Divine conduct towards their nation[2] from the beginning, and to the character of free sovereignty that belongs to the blessings bestowed by God on fallen men;[3] while, as to the infliction on them of such fearful judgments, he puts that on the same footing as the punishment of Pharaoh[4]—as the execution of a righteous sentence of condemnation for a course of rebellion and unbelief, persisted in, in the midst of, and in opposition to, much forbearance and long-suffering.

The vindication of the Divine procedure seems to resolve itself into three parts. (1.) The blessings from which the majority of the Jews were excluded, were blessings never promised to *them*. (2.) These blessings were free gifts, bestowed by God, in the exercise of sovereign grace, on those on whom, in the exercise of the same sovereign grace, he had determined to bestow them. And (3.) the evils inflicted on the unbelieving Jews were the just punishment of long-persevered in disobedience—punishment richly deserved by them—in merciful

[1] Ver. 1–4.
[2] Ver. 5–13, 25–29.
[3] Ver. 11, 14–24.
[4] Ver. 17.

forbearance, long delayed by God. The illustrations of these points sometimes run into each other; for the apostle is not composing a treatise, but writing an epistle. But the keeping in mind that these are the three topics of his complex argument, will greatly assist us in satisfactorily apprehending its meaning and force.

The sum of the statement and argument is, The blessings of the Divine method of justification are intended for *mankind*—not for Jews as Jews, or for Gentiles as Gentiles. They can be received only in the belief of the truth, and in the belief of the truth they shall certainly be received. No unbelieving Jew can obtain them—no believing Gentile remain destitute of them. If any, whether Jew or Gentile, to whom the Gospel comes, remain destitute of *them*, it is because he does not believe *it*. They who refuse to believe are guilty of a great sin, and deserve not only what is the natural, necessary result of their unbelief—exclusion from the blessings of the Christian salvation, but positive punishment for disobedience to the clearly revealed will of God. They who believe, have no merit in believing,—the faith of the Gospel and the blessings in which it interests, being equally the result of the sovereign grace of God.

(1.) *The Divine Procedure, in excluding the unbelieving Jews from the benefits of the Divine Method of Justification, and punishing them for rejecting it, Vindicated.*[1]

a. The Apostle's deep sorrow for his unbelieving brethren.[2]

The thought present to the apostle's mind, in entering on this discussion, seems to have been that so naturally suggested to one of so strong patriotic affections by the vivid representation of the happiness and security of all who, being in Christ Jesus, were interested in the Divine method of justification, contained in the close of the eighth chapter: 'From all this blessedness, the great body of my countrymen, by their un-

[1] Chap. ix. 1–29. [2] Chap. ix. 1–5.

belief, have excluded themselves; and they are bringing down on themselves a load of Divine vengeance proportioned to the value of the blessings they reject, and the guilt necessarily implied in rejecting these blessings. They are not "in Christ," and therefore there is condemnation to them. They have put Him away from them, and He is about to put them away from Him. They are treating Him as if he were an *anathema*—accursed, and He is about to treat them as an anathema. They are filling up their sins daily, and wrath is coming on them to the uttermost. Righteous is Jehovah, and righteous are His judgments. "Yet my heart is turned within me; my repentings are kindled together." "My sighs are many; my heart is faint." "Oh, that they had known, in this their day, the things that belong to their peace!"' These sentiments are very strikingly expressed in the commencement of the ninth chapter:[1]—"I say the truth in Christ, I lie not, my conscience also bearing me witness in the Holy Ghost, that I have great heaviness and continual sorrow in my heart. For I could wish that myself were accursed from Christ for my brethren, my kinsmen according to the flesh: who are Israelites; to whom pertaineth the adoption, and the glory, and the covenants, and the giving of the law, and the service of God, and the promises; whose are the fathers, and of whom, as concerning the flesh, Christ came, who is over all, God blessed for ever."

There is some difficulty in the construction of this passage. The first verse is obviously a very solemn introduction to an assertion about to be made—something apparently equivalent to a double oath. But the question is, what is that assertion? From their version, it is plain that our translators considered the assertion, so solemnly introduced, as that contained in the second verse, "I have great heaviness and continual sorrow of heart;" and they consider the third verse as a proof or evidence of the sincerity of this declaration. But there are two strong objections to this view of the matter. The first is,

[1] Ver. 1–5

the sentence is incomplete: it expresses sorrow, but does not say for what. And the second is, that, though it were complete, the declaration, neither in importance nor in strangeness, seems to correspond with the singularly solemn adjuration by which it is introduced. These difficulties have been felt by interpreters, and various methods adopted to remove them.

Some insist that the apostle is here expressing his sorrow, not for the misery of his unbelieving brethren, but for his own conduct, under the influence of a mistaken patriotism, previously to his conversion. They consider the third verse as assigning, not the proof, but the reason, of the statement made in the second—translating the word rendered "I could wish,"[1] 'I did wish, I was wishing, I once wished' (a rendering the word will certainly bear) 'I say the truth in Christ, I lie not, my conscience also bearing me witness in the Holy Ghost, because for my brethren, my kinsmen according to the flesh, I once wished myself an anathema from Christ, and acted accordingly. Under the influence of a false zeal for the honour of my countrymen, I thought I could not be too far or too obviously removed from the crucified Nazarene. "I verily thought with myself, that I ought to do many things contrary to the name of Jesus of Nazareth."[2] This now fills me with the deepest regret—now that my highest happiness consists in the assurance that nothing can separate me from His love, and from the love of God in Him.' These interpreters consider this passage as parallel to the affecting declaration in the close of the first chapter of the First Epistle to Timothy.[3] To this mode of construing and explaining the passage, there are many objections; but it is unnecessary to mention more than one. An ardent expression of his love to his countrymen was a natural, and indeed necessary, introduction to the statements which he was just about to make respecting their criminal rejection of the manifested Divine method of justification, and the fearful punishment they had thus drawn down on themselves; whereas an expression of regret at his

[1] ηὐχόμην. [2] Acts xxvi. 9. [3] Ver. 13, 14.

own mistaken displays of patriotism, when he thought that, for the honour of Israel and Israel's God, he "ought to do many things against Jesus of Nazareth," seems quite out of place.

Another class of expositors, holding that 'I did wish,' or 'I was wishing,' is the true rendering, have given another, and certainly a more plausible view of the sense which may thus be brought out of the words. They consider the whole passage as an ardent expression of the apostle's love to his Israelitish brethren. They consider the second verse as an incomplete sentence, and find the complement of it in the last clause of the third verse, "for my brethren, my kinsmen according to the flesh;" regarding the rest of that verse as parenthetical. They read it, without the parenthesis, thus: "I say the truth in Christ, I lie not, my conscience also bearing me witness, that I have great heaviness and continual sorrow of heart for my brethren, my kinsmen according to the flesh." The words included in the parenthesis they consider as giving the reason of this intense grief: 'For I myself once wished myself an anathema from Christ. Their condition of obstinate unbelief was once his own. He pitied them for hating Christ, for he once hated Him as cordially as they could do. He knew by experience the horrors of such a state; and, therefore, he could not look on his infatuated brethren without the tenderest emotions of pity. They consider it as expressing the same sentiment as is so beautifully brought out, Tit. iii. 3. It is impossible to deny to this mode of construction and exposition the praise of great ingenuity. It not only removes the difficulty connected with the apparently imperfect state of the second verse, but it keeps clear of considerable difficulties, which every one must perceive to be connected with any explanation of the third verse which makes it the expression of the apostle's wish in the circumstances in which he wrote the Epistle. Yet, notwithstanding all this, it does not appear to me satisfactory. Besides minor considerations, it leaves one objection to the ordinary mode of construing the passage untouched. There is nothing in the strangeness or importance of the statement to account for the uncommon solemnity of the manner in which it is introduced; it requires a leading idea to be supplied by the reader, to make up the continuity of the current of thought: 'I am deeply affected by my brethren's miserable circumstances; they are accursed from Christ, and willing to be so; I also was once as infatuated as they are now; and therefore my heaviness is so great, my sorrow so continual.' It is not natural for the mind, under deep emotion, thus to analyse its own feelings. Besides, it does not seem a natural way of describing the feelings, either of the unconverted Jews or his own before conversion, to say they wished to be anathema from Christ, with whom they were not at all connected. Though the apostle is a parenthetical writer, it would be difficult to find a parenthesis such as this in any of his Epistles; and, what must weigh much in coming to a conclusion on such a question, the Greek Fathers, to whom the language of the New Testament was vernacular, though quite aware of the difficulties connected with the exposition of the passage, never refer to this mode of disposing of them.

The true way of construing the passage seems to me to depend on the rather unusual force that ought to be given to the particle translated *For*, in the beginning of the third verse. That verse, not the second, contains the startling, scarcely credible, declaration, which he found it proper to preface by so solemn a declaration that it was the truth. The word rendered *for* is sometimes, both in the Greek version of the Old Testament and in the New Testament, employed as we use the word *namely*, or *to wit*, to mark strongly what is wished to be particularly attended to. For example, the remarkable passage in Job xix. 23-25, "Oh that my words were now written! oh that they were printed in a book!" etc.; "*for* I know that my Redeemer liveth," etc. *For* here plainly indicates, that what follows were the words which he wished thus written, printed, engraved. And in 2 Tim. ii. 11, "It is a faithful saying: *For* if we be dead with Him, we shall also live with Him: if we suffer with Him, we shall also reign with Him." *For* here, obviously, is just equivalent to *namely;* what follows is the faithful saying referred to. We consider the whole first five verses as one sentence, the second verse being the complement of the last clause of the first; and construe the passage thus: 'I say the truth in Christ, I lie not, my conscience also bearing me witness in the Holy Ghost, that I have great heaviness and continual sorrow of heart. And this is the truth which I say in Christ: I solemnly declare that I utter nothing but truth when I say, I could wish that myself were accursed from Christ for my brethren, my kinsmen according to the flesh: who are Israelites; to whom pertaineth the adoption, and the glory, and the covenants, and the giving of the law, and the service of God, and the promises; whose are the fathers, and of whom, as concerning the flesh, Christ came, who is over all, God blessed for ever.'

The paragraph naturally divides itself into three parts: the solemn introduction, the strange declaration, and the grounds on which that declaration rests. Let us look at these in their order.

And first—The solemn introduction: "I say the truth in Christ, I lie not, my conscience also bearing me witness in the Holy Ghost, that I have great heaviness and continual sorrow in my heart." The words, "I speak the truth in Christ," admit of two expositions. They may signify, I speak the truth as a Christian. The phrase, "in Christ," has often this meaning: as 2 Cor. xii. 2—"I knew a man *in Christ* fourteen years ago;" Rom. xvi. 7—"Who were *in Christ* before me." It may, however, and I rather think it does, signify something else here. It seems a formula of swearing. The declaration is a declaration on oath; and the appeal is made to Christ, the searcher of the hearts, the trier of the reins. The mode of expression here used was commonly used in swearing. —Matt. v. 34–36; Rev. x. 6. The word rendered here *in*, is, in the passages referred to, translated *by*, which, without impropriety, might have been used here also. Assuredly, Paul was no profane swearer; but we find him repeatedly appealing to Christ to attest the truth of his declarations, and the sincerity of his intentions.—2 Cor. xi. 10; 1 Tim. v. 21. He adds, "I do not lie, my conscience also bearing me witness, that I have great heaviness and continual sorrow of heart." "I do not lie," repeats and strengthens the affirmation. For similar modes of expression you may consult John i. 20; Eph. iv. 25; 1 Sam. iii. 18; 2 Tim. ii. 7. The apostle was assured of the reality and depth of his affection for his brethren, of which he was about to give so strange an expression, by the consciousness that the miseries they had brought on themselves by their unbelief, were to him a source of deep abiding sorrow. "I have great heaviness and continual sorrow of heart."

Such a declaration may seem not to harmonize well with the expressions of ecstatic exultation with which the preceding chapter closes. How can the man who so triumphs be in great heaviness and continual sorrow? The incongruity is only apparent. The same man cannot be in the same sense, at the same time, in reference to the same subject, at once joyful and sorrowful. But there is nothing inconsistent, nothing unusual, for the same person to be in different senses, in reference to different subjects, joyful and sorrowful. Paul was happy on his own account—happy on account of all, whether Jews or Gentiles, who had believed the Gospel and become partakers of the common salvation—transcendently happy in Him who loved him, and gave Himself for him—whose he was, whom he served. It is impossible to read Paul's Epistles without perceiving that he was one of the happiest of men out of heaven. But when he turned his attention to the fearful situation, and still more fearful prospects, of his unbelieving brethren, he was filled with a generous sorrow. Never was a human being more fully penetrated with Christian benevolence than the apostle; and this, which was the source to him of some of his sweetest joys, was also the source of some of his deepest sorrows. But even in these sorrows he had a satisfaction, to which the selfish man is a stranger, however great and unmingled may be his enjoyments. The man must be an entire stranger to Paul's spirit, who finds it difficult to conceive how a man may be "sorrowful," very sorrowful, though "always rejoicing."[1]

The only other phrase here which requires to be explained is, "in the Holy Ghost." This, like the corresponding phrase, "in Christ," admits of a two-fold explanation. It may either signify 'my conscience, influenced by the Holy Ghost, who is the Spirit of truth'—or it may intimate an appeal to the Holy Ghost for the truth of what he was about to say. In this case, we have a solemn declaration, as in the presence of Jesus Christ and the Holy Spirit, that what he was about to say was true—the accurate expression of the sincere feelings of his heart.

Now what was the declaration which the apostle ushers in with so much solemnity? It is this—"I could wish that myself were accursed from Christ for my brethren, my kinsmen according to the flesh." That Paul harboured no resentment towards his Jewish brethren, notwithstanding their contemptuous and cruel conduct towards him, might be considered as not a very likely thing; that he should continue to love them as much as ever, might be accounted still less probable; that he loved them more ardently than before they had so treated him, might appear scarcely credible; but that he loved them so well, that he felt that he could wish himself accursed from Christ, whatever that may mean, for them—this statement certainly warranted, and almost required, the utmost possible solemnity of attestation.

The phrase translated "I could wish myself accursed from Christ," *may* mean, as has already been remarked, 'I did wish—I was wishing;' but the reasons which have been given prevent me from acquiescing in either of the modes of interpretation to which such a mode of rendering leads. I have now to state that I am persuaded that our translators have here, as usually, accurately transfused the apostle's meaning into their version. We have instances of the same kind of version in passages where even an English reader

[1] 2 Cor. vi. 10.

can perceive the propriety of the translation :—Acts xxv. 22, "I would"—or I could—"wish to hear the man myself,"—literally, I did wish ; 2 Cor. xi. 4, "Ye might well bear with him,"—literally, 'Ye did well bear;" John viii. 39, "Ye would do,"—literally, 'ye did do.' In all these passages, the course of thought—the scope of the writer—requires a deviation from the strictly literal version of the words; and so is it here.

The apostle's declaration, then, seems to be this—'I could wish myself accursed from Christ for my brethren, my kinsmen according to the flesh.' This is a very strange declaration, and interpreters have been much perplexed in their attempts to explain and vindicate it.

The first thing to be done in order to the elucidation of this passage, "hard to be understood," is to ascertain the meaning of the word translated, "accursed." The best way of doing this, is by attending to the manner in which the word is used in other passages of the New Testament and in the Greek translation of the Old Testament, then in common use among the Jews. It occurs in the New Testament only in five other places:—Acts xxiii. 14, "We have bound ourselves under an oath,"—literally, 'we have cursed ourselves with a curse;' 'we have anathematized ourselves with an anathema;' 1 Cor. xii. 3, "No man speaking by the Spirit of God calleth Jesus accursed"—an anathema; 1 Cor. xvi. 22, "If any man love not our Lord Jesus, let him be anathema"—accursed: "Maranatha,"—the Lord cometh; Gal. i. 8, 9. The word occurs often in the Greek translation of the Old Testament—for example, in Deut. vii. 26, xiii. 17, xx. 17; Josh. vi. 17, 18, vii. 1, 11, 12, 13, 15; 1 Chron. ii. 7; Zech. xiv. 11. The meaning of the word is clearly, to be devoted to destruction.[1] The nature and

[1] "ἀνάθεμα was originally the same as ἀνάθημα; but in more recent times, and in the New Testament also, the latter form was used for what was consecrated, devoted to the gods, in an evil sense, like the Latin *sacer*. It corresponds with κάθαρμα, περίψημα, περικάθαρμα, 1 Cor. iv. 13; that is, a victim for a community—a man upon whom, in the case of pestilence or any other national calamity, the guilt of the community, which is supposed to be the cause of the calamity, is laid."—OLSHAUSEN.

extent of the destruction to which the person or thing, of whom the word is employed, is devoted, must be learned from the circumstances of the case. Let us inquire into these in the case before us.

"I could wish myself devoted to destruction from Christ." To be "devoted to destruction from Christ," is a harsh mode of expression. In none of the instances in which the word occurs, do we find it thus construed. We never read of a thing or a person devoted to destruction, as an anathema from any other thing or person. To get over this difficulty, some have translated the preposition rendered *from*, 'according to,' after the example of;' and have supposed the apostle's reference to be to crucifixion—'I could wish myself to be crucified for my brethren, after the example of Christ.' But this is an unwarranted interpretation. In the only passage quoted in support of it—"God, whom I serve *from* my forefathers,"[1] the word "from" does not mean 'after the manner of;' for Paul did not serve God after the manner of his forefathers: it merely means, Paul worshipped the same God as his forefathers. They worshipped Jehovah, and so did he. The true way of removing the difficulty, is to give the word rendered *from*, the sense of *by*, which it not unfrequently has—as in Mark viii. 31, "Rejected of"—that is, 'by' (the same word as here), "the elders;" Acts ii. 22, "A man approved of"—that is, 'by'—"God;" 1 Cor. i. 30, "Made of God"—*i.e.*, 'by God'—"to us wisdom;" 2 Cor. iii. 18, "As by the Spirit of the Lord;" James i. 13, "Tempted by God:"—"I could wish myself devoted to destruction by Christ."

Why this clause is inserted, becomes plain when we look to the next one—"for my brethren, my kinsmen according to the flesh." The ordinary way of explaining this phrase is, 'for the benefit of my brethren.' It no doubt includes this, but it seems to include more than this. The meaning appears to be—'I could wish to be devoted to destruction by Christ in the room of my brethren. I could wish to take their place—

[1] 2 Tim. i. 3.

to be a victim for them.' That the term rendered *for* will bear this signification, is plain from the way in which it is employed, Philem. 13, in which Paul speaks of retaining Onesimus, that *for* Philemon—that, as our translators well render it, "in his stead"—he might minister to him. The apostle felt as if he could take the place of his brethren, if, by doing so, he could save them from the fearful doom they had brought on themselves from the rejected Messiah. The unbelieving Jews were doomed to destruction—doomed to destruction by Christ. He had said, "Many shall come from the east and west, and sit down with Abraham, and Isaac, and Jacob, in the kingdom of heaven: but the children of the kingdom shall be cast into outer darkness; there shall be weeping and gnashing of teeth."[1] "When the Lord of the vineyard cometh, what will He do to those husbandmen?"[2] "The kingdom of God shall be taken from you." "Whosoever shall fall on this stone"—the stone which the builders rejected, made the head stone of the corner—"shall be broken; but on whomsoever it shall fall, it will grind him to powder."[3] "Your house is left to you desolate."[4] "The blood of all the prophets, which was shed from the foundation of the world, shall be required of this generation."[5] "These be the days of vengeance;" "There shall be great distress in the land, and wrath on this people."[6] "He that believeth not shall be damned."[7] Such was the doom of unbelieving Israel; and such was the ardour of Paul's affection for his brethren, that, if the thing had been possible and proper, he could have wished, by sacrificing his own happiness, to have secured theirs. This appears to me the only satisfactory mode of explaining the words; and if so, what a striking display have we here of the transforming power of Christianity!

Never, perhaps, was the omnipotence of the Gospel more splendidly illustrated than in the thorough revolution it accom-

1 Matt. viii. 11, 12.
2 Matt. xxi. 40.
3 Matt. xxi. 43, 44.
4 Matt. xxiii. 38.
5 Luke xi. 50, 51.
6 Luke xxi. 22, 23.
7 Mark xvi. 16.

plished in the mind and heart of the apostle. When first introduced to our notice by the sacred historian, we find him assisting the murderers of Stephen, the proto-martyr to the faith of Christ, " consenting to *his* death," and taking charge of *their* clothes thrown aside to fit them for their work of blood. Saul was naturally a man of firm character. His modes of thought and feeling were based on principle and strengthened by habit, and were not only different from, but directly opposed to, those which it is the object of the Gospel to generate. A bigoted attachment to Judaism was his ruling passion. This had given a sinister direction to his strong and versatile intellect, and had poisoned with malignity his inmost heart. He hated all who differed from him—Pagans, Samaritans, above all, the Nazarene Impostor, as he deemed Him, and His followers. He cordially approved the course of procedure which had brought *Him* to the cross; and he was "exceedingly mad against *them*," " breathing out threatenings and slaughter" against them, dragging them to prison, and compelling them to blaspheme.

It were a curious and by no means uninstructive speculation, to endeavour, by the application of the general laws of the human mind to the apostle's case, to discover what would have been the probable result of bringing the discipline of the Grecian philosophy to bear on such a spirit. It is not impossible that his attachments might have been transferred from Jewish rites to philosophical subtleties. The Porch or the Grove at Athens might have taken the place occupied in his imagination and affections by the Temple at Jerusalem. The furious bigot might have been converted into a hesitating sceptic or a tenacious dogmatist. His accomplished teachers might in some degree have smoothed the asperity of his temper, and moderated the violence of his passions, but in all the essential ingredients of his character—in the ruling principles of his moral nature—they would have left him unchanged.

Happily for Saul, instead of being sent to the schools of Athens, he was taken under the tuition of Jesus of Nazareth.

The truth, in its meaning and evidence, was, by the agency of the Holy Ghost, presented to his mind; and a thorough change, not merely of conduct but of heart, was the result. The elements of his character, as well as the principles of his faith, underwent a revolution, and here is the proof of it: The man who hated to the death those who differed from him in religious creed, though they never injured him, now declares, that for men not only opposed to him in his faith, but bent on his destruction, he was willing not only to die, but to submit to what to him was worse than ten thousand deaths—to be accursed from Christ, if by this means he could secure their salvation. Could anything but Christianity have done this?

The objections to the mode of interpretation which we have adopted are not so weighty as at first sight they may appear to be. To the question, How could the apostle be willing to be devoted to destruction by Christ in the room of his unbelieving countrymen? it may be answered, that the possibility of his being thus made an anathema is no more implied in what he says here, than the possibility of "an angel from heaven preaching another gospel" is implied in what is said in Gal. i. 8, 9. In both cases, a supposition is made for the purpose of expressing and illustrating a sentiment. The inference, that Paul was willing to submit to the everlasting destruction the unbelieving Jews had incurred, is not warranted by the words before us. If his being cast off by the Saviour could secure the reception and salvation of the whole Jewish people, he expresses his readiness to submit to this. But as such a thing was impossible, and as he well knew that it was so, all we can reasonably infer from the passage is, that such was his attachment to his countrymen, that he was ready to do or suffer anything within the limits of possibility, provided their salvation could be but secured by these exertions and sufferings. This is a remarkable expression for a state of feeling to which the more ordinary forms of language are inadequate.[1] It was intended to express as high a degree of affec-

[1] Stuart.

tion as man can entertain for man. Understanding it in this way, not as the expression of an actual peremptory wish, but a declaration that, were it consistent with the will of God and for the glory of Christ, he could willingly exchange conditions with the wretched unbelieving Jews, who, though his brethren, his kinsmen according to the flesh, were his active, persevering, unrelenting foes,—still we must consider it as the irrepressible bursting out of a generosity and benevolence unexampled but by that which infinitely exceeds it, the love that passeth knowledge, which induced the righteous One not only to wish to become, but actually to become, "a curse for us, that we might be redeemed from the curse," and be "made the righteousness of God in Him."

Let us now inquire what it was that drew out, in so remarkable a manner, the desire of Paul for the salvation of his countrymen. It was (1.) the greatness of the misery they had been doomed to—they were accursed by Christ, anathematised by the Messiah; (2.) the closeness of his relation to them—they were his "brethren, his kinsmen according to the flesh;" and (3.) the high privileges with which they had been invested —they were "Israelites: to whom pertained the adoption, and the glory, and the covenants, and the giving of the law, and the service of God, and the promises; whose were the fathers, and of whom, as concerning the flesh, Christ came, who is over all, God blessed for ever."

The Israelitish people, as a body—the great majority of the nation, was doomed to destruction. They had always been a rebellious and stiff-necked race, though almost all that was really good among men was to be found among them. They had lately filled up the measure of their iniquity by imbruing their hands in the blood of the incarnate Son of God, and madly imprecating that that blood might be on them and on their children. The most dreadful evils that ever befel a people were just about to overwhelm them. Wrath was coming on them to the uttermost. Yet a little while, and overwhelmed in the ruins of their commonwealth—their metropolis sacked and burned—its noblest ornament, the temple, a heap of rubbish—they must fall victims to the famine, the pestilence, and the sword; many of them suffering the accursed punishment which their infuriated malice had brought on Him who came in the name of the Lord to save them, or, driven from their own land, without a country or a home, become enslaved wanderers among the nations. In a spiritual point of view, their condition was still more deplorable. These external evils were but the indications of a wrath which was to *abide* on them. Instead of meeting in the unseen world a refuge from these calamities, they would be found but the prelusive drops of the storm of vengeance which is there to destroy the enemies of God and His Son. And then, though in a distant future, the apostle saw the salvation of Israel, in the conversion of the great body of the nation, strangely preserved, to the faith of the crucified one, yet how many generations of unbelievers must ere then, after having passed away their days in God's wrath in this world, enter on eternity to learn "the power of His anger," and that "according to His fear is His wrath."[1] It was this which produced in the apostle so deep regrets and so intense desire, and which imparted to his language so strange an energy. And had we a clearer view and firmer faith of the truth respecting the doom of unpardoned men, and a larger measure of that benevolence which makes a man love his neighbour as himself, would not we have great heaviness and continual sorrow in our heart; and what sacrifice would we not be disposed to make to rescue our fellow-men from evils so tremendous? The state of the apostle's mind is the natural one. It is the comparative indifference which men who profess to believe these things contrive habitually to entertain, that is strange and unnatural, even to monstrousness. Who can estimate the amount of misery in the loss of one soul? How dreadful to think that that estimate must be multiplied by myriads and millions! One lost immortal must suffer incomparably more than all that has been suffered by all who have ever

[1] Psa. xc. 11.

lived—all that shall be suffered by all who shall yet live, on the earth. What then, in the apostle's estimation, must have been the amount of suffering involved in the event to prevent which he could have wished himself accursed by Christ?

A second circumstance which led the apostle to feel and express so intense a desire for the salvation of the Jews, was his intimate relation to them. They were his "brethren, his kinsmen according to the flesh." Christianity does not unhinge the relations formed by nature; it draws them closer. It does not extinguish the affections which grow out of these relations; it regulates and sanctifies them, and, connecting them with religious duty, secures a healthful strength and a steady operation. Paul, when he became a Christian, became a cosmopolite—a citizen of the world; but he did not cease to be a Jew. He became a philanthropist, but he continued a patriot. Before his conversion, his patriotism manifested itself in his wishes and exertions to promote the worldly prosperity and glory of his race. It is their salvation now that he is chiefly anxious about. For this he lives; for this he is willing to die, aye, to endure what would be more than equivalent to a thousand deaths, accompanied with all conceivable terrors. It is his heart's desire and prayer to God, that all men may be saved; but the salvation of Israel excites a peculiar intensity of desire—draws forth a peculiar fervency of supplication.

The third circumstance which produced in the mind of the apostle so warm an interest in the happiness of the Jews, is to be found in the high privileges with which, as a nation, they had been invested. These are briefly enumerated in the fourth and fifth verses.

They were "Israelites,"—the descendants of him who was the heir of all the privileges conferred on Abraham, the father of the faithful, and who himself, as a prince, had power with God, and prevailed. This was, in the apostle's estimation, the most honourable of all national appellations—a name "above all Greek, above all Roman fame."

Theirs was "the adoption;" not the adoption which secures

an inalienable interest in the Divine favour—that never was, never could be, a national privilege; under every economy it has been the peculiar possession of the individual believer—but the adoption which consisted in separating them from the idolatrous nations, placing them under a peculiar economy, and bestowing on them peculiar privileges. The apostle obviously refers to such passages in the Old Testament Scriptures as Exod. iv. 22: "Israel is My son, My first-born: let My son go, that he may serve Me: if thou refuse, I will slay thy son, thy first-born;" Deut. xiv. 1: "Ye are the children of the Lord your God;" Jer. xxxi. 9: "I am a Father to Israel, and Ephraim is My first-born;" Hos. xi. 1: "When Israel was a child, then I loved him, and called my son out of Egypt."

To them pertained "the glory." The meaning of this phrase is somewhat doubtful. Some interpret it of the dignity which belonged to the Israelites as the people of God, of which Moses speaks in Deut. iv. 6-8: "The nations shall say, Surely this great nation is a wise and understanding people. For what nation is there so great, who hath God so nigh unto them? and what nation is so great, that hath statutes and judgments so righteous?" It seems more natural to suppose that the term refers to something known among the Israelites by the name of "the glory." From a passage in 1 Sam. iv. 21, "The glory is departed from Israel, for the ark of God is taken," some have supposed that this sacred chest was called "the glory." It is more probable that the phrase refers to the miraculous cloud of glory—the symbol of the presence of Jehovah,—the movements of which guided the Israelites through the wilderness, and which occasionally appeared over the tabernacle and temple—if it did not always hover over the mercy-seat. This is very often indeed, in the Old Testament, called "the glory," and "the glory of the Lord," *e. g.*, Exod. xl. 34, 35; 1 Kings viii. 10, 11; 2 Chron. vii. 1; Ezek. i. 28; x. 4. To them pertained the glory: in the midst of them they had what no other nation had, a visible token of the presence and favour of Jehovah.

To them also pertained "the covenants." The covenants here refer to the arrangements, or constitutions, in reference to Israel as a people: That made with Abraham, and renewed to Isaac and Jacob, their progenitors; and those with Israel as a people under Moses at Sinai, of which we have so full an account in the Book of Exodus; and that in the land of Moab, distinguished from the one in Horeb, of which we have an account in the twenty-ninth and thirtieth chapters of Deuteronomy. What a high honour, to have been made the subjects of such Divine arrangements!

Further: to them pertained "the giving of the law." By this expression, some interpreters understand the law itself; but as the law itself was the substance of one of the covenants, mentioned in the preceding clause, it is more probable that it refers to the remarkable Divine dispensation, the giving the law from the summit of Sinai with so awful solemnity. The best commentary on the clause is to be found in the words of Moses: "Ask now of the days that are past, which were before thee, since the day that God created man upon the earth; and ask from the one side of heaven unto the other, whether there hath been any such thing as this great thing is, or hath been heard like it? Did ever people hear the voice of God speaking out of the midst of the fire, as thou hast heard, and live? Out of heaven He made thee to hear His voice, that He might instruct thee; and upon earth He showed thee His great fire; and thou heardest His words out of the midst of the fire."[1]

To them also pertained "the service of God." By "the service of God," we are to understand the appointed, and therefore the acceptable, mode of worshipping God—"the ordinances of Divine service," as the apostle expresses it.[2] While the rest of the nations were left to "seek after the Lord, if haply they might feel after Him, and find Him; and to inquire, Wherewith shall we come before the Lord, and bow ourselves before the Most High God?" Israel had not only a

[1] Deut. iv. 32, 33, 36.

[2] Heb. ix. 1.

revelation made of the only living and true God, but were instructed how to worship Him.[1]

To them also pertained "the promises." There were promises made to, or rather in reference to, the Gentiles. But to Israel were made many exceeding great and precious promises. Those contained in the twenty-sixth chapter of Leviticus and in the twenty-eighth of Deuteronomy may be considered as a specimen. These were promises of peculiar protection, and of continued existence; promises of the Messiah to be raised up from among them; and promises, which remain yet to be fulfilled, of their restoration to the Church in the latter days.

Theirs, too, were "the fathers." The reference here is to their illustrious forefathers, whether nearer or more remote—the patriarchs of their nation—such as Abraham, Isaac, Jacob, Joseph, Moses, David,[2] etc. It is an honour to any nation to have had great, and wise, and good men among the founders and upholders of their state. It is wrong to be proud, but it is right to be thankful that such men as Wallace and Bruce, Knox and Melville, were among our forefathers. But no nation was ever so honoured in this respect as the Jews. No other nation had for its father the friend of God, and the father of all who believe. "Time would fail us," as the apostle says,[3] "to tell of Gideon, and of Barak, and Samson, and Jephthae, and David, and Samuel, and of the prophets."

But a still higher honour belonged to the Israelites than any or all of these: "Of them, as concerning the flesh, Christ"—the Messiah, the great, promised, Divinely-appointed, and Divine Deliverer—"came, who is over all, God blessed for ever." This was the highest honour that could be conferred on a nation, that the Divinity should become incarnate among them. This was the subject of Old Testament prophecy: In Abraham's seed all the nations of the earth were to be blessed; the Great Prophet was to be raised up from among the Israelitish people; the Everlasting King was to be the

[1] Psa. cxlvii. 19, 20. [2] Acts ii. 29. [3] Heb. xi. 32.

Son of David. And the predictions had been fulfilled: "Jesus Christ, the Son of God, was the Son of David, the Son of Abraham."[1]

The apostle plainly intimates in the words, "as concerning the flesh," that the Messiah who was promised, and now had come, was possessed of a nature superior to the human. These words imply that, while "concerning the flesh" He came of the Jews, in some other respects He did not come of them: "His goings forth had been of old, from everlasting." He here repeats what he said in the beginning of the Epistle,[2] that Jesus, who, according to the flesh, was the Son of David, according to the Spirit of Holiness, was, and was proved to be, the Son of God. He who, as concerning the flesh, came of the Jews, is "over all, God blessed for ever."

This is one of the most distinct statements of our Lord's proper deity that is to be found in Scripture; and, therefore, it is not to be wondered at, if, on the part of the enemies of this doctrine, everything which learning and ingenuity can do has been done to explain it away. Some, without proof, in opposition to most abundant evidence, will have it that the word *God* is an interpolation; others, by an utterly unwarranted transposition, would read, 'Of whom, or whose, is God over all, blessed for ever;' while others, in opposition to the uniform usage of Scripture, consider the last clause of the verse as a doxology addressed to God the Father. There can be no reasonable doubt that our version most accurately renders the apostle's meaning.[3]

The doctrine here taught, when he says, "He is over all," is just what the apostle teaches us elsewhere, when he tells us that Jesus Christ is the Prince of the whole creation, before all things; that by Him all things consist; that He upholdeth all things by the word of His power; that He has a name above every name—a name at which every knee is to bow, and every tongue confess that He is Lord.[4]

[1] Matt. i. 1.

[2] Chap. i. 3, 4.

[3] See Wardlaw *On the Socinian Controversy*, Pye Smith's *Scriptural Doctrine*, Moses Stuart *in loc.*

[4] Col. i. 15, 17; Heb. i. 3; Phil. ii. 6-11.

He is not only "over all," but "*God* over all"—God in no inferior or secondary sense, but, as the prophet says, "the mighty God;"[1] as Paul elsewhere says, "the great God our Saviour;"[2] and as John says, "the true God and eternal life."[3]

And He is "blessed for ever." He is the proper object of religious worship, and will be acknowledged to be so for ever. He has been thus blessed by innumerable multitudes ever since these words were written. Who can estimate the numbers of those who at this moment are blessing Him on earth? And the ear of faith can hear the voice of many angels around the throne, and of the living creatures, and of the elders, and the surrounding host of redeemed spirits, "loud as of numbers without number," saying: "Worthy is the Lamb that was slain to receive power, and riches, and wisdom, and strength, and honour, and glory, and blessing." And yet a little while, and every creature that is in heaven, and on the earth, and under the earth, shall be heard saying, Blessing, and honour, and glory, and power, be unto Him that sitteth on the throne, and unto the Lamb, for ever and ever."[4] There can be no reasonable doubt that Jesus Christ is here termed "God over all, blessed for ever;" and as little reasonable doubt that "God over all" means 'supreme God,' and that "blessed for ever" can be applied only to Him who is truly Divine.

Such were the circumstances which excited so deep an interest in the apostle's mind for the salvation of his countrymen! Should they not excite earnest desires in our hearts for the same object? Surely, when we think of the awful severity of the curse under which the great body of them still live and die; when we think of the high privileges which they once possessed; when we think that, through them, salvation has come to us; above all, when we think of them, as not only Paul's kinsmen, but the kinsmen of his and our Lord,—surely we should fervently pray and perseveringly labour for their salvation.

[1] Isa. ix. 6.
[2] Tit. ii. 13.
[3] 1 John v. 20.
[4] Rev. v. 12, 13.

Well does it become us to pray for those whose fathers for so many ages prayed for us. 'God of Abraham, Isaac, and Jacob, look down from heaven, and behold, from the habitation of Thy holiness and Thy glory, the descendants of Abraham Thy friend, still beloved for the father's sake. Pity their miseries; pardon their sins. Doubtless Thou art their Father, their Redeemer: Thy name is from everlasting. Return, for Thy servants' sakes, the tribes of Thine inheritance. O that Thou wouldst rend the heavens, and come down! Be not wroth very sore, O Lord; neither remember iniquity for ever. Let the natural branches be grafted in again to the true olive tree: Let the fulness of the Gentiles come in, and let all Israel be saved; and let them, through our mercy, obtain mercy: And as the casting away of them was the reconciling of us Gentiles, let the receiving of them again be to us life from the dead.'

β. The blessings from which the unbelieving Jews were excluded never promised to them.

Let us proceed to examine somewhat more closely the apostle's vindication of the Divine conduct, in the rejection and punishment of the unbelieving Jews: "Not as though the word of God hath taken none effect."[1] Interpreters have differed as to the reference of the phrase, "the word of God;" and, in consequence of this, as to the rendering of the clause. Some refer "the word of God" to the prophetic threatenings, or to the doom pronounced on the unbelieving Jews for their rejection of Christ, and they would read the clause—'But it cannot be that the Divine word of threatening should not be fulfilled.' They connect this clause either with the apostle's wish, or with his enumeration of the privileges of Israel. In the first case, the force of the assertion is—'I indeed could wish to secure, were it practicable, the happiness of Israel, even by the sacrifice of my own—by becoming a victim for them—but it cannot be. The doom has been pronounced, and it must

[1] Ver. 6.

be executed. The curse was not causeless, and it must come.' In the second, the force is, 'These are indeed great privileges, but they are not such as can bar the fulfilment of the threatenings against those who, abusing them, reject the Messiah.' There can be no doubt that the "word of God" may refer either to the word of threatening or the word of promise; but, had it referred to the word of threatening, we should have expected the apostle to have referred to such passages as Deut. xviii. 19, or Deut. xxviii., xxxii., or such as he quotes at chap. xi. 8, 9, namely, Isa. xxix. 10, vi. 9; Psal. lxix. 22, 23; instead of which we find him immediately referring to a variety of God's promises respecting his ancient people.

I think there is no reasonable doubt that our translators have rightly rendered the words—"Not as though the word of God hath taken none effect." In this case, it is obvious that the sentence is elliptical; and the proper way of supplying the ellipsis seems to be this: 'The Jewish people are, notwithstanding all their privileges, accursed by Christ; but it does not follow from this that the Divine promise has had none effect—fallen to the ground—failed of its accomplishment.' It is just as if the apostle had said, after his usual manner, 'What shall we say then? that the word of God has fallen to the ground? God forbid.' The apostle here reverts to a subject which he had lightly touched on, before, in the commencement of the third chapter, ver. 2, 3—the apparent failure of the Divine promise in reference to the posterity of Abraham, on the supposition that the Jews, if they did not receive the Divine method of justification, would forfeit the Divine favour, and not enjoy the blessings obtained and bestowed by the Messiah. In the passage referred to, he contents himself with strongly *asserting* that, even in this case, the faithfulness of God would remain inviolate; and that *He* would prove true, whoever became liars. In the passage before us, what he had spoken of as a supposition, he now speaks of as a fact; and, not content with *asserting*, he elaborately *proves*, that the rejection of the Jews, on account of their unbelief, was perfectly consistent with the rightly understood declarations of the Divine word respecting Abraham and his seed, and also with the perfections of the Divine character, and the dispensations of the Divine Providence in former ages.

"The word of God" is the promise of God. In this sense, the phrase is often used in the Old Testament, *e.g.* Psal. cvi. 12, cxix. 25. The promise particularly referred to is probably the all-comprehensive promise, "I will be a God to thee, and to thy seed after thee,"—a promise which includes all the blessings to be obtained and bestowed by the Messiah in time and in eternity. This word of promise might seem to have had no effect—to have failed of accomplishment—to have fallen to the ground, according to the Hebrew idiom, if, as the apostle had intimated, the great body of his countrymen, instead of being blessed as the people of God, had, on account of their unbelief, become an anathema—separated from the people of God, accursed by Christ—the Messiah, in whom alone men can be truly blessed. The Jews thought that, on such a supposition, there would undoubtedly be a breach of promise. They held that the blessings under the Messiah were their promised, chartered inheritance; and that, if the Gentiles shared in them at all, it could only be by their becoming Jews; and they, of course, held that Paul's doctrine could not possibly be true. The apostle was ready enough to admit that no doctrine could be true which implied the possibility, far more the fact, of the violation of a Divine promise: but he maintained that the word of promise, both in its meaning and reference, was misapprehended by the Jewish Doctors; and that, when rightly understood, it was perfectly in harmony with his statement. Notwithstanding the lamentable facts of the general rejection of the Messiah by the Jews, and God's rejection of the unbelievers, who formed the great body of the nation, His word of promise to Abraham respecting his seed remained inviolate and inviolable.

The principle which reconciles the word of God with what, at first view, may appear a violation of it, is that stated in the second clause of the 6th verse—"For they are not all Israel who are of Israel." They who are "of Israel" are the natural descendants of Jacob. 'These,' says the apostle, '"are not all Israel"—"the Israel of God"—Israelites indeed—God's peculiar people in the highest sense—"the godly whom he has set apart for Himself"—the people who, like their great ancestor, have power like princes with God.' The apostle's assertion is, not that the whole body of the Israelites did not constitute the whole body of the spiritual people of God, but that the whole body of the Israelites was not included in the body of the people of God. Both are truths. There were those in the true Israel who were not of Israel, and there were those of Israel who were not in the true Israel. But it is the last of these assertions the apostle's argument requires, and which he proceeds to illustrate. According to the apostle, Abraham, Isaac, and Jacob were the spiritual fathers of believers only. To themselves the great promise was made only as *believers;* and this is equally true as to their spiritual seed. So far as this promise is concerned, they were the spiritual fathers of a spiritual posterity—consisting, for many ages, chiefly of individuals from among their natural posterity—but still only of that portion of them who were believers, and embracing also all true believers, though not of Jewish descent. The promises of spiritual blessings were made to Abraham and his seed;[1] but they were made to him and to them, not "through the law, but through the righteousness of faith:"[2] so that Abraham was not only "the father of all who believe, though they be not circumcised," but also "the father of circumcision"—of circumcised persons, only "to them who were not of the circumcision only, but who also walked in the steps of that faith of our father Abraham which he had, being yet uncircumcised."[3] "They which are of faith," they only, "are blessed with faithful Abraham."[4] And when the promised Messiah was come, then they who were *His* by believing in Him—"they," they only, "were Abraham's seed, and heirs according to the promise."[5] The promise was "sure to all this seed," but only

[1] Gal. iii. 16. [2] Rom. iv. 13. [3] Rom. iv. 11, 12.
[4] Gal. iii. 9. [5] Gal. iii. 29.

to them.[1] The word of God did not fall to the ground: it stood fast.

To show that this was not a principle invented to serve a purpose, the apostle proceeds to show that, from the beginning of God's dispensations in reference to the Abrahamic family, this principle of restricting promises, couched in general terms, to a particular class of those to whom they might seem to refer, had been acted on. And first in the case of Abraham's family: "Neither, because they are the seed of Abraham, are they all children." The meaning and force of the apostle's remark here will be more apparent on a slight change in the version, which, according to very good authority, the words admit, if they do not demand,—'Nor that all the *children*, are the *seed*, of Abraham:' or, more in our idiom, 'All of Israel are not Israel; nor are all the *children* of Abraham his *seed*.' The promises are made to Abraham's "seed." But that is a phrase by no means so comprehensive as, or of equivalent meaning with, Abraham's children, his *descendants*. Abraham's *seed* was but a part of his descendants. This is plain from the words of Jehovah to Abraham, referred to by the apostle, "But in Isaac shall thy seed be called." Soon after Abraham's arrival in Canaan, "God appeared to him, and said, Unto thy seed will I give this land."[2] This is the first mention of Abraham's "seed." The promise was repeated on Lot's separating from Abraham.[3] We have an account of a further declaration of the promise in chap. xv. 4, etc. In the course of time, Abraham has a son by Hagar—Ishmael, whom it is likely he considered as the promised seed. Fourteen years after this, the promise is renewed, in a way which showed him that, if he entertained such an expectation, he was mistaken. A son by Sarah is promised; and while God promises to bless Ishmael, He says expressly, "My covenant will I establish with Isaac, whom Sarah shall bear to thee."[4] And when Abraham was grieved at Ishmael's dismissal from his paternal roof, "God

[1] Rom. iv. 16.
[2] Gen. xii. 7.
[3] Gen. xiii. 14-17.
[4] Gen. xvii. 2-21.

said to him," in the words here quoted, "In Isaac shall thy seed be called,"'—*q.d.* 'The descendants of Isaac are those to whom my promise to thee and thy seed is to be performed.'

The import of that declaration is explained by the apostle in the 8th verse: "That is, they who are the children of the flesh, these are not the children of God: but the children of the promise, are counted for the seed." "The children of the flesh," is here obviously not distinctive of spiritual character, but an expression equivalent to natural descendants of Abraham. "The children of the promise," are the individuals to whom the Divine promise refers—children who, but for the Divine promise, would never have existed. And the principle laid down by the apostle is a general one. 'It is not merely as natural descendants of Abraham that men obtain the adoption, or become the children of God, whether in the lower sense in which Israel is said to have been God's son, and to have had the adoption,[2]—or in the higher sense, in which believers are said to be the children of God, and to receive the adoption of sons,[3]—but as persons who are the subjects of a specific promise.' That this was the case in Abraham's family is plain: "for," says the apostle, "this is the word of promise, 'At this time I will come, and Sarah shall have a son.'" In references to the Old Testament occurring in the New, it is no uncommon thing for the whole passage referred to not to be quoted. This seems the case here. The words cited are from Gen. xviii. 10. They are not verbally coincident either with the Hebrew original or the Greek translation, but they are strictly accordant with the meaning of both: "This is the word of promise"—the account of the promise. The full account of the promise is not in the eighteenth, but in the seventeenth chapter. There is first the general promise;[4] and then there is the limitation of the promise to one part of his descendants—his seed.[5]

The appositeness of this reference to the apostle's object is

[1] Gen. xxi. 12. [2] Ver. 4. [3] Gal. iv. 5.
[4] Ver. 1–10. [5] Ver. 15–21.

obvious. The Jews said, 'If, according to your doctrine, the great body of the Israelites are devoted to destruction for their rejection of Jesus Christ—shut out from the blessings to be obtained and conferred by Messiah, then the promises of God to Israel have failed of accomplishment.' 'No,' says the apostle; 'on the same principle you might argue that the promise of God to give Canaan to Abraham and his seed had been violated, because his descendants in the lines of Ishmael and of the sons of Keturah were excluded from the promised possession.' But there is no failure of promise in either case. In neither case is the question, 'Are they the natural descendants of Abraham?' but, 'Are they "the seed"—the particular class of his descendants, natural or spiritual—to which the promise in question refers?'

The apostle produces a second, and a still more striking confirmation of his principle, from the history of the patriarch Isaac: "And not only this; but when Rebecca also had conceived by one, even by our father Isaac"[1]—(for a reason to be given immediately, we pass over at present the 11th verse, which is plainly parenthetic)—"it was said unto her, The elder shall serve the younger. As it is written, Jacob have I loved, but Esau have I hated."[2]

"Not only so," is a common formula of transition with the apostle, and here is equivalent to, 'And not only were not all the children of Abraham his seed—not only in his case were not the children of the flesh counted for the seed, but the children of the promise.' It is equally clear that all Isaac's children were not his seed; not his children of the flesh, but only his children of the promise, were reckoned for the seed. To Isaac, as to Abraham, were given promises, couched in general terms, of blessings to be bestowed on his posterity. Of these promises we have an account, Gen. xxvi. 3, 4, 24: "Unto thee, and unto thy seed, I will give all these countries; and I will perform the oath which I sware unto Abraham thy father: And I will make thy seed to multiply as

[1] Ver. 10. [2] Ver. 12.

the stars of heaven, and will give unto thy seed all these countries." "I am with thee, and will bless thee, and multiply thy seed, for my servant Abraham's sake." Now, a cursory reader might think that these promises secured the blessings to which they referred to the whole of Isaac's posterity. But what is the truth? Isaac had two sons, born at the same time, of the same mother; and, previously to their birth, which was miraculously announced to their mother, it was said, "The elder shall serve the younger,"[1]—a declaration assigning to the younger the birthright, and limiting the fulfilment of the promise to the line of his posterity. The divine oracle is to be found Gen. xxv. 23: "Two nations are in thy womb, and two manner of people shall be separated from thy bowels; and the one people shall be stronger than the other people; and the elder shall serve the younger."

Nothing can be plainer, from the consideration of this passage, than that the oracle had a principal reference, not to Jacob and Esau as individuals, but to the nations which were respectively to descend from them—not directly to spiritual state and character, but to external advantages and privileges. Esau, as an individual, never was a servant to Jacob; on the contrary, he seems to have been possessed of much greater wealth and power than his younger brother. But the Edomites were the servants of the Israelites. The Edomites were not the people of Jehovah; the Israelites were. The Edomites did not inherit the promised land; the Israelites did. The Edomites were reduced to the state of tributaries by

[1] "Vocc. רַב et צָעִיר denotare (ut Job. xxx. 1; xxxii. 9; Gen. xliii. 33; xlviii. 14; Jos. vi. 26; 1 Kings xvi. 34) magnum et parvum ætate, igitur natu majorem et minorem, eaque referenda ad gentes, quæ ex utero Ribcæ prodire dicuntur ita, ut sit aliquando una altera valentior, non solum parallelismus indicat, verum etiam consilium scriptoris, historicè exponendi, jurum primogeniti beneficia ex Dei decreto esse collata in Hebraeos per Jacobum, gentis Hebraeæ patriarcham, neque vero in Edomitas per Esavum, Edomitarum progenitorem. Quocirca non video, cur rectius illa transferenda putaverint Clericus, Dathe, Schott (we may add Morrison), hac ratione: *potentior serviet impotenti*."—SCHUMANN, Genesis Heb. et Graec., p. 380.

David; and though they threw off the yoke in the reign of Jehoram, they were permanently subdued by John Hyrcanus.[1]

This, then, is the apostle's statement. Though a general promise was made to Isaac's posterity, yet all his descendants were not put in possession of the promised blessings. The general promise was limited to a portion of his posterity. To them it was fulfilled, and the word of God did not fail of taking effect, though the Edomites did not enjoy the privileges of the chosen people. They were "children of the flesh"—natural descendants of Isaac, as well as the Israelites,—but they were not "the children of the promise." The promise was not made in reference to them, and therefore to them it could not be broken.

The apostle adds another citation from the Old Testament, as to the different manner in which the two classes of Isaac's natural descendants were treated by Jehovah: "As it is written, Jacob have I loved, but Esau have I hated."[2] This passage is quoted from the prophet Malachi:[3] "I have loved you, saith the Lord; yet ye say, Wherein hast Thou loved us? Was not Esau Jacob's brother? saith the Lord: yet I loved Jacob, and I hated Esau, and laid his mountains and his heritage waste for the dragons of the wilderness." Here, as in the former case, it is plain that the words, Jacob and Esau, are used not to denote the individuals of whom they were the proper names, but the nations which sprung from them, the Israelites and the Edomites; just as Elam is used for the Persians, and Aram for the Assyrians. And the love and hatred here mentioned, are descriptive of the different, and in many respects opposite, characters of the Divine dispensations by which these two nations, in the course of their history, were distinguished. Israel was loved. That nation was blessed with numerous and important privileges, of which we have a comprehensive summary in Deut. vii. 6–8, as well as in the preceding context. Esau—*i.e.* the Edomites, was hated.

[1] 2 Sam. viii. 14; 2 Kings viii. 20, 22; Jos. Ant. xiii. 9, 1.

[2] Ver 13.

[3] Chap. i. 2, 3.

How we are to understand this, we are instructed by the prophet himself. "Their mountains and their heritage were laid waste for the dragons of the wilderness;" and all their attempts to restore their country to a flourishing state were to be abortive. "They shall build," says Jehovah, "but I will throw down; and they shall call them, The border of wickedness, and, The people against whom the Lord hath indignation for ever." The word "hate," does not necessarily signify malignant feeling. Indeed, in this sense, the word is not applicable to the Divinity at all. When God is said to hate individuals, the meaning is, they are the objects of His moral disapprobation, the subjects of His judicial condemnation. When He is said, as here, to *hate* a nation, it signifies either, that for wise and good reasons He does not bestow on them such high favours as, in the exercise of His sovereignty, He bestows on others; or that, on account of their sins, He punishes them. Of the manner in which this word hate, especially when opposed to love, should be understood, an examination of the following passages will help you to form a just judgment:—Gen. xxix. 31–33; Deut. xxi. 15; Prov. xiii. 24; Luke xiv. 26, compared with Matt. x. 37; John xii. 25. The meaning, then, of the passage is obvious. While the Israelites, the descendants of Jacob, were treated as the peculiar favourites of God—the Edomites, the descendants of Esau, were neglected; no revelation was given to them, no covenant formed with them. The Israelites were the Divine commonwealth, and the Edomites were aliens. And the bearing which these facts, stated by Moses and Malachi, have on the apostle's argument, is direct and powerful. The exclusion of the Edomites, though natural descendants of Isaac, from the fulfilment of a promise couched in general terms, but which we know was originally intended only for a part of his natural descendants, did not surely argue any violation of the Divine faithfulness. The Jews would very readily admit this. No more, then, can we conclude that the word of promise which we know was made to Abraham and his seed, "not through the law, but through the righteousness of faith," has "not taken effect," because it has not been fulfilled to men who were Abraham's seed "through the law," but who, by disbelieving the Divine report respecting *Him* who was, on the ground of His expiatory sacrifice, to justify many, showed that they were not His seed "through the righteousness of faith." How could it fail of accomplishment, by the blessing not being bestowed on those to whom it had never been promised? The promise is "sure to all the seed," and it is not violated though the blessing is not bestowed on those who are not the seed.

The apostle's argument does not terminate with the case of Isaac's descendants. It is interrupted by a discussion in reference to what he calls (ver. 11) "the purpose of God according to election," introduced by the notice of two remarkable circumstances in the event in the history of Isaac's family—the fact of Esau and Jacob being twin brothers, and the oracle respecting the different destinies of the nations which should spring from them being uttered previously to their birth; a discussion having, as we shall see, a very important bearing on the apostle's general object. That digression, if it can be so called, reaches down to ver. 24. In ver. 25, I apprehend the apostle resumes his argument, and concludes it with the 29th verse of the chapter.

I am quite aware that the great body of interpreters consider this paragraph of the chapter—ver. 26–29—as an illustration of the 25th verse, and as showing that, according to the prophets, the true Israel under the Messiah should neither be the whole Israelitish people, nor composed only of the natural descendants of Jacob, but should be the "called ones," not of the Jews only, but also of the Gentiles. But to this mode of exposition there are insurmountable objections; for, in the first place, the passages from Hosea, and from Isaiah x. 22, 23, do not refer to the Gentiles at all, but to the ten tribes carried captive into Assyria; and secondly, the passages from Isaiah, with the exception of the last, do not refer to the Messianic times at all. Besides, the formula of quotation in the beginning of ver. 25—"as He saith *also* in Hosea"—is not what would naturally be used in bringing forward the first of a number of Old Testament passages in proof of a position. I therefore am constrained to think this one of the passages to which Mr Locke's sagacious remark applies:—"Paul often breaks off in the middle of an argument to let in some new thought suggested by his own words; which, having pursued and explained as far as conduced to his present purpose, he resumes the thread of discourse, and goes on with it, without taking any notice that he returns again to what he had before been saying; though sometimes it be so far off that it may well have slipped out of his mind, and requires a very attentive reader to observe, and so bring the disjointed members together as to make up the connection, and see how the scattered parts of the discourse hang together in a coherent, well-agreeing sense, that makes it all of a piece."[1]

The discussion about "the purpose of God according to election," commenced in the 11th verse, clearly closes in the 24th verse; and in the 25th, the apostle reverts to the main line of argument. Indeed, the phraseology seems to indicate this: "As he saith also." This is not the way in which a first illustration would be introduced. The word "*also*" naturally leads the mind back to a former quotation, made for a purpose which the writer is still prosecuting. Indeed it deserves notice, that in every case, if we are but sufficiently attentive, we shall find in the apostle's writings, notwithstanding the parentheses in which they abound, something like the loops and taches in the curtains of the tabernacle, which distinctly enough intimate the manner in which the different parts of his discussion are to be connected together. This quotation in the 25th verse, and those which follow, are not meant to prove that the rejection of the Jews and the conversion of the Gentiles were the subjects of Old Testament prediction. This he does abundantly bye and bye. But they are intended to complete the apostle's argument, that God's excluding the great body of the Jews from the blessings procured and bestowed by

[1] Locke's Pref. to Par. and Notes on the Epp. of Paul.

the Messiah, is no violation of God's promise to Abraham, Isaac, and Jacob, and their seed. I therefore leave the whole digression respecting "the purpose of God according to election," as a subject of subsequent consideration, and go on to consider the conclusion of the argument, that "the word of God has not become of none effect, in the general rejection of the Israelitish people, because they are not all Israel who are of Israel."

The apostle has made the history of the family of Abraham and of Isaac bear powerfully on his argument. He now proceeds to show, that in the line of Jacob also, promises, seemingly general, had not been fulfilled, even as to large portions of the natural descendants of that patriarch. His first reference is to the captivity of the ten tribes—the majority of the descendants of Israel—who, for their idolatry, had been rejected by God. To them the quotation from Hosea undoubtedly refers [1] —"As he saith also in Osee" (chap. ii. 23), "I will call them My people, who were not My people; and her beloved, who was not beloved." "And" (chap. i. 10) "it shall come to pass, that in the place in which it was said to them, Ye are not My people, there shall they be called the children of the living God." In these words the apostle intimates to the Jews, in the least offensive way, that the majority of their nation had been for ages regarded by God as not His people; and though a time was coming when they should be again regarded by Him as His people, it had not then come—it has not yet come. We have a very striking account and vindication of this exclusion of a great body of Israelites from the peculiar privileges of God's covenant people in 2 Kings xvii. 7-23. If God's rejection of the ten tribes for their idolatry was no breach of promise, how could His rejection of the majority of the Jews in the Messianic age, for their unbelief, be a proof that His word had become of none effect?

The next quotation made by the apostle, in illustration of

[1] Erasmus, Musculus, Piscator, Camero, Grotius, Limborch, Doddridge, Morus, Terrot, Olshausen, Fritzsche.

his principle that the exclusion of the majority of the Jews from the Messianic blessings did not infer any violation of the Divine promise, is taken from the prophet Isaiah: "Esaias also crieth concerning Israel, Though the number of the children of Israel be as the sand of the sea, a remnant shall be saved: for He will finish the work, and cut it short in righteousness; because a short work will the Lord make upon the earth." These words have been ordinarily explained as if they were a prediction of the small number of the Jews who should embrace the Messiah, and be saved through Him, and of the sudden and dreadful punishment which should fall on the unbelieving and impenitent majority. But that this is not correct interpretation must be evident to every one who reads carefully the passage referred to, as it occurs in the book of the prophet—chap. x. 22, 23. The prediction obviously refers to the Ephraimitish people—Israel, as distinguished from Judah—and to the Assyrian conquest and captivity. The words seem quoted by the apostle from memory. They do not exactly correspond either with the Hebrew original or the Greek translation, but they give the import of both. The meaning of the words is, that although, at the time the oracle was uttered, the Israelites were very numerous, only a small part of them—such as returned to Jehovah, and joined themselves to the kingdom of Judah—should be saved from the impending destruction; the great body of them should be destroyed or carried into captivity, and cease to be the people of the Lord; for God had determined to execute, and that suddenly, His righteous judgment on that guilty people in the midst of the land. The object of the quotation is obvious. If God, without violation of promise, had in a former age treated the majority—almost all the ten tribes, the greater part of the Israelitish nation—as if they had not been his people, surely the strikingly analogous dispensation in reference to the Jews in the primitive age, could not imply that the word of God had become of none effect.

But God had not only dealt in this way with the Ephraimitish people who had, to a great extent, by rebelling against the divinely-appointed family of David, and forsaking the temple at Jerusalem, removed themselves from the protection of His peculiar providence, but He had also dealt in a similar way with the Jewish people. To this fact, of much importance to his argument, the apostle turns our attention by his next quotation :[1] "And as Esaias said *before*," *i.e.* in a part of his book preceding that already quoted,[2] "Except the Lord of Sabaoth had left us a seed, we had been as Sodoma, and had been made like unto Gomorrhah." These words, too, have been considered as a prediction of the conversion of a small portion of the Jews to Christ in the primitive age, and the destruction of the great body of that people. But when we look at the passage as it stands in the Old Testament, it is impossible not to see that it has no reference to these events. It is a description of the miserable state of the kingdom and people of Judah under Ahaz. In that most disastrous reign, not merely did Pekah the Ephraimitish king, but the Syrians, the Idumeans, and the Philistines, lay waste the land. In one day Pekah's army put to death 120,000 men ; and the Assyrians, whom Ahaz called in to his assistance, completed the devastation.[3] To use the words of Hezekiah, "The wrath of God was upon Judah and Jerusalem, and He delivered them to trouble, to astonishment, and to hissing. Our fathers have fallen by the sword; and our sons, and our daughters, and our wives, are in captivity for this."[4] It is with regard to these evils that Isaiah says, "Except the Lord had left to us a very small remnant, we should have been as Sodom, and we should have been like unto Gomorrah." The inference to be drawn from the passage then is, 'If, without the violation of His promise, God has in a former age, for abundantly sufficient reasons, treated the majority of the Jewish people as if they were not in covenant with Him, He may, for equally good reasons, in this age, treat a majority of them as if they were not His peculiar people, without His word of promise becoming of none effect.' Such is the argument, and it seems a thoroughly

[1] Ver. 29.
[2] Chap. i. 6–9.
[3] 2 Chron. xxviii. 5, 6, 7, 17, 18.
[4] 2 Chron. xxix. 8.

sound and conclusive one. Whether we look to the history of Abraham's family, or of Isaac's, or of the Israelites as a nation divided into the kingdoms of Israel and of Judah, we find a promise, which might seem to be universal in its application, fulfilled to only a part, in many cases to only a small part, of those to whom it might seem to refer, while the rest were treated as if no promise had been made to them. In these cases, we do not conclude that the word of God has become of none effect; and why should that conclusion be drawn in the case of the rejection of the Messiah by the great body of His countrymen, and the sad consequences which had resulted from it?—The apostle's statements respecting "the purpose of God according to election," and their bearing on his argument, must now be considered.

But first, let us learn from the apostle's mode of treating his subject, to compare one Divine dispensation with other Divine dispensations, if we would understand the true character of God's moral government—to compare dispensations in which we have a deep, direct, personal interest, with others with which we are not so immediately concerned. By following this course, we shall often find that what we counted an exception from the ordinary mode of Divine procedure, is indeed an exemplification of it; that what we may find it difficult to reconcile with His word or work, with His wisdom or righteousness or mercy, is perfectly consistent with all these; and that, in dealing with us, He acts according to the same great principles of sovereign kindness or strict justice, by which all the operations of His moral government are guided.

We are ready enough to acknowledge the absurdity of the conduct of the Jews in building their hopes upon their natural descent from Abraham and Isaac and Jacob, in supposing themselves secure of final happiness by promises made to Abraham's seed, not through the law, but through the righteousness of faith—to Israel, not after the flesh, but after the spirit, and in calling in question the Divine faithfulness, if these expectations were not realized. But it is to be feared, that an equally presumptuous and dangerous, and still more inexcusable, mistake prevails extensively among nominal Christians. To cherish the hope of salvation merely because we are Christians by profession, is still more absurd than it was in the Israelite to presume that all was safe with him because he was a descendant of Jacob. There were many temporal promises made to Israel after the flesh; and even the spiritual promises, which were restricted to the spiritual Israel, were expressed in language which easily admitted of the false interpretation put upon them. But where is the promise made to men as mere professors of Christianity? Is it not distinctly stated, that the confession with the mouth, connected with salvation, is that which springs from faith in the heart? All are not Christians who are called by the name of Christ. He who is not in Christ is not a Christian. He who has not the Spirit of Christ is none of His. The Jews perished, and perished justly, who rested their hope of salvation on the ground of their natural descent. And the nominal Christian, who is resting his hope of salvation on anything but the free grace of God manifested through the atonement of Christ revealed in the Gospel, and cordially trusted to in the exercise of an enlightened faith, shall, inasmuch as his delusion is still more willful, meet with a severer judgment and a deeper perdition.

Let us guard against the disposition manifested by the unbelieving Jews, to call in question the rectitude of the Divine administration in the method of human salvation. Let us never quarrel with the Divine dispensations, or suffer our hearts to fret against the Lord. Let us never impiously and absurdly call Him before the tribunal of our judgment; but readily owning that destruction is our due, and that it is of His mercies that we have not long ago been consumed, let us submit to the righteousness of God, rejoicing that it is not more certain that he that believeth not shall be damned, than it is that he that believeth shall be saved. Let us accept salvation—full, free salvation—in the only way in which it becomes Him to offer it, and the only way in which it is possible for us ever to receive it—as the gift of sovereign kindness; counting it most meet that every ground of glorying should be cut off from man, the saved sinner, who owes all his miseries to himself, and must owe his salvation to God, and that to Him of whom, and through whom, are all things in the wondrous economy of man's redemption, should be glory undivided and infinite for ever. Amen.

γ. *The Blessings from which the unbelieving Jews were excluded, were Free Gifts, bestowed, in Sovereign Grace, on those who, in Sovereign Grace, were chosen to receive them.*

We now enter on the apostle's illustration of the second principle—that these blessings were free gifts, to which none had, or could have, a claim of right—free gifts bestowed, in sovereign grace, on them who had been chosen in sovereign grace, and prepared to receive them. This principle, along with the *third*—that the evils coming on unbelieving Israel, were but the infliction of richly merited and long deferred punishment —forms the subject of the paragraph, in a great measure parenthetical, from ver. 11–24.

Let us proceed to examine that paragraph, with all the attention in our power. It has been the great battle-field of the two principal parties of philosophical theologians for fourteen centuries. It is here that, under their mighty leaders, Augustine and Calvin, on the one side, and Pelagius and Arminius on the other, numerous, powerful (well-armed with learning and logic), expert, zealous combatants have measured their strength in contests respecting Divine sovereignty and human freedom,—

> "Reasoning high
> Of Providence, foreknowledge, will, and fate,
> Fix'd fate, free will, foreknowledge absolute."

And in many cases

> "Have found no end in wand'ring mazes lost."

We will not say, with our great poet, of such discussions, that they are

> "Vain wisdom *all*, and false philosophy;"[1]

[1] Milton.—*Paradise Lost.*

For we do hold, that the grand characteristic principles of Augustinianism and Calvinism are real wisdom—the true philosophy of Christianity—the theory which best binds together "the facts" (for the doctrines of Christianity are "facts"), in which the substance of our holy religion consists. But it must be admitted that, on both sides in the great conflict, there has often been discovered a greater anxiety to wrest a passage out of the hands of an antagonist, and to convert what he was using as argument for, into an objection against his system, than to discover what was the meaning of the apostle's words, and the design he intended them to serve. The whole paragraph, to a person moderately acquainted with these controversies, looks like a field, whose natural aspect has been much disfigured by a combat between warring armies, and he wishes almost that he could forget all he knows about these controversies, that he might be enabled to look at the passage, just as it would have struck a pious, attentive reader before Pelagius disturbed the Christian world with his pestilent theories, and rendered necessary the elaborate, and on the whole triumphant, refutations by such men as Augustine, Calvin, and Jonathan Edwards. I shall endeavour, in the following observations, to keep myself to my proper duty, that of an interpreter—bringing nothing into the inspired statement, and bringing all out of it that I find in it.

The Jews entertained, in direct opposition to many plain declarations in their own Scriptures, the foolish opinion, that the Divine regards towards them were founded on the merits of their ancestors, and that God, on account of the merits of these great and good men, had bound Himself never to forsake their children. To lay low these proud imaginations, by showing that God has, and has asserted a sovereign right to give, or withhold, or withdraw His favours, as He sees fit, is the apostle's object in the paragraph, on the illustration of which we are about to enter.

For introducing a discussion of this subject, the facts in reference to the limitation of the promise, expressed in general terms, afforded a favourable opportunity. With some appearance of justice, it might be said, that a ground of the preference of the line of Abraham's descendants by Isaac, to that of his descendants by Ishmael, was to be found both in the different conditions of Sarah the free-woman, the wife of Abraham, and Hagar the bond-maid, his concubine, and in the bad disposition of Ishmael, discovered in his treatment of his younger brother. But here an oracle is delivered respecting two nations, to spring from two twin brothers, having the same father and the same mother—an oracle delivered previously to their birth, and, therefore, before their good or bad dispositions and conduct could lay a foundation for treating them differently, on the ground of personal desert. Of the descendants of Esau and Jacob, the twin-sons of Isaac and Rebecca, while they were "not yet born," and had "neither done any good or evil," "it was said"—disregarding the claim of primogeniture—"The elder shall serve the younger"—an oracle, of whose accomplishment we have an account in the words of the Prophet Malachi. Now, says the apostle, all this was so ordered, "that the purpose of God according to election might stand."

"The purpose of God" is His determination. It may either refer to the act of determination, or to the thing determined. It seems here to refer to the fact that God *determines* to do what He does; that He acts according to previous council or decree; that the performance of the promise to a part only of Abraham's posterity, and of Isaac's posterity, was the result of a Divine purpose. This purpose of God is described as being "according to election, not of works, but of Him that calleth." "Election" is a word that sometimes signifies the mental, inward act of choice, by which one person or thing is preferred to another, or the external act of selection, in which this inward act finds expression; and, at other times, the dignity or blessing to which the favoured individuals are chosen; and, at other times also, the objects of choice—the persons preferred. It is used in the place before us as descriptive of the act of choice. It matters little whether you refer it to the inward or the outward act—the one is but the expression of the other; but, in strict propriety, it must be referred to the first, as it is viewed as conjoined with the purpose.

This "election" is said to be "not of works, but of Him who calleth;" for the words, "not of works, but of Him that calleth," qualify and define the term "election." The choice is not founded on the works of the person chosen. The person chosen is chosen, not because he better deserves to be chosen than the person who is not chosen—desert, in the proper sense of the word, has nothing to do with the choice. The choice "is of Him that calleth." "He who calleth," is obviously another name for God; and He is thus designated, because it is by *calling* that God indicates His election. His calling Abraham out of Ur of the Chaldees—His calling Israel out of Egypt, were the acts in which He showed that they were the objects of His choice. The choice does not originate in anything in him that is chosen, but in Him who chooses. It has its cause in the Divine will. It is a choice for which we can assign no reason, but that God willed so to choose. Now, says the apostle, God's purpose to bestow peculiar blessings on certain individuals, was according to this choice—originating, not in any superior claim they had on His preference, but in His own sovereign, though most wise, will.

The order of the Divine decrees is a very high subject of thought. I instinctively shrink from speculating on it. But I confess I cannot bring any other sense out of the words of the apostle than this—that the purpose of God to confer blessings is based on, and regulated by, a choice of individuals—a choice for which we in vain seek for any cause out of Himself. The circumstances in reference to Isaac's posterity, were ordered to be as they were, that this great principle of the Divine conduct, in bestowing blessings on fallen man might *stand*, be upheld—namely, that His purpose to bestow blessings on men is not a mere general determination, but is "according" to a sovereign election of individuals on whom these blessings shall be bestowed—an election, "not of works, but of Him that calleth." The arrangement with regard to Abraham's family really proceeded on this principle; and the corresponding arrangement about Isaac's family was such as made it plain that this was not a peculiarity as to Abraham's family; but that, in this case also, "the purpose of God according to election" stood—remained,—"according to election, not of works, but of Him who calleth."

Indeed, this principle *stands—remains*, as a great characteristic feature of the Divine administration. The principle, that the Divine Being bestows benefits on some and withholds benefits from others—according to a purpose, founded on a selection, for which, ultimately, no reason can be assigned to us but His sovereign will, is manifested not only in His dealings with the Jews, or in reference to blessings connected with the spiritual and eternal interests of men, but in all His dispensations. Why have the inhabitants of Italy a finer climate than the inhabitants of Norway? Why is Europe so highly raised in privilege above Africa and Asia? Why have we a better government than the Turks? Why is one man possessed of higher intellectual powers, or of more extensive property, than another? Why is one nation blessed with the Gospel, while others are destitute of it? Why are different districts of the same country very variously privileged in this respect? Why is one man made the subject of the transforming, saving influence of the Divine Spirit, while another is left to the results of the development of the tendencies of his fallen nature? These are questions to which, when pressed home in reference to the ultimate cause and reason of these events, we are obliged to reply—'We know no reason that can be assigned, but that such is the will of God. That will is not—cannot be, a capricious one; it must ever work in union with love and wisdom; but, in many cases, we know, we can know nothing further than that such is the will of God.' "They err," says Hooker, "who say—who think, that of the will of God to do this or that, there is no other reason but His will. Many times no reason known"—he might have added *knowable*—"to us; but that there is no reason, I judge it most unreasonable to imagine, inasmuch as 'He worketh all things,' not only according to His will, but 'according to the counsel of

His will;' and whatsoever is done of counsel or wise resolution, has of necessity some reason why it should be done, albeit that reason be to us something so secret, that it forceth the wit of man to stand, as the blessed apostle, amazed thereat: 'Oh the depth of the riches, both of the wisdom and knowledge of God; how unsearchable are His judgments, and His ways past finding out!'"

In reference to this purpose of God, based on and regulated by an election, "not of works, but of Him who calleth," as exercised and manifested in the case of Esau and Jacob, and their descendants, the apostle asks, "What shall we say then? Is there unrighteousness with God?" and replies, "God forbid." "The apostle's argument, which we have already considered, vindicates the faithfulness of God in excluding the unbelieving Jews from the Messianic blessings. The argument he is now prosecuting, vindicates the equity of God, and shows that there is no unrighteousness in the dispensation. Is it inconsistent with equity to choose some individuals from among a class of individuals on whom to bestow undeserved blessings, all being equally destitute of claim on God, but for punishment—which is the case of the whole fallen family of man? Is it wrong to have a purpose to follow out this election to its object? Is it wrong actually to fulfil that purpose, and confer on these chosen ones blessings not conferred on those who were not chosen? What is there of unrighteousness in all this? This is what God did in the case of the Israelites and the Edomites. This is what God did with regard to one portion of Jews and Gentiles, and another portion of them. The unbelieving Jews were ready enough to acknowledge that there was nothing iniquitous in not giving to Edom what He gave to Israel; and if they but judged righteous judgment, they would see that, in giving to some Gentiles and Jews what they did not deserve, and in withholding this undeserved benefit from others, there was just as little cause for ascribing unrighteousness to God.

The apostle goes on to give an illustration of the "purpose of God according to election, not of works, but of Him who calleth," in the case of the Israelites themselves. He had already done this in the case of Israel and Edom. But the same principle is asserted and illustrated in the Divine conduct to Israel. The Israelites, immediately after the giving of the law, had committed the gross crime of idolatry, broken the covenant, forfeited its blessings, and exposed themselves to punishment. Moses earnestly besought God to forgive his guilty countrymen. It seems to have been in answer to his prayer that the declaration quoted by the apostle was made. Moses, like Paul, would have had, if possible, all offending Israel pardoned and saved, and would have submitted to any deprivation necessary to secure this. But God intimated to him, that with regard to some of them, He would "visit their sin upon them," and that others He would pardon; not because they were better than those who were punished, but because, in His sovereign kindness, He was disposed and determined to pardon them. "For He saith to Moses, I will have mercy on whom I will have mercy, and I will have compassion on whom I will have compassion."

The original words, both in the Hebrew and Greek, admit of various renderings and interpretations; but the apostle himself, by the inference he draws from them in the 18th verse, shows us how to understand them. The whole nation deserved punishment, and needed mercy, in the form of pardon. Now God was determined to allow justice to have its course with regard to some of them; and He was determined to show mercy to others by pardoning them; and His declaration is, that the reason why *any* are pardoned, and why *these* are pardoned, was to be found in His sovereign grace. "I will have mercy on those on whom I will"—choose, to "have mercy; I will have compassion on those on whom I will"—choose, to "have compassion." The two clauses are nearly, if not altogether, synonymous, and the reiteration is an example of the way in which emphasis is often given to a sentiment in the Holy Scriptures. There was no unrighteousness here. God gave to some what none deserved, and He inflicted on none anything but what all had deserved—and He did all this according to the purpose purposed in Himself—according to the counsel of His own will.

From the facts referred to in the declarations respecting Israel and Esau, and respecting sinning Israel to Moses, the apostle draws this inference[1]—"So then it is not of him that willeth, nor of him that runneth, but of God that showeth mercy." The reason why God bestows benefits on sinful man, is not in *man* but in God—not in man's merits in any form or degree—but entirely in mercy, sovereign mercy. The phrase *it is*, is equivalent to—this, the communication of blessings to men—took place. The peculiar expressions, "he that willeth," and "he that runneth," may possibly have been suggested by the history of Isaac's family. Isaac *willeth* to give Esau the blessing, and Esau *ran* to the field to obtain venison for his father, "that he might eat of it, and that his soul might bless him before his death;"[2] and yet the blessing was not thus obtained—it was given to Jacob. But if so, a mere allusion is meant; the sentiment is a general one. The ultimate reason why God confers benefits on men is not their desires and exertions—for true desires, right exertions, are God's work in man—but His own sovereign good pleasure. This is the origin of the blessing, and also of the desire and the exertion *through* which, though not *for* which, in most instances, the blessing is conferred.

I do not know any passage in the Bible that is better fitted to show the baselessness of the system which seeks the cause of election to salvation, in foreknown good works, than this argument from the case of Jacob and Esau. On that principle the apostle's reasoning has no force. His argument is that since, previously to the birth of Jacob and Esau, the fates of the nations respectively to descend from them, were determined, and proved to be determined by Divine declarations made before the birth of these patriarchs, the determination could not originate in the respective merits of these nations or their founders, but in the purpose of God according to election, —an argument which loses all its force and becomes a silly sophism, if the cause of the determination is to be found in

[1] Ver. 16. [2] Gen. xxvii. 1–5.

His foreknowledge of their respective characters—an argument which, if the apostle had held this view, he could never have used.

While we endeavour to vindicate the apostle's meaning from misrepresentation, let us also guard it against abuse. To conclude from this passage that it is to no purpose to use means in order to obtain Divine blessings, would be most unwarrantable, and, indeed, absurd. The discussion does not refer to the manner in which men are put in possession of Divine blessings, but to the principle in the Divine mind to which the communication of these blessings is to be traced. It is equally true that 'it is not of him that soweth, nor of him that watereth, but of God, that giveth the increase,'—that our harvests come. The fertility of any particular field, or of any particular season, is to be resolved ultimately into the sovereign will of God; but that is certainly no reason why men should not sow or water. There is an established order in the communications of the blessings of grace as well as of nature; but neither the one nor the other at all interferes with the sovereign freedom of His elections and operations, "who worketh all things according to the counsel of His own will."

The principles thus laid down and established clearly show, that the conferring of the Messianic privileges on believing Gentiles, and the exclusion of unbelieving Jews from these privileges, instead of being in any way inconsistent with the Divine character, were but exemplifications of that high sovereignty which God has uniformly exercised in conferring blessings on fallen man; and that on neither of these grounds had the Jews any reason to complain of a want of faithfulness or of equity in the Divine administration.

δ. The Evils inflicted on the Unbelieving Jews were the just Punishment of obstinate Transgression, richly deserved, long deferred.

But unbelieving Israel had not only, according to the apostle, been excluded from the Messianic blessings, but doomed to severe punishment, they had become "accursed." The two principles—that the Messianic blessings were never promised to unbelieving Jews; and that the Messianic blessings were the gifts of sovereign grace, to be conferred on those whom God, in sovereign grace, had chosen to be their possessors—sufficiently account for the giving of these blessings to believing Gentiles, and excluding from their possession unbelieving Jews, and clearly show that on these grounds the Jews had no ground of complaint. But how is it that they are to be so severely punished—to be *now* so severely punished? It is to meet this part of the case, I conceive, that the apostle makes the next citation from Old Testament Scripture: "For the Scripture saith unto Pharaoh, Even for this purpose have I raised thee up, that I might show My power in thee, and that My name might be declared through all the earth."[1] That the design of the apostle, in making this quotation, is to explain the reason of the severe punishment of the unbelieving Jews, seems obvious, from the manner in which he applies it in ver. 22.

"*For*," in this verse, does not import that this is a reason for, or a proof of, what is said in the previous verse. It is parallel with the *for* of the 15th verse, and is a further proof of the statement implied in the 14th verse. "The Scripture saith to Pharaoh" is equivalent to, 'In the Scripture we read that the Lord, by Moses, said to Pharaoh.' The passage quoted is Exod. ix. 16, and was spoken after the plague of boils, and before the plagues of hail, and locusts, and darkness, and the death of the first-born. The words cited immediately follow this threatening: "Thou shalt be cut off from the earth." The question of principal importance for ascertaining the meaning of this passage, which has been much disputed, is, What is the precise force of the expression translated "I have raised thee up?" Some interpret the word as meaning, 'I have brought thee into existence, 'I have created thee;'[2] others, 'I have raised thee to the throne of Egypt;'[3] others, 'I have excited thee,' 'I have given thee a preternatural obstinacy of will'—considered as equivalent to "hardened thy heart."

[1] Ver. 17. [2] Beza, Gomarus.
[3] Theodoret, Vatable, Bengel, etc.

None of these interpretations are satisfactory; for either they give a meaning to the word which usage does not support, or they bring out a sense which does not correspond with the context. The words seem to mean, 'I have raised thee up from the bed of affliction,' 'I have preserved thee.'[1] This is the sense given to the term by the most ancient versions;[2] and this sense suits, and is the only sense that suits, the context, either in Exodus or in the passage before us. The words were uttered after the plague of boils, of which, we cannot doubt, Pharaoh, as well as his people, was a partaker. Jehovah threatens him with still heavier judgments. He declares that the design of these judgments was, that Pharaoh might know that there was none like Jehovah in all the earth.

The words in Exodus which immediately precede those here quoted, have been considered by almost all learned interpreters, whatever their opinions on the Calvinistic question may be, as unhappily rendered in our version. They run thus: "For now will I stretch out My hand, that I may smite thee and thy people with pestilence; and thou shalt be cut off from the earth." Now, we know this did not take place. The words might be, and, according to the highest authority, ought to be, rendered: 'For, should I now stretch forth my hand, and smite thee with pestilence, thou wouldst be destroyed from the earth.'[3] God might have thus punished Pharaoh, but He did not choose to do so. He knew that Pharaoh would continue obstinate, in opposition to means most fitted to subdue his obstinacy; yet He raised him up—He made him stand—while so many about him were falling, "that," says He, "I might show My power in thee—by means of thee, and that My name might be declared throughout all the earth."

In inflicting punishment on Pharaoh, and in the measure of punishment inflicted, God was regulated by justice; but in

[1] Isa. xxxviii. 16; James v. 15.

[2] The LXX.; the Peschito-Syriac, and Ancient Arabic Versions; the Targum of Jonathan.

[3] Fagius, Drusius, Ainsworth, Grotius, Le Clerc, Dathe, Nordheimer.

the time and manner of His punishment there was a display of wise sovereignty. He might have justly punished him when this warning was given; but He thought fit to defer it, and not to inflict the deserved and long-deferred punishment, till, in the overthrow of the proud king and his hosts in the Red Sea, He showed forth His power, and made a display of His character which over all these regions must have drawn out the sentiment expressed by Jethro: "Now know I Jehovah to be greater than all gods; for, in the thing wherein men did proudly, He was above them." The design of the apostle seems to have been to let the Jews see, as in a glass, that the judgments coming on them were but the long deferred execution of righteous punishment for obstinate unbelief and disobedience, and that they had no cause to complain, if Jehovah exercised His sovereignty in the time and manner of the infliction of that punishment.

From this passage in reference to Pharaoh, in conjunction with the other instances of "the purpose of God according to election," the apostle draws a general conclusion in the 18th verse, "Therefore He hath mercy on whom He will have mercy, and whom He wills He hardens." This general conclusion seems to me to amount to this: that both in dispensing mercy and in withholding it, both in bestowing favours and inflicting judgments, God displays "His purpose according to election," or His sovereign free choice. While, in no case, does He violate faithfulness or equity in His dealings with His creatures, He so orders His dispensations, as that it may be apparent that "He works all things according to the council of His own will." While this seems plainly the general meaning of the verse, the phraseology, especially that of the second clause, seems to require some explication.

In the first clause there is no difficulty whatever. From the cases of Isaac and Ishmael, Jacob and Esau, the Israelites who were pardoned, and the Israelites who were punished, it appears that, in bestowing favours or withholding them, God acts out "His purpose according to election." "He has mercy on whom He wills"—chooses—is pleased—"to have mercy." He bestows blessings without reference to the merits of the persons on whom they are bestowed, and entirely according to the good pleasure of His will, which He has purposed in Himself. The last clause admits, and indeed requires a somewhat more extended illustration: "Whom He will He hardeneth." And the first thing to be done here is to ascertain, if possible, the meaning and reference of the term rendered "hardeneth."

It has been common to consider "*harden*" here as equivalent to what has been termed judicial obduration—the making men obstinate in their sins. There can be no doubt that when it is said Pharaoh hardened his heart—the meaning is Pharaoh abused those dispensations which were fitted to produce penitence and obedience, into means of strengthening his determination to oppose the will of God. And there can be as little doubt, that not only is Pharaoh said to harden his heart, but God is said to harden Pharaoh's heart;[1] and the penitent Israelites, when in the latter days they are to "seek the Lord and David their king," are represented as thus expostulating with God: "O Lord, why hast Thou hardened our hearts from Thy fear."[2] It may be asked how can God harden men's hearts? There can be no doubt that it would be utterly inconsistent with the holiness and equity of the Divine nature, by direct influence to produce or excite depraved principle in the mind of man, and then punish him for it. This were to act like a demon rather than a divinity. "Far be it from God that He should do this injustice, and from the Almighty that He should commit this iniquity." We know that Pharaoh hardened his own heart, and the Israelites are cautioned against hardening their hearts: and when God is said to do what men themselves do, and are responsible for doing, the meaning cannot be more than this, that God leaves men to the influence of their own corrupt mind, does not interfere to prevent lust from conceiving, or when it has conceived, from bringing forth sin; or when it is perfected from bringing forth death; that instead of interpos-

[1] Exod. vii. 3, ix. 12, x. 1, 20, 27, xi. 10.

[2] Is. lxiii. 17.

ing by the agency of His Spirit to prevent their thus becoming obstinate, He places them in circumstances which, though naturally fitted to produce a very different effect, are perverted into the means of fostering their obstinacy. And, if this be the meaning of the word, the apostle's assertion is, that God exercises His sovereignty equally in giving and withholding that Divine influence, which, in consequence of the depravity of man, is necessary to true repentance. And, however men may fret and quarrel, it will be difficult to show that there is anything unjust or unreasonable in all this. "May not," to use the language of a very sober-minded defender of this mode of explication, "the Judge of all the earth, when a rebellious creature, from enmity to Him and love of that which He abhors, has closed his own eyes and hardened his own heart, and deliberately preferred the delusions of the wicked one to the truth as it is in Jesus, say to such an one, 'Take thine own choice and its consequences; may He not do this without being any more the author of sin than the sun is the cause of cold and frost and darkness, because these are the results of the withholding of its influence?"[1]

But, while it thus appears that, even if understood in this way, the clause exhibits an important truth; I doubt exceedingly whether the term translated "*harden*" here, has any reference to judicial obduration. And the reasons of my doubt are these:—(1.) The word *harden*, when employed in this sense, is, so far as I have observed, uniformly connected with the word 'neck,' or 'heart,' or 'mind.' The ordinary phrase for making obdurate is not simply to *harden*, but to harden the heart. (2.) It is difficult to account for the introduction of such an idea as judicial obduration here. It does not rise out of the subject which is *punishment;* for though, no doubt, Pharaoh's heart was hardened, and this led to his punishment, yet, unless we consider "I have raised thee up," as equivalent to, 'I have hardened thy heart' (which few judicious interpreters will be inclined to do), the introduction of

[1] Scott—*Remarks on Tomline.*

the subject must seem very abrupt. The facts alluded to in Pharaoh's case are his being spared, not punished when he might have been punished, yet reserved to a time and combination of circumstances, when his deserved punishment would more fully answer its purpose; and (3.) The introduction of the idea of judicial hardening seems to destroy the antithesis. *Hardening* is not the natural antithesis of showing mercy. Had it been, 'whom He wills He melts into penitence, and whom He wills He hardens into impenitence,' the antithesis would have been complete; but the one term in the antithesis, being showing mercy, the other must correspond to it—He does not show mercy; He relents in reference to one, He does not relent in reference to another.

I am therefore disposed to concur with those interpreters[1] (and they are distinguished both for learning and judgment) who consider the word rendered "harden," as equivalent to 'treat with severity' in withholding favours and inflicting deserved punishments. We have seen that the word by itself, as it is here, no where else means judicial obduration. The word is not of frequent occurrence, but there is one passage in the LXX. where a compound is used in the sense which we think should be assigned to it here. In Job xxxix. 16, is a description of the manner in which the ostrich treats her young. Our translators render the clause—"The ostrich is hardened against her young." A literal version of the LXX. is, "She hardeneth her young ones."[2] She treats them harshly or severely by abandoning them to the mercy of accident. Here, if I mistake not, as at the 22d verse of the eleventh chapter, "the goodness and the severity" of God are contrasted, and His "purpose according to election," is affirmed of the displays of both. "Whom He wills He treats kindly"—by having the mercy on them which they do not deserve; and "whom He wills He treats severely," not unjustly but severely, in comparison with those whom He treats kindly; He treats

[1] Ernesti—Bengel. The note of the latter is worth quoting—"Indurat dicit pro *non miseretur* per metonymiam consequentis."

[2] ἀπεσκλήρυνε τὰ τέκνα εαυτης.

them severely, in not bestowing on them mercy and in punishing them when and how He pleases. He chose to confer on Isaac and his posterity blessings that He did not choose to confer on Ishmael and his posterity. He chose to confer on Jacob and his posterity blessings which he did not choose to confer on Esau and his posterity. He chose to have mercy on some of the idolatrous Israelites, and He chose not to have mercy on others of them. And though strict justice gave forth Pharaoh's sentence and fixed the measure of his punishment,—"the purpose of God, according to election stood,"—was manifested, in selecting the time and manner of executing that sentence and inflicting that punishment. "Behold, then, the goodness and the severity of God;" and, in the manifestation of both, see Him "working all things according to the counsel of His own will." The application which the apostle wished to be made of these statements, is not far to seek. If this be a leading law of the government of God, what is there to find fault with, in His bestowing the favours which He confers through Christ Jesus, on such Jews and Gentiles, and in withholding them from such others of both these classes, as He pleases; or in His choosing His own time and way for punishing, long borne with, obstinate transgressors? This is the application which the apostle teaches us to make of these statements in the 22d, 23d, and 24th verses. But, before he does this, he fully answers an objection which a Jew might very probably make to his doctrine—an objection he has already more than once referred to.

The truths we have been considering, if rightly improved, will excite gratitude, repress discontent, and produce a reverential acquiescence in the arrangements of Divine Providence. If we are in possession of benefits, of whatever kind, they must all be traced to sovereign kindness. We do not deserve the least of them, and many not more undeserving than we are without them. Surely, then, we should be grateful for them, and should express our gratitude by employing them for the purposes for which they were conferred. If we are destitute of what others enjoy, let us not complain; we have no claim on these blessings, and let us not envy those who possess them. God has given them what He has withheld from us; and He had an undoubted right both to give and to withhold. He never can inflict on us sufferings which we have not deserved. And "why should a living man complain—a man for the punishment of his sins?" Indeed, when most severely afflicted, we are punished less than our iniquities deserve.

Amid all Divine dispensations, however unaccountable they may be, let us never doubt that "*this* also cometh from the Lord;" and that "whatsoever the Lord pleases, that does He in heaven, and in the earth, in the seas, and all deep places." Though His way be in the sea and His path in the mighty waters, so that we are not able to trace His footsteps, let us still hold that "justice and judgment are the foundation of His throne, and that mercy and truth go before His face."

Let us not be stumbled at the prosperity of the wicked. God will, in His own time and way, show His displeasure at sin—and His time and way will be found to be the best time and way.

Let those who are going on in a course of sin, and yet, at the same time, enjoying a large measure of worldly wealth and honour, think on Pharaoh and tremble. Let them be assured that their sin will find them out, and, if not repented of, forgiven, and forsaken, will bring its wages along with it, Death—everlasting death. Oh that, instead of making their being treated severely necessary to the vindication of the Divine character and the stability of the Divine government, they would but "flee for refuge and lay hold of the hope set before us in the Gospel." The God who delights in mercy will then, according to the good pleasure of His goodness, bless even the worst of them with all heavenly and spiritual blessings in Christ Jesus. Let none of us, hardening our hearts in obstinate unbelief, put away from ourselves these blessings. It is thus only we can come short of them; so that, if we perish we shall have ourselves entirely to blame: and when God punishes us, however much we may, like the

Jews, have to say for ourselves now, we shall have nothing to answer Him then.

ε. *Objection stated and answered.*

To the conclusion to which the apostle comes—from the facts which he brings forward as illustrative of what he terms "the purpose of God according to election, not of works, but of Him who calleth"—"He hath mercy on whom He wills to have mercy, and whom He wills He treats hardly—severely" —does not have mercy—he represents the unbelieving Jews as demurring, and insinuating that the conduct of God, if such as the apostle had described, was unreasonable: "Thou wilt say, then, unto me, why doth He yet find fault, for who hath resisted His will?"[1] It is of primary importance to the understanding of the whole paragraph, that we apprehend distinctly the meaning and force of this objection—that we see clearly what is the precise point of the apostle's doctrine that is objected against, and what are the grounds on which the objection proceeds. It is the more necessary that we consider these points, as, from inattention to them, we conceive, the meaning and design of the passage have been generally misapprehended. It has ordinarily been supposed that the objection is based solely on the concluding statement of the 18th verse, rendered by our translators, "whom He wills He hardeneth," and that its force may be thus expressed:— 'If God hardens whom He wills, and if His will be irresistible, is it not very unreasonable in Him to find fault with, and punish those, who are the unresisting subjects of that hardening influence of which He is the author. If this be the true account of the matter, we are much more to be pitied than blamed; and it were an abuse of words to term our sufferings —equitable punishment.'

Such an objection has often been brought forward, and it is not particularly difficult to answer it. But that this is not the objection here stated, seems evident from two considerations.

[1] Ver. 16.

First, that, as I have showed, there is no reason to think that the idea of judicial obduration, on which the objection is grounded, is brought forward at all by the apostle *here;* for the true meaning of the word rendered "harden," is to treat severely, in opposition to having mercy or treating kindly; and, Second, That if we were to understand the word "harden" as referring to judicial obduration, the answer given by the apostle would not at all suit this view of the case. The true answer to that objection is to be found in the fact, that in what is termed the judicial blinding of the mind and hardening of the heart, there is no direct, positive influence put forth by God: there is merely a withholding of what He is under no obligation to bestow, and an allowing the depraved being, unchecked by the dispensations of God's providence, the declarations of God's word, and the workings of God's Spirit, to follow the guidance of his own wilfully blinded mind and rebellious heart. There is no inconsistency between *thus* hardening men, and finding fault with them and punishing them for being hardened.

The objection here, unless I entirely misconceive the meaning of the apostle, is not taken exclusively against the statement made in the close of the 18th verse, but against the apostle's general doctrine of "the purpose of God according to election, not of works, but of Him that calleth,"—the sum of which is—"Whom He wills He has mercy on"—treats kindly, giving them what they do not deserve, and "whom He wills, He treats severely"—severely, but not unjustly—not giving them what they do not deserve, but giving them what they do deserve. And this seems to me the force of the objection: 'Since everything, according to this doctrine, is dependent on God's will, which is irresistible, and since this will of God, according to which He can do everything, is sovereign—since He can have mercy on whom He wills to have mercy, and can refuse mercy and inflict punishment on whom He chooses to do so—why does He not will to have mercy on all, so as to make them obedient, and thus put finding of fault out of the case altogether? Why does He not have mercy on all? Why does He blame and punish any? If He would but have mercy on all, it is plain all would be well: there would be none to blame or to punish. Why then does He find fault, when none has resisted, none can resist His will?'

This is the objection which seems naturally to rise out of the apostle's statement: this is the objection which best suits the character of an unbelieving Jew, unwilling to admit the awful truth respecting the approaching punishment of his guilty nation; and this is, I apprehend, the objection to which the succeeding verses furnish a complete and satisfactory answer. The objection here somewhat resembles that of the unbelieving Jew adverted to by the apostle in an earlier part of his epistle,[1] "If our unrighteousness commend," set off to advantage, "the righteousness of God, is not God unrighteous, who takes vengeance?" but it is not the same. The apostle's answer to that objection is, that it would at once annihilate God's moral government: God could not punish any man; for every sin of every sinner will be made to conduce to the Divine glory; so that the principle, which is the very quintessence of impiety and absurdity, would become true, and the course it recommends right—"Let us do evil, that good may come."

Let us now examine, somewhat more closely, the apostle's answer to the kindred objection here brought before us: "Nay, but, O man, who art thou that repliest against God? Shall the thing formed, say to him that formed it, Why hast thou made me thus? Hath not the potter power over the clay, of the same lump to make one vessel to honour, and another unto dishonour?"[2] The objection is answered in two ways: first, by showing the absurdity and wickedness of man's denying that God does what He does, or says what He says, or finding fault with what He does or says; and then, by showing that the dispensations objected to were perfectly consistent with the Divine justice and benignity.

The first of these answers is contained in the verses just cited; the second in the 22d, 23d, and 24th verses, the last of which concludes the important parenthetical discussion con-

[1] Chap. iii. 5.

[2] Ver. 20, 21.

cerning "the standing of the purpose of God according to election."

It deserves to be noticed, that the apostle does not deny the principle on which the objection goes. He does not say, either —God does not find fault—or, man may resist His will. He does not go on to explain, or to explain away, the principle which gave occasion to the objection; he does not say, 'You have misapprehended my meaning, when I said, "Whom He wills He treats kindly; whom He wills He treats severely."' But he says, first, 'This is an objection you have no *right* to put;' and then, 'This is an objection you have no *reason* to put.'

First, 'This is an objection you have no *right* to put. You say, Why does God find fault? I say, How darest thou to find fault? for the objection is "a replying against God."' The objection was an utterly inadmissible one, being neither more nor less than a contradiction of, or a finding fault with, the obvious dispensations and declarations of God. To "reply against God," is to argue against what God has done in His providence or said in His word. It is a fact, an undeniable fact, that God treats some kindly, and some severely—that He bestows favours on some, and withholds them from others; and, for His doing so, as well as for the time and manner in which He inflicts merited punishment, it is impossible for us to assign any reason, but that so God wills; "Even so, Father, for so it seemeth good in Thy sight."[1] And as this is the Divine conduct, so the Divine declarations with regard to this subject are most explicit. "He worketh all things according to the counsel of His own will."[2] "He doth according to His will in the army of heaven, and among the inhabitants of the earth: none can stay His hand, or say to Him, What doest Thou?"[3] To argue, then, on any principle which supposes that God does not act in the manner in which we see He does act—that God does not say what we see He does say, is to "reply against God." If these things are so, God is unwise, or unkind, or unjust. He had only to will that

[1] Matt. xi. 26. [2] Eph. i. 11. [3] Dan. iv. 35.

matters should have been otherwise, and all would have been well. Your doctrine cannot, then, be true. 'Take heed,' says the apostle, 'what you are about; for whatever consequences you may draw from the works and the words of God, these are the works and the words of God. He is blind who does not see that God acts in this way—stupid who does not perceive that God speaks in this way. Can anything be clearer than the facts I have stated, and the texts I have quoted? God does act in this way; God has made such declarations; and, in attempting to reason in opposition to these facts and assertions, you are not only arguing against me, you are contradicting Him. You are either saying, 'God has not done what He has certainly done—God has not said what He has undoubtedly said;' or, what, if possible, is still worse—'God has done what He ought not to have done—God has said what He ought not to have said.'

But the apostle not merely states, what is so obviously true, that such an objection is "a replying against God," but he strongly intimates the absurdity and presumption of a creature like man in bringing it forward: "Who art *thou* that repliest against God?" There is no presumption in examining whether the account given of a particular Divine dispensation, be a just representation of what God has actually done—no presumption in examining into the meaning and evidence of what professes to be a Divine revelation. But, when it is quite plain that the Divine Being acts in a particular way—when it is quite plain that a well-accredited revelation gives a distinct deliverance on a particular subject, to object to—to reason against, either the one or the other is in the highest degree presumptuous and impious. Is it fit that man, whose intellect is so feeble, and whose knowledge is so limited, should sit in judgment on the undoubted doings, the well-accredited sayings, of the all-wise—the only wise God? Particular dispensations of His providence—particular declarations of His word, may appear to us very strange and unaccountable, and we may find it difficult or impossible for us entirely to reconcile them with what we know to be the perfections of His character, the principles of His government, and the other declarations of His word; but we are not, on these grounds, to "find fault" with them. We are not, in the face of evidence, to say God does not—He cannot, act so; He does not—He cannot, say so. We are to hold fast both portions of the truth, for which we have equally satisfactory evidence, and rest assured that the difficulty of reconciling them arises, not from any real inconsistency between equally clearly proved truths, but from the weakness of our faculties and the imperfection of our information. God's working all things according to the counsel of His own will, and yet blaming and punishing the violator of His law, to whom, if He had willed, He could have given repentance to the acknowledging of the truth—and whose very violations of the Divine law are the means of accomplishing the Divine counsels—are perfectly reconcilable, though we may not be able to reconcile them. They are both certain truths, resting on equally satisfactory evidence; and nothing can be more absurd than to deny either of them, because I am not able to explain everything with regard to both. The articles of that man's creed must be very few, who believes nothing without being able to explain all the difficulties which are connected with it.

The absurdity of thus "replying against God," is not only strongly asserted by the question, "Who art thou that repliest against God?" it is strikingly illustrated. It is so by the use of the appellation, "O man!" It were presumption in the highest angel thus to "reply against God;" but for *man*—the lowest in the class of intelligent beings—to sit in judgment on, ay, and to condemn God, what language can describe the monstrous incongruity! "Shall mortal man be more just than God? Shall man be more pure than his Maker?" It is still more strongly expressed in the question that follows: "Shall the thing formed say to him that formed it, Why hast thou made me thus?"

In these words, the apostle has a reference to one or other of these passages in the prophecy of Isaiah—either chap. xxix 16, "Shall the work say of him that made it, He made me not? or shall the thing framed say of him that framed it, He had no understanding?" or chap. xlv. 9, "Shall the clay say to him that fashioneth it, What makest thou? or thy work, He hath no hands?" The meaning of these words plainly is—that the Divine Being has a power and authority over His creatures, far superior to that which any human artist can have over his works; and that, could we suppose an artist's work to find fault with its framer, we would be furnished with a just, but still very inadequate, representation of the absurdity and presumption of man in finding fault with any of the doings of the Most High. It is as if the apostle had said—'It is indubitably true that God does all things—confers or withholds benefits according to the counsel of His own will. It is true that that will is uncontrollable. Man may—man does, attempt to resist it; but his attempts to resist only become the means of accomplishing it. It is true that He blames and punishes those who violate His law. And wilt thou, because thou canst not reconcile these facts, pronounce them irreconcilable? Wilt thou pronounce that, if both be true, God is unreasonable and unjust? Remember what thou art—how utterly unfit for judging of the doings of the infinitely wise and powerful Ruler of the universe! His administration, like His nature, is "higher than heaven, what canst thou do? deeper than hell, what canst thou know? the measure thereof is longer than the earth, and broader than the sea." If I am sure that God has done it, I may be sure that it is right, though *how* it is so, I may not comprehend. If I am sure that He has said it, I may be sure that it is true, though I cannot reconcile it with some other things which I know that He has said, and therefore know to be true. I may, without presumption, pronounce unjust what I have no evidence that He has done, though men, no wiser than myself, say that He has done it. I may doubt or deny what I have no evidence that He has said, though they strongly assert, without proving, that He has said it. In acting thus, I am but rightly exercising the faculty of discerning truth which He has given me; but if I contradict what He, in His providence and word, shows to be His work—if I say that He has not done it, or if I find fault with it, and say that He ought not to have done it—no words can express the height of my folly, and the depth of my impiety. "Wo to the man that striveth with his Maker: let the potsherd strive with the potsherds of the earth."[1]

This was well fitted to silence the objector; but it was the apostle's purpose, not only to silence, but to convince him—to show not merely that he was presumptuous and impious, in censuring what, beyond all doubt, was done and said by God, but that the doings and sayings of God, which he dared to censure, were all in perfect consistency with the Divine truth, righteousness, and benignity. In the Divine dispensations of the rejection and punishment of the Jews, in connection with the calling of the Gentiles, he shows that, while the Divine sovereignty was displayed, it was displayed in a manner not merely consistent with, but gloriously illustrative of, "the depth of the riches" of His long-suffering patience and redeeming grace: "Hath not the potter power over the clay, of the same lump to make one vessel unto honour, and another unto dishonour? What if God, willing to show His wrath, and to make His power known, endured with much long-suffering the vessels of wrath fitted to destruction; and that He might make known the riches of His glory on the vessels of mercy, which He had afore prepared unto glory, even us, whom He hath called, not of the Jews only, but also of the Gentiles?"[2]

In the 21st verse, there can be no doubt that there is a reference to a passage in the book of the Prophet Jeremiah,[3] the reading of which will assist us in discovering the meaning and object of the apostle's words. "The word which came to Jeremiah from the Lord, saying, Arise, and go down to the potter's house, and there I will cause thee to hear My words. Then I went down to the potter's house, and behold, he wrought a work on the wheels. And the vessel that he made of clay was marred in the hand of the potter: so he made it

[1] Isa. xlv. 9. [2] Ver. 21–24. [3] Chap. xviii. 1–6.

again another vessel, as seemed good to the potter to make it. Then the word of the Lord came to me, saying, O house of Israel, cannot I do with you as this potter? saith the Lord. Behold, as the clay is in the potter's hand, so are ye in Mine hand, O house of Israel."

The primary object of the parable seems to be, to assert Jehovah's right and power to do what He was about to do—to dissolve the existing constitution of the Israelitish people, and to fashion it after another form—that which it assumed after the captivity. Even in this restricted view of the subject, it has a direct and important bearing on the apostle's object; and naturally suggests the thought, 'Has not Jehovah the power and right to dissolve the present constitution of Israel, as the visible representation of His peculiar people, and form another constitution, in which none but believers shall be reckoned His people—and equally all believers, whether Jews or Gentiles?' But the apostle seems plainly to have had another and more extensive object.

As to the meaning of the words there is nothing difficult. "A vessel unto honour," is a vessel destined to an honourable, important use; "a vessel unto dishonour," is a vessel designed for meaner and less important purposes. And the force of the interrogation is—'Has not the potter both right and power to use the clay, which is his own property, according to his own pleasure? Has he not both right and power, out of the same mass of clay, to form vessels for the most opposite uses?'

In the application of the words, however, there is some difficulty. There is plainly an assertion, and an illustration, by means of a figurative interrogation, of a power and right which God has, in reference to all mankind—in some way analogous to the power and right of the proprietor-potter over the mass of clay that belongs to him. In this general view all interpreters are agreed. But, with regard to the nature and object of the exercise of that power, there is a great diversity of opinion. One class will have it that the question is equivalent to—'Hath not God power and right to determine the fates of nations, and to decree that, out of the general mass of mankind, one portion shall be a great and prosperous nation, and another a nation of slaves, the vilest of all people?' Others consider it as equivalent to—'Has not God the power and right, out of the aggregate body of human beings who are to exist in all ages, to fix the everlasting destinies of individuals—to appoint some to everlasting happiness, and others to everlasting misery?' We apprehend that an affirmative answer to both these questions is the true one; and the words, taken merely by themselves, might convey either of these ideas, or a more general idea embracing both.

Nothing, however, can, I think, be more evident than that the apostle is speaking directly, not of Divine *determinations* respecting either nations or individuals, but of Divine *dispensations*—not of what God *decrees*, but of what He *does*. This is an important distinction; for, though the things decreed and done are the same things, the decreeing of them and the doing of them are two very different things.

The apostle's statement is—'Whom God wills, He treats kindly; whom He wills, He treats severely;' and in opposition to the objection to this doctrine—that, supposing it to be true, it would be unreasonable in God to find fault, and unjust to punish any—the apostle has shown that such an objection is inadmissible; for it contradicts what God, both in deed and in word, has most clearly declared. It goes on the supposition that God has not done as the apostle says He has done; for, if He had done so, He would have done something unreasonable and unjust. 'Now,' says the apostle, 'there is—there can be, no doubt that He has done so, and said that He has done so. Will you contradict Him, or find fault with Him? Such "replying against God" ill becomes the highest of creatures—especially ill becomes man.' In the verse before us, and in those which follow, he appeals, as it were, to the common sense of the objector, if it was not reasonable and proper that God should possess and exercise such a right and authority; and if, in the case referred to, He had not exercised that right in perfect consistency both with justice and benignity.

In this figure, the formation of vessels, to serve various

purposes, does not represent the original formation of mankind, either in a physical or moral point of view; but the treatment of men, viewed as different pieces of the same mass, in different ways; in other words, the treating of some of them kindly—more kindly than they deserved, and the treating others severely, though not more severely than they deserved. The mass, or lump, is not, as many have understood it, the whole mass of mankind, viewed by the Divinity as to be brought into being; but the whole of mankind as they exist, the subjects of the Divine moral government, and both as creatures and sinners, all standing in the same relation to Him—something that is *His*, and of which He may make what use He pleases. All men are God's creatures, and so entirely His property. All men are sinners, and justly exposed to the Divine displeasure. The apostle has shown that, in this last sense, all are one mass: "All have sinned, and lost the Divine approbation. There is none righteous, no, not one. The whole world, both Jews and Gentiles, are brought in guilty before God." Now, hath not God, not merely the power, but the right to deal with this mass as He pleases? Has He not the right to deal kindly, or deal severely, with all or any number of this guilty, condemned race? If He deals kindly with some, is it not sovereign kindness? if He deals severely with others, is it not righteous judgment? And has not He who, as Creator and moral Governor, has the fates of the guilty race entirely at His disposal, the right, in His treatment of them, to display that sovereign power and authority which He possesses? Is He to be shut up to save all or to punish all? If justice is to be the only principle consulted, all must be punished. Is it for man to complain that this has not been the course followed? and if none is punished but those who deserve to be punished, or none punished more severely than he deserves who can find fault?

This, according to the apostle, is the exact state of the case in reference to the subject under consideration: "What if God, willing to show His wrath, and to make His power known, endured with much long-suffering the vessels of wrath fitted to destruction; and that He might make known the riches of His glory on the vessels of mercy, which He had afore prepared unto glory, even us, whom He hath called, not of the Jews only, but also of the Gentiles?"[1] It is quite obvious, to every attentive reader, that the sentence is unfinished. Something must be supplied to bring out the meaning distinctly. Different interpreters have suggested different supplements, but they all come to materially the same thing. The following appears to me the simplest way of expressing what all admit to be the sense of the apostle: "What if God, willing to show His wrath, and to make His power known, endured with much long-suffering the vessels of wrath fitted for destruction, but at last punished them as they deserved, when and how He chose—what room is there to find fault? And what if God, willing to make known the riches of His glory on the vessels of mercy which He had afore prepared for glory, has bestowed on them heavenly and spiritual blessings in Christ Jesus—treating them with undeserved kindness, even us, who are called, not of the Jews only, but also of the Gentiles—what room is there to find fault? Is not His work most honourable, most glorious, and pure, and does not His unspotted righteousness endure for ever?" This brings the matter home, both as to the punishment of the unbelieving Jews, and the salvation of the believing Jews and Gentiles.

There is little in the language that requires explication. They who are dealt severely with are termed "vessels of wrath"—with an obvious allusion to the figurative language of the former verse: the expression is equivalent to, 'subjects of punishment'—persons deserving to be punished, and doomed to punishment. "Vessels of mercy," in the same way, is equivalent to, 'subjects of mercy'—persons to be pardoned and saved.

The "vessels of mercy" are said to have been "prepared afore of God to glory"—by the sovereign, efficacious grace of God, destined to, and fitted for, everlasting happiness.

[1] Ver. 22–24.

The marked difference, however, between the language used in reference to those whom God treats kindly, and those whom He treats severely, deserves notice. With regard to the fitting of the vessels of wrath for destruction, there is not a word of Divine agency: they are fitted—how, and by whom, it is not said. More than one have had a hand in it—their own has been the most effective one; but *God* did not fit them for the destruction to which He doomed them as fitted for it; and not only doomed them to it, but executes it on them. In the other case, it is all Divine agency together. He displays the riches of the glory of His grace, both in destining them to it, fitting them for it, and bestowing it on them.

Let us see, then, the force of the statement, with regard to the unbelieving and impenitent Jews. This is the statement of the truth with regard to them: 'God dealt with them as He did with Pharaoh, whom they resembled in their obstinacy. He bore with them long; He spared them, when He might have destroyed them. He offered them mercy: they contemptuously rejected it, and persevered in unbelief and disobedience. To use the apostle's language, they "killed their own prophets and the Lord Jesus, and they persecuted the apostles; they pleased not God, and were contrary to all men. They forbade the apostles to speak to the Gentiles, that they might be saved; and thus continued "to fill up the measure of their iniquity, till wrath came upon them to the uttermost," in a way well fitted "to show God's wrath, and make His power known."[1] When they had fitted themselves for destruction, they were destroyed.' Now, what room is there for finding fault with God here? Is He to be blamed for forbearing with them so long; or is He to be blamed for punishing them, and punishing when and how best served the great purposes of His holy and benignant government? This is the one side of the dispensation, and the other is equally unimpeachable. God bestows the blessings of the Christian salvation on a portion of men called out from the great body of Jews

[1] 1 Thess. ii. 15, 16.

and Gentiles, and fitted by Him, in the exercise of His grace, for their enjoyment, by being made in faith thankfully to accept of them. This is the only preparation for the first reception of the blessings of salvation. In this we have a glorious display of the riches of His liberality, and the tenderness of His compassion; but in all this there is not a shadow of injustice—not the slightest ground for quarrelling with God. In following out His purpose "according to election, not of works, but of Him who calleth," by treating whom He wills kindly, and treating whom He wills severely, He does nothing that any being can reasonably find fault with; while this view of the matter makes it plain that, in withholding saving blessings from certain of the Jews, He does them no wrong; and, in inflicting on them severe judgments, He only at last inflicts punishment which had long been incurred, but which patience and forbearance had prevented from being sooner executed. Such is the parenthetical argument embosomed in the main argument of this ninth chapter.

The whole argument of the chapter, down to the 30th verse, where a new division commences, may be thus summed up: The rejection of the unbelieving Jews, the admission of the believing Gentiles, and the signal punishment of the Jews for their unbelief, which had all been results of the manifestation of the Divine method of justification, however unlooked for and disagreeable to the Jews, were in no way inconsistent with the character, word, or administration of God. In rejecting the majority of the Jews, there was no breach of promise, for those rejected were persons to whom no promise had been made; there was no violation of equity, for the benefits bestowed were such as none had any claim to, and, if bestowed at all, must be bestowed as the gifts of sovereign mercy; and, in inflicting severe judgments on the unbelieving Jews, there was merely the execution of a righteous sentence long incurred, and which forbearance, on the part of God, had prevented from being sooner executed.

The course of our illustrations, place in a strong point of view the criminality, and danger, of presumptuous speculations on the Divine purposes and dispensations. It is unwise, as Luther says, for the novice to meddle with them. "Take heed that thou drink not wine, when thou art but a sucking babe." Nothing has a greater tendency to confound the understanding, to debauch the conscience, and to harden the heart. Let no man think or talk of these subjects lightly; they concern the character of God, and the eternal interests of mankind. Let us keep close to revelation. "Hidden things belong to God; things that are revealed, to us and to our children." Let us rejoice that the great doctrines of the Divine equity and benignity are written on both His works and His word in characters of light, and let us not allow metaphysical disquisitions to cast a cloud on them. "Touching the Almighty, we cannot find Him out; but He is excellent in power, and in judgment, and in plenty of justice: He will not afflict without cause, or beyond measure." "God is a rock: His work is perfect; all His ways are judgment: a God of truth, and without iniquity; just and right is He." Let us never lose sight of the great, plain, consolatory truths; and when we meet with dispensations of His providence, or declarations in His word, which seem to contradict them, let us explain what is obscure by what is clear—not cast darkness on what is clear by what is obscure. Let us, above all, beware of "replying against God." Humbling ourselves before Him, let us thankfully and hopefully anticipate the period when the shadows, which cover so many of His works, and some, too, of His words, shall be completely dispelled, and when in His light we shall see light clearly. Then, what now troubles us will delight us; and it will be seen that, in working all things according to the counsel of His own will, God has done all things well.

Let us learn the great lesson of humility. Let us look for every blessing we need, entirely on the ground of sovereign mercy.

Let all who have obtained mercy be very grateful; the blessing is invaluable, and all have not received it. Let them be very humble; they did not deserve it. Let them be very submissive and obedient; for this is the end for which God has shown them mercy.

Let those who continue obstinate be warned by the case of the Jews, lest they too "fall after the same example of unbelief." Let them recollect that if, in the face of a freely-offered, full salvation, they, by rejecting it, come short of it, their ruin is completely of themselves; and that, if they will not consent that God should be glorified in their salvation, provision is made that, without their consent, He shall be glorified in their perdition.

(2.) *Particular Statement of the Relations, Present and Future, of Mankind, as divided into Israel and the Gentiles, to the Manifested Divine Method of Justification.*

Having thus effectually removed this stumbling-block out of the way, the apostle now, at the 30th verse of the ninth chapter, proceeds to show how Israel and how the Gentiles stand in reference to "the righteousness of God, now revealed"—the manifested Divine method of justification. The sum of his statement is this: 'The great body of the Jews have excluded themselves, by their unbelief, from the benefits of this Divine method, which they might have enjoyed by believing. A portion of the Jews, having believed, have obtained justification, and all its attendant and consequent blessings. Many Gentiles, by believing, have become fellow partakers with them of these benefits. And there is a period approaching, when the great body, both of Gentiles and Jews, shall, through the faith of the truth, become heirs of the blessings procured and bestowed by Messiah.—"The fulness of the Gentiles shall be brought in, and all Israel shall be saved, to the eternal glory of the wisdom and grace of Him, of whom, and through whom, and to whom, are all things."'

(*a*) *Present Relations—Gentiles believing obtain Justification—Israel, seeking Justification not by believing, but "as it were by the works of the law," do not, and cannot obtain it.*

Let us proceed now to consider the manner in which the apostle brings these important statements before the mind. "What shall we say then? That the Gentiles, which followed not after righteousness, have attained to righteousness, even the righteousness which is of faith: but Israel, which followed after the law of righteousness, hath not attained to the law of righteousness."[1] Some interpreters have considered the interrogation here as the close of the elliptical sentence contained in the 22d and 23d verses, considering all that intervenes as parenthetical. To this interpretation there are many objections. It is enough to say, that in this case the second clause of the sentence would have no connection with the first. The words, therefore, "What shall we say then?" are to be considered as just one of the apostle's usual formulæ of transition, and as equivalent to, 'What is the real state of the matter? How is it that Gentiles obtain, while Israelites are excluded from, the Messianic blessings?' And what follows is the answer to this question: "That the Gentiles, which followed not after righteousness, have attained to righteousness," etc. The language is elliptical, but the ellipsis is easily supplied. 'This is what we will say: this is the true account of the matter, both in reference to the Gentile who is received into, and the Jew who is excluded from, the enjoyment of the Messianic blessings.'

With regard to the first, "The Gentiles, which followed not after righteousness, have attained to righteousness, even the righteousness which is of faith." The term, the Gentiles, is not to be considered as descriptive of all the Gentiles, or even of the great body of the Gentiles. In either of these senses, the declaration that they had attained to righteousness

[1] Ver. 30, 31.

would be inconsistent with the fact. The term should have been rendered 'Gentiles,' not "the Gentiles." The persons referred to are those described in ver. 24 as "called of the Gentiles"—from among the Gentiles. They are 'Gentiles,' in opposition to 'Jews'—and 'Gentiles who followed not after righteousness,' in contradistinction to 'Gentiles who (like Cornelius and others) did seek after righteousness:'—Idolatrous Gentiles, who, not following after righteousness, "attained to righteousness, even the righteousness of faith."

What are we to understand by these Gentiles "not following after righteousness?" "Righteousness" here, as usually throughout the epistle, seems to signify justification, in one or other of the nearly related senses—a state of favour with God, or the way of obtaining that state. From "the righteousness," which was not the object of these Gentiles' desire or pursuit, being plainly distinguished from "the law," or a law "of righteousness," which is represented as the object of the desire and pursuit of Israel, it is probably used in the first of these senses. The Gentiles referred to "knew not God." They could not, therefore, desire or seek His favour. Wide and varied as was the field of desire and pursuit to the Gentiles, and full as it was of eager occupants, there was "none that understood or did seek God." They were seeking anything rather than righteousness or the favour of God. Though they had sinned and become guilty before God—though they had some sense of a superior power—though they were in some measure conscious of guilt, and sought its expiation by sacrifice, they were without God: they knew not His character—how could they desire or seek His favour? Yet some—many of this class, in consequence of the Divine method of justification being manifested—"attained to righteousness"—to justification, "even to the justification that is by faith." The Gospel was preached to them—that Gospel in which the righteousness of God by faith is revealed, in order to faith—*i.e.* to its being believed. They believed "the word of the truth of the Gospel" respecting "the righteousness of God manifested to all," and this righteousness was thus *upon* them believing; for it makes no difference between the idolatrous or the inquiring Gentile, or between the Jew and either. The Gospel was thus "the power of God unto salvation" to them believing it. They were "justified freely by God's grace, through the redemption that is in Jesus Christ." Without submitting to the Mosaic law, they were justified from all things, from which it could not justify them. By simply believing the revelation of mercy, idolatrous Gentiles had become the objects of God's peculiar favour, and were blessed by Him with all spiritual blessings.

This is the one side of the case. But it has another, and a less inviting one: "But Israel, which followed after the law of righteousness, hath not attained to the law of righteousness." "Israel" is here equivalent to Israelites—the great body of Israelites. They are represented as following after the law, or rather *a* law, of righteousness. "Righteousness" is here, as in the preceding verse, justification; but what is "the law," or a law of justification, which Israel is said to follow after—to seek for? The word "law" here seems used in the same way as in the expressions, "law in the members"—"law of the mind"—"law of the spirit of life"—"law of sin and death"—"the law of faith"—"the law of works." It is equivalent to method—established order—way. The heathen did not seek after a *method* of obtaining justification, or the Divine favour: the thing itself was not so the object of intellectual apprehension, as that the way of obtaining it could be an object of desire or pursuit. But it was otherwise with the Jews. The character of the true God, and their relations to Him, had been revealed to them. To possess the favour of Jehovah was, in their estimation, highly desirable: they sought a way of obtaining it, but they did not attain to the way—there is only one—of obtaining it. Of consequence, the great body of them (for "the election did attain," having been led into the right way) came short of it: they did not attain to the way; and how could they reach what it alone could lead to? The necessary consequence was, they remained in a state of condemnation.

But how was it that, while idolatrous Gentiles had found

the way and the end they were not previously seeking, or even thinking of, Israel, who was seeking a way to the end, had not found it? This is the apostle's question, "Wherefore?"[1] Why was it that Israel did not attain to the way of justification, and, by not attaining to it, come short of justification, or, what is the same thing, "the glory"—the approbation "of God?" Was it that the "law of righteousness" was not revealed to them? No; it was "manifested to all;" and He who has justified the uncircumcision was equally disposed to justify the circumcision; for in this matter "neither circumcision availeth anything, nor uncircumcision." The reason, the only reason, was, "they sought it not by faith, but by the works of the law." They sought a way of obtaining the Divine favour by obedience to the requisitions of the law of Moses, and not by believing the testimony in the Gospel concerning Jesus Christ, setting Him forth as a propitiation through faith in His blood. They sought—they pursued a way of justification, as if the way had been by working, not by believing. They turned aside from the only way of justification, through the belief of the truth respecting the work finished by Jesus Christ on the cross as the only ground of man's acceptance with God—the only, the all-sufficient propitiation—a method absolutely needful for the Jew—a method equally open to the Gentile. "For they stumbled at that stumbling stone;"—that is, 'this was the cause of their failing to attain what they sought for. It was presented to them; but, instead of building on it as a foundation, they stumbled over it, and fell and were broken.' Some have supposed that "the stumbling stone" is the principle, 'that justification was to be obtained, not by obedience to the law, but by the faith of the truth respecting Jesus Christ.' Others consider the stumbling stone as 'Jesus Christ himself,' whom God has laid in Zion—has appointed to be the foundation on which men, by believing, are to rest their hopes. It comes substantially to the same thing; though it does seem most likely that, as, in the prophecies referred to, the stone is the

[1] Ver. 32.

emblem of the Messiah, the apostle's idea is, that their mistaken views with respect to the Messiah were the cause of their coming short—their mistaken views as to the blessings He was to procure, the manner in which He was to procure them, the persons for whom they were to be procured, and the way in which these were to obtain possession of them. They stumbled at that stumbling stone of whom the prophet speaks. In consequence of their mistaken views they could not believe the truth, the faith of which was the only means of salvation; and, instead of being among those who, according to the prophet, believing on the Messiah, were to be secured from being ashamed by disappointment, they were among those who were to "stumble and fall, and be broken, and snared, and taken." "As it is written, Behold, I lay in Zion a stumbling stone, and rock of offence: and whosoever believeth on Him shall not be ashamed."[1]

The passages here referred to are—"Therefore thus saith the Lord God, Behold, I lay in Zion for a foundation a stone, a tried stone, a precious corner stone, a sure foundation; he that believeth shall not make haste." "And He shall be for a sanctuary; but for a stone of stumbling, and for a rock of offence, to both the houses of Israel; for a gin and for a snare to the inhabitants of Jerusalem: and many among them shall stumble, and shall fall, and be broken, and snared, and be taken."[2] The portion of these two passages here referred to seems to have been quoted from memory, and does not exactly agree with either the Hebrew text or the ancient Greek version. Both these passages are direct predictions of the Messiah; and they are introduced by the apostle to show that what had taken place, and was about to take place, in reference to the manifested Divine method of justification, however opposed to the anticipations of the Jews, was in exact accordance with what "the prophets had foretold of these days;"[3] so that what might seem, at first sight, to discredit Christianity, actually confirmed it.

[1] Ver. 33. [2] Isa. xxviii. 16; viii. 14. [3] Acts iii. 24.

The relation of the manifested Divine method of salvation to the Jews and to the Gentiles is thus distinctly marked. Its principle is, "whosoever believeth on *Him*"—the Messiah, "shall not be ashamed"—shall obtain in Him what he seeks, justification and salvation. "Whosoever believeth"—none else: the Gentile believing in Him obtains these blessings, the Jew not believing in Him excludes himself from them. It regards them as men—guilty men, equally needing justification and salvation—not as Jew and Gentile, and it treats them accordingly; and in doing this, the manifested Divine method of justification has the testimony of the law and the prophets—all this is in entire accordance with Old Testament predictions. This is the leading thought, which is fully unfolded in the tenth chapter.

Interjecting in ver. 1 a renewed declaration of the deep interest he had in the happiness of his countrymen, expressing itself in prayers for their salvation—"Brethren, my heart's desire and prayer to God for Israel is, that they may be saved;" and mentioning, as one cause of that deep interest, "the zeal of God," the sincere ardent regard to religion, in many of them (for the remark is by no means universally applicable), to which, from his own experience and observation while an unbeliever, he can, and readily does, bear testimony—"For I bear them record, that they have a zeal of God"[1]—they do "follow after a law of righteousness," unlike the idolatrous Gentiles, who do not follow after righteousness;—the apostle proceeds to show how this zeal of God, not being an enlightened zeal, prevented instead of securing their embracing the manifested Divine method of justification; instead of enabling them to attain "a law of righteousness"—a practicable method of justification, it proved an insurmountable obstacle in the way of their attaining it.

"For they, being ignorant of God's righteousness, and going about to establish their own righteousness, have not submitted themselves to the righteousness of God."[2] These

[1] Ver. 2. [2] Ver. 3.

words are an illustration of the statement made at ver. 31, 32 of the last chapter, as well as of the closing idea of the preceding verse—'Israel's zeal of God is not according to knowledge.' It has been common to consider "the righteousness of God," in the beginning of the verse, as signifying the Divine attribute of justice; and the same phrase, in the end of the verse, as signifying either the Divine righteousness, on the ground of which men are justified, or the method of justification through that righteousness. In this case the sentiment is, 'the Jews, not being duly aware of the true nature and extent of the demands of the Divine justice on them as sinners, and, in consequence of this, "going about"—diligently employing themselves, "to establish their own righteousness"—to work out a righteousness which might meet these demands, have not submitted to—on the contrary, have rejected—the surety righteousness of Christ, or the method of justification through that righteousness, when presented to them in the Gospel.' This is the truth; but it cannot, without violence, be in this form brought out of the words. Nothing but absolute necessity should ever induce us to interpret the same word or phrase in two different senses in the same sentence, or even paragraph; and no such necessity exists here.

"Righteousness" throughout this verse seems to me to have what is its ordinary meaning in the epistle. The Jews were ignorant: they did not know—they misconceived, "the righteousness of God"—the Divine method of justification manifested in the Gospel; they did not see its necessity—they did not understand its nature; and they were engaged in establishing—in endeavouring to uphold, "their own righteousness"—a method of justification, not of God's appointment, but of man's invention—the method of justification by the works of the law; and, in consequence of this ignorance, and this seeking to establish their own method of justification, they did not—they could not, submit themselves to the righteousness of God—that Divine method of justification which is apart from law, by the faith of Christ upon *all* that believe—which is free, by God's grace—through the redemption that is in Christ Jesus.

This Divine method of justification, which is indeed the wisdom of God, appeared to them, and was treated by them, as foolishness; and, instead of submitting to it, they "rejected the counsel of God against themselves."

There is something very characteristic in the expression, "have not *submitted* themselves." The Divine method of justification requires nothing, but to be submitted to. There is no great work to be done. Its two radical principles are, that man is restored to the Divine favour, not by his own doings and sufferings, but by the doings and sufferings of another; and that, in these doings and sufferings of the justifying Saviour, he is interested, not by working, but by believing. In believing, he receives forgiveness, acceptance, eternal life, as the gift of God through Jesus Christ our Lord: but while it requires nothing but submission, it does require submission—unqualified submission, of the understanding and of the heart; and this, to unregenerate man, is harder than the most toilsome labours and the most severe penances—so hard, that nothing but Divine influence leading him to see the truth, respecting his own state, condition, and character as a sinner, and respecting this Divine method of justification, will ever induce him to yield it.

The declaration that follows (ver. 4): "For Christ is the end of the law for righteousness to every one that believeth," admits of, and has received, a great variety of interpretations. This is not wonderful; for many of the terms employed are ambiguous. "The law" may be viewed as to its substance—the duties it enjoins; or as to its form—a covenant or method of justification, or a rule of conduct: it may mean law generally, or the Mosaic Law; and, supposing it to mean the latter, it may have especial reference either to its moral or its ceremonial statutes—either to it as an exhibition of duty to the Israelites, or as a temporary economy established for some particular purposes in the great scheme of the Divine moral government of mankind. Then the word "end" may signify termination or conclusion, or it may signify a design or purpose. And then, further, it may be questioned whether the law or

Christ is the subject of the proposition—whether the apostle's declaration is, that the end of the law is Christ, or that Christ is the end of the law; and also whether the expression, "for righteousness," is to be connected with "Christ," or with the phrase, "the end of the law." There can be no reasonable doubt that "the law" is here viewed as a method of justification, in contrast with "the righteousness of God," which is "without law"—apart from law. The words may either signify, the design—the purpose, of the law, viewed as containing in it terms of justification (such as, "If thou wouldst enter into life, keep the commandments"—"The man that doeth these things shall live in them"), "is Christ, for righteousness—for justification, to every one that believeth." The law containing terms of justification—the terms on which angels are justified, on which Adam, had he kept his integrity, would have been justified—was never intended to teach fallen man how to obtain justification. Man, the sinner, is already under the curse: he cannot make adequate atonement, he cannot be profitable to God, he can never exceed the limits of present duty; and his depravity morally incapacitates him from yielding the requisite obedience, while the law makes no provision either for pardon, or for a spiritual influence to secure the obedience required. The law is intended to bring the sinner to Christ, and to prepare him for thankfully embracing Him, by a living faith, as the Lord our righteousness. Or they may signify, "Christ for righteousness to every one that believeth"—*i.e.* substantially, "the righteousness of God without law, by the faith of Christ, on every one that believeth,"—that is the end, the termination of the law, as a method of justification. He who embraces the one, necessarily abandons the other. The former of these interpretations suits well enough with the preceding context. The zeal of God which the Jew possesses, and shows in seeking a way of justification as it were by the works of the law, is not according to knowledge: he acts the part of an ill-informed and foolish person, in going about to establish his own righteousness, and not submitting to the righteousness of God; for the very design of the law, by which he seeks to be justified, in stating the only terms of justification which it can offer, was to lead him, not to attempt to comply with these terms, which is impossible, but to lead him to *One* who of God is "made righteousness to every one that believeth." The latter mode of interpretation accords at least equally well with the preceding context. 'The Israelites, being ignorant of the Divine method of justification, and going about to establish a method of justification of their own, have not submitted themselves to the Divine method of justification; and this is just what might have been expected, for the embracing of Christ for justification to every believer, is submitting to the righteousness of God, and necessarily implies in it the end of the law as a method of justification—the entire abandonment, on the part of the individual, of all seeking justification by the works of the law—the going about to establish a method of justification of his own.' The law personally obeyed for justification to him that obeys it, and Christ trusted in by faith for justification to every one believing, are direct opposites; and he who, like the Jew, takes the first course, cannot take the second, and cannot realize those results which can only be obtained by taking it.

I prefer this method of interpretation, for it agrees naturally not only with what goes before, but with what follows: "For Moses describeth the righteousness which is of the law, That the man which doeth those things shall live by them. But the righteousness which is of faith speaketh on this wise, Say not in thine heart, Who shall ascend into heaven? (that is, to bring Christ down *from above;*) or, Who shall descend into the deep? (that is, to bring up Christ again from the dead.) But what saith it? The word is nigh thee, even in thy mouth, and in thy heart: that is, the word of faith which we preach; that if thou shalt confess with thy mouth the Lord Jesus, and shalt believe in thine heart that God hath raised Him from the dead, thou shalt be saved. For with the heart man believeth unto righteousness; and with the mouth confession is made unto salvation. For the scripture saith, Whosoever believeth on Him shall not be ashamed. For there is no difference between the Jew and the Greek; for the same Lord over all is rich unto all that call upon him. For whosoever shall call upon the name of the Lord shall be saved."[1]

The force of the connective particle "for," in the beginning of this paragraph, seems to be illustrative: 'You need only to look at the two methods of justification, to see that he who clings to the first can have nothing to do with the second, and he that embraces the second must have entirely done with the first. "Christ for righteousness to every one that believeth" must be "the end of the law;" and he who will keep by the law as a method of justification, can have no part or lot in "Christ for righteousness to every one that believeth."'

The method of justification by law cannot be more accurately described than in the words of Moses,[2] "The man that doeth those things shall live by them." The man who does all that the law requires, will obtain all that it promises. According to law, a man is justified by complying with all its demands. This method of justification is by the apostle clearly shown to be an impracticable one to fallen man; Rom. iii. 19, 20, iv. 15; Gal. iii. 10.

The Divine method of justification by believing—"the righteousness which is of faith," is now personified, and introduced as describing itself, partly in words borrowed from a description by Moses of the revelation he had been employed to make to the Israelites. It is only necessary to look at the passage where the description occurs,[3] to see that Moses had no reference to the method of justification revealed in the Gospel. The changes the apostle makes in the words, and the addition he makes to them, further show that he merely borrows some of Moses' expressions as being remarkably suitable for the description of this method.

Some interpreters have supposed that the apostle's object in this passage is merely to assert, that there is no difficulty in obtaining the knowledge of the method of justification by

[1] Ver. 5-13. [2] Lev. xviii. 5. [3] Deut. xxx. 11-14.

faith. There is no need to climb up to heaven, no need to dig down into the depths of the earth, in order to obtain this knowledge: it is at hand, in a plain, well-accredited revelation of the Divine mind. But this, though a truth, does not seem to be what the apostle means, or, at any rate, all that he means. He is comparing, not two revelations, but two methods of justification. The address of the personified method of justification may be thus paraphrased: 'Do not think and act as if this method of justification—the only true method of justification, depended on something yet to be done, or on anything done or to be done by you, or that there is any difficulty in obtaining a knowledge of what is this method, or how to obtain a personal interest in it. The descent of the Messiah from heaven "that He might be delivered for our offences,"[1] was necessary to it—"God's sending His Son in the likeness of sinful flesh."[2] But there is no need to say, "Who shall ascend to heaven, to bring Him down?" He has come, and done the work for which He came: He has died for us. The rising of the Messiah from the grave was necessary to it: this justification is by His resurrection from the dead. But there is no need to say, "Who shall descend into the deep, to bring *Him* up from beneath?" He is risen. "God has raised Him from the dead, and given Him glory." The Gospel, which unfolds the righteousness of faith, does not bid you inquire how these things—the necessary means of justification—are to be done: it tells you they are done. It does not call on you to work out a justifying righteousness for yourselves, or even to seek for one to do this for you: it tells you of an all-accomplished Saviour, and of His completed and accepted work of expiation, on which justification may proceed.'

To the question, How is this work to be available for the justification of the individual? we have a reply in the 8th and 9th verses: "But what saith it?"—*i.e.*, What saith "the righteousness of faith"—the method of justification? How does it describe itself? Not only negatively, but positively. It

[1] Chap. iv. 25. [2] Chap. viii. 3.

says, "The word is nigh thee, even in thy mouth, and in thy heart: that is, the word of faith which we preach." By "the word," we are, as the apostle himself teaches us, to understand "the Gospel, in which the righteousness of God by faith is revealed;"[1] "the word of faith," meaning either the revelation to be believed, or the revelation about faith as the sole means of justification. This word is said to be "nigh us." It is brought near to those to whom it is preached, as the laws to which Moses referred were brought near to the Israelites. There was nothing to prevent their becoming acquainted with it. The phrase, "in thy mouth, and in thy heart," is not strictly exegetical of "nigh thee;" for it is not true that that word is "in the mouth and heart"—*i.e.*, understood, and believed, and professed, of all to whom it is nigh, in the sense of its being preached to them. The phrase seems elliptical: "it is nigh thee," *to be—in order to be—that it may be*, "in thy mouth and thy heart," as the apostle himself explains it. And this is "the word of faith"—this is the description of the method of justification by faith—"That if thou confess with the mouth the Lord Jesus, and believe in thy heart that God raised Him from the dead, thou shalt be saved."[2] To "confess with the mouth the Lord Jesus," is to make an open profession of the truth respecting Jesus Christ, as the divinely appointed, and Divine Saviour; to "believe in the heart that God raised Him from the dead," is to be inwardly persuaded, on the testimony of God, that He has testified His satisfaction with the death of Christ, as the propitiation for the sins of men, by raising Him from the dead. He who thus confesses because he thus believes—he, and he only, shall be saved. Confession is here put before faith, as it is the confession which gives visibility to the faith—Paul following the order suggested by the words of Moses. When we think and speak of the believer only, the natural order is faith and confession. When we think and speak of him in reference to others, the natural order is profession and faith; for it is by the first that the

[1] Chap. i. 16, 17.

[2] Ver. 9.

second becomes known. The statement here is substantially the same as that of our Lord: "He that believeth, and is baptized"—*i.e.*, confesses his faith in the appointed way—"shall be saved."

The 10th verse is explicatory and confirmatory of the 9th: "For with the heart man believeth unto righteousness"—unto justification, so that he is justified; "and with the mouth confession is made unto salvation,"—so that he is saved. 'He that believes shall be justified; and he who, by a consistent profession, proves the reality of his faith—shows that he truly believes the truth—shall be saved.'

It has been very generally supposed that the expression, "with the heart man believes," points out some particular kind of faith—the faith of the heart, in contrast to the faith of the head. But the contrast here is not an implied one between two kinds of faith, but an expressed one between faith and confession. Faith is an inward operation, confession an external act. The notion that the heart is the seat of affection, and the head of intellect, is comparatively a modern one. The Jews spoke of the heart as the seat of all mental activity. The contrast is not between what has been termed speculative belief—which is either mere speculation, or the faith of something which, though it may be true, is not the saving truth—and affectionate faith. If there is any implied contrast, it is between real faith and pretended faith; the expressed contrast is between faith and confession. No controversy can be conceived more absurd and fruitless, than whether saving faith be an act of the intellect or of the will. Belief and will, or affection, are two different modes of mental activity; but belief, in a being constituted as man is, always produces affections corresponding to the truth believed. The faith which leads to salvation, is the faith of the truth respecting Jesus Christ as the Saviour; the confession which leads to salvation, is that which flows from this faith, and is made steady and influential by it.

The apostle finishes his account of "the righteousness of faith" by two citations from Old Testament Scripture, showing that it was as he had asserted, chap. iii. 21, "witnessed by the law and the prophets." "For," says he, "the Scripture saith, Whosoever believeth on Him shall not be ashamed."[1] This passage is from Isaiah xxviii. 16, and had already been quoted, chap. ix. 33. It is a Messianic prophecy, and intimates that, under the Messiah, men were to obtain an interest in His blessings by *believing*, and that "whosoever," whether Jew or Gentile, believed in Him, should possess these blessings. The apostle calls attention to this last truth, as indicated by this passage—"For there is no difference between the Jew and the Greek." It is not *whosoever* of the Jews, but simply "whosoever," be he Jew or Gentile; and it is not "whosoever" is circumcised, or "whosoever" obeys the law; it is, "whosoever believeth on Him." For, adds he, "The same Lord who is over all" mankind—*i.e.*, the Lord Messiah, "is *rich*"—full of benefits, and ready to communicate them "to *all*," whether Jews or Gentiles, "who," believing on Him, "call upon Him"—give Him Divine homage—acknowledge His Lordship, by praying to Him. And this He confirms by another Messianic prophecy: "For whosoever shall call on the name of the Lord shall be saved."[2]

Such, then, is "the righteousness by faith," as opposed to "the righteousness which is of the law." Its substance is, "Christ for righteousness to every one that believeth;" and it plainly is "the end" of that righteousness—that method of justification, which has for its substance, "The man that doeth them shall live in them."

Is it not wonderful that *justification*, presented to the acceptance of man as the gift of God, to be received in the belief of the truth, is not universally, eagerly, gratefully accepted? Yet it is not more wonderful than true. The unbelieving Jews have still but too many imitators. Human nature is materially the same in all countries and in all ages. Wherever the Divine method of justification has been revealed and pressed on the attention of mankind, there have been multi-

[1] Ver. 11. [2] Joel ii. 32.

tudes who, ignorant of God's method of justification, and going about to establish a method of justification of their own, have not submitted themselves to God's method of justification. Are there not many such among ourselves? Are there not many among us as ignorant as the Jews were, with less excuse, of the Divine method of justification? Yes; vast multitudes, who have had Paul's epistles in their hands, and have sometimes read them—who have heard the Gospel preached from their infancy, do yet very imperfectly understand, even as an object of intellectual apprehension, God's method of justification. If they were attempting to state it, they would entirely mis-state it. Are there not many who, being thus ignorant of the Divine method of justification, are going about to establish a method of justification of their own? Some are giving themselves no concern about the matter, and are madly rushing on to eternity without thinking what their relations are to Him whose judgment is to make that eternity to them an eternity of misery or an eternity of happiness. Others are going about, as if it were a matter of some consequence to establish a method of justification of their own. It is not just the Jews' method of justification, but it is a different embodiment of the same principles. Some are trusting to comparative innocence or worth; others, to the absolute benignity of God; others, to penitence and reformation; others, to the doing the best they can, leaving the merits of Christ to supplement the deficiencies. None who are thus ignorant of the Divine method of justification, and are going about to establish their own justification, can—it is in the nature of things impossible that they should—submit to the righteousness of God. And what must the end be? They cannot be justified—they must remain condemned. God will not be dictated to by man: He will justify in his own way, in no other. Meanwhile, the curse remains unremoved, and, not being causeless, must come. Like the unbelieving Jews, they must be anathema, accursed —accursed by Christ, by whom alone there is justification. This is a matter of life or death. Let us see then that we know the Divine method of justification, so plainly exhibited in the word of the truth of the Gospel. If we do this, we will no longer go about to establish a method of justification for ourselves. We will see how needless, how useless, how criminal, how ruinous such a course of conduct is. We will see that there is nothing for us but to submit to the righteousness of God; and we will, with the apostle, count all that we once reckoned gain loss, and say, "Surely in the Lord have I righteousness"—not having, not holding to, our own methods of justification, which are all of the law, but submitting to, laying hold of, clinging close to, God's method of justification through the faith of Christ—the Divine method of justification by believing. Happy are those who are thus "shut up to the faith," and after hard struggling, and much worse than wasted labour, are made to rest from their works, and, in a constant Sabbath of the soul, to sing—

> "No hope can on the law be built
> Of justifying grace;
> The law, that shows the sinner's guilt,
> Condemns him to his face.
> Jesus, how glorious is Thy grace!
> When in Thy name we trust,
> Our faith receives a righteousness
> That makes the sinner just."

"Christ for righteousness to every one that believeth is the end of the law." "Thanks be to God for this unspeakable gift."

The force of the next two verses may be thus given: 'Since, then, according to this method of justification, calling on the Lord is necessary to salvation, it follows, that as, in order to acceptable worship, there must be intelligent faith respecting the object of worship—so, in order to faith, there must be a testimony, spoken or written; and in order to this spoken or written testimony, there must be some qualified to give it; and in order to be qualified to give a testimony on such a subject, these men must be sent of God, for He alone can either qualify or authorise men to give a testimony worthy of belief on such subjects.

"How then shall they call on Him in whom they have not believed? and how shall they believe in Him of whom they have not heard? and how shall they hear without a preacher? and how shall they preach except they be sent?"[1]

An inspired ministry is necessary to gain the object of the Divine method of justification by believing. Such a ministry was the apostolic. "We," says Paul, in the name of all his apostolic brethren,—"We have, by Jesus Christ, received from God grace and apostleship for the obedience of faith among all nations for His name." They were "put in charge with the Gospel," and were commanded, "beginning at Jerusalem," to "go into all nations," to "preach the Gospel to every creature." This passage has often been explained of the Christian ministry generally, as condemning men who ultroneously assume that office. No doubt that is wrong; but the apostle speaks here, not of what is improper, but of what is impossible. There is no room to doubt that the sole meaning is: 'Without a divinely-qualified and authorised ministry, the truth with regard to the way of salvation through the Messiah must be unknown to mankind.' The "righteousness of God," till revealed, was a "mystery"—"what eye had not seen, what ear had not heard, what had never entered into the heart of man to conceive," till God manifested it to the apostles. If men are ignorant of the Messiah, they cannot believe in Him; and if they do not believe in Him, they cannot call on Him as the object of their religious trust; and if they do not thus call on Him, they cannot be saved. And thus the method of justification by believing would be utterly unavailing for the purpose for which it was intended.

The appointment of such a ministry, like everything else about this "righteousness of God," was the subject of Old Testament prediction: "As it is written, How beautiful are the feet of them that preach the Gospel of peace, and bring

[1] Ver. 14, 15.

glad tidings of good things!" The passage is quoted, apparently from memory, from Isa. lii. 7. In the beginning of the prophetic oracle, of which these words form a part, it is declared that Jehovah's "righteousness was near; that His salvation was gone forth—a salvation that was to be for ever, a righteousness which was not to be abolished."[1] And the words cited refer to those who should be employed to announce this great truth to Israel and the nations—to the Church and the world; for in thus establishing this righteousness, in accomplishing this salvation, "the Lord had made bare His holy arm in the eyes of all the nations, and all the ends of the earth were to see the salvation of God."[2] It is just as if the apostle had said, 'The agency of a divinely-qualified and authorised ministry, which is necessary to give effect to this method of justification, by proclaiming the truth about it to all—both Jews and Gentiles, and which was promised before in the Holy Scriptures, is prepared—all things are ready.'

The result of all this should have been the universal belief of the Gospel—the universal submission to the righteousness of God by Jew and Gentile. But how different was the truth! "But," *i.e.*, notwithstanding this provision, "they," *i.e.*, mankind, "have not all obeyed the Gospel."[3] These words are equivalent to a statement that comparatively few believed the report of the divinely-commissioned messengers, and yielded to the influence of their message. This was the fact: the number was *great*, abstractly considered, but *small*, comparatively viewed. Few of either Jews or Gentiles believed, in comparison of those of both classes who did not believe. The form of expression is peculiar. It states an unpleasant thing in the least disagreeable way; just as in Heb. iii. 16, it is said, "But *some*, when they heard, did provoke;" which "some" were "all who came out of Egypt with Moses," with the exception of Caleb and Joshua.

This result, however much to be regretted, was nothing

[1] Isa. li. 4–6. [2] Isa. lii. 10. [3] Ver. 16.

more than had been predicted by the prophets. "For Esaias saith, Lord, who hath believed our report?" This is the first verse of the fifty-third chapter of Isaiah. These seem to be the words of the same persons who are spoken of in the oracle just cited from Isaiah lii. 7. These "publishers of peace and salvation" were to have reason to complain that comparatively few credited their report. The event had corresponded with the prediction; and thus, what might seem an objection becomes a confirmation of the Gospel.

The 17th verse is an exegetical note on the passage just cited, showing that it contained in it a confirmation of what the apostle had just said, that in order to the efficiency of the Divine method of justification, there must be a Divine testimony presented to mankind. "So then faith cometh by hearing"[1] (by a report, for the same word is used here as in the preceding verse), "and hearing"—*i.e.* the report—"by the word of God"—a Divine revelation. 'It appears from this passage that the Messianic blessings are to be obtained through the faith of a testimony which, though delivered by man, is indeed the testimony of God.'

If the Gospel, in which the righteousness of God by faith is revealed in order to be believed, is not universally—is not even generally, believed by either Jews or Gentiles, the cause is not to be sought in any want of the means of their becoming acquainted with it. This is what the apostle states in the 18th verse: "But," though all have not obeyed the Gospel, "I say, Have they not heard?" Has not the Divine method of justification been manifested to all? has it not been revealed in the Gospel—a revelation fitted for all, intended for all? Has it not actually been very extensively proclaimed both to Jews and Gentiles? Has not the commission of the risen Saviour been followed out? Are the Christian evangelists not going to all the world and preaching the Gospel to every creature? "Yea, verily:"—the words originally used by the Psalmist as descriptive of the universal intima-

[1] ἀκοή.

tions given by the visible heavens of the glory of Jehovah, may be applied to their labours, "Their sound went into all the earth, and their words to the end of the world."

This was a state of things on which the Jews had not counted. They had not expected a spiritual Messiah; they had not thought of a method of justification for all mankind, being the great blessing He was to confer; they had not thought of the faith of a Divine revelation being the means of interesting individuals in His benefits; they had especially not thought of these benefits being presented to all men on the same terms, and being received by many of the Gentiles, and rejected by the majority of the Jews. "But," adds the apostle, "I say, Did not Israel know? First, Moses saith, I will provoke you to jealousy by them that are no people, and by a foolish nation I will anger you. But Esaias is very bold, and saith, I was found of them that sought Me not; I was made manifest unto them that asked not after Me. But to Israel he saith, All day long I have stretched forth my hands unto a disobedient and gainsaying people." [1]

"Did not Israel know?" Were not the Jews aware that the events accompanying and following the manifestation of the Divine method of justification were to take place? If they were not, they should have been, for they are distinctly enough announced in the writings of their prophets. "First," their great prophet and legislator predicted what was then taking place. The passage referred to is Deut. xxxii. 21, "They have moved Me to jealousy by that which is not God; they have provoked Me to anger with their vanities: and I will move them to jealousy with those who are not a people; I will provoke them to anger with a foolish nation." That wonderful chapter contains an epitome of the anticipated history of the Israelites, from the times of Moses down to "the latter days." It is an intimation that God would, for the punishment of their sins, withdraw from them the special favours He had bestowed on them, and confer them on those

[1] Ver. 19-21.

who had been destitute of them, and who, as "foolish," which in the prophets is often equivalent to idolatrous, were utterly unworthy of them; thus making those the objects of their jealousy and envy who had previously been the objects of their contempt and hatred. This threatening was fulfilled when the great body of the Jews, having rejected the promised Messiah, were disowned by God, and when He "visited the Gentiles to take out of them a people for His name;"[1] "when many came," according to the prediction of our Lord, "from the east and the west, and sat down with Abraham and Isaac and Jacob in the kingdom of heaven, while the children of the kingdom were cast out into outer darkness."[2]

But there were plainer intimations than those contained in these words of Moses. "But Esaias," says the apostle, "is very bold"—in still stronger and more explicit terms does he speak of the calling of the Gentiles and the rejection of the Jews. The passage referred to is Isa. lxv. 1, 2, "I am sought of them that asked not for Me: I am found of them that sought Me not. . . . I have spread out My hands all the day unto a rebellious people." The apostle keeps to the reading of the Septuagint version, only transposing the clause in the first verse which refers to the calling of the Gentiles. According to Isaiah, a time was coming—plainly under the Messiah, and in the commencement of His era,[3] when Jehovah should be sought, so as to be found, by those who had not previously sought Him, and made manifest to those that had not previously asked after Him. How strikingly was this prediction fulfilled in the conversion of so many idolatrous Gentiles! The second quotation, which is the 2d verse of the same chapter, refers in equally plain terms to the rejection of the Jews. To understand the full force of the passage, however, it is necessary to read the rest of the paragraph down to the 15th verse. "But to Israel"—rather, in reference to Israel, for the words are not an address—"He saith, All day long I have stretched out my hands to a rebellious and gain-

[1] Acts xv. 14. [2] Matt. viii. 11, 12. [3] Ver. 17.

saying people."[1] On the hypothesis that this is a Messianic oracle, which the Jews admitted, nothing can be a more just deduction than that of the apostle, that Israel had the means of knowing that at the period referred to, the commencement of the Messianic era, the wicked descendants of Israel were to be stripped of the privileges they had abused, and the Gentiles so introduced among the people of God, that "of them" Jehovah would "take for priests and for Levites."[2] Even the office-bearers of the Church were to be Gentiles."

Thus has the apostle briefly, but clearly, stated the relations in which the Divine manifested method of justification stood to the Jews and Gentiles. It had been presented to both in a plain revelation, given and proclaimed by a divinely-qualified and authorised class of teachers. It had been embraced by many of the latter; it had been rejected by the majority of the former. Gentiles, ignorant and careless about God, had, on hearing the Gospel, believed it, and been interested in all the benefits secured by the Divine method of justification; while the great body of the Jews, continuing wilfully ignorant of the Divine method of justification, and persevering in endeavouring to establish a method of justification for themselves, had, in rejecting the Gospel, of course shut themselves out from the benefits of the Divine method of justification, which, from its very nature, could be obtained only by believing; and not only so, but had exposed themselves to the Divine vengeance for this last and crowning act of a long course of impenitence and disobedience. Such was the state of things when the apostle wrote.

This state was not, however, so gloomy as at first sight it appeared, in reference even to Israel. Their rejection of the Gospel had not been *universal*, and, therefore, neither was their exclusion from the blessings connected with the Divine method of justification, nor their exposure to penal inflictions, universal; and, ultimately, the great body of the Jewish

[1] Ver. 21. [2] Isa. lxvi. 21.

people were to be brought to believe the Gospel, and, along with the great body of the Gentile nations, converted also to the faith of Christ, to enjoy the Divine special favour, and all the blessings which this of course secures. All Israel was to be saved, and the fulness of the Gentiles was to be brought in. The illustration of these points occupies the whole of the eleventh chapter, and shuts up the doctrinal part of the epistle.

The apostle thus introduces this part of the subject: "I say then, Hath God cast away His people? God forbid. For I also am an Israelite, of the seed of Abraham, of the tribe of Benjamin."[1] God had cast away the greater part of the nation, whom He had afore acknowledged as His people, in consequence of their unbelief and obstinate rejection of the proffered Saviour and salvation. There was no doubt of that awful fact. But, has God cast off the descendants of Israel? has He, viewing them as individuals, cast them *all* off? has He, viewing them as a nation, cast them off *for ever?* That, from the sequel, is plainly the intended force of the apostle's question; and to this question he answers by his strong negative, "God forbid"—'Let it not be'—a form of expression which not only denies the supposed fact, but deprecates the consequences which would flow from it; adding, "For I also am an Israelite, of the seed of Abraham, of the tribe of Benjamin"—I belong to the sacred family, and can trace my lineage. It is as if he had said—'If it had been so, what would have become of me? Blessed be God it is not so.' He had obtained mercy, and so might all Israel have done, if, like him, they would have but submitted to the righteousness of faith. "God hath not cast away His people whom He foreknew."[2]

By "God's people," we must not understand here either the spiritual Israel, consisting of believing Jews and Gentiles, or the believing part of the Jews. It is plain that the Israel he is speaking of is the same Israel mentioned chap. ix. 31, and chap. x. 1, 19, 21—the Israelitish nation, the majority of

[1] Chap. xi. 1. [2] Ver. 2.

which were cast off. What he asserts, and goes on to prove, is—that the Israelitish people were neither universally nor finally abandoned of God. They are termed "His people, whom He foreknew." The word "foreknow," in chap. viii. 29, signifies to foreappoint—to predestinate. But it admits of another rendering, which the context here seems to require. To know, according to the Hebrew idiom, signifies to acknowledge—as Numbers xvi. 5; Amos iii. 2. To foreknow, in this sense, is to have acknowledged formerly. There is an opposition between the words "cast off" and "formerly acknowledged." He has not abandoned the Jews, though most of them have abandoned Him; He has not wholly, or for ever, rejected them. There is still a portion of them, in respect of whom, in all the emphasis of the words, He is "their God," and they are "His people;" and there is a period in futurity, when the great body of the nation shall again acknowledge Him, and be acknowledged by Him. He has not cast off all His people; He has not cast them off, as a people, for ever. These are the two heads of the remaining part of the apostle's discussion.

The first of these he illustrates by a striking incident in the history of Israel in former times: "Wot ye not what the Scripture saith of Elias?"[1]—in the history of Elias—"how he maketh intercession to God against"—how he complaineth of, or accuses—"Israel, saying, Lord, they have killed Thy prophets, and digged down Thine altars; and I am left alone, and they seek my life. But what saith the answer of God to him? I have reserved to Myself seven thousand men, who have not bowed the knee to the image of Baal."[2] This passage is from 1 Kings xix. 10. It is quoted, not verbally, but in an abridged form from the LXX., probably from memory. At the period referred to, the great body of the ten tribes had abandoned the true worship of God, and He could not acknowledge them as His people. But, from among them, He still had a people who acknowledged Him, and whom He

[1] ἐν Ἠλίᾳ.

[2] Ver. 2–4.

acknowledged—a small number in comparison of the apostates, yet still a considerable number, and greatly exceeding what the prophet supposed to exist.

Now comes the application of this fact by the apostle to the case before him: "Even so then at this present time also there is a remnant according to the election of grace."[1] Amid the general rejection of God and His Messiah by the Israelites, and their general rejection by God on this account, there is "a remnant"—a comparatively small number—who have obeyed the command, "Kiss the Son;" "This is My beloved Son, hear Him;" and these are acknowledged and treated by God as His people.

This "remnant" is characterized as a remnant "according to the election of grace"—the gracious election or choice—a choice not founded on man's *merit*, but on God's *mercy*—sovereign grace. A part—a small part, remained faithful, according to—in pursuance of—in virtue of, their being, in sovereign mercy, chosen out from among those who sinfully rejected the Messiah, and who, on that ground, were righteously rejected by God. In the case of the ancient Israelites, it was as idolaters that the body of Israel was disowned—it was as faithful that the remnant were acknowledged. In the case of the Jews in the apostolic age, it was as unbelievers that the majority were cast off, and as believers that the minority were saved. Yet in both cases the difference originated in a sovereign, Divine choice. Left to themselves, all would have been, in the one case, idolaters; in the other, unbelievers.

The words which follow appear to be explanatory of the phrase, "election of grace:" "And if by grace, then is it no more of works; otherwise grace is no more grace. But if it be of works, then is it no more grace; otherwise work is no more work,"[2]—*q.d.*, 'Let us remember, when we say an election *of grace*, how much these words imply—nothing short of the entire exclusion of all human *work* as, foreseen, the

[1] Ver. 5. [2] Ver. 6.

cause of the choice, or as, as actually existing, the cause of the selection. If "by grace" the selection has taken place—if it has originated in sovereign mercy on the part of God, as we know it has—then it is not at all of works; works—merit, anything in man—cannot be its cause, otherwise grace, which is sovereign, self-moved love, would lose its nature; but if it were of works, which we know it is not, then it were no more of grace—the cause would be in man, not in God, otherwise work would be no more work—that which earns reward. There is no mingling the two principles. It must be all earned, or none; none conferred by Divine grace, or all. The two schemes of grace and works cannot be combined without destroying the plain meaning of words, and confounding the nature of things. In the first case, the cause is in God; in the second, in the creature. In the one, the benefit is matter of free favour; in the other, of equitable or stipulated right. If the grace of God is the cause of election, the merit of man is not; if the merit of man is, the grace of God is not. Light and darkness, heat and cold, are not more opposed to one another than grace and merit.

"What then?" says the apostle,[1] resuming the discussion. 'How does the matter stand, as to the "casting off" of Israel now being as like that "casting off" in the time of Elijah, not universal? It stands thus: "Israel hath not obtained that which he seeketh for."' "Israel" is the great body of the Israelites, who have not obtained that which they sought for; and what was that? It was "a law of righteousness"[2]—a method of justification—a way of securing the Divine special favour; and justification, or the special favour of God, by that law, method, or way. This they sought, not in God's way, but in their own; not by the faith of the Gospel, but by the works of the law; and, therefore, they had not attained it.

But, while this was the case with Israel as a body, "the election hath obtained." "The election" here is used as

[1] Ver. 7. [2] Chap. ix. 31.

equivalent to "the elect," just as "the circumcision" is used as equivalent to "the circumcised." The elect, because they were the elect, in consequence of an influence originating in sovereign mercy, believed the Gospel, submitted to "the righteousness of God," and thus attained to the true way of justification, and to justification by that way. All believing Jews were "justified freely by God's grace, through the redemption in Christ Jesus."

Thus God has still a people from among the Israelites. Israel is not totally cast off; but "the rest"—those who are not included in the election—"were blinded, or hardened." The peculiar circumstances in which they were placed, as God's chosen people—the predictions of the prophets respecting the reign of the Messiah—these, which were the work of God, misunderstood by the great body of the Jews in consequence of the carnality of their minds, blinded them, so that they could not see that Jesus Christ was the Messiah; or the heavenly and spiritual salvation offered in the Gospel, the glorious emancipation which they anticipated from Him. God exercised no direct influence in blinding or hardening the unbelieving Jews. He left them, after clearly stating the truth to them, to the natural operation of their depraved hearts, in the circumstances in which they were placed; and the result was, they rejected His Messiah, and salvation through Him, and of course were rejected by Him.

And, in this blindness of the majority of the Israelitish people, there was a striking fulfilment of Old Testament prophecy, and, of consequence, a confirmation of the truth and divinity of that Gospel, on which their rejection might be supposed otherwise to cast a cloud of suspicion. This is what is stated in ver. 8, 9, 10: "According as it is written, God hath given them the spirit of slumber, eyes that they should not see, and ears that they should not hear, unto this day. And David saith, Let their table be made a snare, and a trap, and a stumbling-block, and a recompense unto them: let their eyes be darkened, that they may not see, and bow down their back alway."

The first passage referred to by the apostle is from the Prophet Isaiah[1]—"For the Lord hath poured out upon you the spirit of deep sleep, and hath closed your eyes." The quotation seems, like so many more in the apostle's writings, made from memory. The whole of the twenty-ninth chapter is occupied with a prediction of events which exactly correspond with those of the closing scene of the Jewish polity, and to which no satisfactory correspondence can be found in any other period of their history. To be under the influence of the "spirit of deep sleep," or rather of stupefaction, is to be in a state of delusion—to be under the guidance of what the apostle, in chap. i. 28, calls "a reprobate mind," to which God gave up the idolatrous Gentiles—better rendered in the margin, 'a mind void of judgment;' and by "God giving this," we are to understand God punishing them for their sins, by not interfering with the natural operation of circumstances on their depraved minds to stupify and delude. The word 'to give,' is used in a similar way in Gen. xxxi. 7, and Deut. xviii. 14, where it is rendered 'suffered.'

The remaining words in the 8th verse are an allusion to, rather than a quotation of, either Isa. vi. 9, 10, or Deut. xxix. 4. The first of these passages runs thus: "And he said, Go and tell this people, Hear ye indeed, but understand not; and see ye indeed, but perceive not. Make the heart of this people fat, and make their ears heavy, and shut their eyes; lest they see with their eyes, and hear with their ears, and understand with their heart, and convert, and be healed." The second, thus: "Yet the Lord hath not given you an heart to perceive, and eyes to see, and ears to hear, unto this day." The first of these passages is referred to by our Lord (Matt. xiii. 14; Mark iv. 12; Luke viii. 10); and by the Evangelist John (chap. xii. 40), and by the apostle Paul, to their countrymen, in a manner that leads us to conclude that it was directly prophetic of them. The second plainly is a

[1] Chap. xxix. 10.

description of Moses' contemporaries. The most probable interpretation is, that "as it is written" should be considered as equivalent to 'to use the words of Scripture,' and that the verse is to be considered as the apostle's own description of the unbelieving Jews, clothed in Old Testament language. The meaning seems to be—'The great body of the Jewish people have, according to the description of their legislator and prophets, been all along, and continue to be, a stiff-necked and rebellious race; and though, for this, they have been without doubt entirely to blame, yet still this state of mind, as the natural effect of the Divine arrangements on the depraved minds of the Jews, the Divine Being is considered as having such an agency in producing, that He may, in a sense not implying that He is the author of sin, be said to give, as a punishment for sin, the spirit of stupidity—the eyes and the ears inept to perform their proper functions.'

The last passage referred to is cited from Psalm lxix. 22. There is no reasonable doubt that this psalm is a direct prediction respecting the sufferings of the Messiah, and the glories which were to follow. It has all the characteristics of the Messianic psalms; there is much in it that cannot without violence be applied to any but the Messiah—nothing in it, rightly interpreted, that is not applicable to Him; in its structure, it exactly corresponds to other psalms undoubtedly Messianic; and passages from it are repeatedly cited in the New Testament as predictions. Its awful imprecations by the Messiah are illustrative of what the apostle meant when he represented his kinsmen, his brethren according to the flesh, as an "anathema by Christ." They are a prediction of what should befall the opposers of the Messiah, as the righteous punishment of their opposition to Him. "Their table was to be made a snare, and a trap, and a stumbling-block, and a recompense to them; their eyes were to be darkened, so as not to see, and their back to be bowed down always." The general meaning is that their privileges and advantages, through their abuse of them, should be the occasion of their delusion and punishment. They were to become the victims of delusion, and the subjects of a most degrading spiritual slavery. The prediction was fulfilled in the case of the Jews of the apostle's age, and continues to be fulfilled in the case of their posterity who walk in their footsteps. The Old Testament, through their misinterpretation, confirms them in their unbelief, and they are under the bondage of Talmudic superstition. Indeed, it has been remarked, that the first part of the prophecy was verified even to the letter in the case of the Jews, when, in the destruction of their city, "wrath came on them to the uttermost." "Their table"—their paschal feast, was a snare to take them, a stumbling-block, an occasion of their fall, when, towards the close of the Jewish war under Titus, a vast multitude, collected from all quarters to observe the passover and to supplicate the assistance of their God against their enemies, met, in the crucifixion of thousands of them, with "a recompense"—a most appropriate punishment of their great national sin in having, by the hands of the Romans, crucified and slain the Messiah.[1]

This state of spiritual blindness and obduracy, and dereliction by God, and deep degradation and suffering, into which the Jewish people generally sunk on their rejecting the Messiah, and which still continues—for hitherto it has only been a very small remnant that have attained Messianic blessings—is not to continue always. By means of these awful events, those blessings were communicated more speedily and more extensively to the Gentiles than otherwise they could have been, and a destined period would assuredly arrive, when the great body of the Jews, remaining a distinct people, and the great body of the Gentile nations, should, by submitting to "the righteousness of God," become heirs of the common salvation.

The manner in which the manifested Divine method of justification works out its great intended results, remains unchanged, unchangeable. The Divine testimony respecting it

[1] Joseph. Bell. Jud. vi. 9, 3.

must be believed, in order to its benefits being realized. This testimony, contained in the apostolic writings, must be urged on the attention of mankind, both Jews and Gentiles. As there is nothing restrictive in the revelation itself, it ought to be made known to men of every nation, people, kindred, and tongue—to every human creature under heaven. This is the Church's duty; but, alas! how very imperfectly has it been performed! Where this testimony is made known, no human being remains personally uninterested in the blessings it reveals and conveys, but by his own wilful unbelief. We cannot plead that we have not heard. Yet, is it not true, that not all of us who have heard have believed? What is the reason? Not want of plainness in the testimony, not want of power in the evidence. The true reason, in the case of unbelievers now, as in the case of the Jews then, is, they like neither the Saviour nor the salvation. But we must either have this Saviour or none at all—this salvation or perdition must be our portion—"There is no name given under heaven among men by which we may be saved, but the name Jesus." If any of us at last are found uninterested in the Divine method of justification, and therefore liable to the tremendous evils from which it alone saves, we shall be found, in some respects, even more guilty than the unbelieving Jews in the primitive age; and He who spared not them, assuredly will not spare us.

There are some practical instructions very distinctly, though indirectly, intimated in the commencing paragraph of the eleventh chapter, which I think it right briefly to notice before proceeding to the illustration of the next subdivision of the apostle's argument. (1.) Let us be cautious as to the conclusions we draw from acknowledged and undoubted truths. They by no means warrant all the inferences which have been plausibly drawn from them. (2.) Let us be cautious and charitable in the judgments we form of bodies of men: God may have people where we would not expect to find them. (3.) Let us guard against desponding views with regard to religion. Elijah's mistake has often been committed. (4.) Let us take heed not to resist the fair influence of truth and its evidence. If we do, we need not wonder that we should be delivered over to the hands of the great deceiver—"given up to strong delusions, to believe a lie," and be involved in the condemnation of those who, if they make not lies, love them, and who believe not the truth, just because they loved it not. For, as our Christian poet has it:—

> "He that *will* be cheated: to the last,
> Delusions, strong as hell, shall bind him fast."

β. Future relations—The great body of both Jews and Gentiles are to embrace the Gospel and enjoy the benefits of the Divine Method of Justification.

Such was the state of things when the apostle wrote, and, after eighteen centuries, this substantially remains the state of things still. But it shall not be always so. The actual relation of the manifested Divine method of justification to mankind shall yet better correspond to the wants of the race, on the one hand, and the capabilities and tendencies of the Divine economy, on the other. The general rejection of the Gospel by the Jews was to be subordinate to its more speedy and extensive reception by the Gentiles; the advantages enjoyed by the Gentiles, in consequence of their receiving the Gospel, were to operate in exciting a jealousy on the part of the Jews which would lead to their conversion, which, in its turn, would be, as it were, life from the dead to the Gentiles, and ultimately "the fulness of the Gentiles shall come in," and "all Israel shall be saved." The great body of mankind, both Jews and Gentiles, after being alternately shut up in unbelief, shall become the objects of Divine mercy, and together enjoy the blessings of the Christian salvation, to the praise of the depth of the riches of the wisdom and power and grace of Him of whom are all things, and to whom are all things. Such is an outline of the train of thought to the end of the chapter.

The greater part of what is more fully developed in the sequel of the chapter is presented in a very condensed form in the 11th verse. "I say then, Have they," *i.e.* Israel, "stumbled that they should fall? God forbid: but rather through their fall salvation is come unto the Gentiles, to provoke them to jealousy." Israel's "stumbling" is plainly the rejection of the Messiah by the great body of the Jewish people, and their consequent exclusion from the Messianic blessings: the stumbling includes both the sin and its punishment. The reference seems not to the unbelieving Jews as individuals; for without question *they*, continuing in unbelief, had stumbled so as to fall. The finally impenitent individual, be he Jew or Gentile, so falls as never to rise again. The question of the apostle is (and it naturally rose out of what he had said respecting a portion of the Jews—the election, who through believing had obtained the righteousness which is by faith) —'What is to become of the rest—the great body of the nation?' The question admits of two senses, according as you understand the particle translated "that," as meaning 'so that,' or 'in order that.' In the first case, the meaning is, 'Have the Jews, by rejecting the Messiah, brought themselves into such a state, that they shall never more form a part of the Church of God? In their case, has the harvest come? has the wheat been gathered in, and are "the rest" to be consigned as tares to the fire?' In the second case, the meaning is, 'What was the design of God in permitting this sin, and visiting it with this judgment; was it that the people should be utterly destroyed—that, having fallen, they never might rise?' From the answer given, it would appear that the last is the meaning—a meaning which will be found to include the first. To the question, Is the final cause of what has happened to Israel that they may be destroyed?—to this question, the apostle replies, "God forbid!" The destruction of the Jewish people is not the final cause of what has taken place as a Divine arrangement, nor is it that in which, as a

Divine dispensation, it will issue. The final end is twofold: first, that "through their fall[1] salvation might come unto the Gentiles;" and secondly, "to provoke *them*, that is the Jews, to jealousy." Let us inquire what the two ends thus described are, and endeavour to show how the stumbling of the Jews—their rejection of the Messiah, and the punishment they thus brought down upon themselves—was fitted to serve, and has served, or will serve, these ends.

The first purpose intended to be served by the rejection of the Messiah by the Jews, and their rejection in consequence of this, is, "that through their fall salvation should come unto the Gentiles." The general unbelief of the Jews, and their punishment for it, were the means of the Gentiles becoming more speedily and extensively acquainted with the Gospel, and thus interested in the salvation which it at once reveals and conveys, than otherwise they could have been. Though the Jews had universally embraced Christianity, we have no reason to think that the Gentiles would have been permanently excluded from its benefits: but it seems evident, that such an event, however desirable in itself, would have at once prevented the Gentiles from hearing the Gospel so soon, and would have thrown difficulties in the way of their receiving it when they did hear it.

The command of our Lord was to "preach the Gospel to all nations," but to begin at Jerusalem. "The blessings of the Gospel were to be offered to the Jews first." It every way suited the genius of the economy, whose leading character is sovereign grace, that the murderers of the Son of God should have the first offer of pardon—that they who had struck the rock should be invited to take the first draught of the waters of salvation which flowed from it;[2] that they who had shed the blood of atonement should be urged to become the living proof that it indeed cleanseth from *all* sin. Accordingly, the primitive teachers of Christianity, for a considerable time, confined their evangelical labours to their countrymen,

[1] παράπτωμα.

[2] Grosvenor.

the Jews; and even when they went beyond the boundaries of the Holy Land, the conversion of Jews was the primary object of their exertions. Had the Jews generally discovered a teachable disposition, there would have been opened a wide field to the apostles and evangelists, which would have employed them for a considerable period. But when the Jews, as they generally did, opposed and blasphemed, nothing remained for the propagators of Christianity, but to turn themselves to the Gentiles. The best commentary on this view of the subject is to be found in the facts recorded respecting the conduct of the primitive evangelists, of which we have a specimen, Acts xiii. 14–48; xxviii. 17–28.

But this is not the only, nor perhaps the principal, way in which the general rejection of Christianity by the Jews conduced to the speedier and more extensive conversion of the Gentiles. Christianity, if it had been universally embraced by the Jews, would have been much less likely to be embraced by the Gentiles. This may seem strange; but it is true, and it is not difficult to make its truth evident. There existed, as is well known, an inveterate antipathy between the Jews and the Gentiles. The Jews regarded the Gentiles, and the Gentiles the Jews, with equal contempt and hatred. Had the Jews, as a body, received Christianity, that religion would have worn to the Gentiles the repugnant aspect of the religion of the Jews. In this case, too, it is highly probable that the converted Jewish nation would have continued, as so many of the individual converts from among them did, "zealous for the law of Moses," and not at all unlikely that they would have insisted on proselytes from among the Gentiles submitting to its ritual institutions. It is easy to see what obstacles such a state of things would have placed in the way of the general Christianization of the Gentiles. All the difficulties which lay in the way of a heathen becoming a Jew, would have lain in the way of his becoming a Christian. But when Christianity was embraced only by a small minority of Jews, it became evident that Judaism and Christianity were two very different things; and when it was understood that one great cause why the majority of the Jews rejected Christianity was its liberal character—its placing Jews and Gentiles on a level as to religious privilege, it is easy to see how its rejection by the former would be a powerful recommendation of it to the latter. Thus, in consequence of an event in itself deeply to be deplored, Christianity assumed at once that liberal unencumbered form which fitted it to be the religion of "men of every kindred, and people, and tongue, and nation."

This was the direct primary design of the casting away of the Jews; but it was intended, through the gaining of this end, to gain another one, namely, the restoration of the great body of the Jews to the enjoyment of the blessings only to be found among the people of God. Salvation came to the Gentiles, through the fall of the Jews, "for to provoke *them*," *i.e.* the Jews, "to jealousy," or emulation. The advantages possessed by the Gentiles, in consequence of their having embraced Christianity—especially viewed in connection, both with the wretched circumstances in which they were in their previous state of heathenism, and with the degraded and wretched state into which the Jews have fallen since their rejection of Christ—are obviously fitted to lead the Jews to serious reflection, and to excite in them emulation, envy, jealousy of the Gentiles, which may produce inquiry leading to faith. Who can tell in how many individual cases this has happened since the apostle wrote these words? And when converted Gentiles, both as individuals and as churches, more fully develop the direct and indirect advantages which the reception of Christianity is fitted to communicate than they have ever yet done, which they easily might do, which we doubt not they shall do, then an influence shall go forth which Jewish obstinacy shall not be able to resist, and the glorious event more fully unfolded in the sequel—the general conversion of the Israelitish people, shall take place.

And then this change in the state of Israel will re-act, in its turn, in the most favourable way on the Gentiles. "Now, if the fall of them be the riches of the world, and the diminishing of them the riches of the Gentiles, how much more their fulness?"[1] In this verse emphasis is given to the sentiment by repetition. In the first parallel the sense is incomplete. The full expression is, 'If the fall of them be the riches of the world, how much more their restoration?' Though the temporary unbelief and consequent fall of Israel have greatly conduced to the promotion of the interests of the Gentiles, it does not at all follow that the continuance of this degraded state of Israel is necessary to the continuance of the exalted state of converted Gentiles, or would be indeed at all advantageous to them. The truth is just the reverse. The fall of Israel has served its purpose to the Gentiles. They have derived advantage, great advantage, from it; but they are also to derive advantage, still greater advantage, from their rise. This seems the plain meaning of the words of the apostle. The fall of the Jews is their rejection of the Messiah, and its results to them. The diminution of the Jews is their lessened, degraded state—a state devoid of privileges formerly possessed—a state of spiritual poverty. And the fulness of the Jews is the state of fulness of blessing which shall belong to them when, moved by jealousy, they return to their God, and embrace His Messiah. And what the apostle states is this, 'If the Gentiles have derived so much advantage from the former, what will they derive from the latter? The conversion of the Jews will, directly and indirectly, do more for the advantage of the Gentiles than their unbelief has done.' Such a result may naturally be expected. It is easy to see in how many ways the general conversion of the Jews, were it now to take place, would conduce more to the speedy and extended progress of Christianity, than their unbelief did in the primitive age. And this is quite in accordance with old Testament prediction.

The two following verses,[2] though not, strictly speaking, parenthetical, are an expression of the deep interest the apostle felt in the subject of which he was writing, and the influence it exerted over him, as an object of his labours, as the apostle of the Gentiles. "For I speak to you Gentiles, inasmuch as

[1] Ver. 12. [2] Ver. 13, 14.

I am the apostle of the Gentiles, I magnify my office: if by any means I may provoke to emulation them which are my flesh, and save some of them." These words seem intended to meet a tacit objection: But if the conversion of the Jews be a matter of such importance, why do you not devote yourself to it? The reply is twofold. *First*, The apostleship of the Gentiles is the sphere appointed me by my Master; He said to me, "Depart, for I will send thee far hence unto the Gentiles." For this work he was peculiarly fitted. He who wrought effectually in Peter to the apostleship of the circumcision, the same was mighty in Paul toward the Gentiles; and the apostles at Jerusalem "saw that the Gospel of the uncircumcision was committed to him."[2] And *Secondly*, In executing that commission, he was doing what was fitted to forward the conversion of the Jews, and doing it for that purpose; *q. d.* 'I speak the word to you Gentiles, rather than to the Jews, inasmuch as I am especially appointed to do so: I magnify my office—I make much of my office: it is a wide sphere, and I do what I can to occupy it, and to convert as many Gentiles as possible; but in doing this, I am not forgetful of those whom I regard as a part of myself—my flesh. One great reason why I am so desirous thoroughly to Christianize the Gentiles is, that seeing their holy happiness, some of my deluded countrymen may so emulate this happiness as to seek to share it, and thus I may be the means of their salvation.'

In the 15th verse, the apostle reverts to the idea introduced at the 12th. "For if the casting away of them be the reconciling of the world, what shall the receiving of them be but life from the dead?"[3] The rejection of the great body of the Jews on account of their unbelief, was the means of bringing Gentiles, who were aliens, strangers, enemies from the holy commonwealth, into reconciliation with God through the faith of the Gospel. If so untoward an event produced such happy consequences, how much happier consequences might

[1] Acts xxii. 21. [2] Gal. ii. 7, 8. [3] Ver. 15.

reasonably be anticipated from an event of an opposite character? "What shall the receiving of them"—that is, the restoration of the great body of the Israelites to the privileges of the Church in a far higher state than when they had formerly been members of it—"be but life from the dead?" Some have supposed that the words "life from the dead," refer to the happy change which shall take place on the Israelites. No doubt, Ezekiel's prediction shall be verified in that event.[1] But the construction of the passage constrains us to apply these words to the Gentiles. The restoration of the Jews shall be to the Church, composed chiefly, almost entirely, of Gentiles, as "life from the dead." It shall produce the happiest effects: it is easy to see how it must do so. It is not unlikely that the words are also intended to intimate, what they naturally enough suggest, that the Church, at the period of the conversion of the Jews, shall be in a comparatively dead state, and that this wonderful event, in itself and its effects, is to be the means of a great revival.

The words that follow[2] do not give the reason for the fact, that the conversion of the Jews shall be a great blessing to the Gentile churches; but they give a reason for a statement which that fact supposes, namely, that there is to be a general conversion of the Jews; and it is with the evidence of this that the apostle is chiefly engaged to the end of the chapter. It is as if the apostle had said, 'And we have reason to expect that, as they have been cast away, they shall be again received. "For if the first-fruit be holy, the lump also is holy; and if the root be holy, so are the branches."'

In order to apprehend the force of the apostle's argument, it is necessary, in the first place, that we understand the meaning of the figurative language in which it is expressed. The appellation, "first-fruits," is used in the Old Testament in four different ways. *First*, and principally, of a sheaf of barley, cut, before the harvest commenced, on the second day of the feast of unleavened bread, and solemnly devoted by the

[1] Ezek. xxxvii. 10. [2] Ver. 16.

priest to Jehovah, in the name of the congregation of Israel. *Secondly*, of two loaves of fine flour offered at the end of harvest on the day of Pentecost, also in the name of the congregation. *Thirdly*, of a portion of the first produce of the harvest, the exact measure of which is not fixed, which private individuals presented in the tabernacle or the temple. And *Fourthly*, of the first part of their dough, which individuals were required to give to the Levites, or, if none of these lived near them, to burn in the fire as a devoted thing. The "first-fruits," in all these forms, were "holy"—devoted to God—separated to a sacred use. To which of these forms the apostle refers, will appear in the course of our explication. Lev. xxiii. 10–21; Lev. ii. 14–16; Exod. xxii. 29, xxiii. 19; Numb. xv. 19, 20; Deut. xxvi. 1–15.

The word "lump" has very generally been understood of the rest of the grain or meal, after the first-fruits have been separated. This mode of interpretation is untenable; for (1.) the original word rendered "lump" conveys no such idea. It signifies merely a kneaded mass of any material, such as clay or dough. It has not the meaning of our word *mass*, in the sense of the greater part of a thing. (2.) Supposing that that were its meaning, there would be no truth in the apostle's illustration. The rest of the grain or dough was not holy in the sense in which the first-fruits were holy; on the contrary, the consecrating the first-fruits made it lawful to use the rest for common purposes. No such idea is anywhere to be met with in the law of Moses, as that the offering of the first-fruits sanctified the whole produce. (3.) This view of the meaning of the phrase leads to an interpretation of the apostle's reasoning which renders it destitute of all force. The first-fruits are supposed to signify the converts from among the Jews in the primitive age; and the lump, the great body of the nation, now in a state of unbelief, but ultimately to be converted to the faith of Christ. But could anything in the shape of argument be conceived more completely destitute of force than this? 'Because those converted from among the Jews are holy, they who have not been converted are holy also.' The truth is, the two clauses of the verse are merely two different figurative expressions of the same truth. The sanctity of the *branches*, arising from the sanctity of the *root*, and the sanctity of the *lump*, arising from the sanctity of the first-fruits, are figures of the sanctity which, according to the apostle, belongs to the Israelites as a body, in consequence of the sanctity which belonged to the patriarchs from whom they were descended. The "lump," then, is something that stands in the same relation to the first-fruits that the branches do to the root—something that proceeds from it. The "first-fruits," by way of eminence, refers to the sheaf of barley cut on the second day of unleavened bread. This sheaf was to be stript of its grain; the grain was to be reduced to flour by being beaten in a mortar; the flour thus produced was to be made into a lump, by means of oil, mixed with frankincense, and presented by the priest to Jehovah. This is the *lump* the apostle refers to. And the appropriateness of the figure, and the force of the argument, thus become apparent: If the first-fruits be holy, the lump made of them must be holy also. The force of the second illustration is evident: If the root be holy, so are the branches. A holy root makes a holy tree: the branches take their character from the root.

The sentiment which the apostle means to establish by this figurative proof is this: Abraham, who stands to the Israelitish nation in a relation similar to that of first-fruits to the lump made of them, and of the root to the branches springing out of it, was permanently set apart as the head of a family separated from the rest of mankind to serve certain important purposes; and if so, his descendants are to be viewed as a sacred people, to whom, sooner or later, all the promises made to Abraham and his seed are to be performed—by whom, sooner or later, all the purposes contemplated by their separation are to be gained. If you allow the first part of the proposition, you cannot deny the last; and that cannot be done without giving the lie to a large portion of Old Testament history and prophecy. The sentiment conveyed is the same, though not so clearly expressed, as that contained in the 28th and 29th verses, where the Israelites are said, even in their state of unbelief and rejection, to be " beloved for the fathers' sakes, for the gifts and the callings of God," *i.e.*, in reference to them, " are without repentance." It scarcely requires to be noticed, that the " holiness " here mentioned, is not moral excellence. The moral holiness of men does not necessarily follow from that, either of their immediate or more remote progenitors. The holiness here spoken is merely their separation by God to serve particular purposes—as the Babylonian armies were God's " holy ones."[1] The argument is this, 'If Abraham, not as an individual merely, but as the head of a family destined to become a nation, was separated to serve a purpose, his descendants share in this separation. If this be the true view of the Israelitish people, then must it be utterly wrong to consider them as a people whom, though God once acknowledged, He has now completely cast off. Whatever faults they may commit, whatever judgments they may incur, the nation still retains its sacred character, and will do so, till all that prophecy speaks of them shall be fulfilled.'

Not contented with stating the general principle, the apostle expands the last of these parallel figures into an allegory, exhibiting the mutual relations and duties of Gentile believers, and Jews, both believers and unbelievers: " And if some of the branches be broken off, and thou, being a wild olive-tree, wert graffed in among them, and with them partakest of the root and fatness of the olive-tree; boast not against the branches: but if thou boast, thou bearest not the root, but the root thee."[2] The Church of God is here spoken of under the figure of an olive-tree. This tree, rather than any other, is adopted as the emblem of the Church, on account of its being one of the most common trees in Judea, and remarkable for its beauty, fruitfulness, and usefulness. This mystical olive is represented as growing out of the root of the patriarchs of the Israelitish people, with whom, as believers, the covenant was made, that God would be their God, and the God of their

[1] Isa. xiii. 3. [2] Ver. 17, 18.

seed. The Jews are considered as the natural branches. They were the descendants of these patriarchs; and, till Christ came, the true members of the Church of God were to be found almost exclusively among them. The rejection of a part—of the greater part, of that people, in consequence of their unbelief, is represented as a breaking off of a portion of the natural branches; and the conversion of some of the Gentiles is represented as the graffing in to the mystical olive of a number of branches of a wild olive, so that they become partakers of its root and fatness—so that they are so connected with Abraham as to be his children—heirs with him of the same promise—blessed with faithful Abraham. With us, the ordinary way of engrafting is to insert a branch of a fruitful tree into a wild stock; but we learn that, among the ancients, it was customary to insert grafts from wild trees into fruit-bearing ones, to increase their fruitfulness.[1] The unbelieving Jews were cut off from all spiritually advantageous connection with Abraham, and with that Church of which, as the father of all them who believe, he may be reckoned the root; and Gentiles, naturally in a state of spiritual death and barrenness, by believing, were brought into advantageous spiritual connection both with him and with it.

The conclusion which the apostle draws from this contrasted view of the Jews and Gentiles—the first, the natural branches of a good olive-tree, some of whom had been broken off; the second, branches of a wild olive grafted in to the stock of the good olive, is this—that the converted Gentiles should not think contemptuously of the Jews, whether converted or unconverted: "Boast not against the branches." We have already had occasion to notice the strong antipathy that existed between the Jews and the Gentiles. Conversion to Christianity, though it diminished, did not extinguish this feeling. The converted Jews generally regarded the converted Gentiles as their inferiors. The converted Gentiles resented this, and were in danger, not merely of thinking of

[1] Columella *de re rustica*, v. 9; Palladius *de insit.*, xiv. 53.

the unbelieving Jews as a race utterly abandoned by God, but even of despising the converted Jews, as a set of narrow-minded, superstitious, bigoted men. The apostle here guards the Gentile Roman converts against this unbecoming temper. "Boast not against the branches"—not even against those which have been broken off; "but if thou boast"—there is here plainly an ellipsis, which must be supplied by some such word as 'remember'—"thou bearest not the root, but the root thee." The force of these words is readily apprehended. 'The weight of obligation is all on one side. The Jews are in no way indebted to the Gentiles: the Gentiles are very much indebted to the Jews. "Salvation is of the Jews."'[1] The Gentiles owed everything to their connection with that spiritual society, which had the Jewish Patriarch for its root, and whose principal branches had been his natural descendants. It ill became them to look down on those who had been longer connected with that society than themselves, or to glory over those by whose fall salvation had the sooner come to them.

The apostle, with that thorough knowledge of human nature which he possessed, intimates that this last consideration might possibly be considered by them as warranting something like boasting—at any rate, in regard to the rejection of the unbelieving Jews; but shows them that the true lessons to be learned from that sad event, were caution, humility, and gratitude: "Thou wilt say then, The branches were broken off, that I might be graffed in. Well; because of unbelief they were broken off, and thou standest by faith. Be not high-minded, but fear: for if God spared not the natural branches, take heed lest He also spare not thee. Behold therefore the goodness and severity of God: on them which fell, severity; but toward thee, goodness, if thou continue in His goodness; otherwise thou also shalt be cut off."[2]

To the question, 'Why should not we glory over the branches that were broken off? were they not broken off that we

[1] John iv. 22. [2] Ver. 19-23.

might be graffed in? were they not removed to make room for us? why should we not glory in this token of being preferred to them?' the apostle's answer is—'It is true that the casting off of the Jews was, in the order of Divine providence, among the intended means of the calling of the Gentiles. It was not, however, the reason of their being cast off: that was their own unbelief. Had they believed, they would not have been cast off. But, being unbelieving, their rejection on account of that unbelief was made conducive to the conversion of the Gentiles. In all this there is nothing to excite pride, but much to induce caution. They fell by unbelief; "thou standest by faith."' The Gentiles' place in the church depended entirely on faith—*q.d.*, 'It is not as Gentiles that you enjoy your privileges—it is as believing Gentiles. You have no ground for pride as Gentiles—much ground for gratitude and humility. It is by believing the truth that Gentiles become members of the holy family, and continue so; and "it is of faith, that it may be by grace"—for this "faith is the gift of God;" so that there is no room for boasting.'

It is true of every individual Gentile believer, that "he standeth by faith." Could he entirely fall from faith, he would fall from a state of salvation. But the apostle is here speaking both of unbelieving Jews and believing Gentiles as bodies. This is plain from his speaking of the broken off branches as "graffed in again"—a declaration applicable, not to the individual unbelievers of the primitive age, most of whom never were converted, but the Jewish people, then generally unbelieving. What is here said, though indirectly full of instruction to individual believing Gentiles, is directly spoken of the Gentile Church. That stands entirely by faith. While there are believers among the Gentiles, there will be a Church among them—a body whom God owns as *His;* but if there should cease, in any country, to be believers, the Church there would be annihilated. There does not exist any such body as the Israelitish nation, which, even though in a state of unbelief, stands in a peculiar relation to God.

This statement lays a solid foundation for the caution that follows: "Be not high-minded, but fear." What a force does this caution receive, when we look to regions once thickly planted with flourishing Christian churches—such as Egypt, Barbary, and Asia-Minor—now lying entirely desolate under the withering influence of Mohammedan or Pagan superstitions! These churches stood by faith. Faith departed, and where are they? Instead of boasting against the cast off Jews, the apostle calls on his Gentile readers to "behold therefore the goodness and severity of God: on them which fell, severity; but toward thee, goodness, if thou continue in His goodness; otherwise thou also shalt be cut off."[1] The "severity"—*i.e.*, the strict justice—of God was awfully displayed in the Divine conduct to the unbelieving Jews. When we reflect on the high privileges of which they were deprived—on the variety, and weight, and continuance of the judgments inflicted on them—exiled from a land far dearer to them than his native country can be to a Gentile patriot—scattered among the nations, a degraded, hated, ill-used people, and, as individuals, exposed, in the unseen world, to "wrath to the uttermost;" when we reflect on the prodigious numbers who, as race have followed race, have passed, during 1800 years, into the darkness of the grave and eternity—we must say, It is an awful thing to exhaust the Divine patience: "It is a fearful thing to fall into the hands of the living God." On the other hand, "the kindness of God"—His rich, free, sovereign mercy—was illustriously displayed in the calling of the Gentiles. They had not deserved to be thus distinguished. Deserved it! Read the description of them in the close of the first chapter of the epistle, and say if it was not of the Lord's mercies that such monsters of impiety and impurity, ingratitude and malignity, were not consumed! As they did not deserve, they were not soliciting, any such favour from the Divine hand. And then think of the value of the blessing: the knowledge of the only true God, and of His Son Jesus

[1] Ver. 22.

Christ—the revelation of the only way in which they could escape destruction, and be made truly wise, good, and happy for ever—the means of deliverance from error, guilt, depravity, misery, in all their forms—of obtaining glory, honour, and immortality.

It was of high importance that those belonging to the Gentiles who had believed should ponder these truths. "Behold," says the apostle, that, from a consideration of "the severity of God" to the unbelieving Jews, they might learn to take heed, lest they too, thinking, as the Jews did, that they stood, should fall—"fall after the same example of unbelief;" and to "be not high-minded, but fear;" and that, from a consideration of the high value of the benefits bestowed on them, they might learn gratitude and obedience; and from the gratuitous nature of these blessings, they might learn to repress pride, and to say, "Not to us, not to us, but to sovereign mercy be all the glory."

The apostle now proceeds to intimate, that neither of these dispensations—neither the merciful nor the severe one—were to be considered as necessary, irreversible, and final. Should the Gentiles become unbelievers, their state of privilege would be at an end. Should the Jews become believers, their state of abandonment would be at an end. The first of these sentiments is, briefly, stated in the close of this 22d verse; the second, at considerable length, in the succeeding paragraph.

"To thee, goodness, if thou continue in His goodness; otherwise thou also shalt be cut off." The apostle is here, as throughout the whole paragraph, speaking of the called Gentiles as a body; and he states to them, that the inestimable privilege, for which they were indebted entirely to Divine goodness, benignity, grace, mercy, would be continued only while they improved it; and that, if unimproved or misimproved, it would be taken from them. If they resembled the Jews in their sin, they should resemble them in their punishment. This dispensation would be to the Gentiles, in its ultimate result, as well as in its intrinsic character, "goodness," if they continued in this goodness, not otherwise.

To "continue in God's goodness," is to continue within the sphere in which this particular kind of goodness operates,—*i.e.*, to continue in the faith and profession of the Gospel. The apostle's statement seems to be this—'The blessings which the Gentiles have obtained possession of, through the preaching of the Gospel among them, originate in, and are necessarily connected with, the faith of the Gospel; and should those bodies of men—now Christian churches among the Gentiles, and enjoying, in their true members, all heavenly and spiritual blessings—should those churches fall from the faith of the Gospel—should there cease to be a succession of true believers in them—they would cease to enjoy the advantages conferred on them, and be cut off like the unbelieving Jews—cease to be recognised by God as a part of His people.' The desolations of many generations of once famous Christian churches, in Asia, and Africa, and some portions of Europe, are an awfully impressive commentary on these words.

The other side of the contrasted statement is equally true—Israel, if they abide not in unbelief, shall not abide in abandonment.

The apostle has shown that, as it is by faith that standing in the Church of God under the Messianic economy is enjoyed, the Gentiles, who had found a place in that Church, would lose it if they fell from the faith; and he now goes on to state and prove that the Jews, if they continue not in unbelief, may still obtain a place in that Church: "And they also, if they abide not still in unbelief, shall be graffed in: for God is able to graff them in again."[1] The apostle still uses figurative language, carrying out the metaphor of the mystical olive, but the meaning is obvious: 'If the unbelieving Jews, at any future period, shall lay aside their prejudices against Jesus Christ, and embrace the Gospel, they shall be readmitted into the Church of God, and enjoy its privileges.'

[1] Ver. 23.

This is true of individual Jews, but the apostle is here speaking of the great body of the nation. He first shows that this is by no means an *impossible* thing—"God is able to graff them in again." There is nothing in the nature of things, nothing in the declarations of God, to make this impossible. It may appear to man impossible; but what is impossible with man, is possible with God. He can do anything that does not imply a contradiction. This, when taken in connection with God's promise to restore the Jews, is a triumphant answer to all objections in reference to this event. "Why should it be thought an incredible thing" that God should restore the Jews, any more than that He should raise the dead? The words indicate more than possibility. When God is said to be able to give Amaziah more than he sacrificed at the command of duty[1]—to be able to make a man stand[2]—to be able to make all grace abound to men[3]—to be able to do abundantly above all that we ask or think[4]—to be able to keep from falling,[5]—more than a mere assertion of power adequate to these effects is intended; and so here. Still, possibility is the leading idea.

That, however, is succeeded by *probability* in the sentence following: "For if thou wert cut out of the olive-tree, which is wild by nature, and wert graffed contrary to nature into a good olive-tree; how much more shall these, which be the natural branches, be graffed into their own olive-tree?"[6] The general idea conveyed by these words is, 'The restoration of the Jews is, in some points of view, a more probable event than the conversion of the Gentiles was, previously to its taking place; just as, abstractly considered, it might seem less strange to re-insert into its own stock a branch which had been broken off, than to insert into that stock a branch from another tree, and a tree of another kind.' The heathen nations, previously to their conversion, were utterly ignorant of the true God, and the devoted worshippers of idols:

[1] 2 Chron. xxv. 9. [2] Rom. xiv. 4. [3] 2 Cor. ix. 8.
[4] Eph. iii. 20. [5] Jude 24. [6] Ver. 24.

they were in possession of few means to enable them to understand the meaning and evidence of the Christian revelation. It is otherwise with the Jews. They are worshippers of Jehovah, and they have in their possession, and profess to believe, those sacred books in which Moses and the prophets testify to the Messiah, whom we have found in Jesus. No change of economy is necessary for the restoration of the Jews, as was the case for the conversion of the Gentiles; no wall of partition needs to be taken down; no handwriting of ordinances needs to be blotted out. "The doors of the Church stand wide open for the admission of the Jewish people; nothing is wanting to their entering but their faith."[1]

But the apostle goes further: he represents the restoration of the Jews as not only possible and probable, but as *certain*. "For I would not, brethren, that ye should be ignorant of this mystery, lest ye should be wise in your own conceits, that blindness in part is happened to Israel, until the fulness of the Gentiles be come in. And so all Israel shall be saved: as it is written, There shall come out of Sion the Deliverer, and shall turn away ungodliness from Jacob: for this is my covenant unto them, when I shall take away their sins."[2]

"For" introduces the ground of the apostle's assured hope. The word "mystery," signifies something that has been kept secret. The "Gospel"—"the preaching of Jesus Christ," was "the revelation of a mystery, kept secret since the world began."[3] The restoration of the Jews is termed a mystery, because, concealed under the symbolical and figurative language in which prophecy is generally clothed, it was not commonly known and understood among Gentile Christians. The "mystery" refers not only to the fact generally, but to its circumstances, that, after a defined period of spiritual blindness, the Jews, as a body, were to be restored to the Church of God. "Blindness has happened unto Israel." Israel, here, can mean nothing but the Israelitish people—not the

[1] Fry. [2] Ver. 25-27. [3] Rom. xvi. 25.

mystical Israel, consisting of all believers—not the converted part of literal Israel. The Jewish people have come under the influence of a spiritual blindness or obstinacy. "In part" does not modify the word blindness, as if the expression were equivalent to a partial blindness: it modifies the term Israel; and "Israel in part," in the 25th verse, contrasts with "all Israel" in the 26th. A part of Israel—as we learn, a great part—is, according to the scheme of Divine providence, as unfolded in prophecy, to remain in a state of spiritual blindness and obduracy in reference to the Divine method of justification, during, or down to a period described as "the coming in of the Gentiles."

There is some difficulty in satisfactorily ascertaining the meaning of that expression, as well as of the whole phrase, "*until* the fulness of the Gentiles be come in." The word rendered "fulness," has various significations, and is used with various references. It seems to me to signify here, the totality of Gentile nations—every nation under heaven. Gentiles have been entering into the Church since the primitive age, in part; but there is a period coming when they shall enter "in fulness,"—when "*all* the ends of the earth shall remember and turn to the Lord, and *all* the kindreds of the nations worship before Him."[1] That is the period here referred to. Some suppose the apostle to refer to a period *during* which the blindness of Israel in part shall continue, rendering the words, 'While the fulness of the Gentiles shall enter;' others, with our translators, to the period when that blindness is to terminate. The latter appears, on various accounts, the preferable view. The notion, that the Gentiles must be generally or universally converted to Christianity before the conversion of the Jews can be looked for, does not seem fairly deducible from the words. They seem to mean that the two great events shall go forward together. The words may be rendered, 'Till the fulness of the Gentiles may have entered,'—*i.e.*, till the universal conversion of the Gen-

[1] Psa. xxii. 27.

tile nations shall have commenced. For ages, Christianity was in a great degree stationary. But, almost within our own memory, a movement has begun, which looks like the entering in of the fulness of the Gentiles—the commencement of what is to end in the universal Christianization of mankind. Whenever such a commencement really takes place, the conversion of the Jews is at hand; and, from the ancient predictions, it seems equally plain that the Gentiles are to be active in the restoration of the Jews, and the converted Jews, in the bringing in completely of the fulness of the Gentile nations. In the prediction more immediately in the apostle's view,[1] the general conversion of the world is represented as begun before "the Redeemer came to Zion," but the principal part of that glorious work is represented as following that event. When, then, the fulness of the Gentiles shall have entered—begun to go in, or when it is entering—when a general conversion of Gentile nations shall have commenced, then, or thus, shall "all Israel be saved"—the blindness shall pass away. All Israel is not every individual Israelite, but it is Israel as a body: the great majority of that people shall embrace the Gospel, and by doing so be delivered from all the evils under which they have so long groaned, in consequence of their having rejected it.

The apostle quotes some passages from the prophet Isaiah in confirmation of his declaration. Some have supposed that he refers to Psalm xiv. 7; but it is plain that the first part of the citation is from Isa. lix. 20, 21. He seems to have quoted from memory, as it does not exactly agree either with the Hebrew text or with the Greek version. Like many other quotations, only a part of the passage referred to is given. To make out the full sense, the whole of the 21st verse must be taken in: "As for Me, this is My covenant with them, saith the Lord; My Spirit that is upon thee, and My words which I have put in thy mouth, shall not depart out of thy mouth, nor out of the mouth of thy seed, nor out of the mouth of thy

[1] Isa. lix., lx.

seed's seed, saith the Lord, from henceforth and for ever." The concluding words, "When I shall take away their sins," are apparently taken from chap. xxvii. 9:—the exact words quoted are found in the Greek version,—a prophecy considerably obscure, but certainly referring to events to befal Israel in the latter days. Others have supposed the reference to be to Jeremiah xxxi. 34,—a prediction also of the general conversion of Israel.

Of these facts, which had hitherto been a mystery—not clearly revealed or understood, the apostle was desirous that the Roman Christians, chiefly Gentiles, should not be ignorant, "lest they should be wise in their own conceits,"—lest they should proudly suppose that their notions as to their own importance, and as to the permanent degradation of Israel, were correct. Such a caution was necessary; for even after all that he has said, there are many Gentiles who glory over the cut-off branches, as if they were never to be graffed in—wise in their own conceits, and not submitting to receive the plain testimony both of the prophets and the apostle. How wonderful, how deplorable, how well fitted to make us "cease from man," to hear Luther saying, wise in his own conceit, "A Jewish heart is so stock, stone, devil, iron, hard, that it can in no way be moved. They are young devils damned to hell. To convert those devil-brats (as some fondly ween out of the Epistle to the Romans) is impossible." Surely the good Reformer had forgotten the history of his own conversion, and who it is who hath said, "Is anything too hard for the Lord? With man it is impossible, but with God all things are possible."

In the paragraph that follows, the apostle gives a brief, but very complete, summary of all that he had said respecting the rejection and the restoration of the Jews, and of the bearing of these events on the Gentile nations, in reference to their relation to the manifested Divine method of justification; and shuts up the whole discussion with a striking exhibition of the wisdom of God in these dispensations, terminating in an expression of adoring wonder and devout acknowledgment.

This summary is contained in the 28th verse, "As concerning the Gospel, they are enemies for your sake; but touching the election, they are beloved for the fathers' sakes."

The apostle views the unbelieving, rejected Jewish people in two aspects. In reference to the one, he says they are "enemies;" in reference to the other, they are "beloved." These terms are contrasted, and the meaning of the one term must correspond to the other. The word translated "beloved," is a term of unequivocal meaning, exactly answering to the English word by which it is rendered in our version. It is otherwise with the word translated "enemies." Its ordinary meaning is, one acting like an enemy, the subject of hostile sentiments; but it is also used as signifying, one treated as an enemy, the object of hostile sentiments. In this way it is used in chap. v. 10, where "enemies" means persons regarded and treated by God with hostile sentiments. The Greek word rendered 'enemy,' is in exact opposition to our English word 'friend.' As this signifies either one who loves us, or one whom we love, that signifies either one who hates us, or one whom we hate—one who treats us as an enemy, or one whom we treat as an enemy. The sense here is fixed, by its being contrasted with "beloved;" and the meaning is not, the Jews are hostile, but the Jews are treated as enemies. But by whom are the Jews in one sense treated as "enemies," and in another "beloved?" Obviously by God. The whole discussion is in reference to God's dispensations towards them; and the confirmation of the assertion that they are beloved is, that "the gifts and callings of *God* are without repentance." The phrase, "as concerning the Gospel," is just equivalent to 'In reference to the revelation of mercy through Jesus Christ'—the manifested Divine method of justification. In reference to this, the Jewish people have been treated by God as objects of His displeasure; they have been left to reject it—suffered, as the Gentiles were so long, to walk in their own ways; and, in consequence of this, they have been rejected and punished by God. And this, says the apostle, speaking to converted Gentiles, has taken place "for your sake"—for and to your advantage. The cause why God treated the Jews as enemies, in reference to the Gospel, was their own obstinate unbelief; but His object in permitting their sin, and in punishing it, was the advantage of the Gentiles. How the Jews' rejection of the Gospel contributed to the advantage of the Gentiles, I have already showed in illustrating ver. 11. In addition to what is there stated, it may be remarked, that the judgments which befell the Jews who rejected the Messiah, and still lie heavy on their unbelieving posterity, are calculated to be, and certainly have been, useful in confirming the faith of the Gentile churches. The meaning of the first clause in the antithesis is this, 'In reference to the Gospel revelation, which they have rejected, the Jews have been treated by God as objects of His displeasure; and this dispensation was intended to be, and has been, conducive to the advantage of the Gentiles.'

But there is another aspect in which this wonderful people must be viewed: "As touching the election, they are beloved for the fathers' sakes." "The election" here is not the choice of individuals to eternal life, but the choice of the Israelites to stand in a peculiar relation to God, and to answer peculiar purposes in the development of the great economy of human redemption—the election of which Moses speaks, Exod. xix. 5, and Deut. vii. 6, 7, and elsewhere. "As touching the election," is equivalent to, 'As a people chosen of God to answer particular purposes, all of which are not yet answered.' In this point of view they are still "beloved," or the objects of the peculiar care of God. The Jewish people, in their unconverted state, have been marvellously kept distinct from the nations among whom they dwell—have often experienced very remarkable deliverances; and no Gentile people have ever injured them, without being punished for it. The Divine conduct towards them is strikingly described in Isa. xviii. 4, according to Bishop Horsley's translation, "For so the Lord said unto me, 'I will take my rest, yet I will consider my dwelling place.'" The sentiment is, that notwithstanding a long cessation of extraordinary manifestations of God's power,

His providence is not asleep—He is all the while regarding the conduct and the fortunes of His people; He is not forgetful of His promises to His chosen, but, though often by a silent and secret operation, is at all times directing everything to their ultimate prosperity, and to the universal establishment of the true religion. He has purposes of kindness towards them; and He preserves them till "the time He has set" come. "Doubtless He is their Father, though Abraham be ignorant of them, and Israel acknowledge them not."

The unbelieving Jews are represented as objects of this merciful superintendence "for the fathers' sakes;" *i.e.*, not, as they would be disposed to understand it, from a regard to the virtues of their ancestors, but from a regard to the covenants made with their ancestors. In these covenants are contained promises to them as a people, which were not, when these words were written—which are not yet, fulfilled; and "the faith"—*i.e.*, the faithfulness, "of God cannot become of none effect through their unbelief"—*i.e.*, their unfaithfulness. God will be true, whoever may prove a liar. The meaning of the second part of the antithesis is this—'As a people chosen by God for particular purposes, they are, even in their state of unbelief, the objects of His kind regards—the subjects of His particular providence, from a respect to the covenants entered into with their ancestors.'

In confirmation of this sentiment, the apostle adds,[1] "For the gifts and calling of God are without repentance." "Without repentance," means 'irretractable.' This is not to be understood as an unlimited declaration: for God does withdraw benefits when they are abused. It is to be considered as referring to the subject of discussion—the gifts and calling of Israel as a people, secured in the covenants, and promises made to their fathers. It is true that the gifts and calling of God to the spiritual Israel are irretractable; but they are not spoken of here. To quote this passage as a direct proof of the perseverance of the saints, is to misinterpret it.

[1] Ver. 29.

The promises made to Abraham in reference to his posterity—to his natural posterity as well as to his mystical seed, must all in due time be fulfilled, and they must continue a separate people till they are fulfilled. The sentiment here is the same as that expressed with so majestic an eloquence by the prophet Jeremiah, "Thus saith the Lord, which giveth the sun for a light by day, and the ordinances of the moon and of the stars for a light by night, which divideth the sea when the waves thereof roar; the Lord of Hosts is His name: If those ordinances depart from before Me, saith the Lord, then the seed of Israel also shall cease from being a nation before Me for ever. Thus saith the Lord, If heaven above can be measured, and the foundations of the earth searched out beneath, I will also cast off all the seed of Israel, for all that they have done."[1]

In conclusion, the apostle states, that in the manner in which God had successively treated the Gentiles and Jews, which had been strikingly analogous, His design with regard to both these great divisions of mankind was to make them partakers of a common salvation; and that, in the way of bringing both into possession of this, He had so arranged matters as to make it evident that the whole was the result, not of human merit, but of sovereign, Divine mercy. As the Gentiles, after a long course of ignorance, unbelief, and disobedience, were, by the occasion of the unbelief and consequent rejection of the Jews, brought to the faith of the Gospel, and the enjoyment of the blessings of the Christian salvation—all the result of sovereign mercy—so the Jews, who were permitted, through their own perversity taking occasion from the liberal character of the new dispensation, to fall into a state of unbelief and disobedience, and, in consequence, of rejection and punishment,—shall also, after continuing in that state for a course of ages, become the objects of Divine free mercy, by being led to embrace the Gospel. And thus God, by successively allowing the depravity of human nature

[1] Jer. xxxi. 35–37.

to develop itself in the idolatries of the Gentiles and the apostacy of the Jews, will make it evident, when He brings both these component parts of mankind into the enjoyment of saving blessings, that He acts towards them on the principle of sovereign kindness. This is the substance of what is stated in the 30th, 31st, and 32d verses: "For as ye in times past have not believed God, yet have now obtained mercy through their unbelief; even so have these also now not believed, that through your mercy they also may obtain mercy. For God hath concluded them all in unbelief, that He might have mercy upon all."

"For," in the beginning of this sentence, is either merely connective, or it intimates that the general unbelief of the Jews at that time, was no sufficient reason to doubt of their ultimate conversion. Gentiles, who were formerly disobedient, were now obedient; and Jews, who were now disobedient, would, at the appointed season, become obedient also. The Gentiles in past time "had not believed," or obeyed, "God." The reference is here to the state of the Gentile nations previously to the coming of Christ. They had received a revelation of the truth respecting the Divine character and will—the revelation possessed by and made to Noah—and many of them at least had had an opportunity of becoming acquainted with some later revelations. They had had much truth on these subjects presented to their minds by the frame of nature, and the dispensations of the Divine government, both physical and moral. But they did not improve these advantages. They did not believe the intimations made to them respecting the character of God; they did not obey the intimations made to them respecting their own duties: they became in the highest degree impious and immoral. The best commentary on the words, "Ye in time past have not believed God," is to be found in the closing paragraph of the first chapter of this epistle. On reading it, the thought naturally rises—Surely these men will be made monuments of Divine justice, by having adequate punishment executed on them: surely these men cannot find mercy.

But "God's thoughts are not our thoughts—His ways, not our ways." "Ye have now," says the apostle, "obtained mercy." To "obtain mercy," is to be delivered from deserved punishment, and to be put in possession of undeserved blessings: it is to be "saved by grace." This idea is often implied in the phrase; *e.g.*, "God be merciful to me a sinner;"[1] "But I obtained mercy;"[2] "Not by works of righteousness which we have done, but according to His mercy, hath He saved us."[3] By sending the Gospel to them when they were thinking of nothing less, and rendering it through the operation of His Spirit successful, He had manifested "the riches of His grace," in making many of the disobedient Gentiles partakers of the blessings of His salvation.

This important and undeserved benefit came to them "through the unbelief, or disobedience, of the Jews." "Ye have *now* obtained mercy through their unbelief." We have already showed at length how the unbelief of the Jews had been rendered subservient to the conversion and salvation of the Gentiles, as it had led to a speedier and more extensive preaching of the Gospel than would otherwise have taken place, and removed powerful obstacles out of the way of their embracing it. Such had been God's dispensations to the Gentile world. They had been long "suffered to walk in their own ways." They had been for many ages allowed to continue in a state of unbelief and disobedience; and were at last, in the exercise of sovereign mercy, brought to the faith and obedience of the Gospel, through means of the unbelief and disobedience of the Jews.

Now, says the apostle, there is an analogy between the past and present conduct of God towards the Gentiles, and His present and future conduct toward the Jews. "For as ye in times past have not believed God, yet have now obtained mercy through their unbelief; even so have these also now not believed, that through your mercy they may obtain mercy." This verse admits, and almost requires, a somewhat different ren-

[1] Luke xviii. 13. [2] 1 Tim. i. 16. [3] Tit. iii. 5.

dering from that given in our translation—"Even so have these also now not believed through your mercy—or, even so have these also now, through your mercy, not believed—that they also might find mercy." The apostle, in the words "through your mercy," seems to refer to the cause or occasion of the Jews' unbelief, not to the means through which they were to find mercy. It is true the mercy of the Gentiles is to be rendered ultimately subservient to the conversion of the Jews: this is distinctly stated in the 11th verse of this chapter; but though this is a truth, and an important one, it does not seem to be the truth stated here. The apostle contrasts the former state of the Gentiles with their present state, and the present state of the Jews with their future state. The past state of the Gentiles was a state of disobedience—their present state, a state of gracious salvation. The present state of the Jews is a state of disobedience—their future state is to be a state of gracious salvation. He compares the past state of the Gentiles with the present state of the Jews, and the present state of the Gentiles with the future state of the Jews; and he contrasts the instrument or occasion of the Gentiles' conversion with the instrument or occasion of the Jews' apostacy; and he does all this to show how "the mercy"—the grace, of God is displayed in the salvation of both.

"These," *i.e.* the Jews, "have now not believed," or have now become unbelieving and disobedient. The Gospel—the glad tidings of a full and free salvation for mankind, had been proclaimed to them. They were called to believe it, and God had promised that, in believing it, they should obtain all heavenly and spiritual blessings. But they "rejected the counsel of God against themselves." They would not acknowledge Jesus Christ as their Saviour and Lord.

And one circumstance which greatly tended to harden their minds against conviction, was what the apostle here terms "the mercy of the Gentiles." "They have now not believed through your mercy." By the mercy of the Gentiles here, we are not to understand their actual conversion; for, were that its meaning, we should have the apostle assigning as the occasion of the conversion of the Gentiles, an event which he represents as occasioned by that conversion. The mercy of the Gentiles, is that peculiar character of the Gospel revelation which placed the Gentiles on the same level with the Jews, offering the same salvation to both, to be received in the same way—by believing: its declaring that, in order to obtain the blessings promised and bestowed by Messiah, there was no necessity for them to become Jews, but that "whosoever believed on the name of the Lord Jesus should be saved." This was in direct opposition to the strongest prejudices and expectations of the Israelitish people, and, next to "the offence of the cross," was perhaps the strongest obstacle in the way of their embracing Christianity. The elder brother would not come in, because his prodigal brother had been so readily admitted—so kindly entertained. Thus, the Gentiles obtained mercy through the unbelief of the Jews; and, through the extension of mercy to the Gentiles, the Jews became unbelievers.

But are the Jews fallen into a state of hopeless and permanent unbelief and disobedience? Is this the end of the series of Divine dispensations? No; "they have not believed, that through your mercy they also may obtain mercy"—that they also may become the subjects of such a merciful, gracious interposition as had taken place with regard to the Gentiles. The meaning of this clause will vary according as you render the particle translated *that*.[1] It may be rendered either simply *that*, meaning in order that, indicating intention, or *so that*, indicating merely consequence.

According to the rendering preferred by our translators, the meaning is, God has now permitted the Jews, as a body, to become disobedient, through their misconception of His mercy to the Gentiles, just as He had formerly permitted the Gentiles, as a body, to become disobedient; and He has done this, not that He may utterly destroy them, but that when, according to His purpose and promise, He deals with them as

[1] ἵνα.

He dealt with the Gentiles, in giving them "repentance unto life," it may be evident that, as in the case of the Gentiles, it is a display of pure sovereign grace. The design of God, in allowing this display of human depravity in the case of the Jews as of the Gentiles, was that thus the riches of Divine grace might be the more gloriously manifested. The Jews were, as well as the Gentiles, to be blessed in Him in whom all men are to be blessed; but they were not to be put in possession of these blessings *as* persons who had descended from Abraham, and who were observers of the law of Moses; for, in this case, it might have been thought, and the Jews themselves would have so interpreted it, that it was on those grounds they obtained this blessedness. On the contrary, the principles of their depraved nature were left to manifest themselves in the rejection of the Gospel; and they thus brought themselves into a state, from which deliverance could be attributed to nothing on the part of God but sovereign mercy, and implied in it a glorious manifestation of that Divine attribute.

If we render the particle "so that," it refers not so much to the Divine design in, as to the actual result of, the Jewish people becoming unbelieving and disobedient through the mercy of the Gentiles. "They have become disobedient through your mercy, so that they also shall obtain mercy"—become objects of grace—free favour. When saved, as they shall be, according to the Divine oracle, it shall be plain that, like the Gentiles when saved according to the Divine oracle, they are debtors to free sovereign grace for their salvation. As the Gentiles were saved, not as dutiful observers of the law of nature, but as ungodly idolaters—enormous sinners, so the Jews are to be saved, not as those who had been obedient keepers of the law, but as those who had been obstinate rejecters of the Gospel. It does not materially affect the apostle's argument in whatever way you interpret the particle.

The apostle adds: "For God hath concluded them all in unbelief, that He might have mercy on all." This is illustrative of the great principle of the Divine administration, equally involved in the Divine dispensations to the

Gentiles and to the Jews. The words, "them all," are not to be considered as referring to every individual of the human race, but to the two great bodies of mankind of whom he is discoursing—the Jews and the Gentiles. To "conclude all men, both Jews and Gentiles, in unbelief," is a very uncouth English phrase, and scarcely conveys any very distinct idea. The word rendered "conclude," properly signifies to shut up. To "shut up" in unbelief, or disobedience, may signify, to prove most clearly that a person is unbelieving and disobedient. This, in the opinion of some interpreters, is the meaning of the phrase in Gal. iii. 22 : "The Scripture hath concluded all under sin;"—the Scriptures clearly prove that all men are sinners. I rather think these words are parallel to those before us, and mean, 'The Scripture teaches that all men are under the power of guilt.' To be shut up *in*, or under sin, is to be delivered over to its power and influence, and consequences. This seems the meaning of the expression "shut up" in the only passages of Scripture which can properly be considered as parallel, as Job xvi. 11, margin; Ps. xxxi. 8, in the LXX.; Gal. iii. 22, 23.

The declaration here, then, is, God has delivered up all men, both Gentiles and Jews, to unbelief and disobedience; *i.e.* He has allowed the principles of human depravity to develop themselves; He has given up men to "the lusts of their own heart;" He has permitted them to "walk in their own ways," that they might show what was in their heart; He has, as it were, in succession made two great experiments on fallen humanity—in the case of the Gentiles, and in the case of the Jews; He has left them to themselves, that it might be evident what, in this case, they would make of themselves; He has allowed the Gentiles, by their idolatrous and gross immoralities, and the Jews, by their rejection of the Messiah, and their obstinate unbelief and disobedience, to prove that fallen human nature, as existing in both, is a thoroughly depraved thing.

And God has done this, "that He may have mercy on all." The meaning here, as in the preceding verse, will vary according to the sense you give to the particle "that"—according as you consider it as referring to the *design* or to the *result* of the Divine dispensation. In the first case, the meaning is, 'He has suffered Gentiles and Jews, in succession, to fall into, and continue long in, a state of unbelief and disobedience, that, in the salvation of vast multitudes of both, the riches of His mercy might be equally displayed—that it might be evident that all the saved, whether Jews or Gentiles, owe their salvation to "grace, reigning through righteousness unto eternal life, through Jesus Christ."' If we render the particle 'so that,' the meaning is—'Since Gentiles and Jews have equally, at different periods, been distinguished for unbelief and disobedience—have fallen into, and continued in, a state which makes them the fit objects of God's moral disapprobation—the fit subjects of His penal vengeance—it is plain that all who are saved, of either division of mankind, are equally the monuments of Divine sovereign kindness—are equally deprived of all ground of glorying in themselves, and equally bound, by the ties of duty and gratitude, to the service of their God and Saviour.' It is the mercy of God alone that saves; and that mercy is equally needed by, and equally open to, Jews and Gentiles. His providence has so arranged it, that all have been brought into a state from which nothing but mercy can save any of them, and mercy can save the worst of them. "Extremely gross," says Calvin, "is their folly who hence conclude that all shall be saved. Paul simply means that both Jews and Gentiles do not otherwise obtain salvation but through the mercy of God; and thus he leaves to none any reason for complaint. This mercy is, without any difference, offered to all; but it can be received only in believing."

The contemplation of this series of Divine dispensations, past, present, and future, in reference to the Divine method of justification, filled the mind of the apostle with astonishment, awe, and delight; and he gives utterance to these emotions in the burning words which follow: "O the depth of the riches both of the wisdom and knowledge of God! how unsearchable are His judgments, and His ways past finding out! For who hath known the mind of the Lord? or who hath been His counsellor? or who hath first given to Him, and it shall be recompensed unto him again? For of Him, and through Him, and to Him, are all things: to whom be glory for ever. Amen."[1] It is natural to shrink from attempting to illustrate these words, lest the effect be to weaken rather than to strengthen the impression they are fitted to make on every heart not callous to religious emotion. But there are some things in them which require elucidation; and right impression can only be produced by right apprehension.

The first clause of the 33d verse admits of two translations—that adopted by our translators, and the following: "O the depth of the riches, and of the wisdom, and of the knowledge of God!" Both modes of rendering are according to the analogies of the language, though the last is the more literal. Had such a term as 'the power,' or 'the grace,' been employed instead of the figurative expression "riches," there could have been no doubt of its being the preferable mode of translation. The "riches" of God is properly expressive of the immense possessions of the Divinity—*e.g.*, "The earth is full of Thy riches."[2] But there is nothing said in the context calculated to excite admiration of the "riches" of God, in this sense. Those who prefer this mode of rendering, generally understand by "riches" the exuberant goodness or grace of God. We read of "the riches of God's forbearance,"[3] and repeatedly of "the riches of God's grace;"[4] but there is no instance of "riches" being employed simply to signify goodness in any of its forms. Besides, it is plain, from the context, that it is less the kindness than the wisdom displayed in the Divine dispensations, in reference to the method of justification, that forms the subject of the apostle's devout acknowledgment. I am, therefore, disposed to acquiesce in the

[1] Ver. 33–36. [2] Psal. civ. 24, Sophocles, *Ajax*, 130 (Dind).
[3] Rom. ii. 4. [4] Eph. i. 7, ii. 7.

rendering of our translators, and to consider "the depth of the riches," applied to wisdom and knowledge, as a peculiar and emphatic form of expressing a superlative, as equivalent to, 'O the rich depth, or the deep riches;' *or, more in the* English idiom, 'O the profound abyss! O the unfathomable treasures of the Divine wisdom and knowledge!'

The "wisdom" of God is that attribute by which He chooses the best ends, and seeks these by the best means; the "knowledge" of God, that attribute by which He possesses perfect acquaintance with the nature, properties, and connections of all beings and events. The apostle's exclamation may be thus paraphrased—'What infinite knowledge and wisdom do these Divine dispensations display!'

"How unsearchable are His judgments, and His ways past finding out!" By "the judgments" of God, in contrast with His "ways," I understand His eternal determinations—His plan of procedure—His "purpose purposed in Himself." These judgments are "unsearchable." It is impossible for us to discover them—we cannot know them, if He does not reveal them; and even when He has revealed them, there is a depth of wisdom in them which the human intellect cannot fathom. They have a width of range, and, with perfect unity of principle, an infinite variety of modes of operation, which our limited minds cannot grasp. There does not seem to be any reference here to the difficulty, which from our ignorance we often feel, of reconciling the Divine judgments or decrees with the principles of equity. The idea is, the impossibility of any created intelligence comprehending the variety and extent of the Divine designs.

God's "ways" are the execution of His judgments or purposes—His providential dispensations. These are said to be "past finding out." They are not as our ways, but differ from them as much as the heavens are higher than the earth. In one view, they are "far above—out of, our sight;" in another, "His ways are in the sea, His paths in the mighty waters," so that we cannot trace His footsteps. It is the same thought so strikingly expressed in the book of Job: "Dost thou know the balancings of the clouds? the wonderful works of Him who is perfect in knowledge?" The connections, dependencies, tendencies, and designs, of the Divine dispensations are, and in the present state *can* be, but very imperfectly apprehended by us. How small a portion do we know of Him!

The sentiment contained in this exclamation is obviously just, in a general view of all the dispensations of God, both in the physical and moral government of the world. But the apostle has a particular reference to the dispensations he had been considering. That God should render the idolatry of the Gentiles, and the unbelief of the Jews, subservient to the more illustrious display of the riches and freeness of His sovereign mercy; that He should make the unbelief of the Jews conduce to the conversion of the Gentiles, and the conversion of the Gentiles to the restoration of the Jews; that the whole of His dispensations towards the Gentiles and the Jews—unconnected, and sometimes apparently inconsistent—should be, and ultimately be made to appear to be, parts of one grand plan for illustrating the perfections of His character, in the salvation of an innumerable multitude of the lost race of man, both Jews and Gentiles—all this discovers a depth of wisdom and knowledge which strikes the mind with astonishment, and, when we consider the purposes for which this infinite knowledge and wisdom are employed, fills the heart with delight, and confidence, and joy.

If we consider, as we probably ought, the apostle as in these words referring not merely to the particular subject which he had just been considering, but to that which is the grand theme of the epistle—the righteousness of God—the Divine method of justification, we shall find the devout exclamation resting on a still broader and deeper foundation. A plan of salvation for self-ruined man, which at once humbles and exalts him—restores him, by the same means, to the Divine favour, and to moral excellence—displays at the same time, by the same means, the inflexible rectitude and the inconceivable benignity of the Divine nature,—which not only retrieves the ruins of the fall, but raises man to a dignity and happiness far superior to that which he has lost—which converts the evils of life into the means of moral improvement and ultimate salvation, a plan exactly suited to the constitution, character, and circumstances of mankind—embracing men of every kindred, people, and tongue—and securing their happiness, up to the highest measure of their capacity, during the eternity of their being—this is indeed "the wisdom of God in a mystery," the glories of which can never be adequately apprehended by created intelligences. "Into these things the angels desire to look;" and new discoveries of benignant, wise design, ever opening on their enlarged minds, and those of "just men made perfect," will call forth from them ever new anthems of adoring wonder at "the depth of the riches of the wisdom and knowledge of God."

In the words that follow—"For who hath known the mind of the Lord? or who hath been His counsellor?" there is an obvious allusion to Isaiah xl. 13, 14: "Who hath directed the Spirit of the Lord, or being His counsellor hath taught Him? With whom took He counsel, and who instructed Him, and taught Him in the path of judgment, and taught Him knowledge, and showed to Him the way of understanding?" The question is equivalent to a strong negative. No man, no angel, has known the mind of the Lord, or been His counsellor; and, therefore, none can search His judgments, or find out His ways. This is intended as a rebuke to that temper manifested by the unbelieving Jews, to find fault with the arrangements of the new economy, as being so very different from what they had anticipated—so different from anything which it could have entered into the mind of man to conceive. It is man's business, not to criticise and quarrel with Divine arrangements, but to submit to them; to watch with reverential curiosity the development of the Divine designs; to mark the displays they make of His various perfections—His wisdom and power, His righteousness and His grace; to admire their wisdom, in the degree in which we can perceive their objects, and how well fitted they are to gain them; to adore their depth, when we cannot discover their design; and to hold fast, in all circumstances, an unshaken confidence in Him as "the Rock, whose work is perfect, all whose ways are judgment; a God of truth, and without iniquity," infinite in holiness and in love.

In the next interrogation—"Or who hath first given to Him, and it shall be recompensed unto him again?" there is a reference to Job xli. 3, LXX., 11, E.V.: "Who hath prevented Me, that I should repay him?" or to Joel iii. 4: "Will ye render Me a recompense? and if ye recompense Me, swiftly and speedily will I return your recompense upon your own head;" but it is a mere allusion. The meaning is—'No created being can have a claim of strict right on God for any blessing. The Creator is not, cannot be, under obligation to His creatures. What can they give Him, but what He has previously given them? When He gives, He gives freely. If any creature can make out a claim against Him, it will be sustained. If any man can show that he has been profitable to God, he shall obtain his reward as a matter of desert, not grace.' The question is intended to shame into silence the murmurings of the unbelieving Jews, as if they had been dealt unjustly with in the arrangements of the new economy; and to impress on the minds of men, of every race and age, that blessings to sinful men can be hoped for from nothing but the self-moved, sovereign benignity of God.

The absurdity of the opposite sentiment is involved in the sublime doxology with which the apostle concludes the doctrinal part of the epistle: "For of Him, and through Him, and to Him, are all things: to whom be glory for ever. Amen." This is, perhaps, the most comprehensive account of the Deity, in His relation to His works, that is anywhere to be met with. All things are *of* Him: He is of none; He is the origin of them all; they originate in His will; but for Him they would never have been. All things are *by* Him: He creates—He sustains them all; by Him they were created, by Him they subsist. All things are *to* Him: all things are intended to manifest forth His glory, and will ultimately serve this purpose; He has made all things for Himself. And it is obviously meet that it should be so. It is right that His will should be the law, His glory the end, of the universe, of which he is the creator, supporter, and proprietor.

Well might the apostle add—"To whom be glory for ever. Amen." This is an emphatic expression of conviction that it should be so; his desire that it might be so; his firm belief that it shall be so. In this expression of loyalty to the Sovereign of the universe, every right-hearted, intelligent being—man and angel—throughout creation, will cordially acquiesce. In this region of His dominions, we have to mourn that a world so full of His glory should be so empty of His praise. But a happier period is predicted, when the apostle's call shall be worthily responded to—when the rebellious spirit, which now pervades so many of His rational creatures, shall be quelled for ever—and when "every creature that is in the heavens, and on the earth, and under the earth, shall be heard saying, 'Blessing, and honour, and glory, and power, be to Him that sitteth on the throne, and to the Lamb, for ever and ever.' 'Great and marvellous are Thy works, Lord God Almighty; just and true are all Thy ways, Thou King of saints.' 'Salvation, and glory, and honour, and power, unto the Lord our God; for true and righteous are His judgments.' 'Alleluia! the Lord God omnipotent reigneth.'"[1]

[1] "Such is the conclusion of the doctrinal part of our epistle—a powerful expression of profound wonder, reverence, and adoration, in regard to the unsearchable ways of God in His dealings with men; and an assertion of the highest intensity respecting His sovereign right to control all things, so as to accomplish His own designs, inasmuch as all spring from Him—'live, and move, and have their being in Him'—and are for His glory." "Sovereignty in God does not imply that He does anything without the best of reasons. It only implies that these reasons are often not known to us; and that it is meet that they should be concealed from us, that we may be impressed with a sense of our humble condition, and limited faculties and information, and have room for the exercise of implicit, affectionate, child-like confidence in Him, who so well deserves to

be trusted. If our hearts are ever tempted to rise up against any of His dispensations, let us bow them down to the dust—at once silencing and satisfying them with the humbling, consoling, animating, glorious truth, that 'of God, and through Him, and for Him, are all things.' To Him, then, be the glory, for ever and ever."—(Slightly altered from *Moses Stuart*.)

PART III.

PRACTICAL.

CH. XII. 1–XV. 13.

THE third great division of the Epistle to the Romans, to the consideration of which we now proceed, commences with the twelfth chapter, and terminates with the 13th verse of the fifteenth chapter. It seems naturally to divide itself into four sections, of very unequal length. The first, contained in chap. xii. 1, 2, is occupied with a general exhortation to the performance of Christian duty, viewed as self-sacrifice; and to the cultivation of Christian character, viewed as non-conformity to the world, and transformation, by the renewing of the mind.—The second, contained in chap. xii. 3–8, is a directory to the gifted office-bearers of the Church, how to employ and regulate their gifts, and perform their duties.—The third, contained in chap. xii. 9–xiii. 14, is employed in enjoining and enforcing a variety of particular duties incumbent on Christians, religious and moral, personal and relative, to each other, and to mankind at large.—The fourth, and longest section, contained in chap. xiv. 1–xv. 13, treats of "terms of communion," and illustrates the principles on which the Roman Christians were to regulate their fellowship, with a particular reference to the circumstances in which they were placed, as a body composed of Jews and Gentiles, and, from their previous history, and diversified means of information, entertaining different views of some minute points of doctrine and practice. Let us, then, turn our attention to these leading divisions of the Practical part of the Epistle.

SECTION I.

GENERAL EXHORTATION TO CHRISTIAN DUTY.

CHAPTER XII. 1, 2.—" I beseech you therefore, brethren, by the mercies of God, that ye present your bodies a living sacrifice, holy, acceptable unto God, which is your reasonable service. And be not conformed to this world; but be ye transformed by the renewing of your mind, that ye may prove what is that good, and acceptable, and perfect will of God."

The apostle addresses himself to the whole members of the Roman Church, whether Jews or Gentiles, as "brethren"—possessed of a common relation to God, through Christ; and a common character, rising out of that relation; and a mutual relation and character, resulting from these; and both the appellation, and the exhortation which it introduces, are applicable to all Christians, in all countries and in all ages. The duty enjoined is unreserved devotement of themselves to the service of God; and the language in which the injunction is couched is borrowed from the usages of the Mosaic economy. They are called to "present their bodies to God a sacrifice." We are plainly not to understand the phrase, "your bodies," as contrasted with 'your souls,' or 'spirits,' but as equivalent to, 'yourselves as embodied intelligencies'—just as he calls on them not to let "sin reign in their mortal bodies;"[1] and as the apostle James says, "the tongue defileth the whole body."[2] It is probable that the phrase, "your bodies," was preferred by the apostle to 'yourselves,' for two reasons: first, because he is comparing Christians to sacrificial victims, and it was the bodies of the devoted animals that were presented in sacrifice; and, secondly, because he wished to bring broadly before their minds this truth—that an essential part of Christian duty was keeping themselves from those shameful abuses of the body which prevailed so extensively among the

[1] Chap. vi. 12. [2] Chap. iii. 6.

heathen, and entered even into their religious services.[1] It is of importance to remark, that there is no reference to *expiatory* sacrifice. The person is not considered as making atonement for sin, or presenting a price for blessings to be bestowed, by devoting himself to God. The idea is—'You are entirely God's property—His property by the double claim of creation and redemption. You ought, therefore, to present yourselves as a sacrifice to Him—to hold yourselves bound and ready to be, and do, and suffer, whatever He requires you to be, and do, and suffer.' To "present ourselves a sacrifice to God," is the same thing as the "yielding of ourselves to Him as those who are alive from the dead, and our members to Him as the instruments of righteousness;"[2] "the glorifying of God in our body and in our spirit, which are God's;"[3] "the living to the Lord, and dying to the Lord, because we are not our own, but His."[4]

The apostle calls on the Romans not only to present their bodies to God as "a sacrifice," but as "a living sacrifice." In using this expression, he might perhaps refer to the fact that, under the law, no animal which had died of itself could be offered on God's altar. The victims were to be presented alive before the altar, and there slain.[5] In this case, the force of the injunction is, 'Devote yourselves to God, not in external profession merely, but in spirit and truth: serve God "with your spirits, according to the Gospel of His Son."' Or the reference may be considered as being to the striking contrast between the legal sacrifices and this Christian sacrifice. *They* were the dead bodies of brute animals: *it* is the sacrifice of the animated bodies of rational, immortal men—a sacrifice that shall "please the Lord, better than an ox or bullock that hath both horns and hoofs."[6] In this case the sentiment is, 'Devote yourselves to God; this is a more excellent kind of sacrifice than any offered under the law.'

The apostle further characterizes this sacrifice as "holy."

[1] Chap. i. 24. [2] Chap. vi. 13. [3] 1 Cor. vi. 20. [4] Rom. xiv. 8.
[5] Lev. xvii. 5; 2 Chron. xxix. 21, 22. [6] Psa. lxix. 31.

The bodies, or persons of Christians presented in sacrifice, are said to be "holy." The words may either signify, They are "holy" in the proper sense of the word; they are set apart to a sacred purpose—purchased by the blood, transformed by the Spirit of Christ—thus "set apart by the Lord for Himself;" and, therefore, as sprinkled with atoning blood, washed in the laver of regeneration, should they present themselves: or the word "holy" may be used in its secondary signification, "unblemished;" and then it is expressive not so much of the reason why they should present themselves, as of the moral character of the offering. Let it be unstained, unblemished—a "walking in all the commandments and ordinances of the Lord blameless."[1] Let it be the right thing done in the right way. Still further, the apostle requires them to present themselves an "acceptable sacrifice." The phrase, "to God," may be connected either with "present" or "acceptable;" equally good scholars support each of these modes of connection. I prefer connecting it with "present,"—thus, "present your bodies to God,"—though there can be no question that "acceptable" here is equivalent to 'acceptable to God.' The word either may be intended to denote the fact that such a sacrifice is acceptable to God—this worship in spirit and truth is pleasing to God; "The Father seeketh such to worship Him:"[2] or it may be, and I rather think it is, a hint to take care that the sacrifice be so presented that it shall be acceptable. We and our services can only be "accepted in the Beloved." Religious duty, to be pleasing to God, must be the result of the influence of His Spirit. If we would have our sacrifice accepted, it must be presented in the name of, by the hands of, the great High Priest, and purified by the cleansing power of the Good Spirit.

Now, such a sacrifice of our bodies—ourselves, thus "living, holy, and acceptable, is," says the apostle, "your reasonable service." These words are commonly understood as conveying this idea: Such a sacrifice is most reasonable.

[1] Luke i. 6. [2] John iv. 23.

Everything in the character of God, and in the condition of man, especially of redeemed man, declares it to be so. The man who devotes himself to God acts the part of a reasonable being; the man who does not, behaves most irrationally. This is the truth most sure, but it is not just the truth expressed in the words. The term rendered "service,"[1] is, in the Scriptures, uniformly descriptive of worship.[2] The word rendered "reasonable,"[3] properly signifies what belongs to the reason, mind, or understanding of man, in contrast with what belongs to his animal part. It occurs only in another place in the New Testament, 1 Pet. ii. 2, "the milk of the word,"—properly "the rational milk"—the nourishment suitable to the mind. The apostle's object here seems to be to fix the mind of his readers on the inferiority of the carnal ordinances of divine service under the law to the internal worship of the new economy, which converts all action into duty, and all duty into worship, and makes every part of worship the expression of thought and affection. It is as if he had said, 'The presentation of this sacrifice is not the worship of the body merely, it is, even where there is bodily action, the worship of the mind and heart. This is worship worthy of a rational being to offer—fit for a spiritual Divinity to accept.'

To present this sacrifice, to perform this "reasonable service," this 'spiritual worship,' the apostle "beseeches" the Romans. As an apostle, he might have commanded them; but he chose rather to "beseech" them as a friend who saw how very deeply their happiness was involved in their compliance with his injunctions. And he beseeches them "by the mercies of God." The term is put in the plural, either to indicate the innumerable manifestations which God had made of his mercies to men, or to serve as a superlative in describing the great, the unspeakable, grace of God in Christ Jesus, in unfolding which the previous part of the epistle had been chiefly engaged. The reference is probably to chap. iii. 19–26; v. 1-11; vi. 23; viii. 31-39—as if he had said, 'Such

[1] λατρεία. [2] John xvi. 2; Rom. ix. 4; Heb. ix. 1, 6. [3] λογική.

are the wonders of Divine grace. Should they not produce a corresponding state of mind and heart in those who are the objects of this mercy? God has given His Son for *you*—to *you*, and with Him freely all things necessary to make you perfectly holy and happy for ever. Is it too much that you should give yourselves to *Him*—your whole selves, in all the faculties of your nature, during the whole term of your being?' Nothing but the knowledge and belief of the truth respecting these mercies will ever induce any man thus to present this living, holy, acceptable sacrifice—thus to perform this rational worship; and nothing but the presentation of this sacrifice—nothing but the performance of this worship, can be satisfactory evidence that a man knows this "grace of God in truth." This "grace of God, bringing salvation to all, teaches" every man who knows it—nothing else can—"to deny ungodliness and worldly lusts, and to live soberly, and righteously, and godly in this present world; looking for that blessed hope, the glorious appearing of the great God and our Saviour Jesus Christ; who gave Himself for us, that He might redeem us from all iniquity, and purify unto Himself a peculiar people, zealous of good works."[1]

In the 2d verse, the apostle presents the whole of Christian duty under another phasis. In the preceding verse, Christian duty, as a whole, is viewed in its reference to God; and in this respect it is one spiritual sacrifice—the sacrifice of the person's self—all he is, all he has, all he can do—one continued act of rational worship. Here it is viewed in reference to that system of things seen and temporal, in the midst of which the Christian lives, and is represented as a disconformity to it, and a transformation by the "renewing of the mind." "And be not conformed to this world; but be ye transformed by the renewing of your mind, that ye may prove what is that good, and acceptable, and perfect will of God."[2] These words contain (1.) a description of the Christian's duty, "Be not conformed to this world, but be transformed;" and (2.) an

[1] Tit. ii. 11-14. [2] Ver. 2.

account of the manner in which he is to be enabled to perform this duty, "by the renewing of the mind."

The word here rendered "world,"[1] properly refers to time, and is often translated 'age.' It is very usually in the Holy Scriptures, as here, employed to denote the whole external frame of things existing in time—what the apostle calls "things seen and temporal." It is called *this* world, to distinguish it, as the seen world, from the unseen world—the present temporal world, from the future and eternal world, with which faith makes us acquainted. The word "world" is often interpreted as signifying "the men of this world," worldly men—men supremely interested in, influenced by, and occupied about "things seen and temporal," of whom the Psalmist speaks—"men of the world, who have their portion in this life."[2] Another word rendered world[3] often has this meaning, as John vii. 7; xiv. 22; xv. 18, 19; xvi. 20; xvii. 9; James iv. 4; 1 John iii. 1. But it is very questionable whether the word before us is ever thus employed.[4] It seems to bear here what may be safely called its ordinary scriptural meaning, "the present state of things," including the external frame of nature, and the opinions, tempers, and habits of mankind—the idea of disorder and evil, both moral and physical, being generally obviously implied—Matt. xiii. 22; Luke xvi. 8; xx. 34; 1 Cor. i. 20; ii. 6, 8; 2 Tim. iv. 10; Tit. ii. 12—the world of which John says, "All that is in it, the lust of the flesh, the lust of the eyes, and the pride of life"—*i.e.*, what the flesh desires, what the eyes desire, what living men are proud of—"is not of the Father."[5]

To be conformed to this world, is to be possessed of a character formed entirely by the influences of the present sensible state of things acting on the unchanged principles of fallen humanity, managed by him who is "the prince" and "the god of this world." Unregenerate men are "fashioned" by

[1] αἰών. [2] Psa. xvii. 14. [3] κόσμος.

[4] The only passage adduced by Robinson, Eph. ii. 2, is certainly not to the point.

[5] 1 John ii. 16.

this state of things, through the medium of "their flesh and its lusts." The character thus formed—the truth respecting God and the unseen world being shut out from the mind, the "powers of the world to come" supplanted by the power of the present world—is a character of godlessness and selfishness—of alienation from God, and of disregard to the happiness of others, except so far as it is seen to be identified with their own; and they who possess this character "walk according to the course of this world, fulfilling the desires of the flesh and of the mind"—"mind earthly things."[1] This worldly character admits of almost an infinite variety of shades, according to diversity in the original constitution of the individual, and in the circumstances in which he is placed. In one case, an individual, possessed of strong appetites and passions, destitute of the restraints of education, and so situated that he may readily find the full indulgence of his low propensities, becomes an absolute monster of impiety, selfishness, malignity, and sensuality. In another, a man, blessed with a more happily constituted bodily and mental frame, and with the superadded advantages of careful intellectual culture and moral restraint, becomes an amiable, respectable, useful member of society. Yet the two individuals may be equally "conformed to this world." Everything in the character of both is "of the earth, earthy." Nothing bears the stamp of God and eternity.

The apostle enjoins Christians "not to be conformed to this world;"—not to allow the influences of things seen and temporal to be the forming, regulating principle of their conduct; to seek treasure, not on earth, but in heaven; to mind the things that are above, and not the things that are on the earth; to avoid the modes of thought, feeling, and conduct, which result from looking at things seen and temporal, to the neglect of looking at things unseen and eternal—the modes of thought, and feeling, and conduct—the principles and maxims—which are characteristic of the great mass of mankind, men merely born of the flesh, and who "fashion themselves

[1] Eph. ii. 2, 3; Phil. iii. 19.

according to their lusts in their ignorance," and follow "the vain conversation received by tradition from their fathers." [1]

This is a character which belongs to all men by nature. It was the original character of the Roman Christians—but it must be so no longer; and that it may be "put off," as "the old man," they must be "transformed by the renewing of their mind,"—they must be radically changed. They must learn to think, and feel, and act under the power of that unseen eternal world with which faith has made them acquainted. Instead of being without God, God must be set always before them—His favour the chief good—His will the grand governing, guiding principle—His glory the great end. Instead of minding only their own things, they must mind the things of Christ. Instead of looking every one at his own things, every man is to look also at the things of others. They must become "new creatures: old things must pass away, and all things must be made new." [2]

And this transformation of character is to be sought for "by the renewing of the mind." "The renewing of the mind" is not descriptive of some physical operation—such as the putting a new thinking principle into the individual, or even the superadding of some new, physical capacity of thought and feeling to the intellectual and moral frame of our nature: the mind is renewed when, under the influence of the Spirit, the truth is understood and believed, so as to displace the ignorance and error that previously prevailed. It is the truth, understood and believed, that purifies the heart from the love of the world; and, just in proportion as that truth is understood and believed, are men transformed. It is by men's being formed to a right way of thinking, that they are formed to a right way of feeling and acting with regard to this world and the next—to God, and our brethren of mankind.

Christians are thus not to be conformed to this world, but transformed by the renewing of their mind, "that"—in order that, "they may prove what is that good, and acceptable,

[1] 1 Pet. i. 14, 18. [2] 2 Cor. v. 17.

and perfect will of God,"—or rather, the 'will of God—that which is good, that which is acceptable, that which is perfect.' The will of God here is what, from the Christian revelation it appears, God would have us to be—" This is the will of God, even our sanctification."[1] What He wills for us is "good"—excellent in itself, good for us, good for all: it is "acceptable" —well pleasing to Him, and to all good and wise intelligent beings; and, finally, it is "perfect"—it includes in it everything that is necessary to complete the character, and to make us every way what we ought to be.

To "prove this will," is practically to become acquainted with it—to know its excellence by experiencing it: not merely to know it speculatively, but to realize it. This can only be done by "our being transformed, by the renewing of our mind." The goodness, excellence, and perfection of the will of God can be proved in no other way. The substance of the whole exhortation is—'Seeing God has thus manifested His love to you by giving His Son for you—to you, and with Him all good things, manifest your love to Him by devoting yourselves entirely to His service in the spiritual duties of true Christianity, and seek higher and higher degrees of that disconformity in thought and affection to this world, and of that new and better frame of principles and feelings which is to be obtained by your mind being renewed through the faith of the truth, and by which, by which alone, you can experimentally know how good, acceptable, and perfect is that spiritual state to which it is the will of God that you, as Christians, should attain.'

These statements of Christian duty—this enforcement of it, "by the mercies of God"—and this directory as to how Christians are to be enabled to perform it, "by the renewing of their minds,"—are equally applicable to us as to those to whom they were originally addressed. Let us improve them for self-examination, for stimulus, and for guidance. Let us see that we habitually present ourselves a living sacrifice—that, in our principles, aims, maxims, and habits, we become

[1] 1 Thess. iv. 3.

more and and more "not of the world," even as He whom we call Master was not of the world—that we be steadily transforming ourselves in accordance with His word, under the influence of His Spirit. Let us lay ourselves more and more open to the melting power of "the mercies of God," fitting the various elements of our nature for being poured into the mould of the doctrine of Christ.[1] And let us study, with constantly increasing attention, that word, by which the Divine Spirit quickens and forms men anew in Christ Jesus. Thus will we "*prove*"—thus will we experience, what the will of God, in reference to man, is; and how good, how perfect, how acceptable it is.

The next section of the practical part of the epistle is occupied with a comprehensive exhortation with regard to the right employment of gifts, and the right discharge of duties, by those who held office in the Church.

SECTION II.

EXHORTATION TO OFFICE-BEARERS.

CHAPTER XII. 3-8.—"For I say, through the grace given unto me, to every man that is among you, not to think of himself more highly than he ought to think; but to think soberly, according as God hath dealt to every man the measure of faith. For as we have many members in one body, and all members have not the same office; so we, being many, are one body in Christ, and every one members one of another. Having then gifts differing according to the grace that is given to us, whether prophecy, let us prophesy according to the proportion of faith; or ministry, let us wait on our ministering; or he that teacheth, on teaching; or he that exhorteth, on exhortation: he that giveth, let him do it with simplicity; he that ruleth, with diligence; he that showeth mercy, with cheerfulness."

In illustrating the apostolical epistles, interpreters have run into two opposite extremes: some treating them as if they had an exclusive reference to those to whom they were addressed, and as if their bearing, as a rule of faith and duty, on Chris-

[1] Rom. vi. 17.

tians of other countries and ages were of a very indirect and occasional kind; others applying, without discrimination, and directly, everything contained in them to the Christian Church in all time, and scarcely admitting that they to whom they were addressed had any exclusive interest in them. Both these extremes are based on error, and tend to injury.

The first is the worst extreme: it embodies most error, and is fraught with most mischief. But the second extreme is to be avoided also. The meaning of many passages in the apostolic epistles have been misapprehended, and of course misrepresented, by our coming to the consideration of them with minds full of ideas borrowed from comparatively modern forms of thought and usage, and by our losing sight of the striking peculiarities of the primitive age, and of the particular society to which the epistles are addressed. By far the greater part of every one of the apostolical epistles is as applicable to us as to those to whom they were written; and there is no part of them which, when rightly understood and improved, may not be useful to us. But there are not a few passages (and the occurrence of such passages is a strong corroboration of the authenticity of these writings—entire absence of them would have naturally suggested doubts on this subject) in which the instruction given has a plain reference to something that was peculiar to the primitive age, or to the particular church addressed, and which is not directly applicable to churches in other countries and ages, which may be placed in very different circumstances; though, in every such case, the passage will be found, when rightly understood in reference to its original object, to be indirectly replete with important instruction to Christians of every land, and during all time. And it deserves to be noticed, that such passages as we are referring to are often introduced in the midst of discussions, doctrinal or practical, of unchanging interest, and of perpetual, universal importance.

This is, I apprehend, the case with that section of the Epistle to the Romans, on the exposition of which we are now entering. It does not refer, as a superficial reader may suppose, to *all* Christians, but only to all Christians who are endowed with certain gifts and invested with certain offices; and it does not refer directly even to the Christian ministry in all countries and ages, but to the spiritually-gifted ministry of the Roman Church (the evidence of this will come out by and by); though, at the same time, it will be found indirectly to furnish much important instruction, both to all Christian men, and especially to all Christian ministers.

Owing to this peculiar character of the section, it may serve a good purpose to prefix to its analytical exposition a few preliminary observations respecting the ministry of the Primitive Church. These remarks may be of some use in enabling us to understand aright, not only this paragraph, but many other passages in the apostolical writings.

In the present age, in rightly constituted Christian churches, persons who are judged qualified by their brethren, the body of the faithful, are called to officiate as teachers and ministers; and these office-bearers must seek for fitness to discharge the duties of the stations to which they are called, by exerting their natural talents in the careful study of the doctrine and law of Christ, in dependence on the ordinary enlightening and sanctifying influences of the Holy Spirit, and by the acquisition of such branches of knowledge and habits of mental exercise as are subservient to this study. It was otherwise in the primitive age. When the risen Saviour ascended on high, He conferred gifts on His infant Church suited to her circumstances: "He gave some apostles, and some prophets, and some evangelists, and some pastors and teachers; for the perfecting of the saints, for the work of the ministry, for the edifying of the body of Christ."[1] So far as we can discover, wherever, through the working of the Holy Spirit, the Gospel was believed by a number of individuals, so that a Christian church was formed, a due portion of these individuals were supernaturally endowed with what are called 'spiritual gifts'[2] of various kinds: some being enabled, by the inspiration of the

[1] Eph. iv. 11, 12.

[2] χαρίσματα.

Holy Ghost, clearly to apprehend, and accurately to unfold and explain, the principles of the new religion; others, to attest its Divine origin by speaking "divers tongues,"—*i.e.* apparently, languages which they had not been taught, and by performing other miraculous works; both kinds of gifts not unfrequently being combined in the same individual.

The following is the account of what took place at the foundation of the Corinthian church; and though there may have been more gifted men in that church, and a greater variety of gifts than in some other churches, we have no reason for thinking that the fact of their having gifted men among them was at all peculiar to them: "Now there are diversities of gifts, but the same Spirit. And there are differences of administrations, but the same Lord. And there are diversities of operations, but it is the same God which worketh all in all. But the manifestation of the Spirit is given to every man to profit withal. For to one is given by the Spirit the word of wisdom; to another the word of knowledge by the same Spirit; to another faith by the same Spirit; to another the gifts of healing by the same Spirit; to another the working of miracles; to another prophecy; to another discerning of spirits; to another divers kinds of tongues; to another the interpretation of tongues: but all these worketh that one and the selfsame Spirit, dividing to every man severally as He will."[1]

All these gifted persons were to employ their supernaturally conferred faculties for the advantage of the church with which they were connected; and from these gifted persons it appears that the official men, the teachers and administrators, were always chosen. It seems certain that there were gifted men in some of the primitive churches who were not office-bearers, but it seems at least equally plain that there were no office-bearers who were not gifted men.[2] The circumstances of the

[1] 1 Cor. xii. 4–12.

[2] The whole of this interesting question is very judiciously treated by Mr M'Leod, in his *Essays and Enquiries respecting the Gifts and the Teachers of the Primitive Churches*, Essay iv.: and in his longer and very able work, *A View of Inspiration*, chap. xviii.

primitive Church rendered such qualifications absolutely necessary in her functionaries. Let us take, for example, the most favourable case that can be supposed: a church composed chiefly of Jews. In such a church, few, it may be none, possessed a copy of the Old Testament, and few of them could have read it if they had possessed it. The art of reading was confined to few; and even of those who could read the vernacular tongue, few could read the language in which the Old Testament was written, which had been a dead tongue for many ages. The Old Testament, in Hebrew, was probably not more intelligible to them who could read, than Wicliff's translation is to the great body of those among us who can read English. Whatever knowledge they had of the Jewish Scriptures, had been obtained by hearing them read and interpreted in the synagogue every Sabbath. A minority, who understood Greek, might have an opportunity of perusing the Septuagint version. As to the Scriptures of the New Testament, it is generally held that Matthew wrote his gospel not sooner than eight—it may be not sooner than fifteen—years after the Ascension; and the last of the writings of John was probably written not earlier than sixty years after that event. There existed then few of the facilities which we possess of multiplying and diffusing writings. A few copies, or a single copy of one gospel, or one epistle, might be all the means possessed by a Christian church of deriving instruction in their religion from its written documents; and probably no Christian church, till a time considerably posterior to the death of all the apostles, had a complete copy of the Christian Scriptures. The churches, indeed, occasionally enjoyed the ministrations of an apostle or an evangelist; but the peculiar duties of these functionaries were of such a kind as forbade their becoming stationary, or even remaining long in one place. In such churches as were formed of converts from Judaism, could men have been found fit for teaching Christianity, without supernatural endowments? And if this was the case among Jews, partially prepared for understanding the principles of Christianity by their familiarity with the Old Testament Scriptures, what must have been the state of those churches which were composed almost exclusively of converts from Paganism? In bestowing these gifts, then, so liberally in the primitive age, we see the Divine Being acting on the principle which characterises all His economics. He does nothing by miracle which could be effected by natural means—

"Unlavish Wisdom never works in vain."

It further appears obvious, that the office-bearers in the primitive churches must have been gifted men, from the consideration that, in most, if not in all these churches, gifted men were to be found among the ordinary members. Certainly no grosser incongruity could well be conceived, than that of "a novice," whether of Jewish or Gentile origin, who had no knowledge of Christianity but what he had acquired in the ordinary way, being called to instruct men who had received "the spirit of wisdom and revelation," "the word of wisdom," and "the word of knowledge;" or even to teach in churches where such men were to be found.

These "spiritual gifts" were, in various respects, different from the ordinary, enlightening, sanctifying, and comforting influences of the Holy Spirit, which are essential to vital, personal Christianity; and it does not appear that the possession of the former, even in a large measure, was necessarily connected with the possession of the latter in a corresponding degree, or indeed in any degree. There might be unconverted, inspired men in the primitive age, as well as under the previous economies. Those spiritual gifts, like natural endowments, might be abused—we know that in some cases they were abused; and, when carefully considered, the two classes of facts adverted to, seem to be much on a level as to the difficulty of accounting for them. The persons who were possessed of these gifts were, like naturally, highly gifted men, in danger of being puffed up, and of employing their supernatural faculties for the purpose of personal display, rather than general advantage. This was the case in the Corinthian church; and the twelfth, thirteenth, and fourteenth chapters of the first epistle to that church, are intended to prevent and correct the abuses into which these gifted men had fallen in the exercise of their gifts. The prevention of disorders of this kind, so injurious in various ways to the Christian cause, among the Romans, seems to have been the apostle's object in writing that section of the epistle now before us—which, as we shall see, contains in it clear evidence of being intended as a directory for the gifted office-bearers of that church. And keeping in view these remarks, I trust we shall find little difficulty in understanding its various parts.

The general purport of the advice given by the apostle may be thus stated: 'Since, as in that closely compacted society, the Church of Christ, there is a variety of individuals, endowed with a variety of gifts, and called to a variety of offices, to serve a variety of purposes—all, however, subservient to the advantage of the body which these individuals collectively form, just as in the human body there are a variety of members, endowed with a variety of capabilities, and fitted for a variety of uses—all, however, subservient to the growth, and nourishment, and health, and general well-being of the organised whole which they compose;—since such is the constitution of the Christian Church, no individual, however high in gifts or in office, should entertain an undue sense of his own individual importance, or make an undue display of his own individual endowments or attainments, or intrude into a place that belongs to another, but should seek to promote the welfare of the whole society, by an humble, seasonable, diligent exercise of his gifts, and discharge of the duties of his own place; just as, if we could suppose the different members of the body animated each by a separate intelligence, the limbs must not pride themselves on their speed, and make a useless ostentation of it, nor the hands on their dexterity, nor may one member attempt to perform the appropriate function of another, but all in harmony, each doing its own work, promote its own interest by promoting the welfare of the body of which it forms a part.' This is the general principle. Let us now consider its application.

"For I say, through the grace given unto me, to every man that is among you, not to think of himself more highly than he ought to think; but to think soberly, according as God hath dealt to every man the measure of faith."[1] It is not easy to fix the precise force of the connective particle rendered *for*. By many interpreters it is considered as equivalent to moreover. Perhaps it has its illustrative power—for in nothing is non-conformity to this world, and transformation by the renewing of the mind, more necessary, than in the attainment and exercise of that sober-minded estimate of individual gifts and claims which the apostle here recommends to the official men in the Roman church. "I say,"[2] is equivalent to "I command"—no uncommon use of the term, as Matt. xxiii. 3, "They *say*"—that is, they authoritatively command, "but they do not;" Luke vi. 46; Mark xiii. 37; Matt. v. 44, and often elsewhere. The clause that follows fixes the meaning here: "According to the grace given unto me." The apostle clearly refers to his office as an apostle, and the apostle of the Gentiles. Here we see the difference between the meaning and the reference of a term: the meaning of "the grace given me," is just 'the favour conferred on me;' but the reference is to that "grace" which consisted in the office which he delighted to magnify, and of which he speaks so gratefully: "To me, who am less than the least of all saints, is this grace given, to preach among the Gentiles the unsearchable riches of Christ."[3] The apostle's language, then, is equivalent to, 'In virtue of the apostolic office graciously conferred on me, and in the exercise of the supernatural gifts and authority belonging to that office, I enjoin you.' It is just as when he says to the Thessalonians,[4] "This we say unto you by the word of the Lord."

But to whom is the injunction addressed? At first view, it may appear that it was addressed to every individual in the Roman church; but a little reflection will show that it is

[1] Ver. 3. [2] λέγω.

[3] Eph. iii. 8; Rom. i. 5; xv. 15, 16.; 1 Cor. iii. 10; Gal. ii. 9.

[4] 1 Thess. iv. 15.

addressed only to every individual of a particular class in that church. It is addressed to those who had "gifts:"[1] to the prophets and to the ministers—to those who teach and exhort —and to those who rule and give;[2] and "all were not prophets, or teachers, or rulers, any more than apostles.[3] "Every man" is here used in the same way as in 1 Cor. xii. 7, 11.

The apostle not only thus shows us that he speaks of a limited universality—the whole of a class, but he marks the precise limits of the class he addresses; they are those "to whom God had dealt a measure of faith." The word "faith" is here used, not in a peculiar sense, but with a peculiar reference, to denote that faith which was in the primitive age possessed by those who were endowed with supernatural gifts —what is ordinarily termed by divines 'the faith of miracles.' When God conferred on an individual supernatural gifts, He revealed to the individual, in a way we cannot explain, that He had done so; He made him conscious of it. And the faith which corresponded to this revelation seems to have been that referred to here,—a faith by which gifted men were distinguished, not only from unbelievers, but also from their Christian brethren to whom such a revelation had not been given. This faith must always have corresponded to the nature and measure of the miraculous gift; so that we need not wonder at finding the apostle use as the synonym of the phrase here employed, "the measure of the gift of Christ."[4] The word "faith" seems to be used in a different sense by the apostle when he employs it as the name of a spiritual gift,[5]— probably a degree of confidence and boldness in declaring the truth, and suffering for it, superior to what the individual in the exercise merely of his natural faculties could have exerted. Here it is plainly used as something equally extensive with spiritual gifts —something common to all gifted men.

The phrase translated "to every man among you,"[6] is

[1] *χαρίσματα*. Ver. 6. [2] Vers. 6, 7, 8. [3] 1 Cor. xii. 29.
[4] Eph. iv. 7. [5] 1 Cor. xii. 9. [6] *παντὶ τῷ ὄντι ἐν ὑμῖν.*

somewhat remarkable, and has been considered by some interpreters as equivalent to—'to every man that is of consequence among you,' as in 1 Cor. i. 28, "things that are"[1]—which signifies persons of consequence—as opposed to "things that are not,"[2] insignificant persons. In this case, the limitation is obvious; and "they who *are*" is here a phrase similar in meaning to "those who seemed to be somewhat," in Gal. ii. 6.[3]

Having thus attempted to ascertain the class to whom the apostle addresses himself here, let us inquire into the import of the injunction given them. The gifted and official men are commanded not to "think of themselves more highly than they ought to think; but to think soberly, according as God had dealt to every man the measure of faith."[4] There was a danger that supernatural gifts might, in an imperfectly sanctified mind, engender pride. "Knowledge," however obtained, is an attainment of a kind that, in a being like man, even renewed man, naturally "puffeth up." It is against this evil that the apostle here guards the gifted office-bearers of the Roman church. He cautions them against thinking their intellectual power and attainment, even though derived from supernatural Divine influence, to be greater than they really were; and calls on them to judge of themselves and of their gifts "soberly"—that is, "judiciously," "modestly," "*according as*[5] God had dealt to every man the measure of faith;" that is, either, 'Since God has given to every gifted man his measure of endowment, there is no room for pride, though there is strong reason for gratitude and diligent improvement; and if God has given one a greater measure than another, that is no reason why he should despise or undervalue that other,—who hath made the difference?' or, as our translators have understood it, 'Let the measure of the gift which God has given be

[1] τὰ ὄντα. [2] τὰ μὴ ὄντα. [3] τῶν δοκούντωνί εἶνα τι

[4] Ver. 3. παρὰ is often used as here, Luke xiii. 2; iii. 13; Rom. xiv. 5; Heb. i. 4, 9; iii. 3. There is an obvious παρονομασία in ὑπερφρονεῖν and σωφρονεῖν.

[5] ὡς.

the measure of the opinion you form of yourselves. Beware of supposing you possess gifts which He has not conferred on you, or a higher degree of the gifts you do possess than He has given.' While it seems to us that these words, in their direct reference, are applicable only to the gifted office-bearers of the primitive age, they convey, indirectly, important instruction to all Christians in all ages, whether occupying official station or not. Superior endowments and acquirements, and station, are always apt to excite an undue self-complacency in their possessors; and they need to be sober in their estimate of these, and habitually to remember to whom they are indebted for them, and for what purpose they were bestowed.

The apostle's enforcement of the injunction is contained in the 4th and 5th verses, and in the first clause of the 6th verse: "For as we have many members in one body, and all members have not the same office; so we, being many, are one body in Christ, and every one members one of another, having then"—or rather, 'yet, or but having'—"gifts differing according to the grace that is given to us."[1] With many of the best interpreters, I include the first clause of the 6th verse as necessary to complete the sentence. The statement here made, bearing so directly on the preceding injunction, is this: 'The human body has many members: these members are not independent beings, but together form one whole, and have each its appropriate functions to perform in reference to that whole. In like manner, the Christian Church is formed of many individuals; but these individuals, as "in Christ"—related, united, to Christ—form one society, closely connected with each other, every individual having his appropriate duty to perform to the society.' The somewhat odd phrase, "Every one members one of another," conveys the idea, that as every member of the body has a relation to every other member, from their common relation to the body as a whole, every member of a Christian church is, in the same manner, connected with every other member, from their common connection with the

[1] Ver. 4-6.

society which they collectively form. "According to the grace given to us," is 'according to the favour bestowed on us:' we have "the gift"—"the measure of faith," which it has pleased God to bestow on us. We find the same figure used by the apostle to illustrate the same subject: 1 Cor. xii. 12-27; Eph. iv. 16.

The conclusion to which the apostle wishes to conduct the gifted men is, that they are not to seek the display of their endowments, or the advancement of their reputation; but in a diligent application of their gifts to the advantage of the whole society, to study to gain the great end for which these gifts had been graciously bestowed. In bringing out this conclusion, he appears to divide the gifted men into two classes, according to their offices and the gifts corresponding to them—prophecy, or inspired instruction; and ministry, or the administration of the affairs of the society: and then he seems to advert to the two great branches of instruction, according as it refers to doctrine or practice, teaching and exhortation; and to the three great branches of administration in such a society as the Christian Church—distribution or alms-giving, presidence or government, and caring for the sick and the afflicted; and he exhorts them that, instead of unduly esteeming themselves and intruding on each other's departments, they should diligently exercise their peculiar gifts, and perform the functions of their peculiar offices, to the edification of all.

"Whether prophecy, let us prophesy according to the proportion of faith; or ministry, let us wait on our ministering; or he that teacheth, on teaching; or he that exhorteth, on exhortation; he that giveth, let him do it with simplicity; he that ruleth, with diligence; he that showeth mercy, with cheerfulness."[1] Few paragraphs in our version are so unhappily divided as this. The apostle's comparison does not close till the middle of the 6th verse: there is no break in the meaning at the end of that verse; but there is one, as appears by the change of construction, at the middle of the 7th verse.

[1] Ver. 6-8.

Again, there is no break in the meaning at the end of that verse; but there is one after the first clause of the 8th verse. The language is very elliptical, as the English reader may observe, from the number of supplementary words in the italic character. "If we have received the gift of prophecy, let us prophesy according to the proportion of faith; if we have received the gift of ministry, let us wait on our ministry: the prophet, who has the faculty of teaching, let him exert it; and the prophet, who has the faculty of exhortation, let him do so likewise; the minister, who gives, let him give with simplicity; the minister, who rules, let him do it with diligence; the minister, who showeth mercy, let him do it with cheerfulness." Such seems the apostle's exhortation when the dislocations have been replaced. Let us inquire into the meaning of its various parts.

"Whether prophecy—according to the proportion of faith." This is a literal rendering of the original words. The ellipsis must be thus supplied: 'If we have the gift of prophecy according to the grace given to us, let us prophesy according to the proportion of faith.' The original meaning of the Hebrew word, of which "prophet" is the translation, is a person in any way in intimate relation with God. Thus Abraham was a prophet,[1] and the patriarchs were prophets;[2] Moses was God's prophet, as Aaron was his.[3] The term, however, is more usually employed to signify a person inspired with the knowledge of God's will, and commissioned to declare it to others, and especially those inspired persons whose communications referred to future events. In the New Testament, the corresponding term is used much in the same way. "Prophecy," when spoken of as a separate spiritual gift, distinguished from the "word of wisdom" and "the word of knowledge,"[4] seems to be the supernatural knowledge of future events; but "prophets" appears to denote generally inspired teachers, who rank next to the apostles.[5] "Prophets," however, is not a term

[1] Gen. xx. 7. [2] Psa. cv. 15. [3] Exod. vii. 1.
[4] 1 Cor. ii. 8, 10. [5] Eph. ii. 20; iv. 11.

merely equivalent to teachers, nor is ordinary preaching to be considered as the same thing as prophesying; though, as we have already seen, the teachers in the primitive Church were usually prophets, and *their* preaching was prophesying.

Those who possessed this gift are required by the apostle to use it, and to use it "according to the proportion of faith."[1] "The proportion of faith" is the same thing as "the measure of faith;" and to prophesy according to it, is to make the prophesying or utterance the exact expression of the revelation received—the "measure of their faith," and the measure of the revelation, being obviously coincident. 'Let the prophets not obtrude on the Church their own speculations, but scrupulously deliver the message they have received of the Lord.' The apostle's injunction corresponds with that of Jehovah by the prophet, "He that hath My word, let him speak My word faithfully: what is the chaff to the wheat?"[2]

"Or ministry—on ministering:" that is, supplying the ellipsis, 'If, according to the grace given to us, we have received the gift of "ministry," let us exercise it in performing the offices of ministry.' As the gift of prophecy qualified a man for teaching, the gift of ministry qualified a man for management, or administration. There is no doubt that the word ministry[3] is employed in the New Testament to signify any office in the Christian Church, the apostolic not excepted. —1 Cor. xii. 5; 2 Cor. iv. 1; Rom. xi. 13; 1 Cor. iii. 5. But when distinguished from other gifts or offices, it signifies what is concerned rather with affairs than with doctrines, it refers to management, rather than teaching.—Acts vi. 1–7; Phil. i. 1; 1 Tim. iii. 8, 12. The spiritual gifts of "healing," and "the discerning of spirits,"[4] peculiarly fitted one for the office of a minister in this restricted sense. 'If then,' says the apostle, 'we have the gifts of ministry, let us exercise them in ministration. Let us not intrude into the office of the prophet, for

[1] "Puto *ἀναλογίαν τῆς πίστεως* esse *μέτρον πίστεως*: 'Credidi ergo locutus sum.' Nequis inter prophetandum effutiat quod non revelatum fuit."—CAMERO.

[2] Jer. xxiii. 28.

[3] *διακονία*.

[4] 1 Cor. xii. 9, 10.

which we are not fitted; let us not exercise our gifts ostentatiously, and for no definite object, but let us apply them to the purposes to which they are suited, and for which they are intended.' What these are will appear immediately.

Having thus stated, generally, that they who had the gift of prophecy should exercise it with a strict regard to the limits of the revelation made to them, and they who had the gift of ministry should exercise that gift in ministration, the apostle, if I mistake not, proceeds to give directions as to the manner in which different prophets and different ministers should conduct themselves, according to the "different gifts" which they possessed, "according to the grace given to them."

And, first, with regard to the prophets: "He that teacheth, on teaching; he that exhorteth, on exhortation." 'If any one among the prophets be, according to the grace given him, a teacher peculiarly fitted to unfold the doctrines of Christianity, let him, according to the measure of faith, devote himself to teaching—let him, in the Church, do that for which he is peculiarly qualified.' "He that exhorteth, on exhortation." 'If any one among them is more fitted for practical instruction—for presenting, in an impressive form, the motives and consolations of Christianity, let him employ himself in this particular department.' The gift of prophecy, as communicated to them, might, in the case of some individuals, qualify them not so much for teaching—exhibiting the meaning and evidence of Christian doctrine—expounding the sacred writings, as for warm enforcement of duty. 'Let the two classes of inspired instructors employ their peculiar gifts, and keep to their own province. So shall the edification of the Church be best promoted.'

Now, as to the ministers or deacons: "He that giveth, with simplicity." 'If any one is, by the grace given him, fitted for, and called to, the office of a deacon—has allotted to him the duty of collecting and distributing the voluntary contributions of the Church, let him devote himself to his own work, and perform it "with simplicity"—without seeking selfish or secular ends, with sincerity and uprightness, with a single eye to the honour of Christ and the advantage of His cause.' "He that ruleth, with diligence." 'If any one has the gifts and the office of ruling—of presiding in the assemblies, and superintending the affairs of the Church, let him do the work with the sedulous care and untiring "diligence" which is necessary to its being done well.' "He that showeth mercy, with cheerfulness." In the primitive Church, from its exposure to persecution, there were many of its members placed in circumstances of destitution and distress; and it was the duty of the Church, by her deacons, to relieve these. If any one, then, of the ministers was, from the gifts bestowed on him—such as the gift of healing—peculiarly fitted for this department of duty, it behoved him to devote himself to it with that kind "cheerfulness" which is peculiarly needed in such ministrations, and which gives a double value and efficacy to the relief and consolation afforded.

We are not to suppose that, in the primitive Church, their teachers, who we believe were all prophets, were formally divided into two classes—teachers and exhorters; nor the administrators into three classes—givers, rulers or presidents, and showers of mercy: all that the apostle seems to mean is, that every official and gifted man should do the duties of his own office, and exercise his own gift; for in that way was the welfare of the Church most likely to be promoted;—every gifted and official man forming a just but not exaggerated view of his endowments, and seeking to advance the good of the Christian society, by keeping himself within his own sphere, and diligently performing its appropriate duties.

The paragraph we have illustrated is parallel with 1 Pet. iv. 10, 11, and at once illustrates, and is illustrated by that passage:—"As every man hath received the gift, even so minister the same to one another, as good stewards of the manifold grace of God. If any man speak, let him speak as the oracles of God; if any man minister, let him do it as of the ability which God giveth."[1]

[1] See Exp. of the First Ep. of Pet., vol. ii., p. 320-326.

This section, though directly referring to a state of the Church which, in some of its features, has ceased to exist, is yet full of important instruction to Christian churches in all countries and ages. It teaches us that it is of vital importance to the welfare of a Christian church that its component parts should know their own place and duty, and confine themselves to them, as teachers, elders, brethren. It is the duty of teachers to take care that, in their teaching, they keep close to the Divine word—teach no doctrine, enjoin no law or institution, but what it authorises; and to turn to the greatest advantage the peculiar talents with which they may have been endowed. It is the duty of all official men to devote themselves to that department of official duty for which they are peculiarly qualified. In one word, it is the duty of all the members of the Church, whether they occupy public office or not, to check a spirit of selfishness, in all its forms, and to cherish a regard for the public interest, expressed in a corresponding course of action—to "look not every man on his own things, but every man also on the things of others"—to seek every man not his own things, but the things of Christ. The right man in the right place, doing his own work, is the apostle's idea of a well-organized Christian church; and in the degree in which that idea is realised in any individual Christian society, will the objects intended by its great Author for those within and those beyond its pale be gained.

SECTION III.

EXHORTATIONS TO PARTICULAR CHRISTIAN DUTIES.

CHAPTER XII. 9–XIII. 14.—"Let love be without dissimulation. Abhor that which is evil; cleave to that which is good. Be kindly affectioned one to another with brotherly love; in honour preferring one another; not slothful in business; fervent in spirit; serving the Lord; rejoicing in hope; patient in tribulation; continuing instant in prayer; distributing to the necessity of saints; given to hospitality.

Bless them which persecute you: bless, and curse not. Rejoice with them that do rejoice, and weep with them that weep. Be of the same mind one toward another. Mind not high things, but condescend to men of low estate. Be not wise in your own conceits. Recompense to no man evil for evil. Provide things honest in the sight of all men. If it be possible, as much as lieth in you, live peaceably with all men. Dearly beloved, avenge not yourselves, but rather give place unto wrath: for it is written, Vengeance is mine; I will repay, saith the Lord. Therefore, if thine enemy hunger, feed him; if he thirst, give him drink: for in so doing thou shalt heap coals of fire on his head. Be not overcome of evil, but overcome evil with good.

Let every soul be subject unto the higher powers. For there is no power but of God: the powers that be are ordained of God. Whosoever therefore resisteth the power, resisteth the ordinance of God; and they that resist shall receive to themselves damnation. For rulers are not a terror to good works, but to the evil. Wilt thou then not be afraid of the power? do that which is good, and thou shalt have praise of the same: For he is the minister of God to thee for good. But if thou do that which is evil, be afraid; for he beareth not the sword in vain: for he is the minister of God, a revenger to execute wrath upon him that doeth evil. Wherefore ye must needs be subject, not only for wrath, but also for conscience sake. For, for this cause pay ye tribute also: for they are God's ministers, attending continually upon this very thing. Render therefore to all their dues: tribute to whom tribute is due; custom to whom custom; fear to whom fear; honour to whom honour.

Owe no man any thing, but to love one another: for he that loveth another hath fulfilled the law. For this, Thou shalt not commit adultery, Thou shalt not kill, Thou shalt not steal, Thou shalt not bear false witness, Thou shalt not covet; and if there be any other commandment, it is briefly comprehended in this saying, namely, Thou shalt love thy neighbour as thyself. Love worketh no ill to his neighbour: therefore love is the fulfilling of the law.

And that, knowing the time, that now it is high time to awake out of sleep; for now is our salvation nearer than when we believed. The night is far spent, the day is at hand: let us therefore cast off the works of darkness, and let us put on the armour of light. Let us walk honestly, as in the day; not in rioting and drunkenness, not in chambering and wantonness, not in strife and envying: but put ye on the Lord Jesus Christ, and make not provision for the flesh, to fulfil the lusts thereof."

The third section of the Practical part of the Epistle is occupied with exhortations to the cultivation of particular graces, and the performance of particular duties, which should characterize all Christians. This section reaches from chap. xii. 9 to chap. xiii. 14. There is no general division under which the several injunctions can be brought; but the section is not without internal order—one injunction often, at least, naturally rising out of another. It does not admit of strict logical division; but its contents are not, therefore, to be viewed as unconnected maxims. They follow each other in a natural order, like the result of living thought. First, the apostle enjoins that love to all men, which is the fulfilling of that department of the law which refers to our fellow-men;[1] then the brotherly love which Christians should cherish and manifest towards each other.[2] He then enjoins that "service of the Lord," which embraces all duty, and which should be performed with unwearying diligence and ever ardent zeal.[3] He passes on to the duties which the depressed and persecuted state of Christianity made it especially necessary to attend to. To fit them to meet their trials, he calls on them to cultivate a joyful hope of future happiness, to exemplify steady perseverance amid present afflictions, and to be ardent and constant in prayer to God.[4] He instructs them how they should treat both their suffering brethren and their cruel persecutors—ministering to the necessities of the former, and bringing them to their homes;[5] and imploring blessings—not imprecating vengeance, on the latter.[6] He recommends to them cordial sympathy with the joys and sorrows of their fellow-men, and especially of their fellow-Christians;[7] and calls on them to cherish unity of affection, and, instead of striving who should be the greatest, to be ever ready to perform the humblest offices, by which a brother's best interests may be promoted; and, in order to this, he cautions them against self-conceit.[8] He then gives a number of advices as to their behaviour to the men of the world—calling on them in no case to meet injury by injury; to display tempers and follow courses which were fitted to command the respect even of an unfriendly world;[9] to be ready to do everything but sin in order to preserve peace[10]—repeating again,

[1] Ver. 9. [2] Ver. 10. [3] Ver. 11. [4] Ver. 12.
[5] Ver. 13. [6] Ver. 14. [7] Ver. 15. [8] Ver. 16.
[9] Ver. 17. [10] Ver. 18.

and strongly enforcing, the exhortation not to avenge themselves, but to endeavour to overpower malice by kindness.[1] Finally, he instructs them how to conduct themselves with regard to their civil superiors;[2] and then shuts up the section by showing that all the duties he had enjoined were but various forms and manifestations of love,[3] and by urging on them the circumstances of the times, as a reason why they should carefully perform these duties.[4] Such is an outline of the contents of this section.

The first injunction is to that love, which, including all relative duties, as the apostle shows, chap. xiii. 8–10, naturally takes the lead: "Let love be without dissimulation. Abhor that which is evil; cleave to that which is good."[5] "Love" is not here the peculiar affection Christians should cherish towards each other—that is enjoined in the next verse. It is the Apostle Peter's "charity," which he calls on Christians to add to "brotherly-kindness."[6] It is a cordial good-will—a disposition to make all men with whom we are connected happy—leading us to confer suitable benefits on them, "as we have opportunity." This love must be "without hypocrisy." We must not pretend to love when we do not love; we must not profess more love than we really possess. We must love, sincerely love, all mankind; and this love must "not be in word and tongue only, but in deed and in truth."[7]

The manner in which the existence and prevalence of this principle are to be manifested, is pointed out in the two injunctions in the close of the verse: "Abhor that which is evil; cleave to that which is good." The word translated "evil,"[8] properly signifies "malignant, injurious;" though it is often employed to denote what is morally bad generally; and "good"[9] properly signifies whatever is excellent in its kind; but it is often used to denote what is morally excellent

[1] Ver. 19–21. [2] Chap. xiii. 1–7. [3] Ver. 8–10.
[4] Ver. 11–14. [5] Ver. 9. [6] 2 Pet. i. 7.
[7] 1 John iii. 18. [8] τὸ πονηρόν. [9] τῷ ἀγαθῷ.

in general, and also what is beneficial and useful. The first term is here used in its primary sense of mischievous; the second, whose meaning is fixed by the antithesis, in its secondary sense. "Evil" is equivalent to injurious, and "good" to what is fitted to profit and to please. This is no unwarranted use of the terms. "Evil," in Matt. v. 39, is 'injury;' and "good," in Matt. vii. 11, is 'advantageous,' 'profitable.'[1]

Christians are to "abhor what is injurious." They must not only abstain from inflicting wrong on any human being, but they must so abhor every temper and action that has an injurious tendency, as to keep at the greatest distance from it.

The second injunction is, literally, "be glued to that which is good." The Christian is to be steady and persevering in seeking the advantage of his fellow-men; he must "stick to it." He must eagerly seek, readily embrace, strenuously prosecute, and, in opposition to all attempts to abandon them, firmly, steadily, stand by every right method of promoting the happiness of mankind. This is to "cleave to that which is good." From the duty which Christians owe to all their brethren of mankind, the apostle proceeds to their duty towards one another.

"Be kindly affectioned one to another with brotherly love; in honour preferring one another."[2] Christians are related to each other by a variety of bands, in addition to those which bind man to man. They have common peculiar relations—a common peculiar character. They are all "children of God through faith in Christ Jesus,"[3] and therefore, in a peculiar sense, brethren. They have common principles, common affections of love and hatred, of hope and fear. They have common objects: they have the same hazards—the same interest. They worship the same God and Father; acknow-

[1] Voces *boni et mali* non habent generalem significatum: sed pro maliciosa iniquitate, qua nocetur hominibus, *malum* posuit; *bonum* autem pro benignitate qua ipsi juvantur."—CALVIN.

[2] Ver. 10.

[3] Gal. iii. 26.

ledge the same Lord; trust in the same Saviour; are animated by the same Spirit. They form a holy fellowship, out of which a great variety of duties originates, none of which can be performed without a high degree of a peculiar kind affection. It is the cultivation and display of this affection that the apostle here enjoins. The phrase, "with brotherly love," belongs to the first clause, not, as it is represented in some of the editions of our version, to the second. In the original, the words stand at the beginning of the verse—"With brotherly love, or, in brotherly love, be kindly affectioned one towards another." The word rendered "kindly affectioned,"[1] is one of the strongest which the Greek language furnishes. It expresses the peculiar affection with which parents generally regard their offspring, and the corresponding feeling of the child to the parent. The whole precept may be fairly rendered—'Cherish and display to each other the tenderest affection as being connected by the closest relations.' It condemns apathy, and requires the tide of holy affection, from a purified heart, to flow forth spontaneously, copiously, steadily, perseveringly, towards all Christians, and especially towards those brethren with whom we stand in the relation of fellow church-members.

The apostle adds—"In honour preferring one another." This seems to be the same idea as that expressed by him in his Epistle to the Philippians: "Let each esteem other better than themselves."[2] It is the natural effect of kind affection to lead us to think respectfully of the objects of it. He has not the heart of a son who does not behold the excellencies of his father's character in a stronger light than an indifferent person can see them, and who is not blind, in some measure, to defects which to others may be apparent. The apostle does not here inculcate anything that is inconsistent with truth. He does not mean that a very intelligent Christian should regard, as worthy of more esteem for his knowledge, a very weak and ill-informed brother; still less, if possible, does he

[1] φιλόστοργοι.

[2] Chap. ii. 3.

mean that he should pretend a degree of respect which he does not—which he cannot, feel; but he does mean, that, under the influence of Christian love, we should put the best possible construction on the motives of our brethren; and that, as we have not the same means of judging them as ourselves, and if we know ourselves—know that "in us, that is, in our flesh, dwells no good thing"—we ought to cherish very lowly thoughts of ourselves, and comparatively high and honourable thoughts of them. A Christian is to "*honour* all men," but especially "the brotherhood;" and to show this in the manner in which he treats them—guarding their reputation and credit not less carefully than his own.

In the next verse, the apostle seems to state the Christian's duty to his Lord. All Christian duty is represented as the service of the Lord; and, in performing this service, Christians are required to be diligent and zealous: "Not slothful in business; fervent in spirit; serving the Lord."[1] The first of these clauses has generally been explained as enjoining diligence in our secular business; and the last part of the verse as intimating that, while thus diligent in our worldly affairs, we must not allow our minds and hearts to be engrossed with them, but must be fervently zealous in the duties of religion—by way of eminence called "the service of the Lord." Diligence in secular business is included in the injunction, but only as that forms a part of "the service of the Lord." The general injunction is, "Serve the Lord." Make the law of the Lord your rule in everything. Whatever you do, do it as to Him. Are you engaged in the ordinary affairs of life? remember you are His servant, and act as in His sight, under the motives and for the ends He has enjoined. Are you employed in the duties of religion? still, whatever you do, do it to Him, guided by His authority, animated by His love. Let your whole life be service to the Lord; and let this service have two characters: "Be diligent in business"—*i.e.*, I apprehend, 'Beware of the influence of sloth; be active; do not

[1] Ver. 11.

content yourself with mystical speculation or enthusiastic feeling; be diligent in performing the active duties both of life and of religion.' This is the one character. The other, 'Be fervently zealous: let not the service of the Lord degenerate into a cold formalism—mere bodily service; let all your duties be animated by, and indeed be the expression of, fervent zeal for the honour of your Lord, growing out of a habitual faith of the truth—kept alive by constant supplies of Divine influence.

An expositor[1] of great name would connect "diligent in business," and "fervent in spirit," with the former verse; as if the apostle had said, 'Let your unfeigned love not be sluggish, but active—not cold, but most affectionate; and thus, in love serving one another, serve the Lord.' But we prefer the view we have given. It is right to notice, that some MSS. of considerable authority read, instead of the word rendered properly "the Lord," a word very similar in appearance, signifying "the time, or the occasion."[2] The meaning this gives is a very good one. The injunction is, in this case, equivalent to, "Redeeming the time." There is little doubt, however, that the received reading is the true one; and there can be no doubt that the sense it gives is not only a more important but a more appropriate one.

The apostle having thus enjoined on the Roman Christians the cultivation of a warm and diffusive charity towards all men, and a tender and respectful brotherly affection towards each other, and a diligent and fervent prosecution of the service of their common Lord, proceeds to give them a variety of advices, all of them having a reference to that state of privation, self-sacrifice, and exposure to persecution, in which, as Christians, they were placed. These reach to the end of the chapter. Some of these advices refer to the tempers they should cultivate, and the duties they should perform as individuals, in the circumstances in which they were placed; some refer to the manner in which they should behave to

[1] Olshausen.

[2] καιρῷ instead of κυρίῳ.

their persecuted brethren; and others, to the manner in which they should conduct themselves to their enemies.

The first set of these advices is in ver. 12, Be "rejoicing in hope, patient in tribulation, continuing instant in prayer." First, "Be joyful, or rejoice, in hope." "We rejoice in tribulation," says the apostle in chap. v. 2, 3, because "we rejoice in hope of the glory of God." He here calls on them to do what he there says the faith of the Gospel enables and naturally disposes a man to do. Hope, properly signifies the expectation of future good, though, not unfrequently, it is also employed to denote the future good expected; as "the hope laid up in heaven."[1] The Roman Christians are here supposed to be possessed of a hope of future happiness. Now what is the hope of the Christian—the man who has believed, and been justified by believing? It is, as appears from the preceding part of the epistle, and other parts of the apostles' writings, that "he shall never come into condemnation;"[2] that "sin shall not have dominion over him;"[3] that "all things shall work together for good" to him;[4] that "the God of peace will bruise Satan under His feet shortly;"[5] that his "light afflictions, which are but for a moment, shall work for him a far more exceeding, and an eternal weight of glory;"[6] that nothing shall "separate him from the love of Christ—the love of God which is in Christ;"[7] that "when the earthly house of this tabernacle is dissolved, he shall have a building of God, a house not made with hands, eternal in the heavens;"[8] that when he becomes "absent from the body," he shall be "present with the Lord;"[9] that he shall "attain to the resurrection of the dead;"[10] that "the Saviour, the Lord Jesus, shall change his vile body, and fashion it like unto His own glorious body;"[11] that he shall be "like Him, for he shall see Him as he is;"[12] that he shall be "with Him where he is, that

[1] Col. i. 5.
[2] Rom. viii. 1.
[3] Chap. vi. 14.
[4] Chap. viii. 28.
[5] Chap. xvi. 20.
[6] 2 Cor. iv. 17.
[7] Rom. viii. 35-39.
[8] 2 Cor. v. 1.
[9] 2 Cor. v. 8.
[10] Phil. iii. 11.
[11] Phil. iii. 20, 21.
[12] 1 John iii. 2.

he may behold His glory;"[1] and finally, that he "shall be" thus "for ever with the Lord."[2] This was the hope of the Roman Christians—this is the hope of all Christians. It "comes to them" in consequence of "being heard of in the word of the truth of the Gospel;"[3] and that word coming to them, "not in word only, but in power, in the Holy Ghost, and in much assurance."[4] This hope, resting on the testimony of Him that cannot lie, is fitted to produce "joy," in whatever circumstances he who cherishes it is placed. It is the duty of the Christian to see that nothing takes place that is fitted to shake this hope, and damp the joy which flows from it; for "this joy of the Lord"—this "joy of the Holy Ghost," is his strength. He is to use all proper means to have his faith strengthened, and to avoid whatever, in the way of worldly or sinful disposition or conduct, goes to cast a cloud over his personal interest in the "exceeding great and precious promises." Every Christian should "show diligence to the full assurance of hope, to the end that"—in order that, "he may be not slothful, but a follower of them who, through faith and patience, inherit the promises."[5]

The cultivation of this "joy of hope" was specially necessary to enable Christians patiently to bear the afflictions of life, particularly those rising out of the profession of the faith of Christ; and therefore we find the apostle subjoining an injunction to what was only to be obtained by the strengthening influence of the joy of the Holy Ghost. "Patient"—that is, "be patient, in tribulation." "Tribulation," here, is ordinarily considered as descriptive of affliction, of whatever kind, and "patient" as expressive of the duty of humbly submitting to afflictive dispensations as the result of Divine appointment and agency—bearing the suffering without murmuring, while God is pleased to continue it; using no improper means to escape from it, and calmly waiting for the event. This, I have no doubt, was the duty of the Romans;

[1] John xvii. 24. [2] 1 Thess. iv. 17. [3] Col. i. 5, 6.
[4] 1 Thess. i. 5. [5] Heb. vi. 11, 12.

and it is the duty of all Christians, of all men, in all countries and ages. But I rather think the word "tribulation" here, as in chap. v. 3, refers to the afflictions to which the Roman Christians were exposed for their religion; and the word translated, there and here, "patience," is expressive of that persevering stedfastness in their faith and profession, by which, notwithstanding these afflictions, it was their duty to be distinguished. We have no reason to think that the Christians at Rome had, as yet, been exposed to persecution from the imperial power. But there, as well as everywhere else, Christians had to suffer in a variety of ways as Christians; and a fearful storm was just impending. The apostle therefore calls on them to be stedfast amid tribulation—"To hold fast the profession of their faith without wavering;" "to persevere in running" the race set before them.[1] Nothing was so well fitted to induce and enable them to do this, as a constant reference to the glorious object of their Christian hope. Nothing but the faith of the Gospel, and the hope of eternal life, could keep them firm in the hour of trial; and wherever there was a well-grounded joyful hope of final happiness to be reached only by "a patient continuance in well-doing,"[2] there would be constancy amid sufferings, however severe.

As, in order to persevering steadiness in the faith and profession of the truth amid affliction, and to that joyful hope which renders this practicable and comparatively easy, Divine influence is absolutely necessary; and as prayer is the appointed means of obtaining renewed supplies of that influence, the apostle adds, "continuing instant in prayer." Prayer is at once the proper mode of expressing our entire dependence on God, and of obtaining from Him such blessings as our circumstances require, "Call on Me in the day of trouble," is the command, and the promise, "I will deliver thee."[3] And our prayer must be "instant"—fervent and continued. "Men ought to pray always," *i.e.*, continue praying, "and not to faint."[4] Never do we need more to be fervent and persever-

[1] Heb. x. 23; xii. 1. [2] Heb. ii. 7. [3] Psal. l. 15. [4] Luke xviii. 1.

ing in prayer, than when tempted by afflictions to "make shipwreck of faith and of a good conscience." Then with redoubled eagerness, feeling our own weakness, and aware of the fearful consequences of "casting away our confidence, which has great recompense of reward," we should cry "out of the depths;" and the deeper we sink, the louder we should cry, "Hold Thou me up, and I shall be safe;" "Give to me the joy of Thy salvation;" and, in order to this, "Lord, increase my faith;" "then shall I not be ashamed when I have respect to all Thy commandments."

In the next verse the apostle enjoins certain duties which the Roman Christians owed to their suffering brethren:[1] "Distributing to the necessities of the saints, given to hospitality." It is scarcely worth noticing, that some codices have a word signifying "the memories,"[2] instead of that properly rendered "the necessities,"[3] and read the first clause, 'contributing to the memories or memorials of the saints.' The Latin Vulgate, the authorised version of the Church of Rome, follows this reading. There is no ground for departing from the received text, and, indeed, the other reading does look like an intentional depravation of the text, for the purpose of obtaining from the New Testament something like a sanction of the superstitious respect for the sepulchres and monuments of the saints, which early began to prevail in the Church.

The "saints," are here just another name for Christians, as "Set apart by the Lord for Himself"—His "peculiar people." In the primitive age, Christians were often called to prove the sincerity of their faith, by submitting to "the loss of all things." Many were called to lay down their lives—many more were obliged, after having been "spoiled of their goods," to abandon their native countries, and wander through strange lands, like their Master, not having where to lay their head. It is in direct reference to these persons, many of whom were probably in Rome, that the apostle gives the injunctions before us. To "distribute to the necessities of the saints"—was to commu-

[1] Ver. 13. [2] μνείαις. [3] χρείαις.

nicate to them what was necessary to supply their wants, and relieve their distress. This was a duty which the primitive Christians seem to have performed with exemplary readiness and liberality.[1] The spirit of the command reaches all lands and ages, and requires a Christian, whenever he sees a fellow-Christian in distress, especially if that distress has arisen out of a consistent adherence to his Christian profession, to do all in his power to relieve him.

The second injunction refers to the same class of persons. They were to take home to their houses, and cordially to entertain there, those who had "forsaken houses, or brethren, or sisters, or father, or mother, or lands, for Christ's name sake."[2] "Hospitality," in the common use of the word, means something quite different from this. It is the occasional entertainment in our houses, and at our tables, of those of our fellow-men with whom, in the relations of life, and the intercourse of society, we come to be connected—a very good thing in its own way, but not at all the Christian duty here enjoined. "I was hungry, and ye gave Me meat; thirsty, and ye gave Me drink; naked, and ye clothed Me"—this is "distributing to the necessities of the saints." "I was a stranger, and ye took Me in"—this is Christian hospitality. This form of the manifestation of Christian love, was peculiarly called for in the primitive times—but if a Christian has but the heart, he will not want the opportunity of showing that he is "given to hospitality." The parable of our Lord, Luke xiv. 12–14, well deserves the study of modern Christians.

Having thus stated how the Roman Christians ought to behave to their fellow-sufferers, the apostle proceeds to show how they should conduct themselves to the authors of their sufferings,[3] "Bless them that persecute you; bless, and curse not." These words require little exposition. "Persecutors" are those who, directly, or indirectly, are the authors of these unjust sufferings—especially the former. It is natural for

[1] Acts, iv. 34, 35; xi. 27–30; Rom. xv. 25–27; 2 Cor. viii. 1–4; ix. 1–4. [2] Matt. xix. 29. [3] Ver 14.

man to resent ill-usage, and, if in his power, to avenge it. But the apostle teaches the suffering Christians a more excellent way. His injunction is just an abridgment of what our Lord says in the Sermon on the Mount: "Ye have heard that it hath been said, Thou shalt love thy neighbour, and hate thine enemy; but I say unto you, Love your enemies; bless them that curse you; do good to them that hate you; and pray for them which despitefully use you, and persecute you."[1] The word "bless" is not equivalent in meaning to "do good offices,"—though it is a Christian's duty to do good offices to him who does him evil offices—it strictly means, to speak well of, or for. Here, and in the parallel passage referred to, it means to pray for the authors of our wrongs. This is one of the most effectual ways of promoting their welfare, and where it is genuine, will lead to every other practicable method. "When men persecute you," imitate your Lord, and say, "Father, forgive them; they know not what they do;" and His faithful martyr, Stephen, "Lord, lay not this sin to their charge." He redoubles the injunction, knowing how hard a thing it is for flesh and blood to comply with it: "Bless, and curse not;"—*i.e.*, 'Instead of imprecating vengeance on your persecutors, pray for their salvation.'

The next apostolical command refers to the cultivation and expression of an enlightened tender sympathy, both with the joys and the sorrows of others—"Rejoice with those who do rejoice, and weep with those who weep."[2] The persecution to which the Christian is exposed must not be allowed to produce an ascetic, stoical, monkish spirit. He must not, under the combined influence of his faith and hope in reference to a better world, his convictions of the vanity of this world, and his experience of the unkindness of the men of the world, withdraw from society. He must not go out of the world; he must mingle with his fellow-men and take an interest in their happiness—rejoicing with them when they rejoice, and weeping with them when they weep. This is the duty of

[1] Matt. v. 43, 44. [2] Ver. 15.

Christians in reference to all men. The joys of the worldling are often of a kind in which the Christian cannot, ought not to rejoice; but in all the innocent enjoyments of his fellow-men he is to take a kindly interest. He is to rejoice with others, even when suffering himself. And in every case of suffering he is to pity the sufferer. The character of the sympathy must vary as the suffering is deserved or undeserved; but in every case of suffering there is to be sympathy—genuine sympathy. Are not all men brethren? Is not the humblest—aye, the worst of mankind, connected with me by a bond of brotherhood that nothing can dissolve?

But there can be little doubt that the apostle, in the injunction, had a peculiar reference to the sympathy in enjoyment and in suffering which Christians ought to cultivate and display towards each other. It is natural to have a peculiar interest where there is a peculiar relation. The joys and sorrows, peculiar to Christians, have a common character, which enables them more thoroughly to sympathize with one another. They understand each how others feel, and the love, which is the badge of brotherhood, secures kind sympathy both in enjoyment and suffering. The cultivation and display of this disposition, proper at all times, is peculiarly required in seasons of trial. The joys of the suffering Christian are doubled, and his sorrows are greatly diminished, when he perceives that he is not alone—that many human hearts beat in unison with his. The prevalence of this disposition in an individual Christian society, is one of the best proofs of its spiritual prosperity, and one principal source of genuine happiness to its members. A Christian Church, though few in numbers and depressed in circumstances, if pervaded by Christian sympathy, gives evidence of spiritual vitality, and is the abode of peace, and love, and holy happiness. On a Christian Church, however numerous and flourishing in its external circumstances, where this principle of sympathy among the members is wanting, Ichabod may be inscribed—the glory has departed.

In addition to this kind of sympathy, the apostle recommends unanimity, mutual condescension, and humility. "Be of the same mind one toward another. Mind not high things, but condescend to men of low estate. Be not wise in your own conceits."[1]

The expression "Be of one mind," may, from the force of the original word, signify either 'be united in your sentiments,' or 'be united in your affections.' The two things are closely connected. Union of sentiment, as to the great fundamental doctrines of Christianity, is the only legitimate and solid basis of mutual Christian affection. Christians love one another "in the truth for the truth's sake."[2] The explanatory phrase, "toward each other," seems to fix the meaning here to unity of affection. It is not the duty of every Christian to love every other Christian with the same measure of affection, for all are not equally amiable, and affection should be enlightened as well as warm; but every Christian is to regard every Christian with the same kind of affection—a kind of affection which none but a Christian can cherish, and which *he* can cherish only to a brother Christian.

If Christians would thus love one another, they must guard against an aspiring ambitious spirit, "mind not high things." Christians are, in the most general sense of the word, not "to mind high things,"—they are not to make the attaining a high position in the world their great object. They are to seek first the kingdom—mind the true high things—"the things that are above"—and look down on what the world calls high things as low things. The command to Baruch comes to us all,—"Seekest thou great things for thyself? seek them not."[3] This, as is intimated in the passage referred to, is peculiarly unbecoming in a time of public judgment and persecution. The injunction here seems to have a direct reference to the conduct of Christians in their holy fellowship with each other. They are not to be, like Diotrephes, of whom the Apostle John speaks.[4] They are not to "love to

[1] Ver. 16.
[2] 2 John 1, 2.
[3] Jer. xlv. 5.
[4] 3 John 9.

have the pre-eminence." They are not assiduously to seek office and honour in the Church. They are not to aspire to lordship over the faith or practice of their brethren. "In love they are to serve one another." They are to remember the words of their Lord,—"One is your Master, and all ye are brethren."[1]

Instead of "minding high things," they are to condescend to "men of low estate." The words rendered, "men of low estate," may refer either to persons or to things. As it is "high things" in the previous clause, it is probable that the last is the designed reference of the apostle. Instead of aspiring to the highest places in the Church, to which none has a right but those called by the suffrages of the brethren, they were to be ready to perform the humblest offices for promoting the general edification of the body; remembering that their Lord washed the disciples' feet, and, in doing so, had given them an example that they should do to one another what he had done to all.[2] If we take the view adopted by our translation, then, the meaning is, 'count it not beneath you to associate with the poorest and the most despised and persecuted among the brethren:' and, in this case, the injunction is intended to strike against the abuse, which, we learn from the Epistle of James, early made its appearance, and still exists, in the Christian Church—the paying an undue respect to secular rank and wealth in matters of religion.[3] The other interpretation seems, however, the best supported.

Closely connected with an ambitious spirit is an unduly high estimate of our own powers and acquirements, and its prevalence is equally inconsistent with that harmony of affection which the apostle wished to secure for the Church in Rome: and therefore he adds—"Be not wise in your own conceits." To have a just estimate of our own powers and acquirements, natural and spiritual, is of great importance in various ways; and, if these are really greater than those of many of our

[1] Matt. xxiii. 8. [2] John xiii. 1–17. [3] James ii. 1–7.

brethren, to know this cannot be wrong. But to suppose that we monopolize all the knowledge and wisdom of the society we belong to, to refuse to co-operate in works of importance to the common good of the society, because our plans are not followed, and we have not assigned to us the place which we think due in executing the work, is folly and sin in the most gifted church member. We ought to cherish habitually a deep sense of our own ignorance and fallibility, and preserve a mind ever ready to receive instruction from whatever quarter it may come. This is the way to make progress in personal improvement; and this, too, is the way to promote the peace and prosperity of the Church. What kind of a society would be formed of a set of men all "wise in their own conceits?" It is plain they would not "be of the same mind one towards another," and that, instead of being bound together "in the unity of the Spirit and the bond of peace," there would be nothing but "strife and division," "the biting and devouring of one another," "confusion and every evil work." The apostle now proceeds to instruct the Roman Christians in their duties to the world around them—an ungodly and unfriendly world.

"Recompense to no man evil for evil. Provide things honest in the sight of all men."[1] The first of these injunctions proceeds on the supposition that the Roman Christians would meet, not only with afflictions, but with injuries. Christ and His apostles never imposed on men by concealing the sacrifices they must make, the hazards they must expose themselves to, the sufferings they must endure, if they would act the part and secure the reward of genuine disciples. "In this world," said He, "ye shall have tribulation."[2] "All who live godly," said they, "shall suffer persecution."[3] "We must through much tribulation enter into the kingdom of God."[4] But, though they might receive many injuries, they were to inflict none. They were not even to "*recompense* to any man evil for evil." This command does not prohibit

[1] Ver. 17.
[2] John xvi. 33.
[3] 2 Tim. iii. 12.
[4] Acts xiv. 22.

Christians from availing themselves of the institutions of society to defend their persons, property, and reputation from lawless violence, or to obtain redress when they have been injured, or to secure themselves from a repetition of the injury; but it does forbid everything of the nature of vindictive retaliation. If a man has defamed my character, I not only may, but I ought, to use all fit means to have my reputation cleared, which is so intimately connected with my usefulness and the credit of Christianity; but I must not, though I could do it, in perfect consistency with truth, injure his character further than it is necessarily injured by the exposure of his malignity and falsehood. Instead of recompensing his evil with evil, I must endeavour to overcome his evil by good.

The second injunction is, "Provide things honest in the sight of all men." These words seem a quotation from memory of Prov. v. 4, which, in the Septuagint, runs thus —"Provide honourable things before God and men." Our English translation of this clause has contracted a degree of obscurity from the variations of a living language. The word "honest" here is used in a nearly obsolete sense—that of 'honourable,' 'comely,' 'of good report.' To provide things honest in the sight of all men, is to add to the substantial virtues of Christianity, such as piety, truth, justice, beneficence, chastity, and temperance—a temper and a behaviour fitted to command the respect and esteem of mankind at large. Christians ought assuredly "not to be conformed to the world," in order to avoid the contempt and secure the good will of the worldly. But they are carefully to avoid acting in a way which might necessarily sharpen their dislike and strengthen their prejudice in reference to Christianity and to Christians, and give plausibility to their misrepresentations of both. There should be nothing mean, nothing suspicious, about the character and conduct of a Christian. His strict integrity, his honourable principle, his open—straightforward course, his complete freedom from everything like assumption, trick, and imposture, his sincere kindliness, his disinterested public spirit should be so conspicuous that men may be made "ashamed who falsely accuse his good conversation in Christ."[1] It is a happy thing when worldly men are constrained to say of a Christian what Tertullian makes a heathen say of a Christian in his time, "He is an excellent man, that Caius Servius, only he is a Christian."[2]

A third injunction which the apostle lays on the Christian Romans, in reference to their conduct towards mankind at large, is contained in the 18th verse: "If it be possible, as much as lieth in you, live peaceably with all men." To "live peaceably," is descriptive of that state, in which a man does not disturb others, and is not disturbed by them. The first is always in our own power, the second is not; and hence the limitation of the injunction, "If it be possible, as much as lieth in *you*." Christians ought never to offer an affront or inflict an injury; and they ought, as far as is consistent with the requirements of an enlightened conscience, to avoid everything which may prove the occasion of other men quarrelling with them. They are to act in this way to "all men"—not only to Christians, but to unbelievers; not only to those of their own party or denomination, but to men of all parties and denominations; not only to those who are peaceably disposed, but also to those of a quarrelsome disposition—who seem always on the outlook for an occasion of strife; to those whom we have the power and opportunity of disturbing with impunity, as well as to those who have the corresponding power and opportunity of harrassing us. And, in order to this, we are to do all that lieth in *us*. The emphasis is on *you*. We are to overlook many slights; to put up with many injuries; we are to make many sacrifices. There are two things, quite in our power, which go far towards securing the desirable object of "living peaceably with all men:" the keeping that unmanageable member, the tongue, under a strict rein; and the studying to be quiet, and doing our own business. Foolish tattling, and being "busybodies in other men's matters," are more to blame, than more serious causes of dispeace, in dis-

[1] 1 Pet. iii. 16. [2] Apolog. iii.

turbing society. But there are sacrifices which must not be made, there are things that must not be done, even to secure peace. We must not flatter nor imitate what we think wrong in men's opinions and conduct; we must not purchase peace at the expense of truth or justice; we must not omit duty; we must not commit sin. If men will not be at peace with us but on principles which infer our disloyalty to the Supreme Sovereign—which are inconsistent with our primary and paramount obligations—then peace, however desirable, must be parted with, for the plain reason, that to have God as a friend is a greater good, than to have all the world our enemies is an evil. One great cause of dispeace is men's taking upon themselves to avenge their own wrongs; and, accordingly, the apostle proceeds to prohibit this on the part of the Roman Christians, and to fortify his prohibition by very powerful motives.

"Dearly beloved, avenge not yourselves, but rather give place unto wrath: for it is written, Vengeance is Mine; I will repay, saith the Lord."[1] The cause of the apostle's prefacing this prohibition with the compellation "Dearly beloved," is to be found either in the earnestness which he felt in pressing this matter on their attention—so important to individual Christian improvement, as well as to the credit and progress of the Christian cause—or to impress on their minds that his urging them not to avenge themselves, did by no means proceed from indifference to them and their interest, or want of sympathy under the wrongs done them. It is exceedingly probable that the Christians were involved in the hardships to which the Jews were exposed (being looked on by the government as a Jewish sect), when banished from Rome by Claudius, and that, on that occasion, they had many injuries inflicted on them by their heathen neighbours. It is certain that they had met with injuries; for there is no living in this world—especially there is no "living godly in this world," without meeting with them. In many—in most cases

[1] Ver. 19.

Christians have not the power to avenge their injuries on their enemies; but even when they have the power, they must not exert it. They must not wish that they had it. The command is most express: "Avenge not yourselves." They must not seek the injury of those who have injured them. The good of society may make it necessary for them to prosecute those who have wronged them—even true love to the wrongdoer may dictate this course; but in no case must he do this to gratify ill-will, or to avenge injury. Resentment must not be the impelling cause, nor the suffering of the injurer the ultimate object.

Instead of avenging *themselves*, the apostle enjoins them to "rather give place to wrath." This is an injunction, the meaning of which is by no means self-evident. There is some difficulty in fixing the precise import both of the term "wrath," and of the phrase "give place to." Some suppose that the word "wrath" signifies the human passion of anger; and these are divided into two classes—one supposing that it refers to the furious rage of the inflicter of the injury; the other, that it refers to the natural resentment of him who sustains the injury. Those who explain the word "wrath" of the rage of the injurious person, interpret the injunction, "give place unto wrath," as equivalent to—'Yield to it; do not resist it; allow it to spend itself. Keep out of its way, if possible; but let it run its course. Resistance would, probably, but increase the tempest—give greater intensity to the flame—and make the injurious more and more injurious.' Those who consider "wrath" as referring to the anger of the person injured, explain the injunction as equivalent either to, 'Fly anger; keep out of its way;' or, what seems a more natural interpretation, 'Let the natural emotion have its course. Do not lay up the injury in your heart, as something to be brooded over. Express your feelings, and thus abate them. To borrow the image of the poet, "Do not nurse your wrath to keep it warm;" or, in the words of the apostle, "Be angry and sin not." Do not conceal the conviction and feeling that you have been wronged; and follow this course, as the natural means of preventing the cherishing of malignant feeling, and forming dark plans for future vengeance.'

None of these modes of interpretation seem satisfactory. Some of them are not consistent with the scope of the passage; and others, to speak gently, are not supported by the analogy of Scripture phraseology. "Wrath" appears here to refer to the moral disapprobation—the judicial displeasure of God against all injustice and injury, and the expression of these in righteous punishment. It is not uncommon in Scripture to use the simple word "wrath" to denote the Divine wrath—an expression the meaning of which we have just explained. In 2 Chron. xxiv. 18, it is said, "Wrath came upon Judah and Jerusalem for their trespass;" in Matt. iii. 7, we read of "the wrath to come;" in Rom. ii. 5, we find the sinner represented as "treasuring up to himself wrath against the day of wrath;" in chap. v. 9, we read of men "saved from wrath;" in Eph. ii. 3, unforgiven sinners are represented as "children of wrath;" and, in 1 Thess. ii. 16, we read of "wrath coming on the impenitent Jews to the uttermost." In all these passages, "wrath"—"the wrath"—is the wrath of God. Such seems its meaning here—"Give way to the wrath." 'Leave God to avenge the injury, which is more against Him than against you. You are not the man's judge—He is. Interfere not with His prerogative. Let Him take His own time and way to manifest His displeasure at sin. He will do what is right. Remember that He, whose name alone is Jehovah, is the Judge over all the earth.' This was the course our Lord took: "When He was reviled, He reviled not again; when He suffered, He threatened not; but committed Himself to Him that judgeth righteously."[1]

This mode of explaining the passage is greatly recommended by its entirely harmonizing with the quotation from the Old Testament which follows: "For it is written, Vengeance is Mine; I will repay, saith the Lord." This passage is to be found Deut. xxxii. 35. The words teach two truths: first,

[1] 1 Pet. ii. 23.

that God will ultimately repay all injuries done to His people; and, secondly, that to do this is *His* prerogative. The quotation bears most directly on the injunction, in the way of motive. 'Your avenging yourselves is both unnecessary and improper. The righteous Judge will judge righteously; and it is not for you to show that you doubt this, by attempting to do what He will do, and what He only has a right to do. Vengeance is not work for *you;* it comes within the province of the Supreme Ruler, or of those to whom He has, in some measure, delegated His authority. The great object is to vindicate the cause of truth and right, and He will take care of that. It is yours to suffer and forgive; it is His to judge and to avenge.' Christians are quite inexcusable in cherishing resentment and seeking vengeance. "Their Redeemer is strong, the Lord of hosts is His name, He shall thoroughly plead their cause."[1] This passage throws a striking light on the danger of injuring the people of God. "He that touches them touches the apple of *His* eye;"[2] and, in the ultimate result of things, it will be found that it had been better for their persecutors, however powerful, "that millstones had been hanged about their necks, and they cast into the deeps of the sea, than that they had offended"—injured, by making stumble—"one of these little ones."[3] The Divine faithfulness is pledged to avenge the wrongs done to the faithful.[4]

While Christians are thus to commit themselves and their cause to their "faithful Creator," the kind Father, the righteous Judge, they are not only not to avenge themselves, but on the contrary, they are to do everything in their power to contribute to the welfare of their enemies, by supplying their wants and relieving their distresses. "Therefore, if thine enemy hunger, feed him; if he thirst, give him drink; for in so doing thou shalt heap coals of fire on his head."[5] This is a quotation from Prov. xxv. 21, 22. "Therefore," if understood in its most ordinary sense as indicating an inference—

[1] Jer. l. 34. [2] Zech. ii. 8. [3] Matt. xviii. 6.
[4] Deut. xxxii. 40–43; 2 Thess. i. 6–10; Rev. vi. 9–11. [5] Ver. 20.

'For this reason,' must be considered as looking forward rather than back. The statement that God is the judge, is a good reason why Christians should not seek to avenge themselves, but it does not seem to lay a foundation for the exhortation here. The last clause of the verse does. By acting in this way you will heap coals of fire on the head of thine enemy, therefore so act. The command of our Lord is, "Love thine enemy, do good to them that hate you."[1] The absence of hatred is not love; the abstinence from retaliation of wrong is not doing good. True love is not a merely negative principle; it is positive: not passive merely, but also active. It produces a disposition to do good, which manifests itself in supplying wants, relieving distress, and, in one word, in every proper way seeking to promote the satisfaction and welfare of its object. If the man who has injured me is visited with poverty and affliction, I must not derive enjoyment from his sufferings, I must not pass by on the other side, I must exert myself to soothe his sorrows—to remove their cause. If he is hungry, I must feed him; if he is fainting for thirst, I must give him drink; if he is naked, I must clothe him. If he is, in his comfortless dwelling, laid on a bed of languishing and pain, and destitute of the comforts and means of alleviation and cure which such circumstances require, I must supply him with them, and do all in my power to prolong the life even of him who, it may be, has plotted the shortening of mine. If we see a man who has acted dishonestly toward us, about to be circumvented in business, instead of sitting still, and, not without secret satisfaction, seeing him ruined, we are to exert ourselves to save him from the meshes in which villainy is seeking to entangle him; we must do what we can to unfold the fraud and repel the injustice. If we hear the man who has slandered us calumniated, and charges brought against him which we know to be untrue, we must not silently allow the poisoned arrow to reach its mark and work its purpose, we must stand up for his reputation, who trampled on ours, and

[1] Matt. v. 44.

do justice to his character, who did all in his power unjustly to destroy our reputation. In one word, we must readily embrace, nay, we must sedulously seek, opportunities of conferring favours on those who have inflicted on us injuries.

These exalted maxims the apostle, following in the wake of the Old Testament writer whom he had quoted, enforces by the consideration, that "in so doing they should heap coals of fire on the head" of their enemies. There is some difficulty in discovering and unfolding the precise meaning and incidence of these words. They certainly do not signify what some have supposed them to do, "Heap favours on your enemies, that their ultimate punishment may be more severe." It does not seem very clear how our doing favours to our enemy should increase his punishment for past injuries. And it were strange if he who had just affirmed that vengeance was God's prerogative, and that we must beware of even seeming to usurp it, should immediately proceed to put us upon a way of avenging ourselves on our enemies, more completely than by any personal evil we could inflict, by bringing down on them the vengeance of heaven. He who had just forbidden us to hurt our enemies by our evil deeds, could not surely go on to show us how we might ruin them by our good ones. Nor does it mend the matter much to say that the apostle does not speak of what should be our *intention*, in conferring benefits on our enemies, but of the event of our doing so if they continue in their enmity. The apostle does not insert, does not hint at, any such qualification; and it is obvious that the last clause of the verse is a motive brought forward to enforce the injunction in the first clause. What, in this case, would apparent acts of kindness be but hypocritical malignity, in one of its most hateful forms?

The principal difficulty of interpretation here, arises from the fact, that the figurative expression, "heap coals of fire on the head," occurs only here and in the passage in Proverbs which the apostle quotes. If the figure be considered as directly referring to the person of our enemy, it would seem that it must denote something that would occasion intense pain. Putting coals of fire on the head was one of the tortures which the persecutors inflicted on the ancient confessors, and must have been intolerably agonising. Following out this thought, some have supposed the apostle's meaning to be—By continuing—by increasing kindness to your enemy, awaken shame in him for his base as well as bad conduct—a feeling very painful: you will thus give him pain, but it will be salutary pain. This seems rather too artificial and far-fetched.

The more probable account of the matter seems to be this: The whole phrase is figurative, and borrowed from the art of metallurgy. Fire is used to convert the ore into a metallic state. The fire is heaped on the ore, cast into the furnace, and through its influence the cold and rugged substance is melted and becomes malleable, and fit for being employed for useful purposes. The native tendency of persevering, disinterested goodness, is to produce gratitude, even in a very depraved heart. It is difficult to lodge, by any means, the conviction of disinterested goodness. There must be many coals heaped on the sullen ore—many favours must be done, which will produce little or no effect—but the tendency is to melt; and when once the fact, that the man whom I have unjustly injured really loves me, forces itself on the mind, love takes the place of suspicion and hatred.

> "So artists melt the stubborn ore of lead,
> By heaping coals of fire upon its head,
> In the kind warmth the metal learns to glow,
> And, loose from dross, the silver runs below." [1]

This mode of interpretation is in perfect conformity with the spirit of Christianity, and exactly suits both the preceding and the following context.

The whole duty of Christians in reference to injury is summed up by the apostle in one comprehensive precept, "Be not overcome of evil, but overcome evil with good." [2] "Evil" here is, as at ver. 17, injury. 'Be not overcome of

[1] Parnell. [2] Ver. 21.

injury. Let not the injuries you receive, however numerous, varied, severe, and long-continued they may be, get the better of your Christian principles. Never let the injustice and malignity of man exert an influence superior to the authority of God and the love of Christ. Never let the diabolical pleasure of revenge displace the divine delight of forgiveness.' "But overcome evil with good." "Good," here, is equivalent to kind offices—benefit, in opposition to injury. 'By benefits bestowed on your enemy, overcome his evil. Show him that you are not to be outdone by him; that while he continues to injure, you will continue to forgive, and, so far as is in your power, to render good for evil.'

This noble sentiment is peculiar to Christianity. It is well said, "Nothing like this moral precept is to be found in the heathen classics, and nothing like what it enjoins ever existed among heathen nations. The idea of overcoming evil with good never occurred to men till the Gospel was preached to them: it never has been acted on but under the influence of that Gospel. On this principle, God shows kindness to sinful men; on this principle, the Saviour came into our world, and bled, and died; and on this principle all Christians should act in treating their enemies, and in their attempts to bring the race of man to the knowledge and obedience of the truth as it is in Jesus. If Christians would but show disinterested benevolence sufficiently extensively and perseveringly, evil, all over the world, would be overcome of good. The heathen nations will be converted to Christianity then, and not till then, when Christians shall, generally and habitually, individually and collectively, act on this great practical principle of their religion: "Overcome evil with good."

The apostle now proceeds to instruct the Roman Christians in reference to their duties to the civil authorities, in the paragraph from the beginning of the thirteenth chapter to the end of the 7th verse. To understand this important and much discussed passage aright, it is of primary importance to recollect that it was directly intended to guide the Roman Christians in the circumstances in which they were placed, and to apprehend distinctly what may be termed the logical division of the paragraph, and the bearing its various parts have on each other.

The Christians at Rome were a small handful of men—comparatively few of them, probably, Roman citizens—living under a powerful, absolute monarchy, whose administration was, however, ordinarily conducted according to the principles of a civil and criminal code of law which is admitted to have been one of the best the world has ever seen.

The apostle enjoins the general duty of civil obedience, in very strong terms, in the first clause of the first verse; and he enforces his injunction by an appeal both to the principle of conscience and that of self-love: to the first, by stating that "there is no power but of God;" that "the powers that be are ordained of God;" so that "whosoever resisteth the power, resists the ordinance of God;"—to the second, by stating that they who "resist shall receive to themselves damnation"—punishment; for the Roman rulers, in their ordinary administration, were a terror, not to good works, but to evil;[1] so that, if they wished to live free from fear of the government, they must do what the law enjoined, and what was, in ordinary cases, good—right. In this case they would have protection, not punishment; for the Roman government was, in the ordinations of Divine providence, a minister of God to the Christians for good.[2] But, if they transgressed the law—in doing which they would, generally speaking, do not only what was illegal, but what was wrong, they might rest satisfied that, as the Roman government was a strong, jealous, active government, they would not escape condign punishment. Thus a regard to the will of God, and to their own interests, equally required them to act the part of peaceable, good subjects.[3] The specific duty of paying tribute is enjoined in these words: "For this cause pay you tribute also;"[4] and enforced, first, as a part of that civil obedience already enjoined; and, secondly, by the consideration that the collectors of tribute were

[1] Ver. 3. [2] Ver. 4. [3] Ver. 5. [4] Ver. 6.

in reality as much God's ministers as the "higher powers;" and he concludes by urging them to render what was due to every order of men employed in the complicated machine of civil government, from the publican to the emperor—tribute, custom, fear, and honour, according as they were respectively due.[1] We will find this outline of use in the more close examination of the passage, to which I now proceed.

"Let every soul be subject unto the higher powers."[2] "Powers" signifies persons invested with—possessing, power. It is joined by Luke with "magistrates."[3] We are accustomed to speak of the great "powers" of Europe, meaning the principal governments. The word rendered "higher" has been considered by some as equivalent to 'protecting;' but this is not the import of the term; nor is the injunction confined to such magistrates as protected the Christians; nor does the phrase, "higher powers," seem intended to describe exclusively the supreme authorities. It seems used as a description of all orders of magistracy, "whether," as Peter says, "the king, as supreme, or governors, as sent of him."[4]

Now, in reference to these "higher powers," the command is, "Let every soul be subject" to them. To "be subject," is to be obedient, actively and passively—to do what they command, and to submit to what they appoint. This command, though unlimited in its terms, is yet obligatory only on certain clearly defined conditions. It is to the magistrate acting officially, not to the magistrate personally, that this obedience is owing. Obedience to an inferior magistrate is not due, if he enjoins or exacts anything inconsistent with the declared will of the supreme authority; and, finally, the Divine law must not be violated, in consequence of any command of the civil power: "We must obey God rather than men."

Within these limits, the law is peremptory: "Let every soul be subject unto the higher powers." Every *soul* is a Hebraism for every person,[5] just as every *body* is an Anglicism

[1] Ver. 7. [2] Ver. 1. [3] Chap. xii. 11. [4] 1 Pet. ii. 13, 14.
[5] Gen. xii. 5; Exod. i. 5; Acts ii. 41; 1 Pet. iii. 20.

for the same thing. It is an idiomatic, and, probably here, an emphatic expression. It seems intended to bring the idea of the universality of the obligation more strongly out than the use of the ordinary term, "every one,"[1] would have done. Whether Jew or Gentile—whether a Roman citizen or an alien—whether a freeman or a slave—whether an official Christian, or one in private life—whatever dignity of character he may be clothed with—whatever extent or variety of spiritual gifts he may be endowed with—let every one of you be subject to the ruling authorities. Chrysostom very well expresses the meaning: "Although he be an evangelist, although he be a prophet, although he be an apostle, let every soul be subject."

The apostle proceeds now to unfold the reasons on which this injunction is founded. These are two. The Roman Christians could not violate this law without—(1.) Involving themselves in guilt, and in the consequences of guilt, as despisers of a Divine appointment—violators of a Divine law; and without—(2.) Exposing themselves to punishment by the magistrate for a crime—an offence against the peace and order of society. The first of these grounds is stated in the words: "For there is no power but of God: the powers that be are ordained of God. Whosoever therefore resisteth the power, resisteth the ordinance of God."[2] The second of them is stated in the words: "They that resist shall receive to themselves damnation."[3]

In the first part of the sentence, we have something like a formal argument: the premises, "There is no power but of God;" "The powers that be are ordained of God"—a great principle applied to an individual case; and then the conclusion, "Whosoever resisteth the power, resisteth the ordinance of God."

"Power" here is often understood of magistracy in the abstract. Some who take this view understand the assertion, 'magistracy is of God,' as signifying that it exists, as every-

[1] ἕκαστος. [2] Ver. 1, 2. [3] Ver. 2.

thing does, by the permission of God. It is of God, as war or slavery is of God. These interpreters err by defect; such an assertion lays no ground for the apostle's inference. Others, erring by excess, hold it to mean, 'Magistracy is directly of Divine appointment.' This, as a general truth, is not true: magistracy among the Jews was directly of Divine appointment, but among no other people. It does not stand on the same ground as the priesthood under the law, nor as the Christian ministry under the Gospel. It was not formally instituted like marriage. It occupies similar ground with property, the social state, agriculture, and commerce. It rises out of the constitution of men's minds, which are God's work, and their circumstances, which are the result of His providence; and it is conducive to the security and well-being of mankind, which we know to be agreeable to the "good" will of God. It is thus of God; yet not so of God, as not also to be of man. The Apostle Peter calls it "the ordinance of man."[1] Its elementary principles are Divine; the mixing them up in any particular form of magistracy is human.

I do not, however, consider the word as used abstractly. "No power" is equivalent to 'no man invested with civil rule,' just as "the higher powers"[2] are the governors, and "the powers that be" are 'the existing magistrates.' No man, in society, clothed with civil power—whatever form it may assume, whether he be an arbitrary autocrat, or a limited monarch, or the administrator of an aristocracy or democracy —no such man fills such a place but "of God." The Jewish Theocratic governor is not the only governor who has a right to obedience as a religious duty. Every magistrate, in organized society, occupies his place in consequence of Divine arrangements; and the grand object of the institution, of which he is the organ, is a thing agreeable to God's will.

The apostle now proceeds a step further, and, as a person invested with Divine authority, decides that the existing Roman government was so the ordinance of God to those whom he was

[1] 1 Pet. ii. 13. [2] Ver. 1.

addressing, as that they could not disobey, or resist it, without violating His law, and incurring His displeasure. "The powers that be are ordained of God." The phrase, "the powers that be," has been explained, of rightly constituted governments, as equivalent to 'the authorities that, from their wisdom and equity, are really authorities—the legitimate powers—the magistrates that possess the qualifications and prosecute the ends of their office:' but, though I do not deny that the words in certain conceivable connections might have this meaning, it is plain this is not their meaning here. "The powers that be" are the existing Roman magistracies—including the frame of government and those who administered its functions. These magistracies, says the apostle, are "ordained of God"—literally, are 'arranged, or set in order, under God.'[1] They have originated in circumstances of His arranging; and, as the best government which, all things considered, the inhabitants of the wide regions forming the Roman empire could bear, are so in accordance with His will, that none of their subjects—especially their Christian subjects, after this explicit declaration by an apostle—can rebel against them without disobeying God.

The conclusion follows irresistibly from the premises: "Whosoever therefore resisteth the power, resisteth the ordinance of God." The existing Roman magistrates, from the Emperor to the Ædile, have been put into order under God: whosoever, then—however high his place may be in the Church, or however distinguished by miraculous gifts—sets himself against this divinely marshalled magistracy, not only commits a crime against society in disturbing a useful human arrangement, but is guilty of sin in opposing a Divine arrangement. Disobedience is not only a civil crime, but also a moral delinquency: it is not only a breach of the laws of men, but of the law of God. This is the first and the strongest reason the apostle urges on the Roman Christians, why "every soul should be subject to the higher powers."

[1] ὑπὸ τοῦ Θεοῦ τεταγμέναι.

A second far inferior, yet still powerful, enforcement of the duty of civil obedience, is brought forward in the second clause of the second verse: "And they that resist shall receive to themselves damnation." Almost all interpreters are of opinion that, instead of the word "damnation"—which, though not at the time when our translation was made so exclusively appropriated as now to express the final punishment of the wicked, was even then a very strong word—should be substituted "punishment."[1] The punishment spoken of has ordinarily been interpreted of Divine punishment; and, had the second verse not been immediately followed by the third, I should have concurred in that opinion. But when we consider that the apostle, in summing up his argument, represents it as consisting of two parts—an appeal to conscience, and an appeal to fear;[2] when we find the statement before us immediately followed by another statement giving the reason of it,—I think there can be no doubt that the punishment referred to is the punishment which the Roman government inflicted on violators of the law and disturbers of the public peace.

"And," or moreover, "they that resist" the power—the Roman government—"shall receive damnation"—punishment; "for rulers"—rather, for "the rulers, are not a terror to good works, but to the evil." These words have often been interpreted of rulers in general, and they are true of them; but it is as plain as anything well can be, that the apostle is here speaking of the Roman rulers. The Roman government was a strong and active one: the only way to avoid its vengeance was to obey its laws. To be "a terror not to good works, but to the evil," is to be a reasonable source of alarm, "not to those who do good works, but to those who do evil." Good works, here, are such actions as the Roman law enjoined, which, generally, were really good works—actions fitted to promote the good of society; and evil works, such as it condemned, and which, generally, were really evil works—actions fitted to disturb the order of society, and

[1] Rom. iii. 8; 1 Cor. xi. 29; Gal. v. 10. [2] Ver. 5.

infringe on the rights and happiness of individuals. The Roman law, on the whole, was an admirable specimen of legislation. We know that ere long the Roman magistrates were to legislate, and act on their legislation, in reference to the Christian religion; and, so far as that was concerned, they became a terror to good works, and not to the evil. But the apostle here refers to the general character of the code of the Roman law, and its administration. The laws of the empire were favourable, like the laws of all civilized states, to the peaceable subject, and armed with penalties against the disobedient and rebellious.

"Wilt thou then not be afraid of the power? do that which is good, and thou shalt have praise of the same." 'Would you wish to live secure in the possession of property and life under the Roman government? Be an obedient, peaceable subject; and you will not only be protected, you will "have praise" from it. The government will not only not punish you, but show its approbation of your conduct in protecting you.' "For," says he,[1] going on to illustrate his assertion, "he is the minister of God for good to thee." He refers to the security which Christians possessed as to life and property under the Roman government, when compared with the danger to both in a state of anarchy. But for a regular government, they would, by the infuriated Jews and the Pagan rabble, have been torn to pieces as wild beasts. The apostle very probably had in his mind the instances in which the Roman magistrate—"the power," had been to himself "the minister of God for good."[2]

On the other hand, if the Roman Christians, by conspiracy and revolt, disturbed the public peace, the apostle assures them that they might lay their account with being punished; and that, if they were so, it would be no more than they deserved: "But if thou do that which is evil, be afraid; for he beareth not the sword in vain." "Evil" here is descriptive of what is opposed to the law—what is in its tendency subversive

[1] Ver. 4.

[2] Acts xviii. 14; xix. 35; xxi. 31; xxiii. 12–23; xxv., *passim*.

of the government. If the Christians did anything of this kind, they had good cause to fear; punishment—severe, certain, and sudden—was likely to overtake them. The Roman magistrate "bore the sword"—had the power of life and death, which was emblematised by the sword, or dagger,[1] which formed a part of his official dress; and he was disposed to use it—"he bore it not in vain." The Roman government was not backward in inflicting merited punishment. And, in punishing disobedient, rebellious professors of Christianity, he was equally God's minister, as in protecting them when they acted as dutiful subjects. "He is the minister of God—a revenger, to execute wrath upon him that doeth evil." As, in the case of obedience, the Christians would enjoy security—this would come from God, and, in conferring it, the Roman magistrate would be His minister—so, in the case of disobedience, they would be punished—this punishment would indeed be from God, and, in inflicting it, the Roman magistrate would be His minister.

The conclusion of the whole matter, as to civil obedience, is to be found in the words which follow:—"Wherefore ye must needs be subject, not only for wrath, but for conscience sake."[2] 'It is necessary (such is the import of the apostle's summing up) that ye be subject to the Roman government on two accounts: on account of "wrath," the punishment which disobedience will certainly bring on you; but not only on this account, but for a higher reason—for "conscience sake," from a regard to the Divine authority interposed in this matter, not merely on the evidence, which forces itself on every reflecting mind, that civil government is in accordance with the Divine will, but also in the clear revelation of His will, which I, an inspired apostle, have now made to you.'

The general principles contained in these injunctions are applicable to Christians in all countries and in all ages. This passage clearly teaches us that Christians, in all countries and ages, should respect and obey the civil government under

[1] Pugio. [2] Ver. 5.

which they live; that a Christian who follows a course that leads to anarchy, acts a wicked, as well as an inconsistent and foolish part; that no Christian is warranted to disturb a settled civil government because it is not, in its form and administration, so good as he could desire it; and that all Christians, placed in the same circumstances in reference to the civil government under which they live as the primitive Christians were to the Roman government, are bound to act, not only on the same general principle, but precisely in the same way.

There are a great many questions connected with the limits of civil obedience, and the right, in certain circumstances, of resistance on the part of subjects, which have been dragged into the exposition of this passage; but, so far as I have been able to perceive, the above is the meaning—the whole meaning of the apostle. The questions referred to are deeply interesting, and I have had full opportunity of discussing them, both in a discourse on civil government in the Exposition of the First Epistle of Peter, and in a Treatise "On the Law of Christ respecting Civil Obedience, especially in the Payment of Tribute."

Having stated the law of Christ respecting civil obedience generally, the apostle now applies the general precept to the specific case of payment of tribute: "For, for this cause pay ye tribute also: for they are God's ministers, attending continually on this very thing."[1] This verse resolves itself into two parts—a statement or command respecting the payment of tribute, and a reason for this. The first clause[2] may be viewed either as a statement or as a command; it may be rendered either 'ye pay,' or 'pay ye.' The first view is taken by many interpreters, who consider it as a further enforcement of the duty of civil obedience, drawn from the fact that those to whom he wrote paid tribute. They view it as an appeal to consistency. 'Ye pay tribute: why not yield, generally, civil obedience?' This seems an unnatural exposition. Standing so closely connected with injunctions, it seems more natural to

[1] Ver. 6. [2] φόρους τελεῖτε.

understand the words imperatively than indicatively. An argument from consistency is a feeble one after those already used.

"For" seems equivalent to moreover—or, as an instance of what I mean. "For this cause" may refer either to what goes before in the 5th verse, or to the conclusion of this verse; or it may mean, 'in reference to this thing,'[1]—that is, civil government.

In the 7th verse, "tribute" is employed to signify one kind of impost as distinguished from another. Here it is used as a general name for civil taxes. The duty of Christians in reference to these was, that they should not refuse to pay them—that they should not seek to evade them, or to escape by under-payment. They were conscientiously to give what was required as civil tribute by their governors; and to do this as a matter, not merely of external necessity, but of moral obligation.

Like every other part of civil obedience, this is limited by the paramount claims of Divine law. If a Christian be required to pay a portion of his substance for the express purpose of securing what he, in his conscience, believes to be opposed to the law of God, it would seem that he has no alternative but to decline acting in such a case. If the government enforce such a tribute, he may, in ordinary circumstances he ought, quietly to allow them to take from him what he cannot, in consistency with a higher law, give.

The reason for paying tribute is contained in the second clause of the verse: "For they are God's ministers, attending continually on this very thing." These words may either refer to the magistrates, who impose taxes, or to the officers who collect them. In the first case, their meaning is, The magistrates are agents of the divine providence in promoting the welfare of society; and, as their work requires all their time, they ought both to be supported and furnished with the means of

[1] This seems the meaning of δια τουτο in Matt. xiii. 52; Mark xii. 24; John xix. 11.

doing their work, which can only be done by tribute. In the second, the meaning is, 'You are bound to pay tribute as well as to yield civil obedience; for that department of government which is employed in raising the revenue, is as really a part of the Divine institution as any other. The revenue officers are to be obeyed, in paying them the taxes imposed; for they are doing work agreeable to the will of God, though often, it may be, not in a way agreeable to His will. You cannot refuse compliance with their lawful demands without disobeying God; you cannot cheat them, without robbing Him.' The latter appears to us the preferable exposition.

The apostle shuts up this branch of his exhortation, by enjoining the Christian Romans cheerfully to render to the different orders of the magistracy that kind and degree of obedience and submission which, according to the constitution of the government, they had a right to demand—"their due." "Render therefore to all their dues: tribute to whom tribute is due; custom to whom custom; honour to whom honour; fear to whom fear."[1]

"All," here, is to be understood as expressive of a limited universality—of the whole of the persons spoken of. Render therefore to them all—to all the grades of the administrators of civil authority—"their dues," that which properly belongs to them. "Tribute to whom tribute is due." Tribute, as distinguished from custom, was a species of property-tax—a sum which every individual was called to pay, according to the valuation of his estate by the censor. "Custom to whom custom," included money paid on goods imported and exported, tithes, or a tenth part of the produce of the public lands by those who occupied them, and a rent for the privilege of pasture on the public lands.[2] Let these taxes be paid to those who are authorised to exact them.

"Fear" is reverence—a high degree of respect; and "honour," an inferior degree of the same sentiment. You see the comparative force of the two words in the precept, "Fear God;

[1] Ver. 7. [2] Adam's Antiquities.

honour the king."[1] It is as if the apostle had said, 'Civil authority is a sacred thing: reverence it wherever you meet it, and let your reverence correspond to the degree in which it is possessed by the object of your respect. Reverence the emperor; fear the prætor; respect the quæstor; and beware of treating with contempt even the despised publican.' Just as we might say, 'Reverence the sovereign—the visible emblem of the supreme civil power; respect the High Court of Parliament; honour the municipal or local authorities; and beware of treating with contempt even the constable or policeman. Honour civil rule, as God's ordinance, in all its forms.'

The concluding paragraph of the thirteenth chapter is, I apprehend, the enforcement of the exhortations to particular Christian duties which commence with the 9th verse of the twelfth. It is twofold, derived from the comprehensive nature of love,[2] and from the peculiar circumstances in which the Roman Christians were placed.[3]

The words in the 8th verse may, from a peculiarity in the structure of the original language, be understood either as an injunction or as an assertion, and may, with equal justice, viewed apart, be rendered, as our translators have done, "Owe no man anything,"—or, "Ye owe no man anything, but to love one another." The last appears to me the better rendering. Though it is possible to bring a very good sense out of the apostle's words, viewed as an injunction, there is something harsh and unnatural in the mode of expression, "Owe no man anything, but to love one another,"—'Pay all debts except that which, though you must be constantly paying, you will never be able to discharge or even to diminish.' When considered as an assertion, it conveys an important meaning in natural phraseology. The apostle began his exhortation with "Let love be without dissimulation;" and now that he has finished it, he says, 'This includes everything I have

[1] 1 Pet. ii. 17. [2] Ver. 8-10. [3] Ver. 11-14.

said—everything I can say, as to relative duty.' It is a very strong confirmation of the propriety of this interpretation, that the apostle proceeds immediately to the illustration of the principle, that love is the sum and substance of all relative duties. It is as if he had said, 'All the duties which I have been enjoining on you are nothing more than the natural expressions of that mutual love which you should cherish towards each other. "For he that loveth another, hath fulfilled the law."'

The Roman Christians might think these are very many and heavy burdens; but, says the apostle, 'Reflect; they are all nothing but developments of one principle, nothing but different ways of doing one thing—love. If you but love, you will find it easy to perform them all—you will find it impossible to refrain from performing any of them.' To "fulfil the law," here, is to do all that the law requires. The phrase must clearly be limited by the connection. He who loves his brother, fulfils the law with regard to him. The law has nothing to require of him, in reference to his brother, that is not contained in love.

In the 9th and 10th verses, the apostle shows how these things are so: "For this, Thou shalt not commit adultery, Thou shalt not kill, Thou shalt not steal, Thou shalt not bear false witness, Thou shalt not covet; and if there be any other commandment, it is briefly comprehended in this saying, namely, Thou shalt love thy neighbour as thyself. Love worketh no ill to his neighbour; therefore love is the fulfilling of the law." [1] The sum of the Divine law, with regard to our brethren of mankind—the second great commandment, like unto the first, "Thou shalt love the Lord thy God"—is, "that we love them as we love ourselves;" [2] and the apostle's object is to show that this summary does indeed contain in it all the particular requisitions to relative duty, so that he who keeps *it* cannot break *them*. It is obviously impossible that a man should love his fellow-man as he loves himself, and yet be

[1] Ver. 9, 10. [2] Matt. xix. 19.

guilty of any of the particular offences against him which the law of God forbids. Can a man who loves his brother, violate the honour and purity of the marriage-bed? Can he injure him in his person, or in his property, or in his reputation? Can he murder, or defraud, or defame him? Can he cherish in his bosom any principle leading to practical results inconsistent with his happiness? The thing is plainly impossible —it implies a contradiction. The general injunction of love thus includes all the particular injunctions of the second table, and every other injunction of a similar kind; and if it be reasonable, so are they.

"Love worketh no ill to his neighbour;"—that is, 'The man under the influence of love can do no injury to his fellow-man.' He cannot willingly hurt him; for this is inconsistent with love. He must do all that is in his power to promote his happiness; for this is required by love. "Therefore love is the fulfilling of the law." "The fulfilling"[1] is here, as a similar word[2] in Gal. v. 14, that which comprehends all the rest. He who loves his neighbour will, just in proportion to this love, perform all the duties which he owes to his neighbour; and of course the apostle's declaration is demonstrated to be true. "Ye owe no man anything, but to love one another." You owe nothing to any man which is not included in the love which the law requires—a love like that which a man bears to himself. This is the precise principle of our Lord's beautiful summary of relative duty in the Sermon on the Mount: "Therefore all things whatsoever ye would that men should do to you, do ye even so to them; for this is the law and the prophets."[3] This is reducing the principle to practice. As we are to love our neighbour as ourselves, we are in imagination to change person and circumstances with him, and to treat him just as we could reasonably expect him to treat us. Under the influence of natural and laudable self-love, no one wishes to be injured by another; therefore, under the influence of that love which the law requires, he will ab-

[1] πλήρωμα. [2] πληροῦται [3] Matt. vii. 12.

stain from injuring others. Under the influence of natural and laudable self-love, every one wishes that his neighbour should do him good, not only by doing what in strict justice he cannot refuse to do, or even abstain from doing, but, so far as lies in his power, to do for him what his wants render necessary; therefore, under the influence of that love to his neighbour which the law requires, he will treat him not only equitably, but kindly, up to the full measure of his power to do so. It is obvious that he who acts in this manner, will obey the whole law in reference to his neighbour—will discharge the full amount of relative duty.

What an interesting view of the Christian's rule of duty! How reasonable, how amiable, is the Divine law! What wisdom and harmony pervade its principles and requisitions! The compliance with its various injunctions is but the natural display of one principle, and that the object of the highest approbation of the reason, the fullest sanction of the conscience, and the most cordial concurrence of the heart—a principle, to produce and strengthen which, all the doctrines of revelation are plainly intended and admirably fitted. How spiritual this law, in all its departments,—in what concerns man, as well as in what concerns God! External duties are valuable only as expressions of inward principles.

In the words that follow, the apostle gathers a motive for strict attention to the duties which he had been enjoining, from the present circumstances of those whom he was addressing as compared with their former situation: "And that, knowing the time, that it is now high time to awake out of sleep; for now is our salvation nearer than when ye believed. The night is far spent, the day is at hand."[1] The introductory clause, "and that," is elliptical. We have the same ellipsis in 1 Cor. vi. 8, "And *that*—your brethren." The supplement, as in such cases generally, is to be found in the preceding context. In the passage in the epistle to the Corinthians, it is, and 'ye do *that*—ye defraud your brethren.'

[1] Ver. 11, 12.

Here it is, 'And do that which I have enjoined from the consideration I am now about to press on you.' It is very similar to what the apostle says, Heb. x. 25, "And so much the more, as ye see the day approaching." Attend to these duties, "knowing the time."

"To know the time," is to be so acquainted with the real state of present circumstances, as distinctly to perceive what are the duties which rise out of them. The phrase derives illustration from 1 Chron. xii. 32, where "the men of Issachar are said to have had understanding of the times, to know what Israel ought to do." It seems also to have the force of our Lord's phrase, "to know the signs of the times"[1]—to be aware of the Divine dispensations, which present events intimate to be impending. The phrase seems equivalent to, 'And attend to these duties; for ye are not unaware of the peculiar character of the present period, and of the events which it indicates as near at hand.'

With regard to that character, the apostle states, generally, that it was such as made it evident that "it was high time for them to awake out of sleep." These words, by themselves, might seem to be a universal proposition, and to apply generally to mankind. A state of spiritual ignorance, delusion, and inaction, such as is that of all men in their natural condition, is in Scripture represented as a sleep. "Awake thou that sleepest, and arise from the dead."[2] In this case, the meaning would be, 'From the peculiar character of the present times, it is very obviously the urgent duty of "all men everywhere to repent"[3]—to rouse themselves from their spiritual slumbers, and seek the knowledge of God.'

But what the apostle says is a limited proposition, "It is high time *for us* to awake out of sleep." He plainly does not refer to a state of spiritual death, for from that they had awaked when they were converted. It refers, probably, to that state of spiritual languor which, according to our Lord's prophetical parable, was, previously to His coming, generally

[1] Matt. xvi. 3. [2] Eph. v. 14. [3] Acts xvii. 30.

to affect Christians—not only professed Christians, but true Christians. The five wise virgins, as well as the five foolish, were affected with this spiritual disease; none of them "watched," as they should have done—"They *all* slumbered and slept."[1] The circumstances of the times, and the events which seemed to be approaching, were such as to call for the utmost vigilance, circumspection, and attention, on the part of Christians. It is a turn of thought similar to—"But this I say, brethren, the time is short. It remaineth that—"[2]

What those circumstances were, what the events impending, we learn from the words that follow: "For now is our salvation nearer than when we believed. The night is far spent, the day is at hand."[3] There have been three opinions advanced by interpreters respecting the meaning and reference of the phrase, "our salvation." Some understand by it, the deliverance which Christians were to obtain from persecution by the Jews, on the approaching destruction of their polity; others, the complete and eternal deliverance from evil, in all its forms, to which Christians are looking forward, and to which every day is bringing them nearer; and others still, the general, the universal, diffusion throughout the world of Christianity and its blessings, towards which so great a step was soon to be made in the extension of the Gospel, and the approaching fall of Paganism.

As to the first of these modes of interpretation, it is to be remarked, that though the words, "our salvation," or deliverance, may certainly refer to a deliverance from persecution; yet we have no ground to believe that the Christians at Rome were then suffering persecution in any way from the unbelieving Jews, or that the overthrow of the Jewish polity would be attended by any particular advantages to them. Besides, all the duties enjoined by the apostle, were of a kind equally obligatory in a time of persecution and of peace.

As to the second mode of interpretation, it gives to the phrase, "our salvation," what may be termed its classical,

[1] Matt. xxv. 5. πᾶσαι. [2] 1 Cor. vii. 29. [3] Ver. 12.

normal meaning. But it is not without its difficulties. It is plain that the apostle could not mean to say, that the final and complete deliverance of Christians from evil, when "the last enemy shall be destroyed—death," was at hand. He knew[1] that events were to take place before that, which would occupy a long space of time. If the phrase be referred to the deliverance of individual Christians at death—not only do we not read of "death," in the New Testament, as equivalent to "salvation," but, in this case, as "the night" must signify the present life, and "the day" the state of "the spirits of just men made perfect," it is not easy to make out an interpretation of the phrases—"Put off the works of darkness"—"Put on the armour of light"—"Walk in the day"—that harmonizes with this view of the subject.

The third mode of interpretation, though not without its difficulties, appears to me, upon the whole, the preferable one. The difficulty of chief importance is the unusual acceptation of the phrase rendered "our salvation." We have, in the prophecy of Isaiah, a similar phrase pointed at in the words before us, and referring to the same events as this interpretation looks to. In the passage, where, if I mistake not, we have the source of the apostle's peculiar use of "righteousness"—"the righteousness of God," we find "salvation" mentioned, which is God's salvation, as He is its Author, and "our salvation," as men are its objects: "Hearken unto Me, My people; and give ear unto Me, O My nation: for a law shall proceed from Me, and I will make My judgment to rest for a light of the people. My righteousness is near; My salvation is gone forth, and Mine arms shall judge the people: the isles shall wait upon Me, and on Mine arm shall they trust. Lift up your eyes to the heavens, and look upon the earth beneath; for the heavens shall vanish away like smoke, and the earth shall wax old like a garment, and they that dwell therein shall die in like manner: but My salvation shall be for ever, and My righteousness shall not be abolished. Hearken unto Me, ye that know righteousness, the people in whose

[1] 2 Thess. ii. 1–12.

heart is My law; fear ye not the reproach of men, neither be ye afraid of their revilings. For the moth shall eat them up like a garment, and the worm shall eat them like wool: but My righteousness shall be for ever, and My salvation from generation to generation."[1] In the Apocalypse,[2] a great triumph of Christianity is described in the following terms: "And I heard a loud voice saying in heaven, Now is come salvation, and strength, and the kingdom of our God, and the power of His Christ." The Gospel had made great progress already; but the fall of Jerusalem was the commencing period of a new and still more extensive triumph—to proceed till Paganism fell prostrate, and the religion of the crucified One became the dominant religion of the empire.

"The night is far spent, the day is at hand." "The night," on the first scheme of interpretation, is the season of persecution; "the day," that of deliverance—a period of freedom and security from persecution. On the second plan of interpretation, "the night" is the season of mortal life and its sorrows; and "the day," the state of rest and happiness on which Christians enter at death. According to the third, which seems to us the preferable mode of exposition, "the night" is the season of Pagan ignorance, immorality, and wretchedness; and "the day," the period of Christian knowledge, purity, and happiness. This is quite a common figurative representation of heathenism and Christianity. We find the Prophet Isaiah using the following language in reference to the events here referred to: "Behold, the darkness shall cover the earth, and gross darkness the people: but the Lord shall arise upon thee, and His glory shall be seen upon thee. Arise, shine; for thy light is come, and the glory of the Lord is risen upon thee."[3] The long night in which this world had been plunged for so many ages was coming to an end: the morning had dawned; the Sun of Righteousness had risen on the nations with healing under His wings; and ere long it would be meridian-day over the Roman world.

With a reference to this commenced and progressive state

[1] Isa. li. 4–8. [2] Rev. xii. 10. [3] Isa. lx. 1, 2.

of things, the apostle enjoins the Roman Christians to cultivate a corresponding course of character and conduct: "Let us therefore cast off the works of darkness, and put on the armour of light."[1] "The works of darkness" are those vicious habits of thought, feeling, and action, that are formed by, and correspond to, a state of heathen ignorance and depravity. These are to be "cast off" as a dress, which, however it might suit the darkness of night, in which the coarsest material, foulest spots, and most unsightly rents might be concealed, could not bear to be exhibited before the eye of heaven, amid the brightness and purity of noon-day. These garments of pollution and shame are to be "cast off"—thrown away. These habits are to be abandoned with a feeling of loathing and horror; and, instead of them, is to be "put on the armour of light." The word rendered "armour" has that sense; but it also, when used Hebraistically, signifies "dress."[2] The "dress of light" is a figurative expression for those habits of thought, feeling, and action, which correspond with the knowledge, purity, and holiness of the Gospel. The phrase, denoting a warrior's dress, was not likely to be chosen without the intention of suggesting the idea, that the new life, under "the day," instead of being a life of dissolute revelling, is to be a life of vigorous exertion—the life of a soldier.

The apostle pursues the figure in the 13th and 14th verses: "Let us walk honestly, as in the day; not in rioting and drunkenness, not in chambering and wantonness, not in strife and envying: but put ye on the Lord Jesus Christ, and make not provision for the flesh, to fulfil the lusts thereof." "Let us walk," properly signifies, 'Let us walk about, steadily, actively, like sober, healthy men.' "Honestly" is here used in the nearly obsolete sense of 'respectably, gracefully;' "as in the day"—as every one feels it is right to do in clear daylight, in the presence—under the eye, of our fellow-men—not reeling, most discreditably, to and fro like dissolute men in the night season, who spend the first part of the night in

[1] Ver. 12.

[2] Deut. xxii. 5. Drusius, *Preterita;* Deyling, *Obs. Sac.*, p. iii.

"rioting and drunkenness," and "chambering and wantonness," and then, coming forth from their haunts, "flown with insolence and wine,"[1] fill the streets with deeds of "strife and envy, or hatred, violence and blood." That is the figure; let us examine its signification.

Let your conduct correspond with your privileges. With you, the night of heathenism or degenerate Judaism is past—the true light of Christian knowledge and privilege shines. Improve it for active useful exertion in your proper business—the service of God and man. Go about doing good. The light shines: you know where to go, what to do. Act becomingly, as not only under the inspection of your fellow-men, but compassed about with a cloud of higher witnesses, and especially regarded by the great Witness, soon to be the Judge.[2] Act in a manner directly the reverse of that which characterizes those who live under heathenism, which once characterized yourselves when heathens. "Live the rest of your time in the flesh, not to the lusts of men, but to the will of God;" "not fashioning yourselves according to the former lusts in your ignorance; but, as He who hath called you is holy, be ye holy in all manner of conversation;" reckoning, as ye well may, that "the time past of your life may suffice to have wrought the will of the Gentiles, when ye walked in lasciviousness, lusts, excess of wine, revellings, banquetings, and abominable idolatries," "hateful, and hating one another."[3] Instead of this intemperance, and impurity, and malignity, which characterize the night of Paganism, and which are things of which men may well be ashamed, be distinguished by the moderation, and purity, and benevolence which become the day of Christian, holy light, and benignant influence.

The same figure is carried forward into the 14th verse:—"But put ye on the Lord Jesus Christ, and make not provision for the flesh, to fulfil the lusts thereof." The apostle explains by a figure what he means by the dress of light—the dress suitable to the day of Christian knowledge and privilege:

[1] Milton. [2] Heb. xii. 1.
[3] 1 Pet. i. 14, 15; iv. 2, 3; Tit. iii. 3.

"Put on the Lord Jesus Christ." The same figure is employed by the apostle in the Epistle to the Galatians:—"As many of you as are baptized into Christ have put on Christ."[1] There the meaning seems to be—'All of you who are really related to Christ in the way of which baptism is an emblem, have been so identified with Him, as to be treated by God, not as you deserve, but as He deserves.' It refers to what the apostle is there discussing—justification: here it refers to character. To "put on Christ," is to clothe ourselves with all the graces which adorned His character—to become His living images—to be "in the world as He was in the world"[2]—to reflect His excellencies as mirrors[3]—to speak as He spoke—to act as He acted—to suffer as He suffered—to live as He lived—to die as He died. In order to this, Christ must be in us. The mind that was in Him must be in us. His Spirit must be *in* us, that His likeness may be *on* us. The transformation into His likeness can be effected only by "the renewing of the mind." It is meet that it should be so. Christ put on man in nature and condition; man should put on Christ in disposition and character. He became a partaker of our physical nature: we should become partakers of His moral nature. Christ put on man, that man might put on Christ.[4]

The apostle shuts up this exhortation by exhorting Christians "not to provide for the flesh, to fulfil the lusts thereof." Some interpreters consider "flesh" here as just equivalent to 'the animal part of our nature;' and understand the apostle as saying, 'You may, you must, provide for that; but you must not so provide for it as that the fulfilment of its desires shall be your great object in life. You have something infinitely higher and better to provide for than this.' This is good sense, and sound Christian morality; but it does not seem to be what the apostle says here. "The flesh," with him, generally, means depraved human nature; and there is no reason why we should depart from the ordinary meaning

[1] Gal. iii. 27. [2] 1 John iv. 17. [3] 2 Cor. iii. 18.

[4] The idea of ὅπλα, which is strictly "accoutrements," was likely still in the apostle's mind.

of the term. To provide, or to make provision, for the flesh, is to make it an object of thought and pursuit how to secure what is necessary to the life, and health, and gratification of the flesh, or "the old man." The concluding clause, which, in the original, is just "towards," or "in reference to lusts," is explicatory of the general term, provide, and is equivalent to —in order to excite, or to gratify, its desires. What is forbidden is, the making it the great subject of thought and pursuit how we are to obtain the things that are in the world; for these are the objects of the desires, the lusts, of the old man: how to obtain the lust of the flesh, what the flesh desires—the lust of the eye, what the eye covets—and the pride of life, what men pride themselves in. It is the same thing as laying up treasures on earth—minding earthly things; acting as if we were debtors to the flesh, so as that our great business should be to live to it—to serve it. Here, as in many such cases, more is suggested than expressed—less is said than is meant. Instead of making "provision for the flesh, to fulfil the lusts thereof," we, whose "life is hid with Christ in God," are to "mortify our members which are on the earth;" we, who "have put on Christ," are to "put off the old man, who is corrupt according to the deceitful lusts;" we, who are Christ's, are to "crucify the flesh, with its affections and lusts;"[1] we are to place on the cross those who placed Him there.

These exhortations are as applicable to us as to those to whom they were originally delivered. We live in *times* which have a peculiar character, and we should seek to know that character. Our times, like those of the apostle, are a period of transition, indicating the approach of an important crisis. The salvation of the world, in the sense of the general Christianization of mankind, is plainly approaching; and, in reference to the heathen world, the night is far spent—the day is at hand. The old systems of Paganism are becoming effete, and losing their hold on their votaries. The Mohammedan crescent is dim and waning. The exertions of Romanism are the convulsive

[1] Col. iii. 5; Eph. iv. 22; Gal. v. 24.

movements of an outworn constitution, not the natural action of sound health. Its apparent revival is far more the verdure of the parasite plants, which draw their nourishment from the corruption of the majestic tree to which they give the appearance of life—a life which is the proof of death—than the vigorous shoots which, in the season of spring, tell that the oak of many centuries is still fresh at heart. The rapidly shifting forms of false philosophy and corrupted Christianity indicate a felt want of safe standing ground. Arbitrary power is exhausting the patience of the nations, and must, ere long, cease to exist as the enemy of truth as well as freedom. It becomes Christians, who have long enjoyed the light as we have done, to walk in the light, as the children of light—to shine as lights in the world—to hold forth the word of life to a perishing world—to exhibit it as it is in the Bible—to exhibit it, in living character, in our temper and conduct—and to feel that, in the character of the time, we have new, powerful motives to do all this. The night of the world and of the Church is far spent—the day is at hand. And, for this purpose, we must "put on Christ"—embrace His truth—imbibe His Spirit, that we may exhibit His likeness. Oh! how unworthy our profession and our privileges to be slumberous and slothful when we should be broad awake and active. How carefully should we think on and manifest the things that are *honourable*, decent, becoming, venerable, calculated to command respect for ourselves and for our cause! At what a distance should we keep from everything impure and dishonest, or even doubtful; and, instead of making it the business of life "to provide for the flesh," let us make it the business of life to provide for the health and growth of the spirit, knowing that "we are not debtors to the flesh, that we should live after the flesh; for if we live after the flesh, we shall die; but that we are debtors to the Spirit, so that we should live after the Spirit; for if we, through the Spirit, do mortify the deeds of the body, we shall live;"[1] and not only live ourselves, but be

[1] Rom. viii. 12, 13.

the means of communicating life to a dead Church and world. The prevalence of a worldly, self-seeking, self-indulgent, which is an un-Christ-like spirit, among the professors of Christianity, is one of the most alarming signs of our times. The frame of civil society seems on the verge of being shaken to pieces. Is this the time for Christians to be acting as if it were to be perpetual? Seeing all these things must be dissolved, and give way to the new heavens and the new earth, what manner of persons should we be in all holy conversation and godliness? Is this the time for Christians to be labouring for the meat that perisheth, instead of that which endureth unto eternal life? Is this the time to be laying up treasures on earth, instead of laying them up in heaven? How loud and clear to every heaven-opened ear does the command come forth at this time from Him who sitteth on the throne—"Seek first the kingdom of God and His righteousness, and all things shall be added to you!" All that can be shaken in human institutions must ere long be removed, as things made only in reference to those things which cannot be shaken, and which are on their way to take their abiding place. The hosts, on both sides, are mustering for the battle. Let us take our stand. It will be hazardous, as the decisive engagement comes on, to be found either neutral or on the wrong side. Brethren, this I say to you—"Know the time. It is high time to awake out of sleep."

SECTION IV.

OF TERMS OF COMMUNION.

CHAPTER XIV. 1–XV. 13.—Him that is weak in the faith receive ye, but not to doubtful disputations. For one believeth that he may eat all things: another, who is weak, eateth herbs. Let not him that eateth despise him that eateth not; and let not him which eateth not judge him that eateth; for God hath received him. Who art thou that judgest another man's servant? to his own master he standeth or falleth; yea, he shall be holden up: for God is able to make him stand. One man esteemeth one day above another; another esteemeth every day alike.

Let every man be fully persuaded in his own mind. He that regardeth the day, regardeth it unto the Lord; and he that regardeth not the day, to the Lord he doth not regard it. He that eateth, eateth to the Lord, for he giveth God thanks; and he that eateth not, to the Lord he eateth not, and giveth God thanks. For none of us liveth to himself, and no man dieth to himself. For whether we live, we live unto the Lord; and whether we die, we die unto the Lord: whether we live therefore, or die, we are the Lord's. For to this end Christ both died, and rose, and revived, that He might be Lord both of the dead and living. But why dost thou judge thy brother? or why dost thou set at nought thy brother? for we shall all stand before the judgment-seat of Christ. For it is written, As I live, saith the Lord, every knee shall bow to me, and every tongue shall confess to God. So then every one of us shall give account of himself to God.

Let us not therefore judge one another any more: but judge this rather, that no man put a stumblingblock, or an occasion to fall, in his brother's way. I know, and am persuaded by the Lord Jesus, that there is nothing unclean of itself: but to him that esteemeth any thing to be unclean, to him it is unclean. But if thy brother be grieved with thy meat, now walkest thou not charitably. Destroy not him with thy meat for whom Christ died. Let not then your good be evil spoken of: for the kingdom of God is not meat and drink; but righteousness, and peace, and joy in the Holy Ghost. For he that in these things serveth Christ is acceptable to God, and approved of men. Let us therefore follow after the things which make for peace, and things wherewith one may edify another. For meat destroy not the work of God. All things indeed are pure; but it is evil for that man who eateth with offence. It is good neither to eat flesh, nor to drink wine, nor any thing whereby thy brother stumbleth, or is offended, or is made weak. Hast thou faith? have it to thyself before God. Happy is he that condemneth not himself in that thing which he alloweth. And he that doubteth is damned if he eat, because he eateth not of faith: for whatsoever is not of faith is sin.

We then that are strong ought to bear the infirmities of the weak, and not to please ourselves. Let every one of us please his neighbour for his good to edification. For even Christ pleased not Himself; but, as it is written, The reproaches of them that reproached thee fell on me. For whatsoever things were written aforetime were written for our learning; that we, through patience and comfort of the Scriptures, might have hope. Now the God of patience and consolation grant you to be likeminded one toward another, according to Christ Jesus; that ye may with one mind and one mouth glorify God, even the Father of our Lord Jesus Christ. Wherefore receive ye one another, as Christ also received us, to the glory of God. Now I say, that Jesus Christ was a minister of the circumcision for the truth of God, to confirm the promises made unto the fathers: and that the Gentiles might glorify God for his mercy; as it is written, For this cause I will confess to Thee among the Gentiles, and sing unto Thy name. And again he saith, Rejoice, ye Gentiles, with His people. And again, Praise the Lord, all ye Gentiles; and laud Him, all ye people. And again Esaias saith, There shall be a root of Jesse, and He that shall rise to reign over the Gentiles; in Him shall the Gentiles trust. Now the God of hope fill you with all joy and peace in believing, that ye may abound in hope, through the power of the Holy Ghost.

In the section of the practical part of the Epistle to the Romans, on the illustration of which we are now about to enter, the apostle gives directions in reference to the terms of Christian fellowship, and the manner in which Christians, who are not entirely of one mind in reference to minor points of faith and practice, should treat each other. The section does not seem to have any other connection with what goes immediately before, than what arises out of its general character as a practical exhortation. There is a connection referred to by the apostle in his first epistle to the Corinthians,[1] between "the flesh" and the practices which he here guards against; but this connection does not seem to have been in his view here.

In the Church of Rome, as in most of the primitive churches beyond the limits of Judea, there were two classes clearly distinguished from each other. The first, composed of the Gentile converts and the more enlightened of their Jewish brethren, who considered the ceremonial institutions of the Mosaic law as annulled by the new and better dispensation; and the other, composed of the great body of the Jewish converts, who, though they embraced Jesus as the Messiah, were yet of opinion that the Mosaic law was not repealed—was not, indeed, repealable—and therefore continued to be zealous for it, all of them observing the legal institutions themselves, and some of them desirous of imposing them on the Gentiles. The first class were in danger of despising the second as narrow-minded, bigoted, superstitious men: the second class were in

[1] 1 Cor. iii. 1-3.

danger of judging harshly of the first as latitudinarian freethinkers. The apostle's object is to show that, where there is evidence of genuine faith of the saving truth, such differences of opinion should not in the slightest degree diminish brotherly love, or interrupt their religious fellowship. The particular controversies here referred to have long ceased to be agitated, but the principles in human nature which gave origin to them are as powerful as ever. In all Christian churches there are among the members analogous diversities of endowments and acquirements, which must occasion analogous differences of opinion and of conduct; and the things which the apostle has here written, according to the wisdom given him, will, if rightly understood, be found "written for our learning," and "profitable" for instruction, warning, and reproof to Christian churches in all countries and in all ages.

"Him that is weak in the faith receive ye, but not to doubtful disputations." [1] This is the general law of church-fellowship which the apostle lays down, and in the sequel applies to the peculiar circumstances of the Roman Church. "Faith," here, does not denote the *act*, but the *object*, of belief —the principles of Christian faith and duty. "To be weak in faith," understanding by that word the mental act of believing, is to doubt and hesitate. To be weak in faith, or rather in the faith, understanding by the word the objects of faith—the declarations of Christ and his apostles, is to be but imperfectly acquainted with the Christian system. We say of an individual divine, he is strong in dogmatic, but he is weak in exegesis; or of a philosopher, he is strong in physics, but weak in metaphysics; or of a scholar, he is very strong in Greek and Latin, but very weak in Hebrew. The one kind of weakness does not necessarily infer the other. A man may be but imperfectly acquainted with Christianity as a system, who has a very firm faith in the saving truth; and, on the other hand, a man may have a great extent of knowledge as to Christianity as a system—a subject of mere intellectual ap-

[1] Ver. 1.

prehension, who may have very little, or be altogether destitute of, saving faith. Yet the two things—strength in faith, and strength in the faith—are naturally connected; there is something wrong when they are disjoined, but they do not, as a matter of course, co-exist in proportionable degrees.

The person here described by the apostle is a sincere but weak Christian. He really believes the Gospel; but, at the same time, owing, it maybe, to a deficiency of mental power—it may be, to the deficiencies or the prejudices of education, or to some other cause—he is far from having a distinct, extended, consistent view of all the principles of faith and duty taught by the One Master, whose authority he most cordially recognises. Now, how is such a person to be treated by those who are "strong in the faith"—who have clear, wide, deep views of the Christian system? Is he to be refused, on his professing his faith, admission to the communion of the Church? Is his recognition as a Christian brother to be deferred till he equal "the strong in the faith," in the extent and accuracy of his views? No, says the apostle—himself a strong man in the faith, if ever there was one—No; "Him that is weak in the faith receive ye."

The word translated "receive"[1] admits of two renderings,—'Support—assist,' or 'receive, admit to intimate intercourse.' The context seems plainly to require the meaning adopted by our translators, which is also that which the word ordinarily bears in the New Testament, *e.g.*, Acts xviii. 27; xxviii. 2. The person referred to, if he seemed to be really what he professed to be—a person believing that Jesus Christ is the Saviour and Lord of men, trusting to Him for salvation, and submitting to His authority—though his views on some subjects may be indistinct and even erroneous, was to be admitted to their fellowship. He was to be acknowledged as a brother in Christ—a child of God through faith in Christ Jesus, and treated accordingly.

The apostle adds, "But not to doubtful disputations." This

[1] προσλαμβάνεσθε.

phrase,[1] as rendered by our translators, does not convey any distinct idea. The sentiment it seems to express is this, 'Receive such a man to communion—admit him to the solemnities of Christian worship; but when you engage in discussions about doubtful subjects, do not receive or admit him.' Now we have no reason to suppose that the primitive churches had any meetings for any such purpose as this, or that there was any distinction among them, as afterwards, into the initiated and uninitiated. The Church, in the days of the apostles, had no distinction of exoteric and esoteric doctrines—no meetings from which any of the members were excluded. It is not easy to say with certainty what the phrase precisely means. It may be literally rendered, "Not in order to the discussion or determination of opinions." It describes what ought not to be the object in receiving such persons. They were to be received "to the glory of God,"[2] and to their own edification; but they are not to be received in order to the discussion and determination of their peculiar opinions. These opinions were not to prevent their being admitted to communion; but discussions and determinations about them were not to disturb the peace of the Church. They were not to be admitted that their opinions might be discussed by *them*, for the purpose of bringing their strong brethren to their views; or that they might be discussed by the strong, that the weak might be induced to abandon them. The meaning of the injunction seems to be, 'Readily admit into fellowship every man who appears to be a sincere believer, though his views may on some points be indistinct, and even incorrect; but let care be taken that neither he be harassed about these opinions, nor the Church harassed by him in reference to them.' These opinions must not be the occasion of strife and division, where all should be peace and union.

The apostle now proceeds to apply this principle to the existing circumstances of the Roman Church. There were two points on which diversity of opinion among its members, as

[1] *μὴ εἰς διακρίσεις διαλογισμῶν.*

[2] Chap. xv. 7.

divided into the weak and strong, naturally led to diversity of usage—meats and days: Judaical distinctions about what was lawful in food, and sacred in time. He considers the two cases in succession.

And *first,* with regard to meats. "For one believeth that he may eat all things; another, who is weak, eateth only herbs."[1] Some interpreters have supposed that the apostle here refers to some individuals in the Roman Church, who held the principle which is said to have distinguished the sect of ancient philosophers called Pythagoreans, and the sect of Jewish ascetics called Essenes, a principle revived in our own times, that the use of animal food is unlawful. It seems far more likely that the reference is to the distinction of articles of food made in the Mosaic law. "One"—that is, he who is "strong in the faith," is persuaded that this distinction is abolished; that "nothing is unclean of itself," but that "every creature of God," fit for food, may be eaten. "Another, who is weak" in the faith, "eateth herbs,"—that is, eateth them only. The Jews were not prohibited from eating animal food; but in a heathen country it was so difficult to ascertain that "flesh sold in the shambles" had not been offered to idols, and that the requisitions of the Mosaic law had been observed as to the manner of slaughtering the animal, that the more conscientious Jews among heathens seem to have altogether abstained from the use of animal food, and confined themselves to a vegetable diet; and it would appear that some of the Jewish converts at Rome, supposing the laws respecting the distinction of foods to be unrepealed, on conscientious grounds ate only herbs. Such was the state of the fact. Now, what was to be done in this case? Were the two parties to form two churches, and to remain separate till, coming to be of one mind, they followed the same course as to food? Or were the strong to admit the weak to fellowship, but with the design of arguing them into concurrence with them in opinion and usage? Neither course was to be followed. The weak Christian

[1] Ver. 2.

was to be received; and, when admitted, neither was he to be disturbed as to his own conscientious views and practices, nor was he to be permitted to disturb his brethren in their conscientious views and practices. "Let not him that eateth despise him that eateth not; and let not him that eateth not judge him that eateth: for God hath received him."[1] The enlightened Christian was in danger of looking down with contempt on his less liberal-minded and less perfectly instructed brother, as a bigoted slave of superstition; and the weak, less-informed Christian, was in danger of indulging dark suspicions as to his more enlightened brother, as a person not duly submissive to Divine authority. The apostle cautions against both these unbrotherly modes of thinking and feeling. "Let not him that eateth despise him that eateth not." 'He has no reason to be proud. Who gave him that strength of mind and width of view as to Christian doctrine and law, that enable him to walk at liberty? What has he that he has not received? And as to his weak brother, his weakness calls for pity, and his conscientiousness for respect. To despise him, shows something far wrong with him who does so.' Conscientious principle, even when mistaken, and assuming a form which may easily be turned into ridicule, is a really respectable thing. 'On the other hand, he that eateth not, must not judge him that eateth.' "Judge," is here equivalent to condemn, and to condemn as a conscious violator of a Divine law. A weak man finds it very difficult to understand how another man should see anything in a light different from that in which he sees it, and comes too readily to the conclusion that he who thinks and acts differently from him cannot be thinking and acting with a good conscience. If I think myself right, I must think the man who differs from me wrong; but I must not, without strong evidence, suppose—what indeed I am not called on to judge of—that he is consciously wrong—that he is acting in opposition to his own secret convictions of what is right. 'Let the weak Christian,

[1] Ver. 3.

who eateth not, beware of thus judging—condemning, his stronger brother who eateth; "for," adds the apostle, "God has received him."' The Gentile believers were, equally with those who kept the law, blessed with the influences of the Holy Spirit; and as God had thus given evidence that He had received them as members of His Church, it ill became the Jewish converts to condemn such persons as unfit for communion with them. The best commentary on this passage is to be found in the Acts of the Apostles, x. 44-48; xi. 15-18; xv. 7-11.

The disposition of the less-informed Christians to condemn their really better-informed brethren, because their views of truth and duty on some points were not coincident with theirs, is strongly prohibited, and its absurdity, and indeed impiety, strikingly exposed in the next verse: "Who art thou that judgest another man's servant? To his own master he standeth or falleth; yea, he shall be holden up: for God is able to make him stand." [1] The Christian who, in reference to meats, used the liberty wherewith Christ had made him free, was not the servant of his narrow-minded Jewish brother—they were fellow-servants of God; he was to be judged by their common Lord. In relation to Him he would stand or fall. To stand in the judgment, is to be acquitted; to fall in the judgment, is to be condemned. It is God's prerogative to judge in such matters. 'The conduct of thy brother is subject to judgment—it may become matter of acquittal or of condemnation; but is not subject to thy judgment. God is his judge, not you. It is arrogance in you to ascend the tribunal of judgment.'

But this is not all. 'He is right, and you are wrong: "Yea, he shall be holden up." His conduct will be approved of. He shall be found to have formed the correct judgment, and to have followed the right course: "For God is able to make him stand." Though *you* cannot reconcile the conduct of your brother with a due regard to God's authority, God *can*, and will.' When the time for judgment comes, the conduct

[1] Ver. 4.

of the strong brother shall be found to have arisen from as implicit, while more enlightened, a regard to the Divine authority, as that of the weak brother who condemned him.

It does not follow, from what the apostle says, that such subjects as he refers to are not to be discussed by Christians —discussion is the highway to truth; but it does follow that these discussions are not to be "in the Church,"—they are to take place between individuals; and it also follows that, though the result of the discussion should be, as it often is, that the two disputants remain equally unconvinced, they are not to form condemnatory judgments of one another's characters on that account.

In the verses that follow, the apostle proceeds to apply his principle to differences with regard to sacred times. "One man esteemeth one day above another; another esteemeth every day alike. Let every man be fully persuaded in his own mind."[1] It has been imagined by some that the apostle here refers to the supposed custom of some Jewish converts of abstaining from the eating of animal food on certain days, while others abstained from it at all times, and others allowed themselves in the use of it at all times. It is much more probable that he alludes to the distinction of days made in the Mosaic law, which some of the primitive Christians attended to, and others disregarded. The apostle refers to the same topic in the Epistle to the Galatians, when he says, "Ye observe days, and months, and times, and years."[2] "One man esteemeth one day above another." The new moons, the seventh day Sabbath, the feasts of the Passover, Pentecost, and Tabernacles, continued to be observed by many of the Jewish converts on the principle, that these undoubtedly Divine institutions, having never been formally abrogated, must be considered as continuing obligatory. "Another esteemeth every day alike." The greater part of the Gentile converts, and the more enlightened among the Jewish converts, regarded the injunctions of the Mosaic law on such

[1] Ver. 5. [2] Gal. iv. 10.

subjects as obsolete, and disregarded them. They did not think themselves obliged to make any distinction between the days which had a character of sacredness, in consequence of the appointment of the law given by Moses, and ordinary days. To conclude, from this passage, that the strong in the faith made no distinction between the first day of the week, the day appropriated to Christian worship in commemoration of the resurrection—the form, under the new economy, of the Sabbatical institution, which, more than circumcision or even sacrifice, was "before the law," bearing date in Paradise immediately after the creation of man—is to go beyond the premises. The assertion refers to the matters in controversy—distinctions originating in the law of Moses. If the observance of the first day originated, as we believe it did, in apostolic authority (and it must not be taken for granted that it did not, merely because we have no explicit account of this, for, on that principle, the practice, not only of infant baptism, but of female communion, must be held to be unfounded), there could not well be any controversy among primitive Christians on the subject; and accordingly, though we know that some of them observed the seventh day, we have no evidence that any of them disregarded the first.

To this subject the observations made respecting meats are equally applicable. Indeed, it is substantially the same question under a different form. 'Let not him that observeth not those days despise him who does; and let not him that observeth them condemn him who does not.' The apostle adds: "Let every man be fully persuaded in his own mind." 'Let no man observe those days unless he be persuaded they are of Divine authority. Let no man disregard them unless he be persuaded that, whatever sacredness belonged to them, within certain limits, has, by Divine authority, been taken from them. Let every man act with a religious conscientiousness. If he is persuaded that those days ought to be observed, let not the fear of the contempt of those who entertain an opposite opinion, or the wish to secure their approbation, induce him to trifle with a religious conviction: if he is persuaded that there is no such obligation, let him not persist in their observance to shield himself from the persecution of the unbelieving Jews, far less to harass the minds of his Gentile brethren.'

This passage does not lay the foundation for the conclusion sometimes drawn from it, that conscientiousness is everything in religion—that he who acts conscientiously, of course, acts rightly. It does, however, lay a foundation for the conclusion, that he who, in religion, acts without conscience—still more, against conscience—acts wrong.

All Christian men ought to act according to conscientious conviction, and all Christians are to be held, in the absence of clear evidence to the contrary, to be doing so; and their conduct is to be judged of accordingly.

This is the principle which the apostle lays down and illustrates in the following verses:—"He that regardeth the day, regardeth it unto the Lord; and he that regardeth not the day, to the Lord he doth not regard it. He that eateth, eateth to the Lord, for he giveth God thanks; and he that eateth not, to the Lord he eateth not, and giveth God thanks. For none of us liveth to himself, and no man dieth to himself. For whether we live, we live unto the Lord; and whether we die, we die unto the Lord: whether we live therefore, or die, we are the Lord's. For to this end Christ both died, and rose, and revived, that He might be Lord both of the dead and living."[1] 'Being fully persuaded in his own mind that the day is still sacred, one Christian observes it. Being equally fully persuaded in his own mind that the day is no more sacred, and that to observe it as sacred is to act inconsistently with the will of God, as he apprehends it, another Christian disregards it. The acts are different—indeed, opposite; but they embody the same principle. Each acts as he does from a regard to what appears to him the authority and will of God. If they could exchange convictions, the observer would disregard, the disregarder would observe, the days in question; and, were they both to be brought to see the question in the

[1] Ver. 6–9.

same light, they would both act in the same way. It is not humour on either side that produces the effect: it is conviction—conscientious conviction. In the same way, the conscientious Christian who partakes without scruple of all kinds of wholesome animal food, does so, for he is persuaded that the Lord has put an end to all legal restrictions—that He has made clean what was, under the law, unclean—and that it is not for him to call, or treat, as unclean or common, what God has cleansed—sanctified for use; and, in the use of his liberty, he gives God thanks for His great liberality. On the other hand, the conscientious Christian who refrains from the meats prohibited by the law, does so because he is persuaded that Christ has not given him liberty to partake of them; he knows that the distinction was divinely established—he does not see that the authority that established has annulled it; and, over his dinner of herbs, he gives thanks that he has still abundance of nourishing and pleasant food, and is grateful even for an institution which, rightly improved, was fitted to serve useful moral purposes. The two individuals act under the influence of the same principle—regard to the will of the Lord, a principle which unites them far more than their opposite practices divide them. In the different courses they take, they equally acknowledge the authority of the Lord. And this is what constitutes the essence of Christianity—the practically recognising the Lord's property in us and authority over us.'

"For none of us," if we are really Christians—whether weak or strong, whether we eat flesh or abstain, whether we observe the Jewish sacred days or disregard them—"none of us liveth to himself, and none dieth to himself." 'None of us regard ourselves as our own property, to be regulated by our own reason or humour, and to seek our own objects in life or in death: all of us, from the very fact that we are Christians, consider ourselves as in life and in death the property of the Lord, to act and suffer according to His will, preceptive and providential; seeking that He may be "magnified in our body, whether in life or in death."'[1]

[1] Phil. i. 20.

'And nothing can be more certain than this; for this is the design of the death and of the restored life of our Lord. "For to this end"—to the end that we Christians should be the property of the Lord, entirely guided by His authority, and devoted to His purposes in life and in death—"Christ both died, and rose, and revived, that"—in order that, "He might be the Lord both of the dead and of the living."' It is generally agreed among critics that the words "rose again" do not belong to the text. Even an English reader sees that they are strangely placed—between dead and revived, and that they add nothing to the sense. The design of our Lord's death was, that by giving Himself for them in death, he might obtain for Himself a peculiar people; and of His renewed life, that He might reign in them and over them, and thus save them to the uttermost. This doctrine is very clearly stated in the Epistles to the Corinthians: "Ye are bought with a price: your body, your spirits, are God's."[1] "We thus judge, that if one died for all, then all were dead;"[2] and that He thus "died for all," that they who died "in Him, and revived in Him"—those who are united to Him as having died and now living for evermore—that they living, living in Him, "should live not to themselves, but to Him who died for them and who rose again." And in the Epistle to Titus, chap. ii. 13, 14: "The great God and our Saviour Jesus Christ gave Himself for us, that He might redeem us from all iniquity, and purify unto Himself a peculiar people, zealous of good works." Thus is He "Lord of the dead and of the living." This declaration is true in the most unqualified sense. Jesus Christ is Lord of *all*—of all created beings. He is the Lord of all men, whether in the seen or unseen world. He has all power—in heaven, and earth, and hell. Here, however, the declaration is to be understood in reference to His own people. They are *His*, entirely *His*, unalienably *His*. None must treat them as property but Him. They must acknowledge none but *Him* as their proprietor and Lord, in life and in death. It espe-

[1] 1 Cor. vi. 20. [2] 2 Cor. v. 14.

cially ill becomes them to trespass on His prerogative by attempting to lord it over one another's consciences.

To bring home this practical truth, is the use the apostle makes of this great fundamental principle of Christianity. "But why dost thou judge thy brother? or why dost thou set at nought thy brother? for we shall all stand before the judgment-seat of Christ. For it is written, As I live, saith the Lord, every knee shall bow to Me, and every tongue shall confess to God."[1] The apostle here expostulates with both the classes referred to—the weak and the strong. The first "*thou*" refers to the weak brother—the second to the strong. To the first he says, 'Why—since these things are so, why doest thou judge, condemn, un-Christianize thy brother, because he does something which you could not, ought not, to do, for you think it unlawful, but which he, in equal good conscience, considers as agreeable to the will of the Lord.' And to the second, 'Why dost thou set at nought thy brother—why dost thou despise him, because, from an equally sincere, though it may be, in this case, not so enlightened a regard to the will of the common Lord, he dare not do what thou canst do, and subjects himself to sacrifices—among the rest, that of standing not so well in your opinion as he might wish—merely because he dare not do what he believes, however mistakingly, the Lord disapproves? Remember both of you that we shall *all*—all of us, the weak and the strong—stand before the judgment-seat of Christ. Thou who condemnest—think, What if He should approve what thou hast condemned, and welcome thy brother as a good and faithful servant for doing that for which thou wast disposed to deny his right to the title of Christian? Thou who despisest—remember that, in the estimation of the final Judge, mere correctness of doctrinal view will go but a short way to establish a claim on His approbation. The scrupulously conscientious, weak disciple, will stand higher with Him than he who, with much of the knowledge that puffeth up, has but little of the charity that edifies. Re-

[1] Ver. 10, 11.

member that you both must stand before the judgment-seat of Christ; and remember, too, that your present judgments of each other will form elements of the judgment then to be declared. "By what judgment ye judge, ye shall be judged." '[1]

In support of the principle, that all must stand before the judgment-seat of Christ, the apostle quotes a passage from the Prophecies of Isaiah. The citation is from Isaiah xlv. 23, and seems plainly, from verbal discrepancies both from the Hebrew and Greek texts, to have been quoted from memory. The words are those of Jehovah the Saviour. They do not seem to have any definite reference to what we ordinarily call the last judgment, though that is included in the authority which is here claimed by Him. They describe that universal dominion which belongs to Jehovah the Saviour, in the exercise of which He will, at the appointed day, "judge the world in righteousness." There can be no reasonable doubt that the apostle refers these words to Christ; and there can be as little that He who utters them is Jehovah—"*God*, and none else."

The conclusion drawn by the apostle is contained in ver. 12: "So then every one of us shall give account of *himself* to God." "Himself" is the emphatic word—not one of another, but each of *himself*. The first concern of every man is to see that his own matters be in a safe state—be "good and right," when he comes before the Great King—"the one Lawgiver, who is able to save and to destroy"—for final judgment. I am "my brother's keeper," so as that it is my duty to do all I can to promote his highest welfare; but I have not the charge of his conscience. That, under the Lord of conscience, belongs to himself, and must not be interfered with. I cannot answer for him "in that day:" I shall have enough to do to answer for myself. Almost all unchristian judgments, with regard to Christian brethren, rise from keeping the solemnities of the personal, while universal, judgment out of view. Had controversial writers remembered that "every

[1] Matt. vii. 2.

one of us must give an account of himself to God," could the unnumbered volumes of bitter anathematising controversy have been written, on points respecting which the Holy Scriptures either do not speak at all, or so speak as that inquirers, equally conscientious and diligent, may arrive at different conclusions?

It is to be hoped, notwithstanding much that still indicates, in some quarters, a disposition to exercise over the minds and consciences of men an authority and influence which belong only to God, that the reign of spiritual tyranny—the worst of all tyrannies, is drawing toward a close. Let us determine neither to exercise such domination, nor to submit to it even for an hour. Let us "call no man master;" and let us not seek to be called masters by others. One is our Master, who is Christ the Lord, and we are all His fellow-servants. Let us help each other, but let us leave Him to judge us. He only has the capacity, as He only has the authority, for doing so.

In the remaining part of the section, the apostle is occupied chiefly with the part which the strong should act towards the weak. He cautions them against an unnecessary, ostentatious, and uncharitable display of their Christian liberty from restraints, by which their weak brethren thought themselves bound, and urges them to abstain from what they knew and believed to be lawful, if it was not at the same time obligatory, rather than hazard the most important interests, not only of their less informed brethren, but of their common religion.

"Let us not therefore judge one another any more: but judge this rather, that no man put a stumblingblock, or an occasion to fall, in his brother's way."[1] This verse seems to refer to both classes, though what follows is restricted to the conduct of the strong towards the weak. "Let us therefore not judge one another any more." These words are not a general prohibition against forming a judgment respecting the

[1] Ver. 13.

conduct of our fellow-men, which, if a true judgment, must in many cases be an unfavourable one. We are to form our opinions of men according to the principles of the Divine law—approving of what in them accords with it, and disapproving of what is inconsistent with it. The apostle's injunction refers to the judgments formed by Christians of each other. Yet, even within this limit, it is not an unqualified prohibition to form a judgment—it may be an unfavourable judgment, in regard to an opinion held, or a practice followed, by one who professes to be a Christian brother. We must act according to our Lord's principle—one applicable not only to teachers—"By their fruits shall ye know them."[1] The command before us is limited by the circumstances in which it is given. It refers to persons who apparently are equally in the faith, though not equally strong in it; and it forbids them to form such judgments of each other, as, from the remaining depravity of even regenerated human nature, they are very apt to do. It does not forbid them to disapprove of that in which their brother differs from them. If I am honest in my own conviction—conscientious in my own course, I cannot but think that he who differs from me in sentiment is mistaken—that he who, in conduct, follows an opposite course to mine is wrong. The command refers to general judgments as to character: condemning judgments on the side of the weak—contemptuous judgments on the part of the strong. It is as if the apostle had said—'Let us have no more of such judgments, so unseemly, when our mutual relation to each other, and our common relation to our Proprietor and Judge, are considered; we have had but too much of them already. Instead of these judgments as to one another's character, let us form and act on this judgment, each as to his own conduct—"Let us judge this rather, that no man lay a stumblingblock, or an occasion to fall, in his brother's way." Let us all resolve to do nothing, but what duty absolutely requires, which may prove the means of leading our brother into sin.'

[1] Matt. vii. 20.

'Let the brother who makes a distinction of meats and of days, take care lest, in insisting on making his conviction and conscience a rule to his brother who can see no such distinction as of Divine authority, he excite disgust, and make it all but an impossibility for his brother to regard him with brotherly love. Were such weak brethren to be the majority, and to press their views, they would tempt their stronger brethren to abandon their profession, or, at any rate, to withdraw from the fellowship of those who would impose on them a yoke which, as the Lord had not imposed it, they were not disposed to bear. And, on the other hand, let the brother "who eats all things," and "to whom every day is alike," so far as mere Mosaic legislation is concerned, take care lest, by insisting to do on all occasions what he thinks lawful, though he cannot think it obligatory, he excite unchristian feelings in the heart of his weaker brother towards himself; or (what is the danger the apostle seems to have had chiefly in view) induce, by his example, his weak brother to do what, from his limited views, he cannot do without violating a conscientious conviction. The strong must not neglect any duty—they must not commit any sin, under the pretence of avoiding the leading of their weak brother into temptation or sin; but, if that is likely to be the result of their practically asserting a privilege which undoubtedly belongs to them, but which duty does not call on them thus to assert, the judgment they should form and follow is, that they do not "put a stumblingblock, or an occasion to fall, in their brother's way."' This is the principle which the apostle illustrates and enforces down to the 4th verse of the fifteenth chapter.

"I know, and am persuaded by the Lord Jesus, that there is nothing unclean of itself: but to him that esteemeth anything to be unclean, to him it is unclean. But if thy brother be grieved with thy meat, now walkest thou not charitably. Destroy not him with thy meat for whom Christ died."[1] It is well remarked by Tholuck, that "the spirit which Paul

[1] Ver. 14, 15.

evinces in these exhortations proves what a mighty influence the Christian faith had had in making him indulgent and humble; for, if we reflect on his natural character, we can well suppose that he would have been more disposed to kindle into anger at the weak and scrupulous, and to treat them with severity. But the Spirit of Christ had taught him to be weak with the weak, so that he says, 1 Cor. viii. 13, 'If meat make my brother to offend, I will eat no meat while the world standeth, lest I make my brother to offend.' And in the Christian Church, which is never but composed of those who must bear with, and those who must be borne with, this is the only way in which the bond of perfectness and of peace can subsist; to wit, when the child aspires to manhood, and the man becomes a child. Such mutual subordination and forbearance is a salutary medicine for pride."

The apostle states his full persuasion that the distinction of foods, which had originated entirely in the positive laws of Moses, and not from any essential difference of a moral kind in the different articles of diet, had ceased in consequence of that law having merged in the new dispensation: "I know, and am persuaded by the Lord Jesus, that there is nothing unclean of itself." The Lord—the one Master—had revealed this to him by His Spirit. He had "received of the Lord" "that every creature of God is good, and nothing to be refused, if it be received with thanksgiving; for it is sanctified by the word of God"—by Divine appointment, probably referring to the permission given to Noah (Gen. xix. 3), afterward limited by the law of Moses, but now restored to its pristine extent—"and by prayer."[1]

The apostle here decidedly gives his sanction to the sentiment of those who were strong in the faith. It was this revelation that enabled him to assert so unequivocally that the strong in the faith, though condemned in his practice by his weak brother, would be "held up"—"made to stand," in the judgment by God;[2] but, while this was his conviction,

[1] 1 Tim. iv. 3–5. [2] Ver. 4.

and ought to have been the conviction of all who heard him make such an avowal, yet, notwithstanding, there were persons—sincere Christians too—who esteemed certain articles of food to be unclean; and he declares that "to them they were unclean." They could not eat of them without violating a conscientious conviction—without doing what they thought inconsistent with the will of God—without, in one word, committing sin, the natural effect of which was "destruction." The thing is not wrong in itself; but the scrupulous brother reckons it wrong, and in doing it would violate the regard due to what appears to his mind the will of God. This is the evil which the apostle contemplates as possible, and which he sees that an ostentatious display of liberty, on the part of the strong Christian, may be the means of producing in the weak. To have an unrestricted range of articles of food is, on different grounds, desirable. Now, an unenlightened Jewish Christian feeling this, and seeing many of his brethren —the most distinguished for their intelligence and piety—indulging in this, might, while his mind remains unenlightened, his conscientious convictions unchanged, be induced to follow their example; and thus, though doing nothing materially wrong, in truth contract much guilt, and greatly injure his spiritual character.

To prevent this evil, the apostle would have the strong to be cautious in the practical assertion of their privilege: "But if thy brother be grieved with thy meat, now walkest thou not charitably." The connective particle rendered "but," would have been better translated "and"—there is no contrast between what is stated in the last clause of the 14th verse and the first clause of the 15th. It is just the continuance of the statement of the case—"To him that esteemeth anything to be unclean, to him it is unclean; *and* if such a brother be grieved with thy meat"—*i.e.*, grieved by thine assertion of thy right, by using it, to eat food he thinks unclean. The words, "grieved by thy meat," have been very generally entirely misunderstood. It has been supposed that the meaning is—'If thy eating of things which the law of Moses prohibits makes thy Jewish brother uneasy—displeases him, vexes him, irritates him—you act an uncharitable part if you persist in it.' There is truth in this; but it seems plain that that is not the apostle's meaning. The grieved brother is the brother who, by the conduct of the strong, has been induced to trifle with the convictions of his conscience by imitating that conduct, and has thus involved himself in that sin which naturally leads to destruction—sin which, if it do not lead to destruction, must occasion grief. It is substantially the same case that is detailed 1 Cor. viii. 8–12: "Meat commendeth us not to God: for neither, if we eat, are we the better; neither, if we eat not, are we the worse. But take heed, lest by any means this liberty of yours become a stumblingblock to them that are weak. For if any man see thee which hast knowledge sit at meat in the idol's temple, shall not the conscience of him which is weak be emboldened to eat those things which are offered to idols; and through thy knowledge shall the weak brother perish, for whom Christ died? But when ye sin so against the brethren, and wound their weak conscience, ye sin against Christ."

The injury, then, supposed here inflicted on the weak brother is, as in the case of the Corinthians, the emboldening him by example to do what his conscience forbids him to do: of so much more importance does the apostle reckon the preservation of an undebauched conscience, to strict unity of opinion and of usage in minor matters, among Christians. This remark as to the nature of the grief or injury referred to, must be kept in view to understand the force of what the apostle goes on to say to the strong Christian, which is substantially this: 'If you have reason to think that such will be the effect of your doing what you justly reckon in itself warrantable, but what you must acknowledge is not, except in peculiar circumstances, obligatory, you act an uncharitable part in using your liberty. You are doing what may probably involve your brother in guilt, and in the grief, and, if mercy prevent not, the destruction, which are the natural results of guilt.' "Destroy not thy brother;" that is, 'Do not what may end—what, but for the interposition of Divine grace, must end—in his destruction. The tendency of every sin is to destroy the soul. And will you, to gratify what is itself an innocent, though comparatively low, appetency of your nature, or to make a display of your freedom from prejudices which enslave some of your brethren—will you expose to hazard a brother's salvation—that for which Christ laid down His life? If you can, whatever knowledge you may have, "the mind of Christ is not in you."[1] As Bengel says, "Will you make more of your food, than Christ did of His life?"

But regard to the personal interest of the weak brother is not the only motive which the apostle urges on the strong Christian, to make a cautious use of his liberty. The cause of Christ was implicated in this matter. "Let not your good be evil spoken of."[2] Interpreters are divided as to the reference of the phrase, "your good." It is common to consider it as referring to the liberty of using all kinds of wholesome food, and the freedom from the Judaical restrictions as to time. This was a good thing enjoyed by the strong; and an incautious, uncharitable use of it, was likely to lead the weak especially to "speak evil of it"—to blaspheme and calumniate it. It was the direct way to prevent the enjoyment of this good thing from becoming more extensive among Christians. Every such uncharitable act deepened in hostile minds prejudice against it. This is very good sense, and much to the apostle's purpose. But I prefer the interpretation that considers the phrase, "your good," as descriptive of the Christian cause, for two reasons: *first*, it includes the other; and *secondly*, it seems the same thing that is here termed "your good thing," that in the 17th verse is called "the kingdom of God," and in the 20th verse, "the work of God." From the beginning of the 16th verse, to the end of the first clause of the 20th verse, it is the same motive which the apostle illustrates—the bearing of the conduct referred to on the general interests of Christianity.

[1] Phil. ii. 3-8. [2] Ver. 16.

How well Christianity may be called "the good thing" of Christians, needs no illustration. They are intrusted with the care of this good thing—"the power of God to salvation to mankind." Nothing more hinders its progress, than its being "evil spoken of." Christians, then, are to guard against this, so far as depends on them. It is not, indeed, in their power to prevent their religion from being misrepresented and abused; but they can take care that their conduct shall not give occasion and plausibility to the misconceptions and calumnies of worldly men. "Let not your good be evil spoken of," means, 'Let it not be calumniated through your imprudent or improper behaviour;' just as the apostle's exhortations to Titus and Timothy, "Let no man despise thee," "Let no man despise thy youth,"[1] mean, 'Do nothing that is fitted to produce contempt.' Nothing had a more obvious tendency to make Christianity the object at once of dislike and contempt among those who knew little or nothing of it but from the conduct of its professors, than angry controversies about such points as distinction of days and meats. Nothing was more calculated to repel and disgust an inquirer, and to afford a handle for malignant misrepresentation. Eager contentions about such comparative trifles gave plausibility to the suggestion, that they who engaged in them had nothing better to contend about, and led the surrounding heathen to suppose that Christianity was merely a peculiar form of Judaism, having nothing to recommend it from the intelligence of its adherents, if their controversies were to form the measure of their understandings, and that the Christian doctrines referred, as Festus says, to "certain questions of that superstition."[2] Such contentions, too, had an obvious tendency to produce what Paley calls "contempt before inquiry," and to deter men from connecting themselves with a society so divided on such points, and showing such tempers. This was gross injustice to the good cause intrusted to their care. There was much about it, if rightly exhibited, that had a tendency

[1] Tit. ii. 15; 1 Tim. iv. 12. [2] Acts xxv. 19.

to produce any feeling rather than contempt—much which was fitted to commend it to the respect and admiration of mankind.

This is what the apostle next adverts to, "For the kingdom of God is not meat and drink; but righteousness, and peace, and joy in the Holy Ghost."[1] "The kingdom of God," "of heaven," and "of Christ," are phrases of frequent occurrence in the New Testament, and all refer to the same thing. The better order of things to be introduced by the great promised Deliverer, is often, in the Old Testament predictions, represented as a kingdom of celestial origin, of which Jehovah is the Sovereign, and Messiah, the King and King's Son, the great administrator. The expression sometimes describes this state as begun on earth, sometimes as perfected in heaven. It sometimes refers to its external form, sometimes to its internal organization; sometimes to the privileges enjoyed by, sometimes to the responsibilities laid on, those who are its subjects. In the passage before us, I think there can be no reasonable doubt that it refers to the privileges enjoyed by those who have by faith entered into it. These are not of an external, but of a spiritual kind. This kingdom "is not meat and drink." The being freed from the restrictions of the Jewish law, does not form the grand distinction of those who belong to this kingdom, as one might be apt to suppose from the eagerness of some of the strong, but not wise, Roman Christians, to assert and display this privilege. Its privileges are of a far higher character. They are "righteousness, and peace, and joy in the Holy Ghost." It has been common to suppose that the apostle's meaning here is, 'It is not by either abstaining from, or indulging in, certain articles of diet, that a man is to show that he is in the kingdom of God,—it is by righteousness, by strict justice, by living righteously, by a peaceable disposition, and by a habitual cheerful, happy temper, growing out of a pacified conscience and a purified heart, that he is to prove himself a Christian. Christianity is not

[1] Ver. 17.

occupied about external, but about internal things; not about ceremonial distinctions, but about moral temper and behaviour.' But neither "peace," nor "joy," as used in the text, naturally express the meaning thus given to them, and the word "righteousness," seems to have its ordinary signification in the epistle—'justification.' The apostle's meaning appears to be, 'You give a degrading and false view of Christianity by these contentions, leading men to think that freedom from ceremonial restriction is its great privilege; while the truth is, justification, peace with God, and joy in God, produced by the Holy Ghost—these are the characteristic privileges of the children of the kingdom, as these are the privileges illustrated in the former part of the epistle, especially at the beginning of the fifth chapter. If you would not have your good evil spoken of—if you would wish to recommend the kingdom of God, give prominence, in your representations of it, both in word and in conduct to these grand characteristics. This is the way to recommend your religion to men, as well as to secure the approving smile of God.'

"For he that in these things serveth Christ, is acceptable to God, and approved of men."[1] It is the man who enjoys these privileges, and who, in their enjoyment, "serves Christ" —yields an implicit universal obedience to *His* laws, who is the true Christian. He is the person whom God accepts as a worshipper, whether he observes the law of Moses or disregards it. And he, too, is the man who is "approved of men." His behaviour commands respect and gives a favourable, because a just, view of the religion of Christ, fitted to put to silence the ignorant calumnies of foolish men. An undue attention to lesser matters has injured Christianity; an increasing attention to its greater matters is the way to repair these injuries.

The practical inference which the apostle draws from this statement is, "Let us therefore follow after the things that make for peace, and things whereby one may edify another."[2]

[1] Ver. 18. [2] Ver. 19.

The expression, "Things which make for peace,"[1] describes the opinions, and dispositions, and habits, which are calculated to bind together in holy union the followers of Christ. "Things whereby one may edify another," is another description of the same opinions, dispositions, and habits, derived from their tendency to produce mutual Christian improvement—in knowledge, faith, holiness, usefulness, and comfort. Disputes about meats and days, and similar subjects, and the temper such disputes manifest and strengthen, are not fitted to promote either the peace or the holiness of the Church. Let the strong, instead of outraging the prejudices of their weaker brethren, bear with them, and even yield to them, so far as integrity will permit; and let them, by turning their attention to the great characteristic principles of Christian truth, and by exemplifying the purity and benignity of the Christian character in their temper and conduct, promote their spiritual improvement, bind them in the close bands of holy affection to themselves, and gradually loosen their prejudices, and prepare their minds for more liberal and extended views of those subjects on which they are now mistaken, though conscientiously mistaken.

The force of the apostle's deduction deserves to be noticed: "Let us *therefore*," etc. Since these controversies have a tendency to injure the character of Christianity, and since an opposite course is fitted to recommend it, as the former course leads to division, and the latter to union—as the one is calculated to create stumblingblocks, and the other to promote edification — let us, as we value the honour of Christ, the progress of religion, the prosperity of the Church, the edification of the brethren—let us avoid such "vain janglings," such "strivings about the law which are vain," such "unlearned questions," and follow peace, and truth, and holiness.

The apostle concludes this paragraph in the first clause of the 20th verse (which should either have been the last clause

[1] τὰ τῆς εἰρήνης = τὰ εἰρηνικά.

of the 19th, or have stood alone, like verse 16, which begins the paragraph): "For meat destroy not the work of God."[1] "The work of God" is often understood of the 'work of God in the heart of the weak in the faith.' Of all Christians it may be said, "They are *His* workmanship, created in Christ Jesus unto good works, which God hath before ordained that they should walk in them;"[2] "He worketh in them both to will and to do of His good pleasure;"[3] He begins "a good work in them," and "will perform it until the day of Jesus Christ."[4] In this case, this verse, as to meaning, is synonymous with ver. 16. But it seems more natural, and more agreeable to the context and the flow of thought, to understand "the work of God" to be "the kingdom of God"—the progress and establishment of the religion of Christ among mankind. "This is the work of God, that men believe on Him whom He has sent." To create men anew, through the mediation of His Son, by the operation of His Spirit, through the instrumentality of His Gospel, this is "the work of God." To "destroy," is often equivalent to doing what has a tendency to destroy, as in ver. 15—to do injury to.[5] Few things would have a greater tendency to prevent the progress of the Gospel, among both Jews and Gentiles, than the giving prominence to the controversy here referred to. To decide it in the one way, would offend the Jews; to decide it in the other, would throw great obstacles in the way of the conversion of the Gentiles. The very existence of such a controversy was fitted to prejudice bystanders against Christianity as a system occupied with such trivial contests; and the time and mental activity, worse than wasted in such a strife, otherwise employed, might have told powerfully on the edification of the Church and the conversion of the world.

There is a wonderful energy in the apostle's words: "For *meat* do not destroy the *work of God*." The contrast between the insignificance of the subject in dispute, and the magnitude

[1] Ver. 20. [2] Eph. ii. 10. [3] Phil. ii. 13. [4] Phil. i. 6
[5] Acts v. 38, 39; 2 Mac. ii. 22.

of the evil it was likely to produce, is very striking. 'Will you really do what is so monstrously absurd, as well as obviously wrong—will you, for a question about meats ("meats for the belly, and the belly for meats, but God will destroy both it and them"[1])—will you, so far as lies in your power, prevent the progress of that Gospel which brings "glory to God in the highest," which is fitted to save innumerable souls from everlasting death, and make countless myriads of otherwise hopelessly lost immortals happy for ever?'

The applicableness of this passage to the Church in all ages is very evident. "Woe" has been "to the world" because of the offences—"the stumblingblocks," which unchristian controversies have produced, both in disputes about philosophical dogmas, and questions on which the inspired word gives forth no utterance—controversies on subjects out of the limits of Christianity, properly so called, and controversies within these limits conducted in an unchristian spirit. They have prevented the spread of the Gospel and the conversion of mankind, both by indisposing, and indeed disabling, the Church for making the necessary exertions, and strengthening the prejudices of unconverted men against the truth. How was the progress of the Gospel interrupted, and ultimately stopped, by the controversies of the earlier ages! How did the strivings among the Reformers, especially in the second generation, turn away their attention from their proper work! How has the cause of Christ in our land been, at different periods of its history, injured from similar causes! It is one of the proofs of the celestial vitality of true Christianity, that even the unnatural contests of her true disciples, calculated above all other causes to injure and destroy it, have been prevented from producing what might not be the designed, but what was the natural result. If Christians would but give up strifes which have fully as little to do with genuine Christianity as the controversy about meats and days, we would have reason to hope that the word of the Lord would have a freer course and be

[1] 1 Cor. vi. 13.

more glorified. "When the envy of Ephraim shall cease, and the enemies of Judah shall be cut off"—rather, the hostile ones in Judah; when "Ephraim shall not envy Judah, and Judah shall not vex Ephraim," then they shall, as a united body, soon vanquish a hostile world, and by the weapons not carnal, but mighty through God, subdue the nations to the obedience of Him who is Lord of all. They are His rightful inheritance—"His by ancient covenant, ere nations' birth; and He has made them His by purchase since, and overpaid their value in His blood." "They together will soon fly upon the shoulders of the Philistines towards the west; they shall spoil them of the east together: they shall lay their hand upon Edom; and Moab and the children of Ammon shall obey them."[1] A united Church would soon lead to a converted world. The Lord hasten it in His time.

A new paragraph commences with the second clause of the 20th verse, in which the apostle urges the strong to a prudent and charitable use of their privilege of freedom from the law of Moses, as to prohibited meats and sacred days, from a consideration of the bad consequences which might result from an opposite course, in leading the weaker brethren to act in opposition to their own conscientious convictions; and states strongly, that to persist in doing what is in itself lawful, becomes in these circumstances criminal. "All things are pure; but it is evil for that man who eateth with offence."[2] "All things" refers to all articles of food—those prohibited, as well as those permitted, by the law of Moses. They are all equally pure. No sin is committed by eating any of them. The distinction between different articles of food, as some clean and others unclean, is no more. It originated, not in the nature of things, but in positive appointment. The ends secured by these positive ordinances have been served; the law enjoining them has been repealed by the same authority that enacted it; and no modification of it has been substituted by the

[1] Isa. xi. 13, 14. [2] Ver. 20.

"One Lawgiver" under the new economy. But, while thus there is no harm in—no sin contracted by, the merely eating any kind of food, yet still harm may be done—sin may be contracted, in reference to this matter. It is a just remark, that much sin is committed in the unlawful use of what is itself lawful.

"It is evil to him that eateth with offence"—literally, "evil is to him who eateth with offence." To "eat with or through offence," is a remarkable mode of expression.[1] It may signify either to eat so as to be offended, or stumbled, or led into sin, —or to eat so as to offend, to make others stumble, or lead them into sin. Supposing the first of these senses to be its meaning here, the person described is he who eats what is indeed in itself lawful to be eaten, but with regard to the lawfulness of which he is not convinced, or, it may be, with regard to the unlawfulness of eating which he has a conviction. He, in eating what is in itself lawful, incurs guilt, for he does what he thinks to be wrong; or, at any rate, what he is not sure to be right. This is the person who, in ver. 23, is described as eating "in doubt, and not in faith." Of this being wrong there can be no doubt; for, as the apostle states, in the 14th verse, "To him that esteemeth any thing to be unclean, to him it is unclean." The connection, however, leads us to understand the expression in the other senses—of eating so as to give offence—so as to cast a stumblingblock before a brother—so as to expose him to temptation, perhaps lead him into sin. The person here described is one who personally has no doubts or scruples as to the use of articles of food—a strong Christian, who, with the apostle, is persuaded "that nothing is unclean of itself." Even by this person's eating an article of food prohibited by the law of Moses, harm may be done, and guilt contracted, if he persist in doing this, while he is aware that, in doing so, he is likely to lead some of his weaker brethren to do what, though in itself not wrong, will yet defile their conscience, because

[1] *διὰ προσκόμματος ἐσθίοντι.* For a similar use of the prep. *διὰ*, see Luke viii. 4; Acts xv. 27; 2 Cor. x. 11; Heb. xiii. 22.

not warranted by their convictions of what is right. That this is the just view of the meaning of the clause, seems confirmed by the fact that the apostle, in the words which immediately follow, proceeds, not to exhort the weak Christian to abstain till he be better informed, but the strong Christian to abstain in circumstances in which the use of his liberty might injure his weak brother. To eat every kind of food was lawful; but, if eating a particular kind of it will bring a brother into spiritual hazard, I must not eat *that* kind of food. The use of it is lawful, but it is not obligatory. I do not sin in refraining; and, to prevent sin, I must do every thing but sin.

While it is evil for a man thus to eat with offence, on the other hand—"It is good neither to eat flesh, nor to drink wine, nor anything whereby thy brother stumbleth, or is offended, or is made weak."[1] This is the same sentiment stated still more strongly by the apostle, 1 Cor. viii. 13—"Wherefore, if meat maketh my brother to offend, I will eat no flesh while the world standeth, lest I make my brother to offend." The words rendered "stumble," "offend," "make weak," are, in signification, here nearly synonymous, indicating different forms and degrees of spiritual damage. The general rule laid down is, 'We are bound to abstain from everything which duty does not require, if we have reason to think that, by not doing so, we shall in any way injure the spiritual interests of our brethren.'

In the two succeeding verses, the apostle briefly, but comprehensively, states the duties of both the classes referred to, with regard to the subject under discussion: "Hast thou faith? have it to thyself before God. Happy is he that condemneth not himself in that thing which he alloweth."[2] "Faith" here has its usual meaning, 'belief;' but it refers to the particular point in question. "Hast thou faith?" or, "Thou hast faith"—a settled conviction on this subject. Thou art "fully persuaded in thy own mind;"[3] "thou knowest, and art persuaded."[4] What, then? "Have it to thyself

[1] Ver. 21. [2] Ver. 22. [3] Ver. 5. [4] Ver. 14.

before God." These words are often interpreted as if they were equivalent to—'Keep your faith to yourself; you are not required to surrender it; but conceal it where it may do harm.' I cannot believe this to be the apostle's meaning. He did not keep his faith on this subject to himself; and it would have been strange to require them to conceal what he so plainly declares. Open profession of what we are persuaded to be truth and duty, is one of the first of our obligations as rational, social, religious, accountable beings.[1] No good can come out of concealment on such subjects. Besides, this is not the natural meaning of the apostle's words, which may be rendered, 'Have, or hold, it with regard to thyself before God. Hold fast your conscientious conviction, as to yourself, before God—*i.e.* as under His eye—not attempting to impose it on thy brother.'

This advice is not, in itself, inapplicable to either of the two parties—the weak and the strong. To the weak it might be said, "Hast thou faith?" 'Are you fully persuaded that you ought to abstain from certain meats, to observe certain days, then "hold your faith," with respect to yourself, before God—that is, piously, as in His sight; but do not insist that your faith should be the rule of your brethren's conduct, whose "faith," on this subject, is different from—opposite to, yours.'

It seems clear, however, from what follows, that it is to "the strong" that the apostle here refers; and that his meaning is—'Are you convinced that all legal restrictions are abolished? Hold that comfortable persuasion, with regard to yourself, before God. Be thankful that your mind is relieved from scruples and perplexities, and that you have been made to understand the liberty of the Gospel; but, before your weak brethren, who may be injured by your doing what is rather the availing yourself of a privilege than the discharge of an obligation, while you use all proper means that they

[1] A most satisfactory discussion of this important subject, in all its bearings, is to be found in M. Vinet's masterly work—"Essai sur la Manifestation des Convictions Religieuses."

may become better informed, abstain from that which may probably injure them, and which, though conscience allows it, it by no means prescribes to you. Be thankful for the enlarged views you have obtained; but, in following them out, "let all things be done in charity."'[1]

"Happy is he that condemneth not himself in that thing which he alloweth." He is truly happy who has an enlightened conscience, and acts according to it—who "walks at liberty, keeping God's commandments"—bound with no cords but those of love—no bands but those of a man; and so using his liberty, that he has no cause to condemn himself as inattentive to the demands of love towards his weak brethren. Such a man is far happier than his scrupulous unenlightened brother, who, even although conscientious, exposes himself to needless privations, and involves himself in endless perplexities; and in a still higher degree is he happier than him who does condemn himself in that which he alloweth. Such was the case of the weak Christians, who, while convinced of the continued obligation of the Mosaic restrictions—or, at any rate, not convinced of their being annulled—from whatever motive, practically, even in a single instance, disregarded them.

"And"—rather, 'but'[2]—"he that doubteth is damned if he eat, because he eateth not of faith: for whatsoever is not of faith is sin."[3] "He that doubteth" is opposed to "He who hath faith."[4] The person described is he who is not persuaded that it is lawful to eat of meats prohibited by the law of Moses, and yet does eat of them. This person, in eating them, is "damned." Every one feels that this is a very harsh expression. It was an unduly strong rendering when it was made; though the word 'damn' then was much more nearly, than now, equivalent to 'condemn.' In the present state of the language, where the word is almost exclusively used to describe the final condemnation and punishment of the wicked, it is an incorrect rendering. The meaning is—Such

[1] 1 Cor. xvi. 14. [2] δὲ. [3] Ver. 23. [4] Ver. 22.

a man is the reverse of happy: he is condemned—self-condemned—condemned by his brethren, even by the strong—condemned by God; he does what is wrong, and what he must feel to be wrong. "He eateth not of faith"—he eateth without being persuaded that it is lawful for him to do so: he must, therefore, be condemned in what he does; "for whatsoever is not of faith is sin." These words have often been brought forward as a proof that a man must be a believer in Christ, in order to perform any duty in a manner acceptable to God—as if it were synonymous with the dogma of the English Church, in her thirteenth article, that "works done before the grace of Christ, and the inspiration of His Spirit, are not pleasant to God, but rather have the nature of sin;" or with the declaration in the Epistle to the Hebrews—"For without faith it is impossible to please God: for he that cometh to God must believe that He is, and that He is the rewarder of them that diligently seek Him."[1] But they have no direct bearing on this doctrine. They contain the general principle on which the apostle considers the weak Christian as sinning in eating the prohibited meats. Whatsoever a man doubts the lawfulness of, he ought not to do—while these doubts continue, he cannot do, without sin. This is a principle which admits of no exception, which is far from being the case with the converse proposition—which some would place on the same level as a moral axiom—'Whatsoever is of faith is duty.' A man may be very fully persuaded that a thing is right, while it is wrong. Paul himself is an example: "I verily thought," says he, "that I ought to do many things against Jesus of Nazareth."[2] But was what was of faith here duty? Hear Paul's own opinion: "I was a blasphemer, and a persecutor, and injurious"—"the chief of sinners."[3]

In the first verse of the fifteenth chapter, the apostle draws the conclusion as to the conduct of the Roman Church, composed chiefly of Gentiles, in reference to their Jewish brethren weak in the faith. There plainly should have been no divi-

[1] Heb. xi. 6. [2] Acts xxvi. 9. [3] 1 Tim. i. 13, 15.

sion at the end of the fourteenth chapter. Both the section and the part of the Epistle close at the 13th verse.

"We then that are strong ought to bear the infirmities of the weak, and not to please ourselves."[1] It is right to state, that the verses 25–27 of the next chapter, in the *textus receptus*, are in some MSS. of antiquity and authority inserted here. The reasons of the supposed transposition have been the subject of much investigation. The evidence, both external and internal, seems in favour of the ordinary arrangement. It is quite amazing how much learning and ingenuity have been expended on this question.

The words, "We then that are strong"—or, 'But we who are strong'—"ought to bear the infirmities of the weak, and not to please ourselves," are not a logical inference from what has been just said. They seem connected with the preceding context thus: While it is wrong for the weak Christian to desist from acting on his conscientious views, though mistaken, it is not only not wrong in the strong Christian to desist, in certain circumstances, to act on his conscientious views, though correct, but it is his duty "to bear the infirmities of his weak brother, and not to please himself." The reason of the difference is plain: the conviction of the weak brother is, that he must sin if he disregard the legal restrictions; the conviction of the strong brother is merely that he may, without sin, disregard them.

The strong are the well-informed, enlightened Christians, among whom the apostle ranks himself, and to which class, probably, the greater part of the Gentile converts belonged; the other class—the weak, are the narrow-minded, imperfectly-informed, composed chiefly, if not exclusively, of Jewish converts, and likely including the most of these.

"The infirmities of the weak," are their mistaken views, and the modes of conduct to which they led. These indicated weakness, and their tendency was to increase weakness. They unfitted them both for the degree of Christian enjoyment, and

[1] Chap. xv. 1.

Christian activity and usefulness, to which they otherwise might have attained. It was the duty of the strong Christians to bear *with* these infirmities of their brethren. They were not to attempt to prevent their avowing their convictions, or their following them out to their practical consequences, by threatening, if they did, to renounce communion with them as Christian brethren. They were not to say, as has, in succeeding ages, often been said and acted on, when there was no such strong ground to stand on as the strong brethren had—"Our opinion is undoubtedly true, and yours is undoubtedly false; our practice is certainly right, and yours is certainly wrong. If you do not renounce these false views, and abandon these superstitious practices, we cannot admit you to the Lord's table with us. We are not agreed; how can we walk together?" No; though thinking them mistaken in these points, yet, having evidence that they were sincerely subject to the one Master's authority, as discerned by them—united in the faith, and love, and profession of the grand principles of the Christian faith—they were to walk together in love, even as their common Lord had loved them, in His commandments and ordinances.

But this does not seem to be exactly what the apostle is here enjoining. They must do all this; but they must do more than this. They must not only forbear with their weak brethren, under their infirmities, but they must "*bear* their infirmities." They must patiently submit to such personal inconveniences as may very probably rise out of the infirmities of their weak brethren, so far as this is not inconsistent with their own conscientious views of truth and duty, and is calculated to promote the spiritual interests of these brethren. For example, in the case before us, they must not only allow their weak brethren to regulate their own conduct according to their own convictions—they must not only not require them to eat the forbidden meats, nor disregard the consecrated days, but they must also refrain from the practical display of their own opinions respecting freedom from legal restrictions—they must decline the use of what they know to be their privilege, in circumstances in which they see that this would imperil the spiritual interests of their brethren.

This course is so far from being inconsistent with a distinct avowal—a strong assertion of their sentiments, on the part of the strong, that it seems to imply it. For the strong practically to comply with the weak, without explaining the principles on which they did it, would have been to confirm them in their prejudices, and to lay a foundation for their continuing for ever weak; whereas compliance, so far as conscience permitted, while the true reason of it was assigned, was highly fitted to prepare the minds of the weak for wider and juster views of the truth. The former would have been detestable hypocrisy: if wisdom, that which is of the earth, earthy; the latter was true charity—"the wisdom that cometh from above, pure, peaceable."

To illustrate the subject by a figure, naturally suggested by the terms employed by the apostle: Christians are a band of pilgrims, from the city of Destruction to the Jerusalem that is above. Though none are in perfect health—none without some burden, yet still some are comparatively healthy, strong, and unencumbered; others are weak and sickly, and very heavy laden. The former class are not to form themselves into a separate band, and push forward, regardless of what may become of their less fortunate brethren, leaving them to follow as they may. No, they are to remain, what the Lord of the pilgrims made them, one society—a band of brothers. The strong and unencumbered are to help forward the weak and burdened. They are not, indeed, in order that the whole company may appear alike, to pretend that they also are weak and heavy laden; still less, if possible, are they voluntarily to reduce themselves in these respects to a level with their brethren; but they are patiently to submit to such inconveniences as arise out of their connection with such companions, and while using every means to have their diseases cured, and their strength increased, and their burdens removed or lessened, they must not at present attempt to make them move faster than they are able, as that would be likely to produce stumbling and falling. How happy would it have been, how happy would it be, if all the weak were treated by the strong as Feeblemind, in the *Pilgrim's Progress*, says he was treated by his brethren: "Indeed, I have found much relief from pilgrims, though none was willing to go so softly as I am forced to do: yet still, as they came on, they bid me be of good cheer, and said, that it was the will of the Lord that comfort should be given to the feeble-minded, and so went on their own pace."

Thus they were to bear the burdens of the weak, and not to please themselves by following a course that might be more agreeable to themselves, but would be inconsistent with the welfare of their weak brethren. Strong Christians should be followers of Paul, the very Samson of the faith, and take for their motto his words, "I please all men in all things; not seeking mine own profit, but the profit of many, that they may be saved." [2]

It deserves to be noticed, that the mode of conduct here recommended is not a matter of option, but of duty. The words contain not a counsel only, but a command: "We that are strong *ought* to bear the infirmities of the weak, and not to please ourselves." The apostle proceeds to show them a more excellent way than "pleasing themselves."

"Let every one please his brother for his good to edification." [3] Christians are not only not to "offend" one another, that is, to stumble, to tempt, to give occasion to sin, they are to seek to please each other. The strong Christian is, by every means consistent with truth and duty, to endeavour to keep on good terms with his weak brother. It is only thus that he is likely to be really useful to him. If a man has not confidence in our friendly regards, he is not likely to listen to our counsels. But the command "to please" has its limits. These are indicated by the end to be sought—"For good to edification." The phrase rendered "for good," [4] may either

[1] *Pilgrim's Progress*, Part II.
[2] 1 Cor. x. 33.
[3] Ver. 2.
[4] εἰς τὸ ἀγαθὸν.

signify, 'In reference to that which is good,'—in reference to his religion, "that good thing;" or, 'So far as it is fitted to promote the individual's welfare.' In this last case, the two phrases are nearly synonymous; the second phrase is explanatory of the first. They were to seek to please so far as, and no further than, is consistent with the spiritual improvement of the weak brother. He would have been best pleased by the strong adopting his views, and professing a belief that the Mosaic restrictions were still in force; but this would not have been to "please him for edification." We must not seek to please men by flattering their prejudices. When men can be both pleased and profited, it is very right they should be pleased. But it often happens that the two things are utterly incompatible. Even good men cannot always be pleased and profited at the same time. To please, you must sometimes do what would injure them; and to profit them, you must do what is likely to offend them. The apostle does not here contrast pleasing men with profiting them, but pleasing others with pleasing ourselves. Instead of pleasing ourselves, we are to please others, so far as that is calculated to promote edification.

The injunction is enforced by a most powerful motive: "For even Christ pleased not Himself; but, as it is written, The reproaches which were cast on thee, have fallen on Me."[1] Even our Lord pleased not Himself, sought not self-indulgence, shunned not self-sacrifice—readily bore our griefs, carried our sorrows. If He, the Master, did not, how ill does it become the disciples to please themselves? He sought not His own things, He sought the things of others. His whole work was a great act of self-denial—of disinterested, wise kindness. How did He manifest this in His conduct to the chosen disciples! How strong was He, how weak were they! "How wide the interval," to use the words of Robert Hall, "which separated His religious knowledge and attainments from theirs! He, the fountain of illumination—they, encompassed with infir-

[1] Ver. 3.

mities! But did He recede from them on that account? No, He drew the bond of union closer, imparted successive streams of effulgence, till He incorporated His spirit with theirs, and elevated them into a nearer resemblance with Himself." He sought to please them; but His great end was *edification*—building up the great work of God.

According to his manner, the apostle refers to an ancient prophetic oracle describing this feature in Christ—Messiah the Prince: "As it is written, The reproaches which were cast on thee, fell on Me." The passage is quoted from the sixty-ninth Psalm, which has all the characters of a Messianic oracle. Even though it had not been directly applied to our Lord in the New Testament, there is much in it pointing it out as one of the Psalms in which "it is written of Christ;" and it is directly applied to our Lord, not only here, but in chap. xi. 10, and in John ii. 17; xix. 28. It is not easy to say whether the apostle's object was to illustrate our Lord's disinterestedness, in reference to the sacrifices He made for the individuals He came to save, or in reference to the grand public interest of the Divine glory and the moral order of the universe, with the care of which He was intrusted. But for the sake of saving men, He never needed to have been in circumstances in which He could have been exposed to "such contradiction of sinners against Himself." Had He sought His happiness in self-indulgence, He need never have laid aside "the form of God," nor taken on Him "the form of a servant." Perhaps the passage, however, more directly and naturally describes that noble spirit of the love of right and the hatred of iniquity, which led Him to identify Himself with the cause of God's honour, and the order of His moral government. He overlooked personal insult and injury; but when He saw God dishonoured, the cause of truth and righteousness trampled on, He was full of holy indignation. "The zeal of God's house even consumed Him." It was a want of a truly public spirit, and a little-minded, cold-hearted selfishness, that lay at the foundation of the evils which the apostle wished to prevent or cure—the strong contemning the weak, the weak condemning the strong. Could Christians be brought to forget their insignificant personal and sectarian objects, and steadily contemplate the great objects which, as Christians, they should be supremely seeking—the honour of God, and the salvation of mankind, by the universal diffusion of Christian truth—it would be impossible for them to waste their time and their talents, as they often have done, in agitating unlearned questions—"questions which gender strifes, instead of godly edifying." It is greatly to be feared that a large portion of those controversies which have torn the seamless robe of Christ into shreds, broken His body into fragments, and prodigiously retarded the progress of the Gospel and the conversion of the world, have originated and been prosecuted under the influence of the principle here so strongly condemned—the wish to please ourselves; and nothing is better fitted than a contemplation of the opposite temper, as exemplified by our Lord, to shame us out of our selfishness, and to awake within us a more generous spirit. Ah! had He been influenced by the narrow, illiberal, self-seeking spirit, that has been too conspicuous in the character and conduct even of His genuine disciples, what would have become of the infinitely important interests of the Divine glory and human salvation with which He was intrusted? It would be good for a Christian, especially when placed in circumstances similar to those of the Roman Church when this epistle was written, often to ask himself, 'Am I acting the part Christ would have done, had He been placed in my circumstances? He took good care that, if "the good thing" was evil spoken of, it should not be owing to anything He said or did. What amount, think you, of self-gratification, in the shape of ease, or wealth, or honour, could have induced Him to do anything that by possibility could injure, not to say destroy, the work of God? The temptation, "All the kingdoms of the world, and the glory of them, will I give Thee," is met with the indignant, "Get thee behind me, Satan;" and how willingly did He, "though He was rich, become poor, that men through His poverty might be rich!" The same exhortation substantially, and the same motive, too, are most powerfully urged in the epistle to the Philippians: "Look not every man on his own things, but every man also on the things of others. Let this mind be in you, which was also in Christ Jesus: who, being in the form of God, thought it not robbery to be equal with God; but made Himself of no reputation, and took upon Him the form of a servant, and was made in the likeness of men; and being found in fashion as a man, he humbled Himself, and became obedient unto death, even the death of the cross."[1]

In the 4th verse, the apostle introduces a remark by the way, respecting the important use which the Old Testament Scriptures, from which he had made a quotation, were intended and fitted to serve to Christians: "For whatsoever things were written aforetime were written for our learning; that we, through faith and patience of the Scriptures, might have hope."[2] "For," is here equivalent to—'I make this quotation, that you may be impressed with a sense of the value of the Old Testament Scriptures.' The Gentile churches were in danger of regarding these holy writings as interesting chiefly, if not exclusively, to the Jews, and as referring to a state of things which had passed away. We find the sentiment in the text, repeatedly and strongly stated by the apostle. He tells us that the history of Abraham's justification "was written, not for his sake alone, but for us also;"[3] that what things happened to the Israelites, "happened to them for ensamples, and are written for our admonition, on whom the ends of the world are come;"[4] that "the Holy Scriptures," with which Timothy had been familiar from his infancy, were "able to make him wise to salvation, through faith that was in Christ," and, "given by Divine inspiration, were all profitable for doctrine, and for reproof, and for correction, and for instruction in righteousness, that the man of God might be perfect, thoroughly furnished unto all good works."[5] And the Apostle Peter tells

[1] Phil. ii. 4–8. [2] Ver. 4. [3] Chap. iv. 23, 24.
[4] 1 Cor. x. 11. [5] 2 Tim. iii. 15–17.

us that the prophets ministered "to us rather than to themselves,"[1] and calls on Christians to "give heed to the confirmed word of prophecy, as to a light shining in a dark place, till the day dawned and the day-star arose in their hearts."[2] "Whatsoever things were written aforetime"—*i.e.*, the ancient sacred books of the Jews—"were written for our *learning*." The word "learning" is used here in the sense of "teaching," which is the meaning of the original term.[3] They were written to teach *us*, as well as those to whom they were originally given. The manner in which they were to serve the purpose of practical instruction is thus described: "that we, through patience and comfort of the Scriptures, might have hope." Patience,[4] ordinarily, in the New Testament signifies perseverance. To bring forth fruit *with patience*, is to continue to bring forth fruit.[5] In Rom. ii. 7, it is rendered "patient continuance." "To run with patience," in Heb. xii. 1, is to persevere in running. The patience, or rather perseverance, of the Scriptures, is the perseverance which the Scriptures enjoin, and which the belief of them produces. The word "comfort,"[6] signifies exhortation as well as comfort. It is the word rendered exhortation in verse 8, and often elsewhere; and here, the comfort of the Scriptures expresses that impressive and consolatory instruction which the Scriptures communicate. Now, it is the design of the Old Testament Scriptures so to teach us, that by the persevering cleaving to truth and duty which they enjoin, and when believed, produce, and through the powerful persuasive consolatory exhortation which they give us,—we may have hope." To *have* hope, may mean to obtain hope; but men obtain hope not by persevering under the influence of scriptural instruction in the right way — they must have hope before they can enter on that way; the hope which makes not ashamed is produced "by the love of God shed abroad in the heart by the Holy Ghost"[7]—by knowing the love

[1] 1 Pet. i. 12. [2] 2 Pet. i. 19. [3] διδασκαλίαν. [4] ὑπομονή.
[5] Luke viii. 15. [6] παράκλησις. [7] Chap. v. 5.

which God has to us in Christ Jesus. The word rendered "have,"[4] signifies also to hold, to hold fast, to keep hold of: Rev. i. 16; John xiv. 21; 1 Tim. iii. 9; 2 Tim. i. 13. This seems to be its meaning here. The design of the Old Testament Scriptures is, by their teaching, to enable us, through persevering in faith and duty, and under the influence of their powerful and persuasive exhortations, to hold fast our hope, which cannot be maintained in a course of apostacy or inattention to the exhortation of the Scriptures.

Knowing that "every good gift cometh down from above, from the Father of lights," the apostle presents a prayer that the Romans might be brought into such a state of unity of mind and heart, as should enable them, notwithstanding their partial differences of sentiment, to enjoy the delights and advantages of Christian fellowship: "Now the God of patience and consolation grant you to be like-minded towards one another, according to Christ Jesus; that ye may with one mind and one mouth glorify God, even the Father of our Lord Jesus Christ."[2] "The God of patience," or perseverance, is the God who is the author of patience and perseverance—who, by His Spirit, works the perseverance His word requires; the God of consolation, is the author of that powerful, persuasive instruction contained in His word, and who, by His Spirit, makes it effectual for persuading and comforting men. The apostle prays that, in these characters, He might produce in the Roman Christians such a mutual unity of mind—such a measure of common sentiment and affection—as would enable them to perform the duties of church fellowship, in together observing the ordinances of the Gospel; and in these, "with one mind and with one mouth, might glorify"—praise, honour God as their common Father, because the Father of their common Lord.

The apostle now returns to his exhortation, that, without reference to their minor differences, the strong and the weak —which was a distinction nearly coincident with the Gentile

[1] ἔχω.

[2] Ver. 5, 6.

and the Jewish members of the Roman Church—should live in cordial fellowship with each other; and follows it up by a statement that Jesus Christ was the minister of God both to the Jews and the Gentiles, and that the object of His ministry was to unite these in one holy society to the praise of the faithfulness and mercy of God. This is the substance of ver. 7–12: "Wherefore receive ye one another, as Christ also received us, to the glory of God. Now," or 'and,' "I say, that Jesus Christ was a minister of the circumcision for the truth of God, to confirm the promises made unto the fathers: and that the Gentiles might glorify God for His mercy; as it is written, For this cause I will confess to Thee among the Gentiles, and sing unto Thy name. And again he saith, Rejoice, ye Gentiles, with His people. And again, Praise the Lord, all ye Gentiles; and laud Him, all ye people. And again Esaias saith, There shall be a root of Jesse, and He that shall rise to reign over the Gentiles; in Him shall the Gentiles trust."

The 7th verse does not seem an inference from what goes before. "Wherefore" is equivalent to 'for this reason;' and the reason for the exhortation is to be found in the second part of the verse. The duty enjoined, is receiving one another. The word "receive" is to be understood in the same sense as in chap. xiv. 1: 'Acknowledge and treat one another as Christian brethren. Notwithstanding your differences of opinion, regard one another as servants of the same Lord—children of the same Father. Let not the strong exclude the weak, and let not the weak withdraw from the strong. Let there be "no divisions and offences among you, contrary to the doctrine which ye have learned."'

This exhortation the apostle enforces by a very powerful motive: "As Christ has received *us*," or, according to a more approved reading, '*you*—that is, all of you, both Jews and Gentiles, both weak and strong.' The particle *as* may be considered either as a particle of comparison or of deduction. In the first case, it describes the kind of reception they ought to give each other: It should be *mutual*, *He* had received both;—*cor-*

dial, thus he always receives. "The Holy Ghost," to use Peter's language, " fell on them"—the Gentile converts, "as He did on us"—the Jewish believers, " at the beginning."[1] " God, which knoweth the hearts, bare them witness, giving them the Holy Ghost, even as He did unto us; and put no difference between us and them, purifying their hearts by faith."[2]

I prefer understanding it in the second way, as chap. i. 17; John xvii. 2; Rom. i. 28; 1 Cor. i. 6; v. 7; Eph. i. 4; Phil. i. 7. It introduces the reason why they should receive one another, and that is a powerful one. If they were Christians themselves, it was because Christ had received them: and, if He had received others as Christians, on what ground could they exclude them, as they substantially did, so far as they were able, by refusing to associate with them as brethren? Would not this be to set up their own opinion in opposition to the declared mind of Christ, saying, 'He takes that man to be a Christian, but I do not?' This was the Apostle Peter's view of the subject. As soon as he saw, by the giving of the Holy Ghost, that Christ had received Cornelius and his friends, he said, " Can any man forbid water, that these should not be baptized, which have received the Holy Ghost as well as we?"[3] 'Christ has received them; who dare refuse to receive them?' And, when called to account for what he had done, this was his defence, " What was I, that I could withstand God?"[4]

Christ is the only Head of His Church—the supreme Lord of that spiritual society. It is His prerogative to admit men to be members of his true Church, by giving them His Holy Spirit; and it is equally presumptuous in a Christian, or a Christian Church, to acknowledge as Christians, by admitting to church communion persons who give no evidence that Christ has received them—who obviously have not His Spirit, and therefore are none of His,—and to refuse to admit any individual who gives the requisite evidence that He has re-

[1] Acts xi. 15.
[2] Acts xv. 8, 9.
[3] Acts x. 47.
[4] Acts xi. 17.

ceived him. There may be, certainly there is, more difficulty in applying this test for admission to communion now, than there was in the primitive age; but the rule itself is unaltered and unalterable. Those whom Christ appears to have received are to be received by us, and received by us because we think they have been received by Him.

The concluding phrase, "to the glory of God," may be connected either with the first or with the second clause of the verse: "receive ye one another to the glory of God,"—or, "Christ has received you to the glory of God." If joined to the first clause, it signifies the ultimate end which Christians should have in view in receiving one another as brethren—'that God may be glorified.' The union of Christians greatly tends to honour God. Love, mutual love, is one of the fruits of the Spirit—"the fruits of righteousness, which are to the praise and glory of God." "Herein is my Father glorified, that ye bring forth much fruit."[1] Union among Christians is necessary, both to their own edification, and to the conversion of the world; and it is in these two things that God is specially glorified. If the expression be connected with the last clause, then it refers to the object that Christ had in view in collecting a Church. He receives believing Jews and Gentiles, that God may be glorified. He plants the trees of righteousness in the vineyard which He keeps night and day, that the Lord may be glorified. The glorification of God is the great object of all He did on earth, of all He does in heaven, in order to the receiving men. "I have glorified Thee on the earth." "Glorify Thy Son, that Thy Son also may glorify Thee."[2] There is nothing to prevent our considering the words as belonging to both clauses: 'Receive ye one another to the glory of God, even as Christ has also received you to the glory of God. Both do what He has done, and do it for the same purpose as He has done it. In the thing itself, and in its object, He has set you an example that ye may walk in His steps.' That the primary reference is to Christ's object in re-

[1] John xv. 8.

[2] John xvii. 1, 4, 5.

ceiving both Jews and Gentiles seems probable; for what follows is an illustration of how He is a minister of the circumcision, so as to show forth the truth of God; and how, of the Gentiles, so as to show forth His mercy. The verses that follow are in close connection with what precedes them, and form the conclusion of the section in which the apostle shows what is the term of church fellowship, and how Christians are, in accordance with that term, to treat each other.

The object of the apostle, in these verses, is to show that Christ has indeed received both Jews and Gentiles, in accordance with the declarations of Old Testament Scripture, to the glory of the Divine faithfulness and grace. And, first, with regard to the Jews: "Now," or rather 'And,' "I say, that Jesus Christ was a minister of the circumcision for the truth of God, to confirm the promises made unto the fathers."[1] "I say," is equivalent to 'This is what I say.' "Jesus Christ was a minister of the circumcision." Jesus was the minister of God—appointed by Him, directed by Him, sustained by Him, rewarded by Him. But, while God was the author of His ministry, men were the objects of His ministry—men, both Jews and Gentiles. He was, in the first instance, the "minister of the circumcision"—the circumcised. "He came to His own:" He was "sent to the lost sheep of the house of Israel." To them His personal ministry was in a great measure confined; and His command with regard to His Gospel was, that it should be first preached to the Jews—"Beginning at Jerusalem;" and "to the children of the prophets, and of the covenant which God made with their fathers; to them first, God having raised up His Son Jesus, sent Him to bless them."[2] He gathered the outcasts of Israel to Himself, and made them His people. This was done "for the truth of God, to confirm the promise made to the fathers." The object of our Lord, in doing this, was that the Father's name might be honoured, as "He that keepeth truth for ever, and remembers His cove-

[1] Ver. 8.
[2] John i. 11; Matt. xv. 24; Luke xxiv. 47; Acts iii. 25, 26.

nant to all generations." The apostle notices this, that the Gentiles might learn to regard with respectful affection their Jewish brethren, notwithstanding their weakness.

But our Lord was appointed to be a minister of the uncircumcision as well as of the circumcision. He is not said to be so in so many words, but it is so implied in the apostle's language, which is elliptical, that you must supply the words, 'and a minister of the uncircumcision,' or something equivalent, to complete the sense. He was so, in order "that the Gentiles might glorify God for His mercy." He "gave Himself a ransom for all;" He was "the propitiation for the sins of the whole world;" He ordered His apostles "to go teach all nations," and to preach His Gospel "to every creature." He was "a light to lighten the Gentiles," as well as "the glory of God's people, Israel." He came, in the administration of His Gospel, and in the effusion of His Spirit, "preaching peace" and giving salvation "to them that were far off as well as to them who were nigh." He visited the Gentiles, "to take from among them a people to His name."[1] All this was done that the mercy of God might be glorified through the Gentiles, as His truth had been through the Jews. He received sinners of the Gentiles, so as to set them down with Abraham, and Isaac, and Jacob in the kingdom of God—not making two societies of them, but one; receiving them all on the same principles, and with equal cordiality; "making in Himself of twain one new man, so making peace; reconciling both by the blood of His cross; and giving them all, through Himself, access by one Spirit to the Father."[2] What a glorious display of Divine grace, when such monsters of iniquity as are described in the close of the first chapter of the epistle are "washed, and sanctified, and justified, through the name of the Lord Jesus, and by the Spirit of our God;" and when the "aliens and enemies" are "reconciled," and the "strangers and foreigners" made "fellow-citizens with the

[1] 1 Tim. ii. 6; 1 John ii. 2; Matt. xxviii. 19; Mark xvi. 15; Luke ii. 32; Eph. ii. 17; Acts xv. 14.

[2] Eph. ii. 14–18.

saints and of the household of faith!" Should not the elder brother rejoice to receive back again his poor prodigal brother, "who was dead, and is alive again—was lost, and is found," when the Father and the first-born among the brethren have so cordially received him?

As this was intended chiefly for the Jewish part of the Roman Church, he refers them to their own Scriptures, as witnessing to this character of the Divine method of justification under the Messiah, that it is equally for the Gentiles as for the Jews: "As it is written, For this cause I will confess to Thee among the Gentiles, and sing unto Thy name." This is a quotation from Psalm xviii. 49; one of the Messianic psalms, as I apprehend, in the strictest sense of the term.[1] The Messiah, delivered from all His enemies, and from the power of death, and made Head over the heathen, who, as soon as they heard of Him, obeyed Him, was, on these grounds, by the establishment of the ordinances of Christian worship, and by the providential dispensations by which the establishment was to be effected, preserved, and extended, to show forth the glories of the only true God. A second ancient oracle, referring to the same great event, is (ver. 10) quoted from Deut. xxxii. 43: "Rejoice, ye Gentiles, with His people." This intimates that, at the period referred to, the Gentiles—the heathen nations—should, in the possession of common privileges, along with the Jews, long the peculiar people of God, unite in the joyful acknowledgment of Jehovah as their God. The third quotation (ver. 11) is from Psal. cxvii. 1: "Praise the Lord, all ye Gentiles; and laud Him, all ye people,"—or, as it is in our version, "O praise the Lord, all ye nations: praise Him, all ye people." This is a prediction that, at the time referred to, all nations, and the Jews generally, should unite in praising Jehovah for "His great, merciful kindness," and His "ever enduring faithfulness." The fourth quotation (ver. 12) is from the book of the prophet Isaiah, chap. xi. 10:

[1] See the evidence of this in the introductory discourse to "The Sufferings and the Glories of the Messiah."

"There shall be a *root*"—rather, a shoot—"of Jesse, and He that shall rise to reign over the Gentiles; in Him shall the Gentiles trust." The words, as they stand in our translation of the Old Testament, are—"And in that day there shall be a root of Jesse, which shall stand for an ensign to the people; to it shall the Gentiles seek." The apostle quotes the Septuagint version, apparently from memory. This is another prophetic testimony that, under the Messiah, the Gentiles were to form a part of the peculiar people of God.

Such is the apostle's statement of the law of Christ, as to the manner in which His disciples, whether Jews or Gentiles, should conduct themselves toward each other, and His enforcement of that law by peculiar and powerful motives. It may seem strange that, in this discussion as to the mode of conduct which ought to be followed by the Christians at Rome, divided in their views respecting "meats and days," as well as in his remarks on a similar subject in the First Epistle to the Corinthians,[1] there is no reference to the decision which the council of apostles and elders at Jerusalem had given forth respecting this subject[2]—declaring that the Gentiles were free from the law of Moses, but, from a regard to the prejudices of the Jews, should abstain from eating things strangled and blood. That decree was specially addressed to the brethren of the Gentiles in Antioch, and Syria, and Cilicia; and the apostle seems to have thought it better to base his instructions to the Christians at Rome and Corinth on general grounds. Stating most distinctly that the Jewish distinctions about food and time were abrogated, he lays it down as a principle, that conscientious difference about such points should in no degree interfere with Christian fellowship; and that, where duty did not absolutely require it, the practical assertion of an undoubted privilege should be put in abeyance, if it was likely to lead less informed brethren into sin, or even temptation to sin.

The apostle concludes the Practical part of his Epistle with

[1] Chap. viii.; x. 23–33. [2] Acts xv.

an earnest prayer for the Roman Christians: "Now the God of hope fill you with all joy and peace in believing, that ye may abound in hope, through the power of the Holy Ghost."[1] The reference of this to what immediately precedes it is lost, in our version by the noun's receiving here a different rendering from that of the cognate verb in the 12th verse. Read "in Him shall the Gentiles *hope*," and you at once see why the apostle addresses God as the God of hope, and prays that He would make the Roman Christians abound in hope. "The God of hope" is equivalent to, 'The God who is the Author of Christian hope—who has prepared the blessings which are the objects of hope—who has held them out, in His Gospel, as the objects of hope to us—and who, by His Holy Spirit enabling us to understand and believe that Gospel, awakens and maintains the exercise of hope.

The apostle prays that God, in this character, would fill the Roman Christians "with *all* joy and peace." This is an ordinary mode of strongly expressing the superlative, by the apostle—Col. i. 9–11, iii. 16; 1 Tim. i. 15, 16; and often elsewhere. The phrase is equivalent to the best—the purest kind of joy and peace, and the highest degree of them. He prays that God would thus give them "joy and peace in believing"—through believing. It is by faith, in the exercise of child-like belief of the Divine testimony respecting Jesus Christ and salvation though Him, that true "joy and peace" are obtained and secured. There is no possibility of our having them but by believing; and there is no really believing the true Gospel without our having them "according to the measure of our faith."

The object which the apostle had in view, in wishing the Roman Christians thus to be filled with "joy and peace," was "that they might abound in hope"—that their hope might be steady, influential, and abiding. "Hope" is the great spring of action; hence the anxiety of the apostle that Christians should "show the same diligence, to the full assurance

[1] Ver. 13.

of hope to the end: that they be not slothful, but followers of them who through faith and patience inherit the promises."[1] Faith—proving its power by producing "joy and peace"—is the grand support of hope. All these blessings the apostle expects from "the power of the Holy Ghost." Everything spiritually good is the fruit of the Holy Spirit.[2] It is just in the degree in which this prayer is answered, in reference to the individual Christian, that he is holy, happy, useful, full of love and good works; and just in the degree in which it is generally answered, that the Church grows and is multiplied—is peaceful, and pure, and energetic in common operation for promoting the glory of God and the happiness of mankind.

[1] Heb. vi. 11, 12. [2] Gal. v. 22.

PART IV.

CONCLUDING.

THE Concluding part of the Epistle to the Romans begins with the 14th verse of the fifteenth chapter, and terminates at the close of the sixteenth chapter. It divides itself into eight sections. The first, reaching from chap. xv. 14–21, may be entitled, Apology.—The second, contained in chap. xv. 22–29, is occupied with notices of intended journeys.—The third, chap. xv. 30–33, is a request for an interest in the prayers of the Roman Christians.—The fourth, chap. xvi. 1, 2, contains the certificate of the bearer of the Epistle.—Salutations from the apostle to individual Christians at Rome, chap. xvi. 3–16, form the subject of the fifth section.—The sixth section, chap. xvi. 17–20, is taken up with cautions against dissension and division.—Salutations from Christians with the apostle, to brethren at Rome, chap. xvi. 21–23, occupy the seventh section;—and the eighth section, contained in chap. xvi. 24–27, forms the proper and most appropriate conclusion of the Epistle, in an affectionate benediction and noble doxology.

In this part of the Epistle, we have much pleasing light shed over the apostle's personal character, and over the state of primitive Christianity.

The apostle appears no less remarkable as a man of action here, than he has done as a man of thought in the previous parts of the Epistle. He seems to have possessed the faculty of memory in a very high degree. How many individuals at

Rome, whom he had met with elsewhere, does he mention, and how intimate, obviously, was his knowledge of them! Now, we have no reason to think he knew these better, or thought more about them, than multitudes of other Christian brethren. The remarkable strength of his memory owed something, no doubt, to the power of the affectionate part of his nature. How full is he of love—holy love, and how touchingly delicate are some of his expressions of it! And then, how completely is everything subordinated to Christ and His cause! How plainly written on these chapters the mottoes, "To me to live is Christ"—"One thing I do!"

The view of primitive Christianity exhibited in this part of the Epistle is also very interesting. It is clear that Christianity had made very extensive progress before this Epistle was written. From how many—how distant places, were the individuals collected who are addressed as Christians at Rome! and though we mark the imperfections of our fallen nature in these primitive Christians, it is impossible not to be impressed with the conviction that the great body of them were enlightened believers, strongly influenced by the love of Christ; and all, of every rank and of both sexes, appear practically active in promoting the Christian cause. Let us look, in succession, at the eight sections into which this part divides itself.

SECTION I.

APOLOGY.

CHAPTER XV. 14–21.—"And I myself also am persuaded of you, my brethren, that ye also are full of goodness, filled with all knowledge, able also to admonish one another. Nevertheless, brethren, I have written the more boldly unto you in some sort, as putting you in mind, because of the grace that is given to me of God, that I should be the minister of Jesus Christ to the Gentiles, ministering the Gospel of God, that the offering up of the Gentiles might be acceptable, being sanctified by the Holy Ghost. I have therefore whereof I may glory through Jesus Christ in those things which pertain to God. For I will not dare to speak of any of those things which Christ hath not wrought by me, to make the

Gentiles obedient, by word and deed, through mighty signs and wonders, by the power of the Spirit of God; so that from Jerusalem, and round about unto Illyricum, I have fully preached the Gospel of Christ. Yea, so have I strived to preach the Gospel, not where Christ was named, lest I should build upon another man's foundation: but, as it is written, To whom He was not spoken of, they shall see; and they that have not heard shall understand."

In the previous part of the Epistle, the apostle had clearly stated, and powerfully proved and defended, the great principles of the Christian faith: he had faithfully pointed out, and solemnly warned against, the doctrinal errors into which the Romans were in danger of falling; he had also given a clear exposition of the leading duties incumbent on them, both as individuals and as a society, accompanied with appropriate motives to their performance; and, in addition to this, he had, with great plainness of speech, cautioned them against the practical errors and faults into which they were likely to fall. To prevent all this—coming as it did from one who was personally a stranger to most of them, who had not been their founder, and indeed had never been among them—from being misconstrued, from seeming to arise out of a disposition to intermeddle with matters that belonged not to him, and to betray an unfriendly jealousy of them; and to guard against the production of a feeling which would materially interfere with the gaining of the great objects for which the Epistle was written, he, with equal wisdom and humility, apologizes both for the freedom of his manner and for his having been so long in showing his regard by a personal visit; and, while assuring them that nothing was further from him than a low estimate of their character as a church, he gives the true reason of his plain speaking—an earnest desire to promote their spiritual improvement, and a deep sense of the obligation under which he lay to "fulfil the ministry which he had received of the Lord Jesus," "to preach among the Gentiles the unsearchable riches of Christ."

"And I myself also am persuaded of you, my brethren, that ye also are full of goodness, filled with all knowledge, able also to admonish one another."[1] "Goodness" may here signify either moral excellence in general, as in Eph. v. 9; or kindness—beneficence in particular, as in Gal. v. 22. It seems most natural to understand it here in its most extensive sense. "Knowledge" is to be understood of Christian knowledge; and to be "full of all goodness and all knowledge," is to possess in a high degree Christian excellence, and to have extended and just views of Christian truth. The apostle was of opinion that, by this union of Christian worth and intelligence, the Roman church could, better than many Christian churches, depend on its own internal resources: they were "able to admonish one another." He was "persuaded" of this. He was inclined to think well of all Christians and all Christian churches; but, in their case, he likely had received information—not improbably from Aquila and Priscilla—which had lodged this persuasion in his mind, and made it impossible for him to doubt of the Roman church what he wished true of all churches. It was not, then, the notion that they particularly needed, but the conviction that they were likely to relish and improve, such an Epistle as he was closing, that had induced him to write it to them. He might have addressed them in the words of the Apostle John—"I have not written to you, because ye know not the truth, but because ye know it."[2] Indeed, the Epistle contains in itself abundant evidence that, in the estimation of the writer, they to whom it was addressed were not "babes in Christ," but "men of full age;" not "unskilful in the word of righteousness," but "having their senses exercised to discern both good and evil."[3] In none of his writings does the apostle present more of what may be termed "strong meat;" in none of them does he go deeper into the unfathomable mine of Christian doctrine, or bring up richer treasure. He could pay the heads and hearts of the Roman Christians no higher compliment than by sending them such an Epistle. It was not in Paul's nature to use "flattering words;" but

[1] Ver. 14. [2] 1 John ii. 21. [3] Heb. v. 12–14.

there are occasions on which Christians should be told of the good opinion their instructors have formed of them. It stimulates attention, and encourages exertion, as well as conciliates regard.

In the present state, the most accomplished saint is far from being perfect; and the Roman Christians, though "full of goodness, filled with all knowledge, able also to admonish one another," stood in need of being put in remembrance of the doctrine and of the law of Christ; and, in doing this to them, the apostle was not acting unwarrantably—intruding himself into a place to which he had no right—he was but discharging his duty as the apostle of the Gentiles.

"Nevertheless, brethren, I have written the more boldly unto you in some sort, as putting you in mind, because of the grace that is given to me of God, that I should be the minister of Jesus Christ to the Gentiles, ministering the Gospel of God, that the offering up of the Gentiles might be acceptable, being sanctified by the Holy Ghost."[1] The more "bold speaking" the apostle refers to, may perhaps be found in such passages as chap. vi. 19, in which he says he uses a popular illustration "for the weakness of their flesh;" and chap. vi. 1, where he supposes an objection stated, which could only be brought forward by a person very imperfectly acquainted with the Christian faith. The words, "in some sort"—literally, 'in part,' may either signify, 'in some parts of the Epistle,' or they may somewhat qualify the expression, "more boldly;" or, as Taylor views it, 'in reference to a part of you'—that is, the Gentile part.

In using such freedom, he was not to be considered as acting either an unfriendly or an impertinent part. He was not their enemy, but their friend, in telling them the truth. Nor was he to be viewed as an intruder: he was only discharging a duty imposed on him by their common Lord—performing one of the functions of an office to which he had been divinely called. If he had written to them, and that

[1] Ver. 15, 16

somewhat boldly, it was "because of the grace given him of God, that he should be a minister of Jesus Christ to the Gentiles." He refers to his apostolical commission; and he calls it a "grace," because, notwithstanding all its toils and hazards, he reckoned it no common "grace"—favour bestowed on him, who, in his own estimation, was "less than the least of all saints," "to preach among the Gentiles the unsearchable riches of Christ."

Paul's apostolical commission had a peculiar reference to the Gentiles. The general apostolic commission was, "Go, teach all nations;" "Go into all the world—preach the Gospel to every creature;"[1] but to Paul it was said, "Depart, and go far hence to the Gentiles"—"to whom I now send thee, to open their eyes, and to turn them from darkness to light, and from the power of Satan unto God, that they may receive forgiveness of sins, and inheritance among them which are sanctified by faith that is in Me."[2] In writing, and writing with freedom, to the Roman Christians, though he had never seen them, he was thus doing no more than this commission warranted, and indeed required, him to do.

The nature and design of his ministry among the Gentiles is described in the words which follow: "Ministering the Gospel of God, that the offering up of the Gentiles might be acceptable, being sanctified by the Holy Ghost." The language is figurative; but the meaning is plain. The apostle represents himself as 'acting the part of a priest[3] in reference to the Gospel of Christ;' and, in the exercise of this office, laying on the altar of God the converted Gentiles, as a sacrifice acceptable to God, "being sanctified by the Holy Ghost." In plain language, the design of his apostleship was, that the Gentiles, being converted to the faith of the Gospel through his instrumentality, and by the agency of the Holy Ghost, might devote themselves to God as His peculiar property. There is, probably, here an allusion to Isaiah lxvi. 20. "We

[1] Matt. xxviii. 19; Mark xvi. 15. [2] Acts xxii. 21; xxvi. 18.
[3] ἱερουργοῦντα.

see here the nature of the only priesthood which belongs to the Christian ministry. It is not the office of those who fill it to make atonement for sin—to offer a propitiatory sacrifice to God; but, by the preaching of the Gospel, to bring men, through the influence of the Holy Spirit, to offer themselves as 'a living sacrifice, holy and acceptable to God.'"[1]

The apostle proceeds to state the high estimate he had formed of his office, and the success of his labours in the wide field which had been assigned to him: "I have therefore whereof I may glory through Jesus Christ in those things which pertain to God."[2] These words are equivalent to—'"I magnify my office;" I count it a highly honourable one. Since God has been pleased graciously to make me a minister of Jesus Christ, I have whereof I may glory.' "Those things that pertain to God," is a phrase equivalent to 'religious matters.'[3] 'I may—I do occupy a very humble position in civil society—in matters that pertain merely to man; my place in the Roman Empire is that of a mere citizen; but, in the region of religion, I am an apostle—one of the princes who sit on their thrones "judging the twelve tribes of" the spiritual "Israel."'

"In or through Christ Jesus," may be connected either with "things pertaining to God," in which case the whole phrase is a circumlocution for 'the Christian religion;' or with "I glory," in which case the meaning is, 'It is *through* Christ Jesus that I have obtained *that* in things pertaining to God, in which I glory;' or, 'it is "*in* Christ Jesus"—connected with, united to Him—that I enjoy this office, and glory in it.'

In the discharge of the functions of this honourable office, the apostle had been remarkably successful; and, to conciliate the kind regards of the Roman Christians, he makes them acquainted with his success. "For I will not dare to speak of any of those things which Christ hath not wrought by me, to make the Gentiles obedient, by word and deed, through

[1] Hodge. [2] Ver. 17. [3] Heb. ii. 17; v. 1.

mighty signs and wonders, by the power of the Spirit of God; so that from Jerusalem, and round about unto Illyricum, I have fully preached the Gospel of Christ."[1] Some interpreters consider the apostle as saying—'I will not dare to say anything but what I know to be true, as to the success of the Gospel through my instrumentality—though quite aware I was only the instrument: Christ did the work.' Our translators have rightly rendered the words. They are elliptical: 'I will not dare to speak of those successes of the Gospel in which I have had no hand.' In these Paul rejoiced; but he did not wish the Romans to think of him as having done anything but what he really had accomplished through the help of his Master. "I will not dare to speak of any of those things which Christ hath not wrought by me"—*but I will dare to speak of the things that He has wrought by me*—"to make the Gentiles obedient, in word and deed."

"To make the Gentiles obedient," is to bring them to believe the doctrine and obey the laws of Christ. "Word and deed" have been generally viewed as describing the means by which, through the instrumentality of the apostle, the Gentiles were converted: "word" signifying 'preaching;' "work" signifying 'active exertion.' It seems to me more natural, from the construction of the original (the preposition[2] indicating instrumentality being introduced after the words "word and deed"), to understand the phrase as describing the obedience of the Gentiles: it was obedience "in word"—they made profession of faith in Christ; but it was also obedience "in deed"—they walked in His laws and ordinances." This substantial obedience was brought about "through mighty signs and wonders"—by means of signal miracles, calling the attention to the subject, and attesting the Divine mission of the Christian apostles.[3] "By the power of the Holy Ghost," may refer either to the clause, "to make the Gentiles obedient," or the clause "through mighty signs and wonders." It is true of both, that they were by "the power of the Holy Ghost."

[1] Ver. 18, 19. [2] ἐν. [3] Heb. ii. 4.

In this way, with this success, the apostle had preached the Gospel, not in a few places only, but in a great many—not in one district of country merely, but in many lands, "from Jerusalem round about to Illyricum." The apostle had preached the Gospel in Arabia, lying east from Jerusalem; but he fixes on that city as the eastern term of his labours, from the celebrity of the city, and from the fact that his missionary progress had been chiefly westward; or his labours in the farther east may be intended to be referred to in the phrase, "round about."[1] Illyricum lies on the shores of the Adriatic, beyond Macedonia. It is doubtful if Paul was ever in Illyria. He mentions it as the term of his labours. The distance marked out by the apostle, in a direct line, is more than 1400 miles, and taken by him "round about," in a circle, must have been very much greater. Throughout these wide regions, then, among the most densely peopled in the world, had the apostle, at the date of this epistle, preached the Gospel—"fully preached the Gospel of Christ." The original expression, literally rendered, is "fulfilled."[2] The word occurs with the same meaning in Col. i. 25.

This passage is full of important instruction as to what true conversion to Christianity is, which is materially the same thing in all countries and ages, who is its Author, and by what agency and instrumentality He effects it. (1.) True conversion is "obedience to the truth"—"in *word*," that is, manifested in profession; "in *deed*," that is, proved by conduct corresponding to the profession. (2.) Jesus Christ, by His Holy Spirit, is the Author of conversion. (3.) The grand means of conversion is the exhibition of the truth in its meaning and evidence; and, (4.) The work of ministers in conversion is merely instrumental. They do not convert men; Jesus Christ converts men by them declaring the truth, which the Holy Spirit applies to the mind and heart, thus inducing faith and its native results. All that men can do, is "fully to preach the Gospel of Christ."

[1] κύκλῳ.

[2] πεπληρωκέναι.

The apostle, following out the thought hinted at in the beginning of the 18th verse—his indisposition to take credit to himself for other men's labours, unfolds the principle on which he had hitherto regulated his apostolic labours, a principle which satisfactorily accounts for his not having before this time visited the Roman Church. "Yea, so have I strived to preach the Gospel, not where Christ was named, lest I should build upon another man's foundation: but, as it is written, To whom he was not spoken of, they shall see; and they that have not heard shall understand. For which cause also I have been much hindered from coming to you."[1] The apostle, under the guidance of the Holy Spirit, had usually laboured in regions where no Christian church had been previously planted—*usually*, for it is clear from the Acts of the Apostles that he sometimes both visited and wrote letters to churches of which he was not the founder. He judged the *conversion* of the Gentiles to be his appropriate work, and to that he all but exclusively devoted himself. He left the comparatively easy work of teaching and superintending the converted to others. The apostle, whose mind was overflowing with Old Testament Scripture, quotes from Isaiah, ch. lii. 15, a passage illustrative of his leading object in his apostolical labours—that he might be the means of introducing the true worship of God, through His Son, where previously it was utterly unknown—that in his case, the ancient oracle respecting the Messiah, who after suffering had entered into glory, might be verified: "To whom he was not spoken of, they shall see; and they that have not heard shall understand." The passage is correctly quoted from the Septuagint.

In thus perseveringly following out a wisely-formed and clearly-defined plan of operation, the apostle followed in the steps of his Lord. It would have been well for the Church and for the world, if all Christians, and especially if all Christian ministers, had been in this respect followers of Paul, even as he was of Christ. He only who acts on this principle is

[1] Ver. 20-22.

likely to do *much* good—he who has a plan, a good plan, and who keeps to his plan. But, in order to realize the success which this plan is fitted to secure, he will frequently be obliged to deny himself. He must often give up what may be desirable both to himself and others, just because it would interfere with his fixed plan of operation, and the temporary good is not likely to compensate the evil of introducing irregularity and uncertainty into his plans. This was the course adopted by the apostle. He had long cherished an ardent wish to visit Rome, and confirm the Christian Church formed in that most important station. But so long as, in the regions in which he laboured, he could have access to cities yet unvisited with the light of Christian truth, he considered it his duty to deny himself the satisfaction such a visit was sure to afford him.

"For which cause also I have been much hindered from coming to you."[1] The apostle had already,[2] in very strong terms, expressed his earnest desire to have personal intercourse with his brethren at Rome; and he here assigns the reason why that desire had not yet found accomplishment, and his hope that the long wished-for season of an interview was now at hand. There is no better reason for preferring one course to another than this—inclination draws one way, duty the other.

Having thus apologised to the Romans for what to some of them might appear his undue freedom, and for his delaying so long to visit them, the apostle gives them information respecting his future plans, which were likely ere long to bring them and him together. This forms the subject of the second section.

[1] Ver. 22. [2] Chap. i. 8–15.

SECTION II.

NOTICES OF INTENDED JOURNEYS.

CHAPTER XV. 23–29.—But now having no more place in these parts, and having a great desire these many years to come unto you; whensoever I take my journey into Spain, I will come to you: for I trust to see you in my journey, and to be brought on my way thitherward by you, if first I be somewhat filled with your company. But now I go unto Jerusalem to minister unto the saints. For it hath pleased them of Macedonia and Achaia to make a certain contribution for the poor saints which are at Jerusalem. It hath pleased them verily; and their debtors they are. For if the Gentiles have been made partakers of their spiritual things, their duty is also to minister unto them in carnal things. When therefore I have performed this, and have sealed to them this fruit, I will come by you into Spain. And I am sure that, when I come unto you, I shall come in the fulness of the blessing of the Gospel of Christ.

Some interpreters consider the expression, "having no place in these parts,"[1] as referring to the obstacles put in the way of the apostle's progress by the Jews and the Judaizers. It better harmonizes with the context to consider him as saying, 'There being now no place of importance, no city or town in these regions, in which I have not preached the Gospel.' The peculiar labours he had marked out for himself were finished there; and, like a spiritual Alexander, having made many conquests, he immediately plans more. Following out his principle, he had resolved on a journey into the westermost country in Europe—Spain,[2] where probably the name of Christ had never been heard; and he rejoiced in the thought that, without deviating from his plan, he might soon be able to fulfil his long-cherished desire of visiting the Christians at Rome. Rome was in his way towards Spain. He intimates his entire confidence in their friendship, intimating that he anticipated much pleasure in their society, and telling them he expected to be assisted by them in his missionary enterprize.

[1] Ver. 23. [2] Ver. 24.

He hoped to be "somewhat filled with their company"—refreshed by seeing how holy and happy they were, and that they would furnish him with the means of visiting so remote a country as Spain. There is here a reference to a custom in the primitive times, adverted to in Acts xv. 3; xvii. 14, 15; xx. 38; xxi. 5; 3 John 6, 7. The word "somewhat," marks the delicacy of Paul's mind; he does not say satisfied, but partly satisfied, as if he could never have enough of their society. Paul did come to Rome, but neither at the time, nor in the circumstances, which he here anticipates. He came a prisoner, to have his cause determined before the imperial tribunal: Acts xxvii., xxviii. Some ecclesiastical historians think it probable that, after the first hearing of his cause, he obtained liberty to depart from Rome for a season, and that he availed himself of that opportunity of visiting Spain. But Origen and Eusebius, the oldest authorities in extra-scriptural ecclesiastical history, know nothing of such a journey.

The apostle now states the reason why he did not immediately come to Rome, since he had "no more place in these parts:" "But now I go unto Jerusalem to minister to the saints. For it hath pleased them of Macedonia and Achaia to make a certain contribution for the poor saints that are at Jerusalem. It hath pleased them; and their debtors they are. For if the Gentiles have been made partakers of their spiritual things, their duty is also to minister to them of their carnal things."[1] A large portion of the converts to Christianity in Jerusalem and Judea seem to have been exposed to the "spoiling of their goods," and to have been in circumstances of destitution. They were the proper objects of the liberality of their Gentile brethren, who were placed in happier circumstances. We find the apostles of the circumcision recommending to Paul and Barnabas, the apostles of the uncircumcision, that they "should remember the poor,"—that is plainly, the destitute disciples, in Judea; "which thing," says Paul, "I also was forward to do."[2] In consequence, no doubt, of

[1] Ver 25-27.

[2] Gal. ii. 9, 10.

his recommendation, though he modestly conceals this, the churches of Macedonia had of their free will made a contribution.[1] Of this we have a particular account, 1 Cor. xvi. 1-4; 2 Cor. viii. 1-4; ix. 2.

This contribution is a beautiful display of the genius of Christianity—a proper model for churches in all countries and ages. The apostle hints that, in making this contribution, the Gentile churches might be considered as only paying debt; and very likely meant the Romans to draw the conclusion, that as they were equally indebted to the Jews for their spiritual privileges as the churches of Macedonia and Achaia, they would do well to follow their example. The word "carnal" is an unfortunate rendering,—"temporal," as opposed to "spiritual," expresses the apostle's idea.

It was necessary that this labour of love should be immediately attended to; but the apostle assures the Roman Christians, that as soon as that was accomplished, no time would be lost in his coming to them. "When therefore I have performed this, and have sealed to them this fruit, I will come by you into Spain. And I am sure that when I come to you, I shall come in the fulness of the blessing of the Gospel of Christ."[2] "When I have performed"—that is, completed, finished—"this." It is a matter of great importance to persevere in a good work till it be finished. A great deal of labour is often lost by good, benevolent men, through the forgetting of this. What an amount of fruitless, because half done, work, has the Church and the world to grieve over!

The expression, "sealed this fruit," is rather peculiar. The "fruit," is plainly the Greek contribution—the *fruit* at once of the apostle's labours and of the donors' faith and love. To "*seal*" this fruit, is to secure this contribution—to put the last hand to the good work. "Safely delivered," is probably the idea: 2 Kings xxii. 4. We use the word "consign" in the same way. Paul had pledged himself to this amount to the churches in Greece: 1 Cor. xvi. 3, 4. Ministers ought

[1] κοινωνία. Acts xxiv. 17. [2] Ver. 28, 29.

to be particularly careful in managing pecuniary contributions intrusted to their care, "that the ministry be not blamed." It was Paul's determination "that no man should blame him in the abundance which was administered by him, providing things honest"—honourable—"not only in the sight of the Lord, but also in the sight of men." [1]

When this business was completed, it was Paul's purpose to come by the Romans into Spain. Spain was a country where Christ had not been named, and he *will* come to Rome in order to his getting to Spain. He would not interrupt what he accounted his appropriate work—the laying the foundation of Gentile churches—to visit the already formed and flourishing Church of Rome; but he rejoices that, in the prosecution of his own walk of apostolic labour, he was to have an opportunity of visiting his Roman brethren. The words are merely expressive of intention. Paul was uncertain whether he would ever go to Spain; but it was his purpose to go, and to take Rome in his way. We have no evidence that he ever visited Spain; and when he did come to Rome, it was in circumstances very different from those he now anticipated.

But while the apostle speaks doubtfully of his journey to Spain and his visit to Rome, there is one thing about which he speaks with perfect confidence, and that is, that his visit to the Romans, whenever it took place, would be blessed to their spiritual advantage. "I am sure that, when I come to you, I shall come in the fulness of the blessing of the Gospel of Christ."

"The fulness of the blessing of the Gospel of Christ"—or, as it is in the more approved reading, "the fulness of the Gospel of Christ"—may either signify the blessed fulness of Christ, "the unsearchable riches of Christ," the Gospel message in all the fulness and plainness of its meaning and in all the variety and force of its evidence, or 'the abounding blessing of the Gospel of Christ'—that is, all the heavenly and spiritual blessings that are communicated to men by the Gospel. In the first case, the apostle's meaning is, 'Whenever I come,

[1] 2 Cor. viii. 20.

I am sure that I will lay before you a full and plain statement of the truth as it is in Jesus, and of its evidence; I will "fully preach" to you, as I have done to so many others, the Gospel of Christ.' In the second, the force of the statement is, 'I am fully persuaded that, when I come to you, my ministrations shall be remarkably blessed.' The two things are closely connected. It is only when a minister comes to a people in the first way, that he can be expected to come in the second; and when a minister does come in the blessed fulness of the Gospel, he generally brings along with him the full blessedness of the Gospel: for "the word that goeth forth out of God's mouth shall not return to Him void; but it shall accomplish what He pleases, and it shall prosper in the thing whereunto He sent it."[1] It is the Gospel alone that is the ministration of the Spirit.

SECTION III.

REQUEST FOR AN INTEREST IN THE PRAYERS OF THE ROMAN CHRISTIANS.

CHAPTER XV. 30–33.—Now, I beseech you, brethren, for the Lord Jesus Christ's sake, and for the love of the Spirit, that ye strive together with me in your prayers to God for me; that I may be delivered from them that do not believe in Judea; and that my service which I have for Jerusalem may be accepted of the saints; that I may come unto you with joy by the will of God, and may with you be refreshed. Now the God of peace be with you all. Amen.

The journey which Paul had immediately before him was pregnant with important results, and full of hazards; and he begs the prayers of the Roman Christians, that he might be preserved amidst, and delivered from, these dangers, and that the great objects he had in view might be completely attained. There are here three objects specified, about which the apostle was specially desirous, and which he wished the Roman Christians to make the subject of fervent supplication to God in his behalf.

[1] Isa. lv. 11.

The first is "that he might be delivered from them who did not believe in Judea."[1] These formed the great majority, and they had in their hands both civil and ecclesiastical power. To his unbelieving countrymen, Paul was peculiarly obnoxious. From being one of the ablest and most zealous defenders of Judaism, he had become the ablest and most zealous of its assailants. He who was foremost in opposing Christianity, was now in the very front of the battle in its defence. His liberal opinions respecting the footing of entire equality, on which the New Dispensation treated Jews and Gentiles, seemed to them the worst species of blasphemy. Even in Gentile countries, he had often been exposed to persecution, and involved in danger through their plots and violence. What had he to expect when he went to a country where their influence was so much more extensive and powerful? From what actually occurred when Paul did go to Judea, of which we have a record, Acts xxi.–xxvi., it is plain that he had not overrated his dangers. His enemies repeatedly endeavoured to destroy him in a popular tumult; a party of them bound themselves under a curse to assassinate him; before two successive Roman governors they endeavoured to procure his condemnation; and at last, to free himself from the hazards to which their malignant vigilance exposed him, he found it necessary to carry his cause by appeal to the Imperial tribunal at Rome.

The prospect of such danger could not, however, deter the apostle from going to Judea, when the interests of Christianity called him. He went bound in the Spirit to Jerusalem, not knowing the things that should befall him there; save that the Holy Ghost witnessed in every city, saying, that bonds and afflictions awaited him: "but," says he, "none of these things move me, neither count I my life dear unto myself, so that I might finish my course with joy, and the ministry which I have received of the Lord Jesus."[2] When the disciples at Cesarea, alarmed at the intimations of

[1] Ver. 31. [2] Acts xx. 22–24.

the Prophet Agabus, beseeched him not to go up to Jerusalem, he answered, " What mean ye to weep and break my heart? I am ready not only to be bound, but also to die at Jerusalem for the name of the Lord Jesus."[1]

A second object of desire with Paul was " that his service which he had for Jerusalem might be accepted of the saints."[2] From the nature of the service, it might seem that there was but little danger of its being otherwise than very acceptable; yet, so strong were the prejudices of many of the converted Jews against the uncircumcised Gentile converts, that there was reason to fear that even a pecuniary contribution from such a quarter, and especially coming through such a channel, might excite feelings not very compatible with affectionate gratitude. From the conduct of the elders, on his arrival at Jerusalem, this seems to have been their opinion.[3] It was a favourite object with the wide-minded, large-hearted apostle, to produce a complete amalgamation of the Jewish and Gentile believers —that the Church might be, and might appear to be, " one new man." It was in prosecution of this object that he had been so active in receiving contributions for the " poor saints at Jerusalem" among the Gentile Churches, and his success was a gratifying proof that, so far as the Gentiles were concerned, he had in a good degree gained his end: and nothing surely was better fitted to put down the prejudices of the Jews against the Gentiles, and against himself as the apostle of the Gentiles, than the plan he was now pursuing. This was, according to his own maxim, to seek to " overcome evil with good." It was the obvious tendency of this system to knit together in love the two great component parts of the Christian society which chiefly recommended it to the apostle. " The administration of this service," says he, " not only supplieth the wants of the saints, but is abundant also by many thanksgivings unto God; (while by the experiment of this ministration they glorify God for your professed subjection unto the Gospel of Christ, and for your liberal distribution

[1] Acts xxi. 13. [2] Ver. 31. [3] Acts xxi. 20.

unto them, and unto all men ;) and by their prayers for you, which long after you for the exceeding grace of God in you."[1]

The third object of Paul's desire was "that he might come unto the Romans with joy, by the will of God, and might with them be refreshed."[2] He earnestly wished that he might be brought safe to Rome "by the will of God," subordinating his desire to the Divine will, according to the Apostle James' rule,[3] and that his meeting with the Christians there—his great object in wishing to see the metropolis of the world—might be replete with improvement and comfort to both parties. The three wishes of the apostle were closely connected: the attainment of the objects of the first two was necessary to the attainment of that of the third. If he was not "delivered from them that believed not in Judea," he could not come at all; and if "his service was not acceptable to the saints he could not come with joy."

For the attainment of these desirable objects Paul solicits earnestly the prayers of the Roman Christians. "Now I beseech you, brethren, that you strive with me in your prayers for me."[4] Paul had prayed often and earnestly for the Roman Christians,[5] and he requests them to reciprocate the favour. Christians cannot give each other a better proof of their mutual love than fervent intercession for each other. No man can doubt this who believes the doctrine of the efficacy of believing prayer. Paul is desirous that their prayers should be fervent—"that they should strive"—knowing that, as James says, "it is the effectual fervent prayer of a righteous man which availeth much."[6] And he assures them that *he* would pray along with them. It is absurd to expect that the prayers of others for us are to be answered if we do not pray for ourselves.

The apostle enforces his affectionate request by two very powerful motives. "I beseech you, for the Lord Jesus Christ's sake, and for the love of the Spirit."[7] "I beseech

[1] 2 Cor. ix. 12–14. [2] Ver. 32 [3] James iv. 15. [4] Ver. 30.
[5] Chap. i. 9, 10. [6] James v. 16. [7] Ver. 30.

you, for the Lord Jesus Christ's sake" is equivalent to 'I beseech you, by the regard you have to the Lord Jesus.' The cause of Christ was deeply involved in the safety of the apostle, and in the carrying his plans into accomplishment. Nothing had a more lowering aspect on its success than the continuance of the bitter prejudices between converts from among the Jews and from among the Gentiles. The house divided against itself seemed in danger of falling; and it would have fallen if its builder had not been its upholder. It is as if he had said 'It is more for Christ's sake than my own that I urge this request.' "The love of the Spirit" has been supposed to mean 'the love which the Holy Ghost has to Christians;' and under this view of the phrase Dr M'Crie has given us an interesting and useful discourse on it; but there is no ground to doubt, that the reference is to the peculiar love which Christians have to each other, and that this is termed "the love of the Spirit," either by a Hebraism for spiritual love, in contradistinction to natural affection, or because it is produced in the heart by the operation of "the Spirit" by way of eminence—the Holy Ghost. It is the same thing that the apostle speaks of as "the fellowship of the Spirit" in the Epistle to the Philippians.[1] The two motives may be thus stated 'by the regard you have to Christ, and to me, His servant, I beseech you, deny me not your prayers.'

It is natural to ask how far these objects, for which the apostle was so desirous that the Roman Christians should pray, were gained. The apostle was brought safely to Judea, and very wonderfully preserved amidst, and at last, after two years, delivered from, "them who believed not" there. We have no doubt that, to a considerable extent, "his services were acceptable to the saints;" and we know that, "by the will of God," through extreme perils, he did come to the Roman Christians, "with joy," though in bonds, and "that with them he was refreshed." When the brethren at Rome had heard of the apostle's arrival in Italy, "they came to

[1] Phil. ii. 1.

meet him as far as Appii Forum and The Three Taverns," the one about fifty, the other about thirty miles from the city, and when Paul saw them " he thanked God, and took courage."[1] There is much less said, in the Acts of the Apstles, than we could have expected, or wished, respecting the apostle's intercourse with the Roman Christians. This rises out of the design of the book, which is to give the history of the planting of churches, not of planted churches. We have more said about Paul's intercourse with the unbelieving Jews than with his Christian brethren at Rome; but there can be no reasonable doubt, that there was " a Church" in the hired house in which he " dwelt two whole years," as well as in the house of Aquila and Priscilla, and that there, he not only " preached the kingdom of God" to all inquirers " who came to him," but also " taught the things concerning the Lord Jesus Christ," to them who believed. What would we give for his own illustrations of what is contained in this epistle? He enjoyed a longer stay among them than he likely had anticipated—" imparted to them some spiritual gift"—was " comforted together with them" by their mutual faith[2] —was " somewhat filled with their company" — and was " with them refreshed." The next event in Paul's history, that we are sure of, is " his dying at Rome for the name of the Lord Jesus," probably about six or seven years after the writing of this epistle.

When the apostle requested the prayers of the Roman Christians for himself, he gave them an example to follow by praying for them. " Now the God of peace be with you all. Amen."[3] "The God of peace" may mean the reconciled, the pacified divinity. That I rather think is the meaning of the appellation, Heb. xiii. 20. Here it seems more natural to interpret it on the same principle as the phrases, " the God of patience and consolation,"[4] and " the God of hope."[5] 'May God, the author of peace of reconciliation to Himself—that

[1] Acts xxviii. 15. [2] Chap. i. 11. [3] Ver. 33.
[4] Ver. 5. [5] Ver. 13.

peace which is the fruitful mother of all true peace—peace of mind, peace of conscience, peace of heart, peace with all good beings, and a disposition to be at peace with all beings. May this God, as the Author of peace, be with you all. May He give you constant tokens that He is with you—on your side—near you—supplying all your need, according to His riches and glory. May He "give you peace always by all means."[1]

SECTION IV.

CERTIFICATE TO THE BEARER OF THE EPISTLE.

CHAPTER XVI. 1, 2.—I commend unto you Phebe our sister, which is a servant of the church which is at Cenchrea; that ye receive her in the Lord, as becometh saints, and that ye assist her in whatsoever business she hath need of you: for she hath been a succourer of many, and of myself also."

It is a just remark of Dr Priestley,[2] that "the conclusions of the most of Paul's Epistles, though least valuable as to their direct use, are highly valuable indirectly, and especially as evidence of the truth of Christianity: so many particular persons and circumstances being mentioned, as give them the most unsuspicious appearance of genuine epistles, and exclude all idea of forgery. Indeed, there are no epistles come down to us from ancient times that have such clear evidence of genuineness as these; and, accordingly, it does not appear ever to have been called in question. If this case be considered, it will be found absolutely impossible to admit the genuineness of these epistles, that is, their having been actually written by the Apostle Paul, while he was engaged in preaching the Gospel in the midst of business and so much contention, when all his motions were watched by his enemies and

[1] Chap. xvi. 20; 1 Cor. xiv. 33; 2 Cor. xiii. 11; Phil. iv. 9; 1 Thes. v. 23; 2 Thes. iii. 16.

[2] Notes on all the Scriptures, vol. iv., pp. 334, 335.

false friends, without admitting the truth of the facts which he mentions in them, as at that time known to all, especially the miraculous gift of the Spirit, and such a reception of Christianity in that early period, while the facts were recent and open to every man's examination. And the truth of these imply the truth of Christianity; that is, they necessarily lead to conclude that they were facts admitted by those who were best fitted to examine their truth, and who had every motive for doing it with impartiality — that Christ preached the doctrines ascribed to Him in the Gospel history—that He wrought many miracles in proof of His Divine mission —that He was publicly crucified—and that He actually rose from the dead."

If these concluding paragraphs of the Epistles of Paul are thus greatly corroborative of the Christian evidence, they are also well fitted to illustrate the character of genuine Christianity in the primitive age, as it was exhibited both in the writer and in those to whom his Epistles are addressed. Regarding the Epistle to the Romans as a portrait of the apostle's mind, these paragraphs may be considered as the last softening touches of the artist's pencil, which give harmony and sweetness to the picture. It is impossible to peruse with attention the preceding part of the Epistle, without being impressed with the conviction that Paul was a singularly great and good man; but, had it not been for these concluding remembrances, we could scarcely have imagined that he was so thoroughly amiable a man, and that, while he had a power of intellect, an extent of information, and a purity of principle almost angelic, he had, at the same time, a tenderness of heart and a sensibility of kindness altogether human. On reading the conclusion of the Epistle, assuredly we do not admire him less, but we love him more; and many a fine lesson of Christian kindness, and courtesy, and gratitude, may be learned from a perusal of what, at first sight, may appear little more than a dry list of names of persons of whom we know, and can know, nothing more than that they were the acquaintances and friends of the Apostle Paul.

The sixteenth chapter opens with a recommendation, or what we would call the certificate, of the Christian lady who appears to have been the honoured bearer of the Epistle—Phebe, a deaconess of the church at Cenchrea. "I commend unto you Phebe our sister, which is a servant of the church which is at Cenchrea: that ye receive her in the Lord, as becometh saints, and that ye assist her in whatsoever business she hath need of you: for she hath been a succourer of many, and of myself also."[1] The obviously proper and useful practice of Christians, when removing from one place of residence to another, carrying along with them recommendations[2] from the church with which they had been connected, to the church in the place where they were going to sojourn or to reside, seems to have prevailed from the beginning. We have various examples of this custom on record. When Apollos was disposed to pass from Ephesus into Achaia, "the brethren wrote exhorting the disciples to receive him."[3] Diotrephes is blamed for not duly honouring the commendatory certificates of the apostle;[4] and we find Paul certifying, or recommending, to the churches of Achaia the Macedonian brethren who had been chosen by the churches in that country to accompany him to Jerusalem with their donation for the poor saints.[5] This practice has its origin in the very nature of the case, and is well fitted to express and promote that union which should pervade the whole Church of Christ. The *practice* is founded on a *principle* which has been much lost sight of, namely, that he who is a proper member of any church, may be admitted to the communion of every church; and he who may not be admitted to the communion of every church, ought not to be a member of any church.

Of the good woman whose certificate lies before us, we know little but what it tells us. The name would seem to indicate that she was a converted heathen, not a Jewess—Phœbe being one of the names of the goddess Diana. She is described by the apostle as "our sister." The relations which subsist

[1] Ver. 1, 2.

[2] ἐπιστολαὶ συστατικαί, as the apostle terms them, 2 Cor. iii. 1.

[3] Acts xviii. 27. [4] 3 John 3, 9, 10. [5] 2 Cor. viii. 18–24.

among Christians—from their belief of the same truth, their trust in the same Saviour, their submission to the same Lord —are commonly expressed by the names of the most intimate natural relations. God is their Father, Christ their Elder Brother. Being "children of God through Christ Jesus," all Christian men are brethren, and all Christian women are sisters. Nor are these mere names: as they indicate a real relation, they imply corresponding responsibilities and duties.

But Phebe was not only a Christian, she was an official Christian; she was not only a member, she was an office-bearer in the Christian Church. She was "a servant," or deaconess, "of the church at Cenchrĕæ." Corinth stood on an isthmus, and had two harbours—one looking toward Italy, called Lechæum; the other looking toward Asia, called Cenchrĕæ. In the town built at this port there was a Christian church, of which Phebe was a deaconess. We know that in the primitive Church there were no female preachers. The words of the apostle are express—"I suffer not a woman to speak in the church;"[1] but it seems clear that there were female office-bearers, corresponding to the elders and deacons. The female elders appear to have had the charge of the oversight of the moral behaviour of the female disciples; and their characters and qualifications seem described under the name of the "widows indeed," in 1 Tim. v. 9, 10. The female deacons officiated at the baptism of females, and had the charge of the poor and afflicted female disciples. Of these, I apprehend, the apostle speaks, 1 Tim. iii. 8, where the word translated "wives" should have been rendered "women-deacons"—deaconesses. These female office-bearers continued for a considerable time in the Christian Church. We find them mentioned in the earliest uninspired Christian writings; and in the letter of Pliny to the Emperor Trajan, acquainting him with the manner in which he dealt with the Christians, he says, "I thought it necessary to seek the truth by applying the torture to two females, who were called ministers or

[1] 1 Tim. ii. 12.

deaconesses." From the peculiar state of society in the East, where anything like familiarity between the two sexes, unless intimately related, was considered disgraceful, some institution of this kind was necessary in the Christian Church, for superintending the morals and relieving the wants of the female disciples.[1]

Whether Christian churches in the West, where the same necessity did not exist, acted wisely or warrantably in allowing the institution to go into desuetude, and whether important ends might not be served by its revival, are questions which I do not feel myself called on here to consider. It seems very obvious, however, that Christian females, whether formally invested with office or not—with or without the name of deaconesses—might, when called on by their pastors and elders, without at all going out of their own appropriate sphere, "help" them—aye, help them much, in the Lord.

This Christian deaconess is recommended to the Roman Christians for admission to fellowship with them in church privileges, while resident in their city, and their assistance asked for her in the management of the business which had brought her to Rome. "I commend to you Phebe—that ye receive her in the Lord"—as "in the Lord"[2]—as a Christian —"as becometh saints;" that is, 'as it becomes saints to receive a saint'—as it becomes those who are "not of the world, but chosen out of the world"—separated from the world, to receive one of the same distinctive character—with much affectionate esteem, and respectful kindness—with a disposition to promote her spiritual improvement—in a way worthy of her Christian excellence, and of your Christian hospitality.

But, beside free admission to all the privileges of church fellowship, the apostle requested for Phebe assistance in the management of her secular business: "And that ye assist her in whatsoever business she hath need of you."[3]

What that business was we know not. It is to no purpose

[1] See Suicer, Bingham, Coleman.

[2] 1 Cor. xii. 27; Rom. xii. 5; 1 Cor. x. 17; Eph. i. 22, 23; iv. 12; v. 30; Col. i. 24.

[3] Ver. 2.

for one interpreter to say, that Phebe came to Rome to seek the payment of debts due to her; or another, to complain of undue exactions on the part of under-officers of government; or another, to manage a law-suit. It may have been any or none of these. What is of more importance to remark is, that this passage teaches us that, though the connection between Christians be of a spiritual kind, it should influence their conduct generally, and lead them, on the ground of their being Christians, to endeavour to promote one another's secular interests.

The apostle enforces his recommendation of Phebe, by stating the services she had done himself and other Christians: "For she hath been a succourer of many, and of myself also." The word "succourer"[1] properly signifies 'patroness'—a person who, in the Grecian States, undertook the care of a stranger, and became responsible for his behaviour to the civil authorities. This, and no doubt other good offices, had been performed to Paul and many other Christians by Phebe, who appears to have been a person of considerable property and rank—one of the "not many noble that were called"—or at any rate, one of "the honourable women" spoken of in the Acts of the Apostles.[2]

SECTION V.

SALUTATIONS FROM THE APOSTLE TO CHRISTIANS AT ROME.

CHAPTER XVI. 3–16.—"Greet Priscilla and Aquila my helpers in Christ Jesus; (who have for my life laid down their own necks: unto whom not only I give thanks, but also all the churches of the Gentiles.) Likewise greet the church that is in their house. Salute my well-beloved Epenetus, who is the first-fruits of Achaia unto Christ. Greet Mary, who bestowed much labour on us. Salute Andronicus and Junia, my kinsmen, and my fellow-prisoners, who are of note among the apostles, who also were in Christ before me. Greet Amplias, my beloved in the Lord. Salute Urbane, our helper in Christ, and Stachys my beloved. Salute

[1] προστάτις.

[2] 1 Cor. i. 26; Acts xvii 12

Apelles, approved in Christ. Salute them which are of Aristobulus' household. Salute Herodion my kinsman. Greet them that be of the household of Narcissus, which are in the Lord. Salute Tryphena and Tryphosa, who labour in the Lord. Salute the beloved Persis, which laboured much in the Lord. Salute Rufus, chosen in the Lord, and his mother and mine. Salute Asyncritus, Phlegon, Hermas, Patrobas, Hermes, and the brethren which are with them. Salute Philologus, and Julia, Nereus, and his sister, and Olympas, and all the saints which are with them. Salute one another with an holy kiss. The churches of Christ salute you."

It may serve a good purpose to make a few remarks, in addition to those already casually thrown out, tending to explain the reason why such a catalogue of obscure names as lies before us should find a place in what was intended to be a universal and permanent revelation of the Divine will as to faith and manners. It is obvious to remark, that if the mentioning by name such members of the Roman church as the apostle personally knew, was fitted to answer a good end to that church, for whose advantage the Epistle was primarily intended, that was a sufficient reason why it should be done, though no advantage were to be derived from it in other countries or following ages. Now, such a series of kind remembrances was plainly fitted to knit more closely the bands of Christian love between the apostle and the persons noticed, between him and the church to which they belonged, and even between him and those members of that church that were yet personally unacquainted with him. To the person noticed it must have been a source of gratification, and a stimulus to improvement; while, by elevating them in the estimation of their brethren, it enlarged their sphere of useful influence. It must have been felt by all as a compliment to the church, and have called forth kindly feelings from all toward the apostle.

But, such a passage as that now before us is useful for all time—in all places. It strongly corroborates the evidence of the genuineness of the Epistle. It could not have occurred to a forger to have introduced such a train of salutations, especially as the Epistle proceeds on the supposition that the apostle had never been at Rome. It serves also another very important purpose, in presenting a very lovely picture of living Christianity, both in the writer of the Epistle and in those to whom he sends his greetings. We see how well the principles of that religion harmonize with, and draw forth all that is amiable and tender in the human constitution—how consistent a deep knowledge of Christianity, and ardent zeal for its progress, are with the dignified proprieties of an advanced state of civilisation, and the gentle charities and graceful delicacies of the most refined friendship. He who considers these things, will find no difficulty in coming to the conclusion that this paragraph is not an exception from, but a striking illustration of, the principle that "*all* Scripture is profitable."

This also seems the right place to say a word or two on a question which naturally suggests itself to an intelligent reader of the Epistle. How came Paul to mention by name so many members of the church of Rome, when he had never been in that city; and how came he to be so intimate with them, as his language indicates he was? Some suppose that Aquila and Priscilla, who had lately come from Italy, with whom he lived and laboured so long in Corinth,[1] had given much particular information respecting the members of the Roman church. This is very likely; but it will but imperfectly explain the fact in question. The true account of it seems to be this:—Rome was at that time the metropolis of the known world. There was a constant influx of persons, from all quarters of the empire, to that city. Paul had now, for nearly thirty years, been engaged in propagating Christianity in various parts of the dominions of the imperial power; and it is not at all wonderful that many of his acquaintances and converts should have taken up their residence in the capital. A man who, for thirty years, had travelled and mixed with society throughout the counties and leading cities and towns of England and Scotland, on visiting London for the first

[1] Acts xviii. 2, 3, 11.

time after that period, would be likely to find himself in the midst of friends. Besides the ordinary reasons which make men leave the provinces for the metropolis, a peculiar cause was in operation in drawing Christians to Rome. Till the imperial power became persecuting, which was not for some time after the writing of this Epistle, Christians seem to have been safer at Rome than anywhere else.

The apostle places first, in the class of those to whom he wished his kind Christian greetings conveyed, a worthy pair, well entitled to such a mark of his peculiar regard. "Greet Priscilla and Aquila, my helpers in Christ Jesus, who have for my life laid down their own necks, to whom not only I give thanks, but also all the churches of the Gentiles."[1] The word rendered "greet" is the same that in the other parts of the paragraph is translated "salute." Its literal and proper signification is 'embrace.' It is here equivalent to, 'Express my peculiar affection and regard to them.' Aquila was a Jew by descent, and a Pontian by nation. In the prosecution of his business as a tent-maker, or worker in leather, he had gone to Rome; but on the edict of the Emperor Claudius, banishing all Jews from the metropolis, in consequence of an insurrection raised by some of that nation, he and his wife Prisca, or Priscilla, removed to Corinth.[2] In this city Paul first met with them, and "because they were of the same craft" (for according to the Jewish custom, Paul, though devoted to letters, had acquired a mechanical art by which he could support himself), he took up his residence with them, and seems to have dwelt in the same house, and worked at the same occupation with them, for eighteen months. Whether Aquila and his wife were Christians before meeting with the apostle, or whether they were among "the much people in that city," with the prospect of converting whom, the Lord encouraged Paul in a vision,[3] we cannot say with certainty, though we lean to the former opinion. After remaining a

[1] Ver. 3, 4. [2] Acts xviii. 1-4. [3] Acts xviii. 10.

year and a half in Corinth, Paul went to Ephesus, and his worthy host and hostess accompanied him. It was there that they had the great honour and happiness of instructing the eloquent Apollos "in the way of the Lord more perfectly;"[1] and it seems likely that they there fixed their abode. They were there when Paul wrote his first Epistle to the Corinthians, and they were there, too, many years later, when he wrote his second Epistle to Timothy.[2] In the meantime, however, it would seem that, on the edict of Claudius being repealed, or falling into desuetude, they had returned to Rome and resided there for some time, and that the apostle had been informed of this when he wrote this epistle at Corinth.

These excellent persons Paul terms "his helpers in Christ," that is, his Christian helpers—his assistants in every way in which Christians, and only Christians, can assist each other, in the way in which Christians in private life can and ought to assist the ministers of Christ.

But they not only laboured along with the apostle,—they exposed themselves to great danger in order to secure his safety. That is the meaning of the expression, "Who for my life laid down their own necks." The event or events referred to must have taken place at Corinth or at Ephesus. In both places, it is likely Aquila and Priscilla were exposed to great danger—it is certain Paul was.[3] The kindness of Aquila and Priscilla had made a deep impression on Paul's heart. Years had elapsed since this occurrence, but his gratitude is as fresh and lively as if it had happened yesterday. "To whom not only I give thanks, but all the churches of the Gentiles." In protecting Paul, Aquila and Priscilla did a great public service. The life of an able, active, devoted minister of Christ Jesus, is the most valuable of all public property, and whoever protects it, when in hazard, deserves public thanks.

The apostle adds, "Likewise salute the church that is in their house."[4] The most learned interpreters are divided in

[1] Acts xviii. 24-28.
[2] 1 Cor. xvi. 19; 2 Tim. iv. 19.
[3] Acts xviii. 12-17; xix. 30-35.
[4] Ver. 5.

their opinion respecting the meaning and reference of this phrase. Some have supposed that it intimates that all the members of the family of Aquila and Priscilla were Christians —'the church in their family.' This interpretation is made somewhat probable from the circumstance of the same phrase being used of this worthy pair when at Ephesus,[1] and from its being followed by some of the more judicious of the Greek fathers. At the same time, it appears to me more probable that the phrase expresses the fact, that small bands of Christians met in private houses to observe Christian ordinances, since in the primitive times it was not everywhere they durst assemble in numbers; and if this were, as is probable, the case in Rome at this time, who so likely to open their house for such a purpose as Aquila and Priscilla? There is confirmation given to this view, and a pleasing light shed over the expression, by a passage which Neander quotes from Ruinart's "Acta Martyr." Art. *Justin:* "The Roman prefect Rusticus asked of Justin, 'Where do you Christians assemble?' The martyr replied, 'Where each one can and will. You believe, no doubt, that we all meet together in one place; but it is not so, for the God of the Christians is not shut up in a room, but, being invisible, He fills both heaven and earth, and is honoured everywhere by the faithful.'" Justin adds, that when he came to Rome, he "was accustomed to dwell in one particular spot, and those Christians that were instructed by him, and wished to hear his discourse, assembled at his house."—"He had not visited any other congregations of the Church." The assembly referred to would naturally be called, 'the church which is in Justin's house.'[2]

"Salute my well-beloved Epenetus, who is the first-fruits of Achaia to Christ."[3] To be the "first-fruits" of a country "to Christ," is to be the first person or persons in that country converted to Christianity. The statement that "Epenetus was the first-fruits of Achaia" may seem inconsistent with that made 1 Cor. xvi. 15, where "Stephanas' house," or

[1] 1 Cor. xvi. 19. [2] ἡ κατ' οἶκον τοῦ Ἰουστίνου ἐκκλησία. [3] Ver. 5.

family, receives the same appellation. Some MSS. read Asia instead of Achaia; but, though the latter were undoubtedly the true reading, yet Epenetus may, for ought we know, have been of this honoured household; and though he were not, both he and they might have been among the early converts to whom the figurative expression, "the first-fruits," refer. As the commencement of an abundant harvest, Epenetus' conversion must have been recollected by the apostle with peculiar pleasure, and no wonder he calls him "beloved." Few ties are so tender as those which bind the human instrument of conversion to him whose soul he has saved from death, and whose multitude of sins he has covered.

"Salute Mary, who has bestowed much labour on us."[1] This seems to have been a woman, like Lydia of Thyatira, "whose heart the Lord had opened." She had had it in her power to do good offices to the apostle and his companions, and good offices which cost her much labour. Of her it may be said, as of another Mary, "Wheresoever this Gospel shall be preached in the whole world, there shall also this that this woman has done be told for a memorial of her."[2] Was not Mary richly rewarded for all her "much labour?"

"Salute Andronicus and Junia, my kinsmen, and my fellow-prisoners, who are of note among the apostles, who also were in Christ before me."[3] Junias, or Junia, may be the name either of a man or of a woman. From the circumstance of fellowship in imprisonment, and notoriety among the apostles, being predicated of both Andronicus and Junia, it seems likely that they were both distinguished Christian teachers. They were the apostle's "kinsmen," possibly in the sense of his relatives—more likely in the sense of his countrymen, "his kinsmen according to the flesh." These men were triply dear to the apostle—in the flesh, in the Lord, and in the fellowship of suffering for Christ. They were also "of note among the apostles." Not that they were apostles, as some interpreters strangely hold, but that they were highly es-

[1] Ver. 6. [2] Matt. xxvi. 13. [3] Ver. 7.

teemed among the apostles. It is a probable conjecture, though nothing more, that they may have been among the devout persons from Rome who were present at Jerusalem when the Pentecostal effusion of the Holy Ghost took place,[1] who witnessed the wonders of that scene, and were converted, among so many more, by the preaching of Peter; and that by their means the knowledge of Christianity was first brought to Rome. In this case, we see the wisdom of Paul in noticing these circumstances, in order to confirm and strengthen the regard of the Roman Church to these teachers. Those respected by the apostles should surely be revered by the brethren. He adds, "Who were also in Christ before me." This remark gives additional probability to the conjecture just referred to. How ready is Paul to acknowledge any kind of precedency! He seems to have had a strong habitual wish to fix both his own attention and that of others on the circumstances of his conversion. And no wonder. He could not think of it without finding in it an exhaustless source of powerful motive to humility, gratitude, and activity; they could not think of it without seeing in it a striking proof of the truth of their religion, and of the power and grace of their Saviour. 'When they were "in Christ," I was exceedingly mad against Him, and breathing out slaughter and threatenings against His followers.'

"Salute Amplias, my beloved in the Lord. Salute Urban, our helper in Christ, and Stachys, my beloved."[2] Of "Amplias and Stachys," nothing more is known than that they were "beloved in the Lord" by the apostle; they were the objects of his high Christian esteem and love. There is a day coming when it will be seen that to have been the friend of a Christian apostle was really a higher honour than to be the favourite of a Roman emperor, and when the eulogiums of historians and poets, procured by a lavish expenditure of labour and suffering, would be gladly exchanged for the simple record that Paul loved them because they loved Christ.

[1] Acts ii. 10. [2] Ver. 8, 9.

"Urban" is described as Paul's "helper in Christ"—his assistant in his great work of Christianizing the Gentile world. He probably was an evangelist, then resident at Rome. The most accomplished Christian ministers need helpers in their work. Paul was the better of Urban, and men like Urban; and the most accomplished minister should, like Paul, be ready to accept and acknowledge the services of the humblest of his helpers.

"Salute Apelles, approved in the Lord. Salute them that are of Aristobulus' household."[1] "Apelles" is described as "approved in the Lord"—that is, a tried Christian; one who has been tried, and who has stood the trial. "Tribulation," says the apostle,[2] "worketh patience"—that is, perseverance, and this perseverance "worketh experience"—that is, trial; it proves the individual; it is the test of the reality and strength of his faith; and if he abides the test, he is an approved Christian. Many—alas! how many—do not stand the test, and prove themselves "reprobates,"—unapproved either of God or man. Tried Christians deserve to be honoured.

It deserves notice that the apostle does not send his Christian remembrances to the next person named—"Aristobulus," but to his household. Perhaps he was dead; perhaps he was not a Christian. A Christian man may not have a Christian household. The elders must have "faithful children," else they should not be chosen to their office;[3] but a member of the Christian Church may have nothing but unbelieving children, and a family may be all Christians with the exception of its head. It is not improbable that Aristobulus might be a Greek of rank residing at Rome, some of whose household, children, or slaves, may have been converted by Paul. It is a happy thing when the whole of a family is Christian, not in name merely, but in deed and in truth; when, as in the case of Lydia and of the gaoler of Philippi, "salvation comes" not only to the heads of the family, but "to all their house."[4] It is not always so; and when it is not so, Christians in un-

[1] Ver. 10. [2] Chap. v. 3, 4. [3] Tit. i. 6. [4] Acts xvi 15, 31, 34.

christian families have a peculiar claim on the kind notice of Christian ministers.

"Salute Herodion, my kinsman. Greet them that be of Narcissus' household, who are in the Lord."[1] Herodion is a name derived from Herod, and probably indicates that the person referred to was somehow or other connected with the Herod family. We know that a man very closely connected with that family, being Herod the tetrarch's foster-brother, Manaen, stood in very peculiar relations to the apostle, being one of the prophets and teachers at Antioch, who, by the appointment of the Holy Ghost, separated Saul and Barnabas to the work to which they were called among the Gentiles.[2] It is very likely that Manaen had the surname of Herodion; but, had he been the person referred to, we cannot think that the apostle would have passed him over with so slight a notice.

As in the case of Aristobulus, the salutation is not sent to Narcissus, but to those of his household, and apparently not to all his household, but to that part of it only which was composed of Christians. The meaning, though not very distinctly given in our version, probably is, 'Offer my Christian remembrances to such of the household of Narcissus as are Christians.' It is not at all impossible that the Narcissus here mentioned was the favourite freedman of the Emperor Claudius, of whom Suetonius speaks in his lives of the Cæsars—a very rich, but a very wicked man. Very good men may be domestics in the families of very bad men. Obadiah, who "feared the Lord from his youth," and "feared Him greatly," was the steward of Ahab, one of the worst of the Israelitish kings.[3] A venerable countryman of our own occupied a confidential place in the household of one of the most dissolute of our princes, and might, sixty or seventy years ago, be found at midnight, and after it, in his little chamber, reading Marshall on *Sanctification*, or Boston's *Crook in the Lot*, while waiting the return of his master and his companions from their midnight revels.

[1] Ver. 11. [2] Acts xiii. 1. [3] 1 Kings xviii. 3, 12.

Christians do not act like themselves when they place themselves in ungodly families; but, as in the cases referred to, they may be obviously placed there by Providence, and when they are so, they have peculiar opportunities for "adorning the doctrine of God our Saviour," and "holding forth the word of life," and are specially entitled to kind notice from their minister.

"Salute Tryphena and Tryphosa, who labour in the Lord. Salute the beloved Persis, who laboured much in the Lord."[1] "Tryphena and Tryphosa" are the names of two Christian women who had sustained evil and suffering (for such is the import of the word "labour"[2]) in the cause of Christ. Persons to whom it has been "given not only to believe in the Lord Jesus, but also to suffer for His sake,"[3] deserve in no ordinary degree the esteem and love of their fellow-Christians. We are to give "honour to whom honour is due;" and it is honour "to be counted worthy to suffer" shame, or loss, or death "for His sake;"[4] and we are to give it in the degree in which it is due. Paul bestows a mark of respect on Tryphena and Tryphosa, who laboured in the Lord; but he bestows a higher token of esteem on Persis, a Christian woman who had "laboured much in the Lord." From the name, it seems likely that Persis either was a slave or had been in servitude, and was of Persian origin. At a very early period, the primitive Church began to resemble the Celestial Church as a "great multitude," out of almost "every country, and people, and tongue, and nation."[5] This Christian woman seems to have been very amiable and much loved. There are some Christians distinguished by the loveliness of their character; and such persons, whatever station they fill, are a credit to their religion, and a delight to their Christian connections. This "Persis, the beloved," had laboured much in the Christian cause. Female disciples have often been the most active promoters of the Christian cause, and the most patient suf-

[1] Ver. 12. [2] κοπιώσας. [3] Phil. i. 29.
[4] Acts v. 41. [5] Rev. vii. 9.

ferers on its account; and, however humble their rank, such are "to be held in reputation."

"Salute Rufus, chosen in the Lord, and his mother and mine."[1] Rufus, here mentioned, may perhaps be the same person who is spoken of in Mark xv. 21 as the brother of Alexander, and the son of Simon, the Cyrenian, who had the high, though painful, honour of assisting his Lord to bear the cross to Calvary. He is described as "chosen in the Lord,"—a choice Christian. They seem to have been an excellent family. The influence of the father's singular connection with the Saviour affected his household. His wife is mentioned in a way which shows how strong a hold she had on the Christian affection of the apostle. On mentioning her name, and her relation to the worthy Rufus—"his mother," the kind offices he himself had received from the good woman presented themselves so vividly to his mind, that in the ardour of affection, with a beautiful mixture of delicacy and tenderness, he adds, "and mine"—'My mother by kindness, as well as Rufus' mother by natural relation.' Nothing can be finer than this, except, what far transcends it, the voice from the cross, "Woman, behold thy Son!"—"Behold thy mother!"[2]

"Salute Asyncritus, Phlegon, Hermas, Patrobas, Hermes, and the brethren that are with them. Salute Philologus, and Julia, Nereus and his sister, and Olympas, and all the saints that are with them."[3] Of Asyncritus, Phlegon, Patrobas, and Hermes, we know nothing. Eusebius states, though it is difficult to reconcile the statement with chronology, that the Hermas here mentioned is the author of the small work called *The Shepherd*, still extant,—one of the earliest of uninspired Christian writings. From his work, he appears to have been a pious, but a very weak man. It is in no ordinary degree edifying to see so gigantic a mind as Paul's noticing kindly so feeble a spirit as Hermas. "The saints that are with them," seems equivalent in meaning to "the church

[1] Ver. 13. [2] John xix. 25-27. [3] Ver. 14, 15.

which is in their house." In the list of names in the 15th verse, there is nothing that seems to require to be noticed.

It deserves to be remarked, that a very considerable number of the persons here named are females, and that they are represented as having been very active and useful in promoting the cause of Christ. The female sex owe very much to the Gospel, and in its early age they seem to have been sensibly alive to their obligations. They have of necessity powerful and extensive influence in society, and it is right that it should be exerted in behalf of Christ and of Christianity. To do this in the most effectual way, it is by no means necessary that they should go out of the sphere within which it is plainly the will of God they should ordinarily move—the domestic one. Indeed, generally speaking, it is only in their appropriate sphere that their exertions are likely to do much good. In the cases in which they have left it, however pure their intentions may have been, the result of the experiment has not usually been such as to make it desirable that it should be repeated, or that the practice should become general.

The apostle concludes his salutations by exhorting the Christians at Rome to "salute one another with a holy kiss,"[1] and by assuring them that the churches, in the district where he then was, cherished towards them all Christian regard. "The churches of Christ salute you." These words may be considered, generally, as an exhortation to mutual love, and to all proper manifestations of it; and it is in this general sense that they are undoubtedly applicable to all Christian churches, in all countries and in all ages. But there is no reason to doubt that the apostle meant that the Roman Christians should comply with the injunction, in the plain, literal acceptations of the terms.

Salutation by kissing was the ordinary way of expressing friendly affection in those countries, just as shaking hands is in ours; and the command is not more strange than if the

[1] Ver. 16.

apostle, addressing himself to a Christian church in our country and times, were to say, 'Give each other the right hand of fellowship; let there be a cordial shaking of hands.' We find similar exhortations given to other churches: 1 Thess. v. 26; 1 Cor. xvi. 20; 2 Cor. xiii. 12; 1 Pet. v. 14. That the apostle meant that the Roman Church, at all their meetings for public worship, should thus express their mutual affection, is by no means improbable. That he meant to make this an ordinance for all succeeding time in the Church catholic, though it has sometimes been asserted, cannot be proved, and does not appear to me to be at all probable. But that the practice prevailed extensively, if not universally, in the earlier ages, seems certain. "After the prayers," says Justin Martyr, giving an account in his *Apology*[1] of the customs of the Christians,—"After the prayers, we embrace each other with a kiss." Tertullian[2] speaks of it as a piece of the ordinary service of the Lord's day; and in the *Apostolical Constitutions*, as they are termed, the manner in which the salutation was performed is particularly described: "Then let the men apart, and the women apart, salute each other with a kiss in the Lord."[3] Origen's note on the verse is, "From this passage the custom was delivered to the churches, that, after prayers, the brethren should salute one another with a kiss." This token of love was usual at the administration of the Lord's Supper. Suicer, Bingham, and Coleman may be consulted for further information. It was probably on this custom that the calumnies of the heathen, respecting the licentious practices of the first Christians at their meetings for worship, were founded; and it is not unlikely that, to take away all occasion for such slanderous imputations, the practice, though in itself innocent and becoming, having, through the misconstruction of the heathen, become not for the use of edifying, was discontinued.

Some small sections of the Christian Church still follow the original custom, and even insist on it as a term of communion.

[1] xi. 85. [2] *De Orat.*, c. 14. [3] ii. 57; viii. 7.

There is nothing wrong in the first of these practices: there is something very decidedly wrong in the second. Surely this is not one of the things about which the peace of the Church is to be disturbed, or her union broken. They who observe this custom should not condemn those who observe it not, and they who do not observe it should not despise those who do observe it.[1] In both cases, if they are conscientious, they will be accepted of the Lord. The essential matter is the cultivation of mutual love. The mode of expressing it is a matter of something less than even secondary importance, unless it can be proved, and I think it cannot, to have been fixed by apostolical authority for the Church catholic in all ages. The custom is in itself, as Stuart says, a 'res loci et temporis'—a thing of time and place, like the wearing or the not wearing of long hair at Corinth. Wilson, in his curious *Dialogue Commentary*, says, in his quaint way, "The kiss is called *holy*, to distinguish it from the wanton, and the adulatory, and the proditory, and the dissimulatory kiss."

"The churches of Christ salute you." 'The churches in this district cherish for you a kind regard; and, knowing that I am writing to you, request me to express their affectionate wishes for your welfare.' Distant churches should maintain, so far as it is possible, intercourse with each other. They are all members of the same body—children of the same family. The unchristian introduction of separate communions has in a great measure broken up this intercourse, by destroying the feelings in which it naturally originates. An Episcopalian Christian, in England, is in danger of feeling as if he had as little connection with a Presbyterian, or Congregational Church, in Scotland, as with a set of Mohammedans or Pagans.

How amiable and how powerful a thing is true Christianity when it is allowed to develop itself! How does it mollify and enlarge the heart! How happy would mankind be if they were all Christians! They would be a band of brothers.

[1] Chap. xiv. 3.

And how good a thing it would be, and how becoming well, for such a band of brothers to dwell together in unity! How happy would the Church be if all her members were such as those whose names are here chronicled, and especially if all her ministers were men of the same enlarged minds, and generous spirits, and affectionate hearts, as the apostle Paul! The residue of the Spirit of light and love, of purity and peace, is with the Lord. May He shed it forth abundantly on a divided Church, and make His people to appear to each other and to the world—one body, animated by one spirit.[1]

[1] The signs of the time, in this respect, are decidedly favourable. There are working, widely and powerfully, throughout Christian churches of almost every name, the yearnings of that brotherly affection towards all who know the truth and love the Saviour, of which every new creature becomes the subject. The tendency of the God-inspired, elective affinities of genuine Christianity to rise superior to the separating power of artificial, men-made divisions, both of mind and heart, is daily becoming stronger. These interior movements of the Christian body are obtaining a voice; and, we believe, that voice will become, notwithstanding every attempt to suppress it, more distinct, more loud, more extended. A movement towards union among Christians, based on the faith of the truth, cemented by the love of the Saviour, is sure, sooner or later, to be triumphant. The prayer will be answered, "That they all may be one in the Father and the Son, that the world may know that the Son has indeed been sent of the Father."—John xvii. 21. "Him the Father heareth always." He keepeth covenant for ever—His word cannot fail. "I will surely assemble, O Jacob, all of thee; I will surely gather the remnant of Israel. . . . The breaker is come up before them: they have broken up, and passed through the gate, and are gone out by it; and their King shall pass before them, and the Lord on the head of them."—Micah ii. 12, 13. "Thou shalt arise, and have mercy upon Zion: for the time to favour her, yea, the set time is come. For thy servants take pleasure in her stones, and favour the dust thereof. So the heathen shall fear the name of the Lord, and all the kings of the earth thy glory. When the Lord shall build up Zion, He shall appear in His glory. He will regard the prayer of the destitute, and will not despise their prayer. This shall be written for the generation to come: and the people which shall be created shall praise the Lord."—Psa. cii. 13–18. Instead of being exceedingly grieved, or grieved at all, when we see men

SECTION VI.

CAUTIONS AGAINST DISSENSION AND DIVISION.

CHAPTER XVI. 17–20.—" Now, I beseech you, brethren, mark them which cause divisions and offences, contrary to the doctrine which ye have learned; and avoid them. For they that are such serve not our Lord Jesus Christ, but their own belly; and by good words and fair speeches deceive the hearts of the simple. For your obedience is come abroad unto all men. I am glad therefore on your behalf: but yet I would have you wise unto that which is good, and simple concerning evil. And the God of peace shall bruise Satan under your feet shortly. The grace of our Lord Jesus Christ be with you. Amen."

In the Roman Church, difference of opinion respecting "meats and days" was producing uneasiness, and threatening

come to seek the welfare of the children of Israel (Neh. ii. 10), it becomes us cordially to rejoice and say, " Blessed are the peacemakers; for they shall be called the children of God."—Matt. v. 9. Let us cast in our lot with them. Let us " love the truth and the peace."—Zech. viii. 19. Let us " seek the things that make for peace, and by which we may edify one another." Let us pray that wide-minded, large-hearted lovers equally of truth and peace—like the apostle Paul, who would not have hesitated to call an angel from heaven anathema if he had preached another gospel, and who would not eat flesh while the world stood if it made a brother offend—may, by the Great Head of the Church, be raised up to impel and guide the every-day increasing mass of intellect and affection disposed to Christian union on scriptural principles. " May the Spirit be poured upon us from on high;" and may *He* direct the way of His people, seeking peace in righteousness. Then " the work of righteousness shall be peace; and the effect of righteousness, quietness and assurance for ever. And God's people shall dwell in a peaceable habitation, and in sure dwellings, and in quiet resting-places, when it shall hail, coming down on the forest; and the city," that great city, " shall be low in a low place." Meanwhile, " Blessed are ye that sow beside all waters, that send forth thither the feet of the ox and the ass."—Isa. xxxii. 15–20. " Pray for the peace of Jerusalem: they shall prosper that love thee. Peace be within thy walls, and prosperity within thy palaces. For my brethren and companions' sakes, I will now say, Peace be within thee. Because of the house of the Lord our God I will seek thy good."—Psa. cxxii. 6–9.

to create and aggravate an alienation of affection, which naturally tended towards ecclesiastical disruption. To prevent this, is the object which the apostle prosecutes so earnestly in the fourteenth and fifteenth chapters—forming the last section of the Practical part of the Epistle. But the subject lay very near his heart. He was so much impressed with the disastrous consequences which must result from these heart-burnings, jealousies, contempts, and condemnations running their course, that, in the conclusion, he reverts to it, and in the most affectionate manner warns them against those who, for their own selfish purposes, busily employed themselves in sowing the seeds of dissension among the churches.

"Now, I beseech you, brethren, mark them which cause divisions and offences, contrary to the doctrine which ye have learned; and avoid them."[1] The word translated "divisions,"[2] properly signifies 'factions'—parties opposed to each other in the same society; and the word rendered "offences,"[3] literally signifies 'stumblingblocks'—occasions of falling, referring to the effect which the practices the apostle refers to were likely to have both on those within and those without the pale of the Church. Those "who cause divisions and offences," are not those who, being fully persuaded in their own mind, make no secret of their views of any subject connected with the faith, and who endeavour, in the spirit of meekness, to support their own views by fair argument. Free discussion of this kind, among the members of the Church, is one of the best means of producing union, and preventing division; and, instead of proving a stumblingblock to the world, is fitted to remove its prejudices against Christianity, as a system which fetters men's minds, and seals their mouths. But those cause "divisions and offences" who, entertaining, however conscientiously, particular views on subjects of secondary importance, are not satisfied with stating and defending them, but elevate them into matters of primary consequence, wish to press them on their fellow-Christians as

[1] Ver. 17. [2] διχοστασίας. [3] σκάνδαλα.

terms of communion, and, if they cannot succeed, use their influence to create factions in the Church, or to form a distinct communion. Such was the conduct of the Judaizers, to whom the apostle seems here to have a reference.[1]

These "divisions and offences" are said to be "contrary to the doctrine" which the Roman Church had learned. The doctrine they had learned was the pure religion of Jesus Christ, the tendency of which, in its doctrines, institutions, precepts, and spirit, is to bind those who believe it in the bands of a close and permanent friendship, and, in this way, to hold out an encouragement to mankind at large to join a society which affords "rest from the broils and agitations of secular life"—a peaceful haven, inviting us to retire from the tossings and perils of this unquiet ocean to a sacred inclosure, a sequestered spot, which the storms and tempests of the world are not permitted to invade.

> "Intus aquæ dulces, vivoque sedilia saxo:
> Nympharum domus. Hic fessas non vincula naves
> Ulla tenent; unco non adligat anchora morsu."—VIRG.[2]

The apostle calls upon the Romans to "mark those who cause divisions and offences." Persons of this description often for a season carry on their plans secretly, without being observed. The mischief is done before danger is apprehended. It is of importance that such persons should be marked as soon as their character begins to develop itself, that proper methods may be employed to counteract their efforts and defeat their purposes. It is good to "withdraw from them"—to avoid "the foolish and unlearned questions" they delight in agitating—to "shun their vain babbling." Chrysostom remarks, that the apostle does not advise the Roman Christians to enter into debate with these men, but to mark them, that they may avoid them, and have nothing to do with them.

[1] The reader will be instructed and delighted with a dissertation on the Judaizers in Stanley's "Discourses on the Apostolic Age."

[2] Rob. Hall, "Terms of Communion."

Their end is in some measure gained, if they can get others to dispute with them.

The earnestness of the apostle, in this exhortation, deserves notice—"I beseech you, brethren." Such "divisions and scandals," when they prevail, eat out the very life of religion in individuals and churches. His earnestness was increased by his conviction of the unworthy ends which the individuals he had in view were prosecuting: "For they that are such serve not our Lord Jesus Christ, but their own belly; and by good words and fair speeches deceive the hearts of the simple."[1] The words, "they serve not our Lord Jesus," refer not so much to the *event* as to the *motive* of the conduct of these men. It is clear "divisions and scandals" cannot promote the cause of Christ. They may be overruled for good; but their tendency is unmingled mischief, and their consequence usually serious injury. But, what the apostle points at is this: These men have it not for their object to serve the Lord Jesus: it is not His glory that they are seeking to promote; it is not His Gospel they are endeavouring to propagate. Their designs are of another kind: "they serve their own belly." 'They seek their own ease and advantage; they wish to avoid the offence of the cross; and, by becoming the heads of a party, to secure for themselves ample support.' The Judaizing teachers seem to have been men of this unprincipled character.

The insidious methods which these men adopted to gain their ends, are urged on the attention of the Roman Christians as another reason why they should "mark" them. "By good words and fair speeches they deceive the hearts"—the minds—"of the simple." The "simple"—literally, the 'innocent'[2]—describes that class of men who are more distinguished by honesty of intention than by power of intellect or extended accurate knowledge. These are the natural prey of such designing men as the apostle describes. Meaning no harm themselves, they are backward to suspect others of de-

[1] Ver. 18.

[2] ἀκάκων.

signing mischief; and, from the loose texture of their minds, and the slenderness of their information, they are easily imposed on.

The bait by which these men, like "fishes, are caught in an evil net"—the lure by which, as "birds, they are caught in the snare,"[1] is "good words"—"fair speeches." These are applied in two ways: first, they use "good words and fair speeches" respecting their own dogmas and plans, endeavouring to identify them with the "mind of God" and the "law of Christ;" and then they spare no "good words and fair speeches" in flattering those whom they hope to make their dupes. Andrew Melvill refers the "good, kind words" to blandishment; the "fair, plausible speeches" to affected piety. Flatterers and pretenders to singular sanctity are always to be suspected. It is a good advice given in the old distich—

> "Noli homines blandos nimium sermone, probare,
> Fistula dulce canet, volucrem dum decipit auceps."[2]

It is necessary to remark here, that we are by no means warranted to apply the language, which the apostle here uses in reference to Judaizers, to all who cause divisions and offences in the Church. The present unnatural state of the Church has so confounded men's minds, that not unfrequently in this class are to be found men of most conscientious views, whose design is to serve the Lord Jesus, and who, by the sacrifices they make, render it evident that they do not "serve their own belly." Such persons are to be disapproved of and opposed; but we are neither to speak of them nor feel towards them as the apostle did towards the Judaizers. Yet, even when the men who "cause divisions and offences" are, in the estimation of an enlightened charity, good men—in some points of view, it may be, very good men—it is lamentable to see how unlike themselves they behave, and to what arts and shifts they descend, in the prosecution of their unholy work,

[1] Ecc. ix. 12. [2] Pseud. Cat.

as heads of factions in the Church, or leaders of schisms from the Church.

The apostle urges the high character which the Roman Christians had established for themselves, as a reason why they should be on their guard against those whose plans, if successful, would soon rob them of their honest reputation: "For your obedience is come abroad unto all men. I am glad therefore on your behalf: but yet I would have you wise unto that which is good, and simple concerning evil."[1] The words of the apostle admit of being interpreted in two different ways. He may mean to express this thought—'Your readiness to embrace the Gospel is very generally known. From this very circumstance, which is itself to me an occasion of joy, false teachers may be the more ready to practise their arts on you; but I heartily desire that, while so simple as not to deceive, ye may prove yourselves too wise to be deceived.' Or this may be the idea—'You have obtained a high character among the churches: I am glad of it; see that ye maintain it. Beware lest, by listening to false teachers, you should lose it. Walk worthy of your character. Be not only harmless, but intelligent Christians; but never let your intelligence take the shape or colour of "the cunning craftiness of those who are lying in wait to deceive you."' Either sense is good; but I prefer the latter. There is, probably, a tacit reference to Jer. iv. 22.

To encourage the Roman Christians to resist the attempts likely to be made to deceive and divide them, the apostle assures them that they should, ere long, be delivered from all such evils, and from their author: "And the God of peace will bruise Satan under your feet shortly."[2] There can be no reasonable doubt that there is here an allusion to Gen. iii. 15. Satan—a Hebrew word, which signifies an adversary—without doubt, denotes here the chief of the rebel angels, who is the grand author and promoter of evil, moral and physical, in our world. Wicked men are often

[1] Ver. 19. [2] Ver. 20.

represented as his agents. The Judaizing teachers were under his influence, and doing his work. When their schemes were exposed and effectually counterworked, he was thwarted: he was bruised under the feet of the Roman Christians. The promise was fulfilled to them—" Thou shalt tread upon the lion and the adder."[1] " The God of peace"—' the Author of all blessing, will save and deliver you from these dangers.' Though there can be little doubt the apostle had directly in view the deliverance of the Roman Church from those agents of the wicked one who sought to cause " divisions and offences" among them, his words are a declaration that, ere long—for the longest life is not long—shortly, God would remove them out of the sphere in which Satan operates, and make them, for ever, " more than conquerors through Him that loved them." This is a promise in which Christians of all ages have an equal interest with those to whom it was first given. The section is closed with a benediction: " The grace of our Lord Jesus Christ be with you. Amen." ' May the complacent regard of the Saviour ever rest on you, and may you have constant proof of this, in the manifestation of His grace in His benefits.' It seems as if this had been originally intended to be the close of the Epistle: if it was so, the apostle, under the influence of the Spirit, added the two concluding sections.

SECTION VII.

SALUTATIONS FROM CHRISTIANS WITH THE APOSTLE, TO CHRISTIANS AT ROME.

CHAPTER XVI. 21–23.—" Timotheus my work-fellow, and Lucius, and Jason, and Sosipater, my kinsmen, salute you. I Tertius, who wrote this Epistle, salute you in the Lord. Gaius mine host, and of the whole church, saluteth you. Erastus, the chamberlain of the city, saluteth you, and Quartus a brother."

Some of Paul's companions at Corinth seem to have requested the apostle to communicate to the brethren at Rome

[1] Psalm xci. 13.

the interest they felt in their welfare, though probably, in general, personally strangers to them. The first in this list is a highly honoured name: "Timotheus my work-fellow, and Lucius, and Jason, and Sosipater, my kinsmen, salute you."[1] There is not one, in the second class of primitive Christian teachers, that stands higher than Timothy. His father was a Greek, and his mother a Jewess.[2] Of his father we know nothing, but that he probably was a Greek in religion as well as in origin. Of his mother, Eunice, and of his grandmother, Lois, we know that they were distinguished for their piety, and had imbued the mind of Timothy from an early age with the best of all kinds of knowledge—knowledge of the Holy Scriptures.[3] He was a native of Lycaonia; but whether Derbe or Lystra was his native city, is doubtful.[4] He was probably converted, along with his mother, by the ministry of Paul, during his first missionary tour in Asia Minor.[5] On his second visit, some years later, Timothy being "well reported of by the brethren,"[6] was chosen by Paul to be his companion in his evangelical journeys.[7] Having submitted to the rite of circumcision, as a matter of prudence,[8] "because of the Jews;" and having, by "the laying on of the hands of" the apostle and of "the presbytery"—*i.e.*, the eldership, been solemnly set apart to the office of an evangelist, after having "made a good profession before many witnesses;"[9] and having been endowed with the spiritual gifts necessary to his ministry, he was for many years the constant companion of the apostle in his labours and sufferings, and probably enjoyed the first place among the Christian brethren whom the apostle honoured with the esteem, and love, and confidence of friendship. He calls him his "son"—his "own son in the faith"—his "dearly beloved son." At the time this Epistle was written, Timothy was with the apostle at Corinth. The latter part of the history of Timothy, like that of the most of the primitive ministers of Christianity, is involved in obscurity.

[1] Ver. 21. [2] Acts xvi. 1–3. [3] 2 Tim. i. 5; iii. 15. [4] Acts xvi. 1.
[5] Acts xiv. [6] Acts xvi. 2. [7] Acts xvi. 3. [8] Acts xvi. 3.
[9] 1 Tim. iii. 14; v. 14; 2 Tim. i. 6; ii. 2, 14; iv. 5.

Tradition says—what is in itself highly probable—that he went to Rome on receiving Paul's second Epistle, and attended his venerable friend till he laid down his neck on the block, "for the word of God, and for the testimony of Jesus Christ;" and that, leaving Rome, he returned to Ephesus, where, in the reign of Domitian or Nerva, he too received the crown of martyrdom, and rejoined his spiritual father, never to part again. Paul describes him as his "work-fellow." Nothing endears Christians more to each other than common work in the service of their common Lord.

Who this "Lucius" was, it is difficult to say. Some suppose that he was Luke the Evangelist, to whom, writing to Romans, Paul gives a Latin name. It is doubtful if Luke was with the apostle, at this time at Corinth: besides, not Lucius, but Lucanus, or Lucianus, would have been Luke's Roman name. Others have supposed that the person designated was "Lucius of Cyrene," who is numbered among the prophets and teachers at Antioch.[1] It is plain that he was a man of note among the Christians, whose salutation would be valued by the Roman Christians.

"Jason" is very probably the Thessalonian convert who entertained the apostle in his house, on his first visit to Macedonia, and who was exposed to considerable trouble, danger, and loss, from his hospitality.[2] Paul, in his second visit to Greece, passed through Macedonia, and, though it is not mentioned, not unlikely took Thessalonica in his way; and, in this case, Jason, according to the kindly usage of these times, seems to have accompanied him to Corinth.

"Sosipater" is probably the person who, in Acts xx. 4, is called Sopater—a word of the same meaning, one of the Berean Jews, of whom the inspired writer testifies that "they were more noble than those of Thessalonica, in that they received the word with all readiness, and searched the Scriptures daily, whether those things were so."[3] In his case, and in that of many others, serious inquiry—as it will indeed

[1] Acts xiii. 1. [2] Acts xvii. 5–9. [3] Acts xvii. 11.

always do, if honest and unprejudiced—ended in confirmed faith.

Paul calls Lucius, and Jason, and Sosipater, his "kinsmen," or relations. It is possible they might be relatives, in the stricter sense of the term; but it is more likely that they, as well as those mentioned, ver. 7, were relations only as they were of the same race—"brethren, kinsmen according to the flesh." The hearty salutations of Jewish converts to a Gentile church was calculated to do much good. It tended to show the converted Jews at Rome that their best informed brethren made no difference between Jews and Gentiles in the Church; and it was fitted to do away prejudices against the Jewish converts in general, which the narrow-mindedness of some of the Jewish converts at Rome had produced in their Gentile brethren, by showing them that there were Jews who rose above the prejudices of their nation, and gladly acquiesced in the determination of their Lord, that "the Gentiles should be fellow-heirs with them of the promise," and equally "blessed with faithful Abraham."[1]

This is one of the passages from which a powerful corroborative argument may be drawn for the truth of the history of Paul, as recorded in the Acts of the Apostles, and for the genuineness and authenticity of the Epistle. It is nowhere stated in the Epistle where it was written, or when it was written; but, from a careful comparison of different passages, it is clear that it was written at Corinth, in Greece, after collections had been made both in Macedonia and Achaia for the poor saints at Jerusalem, and previously to the apostle setting out on a journey to Jerusalem to deliver these contributions. In the Acts of the Apostles, where there is not the slightest hint about Paul's writing this Epistle, we find, from the twentieth chapter of that book, that just at the time when, and at the place where, the Epistle was written, two, at least, of the persons here mentioned as with Paul were present with him—Sosipater and Timothy; and that, at this time, he was

[1] Eph. iii. 6; Gal. iii. 9.

preparing for a journey to Jerusalem, with alms from the Gentiles. This is a coincidence too recondite to have been intended, and too exact to have been accidental. The truth of the history, and the genuineness of the Epistle, furnish the only satisfactory account of it. They agree, not because the one borrowed from the other, but because they both wrote from a knowledge of facts.[1]

"I Tertius, who wrote this epistle, salute you in the Lord."[2] It has been conjectured that the person calling himself Tertius is no other than Silas, of whom we read in the Acts of the Apostles.—Acts xv. 22, 27, 34, 40; xvi. 19, 25, 29; xvii. 4, 10; xviii. 5. Tertius, in Latin, and Silas, in Hebrew, are of equivalent signification. Silas's name, however, is not in the catalogue of the brethren who came with Paul into Greece; and his name, when Latinized, seems not to have been Tertius, but Silvanus.—2 Cor. i. 19; 1 Thes. i. 1; 2 Thes. i. 1; 1 Pet. v. 12. Whoever he was, he had the honour of being employed by Paul as his amanuensis. Paul dictated, and Tertius wrote the epistle. It was, comparatively speaking, but an humble service; but, in consequence of his having performed it, his name is honourably recorded in a book which has for ages been already more generally known than any other, is yet to be read throughout all the world, and will last to the end of time. Tertius, by being Paul's amanuensis, has obtained for himself what many of the most powerful human minds have in vain exerted all their energies to acquire.

"I Tertius salute you, who wrote this epistle, in the Lord." Such is the order of the words in the original: and some, connecting the words "in the Lord" with "wrote this epistle," suppose the meaning to be, 'I wrote it in the Lord, as a Christian, for the Lord's sake.' It is more natural to connect the phrase with "salute." 'I Tertius, who have been employed by the apostle to commit this Epistle to writing, send you my Christian regards.' From his name, he probably was a Roman, and might be known to some at Rome.

[1] *Vide* Paley's *Hor. Paul.*

[2] Ver. 22.

Why Paul employed an amanuensis we cannot certainly tell. That he usually did so is undoubted, and only wrote the concluding sentence to show that the Epistle was genuine. —1 Cor. xvi. 21; Col. iv. 18; 2 Thes. iii. 17. It has been supposed that he laboured under a chronic defect of sight, arising from the effect of "the light from heaven above the brightness of the sun," which fell on his astonished eyes "on the way to Damascus," and to which it has been supposed that there are various references in his writings, especially Gal. iv. 13–15. It is not unlikely that, like many literary men, he did not write a very legible hand. Some have supposed that there is a reference to this in Gal. vi. 11. Every man has his own gift, and, in the employment of it, may be useful. Tertius could not have composed this epistle; but he could write it, probably better—more legibly, than its author could have done. The greatest of men has not every qualification, and may be much the better for the assistance of those who are immeasurably his inferiors.

"Gaius mine host, and of the whole church, saluteth you. Erastus, the chamberlain of the city, saluteth you, and Quartus a brother."[1] We read of Gaius, a native of Derbe, and an inhabitant of Macedonia.[2] The name is the Latin Caius Græcised, and was a common one. The person here mentioned was clearly an inhabitant of Corinth; for he is called the host or entertainer, not only of the apostle, but of the whole Church, either because, being a man in wealthy circumstances, he was distinguished for a very extended hospitality to the brethren, or because in his mansion he furnished a meeting-place for the Church to observe the ordinances. He was likely the same person who is mentioned as a leading man in the Corinthian Church, 1 Cor. i. 14, and as among the very few in that church whom the apostle had baptized. Whether it was to this good man that John addressed his third Epistle is uncertain. From the character drawn there, ver. 5–8, it is obvious that, if he was not the Gaius mentioned here, he was a man of a

[1] Ver. 23.

[2] Acts xix. 29; xx. 4.

similar spirit. This good man was very much attached to his own church, but he had a catholic spirit. He entertained the Church at Corinth: he salutes the Church in Rome. Our love to the brethren is to be manifested in correspondence to circumstances; but we are to do "good to *all* the household of faith as we have opportunity."

"Erastus, the chamberlain of the city, saluteth you." There is an Erastus spoken of, Acts xix. 22, and 2 Tim. iv. 20. It seems likely, however, that that Erastus was an Ephesian; at any rate, that he was a Christian preacher,—an itinerant Christian preacher—an occupation scarcely compatible with holding the office and discharging the duties of chamberlain of the large city of Corinth. The chamberlain or steward of a Greek city was an officer of high respectability. Josephus mentions the chamberlain among the rulers. The office seems to have resembled that of recorder, town-clerk, or treasurer in our principal cities. Erastus appears to have been one of the few "noble" who were among "the called to be saints in Corinth." While the great body of Christians, in all ages, have belonged to the middle and lower orders of society, there is nothing in vital Christianity incompatible with high rank and multiplied avocations. The chamberlain of Corinth must have been a man of both.

The only other person whose Christian regards the apostle transmits to the Roman Church, is "Quartus a brother." "The brethren," in contradistinction to "the saints," Phil. iv. 21, 22, seems to denote 'brethren in office'—Christian ministers, evangelists, elders, and deacons. But it is common for the apostle to call the body of the faithful, "brethren." It is impossible to say whether Quartus was an official, or merely a private member of the Church. It seems obvious that he was a warm-hearted Christian, and that Paul thought it meet to gratify and honour him by specifying his name among those who wished to be remembered to the brethren at Rome. It is pleasant to think with how many good men, if we shall have the happiness of a place in the Father's house of many mansions, we are yet to become acquainted, of whom we do not know so much as we do of Quartus, of whom we know only the name.

Here, again, the apostle seems to have intended to conclude the Epistle; and, accordingly, to authenticate the above postscript, he again, with his own hand, wrote, "The grace of our Lord Jesus Christ be with you all. Amen."[1]

SECTION VIII.

CONCLUDING DOXOLOGY.

CHAPTER XVI. 25–27.—"Now to him that is of power to stablish you according to my Gospel, and the preaching of Jesus Christ, (according to the revelation of the mystery, which was kept secret since the world began, but now is made manifest, and by the Scriptures of the prophets, according to the commandment of the everlasting God, made known to all nations for the obedience of faith;) to God only wise, be glory through Jesus Christ for ever. Amen."

In the verses with which our version, following the reading adopted in the received text—which is approved by some of the best later critical interpreters—closes, we have one of the most magnificent doxologies in the New Testament—a worthy devotional peroration to such a doctrinal discussion. "Now to Him that is of power to stablish you according to my Gospel, and the preaching of Jesus Christ, (according to the revelation of the mystery, which was kept secret since the world began, but now is made manifest, and by the Scriptures of the prophets, according to the commandment of the everlasting God, made known to all nations for the obedience of faith;) to God only wise, be glory through Jesus Christ for ever. Amen."[2] I have already[3] had occasion to remark that critics are not agreed as to the place which this doxology should occupy in the Epistle. That it belongs to it, there is no reasonable doubt; but some think its right place is at the end of the fourteenth chapter. In most of the

[1] Ver. 24 [2] Ver. 25–27. [3] Chap. xv. 1.

Greek MSS. now extant, it is found there; but in some of the most ancient versions it is found at the end of the Epistle. On *strictly critical* grounds, the question is not easily determined; but the internal evidence is very strong that it is rightly placed in our version. Unless it had been the intention of the apostle to conclude the discussion about meats and days at the end of the fourteenth chapter, which he does not, its insertion there would interrupt the course of his illustrations. We should have looked for it, not at the end of the fourteenth chapter, for the discussion does not close there, but at the end of the 13th verse of the fifteenth chapter, where the discussion does close. As to there being a peculiar propriety in connecting this ascription of praise to God, as the establisher, the strengthener of His people, with the contents of the fourteenth chapter, I cannot help thinking the doxology abundantly appropriate to the object of the whole Epistle, every part of which was intended and is fitted to "strengthen, stablish, and settle" Christians in their most holy faith.[1] The question, however, *where* the three verses should stand, is one of very secondary moment. Let us proceed to inquire into their meaning.

It is natural to consider, first, the character under which God is here introduced as worthy of praise, and then the ascription of the praise that is due to Him. God is described under two characters: first, as powerful, and then as wise. He is "able to stablish" the Romans—"able to stablish them according to Paul's Gospel, and the preaching of Jesus Christ, according to the revelation of the mystery, which was kept secret since the world began, but had now been made manifest, and by the Scriptures of the prophets, according to the commandment of the everlasting God, made known to all nations for the obedience of faith;" and He is "God only wise."

The first description of the Divine character proceeds on

[1] A very elaborate discussion of the question is to be found in Fritzsche, vol. i., *Prol.* xxxviii–xlix.

the supposition that the Roman Christians stood in need of being "stablished"—"strengthened." There were among them the weak, who needed to be made strong; and the "strong" among them had no strength but what God had given them, and they needed to be kept strong and made stronger. A strong Christian, is a Christian in whom the principles of the new life are vigorous, rendering him intelligent, wise, holy, active, useful, happy; and to strengthen a Christian, is to secure these results. It is God alone who can do this. Christians cannot do it for themselves; their ministers cannot do it for them. They may use the means, but they cannot command the success. But God can do this. He "is able to make all grace abound towards them; that they, always having all sufficiency in all things, may abound to every good work."[1] "His grace is sufficient for them, and His strength is made perfect in weakness."[2] The expression, "who is able," indicates more than mere ability. As used in the New Testament, it often implies disposition and will,—Rom. iv. 21; xi. 23; xiv. 4; Eph. iii. 20; Jude, 24. He who *can* stablish, *will* stablish His people. They shall "wax stronger and stronger"—"strengthened with all might, according to His glorious power, unto all patience and long-suffering with joyfulness."[3]

The words that follow are somewhat perplexed in their construction. They are plainly descriptive of something about this "stablishing"—this "strengthening," which God is able and disposed to give the Roman Christians. "God is able to stablish you according to my Gospel." Paul's Gospel—what does that mean? We find this phrase, "my Gospel," chap. ii. 16, and in 2 Tim. ii. 8. It seems the same thing as "the Gospel I preach"—"the Gospel committed to me," Gal. ii. 2, 7. It is equivalent to—'the statement I have made to you of the good news of salvation through Christ Jesus.' The clause that follows seems explanatory of this—"and the preaching of Jesus Christ." Some understand by these words

[1] 2 Cor. ix. 8. [2] 2 Cor. xii. 9. [3] Col. i. 11.

" what Jesus Christ preached," and suppose the apostle to refer to the fact that the Gospel, as he preached it, was not " after man; for he neither received it of man, neither was he taught it, but by the revelation of Jesus Christ."[1] What " he received of the Lord, that he delivered" to the churches, 1 Cor. xi. 23; xv. 1. The whole description, according to them, is, 'The Gospel which I preached to *you*, which is the Gospel Christ preached to *me*.' But the revelation made to Paul was a revelation *in* him, never represented as preaching. The preaching of Christ is, I apprehend, illustrative of the phrase, " my Gospel"—my Gospel was " the preaching of Jesus Christ." " Of Christ" denotes the subject, rather than the author of the preaching. Paul kept to his determination to know nothing in his preaching but Christ, and Him crucified;—the truth about Christ was the sum and substance of his Gospel.

" According to this Gospel"—this preaching of Christ Jesus, God can, God will " stablish you." " According to" may mean 'in accordance with.' 'In my Gospel I told you so, and you will find it true.' I rather think its import is, 'with a reference to.' 'God will make you strong in reference to this Gospel—this preaching about Jesus Christ. He will make you strong *in* the faith of it—strong *by* the faith of it. He will make you powerful Christians—men in Christ, able for work and warfare.'

" According to the revelation of the mystery, which was kept secret since the world began, but now is made manifest, and by the Scriptures of the prophets, according to the commandment of the everlasting God, made known to all nations." This should not have been in a parenthesis, for it is a further description of Paul's Gospel—the preaching of Jesus Christ. " According to my Gospel, etc. According to the revelation of the mystery, which was kept secret since the world began." " The mystery" was the Divine method of saving men through Christ Jesus. That was a thing which, from its own nature,

[1] Gal. i. 12.

human reason could not discover; that was a thing which, from the beginning of the world down to the coming of Christ, "during the ancient ages,"[1] was kept secret—concealed altogether from the great body of mankind, very dimly revealed to the favoured minority. Of this "mystery" there had been "a manifestation" in the incarnation and work of the Saviour, and in the Gospel which contained the account of it. "Paul's Gospel," "the preaching of Jesus Christ," and "the revelation of the mystery," are all materially the same thing. The manifestation of this mystery is referred to, chap. iii. 21, 25, 26; 1 Cor. ii. 10; Eph. iii. 3–5. The method of salvation through Christ is clearly revealed. This manifested mystery is, "according to the commandment of the everlasting God, to be made known, by the Scriptures of the prophets, to all nations for the obedience of faith."

It is the commandment of the everlasting God that this Gospel—this preaching of the Lord Jesus, this revealed mystery—should be made known to all nations. The word rendered "commandment" may mean 'decree,' 'appointment,' and then the reference is to the many passages in the Old Testament in which "the decree is declared;" such as, "I will give Thee the heathen for Thine inheritance, and the uttermost ends of the earth for Thy possession," Psal. ii. 7; "All the ends of the earth shall see the salvation of God," Psal. xcviii. 3: or, it may mean 'precept,' in which case the reference is to the words of our Lord—" Go ye, therefore, and teach all nations;" "Go into all the world, and preach the Gospel to every creature," Matt. xxviii. 19; Mark xvi. 15. This was indeed the commandment of the everlasting God, both as the Father spoke in Him, and as He is God "manifest in flesh" —"God over all blessed for ever."

This commandment was to be carried into effect "by the Scriptures of the prophets." The "Scriptures of the prophets" are the Old Testament writings, especially the predictions contained in them. Some have explained the words "by the

[1] χρόνοις αἰωνίοις.

Scriptures of the prophets," as equivalent to—'according to the predictions of the prophets,' which interpretation states a truth, but it is not warranted by the words, which intimate that "the Scriptures of the prophets" should be instrumental in making the Gospel known to all nations. This has been actually the case. The apostles made great use of the Old Testament Scriptures in their successful preaching of the Gospel to the Gentiles; and, so long as the world lasts, one of the great evidences on which the belief of men in the Divine origin of the Gospel is demanded, will be derived from the fulfilment of Old Testament prophecy. Some would connect "by the Scriptures of the prophets" with the words "made manifest;" as if the apostle's meaning had been this—'The mystery was kept secret during the ancient ages, down to the time when the Old Testament dispensation commenced; it was then manifested—partially revealed, by the Old Testament writings, and was at length fully published under the Gospel dispensation:' but this obliges us to use freedoms with the text altogether unauthorized.

The design of this revelation's being thus, by Divine command, made known to all nations, is "the obedience of faith." The phrase was explained in the commencement of these illustrations.[1] It is equivalent to—that 'they might believe the Gospel, and experience its practical power in making them obedient to God.'

According, then, to "this Gospel of Paul"—this "preaching of Jesus Christ"—this "revealed mystery, long kept secret, now manifested;" and, according to the decree and command of the great God our Saviour, to be made known by the Scriptures of the prophets to all nations for the obedience of faith;—according to this, God is able and disposed to stablish Christians—to strengthen them to lay hold of it, to keep hold of it, and to use it for all the blessed purposes which it is fitted and intended to accomplish.

The second character under which the apostle offers praise

[1] Chap. i. 5.

to God in this doxology, is "God only wise." God is termed "only wise," because He only is infinitely wise. The wisdom of the wisest of His creatures, compared with His, is folly. "God," as Origen says, "is not made wise by wisdom as it happeneth to men; He is wise Himself—the Author and well-spring of wisdom. He only hath wisdom, as He 'only hath immortality,' in Himself. He is the sole origin and Author, and, in the highest degree, the sole *possessor*, of wisdom; for wisdom, in all other beings, is His gift." His wisdom is remarkably displayed in the scheme of grace which the apostle had unfolded in the Epistle; and this infinite wisdom qualifies Him for giving, in the best way, that "establishment" which the apostle says He "*can*"—is able and willing to bestow on His people. Under no characters, then, more appropriate could the concluding doxology of this Epistle be addressed to God, than the all-powerful, the all-benignant, the all-wise.

The doxology is addressed to God "through Jesus Christ." It is "through Jesus Christ" that all such displays of power, and benignity, and wisdom are made; and it is "through Jesus Christ" that our acknowledgments of them can alone rise with acceptance before God.

This praise is to be ascribed to the God of power, and wisdom, and love, and mercy, through Jesus Christ, "for ever." The anthem is to be begun on earth, but it is to be carried on in heaven, and continued throughout endless duration. The power, grace, and wisdom of God, as manifested in the salvation of men, is an exhaustless theme. It will afford abundant and most delightful employment for the enlarged faculties of glorified men and holy angels for ever and ever.

The apostle adds his hearty "amen" to this doxology. 'Oh, that it may be thus! Thus assuredly it shall be. So let it be —so shall it be.' And he is no loyal subject of the great King—no true-hearted disciple of Him whose never-ceasing prayer is, "Father, glorify Thy name"—who does not, with all his heart, say, Amen, and amen. The power of God is regarded as weakness, the wisdom of God as folly, and the kindness of God is disbelieved and despised, in this present evil world. But it shall not always be so. The time hastens onward, when not only shall a hymn of adoring and grateful admiration rise from all the innocent and all the restored of His intelligent creation, but when the wisdom, and the righteousness, and the benignity of His administration shall be made so evident, that all the murmurs of his irreclaimable enemies shall be for ever hushed in self-condemned speechlessness, and when every creature in the new heaven and the new earth, wherein nothing but righteousness shall dwell, shall, with a voice as the sound of many waters, ascribe "Blessing, and honour, and glory, and power unto Him that sitteth on the throne, and unto the Lamb, for ever and ever."

It seems impossible to be long in close intercourse with the apostle without feeling that "virtue comes out of him." Even the coolest of all commentators, Macknight, is warmed to something like eloquence when he finishes his exposition of this Epistle. "Thus," says he, "endeth the apostle Paul's Epistle to the Romans; a writing which, for sublimity and truth of sentiment, for brevity and strength of expression, for regularity of structure, and, above all, for the unspeakable importance of the discoveries it contains, stands unrivalled by any mere human composition, and as far exceeds the most celebrated productions of the learned Greeks and Romans as the shining of the sun exceedeth the twinkling of the stars."

It is curious to contrast with this stately, measured sentence, the outburst of loving admiration which the contemplation of the Epistle drew forth from the deepest recess of the capacious heart of the great German Reformer. "In this Epistle is treated in the most masterly manner everything that belongeth to the Christian life. Whatever it most concerns a Christian to know—Law, Gospel, Sin, Grace, Justification, Christ, God, Good Works, Faith, Hope, Charity; all wherein true Christianity consisteth, how it becometh a Christian to conduct himself towards his neighbours, whether good or bad, strong or weak, friends or enemies, and towards himself; all this is to be found here in such perfection, that it is impossible to wish anything more or better. So rich a treasure is it of spiritual wealth, that even to him who has read it a thousand times something new will be ever presenting itself. Its study, beyond every other, is found useful; and the longer and the more deeply it is pondered, its excellences grow upon you, and it appears to be constantly becoming more delightful, more valuable, and more copious than itself."

INDEX.

I.—PRINCIPAL MATTERS.

2 R

II.—PASSAGES OF SCRIPTURE QUOTED OR REMARKED ON.

THE END.

MURRAY AND GIBB, PRINTERS, EDINBURGH.

ERRATA.

Page 275, line 11 from the foot, *for* play-string, *read* plaything.

Page 355, line 19 from the foot, *for* consolatory, *read* elementary.

Page 597, line 10, *for* evil, *read* toil.

www.ingramcontent.com/pod-product-compliance
Lightning Source LLC
LaVergne TN
LVHW021052110826
845150LV00001B/52

* 9 7 8 1 4 2 5 5 6 7 3 6 1 *